THE COLLECTIVE DEFINITION OF DEVIANCE

Edited by

**F. James Davis
Richard Stivers**

THE FREE PRESS
A Division of Macmillan Publishing Co., Inc.
NEW YORK

The Free Press
A Division of Macmillan Publishing Co., Inc.
866 Third Avenue, New York, N.Y. 10022

Collier–Macmillan Canada Ltd.

Library of Congress Catalog Card Number: 74–10138

Printed in the United States of America

printing number
1 2 3 4 5 6 7 8 9 10

Library of Congress Cataloging in Publication Data

Davis, Floyd James /date/   comp.
    The collective definition of deviance.

    Includes bibliographies.
    1. Deviant behavior--Addresses, essays, lectures.
I. Stivers, Richard, joint comp. II. Title.
HM291.D29 1975   301.6'2   74-10138
ISBN 0-02-907260-3

TO
Lucile, Elinor, Miriam & Sarah

AND
Janet, Mark & Michael

Contents

Introduction

There is growing agreement that the relative neglect of the collective definition of deviance, as an aspect of sociological work on deviant behavior, represents a serious lack. A fuller understanding would require that close-up studies of deviant actors and subcultures be complemented by studies of the processes of societal definition and redefinition of deviant categories (Becker, 1970: 207). Such studies necessitate theories and methods suitable for relating deviance to institutional structures, to bureaucracies of control, to ideologies, social conflict, power, and social change. A number of significant contributions of this kind are brought together in this book, some of them by students of deviance, some by other sociologists, and some by nonsociologists. They all bear on the problem of collective definition as defined by Karl Mannheim (1946: 19; 1956: 97).

Our aim in designing this book can be clarified in relation to developments in the labeling approach to deviance, the perspective that has guided most sociological work for the past dozen years or more. Some of the selections in this book were written in terms of labeling concepts, but the processes of collective definition have not been emphasized in that perspective. The use of theoretical orientations other than those so far predominant in labeling analysis seem necessary to understand the societal definition of deviant categories, and perhaps these perspectives can be accommodated within the labeling framework.

In laying the foundations for the labeling perspective more than two decades ago, Lemert followed social disorganization theorists in defining deviance as conduct in violation of dominant social norms (Davis, 1970: 34–36). He then defined primary deviation as those norm-violating acts committed by a person before the label of an existing deviant category has been attached to him, and secondary deviation as further norm-violating acts after the label has successfully been affixed (Lemert, 1951: 22–23, 75–76). Despite this clear distinction there has been some conceptual confusion, chiefly concerning the basic idea that behavior is not deviant in itself, that societal definition is required to make behavior deviant. If this refers to the collective defining of deviant categories there should be no conceptual problem; but when it appears to refer to attaching the label to the person (Erikson, 1962: 308; Becker, 1963: 9; Kitsuse, 1962: 253), there is confusion. The latter interpretation departs from the definition of deviance as norm-violating behavior, eliminating primary deviation from consideration (Gibbs, 1966: 13–14; Taylor, Walton and Young, 1973: 144–150).

To illustrate this conceptual problem, let us consider a case of deviation from the legal norm against prostitution. Suppose two young women office workers, partly for excitement and partly for money, accept money on occasional weekends for sexual liaisons with strangers. This is primary deviance, and they do not yet think of themselves as prostitutes. Then they are arrested, booked, fined and warned that another offense means a jail sentence. They have now been officially labeled prostitutes, although the ritual would be more complete if they were jailed. The legal stigmatization will probably affect their behavior, their self-concepts, and the probability of their becoming career prostitutes. If we were now to say that these two people were not deviant until society attached the official label of prostitute to them, we obviously would mean that primary deviance is not deviance. Instead, if we note that the act of accepting money from strangers for sexual favors would not be criminally deviant if society had not defined it as such, we can proceed to study both primary and secondary deviance. Deviance requires norm-defining behavior by agents of society, not just the norm-violating behavior of deviant actors.

The problem of definition is complicated by difficulties in getting valid indexes of deviant behaviors. It is helpful always to ask the question, "deviant from what?" (Schur, 1971: 29). Are the violated norms formally stated ones such as written laws, or are they current enforcement practices (which may include patterned organizational deviations from written norms), or are they dominant informal norms? It is also helpful to specify the amount of deviation from certain norms, thus acknowledging varying degrees of deviance. Finally, it is often necessary to specify the social circumstances of the conduct, since the meanings of acts can vary with different situations (Schur, 1971: 15, 23–27). It is not considered deviant to kill in self defense or under (legitimate) military orders, for instance, or to take even the most dangerous drugs under medical supervision.

Secondary deviance has been the emphasis of the labeling approach. Most of the work has dealt with the effects on the person, especially on the image of self, of having the deviant label attached. The effects of labeling on the development of a deviant identity, and on commitment to a deviant career, have been stressed. There have been many field studies of socialization into drug-using groups, homosexual networks, groups of mental patients, and other deviant subcultures. Attention has been centered on the deviant actor, then, on his role-playing, and on the integration of personality around changing self-conceptions. Although the effects of labeling on the deviant career may have been exaggerated (Taylor, Walton, and Young, 1973: 140–144), explanation of these social psychological processes has been the major contribution of the labeling analysts. Symbolic interaction theory has predominated, and the emphasis is often referred to as the interactionist perspective (Schur, 1971: 8, 41; Davis, 1972: 451–456; Rubington and Weinberg, 1973; Filstead, 1972: 2).

Another influence in the microsociological direction has been the use of sociological variants of existentialism, by ethnomethodologists and other phenomenologists, who concentrate on the subjective experiences, understandings, and intentions of the person (Schur, 1971: 115–136; Taylor, Walton, and Young, 1973: 172–208). Much attention has been devoted to responses to stigmatization and to the outlooks and life styles of deviant groups. Matza, and also the ethnomethodologists, have at least implied that the realities of deviant behavior can be correctly understood only through the eyes of the deviant actor (Matza, 1964: 2; Cicourel, 1968: 331; Sudnow, 1965; Bittner, 1967; Douglas, 1967). Existential approaches, with their commitment to the values of equality and to individual freedom and expression, have also encouraged sympathy for deviants as powerless underdogs (Becker, 1967; Davis, 1972: 459; Thio, 1973: 5–6). Deviant categories have thus often been depicted as so absurd and arbitrary as not to seem deserving of serious study.

Labeling analysis emerged in the 1960's during a time of critical evaluation of a dozen years of studies of deviance (mostly of juvenile delinquency) oriented towards various formulations of Durkheim's anomie thesis (Clinard, 1964; Short and Strodtbeck, 1965). Erikson brought Durkheim's ideas about the functions of societal reactions to deviance into the labeling framework, as we shall see in Part I. This had the potential of encouraging studies relating deviance to institutional structures, but the microsociological emphasis continued to dominate the labeling approach. Perhaps in part this stemmed from Lemert's emphasis on personal disabilities, in his latter-day revision of the social pathology approach (Lemert, 1951).

It is quite as logical within the Lemert framework to study the collective definition of deviant categories as it is to study interpersonal reactions (Schur, 1971: 11–13, 18–19). Becker suggested early that the creation of rules involves political conflict between "moral entrepreneurs" and other groups (Becker, 1963: 147–155). He also pointed to the importance of a second type of moral entrepreneur, the rule enforcers (Becker, 1963: 155–163). Labeling analysts have given some attention to the activities of control organizations, usually with an eye towards the development of the deviant identity, but sometimes including observations about feedback effects on the definition of the categories. A number of significant contributions to understanding collective definition and redefinition have come from outside the ranks of specialists in deviant behavior.

A frequent synonym for the labeling perspective has been "societal response," suggesting concern for the collective definition of deviant categories as well as the labeling of persons (Gibbs, 1966: 12). Recently appeals for greater stress on collective definition have become more frequent and more urgent. Schur calls this a "crucial" emphasis, while maintaining that labeling analysis on different levels is necessary (Schur, 1969: 312–13; 1971: 18–19). Another statement is that deviant labels have usually been taken for granted, so that the processes of constructing and reconstructing them are slighted (Filstead, 1972: 3). How does it happen, for example, that society is preoccupied at one time and place with the label "drinker," at another with "heavy drinker," and at still another with "alcoholic"?

This appeal has sometimes been stated as a call for a social control approach to deviance (Cohen, 1971: 17–18; Davis, 1972: 452–453), and increasingly it has been put in terms of conflict theory. Conflict models involve interest groups, ideologies, political power, and bureaucracies for controlling deviants; they are structural and institutional (Davis, 1972: 462–468). Conflict models, it should be noted, exhibit considerable variety along with their common themes.

Types of theory other than conflict models have also been used to illuminate the collective definition of deviance, as the first part of this book demonstrates. It will be apparent that in addition to being macrosociological these approaches are oriented to historical and comparative data. A major limitation of the interactionist perspective has often been said to be that its focus on deviant behavior is too narrow in time and space, yet a basic idea in the labeling approach is that deviance is relative to the definitions of society (Schur, 1971: 14). The interactionist approach evidently must be complemented by social control perspectives in order to bring out the full implications of the idea of the relativity of labeling.

References

BECKER, HOWARD S.
    1963   Outsiders. New York: The Free Press.
    1967   "Whose Side Are We On?" Social Problems 14 (Winter): 239–247.
    1973   Outsiders (revised edition). New York: The Free Press.
BITTNER, EGON
    1967   "The Police on Skid Row: A Study of Peace Keeping," American Sociological Review 32 (October): 699–715.
CICOUREL, AARON V.
    1968   The Social Organization of Juvenile Justice. New York: John Wiley & Sons, Inc.
CLINARD, MARSHALL B.
    1964   Anomie and Deviant Behavior: A Discussion and Critique. New York: The Free Press.
COHEN, STANLEY
    1971   Images of Deviance. Baltimore: Penguin Books, Inc.
DAVIS, F. JAMES
    1970   Social Problems: Enduring Major Issues and Social Change. New York: The Free Press.
DAVIS, NANETTE J.
    1972   "Labeling Theory in Deviance Research: A Critique and Reconsideration," The Sociological Quarterly 13 (Autumn): 447–474.
DOUGLAS, JACK
    1967   The Social Meanings of Suicide. Princeton, N.J.: Princeton University Press.
ERIKSON, KAI T.
    1962   "Notes on the Sociology of Deviance," Social Problems 9 (Spring): 308.

FILSTEAD, WILLIAM J.
  1972   An Introduction to Deviance: Readings in the Process of Making Deviants. Chicago: Markham Publishing Co.
GIBBS, JACK P.
  1966   "Conceptions of Deviant Behavior: The Old and the New," Pacific Sociological Review 9, 1 (Spring): 9–14.
KITSUSE, JOHN I.
  1962   "Societal Reaction to Deviant Behavior: Problems of Theory and Method," Social Problems 9 (Winter): 247–256.
LEMERT, EDWIN M.
  1951   Social Pathology. New York: McGraw-Hill Book Co., Inc.
MANNHEIM, KARL
  1946   Ideology and Utopia. New York: Harcourt, Brace and Co.
  1956   Essays on the Sociology of Culture. London: Routledge and Kegan Paul Ltd.
MATZA, DAVID
  1964   Delinquency and Drift. New York: John Wiley & Sons, Inc.
RUBINGTON, EARL, and MARTIN S. WEINBERG
  1973   Deviance: The Interactionist Perspective (second edition). New York: The Macmillan Co.
SCHUR, EDWIN M.
  1969   "Reactions to Deviance: A Critical Assessment," American Journal of Sociology 75, 3 (November): 309–322.
  1971   Labeling Deviant Behavior: Its Sociological Implications. New York: Harper & Row.
SHORT, JAMES F., and FRED L. STRODTBECK
  1965   Group Process and Gang Delinquency. Chicago: University of Chicago Press.
SUDNOW, DAVID
  1965   "Normal Crimes: Sociological Features of the Penal Code in a Public Defender Office," Social Problems 12 (Winter): 255–276.
TAYLOR, IAN, PAUL WALTON, and JOCK YOUNG
  1973   The New Criminology: For a Social Theory of Deviance. London and Boston: Routledge and Kegan Paul.
THIO, ALEX
  1973   "Class Bias in the Sociology of Deviance," The American Sociologist 8 (February): 1–12.

I

THEORETICAL PERSPECTIVES
ON THE COLLECTIVE
DEFINITION OF DEVIANCE

Introduction

Grand theory (Mills, 1959: 25–49) is after all only metaphor. The theoretical metaphors of society range from society as a machine to society as a drama. Each theory utilizes its dominant metaphor in the formulation of concepts. For instance, society as drama employs actor, role, stage, and setting as concepts. Theory then organizes our conceptions of reality and in this sense explains reality.

In this section we are dealing with divergent explanations of the collective attempt to define, redefine, or undefine behavior as deviant. These explanations are not theories in the positivistic sense of the term, that is, a set of interrelated propositions amenable to the derivation of hypotheses. They are perhaps better described as theoretical orientations (Merton, 1957: 87–89).

The theoretical orientations included here are variously focused on the form assumed by the collective act of defining an individual or group as deviant, on the origins and derivation of the collective definitions themselves, or on the larger consequences of the application of these definitions. The authors of the articles attempt to answer the question, "What is the meaning of the fact that collectivities arrive at conceptions of the deviant and definitions of deviant behavior and then apply them to certain individuals and groups?"

Erikson (1966) assesses the meaning of this process to be the establishment of cultural boundaries for a community. These boundaries are applied social rules. Rules need to be tested, measured, and tempered in the heat of everyday interaction; they can move only from the abstract to the concrete in their varied application. Together the vast array of social rules and the values underlying them comprise a community's identity. Finally, in the act of labeling rule-violators as deviant the community becomes solidary, achieving a temporary unity.

Gusfield (1963) holds that the creation of rules often implies the advocacy of one group's morality and life-style at the expense of another's. From his perspective the creation of a new law is tantamount to a cultural victory, whereby the increased prestige of the victor implies the decreased prestige of the loser. The formulation of rules then becomes an arena for status politics or the competition for social honor.

Szasz (1970b) provocatively registers the collective act of labeling as one of ritualistic scapegoating. In labeling the deviant, members of a community expel evil from their midst, thereby assuring the inclusion of good. Sin, guilt, and suffering are transferred to a scapegoat who bears this burden, willingly

2

or unwillingly, for the rest of the community. Labeling the other as deviant allows for the institutionalized release of emotions and reassertion of the good.

Quinney (1969) is more concerned in his piece with the origins of laws, especially criminal laws, than with the application of such laws. He maintains that laws reflect the interests of specialized groups rather than a broad consensus. The most powerful groups succeed in writing their interests into law. Thus, in the application of a criminal definition, some powerful interest group is the beneficiary. Ultimately society coalesces about this widespread struggle for power.

Davis, too, is concerned with the origin of rules, but also with their maintenance or change. He identifies cognitive beliefs and value beliefs as variables critical to understanding an individual's or group's satisfaction or dissatisfaction with an extant norm. When the cognitive beliefs and value beliefs are congruent, there is either strong support of or opposition to the existing norm. But a group's commitment or opposition to the norm in question can have significant influence only when it is powerful. Therefore, when powerful interest groups are supportive of a new norm, change will most likely occur; when powerful interest groups are supportive of the established norm, it will be maintained.

Before embarking upon a more detailed analysis of the theoretical orientations in this section, let us make several sets of distinctions to further such explication. The first involves comparing order, conflict, and pluralistic models of society; the second entails distinguishing among instrumental, expressive, and symbolic dimensions of human action.

Differential metaphysical assumptions about the nature of man and of society have often been expressed, albeit not always with conscious reflection, in the debate over two apparently polar models of society. One is variously referred to as an order, consensus, functionalist, integrationist, or system approach; the other as a conflict, coercion, dialectic, or power-conflict approach.

The *order* model focuses on that which is ordered, patterned, or static in social relations and in society. Most order theories have stressed individual agreement upon values, norms, and beliefs (consensus) as the ultimate basis of integration within society. Commonly held beliefs, values, and norms unite the citizenry and result in a legitimation of existing structures of authority. Other order theories have emphasized the co-orientation of group members (Scheff, 1967: 32–34). From this perspective the group's ability to mold the attitudes and beliefs of its members receives major attention. However, both the individual agreement and co-orientation approaches to consensus contain the image of society as a "natural boundary-maintaining system of action" (Horton, 1966: 705) or as a transcendent organism which acts to preserve its members (institutions). Hence, the order model of society stresses the power of society to impose values, beliefs, norms, and status-roles upon individuals, resulting in a more or less cultural uniformity. The order approach, then, because of a lack of emphasis tends to minimize change, especially revolutionary change. In terms of formal sociological schools of thought, functionalism and symbolic interactionism are order-oriented.

The conflict approach, on the other hand, has a primary interest in conflict, change, unanticipated consequences of human action, contradiction, irony, and paradox in social relations. A *conflict* model may underscore class conflict over the control of economic production, or the conflict among classes and among individuals within classes over political authority, or the inevitable conflict between the individual and the larger society. The unifying perspective for the different conflict approaches is the corrosive effect social structure has upon certain social classes and upon the individual.

The conflict model directs our attention to society as subjective reality, that is, "society as the extension of man and the indwellling of man" (Horton, 1966: 705). In this view society is not truly transcendent; it only appears so because men have abdicated their "authorship of the human world" (Berger and Luckmann, 1967: 89). Thus man creates his own social reality, but it in turn comes to be perceived as objective and possessing an existence over and beyond man. Focusing upon society as subjective reality then maximizes the possibility for revolutionary change, for man is reminded of his responsibility and freedom to make of society what he would. A specific conflict approach is often consciously linked to Marxist sociology, to existentialist sociology, or to the work of C. Wright Mills (1956) or Ralf Dahrendorf (1958).

A third model of society sometimes mentioned appears to be intermediate between the polar types of order and conflict. The *pluralistic* model has its historical and intellectual origins in utilitarianism, which contained certain assumptions about inexorable human progress through evolutionary process, a process fraught with conflict. The pluralistic model's seminal idea is that of balance (Mills, 1956: 242–268). Political and economic equilibrium or balance is achieved through the competition of interests regulated by as few legal restraints as possible. Thus, competition for power and economic goods and services was inherently self-regulating because it was assumed that the interest groups in society were independent and relatively equal in actuality or at least before the law. Law was seen as formulated for the common good; it represented pluralistic interests and could even be used to eliminate gross inequalities of wealth, station, and power. Implicit in the amalgam of pluralistic assumptions was the view that there existed a common commitment to capitalistic-democratic sentiments and ideals expressed in law and capable of uniting the diverse interest groups. Although the pluralistic model usually asserts the existence of a plethora of values, beliefs, subcultures, and interest groups, it nevertheless recognizes some bond among competitors, be it a commitment to work within the system or a desire to adhere to the rules of the game. Social change then becomes social reform, a perfecting of the given system. The pluralistic model of society is assumed by some functionalists and by others who, while not usually identifying themselves with a formal school of thought, consider themselves "conflict" theorists (Taylor, Walton, and Young, 1973: 237–267).

Advocates of order and pluralistic approaches, sensitive to the criticism of conflict theorists, have pointed out that their models can deal with conflict and change as central and not merely subsidiary themes (Goode, 1973: 64–94). Thus, some (Durkheim, 1960; Simmel, 1955; Coser, 1956; van den Berghe, 1963) have stressed the functions social conflict can serve for groups and for the larger society. As Durkheim (1960: 102) observed, the individual who violates a criminal law can become the means of making solidary those who repudiate and denounce his action as criminal. Without deviance or sin there could be no normalcy or virtue; the one defines the other.

Paradoxically, many conflict theorists reveal a quest for the reduction or elimination of conflict. The young Karl Marx had an eschatological vision of a classless utopian soceity—a perfectly ordered society. C. Wright Mills anticipated that the amelioration of social institutions could rectify the pathology of a polarized mass society ruled by a power elite. Ralf Dahrendorf viewed pluralistic democratic societies as capable of minimizing conflict over political authority. Only some of the doggedly despairing existentialists cling to a belief in conflict as inevitable and an end in itself. For them there is an inevitable conflict between human growth and freedom and society's insatiable thirst for conformity. In actuality all models of society are blueprints of order, either confirming and ideologically justifying the present social order or attacking and compensating for the present order by advocating a new and future order (Rieff, 1973: 68). In this special sense the existentialist variety of the conflict model of society is not a model of society or social order at all but a model of anti-society, anti-social order—a call to the anarchy of individual (situational) morality.

Some sociologists (Horowitz, 1962; van den Berghe, 1963; Williams, Jr., 1966) have perceived the issue of divergent models of society as one involving conceptions of different existing social processes—consensus or co-orientation and conflict or coercion—capable of being synthesized into a larger body of theoretical propositions. Horton (1966: 705–706), on the other hand, has articulated the differences between the two processes by embodying them in polar ideal types of societies, each characterized by one or the other process. These models of societies, especially when incorporated into analysis of social problems and deviant behavior, contain ideological and normative assumptions about the nature of man and society. Thus, the order model of society conceives the causes of deviant behavior as anomie, social disorganization, a failure of the system to control its members (conservative version) or to provide opportunities for its members to adjust (liberal version). Key themes in this approach are conformity and adjustment.

The conflict model sees deviant behavior either as the result of an alienation from self which individuals suffer at the hands of an unequal, acquisitive, and exploitive society or as an attempt to surmount existing social arrangements.

For Horton, then, the order model of society is conservative in its emphasis on adjusting the individual to the system; the pluralistic model (a variant of the order model) liberal in its suggestions for modification of the system so that individual adjustment can better occur; and the conflict model radical in its avowal of an overturning of the system in the interest of individual growth and autonomy and/or a new social order.

Therefore, theoretical statements on the collective definition of deviance can be categorized as order, pluralistic, or conflict in their assumptions. As well, the theoretical orientations can be typed by which dimension of human action they emphasize.

Gusfield (1963), following the lead of Kenneth Burke (1969), distinguished the symbolic function of human action from its instrumental and expressive functions. Instrumental action is action which becomes the means to an end; it serves to realize a desired goal. The legislature passes a new criminal law in order to prevent undesired behavior. Expressive action is action whose basic motivation is the completion of an emotion—the release of emotional stress or the satisfaction of emotional needs. It is self-contained action, yet perhaps not readily recognizable as such. The expression of strong feelings may be obvious in a temper tantrum but less so in a reaction formation. The passage of a new criminal law may be the vehicle for the expression of contempt, hatred, or envy toward a group of whom this now illegal behavior is thought characteristic. Instrumental action is sometimes conceived of as rational while expressive action is thought to be irrational (Gusfield, 1963: 179).

Symbolic acts, according to Gusfield (1963: 170), are "forms of rhetoric, functioning to organize the perceptions, attitudes and feelings of observers." Symbolic action attempts to pursuade. The performance of a religious ceremony is symbolic activity whereby adherence to religious belief is reaffirmed. The passage of a new criminal law can be seen as an act symbolizing the superiority of one type of morality and life-style over another.

Symbolic action can be manifestly instrumental when symbols are used to achieve some predetermined end. For instance, Hitler used the lyrics and music of certain patriotic songs to insure the people's submission to his grand scheme of conquest (Warren, 1972: 72–78). In like manner expressive action can also be instrumental as when, upon doctor's orders, a man plays golf in order to let go and to release his pent-up emotions.

Social movements to define what is good and evil, normal and deviant, involve all three forms of action (Gusfield, 1963: 180). It becomes a matter of determining which dimension is dominant in a particular movement. Each theoretical orientation in this section can be classified by the model of society it assumes and by which dimension of human action it emphasizes. Looking at the two sets of distinctions concomitantly, we obtain the following set of possibilities:

Theories of the Collective Definition of Deviance by Image of Society and Dimension of Action

Dimension of Action	Image of Society		
	ORDER	PLURALISM	CONFLICT
Instrumental	1	2	3
Expressive	4	5	6
Symbolic	7	8	9

Erikson's approach to the problem of order in society is consensual. He stresses community as expressed in common culture and values. The social classes are held together by reciprocal relationships as well as by similar beliefs. Even the deviant accepts the values of the culture at the same time as he violates community norms. As Erikson (1966: 20) has observed, "The thief and his victims share a common respect for the value of property; the heretic and the inquisitor speak much the same language and are keyed to the same religious mysteries; the traitor and the patriot act in reference to the same political institutions, often use the same methods, and for that matter are sometimes the same person."

Erikson draws our attention to both the instrumental and symbolic aspects of the collective definition of deviance. Defining what is and who are deviant persuades community members what their collective identity is and in what they believe. It helps to establish symbolic boundaries of good and evil, in part through public ceremonies in which the alleged rule-breaker is degraded to the status of deviant (Erikson, 1966: 15–23). Yet at the same time the collective definition of deviance functions to create a solidary community; society needs deviance. Moreover, there are occasions, as with the theory of general deterrence, when it is consciously intended that the moral unification of the community be accomplished through the public punishment of the deviant.

Gusfield assumes a pluralistic orientation in his analysis of the American temperance movement. He acknowledges the conflict of interest among economic classes but is more concerned with status politics, the competition between status collectivities for prestige, honor, and superiority of life style. Gusfield (1963: 183–184), however, acknowledges the fragility of this consensus:

> It is the issue of morals and style, of religious beliefs and ethnic loyalties which searchers for political harmony most often implore be kept out of politics. Such pleas are recognition of the intensity with which status loyalties prevent the operation of the culture of bargaining, compromise, and detached trading so necessary for a pluralistic politics. The introduction of status issues cuts deeply at the sources of political consensus by converting political questions into moral ones.

Gusfield avowedly stresses the symbolic character of status infighting, in that the issues are not just instrumental ones of power and economic interest but more often a question of whose morality and life-style gains ascendency. He observes that social movements such as the American temperance movement, in securing the passage of the Volstead Act, were less interested in preventing drinking (instrumental concern) than in asserting the cultural superiority of a native, Protestant, rural, nondrinking life-style over the immigrant, Catholic, urban, drinking life-style (symbolic concern).

An existentialist conflict approach is offered by Thomas Szasz, who regards the collective act of defining deviance as one of ritualistic scapegoating. Basic to modern social existence is the conflict between the state (and its institutions) and the individual (Szasz; 1970a: 1–11). Szasz (1970b: 63) comments, "The fundamental conflicts in human life are not between competing ideas, one 'true' and the other 'false'—but rather between those who hold power and use it to oppress others, and those who are oppressed by power and seek to free themselves of it." Those in power, whether they be priest, politician, or psychiatrist, impose a morality upon individuals in the interest of social control. Psychiatric control is called rehabilitation, and the "scientific" concepts of mental health and mental illness help to conceal the fact that the psychiatrist functions as an arm of the state in imposing a form of morality upon individuals. This morality is otherwise known as adjustment, conformity, or happiness—and professionally as mental health.

The concept of ritualistic scapegoating combines both symbolic and expressive dimensions of human action. Scapegoating is an expressive act in which others heap their guilt, anxiety, hatred, and sins upon an object or person in order to purify themselves. The scapegoat carries the burden for the rest of the community. However, the scapegoat also stands symbolically for what is evil. Moreover, communities devise regular procedures or ceremonies for the handling of the scapegoat. If scapegoating provides for the expression of emotions, it occurs within a ritualistic framework. For example, the civil commitment proceedings for the mentally ill are seen by Szasz as rites for the expulsion of evil.

Szasz also focuses on the functions the collective definition of deviance serves for the larger society, in much the same manner Erikson does in his article. Defining deviance is instrumental in realizing group solidarity. Szasz's view, then, bridges all three dimensions of human action.

Quinney[1] assumes a pluralistic model of society and stresses the instrumentality of human action. Attempts to create law, or any rule for that matter, center about the particular interests of groups and subcultures competing for power. Law then does not reflect the common good but rather the special interests of dominant groups. These "interests" are never precisely defined, but they appear to be material goods and services. Quinney's analysis of the conflict between interest groups is subsumed under a pluralistic umbrella since, as Taylor *et al.* (1973: 265) observe, despite the prevalence of interest-ridden law, Quinney still looks to "the law as an agency for the protection of rights, liberties, and interests." Quinney, then, observes a pluralistic democracy failing in reality but still possible if only law can be made to protect and not oppress.

Davis' perspective is likewise pluralistic. He suggests that compromise between interest groups may be facilitated through the formation of coalitions and by appeals to common value commitments. Therefore the numerous conflicts among interest groups over power, rules, and values are not irreconcilable. Collective efforts to maintain or change existing law are perceived to be largely instrumental but partly expressive acts; that is, they are attempts to realize both group values and what are regarded as the correct factual beliefs. However, insofar as values are regarded as entities that one adheres to in both an affective and an instrumental (cognitive) manner, then the collective attempt to legislate becomes a vehicle for the expression of values as well as for their realization through social control mechanisms.

This completes our analysis of the theoretical orientations in this section. However, in terms of the previous distinctions made between models of society and dimensions of human action, no theory in this section both assumes

[1] Quinney has recently abandoned this earlier theoretical approach of his in favor of a neo-Marxist conflict perspective. See Richard Quinney, *A Critique of Legal Order: Crime Control in Capitalist Society* (Boston: Little, Brown, 1974); also Richard Quinney (ed.), *Criminal Justice in America: A Critical Understanding* (Boston: Little, Brown, 1974).

an order or pluralistic model of society and also stresses expressive action in its analysis of the collective definition of deviance. The work of Richard Hofstadter (1955a: 16–17; 1955b: 33–35) and Seymour Martin Lipset (1955: 166–234), as mentioned by Gusfield (1963: 17–19, 178–180), are illustrative of this position. Both Hofstadter and Lipset have employed a pluralistic model of society in their interpretation of various social movements generated by status politics. Such movements, e.g., the Communist "witch-hunts" of the 1950's, which involve redefinitions of deviance (Communist sympathizer) are characterized as irrational because they become the public outlet for the expression of hatred and envy through the scapegoating of opposing groups.

References

BERGER, PETER, and THOMAS LUCKMANN
    1967   The Social Construction of Reality. Garden City, N.Y.: Doubleday (Anchor Book).
BURKE, KENNETH
    1969   A Rhetoric of Motives. Berkeley and Los Angeles: University of California Press.
COSER, LEWIS
    1956   The Functions of Social Conflict. Glencoe, Ill.: The Free Press.
DAHRENDORF, RALF
    1959   Class and Class Conflict in Industrial Society. Stanford, Cal.: Stanford University Press.
DURKHEIM, EMILE
    1960   The Division of Labor in Society. Glencoe, Ill.: The Free Press.
ERIKSON, KAI T.
    1966   Wayward Puritans. New York: Wiley.
GOODE, WILLIAM
    1973   Explorations in Social Theory. New York: Oxford University Press.
GUSFIELD, JOSEPH
    1963   Symbolic Crusade. Urbana, Ill.: The University of Illinois Press.
HOFSTADTER, RICHARD
    1955a   The Age of Reform. New York: Vintage Books.
    1955b   "The Pseudo-Conservative Revolt." Pp. 33–55 in Daniel Bell (ed.), The New American Right. New York: Criterion Books.
HOROWITZ, IRVING LOUIS
    1962   "Consensus, Conflict, and Cooperation: A Sociological Inventory." Social Forces 41: 177–188.
HORTON, JOHN
    1966   "Order and Conflict Theories of Social Problems as Competing Ideologies." American Journal of Sociology 71: 701–713.
LIPSET, SEYMOUR MARTIN
    1955   "The Sources of the Radical Right." Pp. 166–234 in Daniel Bell (ed.), The New American Right. New York: Criterion Books.

MERTON, ROBERT K.
  1957   Social Theory and Social Structure. Glencoe, Ill.: The Free Press.
MILLS, C. WRIGHT
  1956   The Power Elite. New York: Oxford University Press
  1967   The Sociological Imagination. New York: Oxford University Press.
QUINNEY, RICHARD
  1974   A Critique of Legal Order. Boston: Little, Brown.
QUINNEY, RICHARD (ed.)
  1969   Crime and Justice in Society. Boston: Little, Brown.
  1974   Criminal Justice in America. Boston: Little, Brown.
RIEFF, PHILIP
  1973   Fellow Teachers. New York: Harper and Row.
SCHEFF, THOMAS
  1967   "Toward a Sociological Model of Consensus." American Journal
         of Sociology 32: 32–46.
SCHNEIDER, LOUIS
  1971   "Dialectic in Sociology." American Sociological Review 36: 667–678.
SIMMEL, GEORG
  1955   Conflict and the Web of Group Affiliations. Glencoe, Ill.: The Free
         Press.
SZASZ, THOMAS
  1970a Ideology and Insanity. Garden City, N.Y.: Doubleday (Anchor
         Book).
  1970b The Manufacture of Madness. New York: Dell (Delta Book).
TAYLOR, IAN, JACK YOUNG, and PAUL WALTON
  1973   The New Criminology. London: Routledge, Kegan Paul.
VAN DEN BERGHE, PIERRE L.
  1963   "Dialectic and Functionalism." American Sociological Review 28:
         695–705.
WARREN, ROLAND L.
  1972   "The Nazi Use of Music as an Instrument of Social Control." Pp.
         72–78 in R. Serge Denisoff and Richard A. Peterson (eds.), The
         Sounds of Social Change. Chicago: Rand McNally.
WILLIAMS, JR., ROBIN M.
  1966   "Some Further Comments on Chronic Controversies." American
         Journal of Sociology 71: 717–721.

KAI T. ERIKSON

On the Sociology of Deviance

In 1895 Emile Durkheim wrote a book called *The Rules of Sociological Method* which was intended as a working manual for persons interested in the systematic study of society. One of the most important themes of Durkheim's work was that sociologists should formulate a new set of criteria for distinguishing between "normal" and "pathological" elements in the life of a society. Behavior which looks abnormal to the psychiatrist or the judge, he suggested, does not always look abnormal when viewed through the special lens of the sociologist; and thus students of the new science should be careful to understand that even the most aberrant forms of individual behavior may still be considered normal from this broader point of view. To illustrate his argument, Durkheim made the surprising observation that crime was really a natural kind of social activity, "an integral part of all healthy societies."[1]

Durkheim's interest in this subject had been expressed several years before when *The Division of Labor in Society* was first published.[2] In that important book, he had suggested that crime (and by extension other forms of deviation) may actually perform a needed service to society by drawing people together in a common posture of anger and indignation. The deviant individual violates rules of conduct which the rest of the community holds in high respect; and when these people come together to express their outrage over the offense and to bear witness against the offender, they develop a tighter bond of solidarity than existed earlier. The excitement generated by the crime, in other words, quickens the tempo of interaction in the group and creates a climate in which the private sentiments of many persons are fused together into a common sense of morality.

> Crime brings together upright consciences and concentrates them. We have only to notice what happens, particularly in a small town, when some moral

[1] Emile Durkheim, *The Rules of Sociological Method,* trans. S. A. Solovay and J. H. Mueller (Glencoe, Ill.: The Free Press, 1958), p. 67

[2] Emile Durkheim, *The Division of Labor in Society,* trans. George Simpson (Glencoe, Ill.: The Free Press, 1960).

Source: Kai T. Erikson, "On the Sociology of Deviance," pp. 3–19 in *Wayward Puritans* (New York: John Wiley & Sons, Inc., 1966). Copyright © 1966 by John Wiley & Sons, Inc., Publishers. Reprinted by permission of John Wiley & Sons, Inc.

11

scandal has just been committed. They stop each other on the street, they visit each other, they seek to come together to talk of the event and to wax indignant in common. From all the similar impressions which are exchanged, for all the temper that gets itself expressed, there emerges a unique temper . . . which is everybody's without being anybody's in particular. That is the public temper.[3]

The deviant act, then, creates a sense of mutuality among the people of a community by supplying a focus for group feeling. Like a war, a flood, or some other emergency, deviance makes people more alert to the interests they share in common and draws attention to those values which constitute the "collective conscience" of the community. Unless the rhythm of group life is punctuated by occasional moments of deviant behavior, presumably, social organization would be impossible.[4]

This brief argument has been regarded a classic of sociological thinking ever since it was first presented, even though it has not inspired much in the way of empirical work. The purpose of the present chapter is to consider Durkheim's suggestion in terms more congenial to modern social theory and to see if these insights can be translated into useful research hypotheses. The pages to follow may range far afield from the starting point recommended by Durkheim, but they are addressed to the question he originally posed: does it make any sense to assert that deviant forms of behavior are a natural and even beneficial part of social life?

One of the earliest problems the sociologist encounters in his search for a meaningful approach to deviant behavior is that the subject itself does not seem to have any natural boundaries. Like people in any field, sociologists find it convenient to assume that the deviant person is somehow "different" from those of his fellows who manage to conform, but years of research into the problem have not yielded any important evidence as to what, if anything, this difference might be. Investigators have studied the character of the deviant's background, the content of his dreams, the shape of his skull, the substance of his thoughts—yet none of this information has enabled us to draw a clear line between the kind of person who commits deviant acts and the kind of person who does not. Nor can we gain a better perspective on the matter by shifting our attention away from the individual deviant and looking instead at the behavior he enacts. Definitions of deviance vary widely as we range over the various classes found in a single society or across the various cultures into which mankind is divided, and it soon becomes apparent that there are no objective properties which all deviant acts can be said to share in common—even within the confines of a given group. Behavior which qualifies one man for prison may qualify another for sainthood, since the quality of the act itself depends so much on the circumstances under which it was performed and the temper of the audience which witnessed it.

This being the case, many sociologists employ a far simpler tactic in

[3] *Ibid.*, p. 102.
[4] A similar point was later made by George Herbert Mead in his very important paper "The Psychology of Punitive Justice," *American Journal of Sociology*, XXIII (March 1918), pp. 577–602.

their approach to the problem—namely, to let each social group in question provide its own definitions of deviant behavior. In this study, as in others, dealing with the same general subject,[5] the term "deviance" refers to conduct which the people of a group consider so dangerous or embarrassing or irritating that they bring special sanctions to bear against the persons who exhibit it. Deviance is not a property *inherent in* any particular kind of behavior; it is a property *conferred upon* that behavior by the people who come into direct or indirect contact with it. The only way an observer can tell whether or not a given style of behavior is deviant, then, is to learn something about the standards of the audience which responds to it.

This definition may seem a little awkward in practice, but it has the advantage of bringing a neglected issue into proper focus. When the people of a community decide that it is time to "do something" about the conduct of one of their number, they are involved in a highly intricate process. After all, even the worst miscreant in society conforms most of the time, if only in the sense that he uses the correct silver at dinner, stops obediently at traffic lights, or in a hundred other ways respects the ordinary conventions of his group. And if his fellows elect to bring sanctions against him for the occasions when he does misbehave, they are responding to a few deviant details scattered among a vast array of entirely acceptable conduct. The person who appears in a criminal court and is stamped a "thief" may have spent no more than a passing moment engaged in that activity, and the same can be said for many of the people who pass in review before some agency of control and return from the experience with a deviant label of one sort or another. When the community nominates someone to the deviant class, then, it is sifting a few important details out of the stream of behavior he has emitted and is in effect declaring that these details reflect the kind of person he "really" is. In law as well as in public opinion, the fact that someone has committed a felony or has been known to use narcotics can become the major identifying badge of his person: the very expression "he is a thief" or "he is an addict" seems to provide at once a description of his position in society and a profile of his character.

The manner in which a community sifts these telling details out of a person's overall performance, then, is an important part of its social control apparatus. And it is important to notice that the people of a community take a number of factors into account when they pass judgment on one another which are not immediately related to the deviant act itself: whether or not a person will be considered deviant, for instance, has something to do with his social class, his past record as an offender, the amount of remorse he manages to convey, and many similar concerns which take hold in the shifting mood of the community. Perhaps this is not so apparent in cases of serious crime or desperate illness, where the offending act looms so darkly that it obscures most of the other details of the person's life; but in the day-by-day sifting processes which take place throughout society this feature is always present. Some men who drink heavily are called alcoholics and others are not, some men

[5] See particularly the works of Edwin M. Lemert, Howard S. Becker, and John I. Kitsuse.

who behave oddly are committed to hospitals and others are not, some men with no visible means of support are charged with vagrancy and others are not—and the difference between those who earn a deviant title in society and those who go their own way in peace is largely determined by the way in which the community filters out and codes the many details of behavior which come to its attention.

Once the problem is phrased in this manner we can ask: how does a community decide which of these behavioral details are important enough to merit special attention? And why, having made this decision, does it build institutions like prisons and asylums to detain the persons who perform them? The conventional answer to that question, of course, is that a society creates the machinery of control in order to protect itself against the "harmful" effects of deviation, in much the same way that an organism mobilizes its resources to combat an invasion of germs. Yet this simple view of the matter is apt to pose many more problems than it actually settles. As both Emile Durkheim and George Herbert Mead pointed out long ago, it is by no means evident that all acts considered deviant in society are in fact (or even in principle) harmful to group life. It is undoubtedly true that no culture would last long if its members engaged in murder or arson among themselves on any large scale, but there is no real evidence that many other of the activities considered deviant throughout the world (certain dietary prohibitions are a prominent example) have any relationship to the group's survival. In our own day, for instance, we might well ask why prostitution or marihuana smoking or homosexuality are thought to endanger the health of the social order. Perhaps these activities *are* dangerous, but to accept this conclusion without a thoughtful review of the situation is apt to blind us to the important fact that people in every corner of the world manage to survive handsomely while engaged in practices which their neighbors regard as extremely abhorrent. In the absence of any surer footing, then, it is quite reasonable for sociologists to return to the most innocent and yet the most basic question which can be asked about deviation: why does a community assign one form of behavior rather than another to the deviant class?

The following paragraphs will suggest one possible answer to that question.

Human actors are sorted into various kinds of collectivity, ranging from relatively small units such as the nuclear family to relatively large ones such as a nation or culture. One of the most stubborn difficulties in the study of deviation is that the problem is defined differently at each one of these levels: behavior that is considered unseemly within the context of a single family may be entirely acceptable to the community in general, while behavior that attracts severe censure from the members of the community may go altogether unnoticed elsewhere in the culture. People in society, then, must learn to deal separately with deviance at each one of these levels and to distinguish among them in his own daily activity. A man may disinherit his son for conduct that violates old family traditions or ostracize a neighbor for conduct that violates some local custom, but he is not expected to employ either of these standards when he serves as a juror in a court of law. In each of the three situations he is required to use a different set of criteria to decide whether or not the behavior in question exceeds tolerable limits.

In the next few pages we shall be talking about deviant behavior in social units called "communities," but the use of this term does not mean that the argument applies only at that level of organization. In theory, at least, the argument being made here should fit all kinds of human collectivity—families as well as whole cultures, small groups as well as nations—and the term "community" is only being used in this context because it seems particularly convenient.[6]

The people of a community spend most of their lives in close contact with one another, sharing a common sphere of experience which make them feel that they belong to a special "kind" and live in a special "place." In the formal language of sociology, this means that communities are boundary maintaining: each has a specific territory in the world as a whole, not only in the sense that it occupies a defined region of geographical space but also in the sense that it takes over a particular niche in what might be called cultural space and develops its own "ethos" or "way" within that compass. Both of these dimensions of group space, the geographical and the cultural, set the community apart as a special place and provide an important point of reference for its members.

When one describes any system as boundary maintaining, one is saying that it controls the fluctuation of its constituent parts so that the whole retains a limited range of activity, a given pattern of constancy and stability, within the larger environment. A human community can be said to maintain boundaries, then, in the sense that its members tend to confine themselves to a particular radius of activity and to regard any conduct which drifts outside that radius as somehow inappropriate or immoral. Thus the group retains a kind of cultural integrity, a voluntary restriction on its own potential for expansion, beyond that which is strictly required for accommodation to the environment. Human behavior can vary over an enormous range, but each community draws a symbolic set of parentheses around a certain segment of that range and limits its own activities within that narrower zone. These parentheses, so to speak, are the community's boundaries.

Now people who live together in communities cannot relate to one another in any coherent way or even acquire a sense of their own stature as group members unless they learn something about the boundaries of the territory they occupy in social space, if only because they need to sense what lies beyond the margins of the group before they can appreciate the special quality of the experience which takes place within it. Yet how do people learn about the boundaries of their community? And how do they convey this information to the generations which replace them?

To begin with, the only material found in a society for marking boundaries is the behavior of its members—or rather, the networks of interaction which link these members together in regular social relations. And the interactions which do the most effective job of locating and publicizing the group's

---

[6] In fact, the first statement of the general notion presented here was concerned with the study of small groups. See Robert A. Dentler and Kai T. Erikson, "The Functions of Deviance in Groups," *Social Problems*, VII (Fall 1959), pp. 98–107.

outer edges would seem to be those which take place between deviant persons on the one side and official agents of the community on the other. The deviant is a person whose activities have moved outside the margins of the group, and when the community calls him to account for that vagrancy it is making a statement about the nature and placement of its boundaries. It is declaring how much variability and diversity can be tolerated within the group before it begins to lose its distinctive shape, its unique identity. Now there may be other moments in the life of the group which perform a similar service: wars, for instance, can publicize a group's boundaries by drawing attention to the line separating the group from an adversary, and certain kinds of religious ritual, dance ceremony, and other traditional pageantry can dramatize the difference between "we' and "they" by portraying a symbolic encounter between the two. But on the whole, members of a community inform one another about the placement of their boundaries by participating in the confrontations which occur when persons who venture out to the edges of the group are met by policing agents whose special business it is to guard the cultural integrity of the community. Whether these confrontations take the form of criminal trials, excommunication hearings, courts-martial, or even psychiatric case conferences, they act as boundary-maintaining devices in the sense that they demonstrate to whatever audience is concerned where the line is drawn between behavior that belongs in the special universe of the group and behavior that does not. In general, this kind of information is not easily relayed by the straightforward use of language. Most readers of this paragraph, for instance, have a fairly clear idea of the line separating theft from more legitimate forms of commerce, but few of them have ever seen a published statute describing these differences. More likely than not, our information on the subject has been drawn from publicized instances in which the relevant laws were applied—and for that matter, the law itself is largely a collection of past cases and decisions, a synthesis of the various confrontations which have occurred in the life of the legal order.

It may be important to note in this connection that confrontations between deviant offenders and the agents of control have always attracted a good deal of public attention. In our own past, the trial and punishment of offenders were staged in the market place and afforded the crowd a chance to participate in a direct, active way. Today, of course, we no longer parade deviants in the town square or expose them to the carnival atmosphere of a Tyburn, but it is interesting that the "reform" which brought about this change in penal practice coincided almost exactly with the development of newspapers as a medium of mass information. Perhaps this is no more than an accident of history, but it is nonetheless true that newspapers (and now radio and television) offer much the same kind of entertainment as public hangings or a Sunday visit to the local gaol. A considerable portion of what we call "news" is devoted to reports about deviant behavior and its consequences, and it is no simple matter to explain why these items should be considered newsworthy or why they should command the extraordinary attention they do. Perhaps they appeal to a number of psychological perversities among the mass audience, as commentators have suggested, but at the same time they constitute one of our main sources of information about the normative outlines of society. In a figurative sense, at least, morality and immorality meet at the public scaffold, and it is during this meeting that the line between them is drawn.

Boundaries are never a fixed property of any community. They are always shifting as the people of the group find new ways to define the outer limits of their universe, new ways to position themselves on the larger cultural map. Sometimes changes occur within the structure of the group which require its members to make a new survey or their territory—a change of leadership, a shift of mood. Sometimes changes occur in the surrounding environment, altering the background against which the people of the group have measured their own uniqueness. And always, new generations are moving in to take their turn guarding old institutions and need to be informed about the contours of the world they are inheriting. Thus single encounters between the deviant and his community are only fragments of an ongoing social process. Like an article of common law, boundaries remain a meaningful point of reference only so long as they are repeatedly tested by persons on the fringes of the group and repeatedly defended by persons chosen to represent the group's inner morality. Each time the community moves to censure some act of deviation, then, and convenes a formal ceremony to deal with the responsible offender, it sharpens the authority of the violated norm and restates where the boundaries of the group are located.

For these reasons, deviant behavior is not a simple kind of leakage which occurs when the machinery of society is in poor working order, but may be, in controlled quantities, an important condition for preserving the stability of social life. Deviant forms of behavior, by marking the outer edges of group life, give the inner structure its special character and thus supply the framework within which the people of the group develop an orderly sense of their own cultural identity. Perhaps this is what Aldous Huxley had in mind when he wrote:

> Now tidiness is undeniably good—but a good of which it is easily possible to have too much and at too high a price. . . . The good life can only be lived in a society in which tidiness is preached and practised, but not too fanatically, and where efficiency is always haloed, as it were, by a tolerated margin of mess.[7]

This raises a delicate theoretical issue. If we grant that human groups often derive benefits from deviant behavior, can we then assume that they are organized in such a way as to promote this resource? Can we assume, in other words, that forces operate in the social structure to recruit offenders and to commit them to long periods of service in the deviant ranks? This is not a question which can be answered with our present store of empirical data, but one observation can be made which gives the question an interesting perspective—namely, that deviant forms of conduct often seem to derive nourishment from the very agencies devised to inhibit them. Indeed, the agencies built by

[7] Aldous Huxley, *Prisons: The "Carceri" Etchings by Piranesi* (London: The Trianon Press, 1949), p. 13.

society for preventing deviance are often so poorly equipped for the task that we might well ask why this is regarded as their "real" function in the first place.

It is by now a thoroughly familiar argument that many of the institutions designed to discourage deviant behavior actually operate in such a way as to perpetuate it. For one thing, prisons, hospitals, and other similar agencies provide aid and shelter to large numbers of deviant persons, sometimes giving them a certain advantage in the competition for social resources. But beyond this, such institutions gather marginal people into tightly segregated groups, give them an opportunity to teach one another the skills and attitudes of a deviant career, and even provoke them into using these skills by reinforcing their sense of alienation from the rest of society.[8] Nor is this observation a modern one:

> The misery suffered in gaols is not half their evil; they are filled with every sort of corruption that poverty and wickedness can generate; with all the shameless and profligate enormities that can be produced by the impudence of ignominy, the rage of want, and the malignity of dispair. In a prison the check of the public eye is removed; and the power of the law is spent. There are few fears, there are no blushes. The lewd inflame the more modest; the audacious harden the timid. Everyone fortifies himself as he can against his own remaining sensibility; endeavoring to practise on others the arts that are practised on himself; and to gain the applause of his worst associates by imitating their manners.[9]

These lines, written almost two centuries ago, are a harsh indictment of prisons, but many of the conditions they describe continue to be reported in even the most modern studies of prison life. Looking at the matter from a long-range historical perspective, it is fair to conclude that prisons have done a conspicuously poor job of reforming the convicts placed in their custody; but the very consistency of this failure may have a peculiar logic of its own. Perhaps we find it difficult to change the worst of our penal practices because we *expect* the prison to harden the inmate's commitment to deviant forms of behavior and draw him more deeply into the deviant ranks. On the whole, we are a people who do not really expect deviants to change very much as they are processed through the control agencies we provide for them, and we are often reluctant to devote much of the community's resources to the job of rehabilitation. In this sense, the prison which graduates long rows of accomplished criminals (or, for that matter, the state asylum which stores its most severe cases away in some back ward) may do serious violence to the aims of its founders, but it does very little violence to the expectations of the population it serves.

[8] For a good description of this process in the modern prison, see Gresham Sykes, *The Society of Captives* (Princeton, N.J.: Princeton University Press, 1958). For discussions of similar problems in two different kinds of mental hospital, see Erving Goffman, *Asylums* (New York: Bobbs-Merrill, 1962) and Kai T. Erikson, "Patient Role and Social Uncertainty: A Dilemma of the Mentally Ill," *Psychiatry*, XX (August 1957), pp. 263–274.

[9] Written by "a celebrated" but not otherwise identified author (perhaps Henry Fielding) and quoted in John Howard, *The State of the Prisons*, London, 1777 (London: J. M. Dent and Sons, 1929), p. 10.

These expectations, moreover, are found in every corner of society and constitute an important part of the climate in which we deal with deviant forms of behavior.

To begin with, the community's decision to bring deviant sanctions against one of its members is not a simple act of censure. It is an intricate rite of transition, at once moving the individual out of his ordinary place in society and transferring him into a special deviant position.[10] The ceremonies which mark this change of status, generally, have a number of related phases. They supply a formal stage on which the deviant and his community can confront one another (as in the criminal trial); they make an announcement about the nature of his deviancy (a verdict or diagnosis, for example); and they place him in a particular role which is thought to neutralize the harmful effects of his misconduct (like the role of prisoner or patient). These commitment ceremonies tend to be occasions of wide public interest and ordinarily take place in a highly dramatic setting.[11] Perhaps the most obvious example of a commitment ceremony is the criminal trial, with its elaborate formality and exaggerated ritual, but more modest equivalents can be found wherever procedures are set up to judge whether or not someone is legitimately deviant.

Now an important feature of these ceremonies in our own culture is that they are almost irreversible. Most provisional roles conferred by society—those of the student or conscripted soldier, for example—include some kind of terminal ceremony to mark the individual's movement back out of the role once its temporary advantages have been exhausted. But the roles allotted the deviant seldom make allowance for this type of passage. He is ushered into the deviant position by a decisive and often dramatic ceremony, yet is retired from it with scarcely a word of public notice. And as a result, the deviant often returns home with no proper license to resume a normal life in the community. Nothing has happened to cancel out the stigmas imposed upon him by earlier commitment ceremonies; nothing has happened to revoke the verdict or diagnosis pronounced upon him at that time. It should not be surprising, then, that the people of the community are apt to greet the returning deviant with a considerable degree of apprehension and distrust, for in a very real sense they are not at all sure who he is.

A circularity is thus set into motion which has all the earmarks of a "self-fulfilling prophesy," to use Merton's fine phrase. On the one hand, it seems quite obvious that the community's apprehensions help reduce whatever chances the deviant might otherwise have had for a successful return home. Yet at the same time, everyday experience seems to show that these suspicions are wholly reasonable, for it is a well-known and highly publicized fact that many if not most ex-convicts return to crime after leaving prison and that large numbers of mental patients require further treatment after an initial hospitalization. The common feeling that deviant persons never really change,

[10] The classic description of this process as it applies to the medical patient is found in Talcott Parsons, *The Social System* (Glencoe, Ill.: The Free Press, 1951).
[11] See Harold Garfinkel, "Successful Degradation Ceremonies," *American Journal of Sociology*, LXI (January 1956), pp. 420–424.

then, may derive from a faulty premise; but the feeling is expressed so frequently and with such conviction that it eventually creates the facts which later "prove" it to be correct. If the returning deviant encounters this circularity often enough, it is quite understandable that he, too, may begin to wonder whether he has fully graduated from the deviant role, and he may respond to the uncertainty by resuming some kind of deviant activity. In many respects, this may be the only way for the individual and his community to agree what kind of person he is.

Moreover this prophesy is found in the official policies of even the most responsible agencies of control. Police departments could not operate with any real effectiveness if they did not regard ex-convicts as a ready pool of suspects to be tapped in the event of trouble, and psychiatric clinics could not do a successful job in the community if they were not always alert to the possibility of former patients suffering relapses. Thus the prophesy gains currency at many levels within the social order, not only in the poorly informed attitudes of the community at large, but in the best informed theories of most control agencies as well.

In one form or another this problem has been recognized in the West for many hundreds of years, and this simple fact has a curious implication. For if our culture has supported a steady flow of deviation throughout long periods of historical change, the rules which apply to any kind of evolutionary thinking would suggest that strong forces must be at work to keep the flow intact—and this because it contributes in some important way to the survival of the culture as a whole. This does not furnish us with sufficient warrant to declare that deviance is "functional" (in any of the many senses of that term), but it should certainly make us wary of the assumption so often made in sociological circles that any well-structured society is somehow designed to prevent deviant behavior from occurring.[12]

It might be then argued that we need new metaphors to carry our thinking about deviance onto a different plane. On the whole, American sociologists have devoted most of their attention to those forces in society which seem to assert a centralizing influence on human behavior, gathering people together into tight clusters called "groups" and bringing them under the jurisdiction of governing principles called "norms" or "standards." The questions which sociologists have traditionally asked of their data, then, are addressed to the uniformities rather than the divergencies of social life: how is it that people learn to think in similar ways, to accept the same group moralities, to move by the same rhythms of behavior, to see life with the same eyes? How is it, in short, that cultures accomplish the incredible alchemy of making unity out of diversity, harmony out of conflict, order out of confusion? Somehow we often act as if the differences between people can be taken for granted, being too natural to require comment, but that the symmetry which human groups manage to achieve must be explained by referring to the molding influence of the social structure.

[12] Albert K. Cohen, for example, speaking for a dominant strain in sociological thinking, takes the question quite for granted: "It would seem that the control of deviant behavior is, by definition, a culture goal." See "The Study of Social Disorganization and Deviant Behavior" in Merton, et al., *Sociology Today* (New York: Basic Books, 1959), p. 465.

But variety, too, is a product of the social structure. It is certainly remarkable that members of a culture come to look so much alike; but it is also remarkable that out of all this sameness a people can develop a complex division of labor, move off into diverging career lines, scatter across the surface of the territory they share in common, and create so many differences of temper, ideology, fashion, and mood. Perhaps we can conclude, then, that two separate yet often competing currents are found in any society: those forces which promote a high degree of conformity among the people of the community so that they know what to expect from one another, and those forces which encourage a certain degree of diversity so that people can be deployed across the range of group space to survey its potential, measure its capacity, and, in the case of those we call deviants, patrol its boundaries. In such a scheme, the deviant would appear as a natural product of group differentiation. He is not a bit of debris spun out by faulty social machinery, but a relevant figure in the community's overall division of labor.

JOSEPH R. GUSFIELD

A Dramatistic Theory of Status Politics

Political action has a meaning inherent in what it signifies about the structure of the society as well as in what such action actually achieves. We have argued that Prohibition and Temperance have operated as symbolic rather than as instrumental goals in American politics. The passage of legislation or the act of public approval of Temperance has been as significant to the activities of the Temperance movement as has the instrumental achievement of an abstinent society. The agitation and struggle of the Temperance adherents has been directed toward the establishment of their norms as marks of social and political superiority.

The distinction between political action as significant per se and political action as means to an end is the source of the theory underlying our analysis of the Temperance movement. We refer to it as a dramatistic theory because, like drama, it represents an action which is make-believe but which moves its audience. It is in keeping with Kenneth Burke's meaning of dramatism, "since it invites one to consider the matter of motives in a perspective that, being developed from the analysis of drama, treats language and thought primarily as modes of action."[1] It is make-believe in that the action need have no relation to its ostensible goal. The effect upon the audience comes from the significance which they find in the action as it represents events or figures outside of the drama.

Throughout the analysis of Temperance we have referred to the symbolic nature of Temperance goals. Our theory is further dramatistic in its perspective on political action as symbolic action, as action in which "the object referred to has a range of meaning beyond itself."[2] As we have pointed

[1] Kenneth Burke, *A Grammar of Motives* (New York: Prentice-Hall, 1945), p. xxii.
[2] M. H. Abrams, quoted in Maurice Beebe (ed.), *Literary Symbolism* (San Francisco: Wadsworth Publishing Co., 1960), p. 18.

Source: Joseph R. Gusfield, "A Dramatistic Theory of Status Politics," pp. 167–188 in *Symbolic Crusade: Status Politics and the American Temperance Movement* (Urbana: The University of Illinois Press, 1963). Copyright © 1963 by The University of Illinois Press. Reprinted by permission of The University of Illinois Press and Joseph R. Gusfield.

out in Chapter 1, this is the literary sense of the symbol as distinguished from the linguistic. It is in this sense that we refer to the flag as a symbol of national glory, to the cross as a symbol of Christianity, or the albatross as a symbol of charity in *The Rime of the Ancient Mariner*.

The dramatistic approach has important implications for the study of political institutions. These will be analyzed in this chapter, in the light of our study of the Temperance movement. Governments affect the distribution of values through symbolic acts, as well as through the force of instrumental ones. The struggle to control the symbolic actions of government is often as bitter and as fateful as the struggle to control its tangible effects. Much of our response to political events is in terms of their dramatic, symbolic meaning.

This is especially the case where elements of the status order are at issue. The distribution of prestige is partially regulated by symbolic acts of public and political figures. Such persons "act out" the drama in which one status group is degraded and another is given deference. In seeking to effect their honor and prestige in the society, a group makes demands upon governing agents to act in ways which serve to symbolize deference or to degrade the opposition whose status they challenge or who challenge theirs. We have seen this in the ways that Temperance goals symbolized victory or defeat for the devout native American Protestant.

This view of social status as a political interest enables us to solve some of the ambiguities about noneconomic issues and movements with which we began our study. It also provides us with a useful addition to the economic and the psychological modes of analysis current in the study of political and social movements.

Symbolic Issues in Politics

The State and the Public

Following Max Weber, it has become customary for sociologists to define the state as the legitimate monopolizer of force.[3] A major defect of this view, however, is that it minimizes the extent to which governments function as representatives of the total society. Other organizations or institutions claim to represent the values and interests of one group, subculture, or collectivity within the total social organization. Government is the only agency which claims to act for the entire society. It seeks its legitimation through the claim that it is effected with a "public interest" rather than with a special, limited set of goals. Much of the effective acceptance of government as legitimate

[3] Max Weber, *Theory of Social and Economic Organization*, tr. A. M. Henderson and Talcott Parsons (New York: Oxford University Press, 1947), p. 156. "The claim of the modern state to monopolize the use of force is as essential to it as its character of compulsory jurisdiction and of continuous organization." This definition is open both to the objection discussed above and to the inadequacy of singling out "force" as a major method of compulsion. Other institutions compel behavior by effective means other than violence, such as the ecclesiastical controls of a priesthood or the employment powers of management. The phenomena of "private governments" is not included in Weber's definition but the only ground of exclusion which is sociologically significant is the public character of governing bodies.

rests upon the supposition that it is representative of the total society, that it has the moral responsibility "to commit the group to action or to perform coordinated acts for its general welfare."[4]

The public and visible nature of governmental acts provides them with wider consequences for other institutions than is true of any other area of social life. The actions of government can affect the tangible resources of citizens but they can also affect the attitudes, opinions, and judgments which people make about each other.

It is readily apparent that governments affect the distribution of resources and, in this fashion, promote or deter the interest of economic classes. The passage of a minimum wage law does affect the incomes of millions of laborers and the profits of thousands of owners of capital. The Wagner Labor Relations Act and the Taft-Hartley Act have changed the conditions of collective bargaining during the past 26 years. Tariff laws do influence the prices of products. While these legislative actions may not direct and control behavior as much as was contemplated in their passage, they nevertheless find their *raison d'être* as instruments which have affected behavior to the delight of some and the dismay of others. They are instruments to achieve a goal or end through their use.

That governmental acts have symbolic significance is not so readily appreciated, although it has always been recognized. We see the act of recall of an ambassador as an expression of anger between one government and another. We recognize in the standardized pattern of inaugural addresses the gesture toward consensus after the strain of electoral conflict. These acts, of ambassadorial recall and of presidential oratory, are not taken at face value but as devices to induce response in their audiences, as symbolic of anger or of appeal for consensus.

Not only ritual and ceremony are included in symbolic action. Law contains a great deal which has little direct effect upon behavior. The moral reform legislation embodying Temperance ideals has largely been of this nature, as have other reforms, such as those directed against gambling, birth control, and prostitution. The impact of legislation on such problems as civil rights, economic monopoly, or patriotic loyalties is certainly dubious. While we do not maintain that Temperance legislation, and the other legislation cited, has had no effect on behavior, we do find its intrumental effects are slight compared to the response which it entails as a symbol, irrespective of its utility as a means to a tangible end.

Nature of the Symbol

In distinguishing symbolic from instrumental action we need to specify the way in which a symbol stands for something else. It is customary in linguistic analysis to distinguish between "sign" and "symbol."[5] The former

---

[4] Frances X. Sutton, "Representation and the Nature of Political Systems," Comparative Studies in Society and History, 2 (October, 1959), 1–10, at 6. Sutton points out that in primitive societies the political officers are often only representatives to other tribes rather than agents to enforce law.

[5] See the discussion of signs and symbols in Susanne K. Langer, *Philosophy in a New Key* (Baltimore, Md.: Penguin Books, 1948), pp. 45–50.

points to and indicates objects or experiences to our senses. The latter represents objects and events apart from any sensory contacts. Thus the ringing of the doorbell is a sign that someone is at the front door. The word "doorbell" is a symbol, as is the concept of "democracy." Our usage is not linguistic in this sense,[6] but literary. We are concerned with the multiplicity of meanings which the same object or act can have for the observer and which, in a society, are often fixed, shared, and standardized. The artist and the writer have developed language and visual art with the use of symbols as major tools of communication. Religious institutions have developed a rich culture around the use of objects whose meanings are symbolic. The wine and wafer of the Mass are but one example of objects which embody a multiple set of meanings for the same person at the same time.

This distinction between instrumental and symbolic action is, in many ways, similar to the difference between denotative and connotative discourse. In denotation, our eyes are on the referent which, in clear language, is the same for all who use the term. Instrumental action is similar in being oriented as a means to a fixed end. Connotative references are more ambiguous, less fixed. The symbol is connotative in that "it has acquired a meaning which is added to its immediate intrinsic significance."[7]

It is useful to think of symbolic acts as forms of rhetoric, functioning to organize the perceptions, attitudes, and feelings of observers. Symbolic acts "invite consideration rather than overt action."[8] They are persuasive devices which alter the observer's view of the objects. Kenneth Burke, perhaps the greatest analyst of political symbolism, has given a clear illustration of how a political speech can function rhetorically by the use of language to build a picture contradicting the instrumental effects of political action. For example, if action is proposed or performed which will offend the businessman, language is produced in speeches which glorify the businessman. In this context, language functions to persuade the "victim" that government is not really against him. It allays the fears and "softens the blow." Burke refers to this technique as "secular prayer." It is the normal way in which prayer is used, "to sharpen up the pointless and blunt the too sharply pointed."[9]

[6] Neither is our usage to be equated with the discussion of symbolic behavior used in the writings of the symbolic interaction school of social psychology, best represented by the works of George H. Mead. The idea of symbolic behavior in that context emphasizes the linguistic and imaginative processes as implicated in behavior. It is by no means contrary to our usage of symbols but the context is not specifically literary. The symbolic interactionists call attention to the fact that objects are given meanings by the systems of concept formation. We emphasize one aspect of this process.

[7] Talcott Parsons, *The Social System* (Glencoe, Ill.: The Free Press, 1954), p. 286.

[8] Phillip Wheelwright, *The Burning Fountain* (Bloomington: Indiana University Press, 1954), p. 23.

[9] Burke, *op. cit.,* 393. My debt to Burke's writings is very great. He has supplied the major conceptual and theoretical tools for bridging literary and political analysis. In addition to *A Grammar of Motives,* see his *Attitudes Toward History* (Los Altos, Calif.: Hermes Publications, 1959), and *Permanence and Change* (New York: New Republic, Inc., 1935). Two sociologists, heavily influenced by Burke, have been extremely useful in developing attention to symbolic behavior in the sense used here. They are Erving Goffman, whose works are cited throughout this study, and Hugh D. Duncan, *Language and Literature in Society* (Chicago: University of Chicago Press, 1953).

It is not only langauge which is utilized in symbolic fashion by political agents. Any act of government can be imbued with symbolic import when it becomes associated with noninstrumental identifications, when it serves to glorify or demean the character of one group or another. Ceremony and ritual can become affected with great significance as actions in which the political agent, as representative of the society, symbolizes the societal attitude, the public norm, toward some person, object, or social group. Law, language, and behavior can all function ceremonially. They persuade men to a form of thought or behavior rather than force them to it. "The officer who doubts the obedience of his men may meet the situation by raising his voice, adopting a truculent tone, and putting on a pugnacious swagger."[10] This, too, is a form of rhetoric, of persuasive art.

Types of Political Symbolism

We find it useful to distinguish between two forms of political symbolism: *gestures of cohesion* and *gestures of differentiation*. The first type, gestures of cohesion, serves to fix the common and censensual aspects of the society as sources of governmental support. They appeal to the unifying elements in the society and the grounds for the legitimacy of the political institution, irrespective of its specific officeholders and particular laws. They seek to mobilize the loyalties to government which may exist above and across the political conflict of parties, interest groups, and factions. National holidays, inaugural addresses, and the protocols of address and behavior are ways in which the President of the United States attempts this function in his actions and words. The coronation of the monarch in Great Britain represents a highly ritualized method of symbolizing legitimacy.[11]

Gestures of differentiation point to the glorification or degradation of one group in opposition to others within the society. They suggest that some people have a legitimate claim to greater respect, importance, or worth in the society than have some others. In such gestures, governments take sides in social conflicts and place the power and prestige of the public, operating through the political institution, on one side or the other. The inauguration ceremonies of two presidents can be used as illustrations. In his 1953 inaugural, Dwight Eisenhower prefaced his address with a short, personally written prayer. Commenting on this freely, a WCTU officer remarked approvingly, "Imagine that prayer written in the morning in an offhand way! It's the finest thing we've

10 Harold Lasswell, "Language of Politics," in Ruth Anshen (ed.), *Language* (New York: Harper and Bros., 1957), pp. 270–284, at 281.

11 Edward Shils and Michael Young have studied the consensual effects of the coronation ceremony in England. See their "The Meaning of the Coronation," *Sociological Review*, 1, n.s. (December, 1953), 63–81. The use of ritual and ceremony to establish cohesion and social control through historical pagents and holidays in modern society is studied empirically in W. Lloyd Warner, *The Living and the Dead* (New Haven, Conn.: Yale University Press, 1959), esp. Pts. I and II. These aspects of "political religion" have received comparatively little attention from students of modern societies although most recognize the importance of such rituals and would agree with Hugh Duncan that "Any institution can 'describe' the way it wants people to act but only as it develops rites, ceremonies and symbols for communication through rite in which people can act does it rise to power." Duncan, *op. cit.,* p. 18.

had in years from a president's lips." This gesture placed government on the side of the traditionalist and the devout and separated it from identification with the secularist and freethinker. In the inaugural of John F. Kennedy, the appearance of the poet Robert Frost was greeted as a symbol of respect and admiration for art, conferring prestige upon the poets by granting them places of honor in public ceremonies.

Such gestures of differentiation are often crucial to the support or opposition of a government because they state the character of an administration in moralistic terms. They indicate the kinds of persons, the tastes, the moralities, and the general life styles toward which government is sympathetic or censorious.[12] They indicate whether or not a set of officials are "for people like us" or "against people like us." It is through this mechanism of symbolic character that a government affects the status order.

Status as a Public Issue

Deference Conferral

In what sense can the prestige of a status group be a matter at issue? Conflicts about the appropriate deference to be shown can, and do, exist. Currently the relations between whites and Negroes in the United States are examples of a status system undergoing intensive conflict. An issue, however, is a proposal that people can be for or against. A public issue has status implications insofar as its public outcome is interpretable as conferring prestige upon or withdrawing it from a status group.

Desegregation is a status issue par excellence. Its symbolic characteristics lie in the deference which the norm of integration implies. The acceptance of token integration, which is what has occurred in the North, is itself prestige-conferring because it establishes the public character of the norm supporting integration. It indicates what side is publicly legitimate and dominant. Without understanding this symbolic quality of the desegregation issue, the fierceness of the struggle would appear absurd. Since so little actual change in concrete behavior ensues, the question would be moot if it were not for this character as an act of deference toward Negroes and of degradation toward whites.

---

[12] Another example of this symbolic process in political issues can be found in the conflicts over city manager plans. Development of city manager government is usually supported by middle-class voters and opposed by the lower socioeconomic groups. The impersonal, moralistic, and bureaucratized "good government" is much closer to standards of conduct typical in middle classes. The machine politician is closer to the open, personalized, and flexible government that represents the lower-class systems of social control. The issue of the city manager poses the two subcultures against each other. One study of the advent of city manager government reported that the first thing the new council did was to take away jobs from Catholic employees and, under merit employment, give them to Protestants. The city manager people celebrated their political victory with a banquet at the Masonic hall. See the discussion in Martin Meyerson and Edward Banfield, *Politics, Planning and the Public Interest* (Glencoe, Ill.: The Free Press, 1955), pp. 290–291.

Unlike the desegregation question, many public issues are confrontations between opposed systems of moralities, cultures, and styles of life. Examples of these are issues of civil liberties, international organizations, vivisection, Sunday "blue laws," and the definition and treatment of domestic Communism. Probably the clearest of such issues in American public life has been the one studied in this book, the issue of restrictive or permissive norms governing drinking. Status issues indicate, by their resolution, the group, culture, or style of life to which government and society are publicly committed. They answer the question: On behalf of which ethnic, religious, or other cultural group is this government and this society being carried out? We label these as *status issues* precisely because what is at issue is the position of the relevant group in the status order of the society. Such issues polarize the society along lines of status group differentiation, posing conflicts between divergent styles of life. They are contrasted with *class issues,* which polarize the society along lines of economic interests.[13]

Status issues function as vehicles through which a noneconomic group has deference conferred upon it or degradation imposed upon it. Victory in issues of status is the symbolic conferral of respect upon the norms of the victor and disrespect upon the norms of the vanquished. The political institution or public is thus capable of confirming or disconfirming the individual's conception of his place in the social order.[14] Such actions serve to reconstitute the group as a social object by heaping shame or honor upon it through the support or rejection displayed toward its tastes, values, and customs. When the indignation of the abstinent toward the drinker is publicly confirmed by prohibitory legislation it is, in Harold Garfinkel's analysis of degradation ceremonies, an act of public denunciation: "We publicly deliver the curse: 'I call upon all men to bear witness that he is as he appears but is otherwise and *in essence* of a lower species.' "[15]

Symbolic properties of deference and degradation can be involved in a wide range of issues and events. They may be implicated as a major theme in some issues or as a peripheral element in other issues, where the groups and themes are more directly those of specific economic interests. David Riesman and Ruel Denney have given us an excellent analysis of American football as a carrier of symbols which served to heighten the prestige of some social

[13] Essentially the same distinction is made by students of the voting process. Berelson, Lazarsfeld, and McPhee distinguish between issues of style ("ideal" issues) and issues of position ("material" issues). Bernard Berelson, Paul Lazarsfeld, and William McPhee, *Voting* (Chicago: University of Chicago Press, 1959), p. 184.

[14] ". . . the individual must rely on others to complete the picture of him . . . each individual is responsible for the demeanour image of himself and deference image of others, so that for a complete man to be expressed, individuals must hold hands in a chain of ceremony, each giving deferentially with proper demeanor to the one on the right what will be received deferentially from the one on the left." Erving Goffman, "The Nature of Deference and Demeanor," *American Anthropologist,* 58 (June, 1956), 473–502, at 493. Goffman's writings constitute an important discussion of deference and degradation ceremonies in interpersonal interaction. In addition to the article cited above see *The Presentation of Self in Everyday Life* (New York: Doubleday Anchor Books, 1959), and *Encounters* (Indianapolis, Ind.: Bobbs-Merrill, 1961).

[15] Harold Garfinkel, "Conditions of Successful Degradation Ceremonies," *American Journal of Sociology,* 61 (March, 1956), 420–424, at 421.

groups at the expense of the degradation of others.[16] The victories of Knute Rockne and Notre Dame over the previously championship teams of the Ivy League symbolized the growing social and educational equality of the non-Protestant middle-class Midwest vis-à-vis the Protestant upper-class East. Fans could identify themselves with football teams as carriers of their prestige, whether or not they were college graduates themselves. Knute Rockne was football's equivalent of Al Smith in politics.

Status Interests

Precisely because prestige is far from stable in a changing society, specific issues can become structured as tests of status when they are construed as symbols of group moralities and life styles. A civil liberties issue, such as domestic Communism, takes much of its affect and meaning from the clashes between traditionalized and modernistic groups in American culture. Elements of educational sophistication, religious secularism, or political liberalism may appear as alien, foreign, and in direct contradiction to the localistic ways of life of the traditional oriented culture. Issues of civil liberties become fields on which such cultural and educational groups fight to establish their claims to public recognition and prestige.

In his analysis of McCarthyism, Peter Vierick has referred to just this kind of process in characterizing the attack on officials in the State Department. Vierick placed one source of this attack in the feeling of degradation which the Midwestern, agricultural, middle class felt at political domination by the aristocracy of the Eastern seaboard, educated at Ivy League schools and so prominent in State Department affairs. They symbolized the State Department personnel as "striped-pants diplomats" and "cookie-pushers." "Against the latter (the Foreign Service—ed.) the old Populists and La Follette weapon against diplomats of 'you internationalist Anglophile snob' was replaced by 'you egghead security risk.' "[17]

In the struggle between groups for prestige and social position, the demands for deference and the protection from degradation are channeled into government and into such institutions of cultural formation as schools, churches, and media of communication. Because these institutions have power to affect public recognition, they are arenas of conflict between opposing status groups. Their ceremonial, ritual, and policy are matters of interest for status groups as well as for economic classes.

It is in this sense that status politics is a form of interest-oriented politics. The enhancement or defense of a position in the status order is as much an interest as the protection or expansion of income or economic power. The activities of government, as the most public institutions, confer respect upon a given style of life or directly upon a specific group. For this reason questions of institutional support of tastes, morals, and other aspects

[16] David Riesman and Ruel Denney, "Football in America," *The American Quarterly,* 3 (Winter, 1951), 309–325.
[17] Peter Vierick, "The Revolt Against the Elite," in Daniel Bell (ed.), *The New American Right* (New York: Criterion Books, 1955), pp. 91–116, at 103.

of life styles have consequences for the prestige of persons. Where status anxieties exist, they are then likely to be represented in the form of symbolic issues through which they are resolved.

To see that government, as do other institutions, is a prestige-granting agency is to recognize that status politics is neither extraordinary nor an irrational force in American history. Seymour Lipset appears to be quite mistaken when he writes, "Where there are status anxieties, there is little or nothing which a government can do."[18] Governments constantly affect the status order. During the 1930's the Democratic Party won many votes by increasing the number of Jews and Catholics appointed to state and federal judgeships. Such jobs did little to increase the total number of jobs open to these ethnic and religious groups. They did constitute a greater representation and through this a greater recognition of the worth of these groups. In this sense they were rituals of prestige enhancements, just as Andrew Jackson's inauguration symbolized the advent of the "common man" to power and prestige by the fact that rough men in boots strode across the floors of the White House.

It is just this consequence of the Temperance movement for the public designation of respectability that we have seen throughout this study. We have been interested in the efforts of Temperance people to reform the habits of others. While such efforts have indeed been motivated by the desire to perfect others in accordance with the reformer's vision of perfection, they have also become enmeshed in consequences affecting the distribution of prestige. Temperance issues have served as symbols around which groups of divergent morals and values have opposed each other.[19] On the side of Temperance there has been the rural, orthodox Protestant, agricultural, native American. On the side of drinking there has been the immigrant, the Catholic, the industrial worker, and the secularized upper class. In more recent years the clash has pitted the modernist and the urbanized cosmopolitans against the traditionalists and the localites, the new middle class against the old.

When Temperance forces were culturally dominant, the confrontation was that of the social superior. He sought to convert the weaker members of the society through persuasion backed by his dominance of the major institutions. Where dominance of the society is in doubt, then the need for positive governmental and institutional action is greater. The need for symbolic vindication and deference is channeled into political action. What is at stake is not so much the action of men, whether or not they drink, but their ideals, the moralities to which they owe their public allegiance.

---

[18] Seymour Lipset, "The Sources of the Radical Right," in *ibid.*, pp. 166–234, at 168.

[19] This is evident in Lee Benson, *The Concept of Jacksonian Democracy* (Princeton, N.J.: Princeton University Press, 1961), esp. Ch. 9. Benson's work appeared too late to have been used in earlier sections of the book. It provides valuable evidence for the role of moral issues, and especially Temperance, in developing party loyalties in New York state in the 1840's. Using the concept of negative reference groups, Benson shows that economic interests played less of a role than did religious, cultural, and moral differences as influences on voting. Voters tended to see the two major parties as linked to one or another ethnocultural group.

Political Models and Status Politics[20]

Our analysis of symbolic acts has implications for traditional theories of American politics. In attempting to understand political processes and movements sociologists, political scientists, and psychologists have operated with two major models of political motivation. One model has been drawn from economic action and reflects the struggle for economic interests. This model we have designated *class politics*. The other model has been drawn from clinical psychology and reflects a view of politics as an arena into which "irrational" impulses are projected. The latter model, which we have called *psychological expressivism,* has been utilized by others to describe movements of status politics. Our use of a model of symbolic action has been intended to distinguish movements of status politics from both economic interest on the one hand, and psychological expressivism on the other. This section of the chapter indicates the implications of our analysis for theoretical political sociology.

Class Politics and the Pluralistic Model

The view of the political process as a balance of economic forces organized as classes has led to a compromise model of political actions. The pluralistic model assumes a multiple number of specific interest groups whose demands conflict with and contradict each other. Farmers, bankers, skilled workers, unskilled workers, and professionals are represented through pressure groups and occupational associations. Political decisions are resultants of the compromises mediated between the various groups in accordance with the distribution of political power. Each group tries to get as much as they can but accepts partial losses in return for partial gains.

Compromise and the model of the political arena as one of mutually cooperating yet antagonistic groups presupposes a "political culture" in which victory and defeat are only end points on a continuum. An expediential attitude of calculation and exchange must govern the trading and bargaining. The language and imagery of compromise is drawn to a considerable extent from the marketplace, where monetary transactions enable interaction to be expressed in measurable quantities and mutual advantages. We "meet people halfway," develop political programs that are "deals," and operate through political parties talked about as "brokers of interests."

The "rules of the game" governing pluralistic politics are sharply antithetical to the "poor loser," the "sorehead," the intolerant ideologue who considers himself morally right and all others morally evil. He cannot accept the legitimacy of an institution in which even partial defeat occurs. For him politics is not a search for benefits in his work and life but a battleground between forces of good and evil. He reacts with passion in ways which contradict the rules of pluralistic politics. He rejects the presupposition that everybody in the political arena has a legitimate right to get something and

---

[20] Some of the matters discussed in this section are treated in greater detail in my "Mass Society and Extremist Politics," *American Sociological Review,* 27 (February, 1962), 19–30.

nobody has a legitimate right to get everything. He typifies the moralizer in politics, described by Riesman and discussed in connection with the contemporary Temperance movement in Chapter 6.

Psychological Expressivism as a Model of Status Politics

The analytical scheme of pluralistic politics is most applicable to movements of class politics and instrumental action. Movements such as Prohibition, civil rights, religious differences, and educational change are puzzles to the sociologist and political scientist precisely because they cannot be analyzed in instrumental terms. Their goals and major images appear "irrational" and unrelated to the content of their aims. Being puzzles, a resort is often made to schemes which stress the impulsive, uncontrolled elements of spontaneous and unconscious behavior. Thus Lipset writes of status discontents as one source of rightist extremism: "It is not surprising therefore that political movements which have successfully appealed to status resentments have been irrational in character and have sought scapegoats which conveniently serve to symbolize the status threat."[21]

The essential idea in psychological expressivism is that the adherence to the movement is explainable as an expression of the adherent's personality. "Thus the mass man is vulnerable to the appeal of mass movements which offer him a way of overcoming the pain of self-alienation by shifting attention away from himself and by focussing it on the movement."[22] Unlike instrumental action, which is about conflicts of interest, the substance of political struggles in expressive politics is not about anything because it is not a vehicle of conflict but a vehicle of catharsis—a purging of emotions through expression. The analysis of politics as expressive takes on the attributes of magic, as in Malinowski's classic definition: "Man, engaged in a series of practical activities, comes to a gap . . . passive inaction, the only thing dictated by reason, is the last thing in which he can acquiesce. His nervous system and his whole organism drive him to some substitute activity."[23]

If we utilize only the two models of instrumental actions and psychological expressivism we tend to divide political and social movements into two categories—the rational and the irrational. Status politics, as we have seen in both Lipset and Hofstadter, gets readily classified as "irrational": "Therefore, it is the tendency of status politics to be expressed more in vindictiveness, in sour memories, in the search for scapegoats, than in realistic proposals for concrete action."[24] Between instrumental and expressive politics there is no bin into which the symbolic goals of status movements can be analytically placed. Our usage of symbolic politics is an effort to provide such a bin.

21 Lipset, *op. cit.*, p. 168.
22 William Kornhauser, *The Politics of Mass Society* (Glencoe, Ill.: The Free Press, 1959), p. 112.
23 Bronislaw Malinowski, *Magic, Science and Religion* (New York: Doubleday Anchor Books, 1954; orig. pub., 1925), p. 79.
24 Richard Hofstadter, "The Pseudo-Conservative Revolt," in Bell (ed.), *op. cit.*, pp. 33–55, at 44.

Symbolic Politics and Status Interests

The consequences of interpreting status movements in the language of psychological expressivism is that the analyst ignores the reality of the status conflict. Expressive politics cannot be referred back to any social conflict which is resolved by the action taken. It is not a vehicle through which conflicts are mediated or settled. We have tried to show, in the instance of the Temperance movement, that the attempt to utilize political action was not only expressive but was a way of winning a concrete and very real struggle over the distribution of prestige in American society.

Discontents that arise from the status order are often as sharp and as powerful as those that emerge in the struggles over income and employment. In a society of diverse cultures and of rapid change, it is quite clear that systems of culture are as open to downward and upward mobility as are occupations or persons. Yesterday's moral virtue is today's ridiculed fanaticism. As the cultural fortunes of one group go up and those of another group go down, expectations of prestige are repulsed and the ingredients of social conflict are produced.

The dramatistic approach we have used in this study includes language but is by no means only a linguistic analysis. It is applicable to acts of legislation, such as Prohibition or fluoridation, to court decisions, and to official ceremony. Arguments about symbolic action are real in the sense that men's regard for respect, honor, and prestige is real. We do live in a forest of symbols, and within that forest there is disagreement, conflict, and disorder.

We are not maintaining a symbolic approach to politics as an alternative to instrumental or expressive models. We conceive of it as an addition to methods of analysis but an addition which can best help us understand the implications of status conflicts for political actions and, vice versa, the ways in which political acts affect the distribution of prestige. Most movements, and most political acts, contain a mixture of instrumental, expressive, and symbolic elements. The issues of style, which have troubled many social scientists in recent years, have not lent themselves well to political analysis. Those issues which have appeared as "matters of principle" now appear to us to be related to status conflicts and understandable in symbolic terms.

An example of what we have in mind can be seen in the political issues presented by controversies over school curricula in American municipalities. During the 1950's there has been much agitation to force American schools and universities to require more American history or courses on Communism as ways to establish patriotic loyalties among students and oppose Communist doctrine. Observers of American life are likely to deride these actions as pathetic attempts to control a situation with ineffective weapons or denounce such actions as coercion over the content of education. Beneath these programs, however, is the assumption that the school personnel are not succeeding in transmitting some value which the pressure groups feel important. The symbols of "Communism" are related to the cultural conflicts between fundamentalist and modernizing forces in American life, as well as the foreign policy conflicts between Russia and the United States. Cultural conflicts become easily centered upon school curricula because the content of education

depends upon cultural assumptions. As our schools are increasingly manned
by professionalized, college-trained personnel, they come to represent modern,
cosmopolitan values against which fundamentalists struggle.[25] Whose values
shall the school system enunciate? Whose values shall be legitimized and
made dominant by being the content of education? The manifest intent of
such curricular changes may be inducement of patriotic feeling, but the latent,
symbolic issue is not so directly educational. Psychologists may show that
the pledge of allegiance every morning has no discernible effect upon patriotic
feeling, but this is not the issue as status elements are involved. What such
curricular changes "bear witness" to is the domination of one cultural group
and the subordination of another. As most educators know, schools are run
for adults, not for children. There is more than expression of feeling in such
demands. There is an effort to dominate the rituals by which status is
discerned.

A political model that ignores symbolic action in politics would exclude
an important category of governmental action. It is a major way in which
conflicts in the social order are institutionalized as political issues. Groups
form around such issues, symbols are given specific meaning, and opposing
forces have some arena in which to test their power and bring about compromise and accommodation, if possible. This is precisely what the issues of
Prohibition and Temperance have enabled the status groups involved as Wets
and Drys to accomplish. Turning status conflicts into political conflicts is
precisely what Lasswell seems to have meant when he described politics as
"the process by which the irrational bases of society are brought out into
the open."[26]

Our approach also differs somewhat from that of Murray Edelman, who
has been the most salient political scientist to recognize the role of symbolic
action in legislative acts. He has pointed out that groups frequently seem
satisfied by the passage of legislation, even though the execution of the acts
often contradicts the intent of the legislation. This has been true in cases
such as antitrust laws, the work of the Federal Communications Commission
and other regulatory commissions, and in much civil rights legislation. "The
most intensive dissemination of symbols commonly attends the enactment
of legislation which is most meaningless in its effects upon resource alloca-

[25] For an analysis of one such school controversy in which "Communism," "human
relations," "progressive education," and UNESCO were symbols of a feared cosmopolitanism see National Education Association of the United States, *The Pasadena Story*
(Washington, D.C.: National Education Association, 1951). This same use of these
symbols is linked to group conflict in many of the speeches and pamphlets of the extreme
right wing in the 1950's and early 1960's. They underline the cultural values which are
the center of the struggle. One example is the following from a reprinted speech: "Our
most dangerous enemies are the thousands and thousands of disguised vermin who crawl
all around us and, in obedience to orders from their superiors in the conspiracy, poison
the minds of those about them with glib talk about 'social justice,' 'progressive education,'
'civil rights,' 'the social gospel,' 'one world' and 'peaceful coexistence.' You will find
them everywhere; in your clubs, in your schools, in your churches, in your courts." R. P.
Oliver, "Communist Influence in the Federal Government," speech to the fifth annual
convention of We, the People! Chicago, September, 1959.

[26] Harold Lasswell, *Psychopathology and Politics* (Chicago: University of Chicago
Press, 1930), p. 184.

tion."[27] Edelman's analysis assumes, however, that this discrepancy is a result of the "psychological reassurance" given to such groups that their interests are being protected. We suggest that while this is a credible theory, especially in economic issues, there are some real interests at stake as well.

These can be specified as two different types of ways in which status interests enter into political issues. First, any governmental action can be an act of deference because it confers power on one group and limits some other group. It bolsters or diminishes the claims of a group to differential treatment. Second, the specific status order, as distinct from the constellation of classes, is affected by actions which bear upon styles of life. The issues of Temperance and Prohibition have had particular relevance to the prestige of old and new middle-class ways of life.

We live in a human environment in which symbolic gestures have great relevance to our sense of pride, mortification, and honor. Social conflicts and tensions are manifested in a disarray of the symbolic order as well as in other areas of action. Dismissing these reactions as "irrational" clouds analysis and ignores the events which have significance for people. Kenneth Burke has pointed out the pejorative implications which emerge when non-instrumental usages are described as "magical." He distinguishes between poetic language, which is action for its own sake, scientific language, which is a preparation for action, and rhetorical language, which is inducement to action or attitude. If you think of acts as either magical or scientific there is no place to classify symbolic acts of the kind we have been considering, where an interest conflict is resolved but in noninstrumental symbolic terms. Consequently, a great deal of political activity is dismissed as ritual, magic, or irrational waste when "it should be handled in its own terms as an aspect of what it really is: Rhetoric."[28]

The Volatility of Status Politics

Issues invested with status interests are not easily handled by political institutions oriented to the model of a pluralistic class politics. In American politics such issues are likely to be most difficult to regularize within the structure of the American political framework. Their volatile nature is further accentuated by recent changes in American culture and society which make such issues emerge even more explosively than they have in the past.

Status Conflict and the Political Process

It is the issues of morals and style, of religious belief and ethnic loyalties which searchers for political harmony most often implore be kept out of politics. Such pleas are recognition of the intensity with which status loyalties and aspirations prevent the operation of the culture of bargaining, compromise, and detached trading so necessary for a pluralistic politics. The intro-

[27] Murray Edelman, "Symbols and Political Quiescence," *American Political Science Review,* 54 (September, 1960), 695–704, at 697.
[28] Kenneth Burke, *A Rhetoric of Motives* (New York: Prentice-Hall, 1950), p. 42.

duction of status issues cuts deeply at the sources of political consensus by converting political questions into moral ones.

The language of status issues, essential to their symbolic import, is the language of moral condemnation. In the confrontation of one culture with another, each seeks to degrade the other and to build its own claims to deference. The sources of conflict are not quantitative ones of the distribution or resources. Instead they are differences between right and wrong, the ugly and the beautiful, the sinful and the virtuous. Such issues are less readily compromised than are quantitative issues. When politicians argue about the definition of sin instead of being uniformly opposed to it, then the underlying political consensus is itself threatened.

The discontents generated by social change become fixed upon groups which are in status opposition. Each becomes the symbol of the other's obstacle in objectifying its view of its proper position. Each seeks to wrest from the other the admission of its place in the order. An issue like fluoridation, for example, carries the status struggle between the culturally modern and cosmopolitan middle classes and the culturally fundamentalist and localistic old middle classes.

The association of an issue with the styles of life of its supporters enhances the tendency of political issues to turn into matters of "face," freezing the adherents to a given program and further diminishing the possibilities of compromise or graceful defeat. When participants have become committed to a "line" which makes retreat and compromise immoral, discontinuance of the stance will be more painful than if they had entered with a bargaining orientation. In the former case, they invested their egos. In part, compromise is possible at all because the parties to the action will help each other maintain the illusion that a victory has been achieved. In human encounters, as Goffman has shown, parties to the interaction help maintain each other's "face." People mutually accept each other's lines—the consistent pattern of acts expressing the actor's evaluation of himself and the participants. The hostess covers over the embarrassment of the guest who has just broken a new and expensive piece of glassware by minimizing the importance of the breakage. She maintains the guest's "face' as a considerate person and permits him to "erase" the act by mumbling apologies. "Should the person radically alter his line, or should it become discredited, then confusion results, for the participants will have prepared and committed themselves for actions that are now unsuitable."[29]

Status conflicts, however, involve just such "face-smashing" operations. The pretense that one's values and morals are prestigious and powerful is undermined whenever public actions contradict such assertions. Loss of face becomes degrading. Since status conflicts involve opposition between styles of life, it is necessary to break the "face" of the opponent by degrading his cultural content. Ego is invested in status claims and degradation is keenly felt. The inability of the forces of North and South to reach compromise on

---

[29] Erving Goffman, "On Face-Work," *Psychiatry,* 18 (August, 1955), 213–231, at 216.

the eve of the Civil War is a good illustration of how investment in a line made compromise less possible. ". . . after years of strife the complex issues between the sections assumed the form of a conflict between *right* and *rights*. . . . They suggested things which cannot be compromised."[30]

Political Structure and Status Politics

The institutionalization of status conflicts occurs less frequently than the institutionalization of class conflicts. Class organization develops out of stable, institutional positions in the occupational and economic structures. Labor unions, businessmen's associations, professional organizations are constructed on the basis of institutional roles and statuses. The organization of conflict associations is a necessary step in the structuring of conflict relationships. It enables political accommodations to be worked out among contending groups. Institutional ties operate both to promote the formation of "pressure groups" and to integrate the occupant into organizations on this basis.

Some historians have recently suggested that American politics has displayed a higher degree of consensus than has been true in Europe.[31] The sharp antagonisms between economic and social classes described by Marx have been avoided in the United States, with its higher available level of resources and the absence of a feudal past. Because economic conflicts have been less salient, American politics has been open to the interjection of status issues to a very great degree.[32]

We lack the techniques to measure accurately the degree to which European politics displays more or less conflict than American politics. Certainly issues of cultural conflict have often been significant in European politics. ". . . every significant stratum (in Europe) is divided between support for a modern, secular, industrial society and preference for the values, if not the fact, of a clerical, non-industrial order."[33] The presence of a multiple party system, however, enables such elements to be introduced into politics within the structure of political institutions.

In American politics, especially in recent decades, issues involving cultural conflict appear to find less place in the structure of the two-party system than was the case in past historical periods. The designation of either major party as predominantly Catholic or immigrant or the voice of Puritan morality is less accurate today than it might have been in the nineteenth century and even in the first third of the twentieth. The studies of national voting behavior during the last 20 years indicate the saliency of economic differences between Republicans and Democrats and the lack of any sharp relation

[30] Avery O. Craven, "The Civil War and the Democratic Process," in Kenneth Stampp (ed.), *The Causes of the Civil War* (Englewood Cliffs, N.J.: Prentice-Hall, 1959), pp. 150–152, at 152.

[31] See the presentation of this point of view with additional references in Benson, *op. cit.,* pp. 272–277.

[32] *Ibid.,* p. 275.

[33] Seymour Lipset, "Party Systems and the Representation of Social Groups," *European Journal of Sociology,* 1 (1960), 50–85, at 60.

between party preference and orientations toward such issues as civil liberties, race relations, internationalism, and religious education.[34]

The exclusion of status elements from institutionalized politics imparts an erratic, highly emotional, and disturbing character to such issues when they do find their way into politics. They emerge in highly diffuse forms. The separation of the issue from any specific party location destroys the control of the institution, the political party system, over it. Support in the form of sentiments are just as likely to come from one class as another, from Republicans as well as Democrats. Since status issues are likely to be highly symbolic, the absence of fixed political connotations enables people to provide their own connotations. In this fashion a bewildering array of diverse groups can become attached to any set of symbols when they lack clear location in the political spectrum. Almost every major social segment in the United States has been included by some writer as one of the major supports of Senator Joseph McCarthy. Pro-McCarthyism has been attributed to highly diverse and often conflicting groups, sometimes by the same author. Neo-Populists, Catholics, anti-Catholics, isolationists, downwardly mobile people, upwardly mobile people, Protestant fundamentalists, small businessmen, and industrial workers have all been held "responsible" for McCarthyism.[35] This "looseness" is seldom the case with economic issues.

Status constituencies, however, are looser collections of adherents than are economic interest groups. Formed out of sentiments rather than concrete, objectified interests, commitment is less structured. The organization is less able to speak for its constituency, less able to "deal" with opposing groups in the negotiations on which the model of class politics has been built. The constituency of doctors is more clearly represented by the American Medical Association than the constituency of birth control adherents is represented by the Association for Planned Parenthood.

We have pointed out in the previous chapter that the institutional and communal differences of the past are becoming muted in American life. They are replaced by conflict between characterological and cultural groups within the same institution and community. In our terminology, status communities are breaking up and cultural conflicts emerging in the form of status collectivities. This means that the differences in life styles between Protestants and Catholics or between urban and rural people are lessened. Differences between cosmopolitan and local, between fundamentalist and modernist remain but they are not connected to specific institutions, such as the church or the local community.

Ethnic and religious groups are better structured than social classes, generations, or stylistic groups. Catholics, Jews, Negroes, Protestants, Italians, rural people, or urban people possess stable relationships to churches, communities, or political units which serve to structure their relation to the political institutions. The effectiveness of the Anti-Saloon League as a "pres-

[34] Berelson, Lazarsfeld, and McPhee, op. cit., pp. 189 ff.; Samuel Lubell, The Future of American Politics (New York: Doubleday and Co., Inc., 1956); Angus Campbell, Philip E. Converse, and Warren Miller, The American Voter, (New York: John Wiley, 1960), Ch. 9, esp. pp. 194–195.

[35] See the array of theories and groups in Bell, op. cit.

sure group" rested on the consensus within the Protestant churches on the Temperance issue. As social and cultural cleavages cease to be superimposed on religious, residential, and communal groups the institutional basis for status group representation is lessened.

The isolation of status collectivities from the political party structure is double-edged. We have seen how it operates to push some elements of the Temperance movement toward an extremist response in political programs. On the other hand, as status communities are less salient as political forces, the volatility of status issues cuts across party lines and minimizes the bitterness of party differences. Had the Democrats been clearly pro-McCarthy and the Republicans clearly anti-McCarthy the issues surrounding his actions would have generated as intense conflict as did the nominations of Al Smith and Abraham Lincoln.

Temperance has receded as an issue of paramount significance in American life. It is highly doubtful that the status conflicts which it represented have disappeared from the American scene. The quest for an honored place in society is likely to persist. Social changes are likely to continue to upset old hierarchies and develop new aspirations. Cultural transformations are to be expected and resistance to them is almost certain. Status politics is neither a new nor a transient aspect of American society.

RICHARD QUINNEY

A Sociological Theory
of Criminal Law

In spite of considerable research in recent years, a theory of criminal law
has not developed. We do not yet have the theoretical means to generalize
beyond the research studies or to formulate research hypotheses. In what follows, I will propose a sociological theory of criminal law to assist in these
tasks. This theory is based upon a particular theoretical orientation within
sociology and incorporates the research in the sociology of criminal law.

From Sociological Jurisprudence
to Sociology of Criminal Law

The paradox today is that in the convergence of law and social science the
theoretical orientation to legal matters is no more apparent than it was half
a century ago. From a historical point of view, the rapprochement of law and
social science that we are currently witnessing is not novel. There was a similar occurrence in the United States shortly after the turn of the century. At
that time social scientists, the early American sociologists in particular, were
incorporating law into their scheme of things. E. A. Ross referred to law as
"the most specialized and highly furnished engine of control employed by society."[1] Lester F. Ward, an advocate of government control and social planning, foresaw a day when legislation would undertake to solve "questions of
social improvement, the amelioration of the condition of all the people, the
removal of whatever privations may still remain, and the adoption of means
to the positive increase of the social welfare, in short the organization of hu-

[1] E. A. Ross, *Social Control* (New York: Macmillan, 1922), p. 106 (originally
published in 1901).

Source: Richard Quinney, "A Sociological Theory of Criminal Law," pp. 20–30 in
Crime and Justice in Society (Boston: Little, Brown and Company [Inc.], 1969). Copyright © 1969 by Little, Brown and Company Inc.). Reprinted by permission.

man happiness."[2] The possibility of social reform, through legal means available to the state, was also emphasized by Albion W. Small.[3]

The ideas of the early sociologists directly influenced the development of the school of legal philosophy that became a major force in American legal thought—sociological jurisprudence. Roscoe Pound, the principal figure in sociological jurisprudence, drew from the early sociologists in asserting that law should be studied as a social institution.[4] Pound saw law as a specialized form of social control which brings pressure to bear upon each man "in order to constrain him to do his part in upholding civilized society and to deter him from anti-social conduct, that is, conduct at variance with the postulates of social order."[5]

Central to Pound's sociological jurisprudence was his theory of interests, according to which the law functions to accomplish socially worthwhile purposes. Besides the programmatic and teleological aspects of his work, Pound provided in his theory of interests one of the few starting points for the study of law as a social phenomenon.

A vast amount of writing and research has accumulated in recent years documenting the role of interest groups in the political process. There have been discussions on the techniques and tactics of interest groups, relations between groups, internal organization and politics of interest groups, and overlapping group membership.[6] In addition, studies have been conducted on the operation of specific interest groups.[7] In spite of all these efforts, research

[2] Lester F. Ward, *Applied Sociology* (Boston: Ginn, 1906), p. 339.

[3] Albion W. Small, *General Sociology* (Chicago: University of Chicago Press, 1925).

[4] The relation between early American sociologists and the development of Pound's sociological jurisprudence is discussed in Gilbert Geis, "Sociology and Jurisprudence: Admixture of Lore and Law," *Kentucky Law Journal*, 52 (Winter, 1964), pp. 267–293. Also see Edwin M. Schur, *Law and Society* (New York: Random House, 1968), pp. 17–50.

[5] Roscoe Pound, *Social Control Through Law* (New Haven: Yale University Press, 1942), p. 18. Earlier statements by Pound are found in Roscoe Pound, *An Introduction to the Philosophy of Law* (New Haven: Yale University Press, 1922); Roscoe Pound, *Outline of Lectures on Jurisprudence* (Cambridge: Harvard University Press, 1928).

[6] Donald C. Blaisdell, *American Democracy Under Pressure* (New York: Ronald Press, 1957); V. O. Key, Jr., *Politics, Parties, and Pressure Groups* (New York: Thomas Y. Crowell, 1959); Earl Latham, *Group Basis of Politics* (Ithaca, N.Y.: Cornell University Press, 1952); David B. Truman, *The Governmental Process* (New York: Alfred A. Knopf, 1951); Henry W. Ehrmann (ed.), *Interest Groups on Four Continents* (Pittsburgh: University of Pittsburgh Press, 1958); Henry A. Turner, "How Pressure Groups Operate," *Annals of the American Academy of Political and Social Science*, 319 (September, 1958), pp. 63–72; Richard W. Gable, "Interest Groups as Policy Shapers," *Annals of the American Academy of Political and Social Science*, 319 (September, 1958), pp. 84–93; Murray S. Stedman, "Pressure Groups and the American Tradition," *Annals of the American Academy of Political and Social Science*, 319 (September, 1958), pp. 123–129

[7] Robert Engler, *The Politics of Oil* (New York: Macmillan, 1961); Oliver Garceau, *The Political Life of the American Medical Association* (Cambridge: Harvard University Press, 1941); Charles M. Hardin, *The Politics of Agriculture: Soil Conservation and the Struggle for Power in Rural America* (New York: The Free Press of Glencoe, 1962); Grant McConnell, *Private Power and American Democracy* (New

on the role of interests in formulating and administering law has been almost nonexistent.[8] Moreover, few have attempted to revise Pound's theory of interests to reflect recent sociological developments. As Geis has commented, "Sociologists to date have paid virtually no attention to Pound's doctrine, either in terms of rejecting it, refining it for their purposes, or supplementing it with sociological material of more recent vintage."[9]

In the current movement toward research into law by social scientists and the use of social science research by lawyers, the role of interests might well be considered in an attempt to construct a theory of criminal law that would integrate the existing research findings and provide direction for future research. For sociological purposes, however, Pound's approach necessarily requires reformulation and extension into a sociological theory of criminal law.

Law is not merely a complex of rules and procedures; Pound taught us that in his call for the study of "law in action" as distinguished from the study of law in the books. For some purposes it may be useful to view law as autonomous to society, developing according to its own internal logic and proceeding along its own lines. But law also operates simultaneously as a reflection of society and as an influence in society. Thus, in a social sense, law is both social product and social force. In Pound's juristic approach, however, law as both a product and a force was viewed in a very special way. In jurisprudence, law as a social product is conceived as law which reflects the consciousness of the total society. This *consensus* model of law, regarding criminal law, is described thus: "The state of criminal law continues to be— as it should—a decisive reflection of the social consciousness of a society. What kind of conduct an organized community considers, at a given time, sufficiently condemnable to impose official sanctions, impairing the life, liberty, or property of the offender, is a barometer of the moral and social thinking of a community."[10] Similarly, Pound, in formulating his theory of interests, looked upon law as reflecting the needs of the well-ordered society. In fact, the law was a form of "social engineering" in a civilized society:

York: Alfred A. Knopf, 1966); Harry A. Millis and Royal E. Montgomery, *Organized Labor* (New York: McGraw-Hill, 1945); Warner Schilling, Paul Y. Hammond, and Glenn H. Snyder, *Strategy, Politics and Defense* (New York: Columbia University Press, 1962); William R. Willoughby, *The St. Lawrence Waterway: A Study in Politics and Diplomacy* (Madison: University of Wisconsin Press, 1961).

[8] Other social orientations to the law may be found among sociological jurists, among the so-called legal realists, and among current legal historians. See, in particular, Oliver Wendell Holmes, "The Path of the Law," *Harvard Law Review,* 10 (March, 1897), pp. 457–478; Thurman W. Arnold, *Symbols of Government* (New Haven: Yale University Press, 1935); Jerome Frank, *Courts on Trial* (Princeton: Princeton University Press, 1949); K. N. Llewellyn and E. Adamson Hoebel, *The Cheyenne Way: Conflict and Case Law in Primitive Jurisprudence* (Norman: University of Oklahoma Press, 1941); J. Willard Hurst, *Law and Economic Growth: The Legal History of the Lumber Industry in Wisconsin, 1836–1915* (Cambridge, Mass.: The Belknap Press, 1964).

[9] Geis, "Sociology and Sociological Jurisprudence: Admixture of Lore and Law," p. 292.

[10] Wolfgang Friedmann, *Law in a Changing Society* (Harmondsworth, England; Penguin Books, 1964), p. 143. A similar statement is found in Michael and Adler, *Crime, Law and Social Science,* pp. 2–3.

For the purpose of understanding the law of today I am content to think of law as a social institution to satisfy social wants—the claims and demands involved in the existence of civilized society—by giving effect to as much as we may with the least sacrifice, so far as such wants may be satisfied or such claims given effect by an ordering of human conduct through politically organized society. For present purposes I am content to see in legal history the record of a continually wider recognizing and satisfying of human wants or claims or desires through social control; a more embracing and more effective securing of social interests; a continually more complete and effective elimination of waste and precluding of friction in human enjoyment of the goods of existence—in short, a continually more efficacious social engineering.[11]

Thus, the interests Pound had in mind were those which would maintain and, ultimately, improve the social order. His was a *teleological* as well as consensus theory of interests: There are interests which man and society must fulfill for the good of the whole society. These interests are to be achieved through law. In Pound's theory, only the right law could emerge in a civilized society.

Jurisprudence has generally utilized a *pluralistic* model with respect to law as a social force in society. Accordingly, law regulates social behavior and establishes social organization. Law orders human relations by restraining individual actions and by settling disputes in social relations. In recent juristic language, law functions "first, to establish the general framework, the rules of the game so to speak, within and by which individual and group life shall be carried on, and secondly, to adjust the conflicting claims which different individuals and groups of individuals seek to satisfy in society."[12] For Pound, the law adjusts and reconciles conflicting interests:

Looked at functionally, the law is an attempt to satisfy, to reconcile, to harmonize, to adjust these overlapping and often conflicting claims and demands, either through securing them directly and immediately, or through securing certain individual interests, or through delimitations or compromises of individual interests,' so as to give effect to the greatest total of interests or to the interests that weigh most in our civilization, with the least sacrifice of the scheme of interests as a whole.[13]

In Pound's theory of interests, therefore, it is assumed that the legal order is created in society to regulate and adjust the conflicting desires and claims of men. The law provides the general framework within which individual and group life is carried on, according to the postulates of social order. Moreover, as a legal historian has written, "The law defines the extent to which it will give effect to the interests which it recognizes, in the light of other interests and of the possibilities of effectively securing them through

[11] Pound, *An Introduction to the Philosophy of Law,* pp. 98–99.
[12] Carl A. Auerbach, "Law and Social Change in the United States," *U.C.L.A. Law Review,* 6 (July, 1959), pp. 516–532. Similarly, see Julius Stone, *The Province and Function of Law* (Cambridge: Harvard University Press, 1950), Part III; Julius Stone, *Social Dimensions of Law and Justice* (Stanford: Stanford University Press, 1966), chaps. 4–8.
[13] Roscoe Pound, "A Survey of Social Interests," *Harvard Law Review,* 57 (October, 1943), p. 39.

law; it also devises means for securing those that are recognized and prescribes the limits within which those means may be employed."[14] In the interest theory of sociological jurisprudence, then, law is regarded as an instrument which controls interests according to the requirements of social order.

Pound's theory of interests included a threefold classification of interests: (1) individual interests, (2) public interests, and (3) social interests. "Individual interests are claims or demands or desires involved immediately in the individual life and asserted in the title of that life. Public interests are claims or demands or desires involved in life in a politically organized society and asserted in the title of that organization. They are commonly treated as the claims of a politically organized society thought of as a legal entity. Social interests are claims or demands or desires involved in social life in a civilized society and asserted in the title of that life. It is not uncommon to treat them as the claims of the whole social group as such."[15] While Pound delineated three kinds of interests secured by the legal order, he warned that the types are overlapping and interdependent and that most claims, demands, or desires can be placed in all the categories, depending upon one's purpose. However, he argued that it is often expedient to put claims, demands, and desires in their most general form; that is, into the category of social interests.

Surveying the claims, demands, and desires found in legal proceedings and in legislative proposals, Pound suggested that the most important social interest appears to be the interest in security against actions that threaten the social group.[16] Other social interests consist of the interest in the security of social institutions, including domestic, religious, economic, and political; the interest in morals; the interest in conservation of social resources; the interest in general progress, including the development of human powers and control over nature for the satisfaction of human wants; and the interest in individual life, especially the freedom of self-assertion. According to Pound, the nature of any legal system depends upon the way in which these interests are incorporated into law.

Although the *sociological theory of interests* that I am developing is in the general tradition of the interest theory of sociological jurisprudence, it departs from that tradition in a number of ways. First, the interest theory I am proposing is based on a particular conception of society. Society is characterized by diversity, conflict, coercion, and change, rather than by consensus and stability. Second, law is a *result* of the operation of interests, rather than an instrument which functions outside of particular interests. Though law may operate to control interests, it is in the first place *created* by interests. Third, law incorporates the interests of specific persons and groups in society. Seldom is law the product of the whole society. Rather than representing the

[14] George Lee Haskins, *Law and Authority in Early Massachusetts,* p. 226.

[15] Pound, "A Survey of Social Interests," pp. 1–2.

[16] Pound, "A Survey of Social Interests," 1–39. Other aspects of the theory of interests are discussed by Pound in the following publications: *The Spirit of the Common Law* (Boston: Marshall Jones, 1921), pp. 91–93, 197–203; *An Introduction to the Philosophy of Law,* pp. 90–96; *Interpretations of Legal History* (New York: Macmillan, 1923), pp. 158–164; *Social Control through Law,* pp. 63–80.

interests of all members of society, law consists of the interests of only specific segments of the population. Law is made by men, particular men representing special interests, who have the power to translate their interests into public policy. In opposition to the pluralistic conception of politics, law does not represent the compromise of the diverse interests in society, but supports some interests at the expense of others. Fourth, the sociological theory of interests is devoid of teleological connotations. The social order may require certain functions for its maintenance and survival, but such functions will not be considered as inherent in the interests involved in formulating particular substantive laws. Fifth, the theory proposed here includes a conceptual scheme for analyzing interests in the law. Sixth, the theory is systematically constructed according to an arrangement of propositions. Finally, construction of the sociological theory of interests is based on findings from current social science research.

A Sociological Theory of Interests

These characteristics of a sociological approach to law serve as the basis for constructing a sociological theory of interests. The theory consists of four propositions. Each proposition is presented with supporting rationale.

Law is the creation and interpretation of specialized rules in a politically organized society.

Authority relationships are present in all social collectivities: some persons are always at the command of others. In establishing order in a society, several systems of control develop to regulate the conduct of various groups of persons. Human behavior, thus, is subject to restraint by varied agencies, institutions, and social groupings—families, churches, social clubs, political organizations, labor unions, corporations, educational systems, and so forth.

The control systems vary considerably in the forms of conduct they regulate, and most of them provide means for assuring compliance to their rules. Informal means, spontaneously employed by some persons, such as ridicule, gossip, and censure, may ensure conformity to some rules. Control systems may, in addition, rely upon formal and regularized means of sanction.

The *legal system* is the most explicit form of social control. The law consists of (1) specific rules of conduct, (2) planned use of sanctions to support the rules, and (3) designated officials to interpret and enforce the rules.[17] Furthermore, law becomes more important as a system of control as societies increase in complexity. Pound wrote that "in the modern world law has become the paramount agent of social control. Our main reliance is upon force of a politically organized state."[18]

Law is not only a system of formal social control but also a body of spe-

[17] F. James Davis, "Law as a Type of Social Control," in F. James Davis, Henry H. Foster, Jr., C. Ray Jeffery, and E. Eugene Davis, *Society and the Law* (New York: The Free Press of Glencoe, 1962), p. 43.

[18] Pound, *Social Control through Law,* p. 20.

cialized rules created and interpreted in a *politically organized society*. Politically organized society, or the state, is a territorial organization with the authorized power to govern the lives and activities of all the inhabitants. Though other types of organized bodies may possess formal rules, only the specialized rule systems of politically organized societies are regarded here as systems of law.[19]

Law, as a special kind of institution that exists in particular societies, is more than an abstract body of rules. Rather than being autonomous to society and developing according to its own internal logic, law is an integral part of society, operating as a force in society and as a social product. The law is not only that which is written as statutes and recorded as court opinions and administrative rulings, but is also a method or *process* of doing something.[20] As a process, law is a dynamic force that is continually being *created* and *interpreted*. Thus, law in action involves the making of specialized (legal) decisions by various *authorized agents*. In politically organized society, human actions are regulated by those invested with the authority to make certain decisions in the name of the society.

Furthermore, law in operation is an aspect of politics. That is, law is one of the methods in which *public policy* is formulated and administered for governing the lives and activities of the inhabitants of the state. As an act of politics, law does not represent the norms and values of all persons in the society. Legal decisions, rather, incorporate the interests of only some persons. Whenever a law is created or interpreted, the values of some are necessarily assured and the values of others are either ignored or negated. The *politicality of law* is basic to the sociological theory of interests.

Politically organized society is based on an interest structure.

Modern societies are characterized by an organization of differences. The social differentiation of society, in turn, provides the basis for the political life of the state. To be specific, the governing process in a politically organized society operates according to the interests that characterize the socially differentiated positions. Because various kinds of interests are distributed among the positions, and because the positions are differently equipped with the ability to command, public policy represents certain interests in the so-

[19] The rule systems of other than politically organized society may be adequately referred to, for comparative purposes, in any number of quasi-legal ways, such as non-state law, primitive law, or lawways. Perhaps, even better, such systems of rules could be described simply as tradition, normative system, or custom. The concept of law is expanded to include the control systems of other than politically organized society among such writers as Bronislaw Malinowski, *Crime and Custom in Savage Society* (London: Routledge and Kegan Paul, 1926); E. Adamson Hoebel, *The Law of Primitive Man* (Cambridge: Harvard University Press, 1954); William M. Evan, "Public and Private Legal Systems," in William M. Evan (editor), *Law and Sociology* (New York: The Free Press of Glencoe, 1962), pp. 165–184; Philip Selznick, "Legal Institutions and Social Controls," *Vanderbilt Law Review,* 17 (December, 1963), pp. 79–90.

[20] For this conception of law, as applied to criminal law, see Henry M. Hart, Jr., "The Aims of the Criminal Law," *Law and Contemporary Problems,* 23 (Summer, 1958), pp. 401–441.

ciety. Politically organized society, therefore, may be viewed as a differentiated *interest structure*.

Each *segment* of society has its own values, norms, and ideological orientations. When these concerns are considered as important for the existence and welfare of the respective positions, they may be defined as *interests*.[21] Further, interests can be categorized according to the ways in which activities are generally pursued in society; that is, according to the *institutional orders* of society. The following may then serve as a definition of interests: *the institutional concerns of the segments of society*. Thus, interests are grounded in the segments of society and represent the institutional concerns of the segments.

The institutional orders within which interests operate may be classified into fairly broad categories.[22] For our purposes, these orders will be delimited: (1) *the political order,* which regulates the distribution of power and authority in society; (2) *the economic order,* which regulates the production and distribution of goods and services; (3) *the religious order,* which regulates the relationship of man to a conception of the supernatural; (4) *the kinship order,* which regulates sexual relations, family patterns, and the procreation and rearing of children; (5) *the educational order,* which regulates the formal training of the members of society; and (6) *the public order,* which regulates the protection and maintenance of the community and its citizens. Each segment of society has its own orientation to these institutional orders. Some segments, because of their authority position in the interest structure, are able to have their interests represented in public society.

The segments of society differ in the extent to which their interests are organized. The segments themselves are broad statistical aggregates containing persons of similar age, sex, class, status, occupation, race, ethnicity, religion, or the like. All these segments have *formal interests;* that is, interests which are advantageous to the segment but which are not consciously held by the incumbents and are not organized for action. *Active interests,* on the other hand, are interests that are manifest to persons in the segments and are sufficiently organized to serve as the basis for representation in policy decisions.[23]

Within the segments, groups of persons may organize to promote their common interests. These groups may be simply called *interest groups.* Thus, it is within the broad segments of society that groups become aware of their common concerns and organize to promote their interests. Public policy, in turn, is the result of the success of these groups. These are the dynamics of the interest structure in a politically organized society.

[21] The view here that interests are not distributed randomly in society but are related to one's position in society follows Marx's theory of economic production and class conflict. See Ralf Dahrendorf, *Class and Class Conflict in Industrial Society* (Stanford: Stanford University Press, 1959), especially pp. 3–35.

[22] The conception of institutional orders closely follows that of Hans Gerth and C. Wright Mills, *Character and Social Structure* (New York: Harcourt, Brace, 1953), especially pp. 25–26.

[23] The distinction between formal interests and active interests is similar to the distinction Dahrendorf makes between latent and manifest interests. See Dahrendorf, *Class and Class Conflict in Industrial Society,* pp. 173–179.

The interest structure of politically organized society is characterized by unequal distribution of power and by conflict.

Basic to the interest structure is a conception of unequal distribution of *power* and *conflict* between the segments of politically organized society. The interest structure is differentiated not only by diverse interests, but also according to the ability of the segments to translate their interests into public policy. Furthermore, the segments are in continual conflict over their interests. Thus, interests are structured according to differences in power and are in conflict.

Power and conflict are inextricably linked in this conception of interest structure. Power, as the ability to shape public policy, produces conflict between the competing segments, and conflict, in turn, produces differences in the distribution of power. Coherence in the interest structure is thus assured by the exercise of force and constraint by the conflicting segments of the interest structure.[24] In the conflict-power model of interest structure, therefore, politically organized society is held together by conflicting elements and functions according to the coercion of some segments by others.

The conflict-power conception of interest structure implies that public policy results from differential distribution of power and conflict between the segments of society. Diverse segments with specialized interests become so highly organized that they are able to influence the policies that affect all persons in the state. Groups that have the power to gain access to the decision-making process are able to translate their interests into public policy. Thus, the interests represented in the formulation and administration of public policy are those treasured by the dominant segments of the society. Hence, public policy is created because segments with power differentials are in conflict with one another. Public policy itself is a manifestation of an interest structure in politically organized society.

Law is formulated and administered within the interest structure of a politically organized society.

Law is a form of public policy that regulates the behavior and activities of all members of a society. Law is *formulated* and *administered* by the segments of society that are able to incorporate their interests into the creation and interpretation of public policy. Rather than representing the institutional concerns of all segments of society, law secures the interests of particular segments. Law supports one point of view at the expense of others.

Thus, the content of the law, including the substantive regulations and the procedural rules, represents the interests of segments of society that have the power to shape public policy. Formulation of law allows some segments of society to protect and perpetuate their own interests. By formulating law, some segments are able to control others to their own advantage.

[24] The sociological theory of interests is based upon the coercion model of society as opposed to the integrative model. See Ralf Dahrendorf, "Out of Utopia: Toward a Reorientation in Sociological Analysis," *American Journal of Sociology,* 67 (September, 1958), pp. 115–127.

The interests that the power segments of society attempt to maintain enter into all stages of legal administration. Since legal formulations do not provide specific instructions for interpreting law, administration of law is largely a matter of discretion on the part of *legal agents* (police, prosecutors, judges, juries, prison authorities, parole officers, and others). The decisions reached tend to support the interests of some segments of society while impeding the interests of others. Though implementation of law necessarily is influenced by such matters as localized conditions and the occupational organization of legal agents, the interest structure of politically organized society is responsible for the general design of the administration of justice.

Finally, since law is formulated and administered within the interest structure of politically organized society, it follows that law changes with modifications in that structure. New and shifting demands require new laws. When the interests that underlie a law no longer are relevant to groups in power, the law will be reinterpreted or changed to incorporate the dominant interests. The social history of criminal law can be described according to alterations in the interest structure of society.

Conclusion

The scope of criminology has been broadened in recent years to include the process by which persons and behaviors become defined as criminal. That is, the criminal law—including its formulation and administration—no longer is taken for granted, but serves as a major orientation for the study of crime. Research in the last decade has substantiated the importance of criminal law in criminology. Much of the research is presented in this book.

In order to provide a theoretical perspective for presenting and interpreting the research in the sociology of criminal law, a theory of law has been constructed. This theory, a sociological theory of interests, has been inspired by Roscoe Pound's juristic approach. It departs from Pound's approach by postulating, among other things, that law is created by interests, by assuming a conflict-power model of society, and by proposing a conceptual scheme for analyzing the relationship between law and interests.

Most important, the sociological theory of interests has been systematically constructed according to propositions which state that law consists of specialized rules that are created and interpreted in politically organized society, that such a society is based on an interest structure, that an interest structure is characterized by unequal distribution of power and by conflict, and that law is formulated and administered within the interest structure of politically organized society. This theory is consistent with and is supported by findings from current empirical investigations of crime, law, and administration of justice.

F. JAMES DAVIS

Beliefs, Values, Power, and Public Definitions of Deviance

Perceived Threats and Definitions of Deviance

Many departures from dominant norms are treated casually, but those that are considered a threat to the community are subjected to careful definition. Both underconformity and overconformity to group norms may be regarded as deviant (Cavan, 1961), but the latter is not likely to be considered dangerous unless it is extreme. The rigid moralist or the superpatriot are likely to appear dangerously deviant themselves when they advocate measures for controlling deviance that seriously underconform to such widely supported values as individual freedom or democratic government (Lipset, 1963). This response is especially probable when the public is divided as to the seriousness of the deviant behavior the overconformist seeks to control, as when book banning or burning are proposed to control pornography.

Most collective concern over deviance is with underconforming acts. Much minor, occasional underconformity is regarded as harmless and normal, but deviations need not be extreme to call forth organized sanctions or at least allegedly therapeutic activities. As in treatment programs mild departures are often considered symptomatic of potentially more dangerous deviance, a wide range of underconformity comes under official surveillance in the name of preventive rehabilitation (Kittrie, 1971).

There is fear of direct physical or financial harm to oneself or loved ones from some kinds of deviance. Much of the concern, however, especially that over "crimes without victims" such as drug use and sexual deviance (Schur, 1965), appears to be fear that the society is disintegrating. Public comment often seems congruent with the view of disorganization theorists that deviant acts, as violations of established norms, are indexes of social disorganization. Erikson (1966) has developed Durkheim's view that collective definitions of deviance call attention to official norms that define the limits of nonconformity, thus furthering social cohesion. A major reason why deviance is threatening, according to Lofland (1969), is that it produces ambiguity. In conflict perspectives, groups define as deviant whatever conduct is believed to threaten their power in the struggle against other groups for control of society.

Deviance and Value Priorities

Evidently a group defines deviant acts as dangerous when they are perceived as serious threats to its cherished values. Groups (and persons) with different value priorities may understandably differ as to whether a particular kind of deviance is dangerous, harmless, or socially desirable. Groups that rate health and longevity as paramount values tend to define smoking and heavy drinking as serious deviance, while those giving a higher priority to individual choice do not. Those that rank sexual equality and female autonomy as lesser values than the life of the human fetus tend to define abortion as dangerous deviance, while those with the opposite priority do not. These examples no doubt oversimplify such choices, as additional values are likely to be weighed.

The proposition that definitions of unacceptable deviance reflect priorities of value is derived from the more general premise that all social norms rest on values. Our legal norms against theft of various kinds, for instance, rest chiefly on the value of private ownership of property. The norm against truancy appears to rest on many values, among which are obedience to authority, constructive use of time, child welfare, self-reliance, economic prosperity, participation in government, and knowledge as an end in itself. Perhaps some of these are more crucial than others as supports for truancy laws. In order to investigate such relationships it is essential to use separate indexes of values and norms rather than to infer values from norms or to infer both from behavior.

When value priorities are changing there is pressure on established norms to change also, and groups with different pyramids of value disagree as to what norms should prevail. Sometimes only relative shifts in the rank order of preexisting values are involved. The sharp rise and broader application in the twentieth century of the value of the welfare and happiness of the individual have lowered family stability from the position of an absolute to a relative value. Debates continue as to the relative emphasis, but most people, including marriage educators and counselors, seem to want to have as much as possible of both sets of values. With this value shift the tendency has declined to define a number of behaviors as dangerously deviant, including divorce, adultery, premarital sex, public discussion of sex, contraception, abortion, and failure of the family to care for aging parents. With the rise of person-oriented values such new areas of deviance have increasingly been defined as child-beating, child neglect, contributing to the delinquency of a minor, and various forms of unequal treatment on the basis of sex.

Sometimes new values are included in changing pyramids of value. The emergence of the humanitarian value that everyone is entitled to the minimum standard of living challenged laissez-faire values and norms. Controversial new norms have legitimized a wide range of public responsibilities for economic security and have often shifted the burden of deviance. Labor leaders, long treated by the courts as criminal offenders for attempting to organize unions, could in the 1930's point to employers as the deviants if they interfered with the new rights to organize, to bargain collectively, and to strike and if they failed to help finance such programs as workmen's compensation and social security. These deviations were to be controlled by norms of administrative law, of course, not by criminal sanctions.

The less the consensus on relevant value priorities, the greater the controversy over what norms should govern in defining deviance. Thus, when old orders of value are changing, new definitions of deviance do not emerge smoothly and unambiguously. Conflict often continues in various arenas for decades, sometimes even centuries, and controversies are often redefined and some become a complex of sub-issues. In short, issues over the definitions of deviance very often become social problems, if by this we mean ongoing dilemmas of society. Conflicts of values prevent the issues from being quickly resolved into purely technical (means-ends) problems, so the debates go on (Davis, 1970: 21–23, 29–32). These controversies may be over either the end values or the values involved in choosing the means to reach the ends. Many social problems do not involve deviance as the primary issue, but many do.

This view of deviance and other social problems is derive⌐ ⬛on ⬛ lective behavior reasoning. When existing formal or traditional norms fail to provide adequate guides for conduct, one or more collective actions oriented towards the emergence of new norms takes place. New value priorities may result in rumors, emotional outbursts, protests, social movements, public discussions, fads, panics, or still other forms of collective behavior. If the norms become problematic to at least a considerable segment of the society, a process of public discussion is set in motion, whatever other forms of collective interaction occur. If normative agreement is not reached the public opinion process continues, along with competing social movements and often other collective behaviors (Davis, 1970: 15–21).

Deviance and Cognitive Beliefs

A second basic premise in this analysis is that norms rest on cognitive or fact beliefs, not on values only. Norms are rules of conduct based not only on what people want or don't want but also on what they think will obtain their desired ends. People who agree on values may differ on fact beliefs. Value beliefs are convictions about what is desirable or undesirable, and value statements typically include such words as "good," "bad," "should," "terrible," or "preferable." Fact (cognitive) beliefs are convictions about what exists in reality, and they may or may not be correct. It is a fact judgment to say, "There is more open discussion of sex than there was a generation ago;" but a value judgment to say, "Open discussion of sex is a healthy thing." Someone else may agree with the cognitive belief but make the value judgment that, "Open discussion of sex is disgusting." For convenient reference, let us henceforth reserve the term "beliefs" for cognitive beliefs and refer to value beliefs or judgments simply as "values."

Persons or groups with similar value priorities may disagree as to what norms should govern because they hold different beliefs. For example, groups A, B, and C all strongly deplore alcoholism. Group A supports the norm of lifelong abstinence because of its belief that some people have a biochemical weakness and, lacking the capacity to control their drinking, are certain to become alcoholics if they ever take one drink. Group B supports legal norms that prohibit drinking of any alcoholic beverage until age twenty-one, believing that most people can control their drinking if they do not begin until they are legal adults. Group C supports legalizing the sale of beer and wine to older youth and the norm of giving children small amounts of wine or beer with meals, believing that alcoholism is caused primarily by failing to learn how to drink moderately.

Prosecutions for witchcraft in England declined early in the eighteenth century because the general belief waned that there are people with the alleged powers of witches. Even before the laws against witchcraft were repealed in 1736, judges were refusing to execute convicted witches (Currie, 1968). Legal norms defining dangerous deviance depend both on beliefs and values. Thus it is that lobbyists feed statistics and interpretations of "the facts" to legislators, and lawyers to judges, because differences in beliefs affect which legal norms will be supported.

Existing norms are perceived as inadequate when changes are occurring in either their supporting values or beliefs. Support for new norms does not require new value priorities, then, and may reflect new beliefs about the existence or frequency of certain conditions, about the causes of deviant behavior or other events, or about how human conduct or other conditions can be modified. The diffusion of new knowledge is a major cause of collective searches for new norms in the modern world. The germ theory undermined a great many health norms in the late nineteenth century, resulting in new laws requiring innoculation for many contagious diseases, isolation for some, and a plethora of sanitary regulations. It also produced one of those rapidly accelerating curves of belief in what is possible that de Tocqueville (1956) earlier called "revolution of rising expectations." People came to believe that medical miracles like those that had controlled contagious diseases were possible for the much more intractable diseases of physical deterioration and even that "insanity," drug addiction, and alcoholism were illnesses that could be cured.

Evidently changes in beliefs can influence changes in value priorities, and vice versa (Rokeach, 1968). The great drop in deaths achieved by applying the germ theory affected changes not only in health beliefs, but also in the importance of the value of life itself and of physical and mental health. Negative evaluation two centuries ago of the widespread use of the death penalty and corporal punishments apparently fostered acceptance of the belief of positivistic criminologists that rehabilitation is often possible. Deviance offers many opportunities for investigating the interaction between beliefs and values.

One way in which beliefs influence values deserves particular attention. A very frequent type of cause-and-effect belief is that a given value is instrumental in achieving another value. Many people have believed that character training leads to law-abiding behavior, for example. The belief that one negative value leads to another finds much acceptance in public discussions of deviance. Examples are the belief that marihuana leads to the use of addicting drugs, that prostitution and homosexuality contribute to family instability, and that mental illness produces crime. It is important to note that ideas about instrumental values are beliefs, and whether or not a value actually facilitates another value is an empirical question. Values considered instrumental to achieving major values may themselves become highly prized, and then the fact beliefs involved can become sacred. How many people rationally examine the beliefs supporting our prison system, our schools, or the more established welfare agencies?

Dilemmas regarding deviance and other social problem conditions continue when major disagreement goes on over the beliefs underlying disputed norms, not just when conflicting values persist (Davis, 1970: 16, 32–33). There is a strong value consensus against the nonmedical use of hard drugs, for instance, but much disagreement over the means for its elimination. The basic list of felonious crimes has long reflected well-accepted value priorities, yet a complex of issues about how to control crime are discussed endlessly, and a common complaint is that no single approach ever gets an adequate test. Such dilemmas occur in a context of contending groups with different amounts of power.

Power and Definitional Outcomes

The chance that a group will get community support for its definition of unacceptable deviance depends on its relative power position. The greater the group's size, resources, efficiency, unity, articulateness, prestige, coordination with other groups, and access to the mass media and to decision-makers, the more likely it is to get its preferred norms legitimated. But even groups with a good deal of power on many issues are unlikely to wield much influence for a given norm if they go against a widely held value position. Members of the medical profession were punished for clinical treatment of drug addicts in the 1920's, and only recently have the legal sanctions for performing abortions declined. Other factors are the extent and nature of the connection of the normative issue with the group's dominant interests and the relation to the basis for alignments with other groups. Concerning the last, lawyers, judges, probation officers, and police officers work together on many issues, but at least in California the lawyers met strong opposition from the other three groups in the movement to protect Constitutional rights in delinquency cases in the juvenile court (Lemert, 1970).

Normative issues involve the competition and conflict of groups, acting to protect prized values and on the basis of beliefs about how this can best be done. In order to clarify and justify their convictions and to make convincing arguments, groups develop statements of idea systems that incorporate the desired norms, value priorities, beliefs regarding the means proposed, and efforts to explain apparent inconsistencies and to meet other criticisms with persuasive rhetoric. Group influence is increased the more the ideology can successfully be identified with widely held values and beliefs. Groups favoring legalized abortion have had to develop some very persuasive ideology to counter the Right to Life groups' appeal to the values of life, the worth of the human individual, and naturalness. As groups struggling to legitimize their definitions of homosexuality, sexism, racism, drug use, and pornography well know, power is enhanced by persuasive ideologies, both those designed to justify existing norms and those supporting new norms.

This brief consideration of group power struggles in the public opinion process and in social movements is a pluralist view that seems apt at least in the United States and other Western-style democracies, since no group appears to have a monopoly on even a single issue in deviant behavior, let alone all of them. However, in conflict theory the controlling groups may be regarded as having the power to impose their norms and supporting values and beliefs on powerless groups, much of whose preferred conduct and norms are officially defined as deviant. In terms that might be incorporated into functionalist perspectives, societal norms are undergirded by normally strong agreement on both values and beliefs, and a sufficient lowering of consensus on either jeopardizes societal integration. Thus the essentials of this analysis, in terms of relationships between values, beliefs, group power, and deviance-defining norms, should apply in any society and in any type of theory.

Control Agencies and
Definitions of Deviance

The adoption of official norms defining nontolerated deviance does not end the group struggles over them. Ambiguities characteristically crop up in even the most carefully drafted rules of conduct when they must be applied to concrete situations, and the groups previously involved in the debate continue to try to influence enforcement activities and oftentimes seek changes in the formal norms. Thus the power struggle goes on, influencing the activities of deviance-controlling organizations and public reactions to them. As formal definitions of deviance are thus often uneasy compromises rather than definitive resolutions of the issues, the social problems endure.

People who occupy positions in deviance-controlling agencies have their own value priorities and beliefs, often reflecting views of professional or other reference groups. Sometimes there are deep differences among staff members within the same organization, as in the classic case of the custody versus rehabilitation orientations in correctional institutions. Dominant agency values and beliefs can narrow or broaden collective definitions of deviance. The role of values is perhaps more obvious, but beliefs held by control agents also affect their outlook on what actions they should take (Stoll, 1968). For example, agents who believe deviance is a result of illness are less inclined toward punitive sanctions than are those who consider the deviant actor willfully responsible (Aubert and Messinger, 1958; Nettler, 1959).

Agency officials develop procedures for identifying and processing deviants and for keeping the necessary information to account for their actions. In this sense they produce the deviant populations and count them (Kitsuse and Cicourel, 1963). They and the public may come to believe in the validity of their indexes of deviance, as illustrated by the F.B.I. Crimes Known to the Police Index. Although better than most alternative indexes, it is far from being a complete measure of total crime; officials can produce ups and downs (usually ups) in officially recorded crime by variations in law enforcement activities. Statistics on deviance are often crucial to the maintenance of budgets and other support for control organizations and to elections, appointments, promotions, and tenure. Belief in the need for preventive treatment expands agency surveillance, thus swelling the statistics.

There are other ways in which people in control organizations protect their vested interests and influence public definitions of deviance, including mutual-support arrangements with other agencies and public relations activities. A further method is to select and handle clients in such a way that a particular image of the deviants is fostered, together with the appropriate beliefs about their typical traits and needs. Spradley (1970) maintains that policemen run city drunk tanks in a manner that forces those arrested to accept the status of powerless, immoral, transient, unkempt, worthless bums. Arrests are not just for drunkenness, since well-dressed drunks are rarely detained. Apparently many police officers accept as true the beliefs involved in the stereotype of the bum; but by beatings, confiscation of property, and other means the arrested "drunk" is forced to behave like the powerless bum he must be in order to justify the whole drunk tank process. As city fathers can be convinced that the apparently substantial numbers of disreputable persons must be kept off the streets, the prophecy is self-fulfilling. Since over half of all urban arrests in the United States are for drunkenness, this is a bread-and-butter category when it comes time to justify the budget. Thus police departments have developed a vested interest in the collective definition of the drunken bum.

An example of organizational activity that allegedly encourages a restricted image of deviants is the selection by agencies for the blind of the educable young and employable adult clients (Scott, 1967). Most agencies actually compete for them, according to Scott, while ignoring services to the elderly blind and to multiply-handicapped children. These agencies are given the mandate to serve the needs of the blind, and there is no shortage of funds for this cause. Over two thirds of the blind are elderly, yet Scott maintains that less than one tenth of the agencies attempt to serve them. The chief emphasis is on serving those for whom "success" is most probable, an approach that apparently meets the needs of the agency people and reinforces stereotyped beliefs about blindness in terms of youth, hope, education, and work. So, by fostering what Scott sees as false beliefs, the agencies contribute to a narrow public definition of blindness rather than one that fits the typical needs of today's blind.

Employability of the blind has evidently been the typical agency emphasis throughout the century (Scott: 252–253). Straus (1966: 30–31) contends that public concern for the disabled and other dependents was long characterized by avoidance and grudging provisions for survival, thus exclusion from efforts at rehabilitation. Scott is apparently maintaining that the agency emphasis on education and employability is still denying help to a great many blind people whose performance in family and other roles could benefit from rehabilitation services, for which plentiful public and private funds are available.

Conclusion

Thomas Szasz, redoubtable psychiatrist, has maintained that people have a deep-seated unwillingness to distinguish between the is and the ought, between descriptive and prescriptive statements (Szasz, 1961: 133–163; 1970: 272). In this paper that human weakness has been conquered, and the collective definition of deviant behavior has been analyzed in terms of the influences of value judgments and fact beliefs on deviance-defining norms. If psychiatrists and other agents who control deviants have too long passed off their value judgments as scientific fact beliefs, sociologists have too long attributed social norms to values alone, ignoring or making only passing comments about the ways in which cognitive beliefs affect preferences for one norm over another.

An attempt has been made to show how both values and beliefs support existing norms that define dangerous deviance, but especially how changes in either values or beliefs (or both) bring challenges to existing definitions and collective interaction towards new norms for deviant behavior. The framework outlined also provides an explanation for the persistence of dilemmas about deviance and other social problem conditions. It includes attention to the effects of control organizations on public definitions of deviance, since even formal legislation does not complete the task of definition.

This framework takes account of the competition and conflict of contending groups in the collective behavior processes of defining deviance. The analysis seems to fit most comfortably into a pluralist perspective, but the essentials of the approach seem adaptable to the assumptions of either conflict or consensus theories and to the empirical circumstances of various societies. The root propositions are:

1. Deviance-defining norms rest on both value and cognitive beliefs.
2. Collective definitions of deviance depend on the power of groups to legitimate their preferred norms.

The more important of the further propositions discussed are:

3. A group defines deviance as dangerous when it is perceived as a direct or potential threat to its cherished values.
4. Changes in either pertinent value priorities or beliefs bring challenges to existing deviance-defining norms.
5. Changes in deviance-related values influence changes in relevant beliefs, and vice versa.
6. Group struggles for legitimation of deviance-defining norms take the form of a public discussion process, at least in Western democracies, typically accompanied by social movements and other forms of collective behavior.

7. Effective communication of the group's ideological position on the deviance issue is one of several important factors affecting the degree of the group's influence on the collective definition.
8. Deviance issues persist as societal dilemmas, or social problems, when there are irreconcilable conflicts in either the relevant values or the beliefs or both.
9. When formal adoption of deviance-defining norms does not resolve the underlying dissensus on values or beliefs, the group struggle continues and the activities of control agencies are affected by the ongoing cross-pressures regarding the application of the norms to specific situations and persons.
10. The values, beliefs, and vested interests of people in deviance-controlling agencies result in significant influences on the collective definition of deviance.

References

AUBERT, VILHELM, and SHELDON MESSINGER
    1958   "The Criminal and the Sick." Inquiry 3 (1958): 137–160.
CAVAN, RUTH SHONLE
    1961   "The Concepts of Tolerance and Contraculture as Applied to Delinquency." Sociological Quarterly 2, 4 (October): 243–258.
CURRIE, ELLIOTT P.
    1968   "Crimes Without Criminals: Witchcraft and Its Control in Renaissance Europe." Law and Society Review III, 1 (August): 7–32.
DAVIS, F. JAMES
    1970   Social Problems: Enduring Major Issues and Social Change. New York: The Free Press.
DE TOCQUEVILLE, ALEXIS
    1856   The Old Regime and the French Revolution. New York: Harper and Bros.
ERIKSON, KAI T.
    1966   Wayward Puritans. New York: John Wiley and Sons, Inc.
KITSUSE, JOHN I., and AARON V. CICOUREL
    1963   "A Note on the Use of Official Statistics." Social Problems 12 (Fall): 131–139.
KITTRIE, NICHOLAS N.
    1971   The Right to be Different: Deviance and Enforced Therapy. Baltimore: The Johns Hopkins Press.
LEMERT, EDWIN M.
    1970   Social Action and Legal Change: Revolution Within the Juvenile Court. Chicago: Aldine Publishing Co.
LIPSET, SEYMOUR MARTIN
    1963   "Three Decades of Radical Right: Coughlinites, McCarthyites and Birchers." In Daniel Bell (ed.), The Radical Right. Garden City, N.Y.: Doubleday and Co.
LOFLAND, JOHN
    1969   Deviance and Identity. Englewood Cliffs, N.J.: Prentice-Hall, Inc.

NETTLER, GWYNN
    1959   "Cruelty, Dignity and Determinism." American Sociological Review 24 (June): 375–384.

ROKEACH, MILTON
    1968   Beliefs, Attitudes and Values. San Francisco: Jossey-Bass Inc., Publishers.

SCHUR, EDWIN M.
    1965   Crimes Without Victims. Englewood Cliffs, N.J.: Prentice-Hall, Inc.

SCOTT, ROBERT A.
    1967   "The Selection of Clients by Social Welfare Agencies: The Case of the Blind." Social Problems 14 (Winter): 248–257.

SPRADLEY, JAMES P.
    1970   You Owe Yourself a Drunk. Boston: Little, Brown and Co.

STOLL, CLARICE S.
    1968   "Images of Man and Social Control." Social Forces 47 (December): 119–127.

STRAUS, ROBERT
    1966   "Social Change and the Rehabilitation Concept." Chapter One in Marvin B. Sussman (ed.), Sociology and Rehabilitation. Washington, D.C.: American Sociological Association and the Vocational Rehabilitation Administration of the United States Department of Health, Education and Welfare.

SZASZ, THOMAS S.
    1961   The Myth of Mental Illness. New York: Dell Publishing Co.
    1970   The Manufacture of Madness. New York: Dell Publishing Co.

THOMAS S. SZASZ

The Expulsion of Evil

Perversions of the sacrificial principle (purgation by scapegoat, congregation by segregation) are the constant temptation of human societies, whose orders are built by a kind of animal exceptionally adept in the ways of symbolic action.

—*Kenneth Burke*[1]

I have argued that both the medieval witch and the modern mental patient are the scapegoats of society. By sacrificing some of its members, the community seeks to "purify" itself and thus maintain its integrity and survival. Implicit in this thesis is the premise that communities of men are often in need of venting their frustration on scapegoats. What is the evidence for this assumption? And what social and psychological functions does the destruction of scapegoats fulfill? In this chapter, I shall offer some answers to these questions.

The ritual destruction of men and animals is a prevalent custom among primitive people. "The notion that we can transfer our guilt and sufferings to some other being who will bear them for us is familiar to the savage mind," writes Frazer. "It arises from a very obvious confusion between the physical and the mental, between the material and the immaterial. Because it is possible to shift a load of wood, stones, or what not, from our own back to the back of another, the savage fancies that it is equally possible to shift the burden of his pains and sorrows to another, who will suffer them in his stead. Upon this idea he acts, and the result is an endless number of very unamiable devices for palming off upon someone else the trouble which a man shrinks from bearing himself."[2]

Anthropological accounts abound in such "unamiable devices." An

---

[1] Kenneth Burke, Interaction: III. Dramatism, in David L. Sills (Ed.), *International Encyclopedia of the Social Sciences,* Vol. 7, pp. 445–452; p. 451.

[2] James George Frazer, *The Golden Bough,* p. 539.

ancient Hebrew custom is one of the best-known examples of the ritual of transfer of personal guilt to a scapegoat.[3] I refer to the ceremony of Yom Kippur, the Jewish High Holy Day. When the Temple stood in Jerusalem, the scapegoat was a real goat. His duty was to be the embodiment, the symbol, of all the sins the people of Israel had committed over the past year, and to carry those sins with him out of the community. "And when he has made an end of atoning," we read in Leviticus, ". . . he shall present the live goat; and Aaron shall lay both his hands upon the head of the live goat, and confess over him all the iniquities of the people of Israel, and all their transgressions, all their sins; and he shall put them upon the head of the goat, and send him away into the wilderness by the hand of a man who is in readiness. The goat shall bear all the iniquities upon him to a solitary land; and he shall let the goat go into the wilderness."[4]

The same theme is repeated—but with the significant variation that the scapegoat is a person, not a goat—in Isaiah: "Who has believed what we have heard? And to whom has the arm of the Lord been revealed? For he grew up before him like a young plant, and like a root out of dry ground; he had found no form or comeliness that we should look at him, and no beauty that we should desire him. He was despised and rejected by men; a man of sorrows, and acquainted with grief; and as one from whom men hide their faces, he was despised, and we esteemed him not. Surely he has borne our griefs and carried our sorrows . . . he was wounded for our transgressions, he was bruised for our iniquities; upon him was the chastisement that made us whole, and with his stripes we are healed. All we like sheep have gone astray; and the Lord has laid on him the iniquity of us all."[5]

These passages hint at the Christian ethic, preached but not practiced, that it is better to be wronged than to do wrong, to be a victim than an aggressor. They presage the legend of Jesus,[6] mankind's most illustrious scapegoat, who suffered for and redeemed all men for all time.[7] This imagery of good men suffering for bad, though no doubt lofty in its aim, has probably done mankind little good, and perhaps much harm. It is fruitless to exhort men to be self-sacrificing. Indeed, the more the scapegoat suffers and the more blame he takes upon himself, the more guilt he may engender in those who witness his suffering, and the more onerous is the task he imposes on those who aspire to justify his sacrifice. Christianity thus asks more of man than he can do. In the few, it inspires saintliness; in the many, it often promotes intolerance.[8] The moral aim of Christianity is to foster identification

[3] The scapegoat is so named because, by means of it, man escapes from guilt and sin; the term is a contraction of "escape goat." (Wilfred Funk, *Word Origins,* p. 276.)
[4] Leviticus, 16: 20–22.
[5] Isaiah, 53: 1–6.
[6] See also Isaiah, 53: 7–12.
[7] This scriptural passage also foreshadows the destiny of the Jews, who both chose the role of scapegoat and were cast into it. Zionism may perhaps be looked upon as, among other things, a collective Jewish rejection of the role of scapegoat—just as conversion may be an individual rejection of it.
[8] "Of all the religions," observed Voltaire, "Christianity should of course inspire the most toleration, but till now the Christians have been the most intolerant of all men." (Voltaire, *Philosophical Dictionary,* p. 485.)
Mutatis mutandis, the same should be true for psychiatry, but today psychiatrists are as intolerant as priests were formerly. Illustrative is the following statement by one

with Jesus as a model; its effect is often to inspire hatred for those who fail—because of their origins or beliefs—to display the proper reverence toward Him. The Judeo-Christian imagery of the scapegoat—from the ritual of Yom Kippur to the Crucifixion of Jesus as the Redeemer—thus fails to engender compassion and sympathy for the Other. Those who cannot be saints, and who cannot transcend this awesome imagery, are thus often driven, in part by a kind of psychological self-defense, to identifying with the aggressor.[9] If man cannot be good by shouldering blame for others, he can at least be good by blaming others. Through the evil attributed to the Other, the persecutor authenticates himself as virtuous.

The theme of the scapeogoat is, of course, not confined to Jewish and Christian religion and folkways. Similar practices are described for other times and places. Frazer tells us that among the Caffres of South Africa, for example, "natives sometimes adopt the custom of taking a goat into the presence of a sick man, and confess the sins of the kraal over the animal. Sometimes a few drops of blood from the sick man are allowed to fall on the head of the goat, which is then turned out into an uninhabited part of the veld."[10] In Arabia, "when the plague is raging, the people will sometimes lead a camel through all the quarters of the town in order that the animal may take the pestilence on itself. They then strangle it in a sacred place and imagine that they have rid themselves of the camel and of the plague at one blow."[11] These ceremonies are at once religious and medical; they seek to insure spiritual harmony and protection from illness.

The ceremonial destruction of scapegoats for "therapeutic" purposes was also a common practice in ancient Greece. Together with Jewish customs, these rituals constitute the origin of many later Western medicomoral beliefs and practices. In sixth-century B.C. Greece, the custom of the scapegoat was as follows: "When a city suffered from plague, famine, or other public calamity, an ugly or deformed person was chosen to take upon himself all the evils which afflicted the community. He was brought to a suitable place, where dried figs, a barley loaf, and cheese were put into his hands. These he ate. Then he was beaten seven times upon his genital organs with squills . . . while the flutes played a particular tune. Afterwards he was burned on a pyre . . ."[12]

In first-century A.D. Greece, the custom of the scapegoat was of two kinds. One was recorded by Plutarch (C. 46–120), and is described by Harrison as follows: "The little township of Chaeronea in Boeotia, Plutarch's birthplace, saw enacted year by year a strange and very ancient ceremonial. It was called 'The Driving out of the Famine.' A household slave was driven

---

of the leading forensic psychiatrists in the United States and a recipient of the American Psychiatric Association's prestigious Isaac Ray Award: "If it is considered the will of the majority that large numbers of sex offenders . . . be indefinitely deprived of their liberty and supported at the expense of the state, I readily yield to that judgment." (Manfred S. Guttmacher, *Sex Offenses,* p. 132.)

[9] I believe that intelligent self-interest, conscientious self-restraint, and sympathetic identification with others would engender less inclination to hatred than traditional religious teachings based on the promise of redemption through the sacrifice of scapegoats.

[10] Frazer, p. 540.
[11] Ibid.
[12] Ibid., p. 579.

out of doors with rods of *agnus castus,* a willow-like plant, and over him were pronounced the words, 'Out with Famine, in with Health and Wealth.' "[13] When Plutarch held the office of chief magistrate of his native town, he performed this ceremony, and he has recorded the discussion to which it afterward gave rise.

There was another, darker, form of this practice, which is described by Frazer. Whenever an important locality would be ravaged by the plague, "a man of the poorer classes used to offer himself as a scapegoat. For a whole year he was maintained at public expense, being fed on choice and pure food. At the expiry of the year he was dressed in sacred garments, decked with holy branches, and led through the whole city, while prayers were uttered that all the evils of the people might fall on his head. He was then cast out of the city or stoned to death by the people outside of the walls."[14] In Athens, this practice was institutionalized. The Athenians maintained "a number of degraded and useless beings at public expense; and when any calamity . . . befell the city, they sacrificed two of these outcast scapegoats."[15] One of the victims was sacrificed for the benefit of men, the other for that of women. Sometimes the victim sacrificed for women was a woman.[16]

Such sacrifices, moreover, were not confined to extraordinary occasions but became regular, religious ceremonials, similar to the Jewish Yom Kipper. Every year, Frazer tells us, "at the festival of the Thargelia in May, two victims, one for the men and one for the women, were led out of Athens and stoned to death. The city of Abdera in Thrace was publicly purified once a year, and one of the burghers, set apart for the purpose, was stoned to death as a scapegoat or vicarious sacrifice for the life of all the others; six days before his execution he was excommunicated, in order that he alone might bear the sins of all the people."[17]

These examples should suffice to illustrate the ancient origins of scapegoat sacrifices and their far-reaching social significance.[18] They are sobering reminders, too, of the darker underside of classical Greece. There was more

[13] Jane Ellen Harrison, *Epilegomena to the Study of Greek Religion and Themis,* p. xvii.

[14] Frazer, pp. 578–579.

[15] Ibid., p. 579.

[16] The Athenians maintained a stable of *persons* to be used in such emergencies; we maintain a stable of *words* (and *roles*). Thus when the calamity of an especially horrible crime befalls our society, we reach into our stable of words (and roles) and, instead of coming to grips with the moral problem posed by the crisis, we sacrifice a Symbolic Offender who may be called a "madman," a "schizophrenic," a "homicidal paranoiac," or a "sex-offender." Although these sacrifices are quite ineffective in dealing with the problems that beset our society, they are, because they are fervently believed in, effective in at least temporarily tranquilizing social anxieties.

[17] Ibid.

[18] Many authors consider it a sign of moral progress when man ceases to sacrifice his fellow man and uses animals as scapegoats. For the victim, this is no doubt true; for the persecutor, however, it may not be. The motives for animal and human sacrifices are the same. The individuals who make use of these practices display the same inability or unwillingness to shoulder moral responsibility for their conduct. The psychological significance of replacing human scapegoats by animal sacrifices has thus been generally overestimated. So long as men engage in the ceremonial destruction of symbolic enemies—whether these be animals, alien peoples, or individuals who formerly belonged to the group—man will not be safe from his fellow predators.

to ancient Greek democracy, the cradle of Western liberties, than the *polis,* with its great orators, philosophers, and playwrights; there was also Greek slavery, misogyny, and the ceremonial sacrifice of human beings. These beliefs and practices, no less than others of which we are more proud, we have inherited from them and adapted to our own uses.

The ancient Greeks persecuted scapegoats for reasons which, as they saw them, were religious; we do so for reasons which, as we see them, are medical. The differences between these two perspectives, one theological, the other therapeutic, are ideological and semantic, rather than operational or social. Indeed, the similarities between them—which I emphasize throughout this volume by comparing the Inquisition with Institutional Psychiatry, witches with madmen, religious justifications for violence with medical—are demonstrated by Harrison's excellent analysis of the social function of the ritual expulsion of evil. Choosing as paradigm the ceremony of "The Driving out of Famine" as practised by Plutarch, because "it expresses with singular directness and simplicity . . . the very pith and marrow of primitive religion," Harrison identifies the end goal of the ritual as "the conservation and promotion of life."[19] This end, she notes, "is served in two ways, one negative, one positive, by the riddance of whatever is conceived to be hostile and by the enhancement of whatever is conceived of as favorable to life. Religious rites are primarily of two kinds and two only, of *expulsion* and *impulsion*."[20]

What is considered good must be included in the body, the person, the community; and what is considered bad, must be excluded from them. When medical values replace religious, the same principle continues to operate: whatever promotes health—good food, good heredity, good habits—must be incorporated or cultivated; whatever promotes illness—poisons, microbes, tainted heredity, bad habits—must be eliminated or rejected. Ancient religious rituals are thus restored in new psychiatric ceremonies of inclusion and exclusion, validation and invalidation, exaltation and degradation. That which is considered good, now defined as mentally healthy, is embraced; that which is considered bad, now defined as mentally sick, is repudiated.

In order that he may live, "Primitive man has before him," says Harrison ". . . the old dual task to get rid of evil, and secure good. Evil is to him of course mainly hunger and barrenness. Good is food and fertility. The Hebrew word for 'good' meant originally good to eat."[21] With changing cultural conditions, physical and social survival comes to depend on different things: valor in battle, obedience to authority, sexual asceticism; these, then, become dominant moral values, and their antitheses, mortal sins.

From this perspective, the religious, social, and psychiatric functions of the scapegoat ritual merge into a single conceptual framework. To Plutarch, says Harrison, the Chaeronea rite was "religious, yet it contained and implied no god. The kindred rite at Athens, the expulsion of the scapegoat, became associated with the worship of Apollo, but Apollo is no integral part of it."[22] As Harrison here uses it, the concept of religion does not require a

---

[19] Harrison, p. xvii.
[20] Ibid.
[21] Ibid.
[22] Ibid., p. xxi.

godhead. Buddhism, for example, is universally recognized as a religion, yet it is godless. "That the Chaeronea rite is godless and priestless is clear enough. The civil officer, the Archon [or magistrate], expels the slave and pronounces the expulsion of Famine and the incoming of Health and Wealth. . . . The action is what we call 'magical.' "[23] In this usage, "religion" is a collective, and "magic" an individual, activity of a ceremonial or non-technical type.

It is important that we clearly understand the nature of this kind of ritual action, and not confuse it with technical action. Otherwise, we shall be in grave danger of believing—as indeed we so often believe—that our social behavior, unless explicitly labeled as religious, is always technical. Nothing could be further from the truth.

Until recent decades, much of medical practice was a series of magical acts.[24] This was even truer of psychiatry. Until the turn of the century, psychiatric practice was a mixture of ceremonial and technical acts, the former predominating over the latter like horsemeat over rabbit in the proverbial Hungarian stew made of equal portions of horse and rabbit: one each. What was medical, was ceremonial; what was punitive, was technical. Freud changed the proportions but not the basic character of the mixture: he enlarged the technical at the expense of the ceremonial. At the same time, he added fresh rituals to those of traditional psychiatric practice—for example, the couch, free association, the voyage through the "depths" of the unconscious, and so forth.[25]

The point of this discussion is to re-emphasize that Institutional Psychiatry is largely medical ceremony and magic. This explains why the labeling of persons—as mentally healthy or diseased—is so crucial a part of psychiatric practice. It constitutes the initial act of social validation and invalidation, pronounced by the high priest of modern, scientific religion, the psychiatrist; it justifies the expulsion of the sacrificial scapegoat, the mental patient, from the community. Doomed to failure are attempts to understand this performance as a technical act—for example, to analyze in logical and rational terms why aliens labeled as homosexuals should be excluded from

[23] Ibid.

[24] It was not until "Somewhere between 1910 and 1912," remarked famed Harvard physiologist Lawrence J. Henderson (1878–1942), "[that] in this country, a random patient, with a random disease, consulting a doctor chosen at random had, for the first time in the history of mankind, a better than fifty-fifty chance of profiting from the encounter." (Quoted in Maurice B. Strauss [Ed.], *Familiar Medical Quotations*, p. 302.)

[25] My analysis of the distinction between ritual and technical acts follows closely the standard anthropological view. See especially Bronislaw Malinowski, *Magic, Science, and Religion*.

The English anthropologist Radcliffe-Brown puts it this way: "In any technical activity an adequate statement of the purpose of any particular act or series of acts constitutes by itself a sufficient explanation. But ritual acts differ from technical acts in having in all instances some expressive or symbolic element in them. . . . My own view is that the negative and positive rites of savages exist and persist because they are part of the mechanism by which an orderly society maintains itself in existence, serving as they do to establish certain fundamental social values." (A. R. Radcliffe-Brown, On Taboo, in Talcott Parsons, et al. [Eds.], *Theories of Society*, Vol. II, pp. 951–959; pp. 954, 958.) For a discussion of the distinction between ritual and technical action in psychoanalysis, see Thomas S. Szasz, *The Ethics of Psychoanalysis*, especially pp. 9–77.

citizenship in this country, or what criteria should govern such labeling.[26] Indeed, by confusing ritual acts with technical acts, such efforts distract us from frankly confronting the moral problems which our psychiatric rituals create and pose for us.

Ritual is the product of moral repression. The aim of analyzing ritual is to re-create the moral problem "solved" by it; such analysis is therefore bound to create social anxiety and is likely to be ill-received. When "advanced" societies insist on maintaining the fiction that they engage in no ritual acts; or, more narrowly, that some particular performance of theirs categorized as ritual by their critics is in fact technical—they act like "benevolent" individuals who insist on maintaining the fiction that they engage in no harmful acts; or, more narrowly, that some particular behavior of theirs, categorized as injurious by their victims, is, in fact, beneficial for them. Like individuals, groups prefer to analyze and change others, rather than themselves. It is easier on their self-esteem, and less trouble, too.

The gist of Harrison's interpretation of ritual, then, is that, by expelling evil and incorporating good, it protects and perpetuates life. The scapegoat is necessary as a symbol of evil which it is convenient to cast out of the social order and, which, through its very being, confirms the remaining members of the community as good. It makes sense, too, that man—the animal distinguished by his capacity to make symbols, images, and rules—should employ by his capacity to make symbols, images, and rules—should employ such a practice. For the animal predator in the jungle, the rule of life is: kill or be killed. For the human predator in society, the rule is: stigmatize or be stigmatized. Because man's survival depends on his status in society, he must maintain himself as an acceptable member of the group. If he fails to do so, if he allows himself to be cast into the role of scapegoat—he will be cast out of the social order, or he will be killed. We have seen the way this rule was enforced in the Middle Ages, in the Age of Faith; and the way it is enforced in the modern world, in the Age of Therapy. Religious classification in the former and psychiatric classification in the latter form the bases for processes of social inclusion (validation) and exclusion (invalidation); for methods of social control (banishment, commitment); and for ideological justifications for the destruction of human differences ("sin," "mental illness").

We have had occasion to see what man has done to man by invalidating him on religious grounds, as bewitched (or unbaptized), and on psychiatric grounds, as mad (or psychologically unfit). In keeping with Frazer's and Harrison's anthropological scheme, which pictures societies (and individuals) as introjecting the goods, and expelling the bad, the struggle of (good) Christians against (bad) Jews becomes the essential dynamics of anti-Semitism. This is not merely a hypothesis or a metaphor; it is historical reality. In the Middle Ages, the God of the European was a Christian; his Devil was a Jew.[27] In the modern world, the source of security for the group has been

[26] See Chapter 13.

[27] Satan was an explicitly Jewish demon, often depicted wearing a Jew's hat or yellow badge. For a fine historical study of Satan as a Jew, and the Jews as the devil's disciples, see Joshua Trachtenberg, *The Devil and the Jews.*

displaced from God and Pope to nation and leader, from religion to science; its symbols of insecurity have shifted accordingly from witch and Jew to traitor and madman. The Jew remains a scapegoat, not because he is Antichrist, but because he has been rediagnosed as traitor (as in French anti-Semitism during the Dreyfus affair), and as hygienic threat (as in modern German anti-Semitism). As before, by valiantly struggling against the Other as the Symbolic Offender, the Just Man validates himself as good.

Sartre views anti-Semitism as I view the persecution of witches and madmen. His analysis will help to deepen our understanding of oppressor-victim relationships in general, and of the institutional psychiatrist-involuntary patient relationship in particular.

In Sartre's short story, "The Childhood of a Leader,"[28] we encounter Lucien, the only son of a prosperous manufacturer, struggling for direction and meaning in his life. He meets Lemordant, a young man of conviction. Lemordant knows *who he is* and this charms Lucien. Soon Lemordant introduces Lucien to anti-Semitism—its ideology, its literature, its ardent believers —just as an older man might introduce a younger to homosexuality or heroin. The result is a "cure" of Lucien's identity crisis. "Lucien studied himself once more," writes Sartre; "he thought 'I am Lucien! Somebody who can't stand Jews.' He had often pronounced this sentence but today was unlike all other times. . . . Of course, it was apparently a simple statement, as if someone had said 'Lucien doesn't like oysters' or 'Lucien likes to dance.' But there was no mistaking it: love of dancing might be found in some little Jew who counted no more than a fly: all you had to do was look at that damned kike to know that his likes and dislikes clung to him like his odor, like the reflection of his skin, . . . but Lucien's anti-Semitism was of a different sort: unrelenting and pure. . . . 'It's sacred,' he thought."[29]

Lucien's anti-Semitism makes him feel good in the same way that the war on mental illness makes the supporters of the Mental Health Movement feel good. Jurists, legislators, physicians, society matrons—the pillars of society—thus imbue their lives with meaning; to be sure, they do so at the expense of unemployed Puerto Ricans addicted to heroin, illiterate Negroes committing petty crimes, and the poor of all kinds who drink too much— whom they declare mentally sick to the last man.

In his book, *Anti-Semite and Jew,* Sartre correctly notes that the role of hatred in anti-Semitism may easily be overestimated: "Anti-Semitism is not merely the joy of hating; it brings positive pleasures too. By treating the Jew as an inferior and pernicious being, I affirm at the same time that I belong to the elite. This elite, in contrast to those of modern times which are based on merit or labor, closely resembles an aristocracy of birth. There is nothing

---

Believing in the reality not only of Christ but also of Antichrist, the medieval mind, Trachtenberg notes, climaxed this parallel by making the latter "the child of a union between the devil and a Jewish *harlot*—in deliberate contrast to that other son of God and a Jewish *virgin*." (Ibid., p. 35.) Trachtenberg reproduces a number of engravings from the fifteenth, sixteenth, and seventeenth centuries, showing Satanic figures identified with the Jew badge (Ibid., Frontispiece and pp. 30, 195.)

[28] Jean-Paul Sartre, The Childhood of a Leader, in *Intimacy and Other Stories,* pp. 81–159.

[29] Ibid., p. 156.

I have to do to merit my superiority, and neither can I lose it. It is given once and for all."[30] We encounter the same superiority in the mentally healthy toward the mentally sick. Once a Presidential assistant is defaced as a homosexual, or an Ezra Pound as mad, even the lowliest of "normal" men can feel superior to him. Indeed, men so defaced through the degradation ceremonies of modern psychiatry are like the dead: the survivors congregate at the cemetery and secretly congratulate themselves for being alive, while their poor luckless "friend" is already finished.

For the true anti-Semite, there can be no good Jew. "The Jew," Sartre acutely observes, "is free *to do evil,* not good; he has only as much free will as is necessary for him to take full responsibility for the crimes of which he is the author; he does not have enough to achieve a reformation."[31] (Italics in the original.) For the conscientious mental health worker there can be no mental illness useful to the patient or society, nor any mental patient capable of achieving his own self-transformation. This justifies the debasement of *all* persons labeled mentally ill, and the imposition of treatment on *any* of them by the authorities (whether such "treatment" exists or not).

Another of the scapegoat's functions is to help the Just Man (as Sartre calls the person we might call the Normal Man) avoid confronting the problem of good and evil. "If all he [the anti-Semite] has to do is to remove Evil," writes Sartre, "that means that the Good is already given. He has no need to seek it in anguish, to invent it, to scrutinize it patiently when he has found it, to prove it in action, to verify it by its consequence, or, finally, to shoulder the moral choice he has made."[32] Just so for the mental health worker: all he has to do is convert the addict into the ex-addict, the homosexual into the heterosexual, the agitated into the tranquil—and the Good Society will be here.

Because the anti-Semite fights evil, his goodness and the goodness of the society he is fighting for cannot be questioned. This makes it possible for him to use the most ignoble methods, which will be justified by the ends he seeks. The anti-Semite "bathes his hands in ordure,"[33] Sartre writes. The institutional psychiatrist treating involuntary patients is similarly engaged in a task whose goodness is considered so self-evident that it justifies the vilest of means. He deceives, coerces, and imprisons his victims, drugs them into stupor, and shocks them into brain damage. Does this lessen the goodness of his work? Not at all. He is fighting evil.

Combating evil also helps to consolidate the fighters into a well-knit, harmonious group. Thus, all the lonely and incompetent men who lead dull lives may gain admittance, "by repeating with eager emulation the statement that the Jew is harmful to the country . . . to the fireside of social warmth and energy. In this sense, anti-Semitism has kept something of the nature of human sacrifice."[34] Today, in the United States, anti-Semitism will not gain one admittance to such social warmth and energy; but the solemn incantation

[30] Jean-Paul Sartre, *Anti-Semite and Jew,* pp. 26–27.
[31] Ibid., p. 39.
[32] Ibid., p. 44.
[33] Ibid., p. 45.
[34] Ibid., p. 51.

of slogans like "Mental illness is the nation's number one health problem" or "Mental illness is like any other illness" will.[35]

Can the problem of anti-Semitism be solved by converting Jews to Christianity? (Or that of mental illness by restoring madmen to mental health?) In the classic tradition of humanism, Sartre argues that this solution does not differ greatly from that proposed by the anti-Semite: both result in the elimination of Jews! Identifying the proponent of Jewish conversion as "the democrat," Sartre writes: ". . . there may not be so much difference between the anti-Semite and the democrat. The former wishes to destroy him as a man and leave nothing in him but the Jew, the pariah, the untouchable; the latter wishes to destroy him as a Jew and leave nothing in him but the man, the abstract and universal subject of the rights of man and the rights of the citizen."[36] In psychiatry we encounter a rivalry between these same two positions, as if none other were conceivable or possible.

As the anti-Semite wants to solve the Jewish problems by destroying the Jew, so the Nazi psychiatrist tries to solve the mental health problem by destroying the mentally sick. In a moral revolt against this, the democrat, as Sartre puts it (or the liberal, as we might put it in our contemporary, psychiatric-political jargon), wants to solve the former problem by conversion, and the latter by treatment. Thus, when the liberal defines certain individuals or groups as sick, he does not mean that they have a right to be sick—any more than, in the eye of the anti-Semite, the Jew has a right to be a Jew. Indeed, the diagnosis is but a semantic lever to justify the elimination of the (alleged) "illness."[37] In both cases, the oppressor is unwilling to recognize and accept

[35] It is difficult to pick up a newspaper or medical journal without coming across expressions of this cant. Here is a recent example: "After a quarter of a century in which neurology and psychiatry have been going their separate ways, . . . the boundaries between them are becoming less definable." (Melvin Yahr, Neurology [Annual review], *Med. World News*, Jan. 12, 1968, p. 129.) Dr. Yahr is a professor of neurology and associate dean, Columbia University College of Physicians and Surgeons.

Why this blurring of the boundaries between neurology and psychiatry is a good thing we are not told; it must be self-evident. The ceremonial character of such utterances becomes clear when we stop to think that they are always made by those who most insist that psychiatry is a medical specialty like any other. Of course, none of these men would declare that the boundaries between proctology and ophthalmology, or gynecology and neurosurgery, "are becoming less definable," or be proud that they are.

[36] Ibid., p. 57.

[37] At bottom, we deal here with a deep-seated confusion, or unwillingness to distinguish, between descriptive and prescriptive statements, between what is and what ought to be, between being informed of something and being commanded to do something. I have discussed the importance of this distinction for psychiatry in several works; see, for example, Thomas S. Szasz, *The Myth of Mental Illness,* especially pp. 133–163.

Hannah Arendt has identified the inability or unwillingness to make a distinction between these two categories and linguistic forms as an important characteristic of totalitarian, and especially Nazi, ideologists. "Their superiority," she writes, "consists in their ability immediately to dissolve every statement of fact into a declaration of purpose. In distinction to the mass membership which, for instance, needs some demonstration of the inferiority of the Jewish race before it can safely be asked to kill Jews, the elite formations understand that the statement, all Jews are inferior, means all Jews should be killed . . ." (Hannah Arendt, *The Burden of Our Time,* p. 372.)

What is true for the fascist or communist ideologist, is true as well for the psychiatric. He understands that the statement "John Doe is mentally ill," really means "Commit John Doe to a mental hospital" (or "Take away his driver's license, his job,

a human difference. What the self-righteous person cannot tolerate is inaction toward evil. "To live and let live" is, for him, not a prescription for decent human relations but a pact with the Devil.

Sartre's existentialist interpretation of anti-Semitism closely resembles the sociologic interpretation of deviance:[38] in both, the deviant—scapegoat or victim—is regarded as partly the creation of his persecutors. Although Sartre recognizes that Jews exist in the same way as homosexuals or depressed people exist, he asserts that "The Jew is one whom other men consider a Jew: that is the simple truth from which we must start. . . It is the anti-Semite who makes the Jew."[39] Now, of course, Sartre knows as well as anyone else that Jews may exist without anti-Semites. In saying that the anti-Semite "makes" the Jew, he means the Jew *qua* social object upon whom the anti-Semite proposes to act in his own self-interest. This point cannot be emphasized too strongly about mental illness. It is one thing for an observer to say that someone is sad and thinks of killing himself—and do *nothing* about it; it is quite another to describe such a person as "suicidal" or "dangerous to himself"—and *lock him up in a hospital* (to cure the disease of depression, of which he considers suicidal ideas but a symptom). In the former sense, mental illness may be said to exist without the intervention of the psychiatrist; in the latter, it is created by the psychiatrist. As in the case of anti-Semitism, moreover, the psychiatrist creates mental patients as social objects so that he can act upon them in his own self-interest. That he conceals his self-interest as altruism need not detain us here, as it is but a fresh "therapeutic" justification of interpersonal coercion.

To the extent that people have characteristics that set them apart from others, the truly liberal and humane attitude toward these differences can only be one of acceptance.[40] Sartre describes this in terms equally applicable to so-called mental patients. "In societies where women vote," he writes, "they are not asked to change their sex when they enter the voting booth. . . . When it is a question of the legal rights of the Jew, and of the more obscure but equally indispensable rights that are not inscribed in any code, he must enjoy those rights not as a potential Christian but precisely as a French Jew. It is with his character, his customs, his tastes, his religion if he has one, his

---

his right to stand trial, etc."). Nearly all the deprivations of human rights which so-called mental patients suffer are traceable to this source.

[38] See Chapter 15.

[39] Sartre, *Anti-Semite and Jew,* p. 69.

[40] However, such tolerance of differences, and the conflicts they engender, is contrary to the order of human societies, at least so far as we are familiar with them. Kenneth Burke believes that "the sacrificial principle of victimage (the 'scapegoat') is intrinsic to human congregation." He sums up his argument for this as follows: "If [social] order, then guilt; if guilt, then need for redemption; but any such 'payment' is victimage. Or: If action, then drama; if drama, then conflict; if conflict, then victimage." (Kenneth Burke, Interaction: III. Dramatism, in D. L. Sills [Ed.], *Int. Enc. Soc. Sci.,* Vol. 7, p. 450.)

The deep-seated conviction that victims must somehow be guilty and deserving of their fate—in other words, that, because they have been punished, they must have been guilty of disrupting the social order—is illustrated by Hannah Arendt's observation that "Common sense reacted to the horrors of Buchenwald and Auschwitz with the plausible argument: 'What crime must these people have committed that such things were done to them!' " (Arendt, *The Burden of Our Time,* p. 418.)

name, and his physical traits that we *must* accept him."[41] To apply this attitude to the so-called mentally ill is not an easy task. Present-day American society shows not the slightest interest in even seeing the problem in this light, much less in so resolving it. It prefers the model of conversion and cure: As Benjamin Rush sought the solution of Negritude in vitiligo, we seek the solution of fear and futility, rage and sadness in Community Mental Health Centers.[42]

Man's basic striving to solve problems is at once the source of his supreme glory and of his ignominious shame. If he cannot solve his problems by instrumental, technical means, he tries institutional, ceremonial performances. As the wheelbarrow is necessary for the former, so the scapegoat is for the latter. Technical artifacts or tools may thus be viewed as the symbols of the problems man has endeavored to solve; and so may animal and human sacrifices. What are these problems? One is disease, which endangers the survival of the body biologic; the other is sin, which endangers the survival of the body politic. In their concrete manifestations, these threats pose vast, well-nigh insoluble, problems. Perhaps because of this, throughout history, men have endeavored to simplify their tasks by drawing nonexistent connections between health and virtue, illness and sin. It is as if men could not accept, and still cannot accept, that good men may be sick and evil men healthy; or that healthy men may be evil, or sick men good. The same intolerance of moral complexity and of human differences has led men to reject the image of a just godhead, who loves all his creations equally: Jews and Christians, whites and blacks, men and women, healthy and sick. Repressing the pluralism inherent in such a world view, men have created, instead, the image of an orderly universe, ruled in a hierarchical fashion by God and his vicars on earth; or, if not by God, by men who govern in the name of the common good. Immersed in this perspective, men naturally come to value unity over diversity, control of the Other over self-control; and they construct appropriate methods for stabilizing this "social reality." Validating themselves by invalidating others, as taught by religious and national mythologies and sanctioned by laws, is one such method. In the past, societies entrusted the implementation of this social mechanism for validation and invalidation to their priests; today, they entrust it to their psychiatrists.

Furthermore, since magical methods are easier to come by than technical, it is not surprising that man has shown remarkable resourcefulness in displacing material problems to the spiritual plane, and spiritual problems to the material plane—treating each institutionally and ceremonially rather than instrumentally and technically. For centuries, man attributed disease to sin,

---

[41] Ibid., pp. 146–147.

[42] Not very long ago, when the critics of psychiatry declared that its aims was social conformity, its practitioners generally denied this charge, defining the aim of their "science" as the promotion of mental health or human well-being. This is no longer true. Institutional psychiatrists now blandly acknowledge that their aim is to adjust the human cog to the social machine. "It is the concern of psychiatry to adjust people to the social environment," is the way John Downing, director of the San Mateo County Mental Health Services, and a prominent figure in the community mental health movement, puts it. (Quoted in Leo Litvak, A trip to Esalen Institute: Joy is the prize, *New York Times Magazine*, Dec. 31, 1967, pp. 8, 21–28; p. 8.)

and endeavored to rid himself of illness by attending to his moral conduct. Today, he attributes sin to disease, and endeavors to rid himself of evil by attending to his health.

When it was in power, the Church was worshiped for promising, through its false prophets, the priests, perpetual life in heaven. When it fell out of power, it was reproached for having retarded medical progress. Today, Medicine is worshiped for promising, through its false prophets, the psychiatrists, moral tranquility on earth. When it falls out of power, it will, I think, be similarly reproached for having retarded moral progress. But, since the retardation of moral progress, while it is actually taking place, is invariably hailed as itself moral progress, genuine advancement in our spirituality must depend on the proper resolution of psychological and social problems which we have not even confronted, much less mastered. In the meantime we ought to judge all Great Moral Programs, especially if backed by the power of Churches or States, by the inverse of the Anglo-American decision-rule for judging defendants: immoral until proven otherwise.

II

LIVED MORALITY
AND CONCEPTIONS
OF · DEVIANCE

Introduction

American sociology traditionally has both overemphasized and neglected values and morality. It has explained much of social reality by treating values and morality as the basis of collective motivation. It has utilized values and morality as explanatory variables in empirical research, as well as in numerous theoretical statements. But with a few notable exceptions such as Marx, it has not systematically examined values and morality in any depth as themselves variables to be accounted for (Gouldner, 1970: 140–141).

Even the labeling approach to the study of deviance, though it focuses on rule-makers, rule-enforcers, and rules (norms), has not turned its attention to "lived morality," morality located at the popular level of a particular society (Ellul, 1969; 112–126, 159–171). In actuality it is the totality of cultural demands made upon members of society at a particular moment in time. Lived morality is a reflection of actual social conditions and structures experienced by the group as necessary for survival. Lived morality "expresses the structures in terms of obligation and duty, with a view to preserving them, perpetuating them, and regulating man with respect to them" (Ellul, 1969: 164–165; Marx and Engels, 1970). This morality also functions as justification for the historical and material development of a society.

Lived morality is organized around a "central motif":

> In every society there is an essential motif, a chief center of interest, an undisputed assumption, a good recognized by all. It can be said, for example, that Christianity was this principal motif in the twelfth and thirteenth centuries, as was the proletarian revolution in Communist countries, the idea of the city-state in Greece of the fifth century before Christ, and technology today. The principal motif is always both ideological and material. It is bound up with a certain structure and it expresses itself in an aspiration. It is not a belief alone, nor is it a fact alone. It involves a combination of the two. It is in relation to this principal motif that the group's hierarchy of "values" is arranged, and that the striving toward the desirable and the imperatives of the obligatory are established. By a sort of tacit convenant, the members of the group undergo this moral organization around the principal motif which they approve of by consensus. But this principle motif is always bound up with the various group structures, and the morality takes shape out of these structures: economic, technological, religious, political, cultural, and demographic (Ellul, 1969: 164).

The various imperatives and prohibitions that labeling theorists study are specifications of the more general lived morality. Also resonant of motif, structure, and morality are conceptions of deviance, that is, public images

74

and stereotypes of the deviant, commonplace theories of deviant behavior, and attitudes toward the means and ends of social control.

In "Technological Morality" Ellul (1969: 185–198) identifies three dominant societal moralities of the past five centuries in the Western world: Christian, bourgeois, and technological. Bourgeois (middle-class) morality, still dominant in the West, is a synthesis of individual Christian morality and collective technological morality. These two moral components of bourgeois morality are actually not contradictory, for it has been Christian morality after the Reformation that has paved the way for the eventual emergence of a technological morality stripped of its Christian trappings.

The Christian morality of the Middle Ages, later refurbished in the six-teenth and seventeenth centuries, extolled the individual virtues, especially charity and good works. In a certain sense, Christianity of the Middle Ages held this world in disdain and regarded public life, especially the economic and political, as a necessary evil. However, little distinction was made between the private and public spheres because the individual Christian's beliefs were to inform the whole of his existence.

Out of the Protestant Reformation came new formulations of Christian morality (Weber, 1958). Eschewing an other-worldly orientation, Christians began to regard man's work as a calling from God. The collective anxiety which a belief in predestination spawned gave rise to rational formulations of what constituted a demonstration of one's election to heaven. Gradually the now-famous bourgeois equation of economic success with moral virtue pene-trated to the core of Christian morality. Christianity then accommodated itself to the exigencies of a developing capitalistic civilization, resulting in its moral entrapment within bourgeois society. Furthermore, the Reformation sharply distinguished the public from the private sphere of life, thereby engendering "a sort of spiritual indifference to socio-political questions" (Ellul, 1969: 186). The Reformation then relegated the political, economic, and social to man (earlier they had been subject to God's will) and conse-quently fostered a view of the world as something to be conquered by man's reason.

The eighteenth and nineteenth centuries witnessed the transformation of Christian morality into a bourgeois morality. Utilitarianism (Gouldner, 1970: 61–73) became the philosophical statement of man's relation to the de-veloping structures of bourgeois society, especially of how the common good could be realized by each individual pursuing his own interests. An individual's worth was to be measured by what he did rather than what he was. Men were now to be rewarded (by money, property, and the like), not for their ancestry or inherited station but for their accomplishments. Things and even people were regarded as useful (good) if they were success-ful in helping man attain happiness (materialistically defined, of course).

Moreover, what a man did for himself was equated, by a perverse logic, with what contribution he had made to the collective good. As Niebuhr (1960: 261) has pointed out, utilitarianism "assumes a premature identity between self-interest and social interest and established a spurious harmony between egoism and altruism." That is, bourgeois morality attempted to make compatible inner personal morality and outer public (collective) morality and, as well, man's egoistic tendencies and his altruistic potentialities. It led to the paradoxical conclusion that both less personal control and less social control would result in an harmonious collective existence. It likewise failed to recognize that man's egregious tendencies become exacerbated within the collectivity (as Hobbes duly noted), especially one so competitively organized that it induced a degree of social anarchy (Niebuhr, 1960: xi–xxv).

By concentrating on the consequences of human action (specifically their usefulness), the bourgeoisie de-emphasized the morality of an action in and of itself and thus separated the means from the end of an action. In the bourgeois formula the end justified the means, especially if the end were useful and the means efficacious.

In addition there was the intensified separation of the private from the public sphere of life (already begun in the Reformation). In the public sphere, in constitutions and in other legal formulations, the rights of man, freedom, justice, and equality were extolled while in the private domain Christian belief and man's reliance upon God were still stressed. Thus, man was free to pursue egoistic interests in his economic and political dealings but restrained in his interaction with wife, child, and neighbor in the private sphere, which, however, was rapidly shrinking.

The nexus between individual and collective morality was the family, with the father the center of authority. If bourgeois society advocated a weakly organized state with a minimum of law, yet enough to preserve human freedom, then the locus of social control would reside in the nuclear family. Children would be socialized according to Christian virtues and natural morality (the rights of man) and concomitantly trained to compete in an indutsrialized world where power, wealth, and property were increasingly paramount.

Work with its ancillary virtues of diligence, prudence, thrift, and self-control became the principal bourgeois virtue; laziness its unforgivable vice. It is, of course, no accident that these virtues were advocated, for they were precisely those a production-oriented economy needed to maintain a well-disciplined labor force. The merger of Christian and technological moralities in bourgeois thought is aptly illustrated by the Christian dictum that "work is prayer" (Ellul, 1966: 153). Of course Christianity had paved the way for the triumphant individualism of bourgeois thought by its insistence upon the dignity of the individual before God (Niebuhr, 1964: 66) and by the Reformation's emphasis on man's personal relationship to God by means of private prayer.

The resultant irony is that the more man is called upon to pursue egoistic interests and engage in invidiously competitive practices, the more addicted he becomes to their ideological justification in altruistic terms.

Technological morality, not completely institutionalized as yet, is a morality of behavior, one to bring man into harmony with an efficiency-ordered society. It is bourgeois morality without its Christian basis. Technology (actually technique) or man's happiness (they become interchangeable as the means become the end) is the good in this morality. Ellul (1969: 198) has described technological morality:

As a whole, it is a morality of occupation, of well-doing, which become a total, all-embracing morality for the whole society. It is an essentially total, even totalitarian, collective morality.

. . . In the last analysis, it appears as a suppression of morality through the total absorption of the individual into the group.

The technological morality contains a scale of widely accepted values: technology, the normal, and success. Technological progress is deemed necessary for the creation of the "good society," which assures man's happiness. Technique, "the totality of methods rationally arrived at and having absolute efficiency (for a given stage of development) in every field of human activity" (Ellul, 1964: xxv), which is the real infrastructure of modern society, reduces behavior to the normal (adjusted behavior) and guarantees success (an efficient and effective outcome). The normal replaces the older concept of virtue or the moral; it is statistically determined, average behavior. Social science research techniques such as public opinion polls and questionnaires supply us with statistical norms (Boorstin, 1973: 238–244). In fact the use of such quantitative techniques presupposes a mass society, paradoxically a society of individuals, yet one whose members are sufficiently similar that their common characteristics can be readily abstracted (Ellul, 1964: 286). Success is an additional criterion of the good: success (the efficient and effective) is good; failure (the inefficient and ineffective) is the evil. As work and leisure become replete with techniques, then success implies the use of technique, which in turn assures an efficient and efficacious outcome. The normal is determined by statistical techniques, and the successful is assured by the application of technique. Technique is the realm where the normal and the successful become intertwined.

The growth of and centralization of power within the state and the onslaught of technology, of which technique is the purest expression, coalesce to produce collectivistic societies and an increasingly "monolithic world culture" (Wilkinson, 1964: x). Technological societies tend toward the complete adjustment of the individual to the collectivity, in part through a technological morality which "informs the whole of public, professional, and private life."

In summary, Christian morality is a morality of the individual, technological morality a morality of the collectivity, and bourgeois morality a morality of the collectivized individual.

If Christian morality gave rise to the conception of deviant behavior as sinful behavior of the individual, then technological morality spawns a conception of evil residing within the collectivity, the social environment, and expresses it as illness or maladjustment. Thus, the pathology or maladjustment is actually of the social environment and the illness of the individual only its indicator. A maladjusted environment produces maladjusted individuals. But the complete scientism (Hayek, 1952) of the pathology perspective does not allow for a sharp distinction between individual man and the social collectivity or environment. The social environment determines individual behavior; yet, the social environment is composed of individuals, albeit organized into masses or collectivities. Each individual as part of the social environment determines the behavior of others but never his own behavior. In a certain sense then, both the individual and the collectivity are maladapted, each to the other, in the conception of social maladjustment (pathology).

However, bourgeois morality, a synthesis of Christian and technological moralities, conceptualizes the illness as within the individual even when its theoretical formulations sometimes perceive the cause of the problem to be the social environment. Yet the resolution of the problem involves reforming the individual—to help him adapt to his immediate environment. The bourgeois synthesis does not take the deterministic premises of its pathology orientation to their logical conclusion as does the collectivistic technological morality. Therefore, it holds the individual responsible by focusing on his problems in his relations to others, his inability to adapt. The individualistic bias of Christian morality is retained in the bourgeois synthesis.

Some of the articles in this section are concerned with conceptions of mental illness and mental health that originated in the late eighteenth century and were only fully institutionalized in the nineteenth and twentieth centuries. It is perhaps easier to grasp the morality and values underlying these conceptions if one first examines the concept of mental health, as it represents the ideal—what man ought to do and become.

Davis (1938) attempted to ferret out the values and moral implications of the mental hygiene movement of the early twentieth century. He described the values and the morality underlying the mental hygiene movement as fundamentally supportive of the Protestant ethic and an open-class (bourgeois) society; it was:

1. *Democratic* in the sense of favoring equal opportunity to rise socially by merit rather than by birth
2. *Worldly* in emphasizing earthly values such as the pursuit of a calling, accumulation of wealth, and achievement of status
3. *Ascetic* in stressing physical abstinence and stern sobriety, thrift, industry, and prudence
4. *Individualistic* in placing responsibility upon the individual himself for his economic, political, and religious destiny, and in stressing personal ambition, self-reliance, private enterprise, and entrepreneureal ability
5. *Rationalistic* and empirical in assuming a world order discoverable through sensory observation of nature
6. *Utilitarian* in pursuing practical ends with the best available means, and conceiving human welfare in secularized terms as attainable by human knowledge and action (Davis, 1938: 56)

The mental hygiene movement's "psychologistic" approach (conceptualizing human behavior as a product of individual characteristics) led it to conceive of the prevention of mental illness in individualistic terms, i.e., by educating the individual and assisting his adjustment to the environment. It is only with the growth of community psychiatry and behavior modification movements that we seriously cast prevention in terms of a massive restructuring of the environment.

Wootton (1959) following the lead of Davis (1938) analyzed numerous theoretical definitions of mental health and mental illness. She found that mental health was almost invariably equated with one or more of the following themes: (1) happiness, (2) vigor, (3) full use of one's capabilities, (4) adjustment, and (5) integration or freedom from conflict within oneself (Wootton, 1959: 214). Scott (1961: 33–34) surveyed research definitions of mental health and mental illness and discovered that the definition of mental health as adjustment (conformity to one's immediate situation) was widespread in itself and appeared to be implicit in most of the other definitions of mental health as well. All of these themes, insofar as they are represented as universal criteria, assume that environments are constantly benign, inherently good, and worthy of man's happiness, adjustment, and so on. If environments differentially promote the above values, then the conception of mental health becomes relative to culture and social structure as well as to values. Szasz (1971: 27) notes, "the healing arts—especially medicine, religion, and psychiatry—operate within society; not outside it. Indeed they are an important part of society. It is not surprising therefore, that these institutions reflect and promote the primary moral values of the community."

Let us remember too that happiness, vigor, adjustment, and the rest are values. It has only been the past three centuries in which man has proffered his own happiness as the goal of civilization (Ellul, 1969: 190). Some (Jahoda, 1953) have even advocated the explicit formulation of values as mental health criteria, as a means of confronting this issue head-on.

What then about the concept of mental illness? Superficially it would appear to have eliminated the Christian component of bourgeois morality by negating individual moral responsibility. One is no longer a sinner, a transgressor against God's commandments, but is instead mentally or emotionally sick. Just as bourgeois morality made success and failure (actually dependent upon one's relationship to historically structured inequalities of power and wealth and therefore collective and public enterprise) contingent upon individual private initiative, so too the conception of mental illness formulates expressions of collective stress and strain in terms of individual illness. Yet what really occurred was that deviations from ethical norms (bourgeois morality) were overlayed with a disease format. An individual was still held responsible for his deviant behavior in that he was to be reformed. This made sense only if his deviation were the result of an physiological, anatomical, or genetic defect. Then his "illness" could be operated on as with the removal of a brain tumor. But when he suffered from functional mental illness (illness without an apparent physical base) then the determinism of the disease concept implied that his environment should be reformed, even if the patient needed to be restrained to protect others (a greatly exaggerated danger).

Through a curious reversal, so typical of the nineteenth century, the individual was to be reformed within an asylum which in turn would "rub off on" and revitalize the larger environment that had been conceptualized as the ultimate cause of his illness. That is to say, the asylum was to be the model for good family life on the outside (Rothman, 1971).

In a brilliant sociohistorical analysis of conceptions of madness, Foucault (1965: 274) has suggested that the mental asylum in the eighteenth and nineteenth centuries was "a structure that formed a kind of microcosm in which were symbolized the massive structures of bourgeois society and its values." The asylum attempted to emulate the bourgeois family: the psychiatrist (father) instilled moral values (discipline, obedience, work) into the patient (child). The asylum, as an effort to create a moral order within, was also expected to shore up concurrently the larger social order. However, the asylum was more in keeping with the values of an industrializing society than with those of a traditional community and functioned more as a bureaucratically organized factory than as a traditional extended family (Rothman, 1971: 79–108). The asylum was simply the portent of society's future direction. The family too would come to embody the tensions and anxieties of a technological society.

So in reality the patient was asked to adjust to and conform to his own family environment or its surrogate within the asylum even when it had not been revitalized according to expectation. Environment is worth adjusting to even if it still remains a cause of the problem; it is both problem and solution.

As Foucault (1965: 254) observes, in the liberal economy of the eighteenth and nineteenth centuries, the family was given responsibility to care for the madness of one of its members (by institutionalization if necessary), even when the madness represented an inability of the individual and his family to coexist peacefully. For the bourgeoisie, then, mental illness served the function of obfuscating their responsibility in the patient's "illness" while not appearing to condemn and punish him (an illness that needed treatment).

Furthermore, the conception of illness serves to disguise the morality from which mental illness constitutes a deviation. "The concept of illness," as Szasz (1970: 15) observes, "whether bodily or mental, implies deviation from some clearly defined norm." And the norm is either physical health or mental health. Physical health is conceptualized in physiological and anatomical terms; mental health in ethical, psychosocial, and legal terms which contain judgments about how one *should* lead his life. Deviation from a psychosocial norm, i.e., a phobia (neurotic fear of some thing, place, or event), is not normal in that the "average" person can place the danger in perspective. Deviation from an ethical norm, i.e., chronic hostility or repressed envy, indicates that one should be loving and altruistic in personal relations with others. Deviation from a legal norm, i.e., homicide, occurs when the homicide is seen as the result of mental illness or as its indicator. Thus, mental illness is either indicated by, becomes the cause of, or is deviation from the normal, the moral, or the legal.

The psychiatric description of the simple schizophrenic illustrates this point especially well because all three types of norms are indicated:

> After a steady downward course, the decline may come to a halt at some relatively low level of adaptation Here the patient often lives an idle, ineffectual and apparently meaningless life. If his level of adaptation is very low, or his behavior too unpredictable, he may require permanent institutional care. If not, he may lounge about the house or the neighborhood as an irresponsible idler, or wander aimlessly from place to place as a vagrant (Cameron, 1963: 587).

The simple schizophrenic is often an irresponsible idler (moral judgment) who is apathetic and does not live up to his potential (maladjusted, as it is normal to want to get ahead) and may become a vagrant (a legal category). In short, the simple schizophrenic is not normal, is immoral, and might even be a petty criminal. His major offenses would appear to be laziness and indifference, two immoralities severely sanctioned by bourgeois morality.

The transition from bourgeois morality to technological morality and the resultant changes in the conceptions of deviance can perhaps best be grasped by analyzing the differences between the mental hygiene movement on the one hand and the community psychiatry (social psychiatry, preventive psychiatry) and behavior modification movements on the other hand. Szasz (1970: 40) sees a continuity between the two movements but has not fully explicated their underlying moralities. Nonetheless, there do exist great similarities (remember that technological morality is a component of bourgeois morality). Community psychiatry and behavior modification as social movements represent almost pure expressions of the technological morality.

The mental hygiene movement of the early twentieth century was highly reflective of bourgeois morality in its emphasis on thrift, industry, prudence, and self-control, virtues necessary to maintain a highly disciplined workforce in an industrializing economy. Mental illness was within the individual, and prevention usually entailed working with the individual before the stress he was experiencing became unmanageable.

Community psychiatry focuses more on the causes of the problem (family, community, society) than on the individual whose behavior constitutes the problem. In fact it is often claimed that mental illness exists in a family, a neighborhood, or a community. These are mentally ill, but so is the patient as a part of these environments. But the individual and his immediate environment must be treated concurrently. In the mental hygiene movement environment was often perceived as the cause of mental illness, but with community psychiatry the environment becomes the locus of the problem and the "mental illness" only its indicator. Thus, social environment must be so revamped that mental illness (within the individual) cannot occur. This is the fullness of prevention. If mental illness resides both within the individual and his social environment, then the distinction between the individual and social environment cannot be made (something Marx and other utopians have also suggested). Community psychiatry and its bedfellows, urban planning, community organization, and behavior modification share much in common: coordination, planning, prevention. To its supporters community psychiatry is man's best chance for happy, peaceful co-existence; to its opponents it is a totalitarian movement (Leifer, 1970).

Behaviorism as a social movement (Goodall, 1972: 53–54, 56–63, 133–138) is not a product of psychiatry but of the academic human sciences, especially psychology (Boorstin, 1973: 227–237). It has become an orthodoxy. Because man as man cannot be studied according to a natural science format, he is reduced to object, his behavior, and analyzed according to strictly deterministic premises. Man's behavior is controlled by positive and negative reinforcers and punishments in his environment. B. F. Skinner, behaviorism's foremost spokesman, once claimed that he did not object to utilizing the concept of mental illness if it could be readily translated into behavioristic terms, i.e., "undesired" behavior which environment has shaped.

Behavior modification itself contains at least two branches: behavior therapy and applied behavior analysis (Goodal, 1972: 57). The critical difference between the two is that behavior therapy is largely engaged in one-to-one therapy often involving aversive conditioning methods, while applied behavior analysis concerns itself more with positive conditioning by means of the restructuring of environments (family, school, business, city). Behavior therapy contains a similar orientation with mental hygiene toward the individual, while community psychiatry and applied behavior analysis work on environments as their clients. Skinner and others have noted that behavior modification works most effectively in a totally controlled environment, hense the superior efficiency of applied behavior analysis and community psychiatry.

The totalitarian aims of both movements, which greatly overlap and are ideological by-products of our technological society, are evidenced by the scope of their endeavors. Leifer (1970: 231) quotes a leading spokesman (Visotsky, 1965: 692) for community psychiatry:

> Juvenile delinquency, school problems, problems of urban areas, community conflicts, marriage and family counseling, and well-being programs all can be seen as reasonably in the province of the psychiatrist, who formerly limited his interest to psychopathology.

Caplan (1965: 3) describes the psychiatrist interested in prevention as one who "cannot wait for patients to come to him, because he carries equal responsibility for all those who do not come."

The expansionist goals of community psychiatry, however, are rather pale beside those of Skinner (1971). In a chapter entitled, "The Design of a Culture," Skinner paints in rather broad strokes a planned environment, social and cultural, in which everyone shapes the behavior of everyone else to produce good behavior, that is, behavior conducive to the survival of the human species:

> The intentional design of a culture and the control of human behavior it implies are essential if the human species is to continue to develop. (Skinner, 1971: 177) Leisure is one of the great challenges to those who are concerned with the survival of a culture because any attempt to control what a person does when he does not need to do anything is particularly likely to be attacked as unwarranted meddling. Life, liberty, and pursuit of happiness are basic rights. But they are the rights of the individual and were listed as such at a time when the literatures of freedom and dignity were concerned with the aggrandizement of the individual. They have only a minor bearing on the survival of a culture (Skinner, 1971: 180). The technology of behavior which emerges is ethically neutral, but when applied to the design of a culture the survival of the culture functions as a value (Skinner, 1971: 182).

Thus, Skinner does not eliminate freedom and dignity as values but equates them with the survival of culture and society. Moreover, survival, for Skinner, implies an efficient social and cultural order. Only when the individual is so encapsulated by his environment that he cannot be a threat to his society's survival will we possess happiness and security. Here we see the workings of self-fulfilling prophecy. Historically, living concrete man has proved inconsistent, often unpredictable, and hence not perfectly controllable. But in the interest of survival we now reduce him to an abstraction, normal and standardized behavior, and utilize techniques of control contingent upon this premise, which help to make man the abstraction a living reality. Culture becomes the generalized abstraction of man as normal, average, adjusted; society, its institutionalized fulfillment.

Skinner's insistence upon furthering the technology of behavior we now possess and his advocacy of universal schedules of reinforcement is a statement of technological morality, a morality which governs the whole of private, professional, and public life. In the final analysis behaviorism *is* technological morality and only remains to be fully institutionalized.

References

BOORSTIN, DANIEL J.
  1973 The Americans: The Democratic Experience. New York: Random House.
CAMERON, NORMAN
  1963 Personality Development and Psychopathology. Boston: Houghton Mifflin.
CAPLAN, GERALD
  1965 "Community Psychiatry—Introduction and Overview." Pp. 3–18 in Concepts of Community Psychiatry: A Framework for Training. United States Department of Health, Education, and Welfare, Public Health Service Publication No. 1319.
DAVIS, KINGSLEY
  1938 "Mental Hygiene and the Class Structure." Psychiatry 1: 55–65.
ELLUL, JACQUES
  1964 The Technological Society. New York: Vintage Books.
  1968 A Critique of the New Commonplaces. New York: Alfred A. Knopf.
  1969 To Will and To Do. Philadelphia and Boston: Pilgrim Press.
FOUCAULT, MICHEL
  1965 Madness and Civilization. New York: Random House.
GOODAL, KENNETH
  1972 "Shapers at Work." Psychology Today 6: 53–63, 132–138.
GOULDNER, ALVIN
  1970 The Coming Crisis of Western Sociology. New York: Basic Books.
HAYEK, F. A.
  1952 The Counter-Revolution of Science. Glencoe, Ill.: The Free Press.
JAHODA, MARIE
       "Social Psychology." In Interrelations Between the Social Environment and Psychiatric Disorders. New York: Milbank Memorial Fund.
LEIFER, RONALD
  1970 "Community Psychiatry and Social Power." Pp. 227–238 in Jack Douglas (ed.), Freedom and Tyranny. New York: Alfred A. Knopf.
MARX, KARL, and FREDERICK ENGELS
  1970 The German Ideology. New York: International Publishers.
NIEBUHR, REINHOLD
  1960 Moral Man and Immoral Society. New York: Charles Scribner's Sons.

1964　The Nature and Destiny of Man. Vol. 1: Human Nature. New York: Charles Scribner's Sons.

ROTHMAN, DAVID
1971　The Discovery of the Asylum. Boston: Little, Brown.

SCOTT, WILLIAM A.
1971　"Some Research Definitions of Mental Health and Mental Illness." Pp. 16–39 in Peter Hountras (ed.), Mental Hygiene. Charles E. Merrill Books.

SKINNER, B. F.
1971　Beyond Freedom and Dignity. New York: Alfred A. Knopf.

SZASZ, THOMAS
1970　Ideology and Insanity. Garden City, New York: Anchor Books.

VISOTSKY, HAROLD M.
1965　"Community Psychiatry: We Are Willing to Learn." American Journal of Psychiatry 122: 692–693.

WEBER, MAX
1958　The Protestant Ethic and the Spirit of Capitalism. New York: Charles Scribner's Sons.

WILKINSON, JOHN
1964　"Jacques Ellul as the Philosopher of the Technological Society." Pp. ix–xx in Jacques Ellul, the Technological Society. New York: Vintage Books.

WOOTTON, BARBARA
1959　Social Science and Social Pathology. London: George Allen and Unwin.

JOSEPH R. GUSFIELD

Moral Passage: The Symbolic Process in Public Designation of Deviance

Recent perspectives on deviant behavior have focused attention away from the actor and his acts and placed it on the analysis of public reactions in labelling deviants as "outsiders."[1] This perspective forms the background for the present paper. In it I will analyze the implications which defining behavior as deviant has for the public designators. Several forms of deviance will be distinguished, each of which has a different kind of significance for the designators. The symbolic import of each type, I argue, leads to different public responses toward the deviant and helps account for the historical changes often found in treatment of such delinquents as alcoholics, drug addicts, and other "criminals," changes which involve a passage from one moral status to another.

Instrumental and Symbolic Functions of Law[2]

Agents of government are the only persons in modern societies who can legitimately claim to represent the total society. In support of their acts, limited and specific group interests are denied while a public and societal

[1] Howard S. Becker, *Outsiders: Studies in the Sociology of Deviance,* Glencoe: The Free Press, 1963, Chap. 1. A similar view is presented in John Kitsuse, "Societal Reaction to Deviant Behavior," *Social Problems,* 9 (Winter, 1962), pp. 247–56; Kai Erikson, "Sociology of Deviance," in E. McDonagh and J. Simpson, editors, *Social Problems,* New York: Holt, Rinehart and Winston, Inc., 1965, pp. 457–464, p. 458.

[2] The material of this section is more fully discussed in my book *Symbolic Crusade: Status Politics and the American Temperance Movement,* Urbana: University of Illinois Press, 1963, esp. Chap. 7.

Source: Joseph R. Gusfield, "Moral Passage: The Symbolic Process in Public Designations of Deviance," *Social Problems,* 15, II (Fall, 1967), pp. 175–188. Copyright © 1967 by The Society for the Study of Social Problems. Reprinted by permission of the Society and Joseph R. Gusfield.

interest is claimed.[3] Acts of government "commit the group to action or to perform coordinated acts for general welfare."[4] This representational character of governmental officials and their acts makes it possible for them not only to influence the allocation of resources but also to define the public norms of morality and to designate which acts violate them. In a pluralistic society these defining and designating acts can become matters of political issue because they support or reject one or another of the competing and conflicting cultural groups in the society.

Let us begin with a distinction between *instrumental* and *symbolic* functions of legal and governmental acts. We readily perceive that acts of officials, legislative enactments, and court decisions often affect behavior in an instrumental manner through a direct influence on the actions of people. The Wagner Labor Relations Act and the Taft-Hartley Act have had considerable impact on the conditions of collective bargaining in the United States. Tariff legislation directly affects the prices of import commodities. The instrumental function of such laws lies in their enforcement; unenforced they have little effect.

Symbolic aspects of law and government do not depend on enforcement for their effect. They are symbolic in a sense close to that used in literary analysis. The symbolic act "invites consideration rather than overt reaction."[5] There is a dimension of meaning in symbolic behavior which is not given in its immediate and manifest significance but in what the action connotes for the audience that views it. The symbol "has acquired a meaning which is added to its immediate intrinsic significance."[6] The use of the wine and wafer in the Mass or the importance of the national flag cannot be appreciated without knowing their symbolic meaning for the users. In analyzing law as symbolic we are oriented less to behavioral consequences as a means to a fixed end; more to meaning as an act, a decision, a gesture important in itself.

An action of a governmental agent takes on symbolic import as it affects the designation of public norms. A courtroom decision or a legislative act is a gesture which often glorifies the values of one group and demeans those of another. In their representational character, governmental actions can be seen as ceremonial and ritual performances, designating the content of public morality. They are the statement of what is acceptable in the public interest. Law can thus be seen as symbolizing the public affirmation of social ideals and norms as well as a means of direct social control. This symbolic dimension is given in the statement, promulgation, or announcement of law unrelated to its function in influencing behavior through enforcement.

[3] See the analysis of power as infused with collective goals in Parsons' criticism of C. Wright Mills, *The Power Elite:* Talcott Parsons, "The Distribution of Power in American Society," *World Politics,* 10 (October, 1957), p. 123, 144. [See his book, *Structure and Process,* Glencoe, Illinois: Free Press, 1960.]

[4] Francis X. Sutton, "Representation and the Nature of Political Systems," *Comparative Studies in Society and History,* 2 (October, 1959), pp. 1–10. In this paper Sutton shows that in some primitive societies, political officials function chiefly as representatives to other tribes rather than as law enforcers or policy-makers.

[5] Phillip Wheelwright, *The Burning Fountain,* Bloomington: Indiana University Press, 1964, p. 23.

[6] Talcott Parsons, *The Social System,* Glencoe: The Free Press, 1954, p. 286.

It has long been evident to students of government and law that these two functions, instrumental and symbolic, may often be separated in more than an analytical sense. Many laws are honored as much in the breach as in performance.[7] Robin Williams has labelled such institutionalized yet illegal and deviant behavior the "patterned evasion of norms." Such evasion occurs when law proscribes behavior which nevertheless occurs in a recurrent socially organized manner and is seldom punished.[8] The kinds of crimes we are concerned with here quite clearly fall into this category. Gambling, prostitution, abortion, and public drunkenness are all common modes of behavior although laws exist designating them as prohibited. It is possible to see such systematic evasion as functioning to minimize conflicts between cultures by utilizing law to proclaim one set of norms as public morality and to use another set of norms in actually controlling that behavior.

While patterned evasion may perform such harmonizing functions, the passage of legislation, the acts of officials, and decisions of judges nevertheless have a significance as gestures of public affirmation. First, the act of public affirmation of a norm often persuades listeners that behavior and norm are consistent. The existence of law quiets and comforts those whose interests and sentiments are embodied in it.[9] Second, public affirmation of a moral norm directs the major institutions of the society to its support. Despite patterned practices of abortion in the United States, obtaining abortions does require access to a subterranean social structure and is much more difficult than obtaining an appendectomy. There are instrumental functions to law even where there is patterned evasion.

A third impact of public affirmation is the one that most interests us here. The fact of affirmation through acts of law and government expresses the public worth of one set of norms, of one sub-culture vis-à-vis those of others. It demonstrates which cultures have legitmacy and public domination, and which do not. Accordingly it enhances the social status of groups carrying the affirmed culture and degrades groups carrying that which is condemned as deviant. We have argued elsewhere that the significance of Prohibition in the United States lay less in its enforcement than in the fact that it occurred.[10] Analysis of the enforcement of Prohibition law indicates that it was often limited by the unwillingness of Dry forces to utilize all their political strength for fear of stirring intensive opposition. Great satis-

[7] Murray Edelman has shown this in his analysis of the discrepancy between legislative action and administrative agency operation. Murray Edelman, *The Symbolic Uses of Politics*, Urbana: University of Illinois Press, 1964.

[8] Robin Williams, *American Society*, New York: A. A. Knopf, 1960, pp. 372–96. Hyman Rodman's analysis of "lower-class value stretch" suggests yet another ambiguity in the concept of norm. He found that in Trinidad among lower-class respondents that *both* marriage and non-legal marital union are normatively accepted, although marriage is preferred. Hyman Rodman, "Illegitimacy in the Caribbean Social Structure," *American Sociological Review*, 31 (October, 1966), pp. 673–683.

[9] Edelman, *op. cit.*, Chap. 2. The author refers to this as a process of political quiescence. While Edelman's symbolic analysis is close to mine, his emphasis is on the reassurance function of symbols in relation to presumed instrumental affects. My analysis stresses the conflict over symbols as a process of importance apart from instrumental effects.

[10] Gusfield, *op. cit.*, pp. 117–126.

faction was gained from the passage and maintenance of the legislation itself.[11]

Irrespective of its instrumental effects, public designation of morality is itself an issue generative of deep conflict. The designating gestures are dramatistic events, "since it invites one to consider the matter of motives in a perspective that, being developed in the analysis of drama, treats language and thought primarily as modes of action."[12] For this reason the designation of a way of behavior as violating public norms confers status and honor on those groups whose cultures are followed as the standard of conventionality, and derogates those whose cultures are considered deviant. My analysis of the American Temperance movement has shown how the issue of drinking and abstinence became a politically significant focus for the conflicts between Protestant and Catholic, rural and urban, native and immigrant, middle class and lower class in American society. The political conflict lay in the efforts of an abstinent Protestant middle class to control the public affirmation of morality in drinking. Victory or defeat were consequently symbolic of the status and power of the cultures opposing each other.[13] Legal affirmation or rejection is thus important in what it symbolizes as well or instead of what it controls. Even if the law was broken, it was clear whose law it was.

Deviant Nonconformity and Designator Reaction

In Durkheim's analysis of the indignant and hostile response to norm-violation, all proscribed actions are threats to the existence of the norm.[14] Once we separate the instrumental from the symbolic functions of legal and governmental designation of deviants, however, we can question this assumption. We can look at norm-violation from the standpoint of its effects on the symbolic rather than the instrumental character of the norm. Our analysis of patterned evasion of norms has suggested that a law weak in its instrumental functions may nevertheless perform significant symbolic functions. Unlike human limbs, norms do not necessarily atrophy through disuse. Standards of charity, mercy, and justice may be dishonored every day yet remain important statements of what is publicly approved as virtue. The sexual behavior of the human male and the human female need not be a

[11] Joseph Gusfield, "Prohibition: The Impact of Political Utopianism," in John Braeman, editor, The 1920's Revisited, Columbus: Ohio State University Press, forthcoming; Andrew Sinclair, The Era of Excess, New York: Harper Colophon Books, 1964, Chap. 10, pp. 13–14.

[12] Kenneth Burke, A Grammar of Motives, New York: Prentice-Hall, 1945, p. 393. Burke's writings have been the strongest influence on the mode of analysis presented here. Two other writers, whose works have been influential, themselves influenced by Burke, are Erving Goffman and Hugh D. Duncan.

[13] Gusfield, Symbolic Crusade, op. cit., Chap. 5.

[14] Emile Durkheim, The Division of Labor in Society, trans. George Simpson, Glencoe: The Free Press, 1947, especially at pp. 96–103. For a similar view see Lewis Coser, "Some Functions of Deviant Behavior and Normative Flexibility," American Journal of Sociology, 68 (September, 1962), pp. 172–182.

copy of the socially sanctioned rules. Those rules remain as important affirmations of an acceptable code, even though they are regularly breached. Their roles as ideals are not threatened by daily behavior. In analyzing the violation of norms we will look at the implications of different forms of deviance on the symbolic character of the norm itself. *The point here is that the designators of deviant behavior react differently to different norm-sustaining implications of an act.* We can classify deviant behavior from this standpoint.

The Repentant Deviant

The reckless motorist often admits the legitimacy of traffic laws, even though he has broken them. The chronic alcoholic may well agree that both he and his society would be better if he could stay sober. In both cases the norm they have violated is itself unquestioned. Their deviation is a moral lapse, a fall from a grace to which they aspire. The homosexual who seeks a psychiatrist to rid himself of his habit has defined his actions similarly to those who have designated him as a deviant. There is a consensus between the designator and the deviant; his repentance confirms the norm.

Repentance and redemption seem to go hand-in-hand in court and church. Sykes and Matza have described techniques of neutralization which juvenile delinquents often use with enforcement agencies.

> The juvenile delinquent would appear to be at least partially committed to the dominant social order in that he frequently exhibits guilt or shame when he violates its proscriptions, accords approval to certain conforming figures and distinguishes between appropriate and inappropriate targets for his deviance.[15]

A show of repentance is also used, say Sykes and Matza, to soften the indignation of law enforcement agents. A recent study of police behavior lends support to this. Juveniles apprehended by the police received more lenient treatment, including dismissal, if they appeared contrite and remorseful about their violations than if they did not. This difference in the posture of the deviant accounted for much of the differential treatment favoring middle-class "youngsters" as against lower-class "delinquents."[16]

The Sick Deviant

Acts which represent an attack upon a norm are neutralized by repentance. The open admission of repentance confirms the sinner's belief in the sin. His threat to the norm is removed and his violation has left the norm intact. Acts which we can perceive as those of sick and diseased people are irrelevant to the norm; they neither attack nor defend it. The use of morphine by hospital patients in severe pain is not designated as deviant behavior.

[15] Gresham Sykes and David Matza, "Techniques of Neutralization: A Theory of Delinquency," *American Sociological Review,* 22 (December, 1957), pp. 664–670, at p. 666.

[16] Irving Piliavin and Scott Briar, "Police Encounters with Juveniles," *American Journal of Sociology,* 70 (September, 1964), pp. 206–214.

Sentiments of public hostility and the apparatus of enforcement agencies are not mobilized toward the morphine-user. His use is not perceived as a violation of the norm against drug use, but as an uncontrolled act, not likely to be recurrent.[17]

While designations of action resulting from sickness do not threaten the norm, significant consequences flow from such definitions. Talcott Parsons has pointed out that the designation of a person as ill changes the obligations which others have toward the person and his obligations toward them.[18] Parson's description sensitizes us to the way in which the sick person is a different social object than the healthy one. He has now become an object of welfare, a person to be helped rather than punished. Hostile sentiments toward sick people are not legitimate. The sick person is not responsible for his acts. He is excused from the consequences which attend the healthy who act the same way.[19]

Deviance designations, as we shall show below, are not fixed. They may shift from one form to another over time. Defining a behavior pattern as one caused by illness makes a hostile response toward the actor illegitimate and inappropriate. "Illness" is a social designation, by no means given in the nature of medical fact. Even lefthandedness is still seen as morally deviant in many countries. Hence the effort to define a practice as a consequence of illness is itself a matter of conflict and a political issue.

The Enemy Deviant

Writing about a Boston slum in the 1930's, William F. Whyte remarks:

> The policeman is subject to sharply conflicting pressures. On one side are the "good people" of Eastern City, who have written their moral judgments into law and demand through their newspapers that the law be enforced. On the other side are the people of Cornerville, who have different standards and have built up an organization whose perpetuation depends upon the freedom to violate the law.[20]

Whyte's is one of several studies that have pointed out the discrepancies between middle-class moralities embodied in law and lower-class moralities which differ sharply from them.[21] In Cornerville, gambling was seen as a

---

[17] This of course does not mean that the patient using morphine may not become an addict.

[18] Talcott Parsons and Renée Fox, "Illness, Therapy and the Modern Urban Family," *Journal of Social Issues,* 8 (1952), pp. 31–44.

[19] A somewhat similar distinction as that presented here can be found in Vilhelm Aubert and Sheldon Messinger, "The Criminal and the Sick," in V. Aubert, *The Hidden Society,* New York: The Bedminister Press, 1965, pp. 25–54.

[20] William F. Whyte, *Street-Corner Society,* Chicago: University of Chicago Press, 2nd edition, 1955, p. 138.

[21] See William Westley's analysis of the differences between the morality shared by the lower class and the police in contrast to that of the courts over such matters as gambling, prostitution, and sexual perversion. The courts take a sterner view of gamblers and prostitutes than do the police, who take a sterner view of the sexual offender. William Westley, "Violence and the Police," *American Journal of Sociology,* 59 (July, 1953), pp. 34–42.

"respectable" crime, just as antitrust behavior may be in other levels of the social structure. In American society, conflicts between social classes are often also cultural conflicts reflecting moral differences. Coincidence of ethnic and religious distinctions with class differences accentuates such conflicts between group values.

In these cases, the validity of the public designation is itself at issue. The publicly-defined deviant is neither repentant nor sick, but is instead an upholder of an opposite norm. He accepts his behavior as proper and derogates the public norm as illegitimate. He refuses to internalize the public norm into his self-definition. This is especially likely to occur in instances of "business crimes." The buyer sees his action as legitimate economic behavior and resists a definition of it as immoral and thus prohibitable. The issue of "off-track" betting illustrates one area in which clashes of culture have been salient.

The designation of culturally legitimate behavior as deviant depends upon the superior power and organization of the designators. The concept of convention in this area, as Thrasymachus defined Justice for Socrates, is the will of the stronger. If the deviant is the politically weaker group, then the designation is open to the changes and contingencies of political fortunes. It becomes an issue of political conflict, ranging group against group and culture against culture, in the effort to determine whose morals are to be designated as deserving of public affirmation.

It is when the deviant is also an enemy and his deviance is an aspect of group culture that the conventional norm is most explicitly and energetically attacked. When those once designated as deviant have achieved enough political power they may shift from disobedience to an effort to change the designation itself. This has certainly happened in the civil rights movement. Behavior viewed as deviant in the segregationist society has in many instances been moved into the realm of the problematic, now subject to political processes of conflict and compromise.

When the deviant and the designator perceive each other as enemies, and the designator's power is superior to that of the deviant, we have domination without a corresponding legitimacy. Anything which increases the power of the deviant to organize and attack the norm is thus a threat to the social dominance symbolized in the affirmation of the norm. Under such conditions the need of the designators to strengthen and enforce the norms is great. The struggle over the symbol of social power and status is focused on the question of the maintenance or change of the legal norm. The threat to the middle class in the increased political power of Cornerville is not that the Cornerville resident will gamble more; he already does gamble with great frequency. The threat is that the law will come to accept the morality of gambling and treat it as a legitimate business. If this happens, Boston is no longer a city dominated by middle-class Yankees but becomes one dominated by lower-class immigrants, as many think has actually happened in Boston. The maintenance of a norm which defines gambling as deviant behavior thus symbolizes the maintenance of Yankee social and political superiority. Its disappearance as a public commitment would symbolize the loss of that superiority.

The Cynical Deviant

The professional criminal commits acts whose designation as deviant is supported by wide social consensus. The burglar, the hired murderer, the arsonist, the kidnapper all prey on victims. While they may use repentance or illness as strategies to manage the impressions of enforcers, their basic orientation is self-seeking, to get around the rules. It is for this reason that their behavior is not a great threat to the norms although it calls for social management and repression. It does not threaten the legitimacy of the normative order.

Drinking as a Changing Form of Deviance

Analysis of efforts to define drinking as deviant in the United States will illustrate the process by which designations shift. The legal embodiment of attitudes toward drinking shows how cultural conflicts find their expression in the symbolic functions of law. In the 160 years since 1800, we see all our suggested types of non-conforming behavior and all the forms of reaction among the conventional segments of the society.

The movement to limit and control personal consumption of alcohol began in the early nineteenth century, although some scattered attempts were made earlier.[22] Colonial legislation was aimed mainly at controlling the inn through licensing systems. While drunkenness occurred, and drinking was frequent, the rigid nature of the Colonial society, in both North and South, kept drinking from becoming an important social issue.[23]

The Repentant Drinker

The definition of the drinker as an object of social shame begins in the early nineteenth century and reaches full development in the late 1820's and early 1830's. A wave of growth in Temperance organizations in this period was sparked by the conversion of drinking men to abstinence under the stimulus of evangelical revivalism.[24] Through drinking men joining together to take the pledge, a norm of abstinence and sobriety emerged as a definition of conventional respectability. They sought to control themselves and their neighbors.

The norm of abstinence and sobriety replaced the accepted patterns of heavy drinking countenanced in the late eighteenth and early nineteenth century. By the 1870's rural and small-town America had defined middle-class morals to include the Dry attitude. This definition had little need for legal embodiment. It could be enunciated in attacks on the drunkard which as-

---

[22] The best single account of Temperance activities before the Civil War is that of John Krout, *The Origins of Prohibition,* New York: A. A. Knopf, 1925.

[23] *Ibid.,* Chapters 1 and 2; also see Alice Earle, *Home Life in Colonial Days,* New York: Macmillan and Co., 1937, pp. 148–149; 156–165.

[24] Gusfield, *Symbolic Crusade, op. cit.,* pp. 44–51.

sumed that he shared the normative pattern of those who exhorted him to be better and to do better. He was a repentant deviant, someone to be brought back into the fold by moral persuasion and the techniques of religious revivalism.[25] His error was the sin of lapse from a shared standard of virtue. "The Holy Spirit will not visit, much less will He dwell within he who is under the polluting, debasing effects of intoxicating drink. The state of heart and mind which this occasions to him is loathsome and an abomination."[26]

Moral persuasion thus rests on the conviction of a consensus between the deviant and the designators. As long as the object of attack and conversion is isolated in individual terms, rather than perceived as a group, there is no sense of his deviant act as part of a shared culture. What is shared is the norm of conventionality; the appeal to the drinker and the chronic alcoholic is to repent. When the Woman's Anti-Whiskey Crusade of 1873–1874 broke out in Ohio, church women placed their attention on the taverns. In many Ohio towns these respectable ladies set up vigils in front of the tavern and attempted to prevent men from entering just by the fear that they would be observed.[27] In keeping with the evangelical motif in the Temperance movement, the Washingtonians, founded in 1848, appealed to drinkers and chronic alcoholics with the emotional trappings and oratory of religious meetings, even though devoid of pastors.[28]

Moral persuasion, rather than legislation, has been one persistent theme in the designation of the drinker as deviant and the alcoholic as depraved. Even in the depictions of the miseries and poverty of the chronic alcoholic, there is a decided moral condemnation which has been the hallmark of the American Temperance movement. Moral persuasion was ineffective as a device to wipe out drinking and drunkenness. Heavy drinking persisted through the nineteenth century and the organized attempts to convert the drunkard experienced much backsliding.[29] Nevertheless, defections from the standard did not threaten the standard. The public definition of respectability matched the ideals of the sober and abstaining people who dominated those parts of the society where moral suasion was effective. In the late nineteenth century those areas in which temperance sentiment was strongest were also those in which legislation was most easily enforceable.[30]

[25] *Ibid.*, pp. 69–86.

[26] *Temperance Manual* (no publisher listed, 1836), p. 46.

[27] See the typical account by Mother Stewart, one of the leaders in the 1873–74 Woman's War on Whiskey, in Eliza D. Steward, *Memories of the Crusade,* Columbus, Ohio: W. G. Hibbard, 2nd edition, 1889, pp. 139–143; also see *Standard Encyclopedia of the Alcohol Problem,* 6 (Westerville, Ohio: American Issue Publishing Co., 1930), pp. 2902–2905.

[28] Krout, *op. cit.,* Chap. 9.

[29] See the table of consumption of alcoholic beverages, 1850–1957, in Mark Keller and Vera Efron, "Selected Statistics on Alcoholic Beverage," reprinted in Raymond McCarthy, editor, *Drinking and Intoxication,* Glencoe: The Free Press, 1959, p. 180.

[30] Joseph Rowntree and Arthur Sherwell, *State Prohibition and Local Option,* London: Hodden and Stoughton, 1900, using both systematic observation and analysis of Federal tax payments, concluded (p. 253) that ". . . local veto in America has only been found operative outside the larger towns and cities."

The Enemy Drinker

The demand for laws to limit alcoholic consumption appears to arise from situations in which the drinkers possess power as a definitive social and political group and, in their customary habits and beliefs, deny the validity of abstinence norms. The persistence of areas in which Temperance norms were least controlling led to the emergence of attempts to embody control in legal measures. The drinker as enemy seems to be the greatest stimulus to efforts to designate his act as publicly defined deviance.

In its early phase the American Temperance movement was committed chiefly to moral persuasion. Efforts to achieve legislation governing the sale and use of alcohol do not appear until the 1840's. This legislative movement had a close relationship to the immigration of Irish Catholics and German Lutherans into the United States in this period. These non-evangelical and/or non-Protestant peoples made up a large proportion of the urban poor in the 1840's and 1850's. They brought with them a far more accepting evaluation of drinking than had yet existed in the United States. The tavern and the beer parlor had a distinct place in the leisure of the Germans and the Irish. The prominence of this place was intensified by the stark character of the developing American slum.[31] These immigrant cultures did not contain a strong tradition of Temperance norms which might have made an effective appeal to a sense of sin. To be sure, excessive drunkenness was scorned, but neither abstinence nor constant sobriety were supported by the cultural codes.

Between these two groups—the native American, middle-class evangelical Protestant and the immigrant European Catholic or Lutheran occupying the urban lower class—there was little room for repentance. By the 1850's the issue of drinking reflected a general clash over cultural values. The Temperance movement found allies in its political efforts among the nativist movements.[32] The force and power of the anti-alcohol movements, however, were limited greatly by the political composition of the urban electorate, with its high proportion of immigrants. Thus the movement to develop legislation emerged in reaction to the appearance of cultural groups least responsive to the norms of abstinence and sobriety. The very effort to turn such informal norms into legal standards polarized the opposing forces and accentuated the symbolic import of the movement. Now that the issue had been joined, defeat or victory was a clear-cut statement of public dominance.

It is a paradox that the most successful move to eradicate alcohol emerged in a period when America was shifting from a heavy-drinking society, in which whiskey was the leading form of alcohol, to a moderate one, in which beer was replacing whiskey. Prohibition came as the culmination of the movement to reform the immigrant cultures and at the height of the immigrant influx into the United States.

Following the Civil War, moral persuasion and legislative goals were

31 See the accounts of drinking habits among Irish and German immigrants in Oscar Handlin, *Boston's Immigrants,* Cambridge, Massachusetts: Harvard University Press, 1941, pp. 191–192, 201–209; Marcus Hansen, *The Immigrant in American History,* Cambridge, Massachusetts: Harvard University Press, 1940.

32 Ray Billington, *The Protestant Crusade, 1800–1860,* New York: Macmillan, 1938, Chap. 15; Gusfield, *Symbolic Crusade, op. cit.,* pp. 55–57.

both parts of the movement against alcohol. By the 1880's an appeal was made to the urban, immigrant lower classes to repent and to imitate the habits of the American middle class as a route to economic and social mobility. Norms of abstinence were presented to the non-abstainer both as virtue and as expedience.[33] This effort failed. The new, and larger, immigration of 1890–1915 increased still further the threat of the urban lower class to the native American.

The symbolic effect of Prohibition legislation must be kept analytically separate from its instrumental, enforcement side. While the urban middle class did provide much of the organizational leadership to the Temperance and Prohibition movements, the political strength of the movement in its legislative drives was in the rural areas of the United States. Here, where the problems of drinking were most under control, where the norm was relatively intact, the appeal to a struggle against foreign invasion was the most potent. In these areas, passage of legislation was likely to make small difference in behavior. The continuing polarization of political forces into those of cultural opposition and cultural acceptance during the Prohibition campaigns (1906–1919), and during the drive for Repeal (1926–1933), greatly intensified the symbolic significance of victory and defeat.[34] Even if the Prohibition measures were limited in their enforceability in the metropolis there was no doubt about whose law was public and what way of life was being labelled as opprobrious.

After Repeal, as Dry power in American politics subsided, the designation of the drinker as deviant also receded. Public affirmation of the temperance norm had changed and with it the definition of the deviant had changed. Abstinence was itself less acceptable. In the 1950's the Temperance movement, faced with this change in public norms, even introduced a series of placards with the slogan, "It's Smart *Not* to Drink."

Despite this normative change in the public designation of drinking deviance, there has not been much change in American drinking patterns. Following the Prohibition period the consumption of alcohol has not returned to its pre-1915 high. Beer has continued to occupy a more important place as a source of alcohol consumption. "Hard drinkers" are not as common in America today as they were in the nineteenth century. While there has been some increase in moderate drinking, the percentage of adults who are abstainers has remained approximately the same (one-third) for the past 30 years. Similarly, Dry sentiment has remained stable, as measured by local opinion results.[35] In short, the argument over deviance designation has been largely one of normative dominance, not of instrumental social control. The process of deviance designation in drinking needs to be understood in terms

[33] William F. Whyte, *op. cit.,* p. 99. Whyte has shown this as a major attitude of social work and the settlement house toward slum-dwellers he studied in the 1930's. "The community was expected to adapt itself to the standards of the settlement house." The rationale for adaptation lay in its effects in promoting social mobility.

[34] Although a well-organized Temperance movement existed among Catholics, it was weakened by the Protestant drive for Prohibition: See Joan Bland, *Hibernian Crusade,* Washington, D.C.: Catholic University Press, 1951.

[35] See my analysis of American drinking in the post-Repeal era. Gusfield, "Prohibition: The Impact of Political Utopianism," *op. cit.*

of symbols of cultural dominance rather than in the activities of social control.

The Sick Drinker

For most of the nineteenth century, the chronic alcoholic as well as the less compulsive drinker was viewed as a sinner. It was not until after Repeal (1933) that chronic alcoholism became defined as illness in the United States. Earlier actions taken toward promotion of the welfare of drinkers and alcoholics through Temperance measures rested on the moral supremacy of abstinence and the demand for repentance. The user of alcohol could be an object of sympathy, but his social salvation depended on a willingness to embrace the norm of his exhorters. The designation of alcoholism as sickness has a different bearing on the question of normative superiority. It renders the behavior of the deviant indifferent to the status of norms enforcing abstinence.

This realization appears to have made supporters of Temperance and Prohibition hostile to efforts to redefine the deviant character of alcoholism. They deeply opposed the reports of the Committee of Fifty in the late nineteenth century.[36] These volumes of reports by scholars and prominent men took a less moralistic and a more sociological and functional view of the saloon and drinking than did the Temperance movement.

The soundness of these fears is shown by what did happen to the Temperance movement with the rise of the view that alcoholism is illness. It led to new agencies concerned with drinking problems. These excluded Temperance people from the circle of those who now define what is deviant in drinking habits. The National Commission on Alcoholism was formed in 1941 and the Yale School of Alcoholic Studies formed in 1940. They were manned by medical personnel, social workers, and social scientists, people now alien to the spirit of the abstainer. Problems of drinking were removed from the church and placed in the hands of the universities and the medical clinics. The tendency to handle drinkers through protective and welfare agencies rather than through police or clergy has become more frequent.

"The bare statement that 'alcoholism is a disease' is most misleading since . . . it conceals what is essential—that a step in public policy is being recommended, not a scientific discovery announced."[37] John Seeley's remark

[36] The Committee of Fifty, a group of prominent educators, scientists, and clergymen sponsored and directed several studies of drinking and the saloon. Their position as men unaffiliated to temperance organizations was intended to introduce unbiased investigation, often critical of Temperance doctrine. For two of the leading volumes see John Shaw Billing's, *The Physiological Aspects of the Liquor Problem,* Boston and New York: Houghton, Mifflin and Co., 1903; Raymond Calkins, *Substitutes for the Saloon,* Boston and New York: Houghton, Mifflin and Co., 1903.

[37] John Seeley, "Alcoholism Is a Disease: Implications for Social Policy," in D. Pittman and C. Snyder, editors, *Society, Culture and Drinking Patterns,* New York: John Wiley and Sons, 1962, pp. 586–593, at p. 593. For a description of the variety of definitions of alcoholism and drunkenness, as deviant and non-deviant, see the papers by Edwin Lemert, "Alcohol, Values and Social Control" and by Archer Tongue, "What the State Does About Alcohol and Alcoholism," both in the same volume.

is an apt one. Replacement of the norm of sin and repentance by that of illness and therapy removes the onus of guilt and immorality from the act of
drinking and the state of chronic alcoholism. It replaces the image of the
sinner with that of a patient, a person to be helped rather than to be exhorted. No wonder that the Temperance movement has found the work of the
Yale School, and often even the work of Alcoholics Anonymous, a threat
to its own movement. It has been most limited in its cooperation with these
organizations and has attempted to set up other organizations which might
provide the face of Science in league with the tone of the movement.[38]

The redefinition of the alcoholic as sick thus brought into power both
ideas and organizations antithetical to the Temperance movement. The norm
protected by law and government was no longer the one held by the people
who had supported Temperance and Prohibition. The hostility of Temperance
people is readily understandable; their relative political unimportance is
crucial to their present inability to make that hostility effective.

Movements of Moral Passage

In this paper we have called attention to the fact that deviance designations
have histories; the public definition of behavior as deviant is itself change-
able. It is open to reversals of political power, twists of public opinion, and
the development of social movements and moral crusades. What is attacked
as criminal today may be seen as sick next year and fought over as possibly
legitimate by the next generation.

Movements to redefine behavior may eventuate in a moral passage, a
transition of the behavior from one moral status to another. In analyzing
movements toward the redefinition of alcohol use, we have dealt with moral
crusades which were restrictive and others which were permissive toward
drinking and toward "drunkards." (We might have also used the word
"alcoholics," suggesting a less disapproving and more medical perspective.)
In both cases, however, the movements sought to change the public designation. While we are familiar with the restrictive or enforcing movements, the
permissive or legitimizing movement must also be seen as a prevalent way
in which deviants throw off the onus of their actions and avoid the sanctions
associated with immoral activities.

Even where the deviants are a small and politically powerless group they
may nevertheless attempt to protect themselves by influence over the process of designation. The effort to define themselves as ill is one plausible
means to this end. Drug addiction as well as drunkenness is partially undergoing a change toward such definition.[39] This occurs in league with powerful

[38] The WCTU during the 1950's persistently avoided support to Alcoholics Anonymous. The Yale School of Alcohol Studies was attacked and derogated in Temperance literature. A counter-organization, with several prominent pro-Dry scientists,
developed, held seminars, and issued statements in opposition to Yale School publications.

[39] Many of the writings of sociologists interested in drug addiction have contained
explicit demands for such redefinitions. See Becker, *op. cit.*; Alfred Lindesmith, *The
Addict and the Law,* Bloomington: Indiana University Press, 1965, and David Ausubel,

groups in society, such as social workers, medical professionals, or university professors. The moral passage achieved here reduces the sanctions imposed by criminal law and the public acceptance of the deviant designation.

The "lifting" of a deviant activity to the level of a political, public issue is thus a sign that its moral status is at stake, that legitimacy is a possibility. Today the moral acceptance of drinking, marijuana and LSD use, homosexuality, abortion, and other "vices" is being publicly discussed, and movements championing them have emerged. Such movements draw into them far more than the deviants themselves. Because they become symbols of general cultural attitudes they call out partisans for both repression and permission. The present debate over drug addiction laws in the United States, for example, is carried out between defenders and opposers of the norm rather than between users and nonusers of the drugs involved.

As the movement for redefinition of the addict as sick has grown, the movement to strengthen the definition of addiction as criminal has responded with increased legal severity. To classify drug users as sick and the victims or clients as suffering from "disease" would mean a change in the agencies responsible for reaction from police enforcement to medical authorities. Further, it might diminish the moral disapproval with which drug use, and the reputed euphoric effects connected with it, are viewed by supporters of present legislation. Commenting on the clinic plan to permit medical dispensing of narcotics to licensed addicts, U.S. Commissioner of Narcotics Anslinger wrote:

> This plan would elevate a most despicable trade to the avowed status of an honorable business, nay, to the status of practice of a time-honored profession; and drug addicts would multiply unrestrained, to the irrevocable impairment of the moral fiber and physical welfare of the American people.[40]

In this paper we have seen that redefining moral crusades tends to generate strong counter-movements. The deviant as a cultural opponent is a more potent threat to the norm than is the repentant, or even the sick deviant. The threat to the legitimacy of the norm is a spur to the need for symbolic restatement in legal terms. In these instances of "crimes without victims" the legal norm is *not* the enunciator of a consensus within the community. On the contrary, it is when consensus is least attainable that the pressure to establish legal norms appears to be greatest.

Drug Addiction, New York: Random House, 1958. The recent movement to redefine marijuana and LSD as legitimate is partially supported by such writings but is more saliently a movement of enemy deviants. The activities of Timothy Leary, Allen Ginsberg, and the "hipsters" is the most vocal expression of this movement.

[40] Harry Anslinger and William Tompkins, *The Traffic in Narcotics*, New York: Funk and Wagnall's Co., Inc., 1953, p. 186.

KINGSLEY DAVIS

Mental Hygiene and the Class Structure

Mental hygiene constitutes for the sociologist a two-fold interest, first as a social movement (preparing now to celebrate its twenty-ninth anniversary), and second as an applied science (drawing upon several pure sciences of which sociology is one). Both sides of this interest fit with our present subject—the relation of mental hygiene to the vertical dimension of society—because any phenomenon which is at once a social movement and an applied human science cannot escape on two counts having some connection, however obscure it may seem, with the invidious, discriminatory aspect of social life.

We should like to define mental hygiene in terms of its chief aim, but the general goal as usually stated—improvement of mental health in the community, promotion of personal efficiency, or provision for personality expression and happiness—is ambiguous. It is difficult to determine whether mental hygiene practises are really conducive to such a goal, or whether the practises of any well-intentioned movement are not equally conducive to it. Our conception of mental hygiene, then, will embrace simply the movement and the point of view called by that name. The diffuseness of its main goal and the proliferation of subsidiary ends[1] will be viewed as symptomatic of its social role and function.

[1] "The ultimate in mental hygiene means mental poise, calm judgment, and an understanding of leadership and fellowship—in other words, cooperation, with an attitude that tempers justice with mercy and humility."—Dr. M. J. Rosenau, "Mental Hygiene and Public Health," *Mental Hygiene*, xix (Jan. 1935): 9. Bromberg attributes to a prominent spokesman of the movement the following statement: "Mental hygiene . . . presents many wider aspects. Industrial unrest to a large degree means bad mental hygiene, and is to be corrected by good mental hygiene. The various antisocial attitudes that lead to crime are problems for the mental hygienist. Dependency, insofar as it is social parasitism not due to mental or physical defect, belongs to mental hygiene. But mental hygiene has a message also for those who consider themselves quite normal, for, by its aims, the man who is fifty per cent efficient can make himself seventy per cent efficient. . . ."—W. Bromberg, *The Mind of Man*, New York, 1937, p. 217. So

Source: Kingsley Davis, "Mental Hygiene and the Class Structure," *Psychiatry*, 1 (1938), pp. 55–65. Reprinted by special permission of the copyright holder, The William Alanson White Psychiatric Foundation, Inc., and Kingsley Davis.

Now let us turn briefly to the vertical dimension in society. Its essence is the relative inferiority and superiority of persons in one another's eyes. It is manifest on the one hand in a *crystallized hierarchy* of positions (offices and statuses) which is supported by a correlative system of sentiments and a constraining set of legal and moral sanctions; and on the other hand in *interpersonal relations* where (in rough accord with the crystallized attitudes) every act, word and thought of the person is unremittingly subjected to the praising and condemning scrutiny of others. The vertical dimension is thus not limited to the wider or smaller circles; it is coextensive with the social.

Persons occupying similar positions in the hierarchy constitute a social class, in most cases a statistical rather than a real group. Class implies the division of persons into broad strata according to their final score in the summation of estimable tallies—the precipitate of all the countless criteria of invidious distinction. The strata may be so organized with reference to one another that movement up or down the scale is facilitated or blocked. The first type we call a system of mobile classes, the second a system of immobile castes. Each type possesses its appropriate world philosophy common to its members, absolutistic in expression, and conceived as an order of justice. Its principles penetrate to every phase and aspect of life, taking hold of the person in the dynamic maze of communicative, especially interpersonal and primary, contacts.

Our interest lies in our own mobile class system and its accompanying world philosophy. The latter, which may conveniently be called the Protestant ethic, and which receives its severest expression in Puritanism, is: (1) *Democratic* in the sense of favoring equal opportunity to rise socially by merit rather than by birth. (2) *Worldly* in emphasizing earthly values such as the pursuit of a calling, accumulation of wealth, and achievement of status. (3) But at the same time *ascetic* in stressing physical abstinence and stern sobriety, thrift, industry, and prudence. (4) *Individualistic* in placing responsibility upon the individual himself for his economic, political, and religious destiny, and in stressing personal ambition, self-reliance, private enterprise, and entrepreneurial ability.[2] (5) *Rationalistic* and *empirical* in

---

many similar statements can be found in mental hygiene texts, articles, and credos, that these quotations are typical.

Mental hygiene thus possesses a characteristic that is essential to any social movement—namely, that its proponents regard it as a panacea. Since mental health is obviously connected with the social environment, to promote such health is to treat not only particular minds but also the customs and institutions in which the minds function. To cure so much is to cure all.

A sane way to discuss mental hygiene is to assume that the purpose of mental hygiene is the prevention of positive mental disorder, and that it is therefore a branch of the public health movement, which intends not so much to make everybody bouncingly robust as to prevent the onset and spread of definite diseases. But since mental hygienists dub this limited goal as old fashioned, our realistic treatment cannot make the assumption.

[2] The individualistic and worldly-ascetic qualities were delineated by Max Weber. See his *General Economic History,* trans. by F. H. Knight, Part IV; and *The Protestant Ethic and the Spirit of Capitalism*, trans. by Talcott Parsons, London, 1930.

assuming a world order discoverable through sensory observation of nature.[3] (6) *Utilitarian* in pursuing practical ends with the best available means, and conceiving human welfare in secularized terms as attainable by human knowledge and action.

It can be demonstrated, we think, that this ethic is functionally related to an open-class society. Not only are the two historically connected, but it seems that an open-class society could scarcely work without such a philosophy.[4]

But what has this Protestant ethic, plus the underlying system of mobile classes, to do with mental hygiene? Our discussion of this point, suggestive rather than conclusive, will embrace the following propositions: first, that mental hygiene, being a social movement and a source of advice concerning personal conduct, has inevitably taken over the Protestant ethic inherent in our society, not simply as the basis for conscious preachment but also as the unconscious system of premises upon which its "scientific" analysis and its conception of mental health itself are based. Second, that this unconscious incorporation of the open-class ethic has made mental hygiene doubly susceptible to the psychologistic approach to human conduct, though the latter has represented, in part, a contradictory feature. Third, that the unconscious assumption of the dominant ethic, together with the psychologistic interpretation, has served to obscure the social determinants of mental disease, and especially the effects of invidious or emulative relationships. And finally, that mental hygiene will probably fail as a preventive movement because it cannot overcome its defects, the free analysis and manipulation of invidious social elements never being permitted in an integrated society.

The relation between mental hygiene and the open-class ethic is an unconscious one. Tacitly the textbooks for teachers and practitioners of the subject assume the existence of a mobile class structure and teach by implication the congruent moral norms. Frequently they interpret these norms as somehow given in the individual, and in the last analysis always define mental health itself in terms of them.[5]

[3] R. K. Merton, "Puritanism, Pietism, and Science," *Sociological Review*, xxviii (Jan. 1936): 1–30. Max Weber, *op. cit.*, also points out the rationalistic character of Protestantism, as does W. Sombart in his *Quintessence of Capitalism*, trans. by M. Epstein, London, 1915, in his article on "Capitalism" in *Ency. Soc. Sciences*, 1930, and in his *Jews and Modern Capitalism*, London, 1913. Sombart, in the article cited, sums up the capitalist spirit in the concepts: acquisition, competition, and rationality. Following this lead we could regard capitalism as the competition for social status in terms of the acquisition of goods by rational manipulative processes.

[4] The Protestant ethic was perhaps most characteristic of early capitalism, and it has doubtless fallen into some desuetude with subsequent social changes, but it still tends to form the unconscious premises of our thinking about conduct, even when in practice we do not follow its precepts. Veblen was particularly impressed with the archaic character of our present 18th Century moral philosophy. (See his *Vested Interests and the Common Man*, N.Y., 1920). The Protestant ethic is still the living message of our departed moral authorities—Jefferson, Franklin, Lincoln, and Emerson— and is woven into poetry, song, and precept.

[5] Our generalizations are based upon a systematic study of selected literature in the field, chosen from a list sent out by the National Committee for Mental Hygiene, Inc. In addition, a few other standard works were read with a view to sampling. All told,

Vertical mobility, for example, is taken for granted, and social advancement accepted as a natural goal. Democracy, in the form of equal opportunity to advance, is regarded as desirable. Lack of ambition is felt to represent a definite symptom of maladjustment, to be eliminated if possible. The normal person is considered to be one who chooses a calling and tries to distinguish himself in it, while the mentally sick person is one who needs occupational therapy.[6]

Likewise *competition* is assumed, life being regarded as a battle or a game in which victory goes to him who uses wit and strength to best advantage.[7] Since the morality of the competitive system requires that we not violate the rules of the game, and that we not envy the other fellow his accomplishments or gloat over his failures, this morality is incorporated into the mental hygiene teaching—the prevention of mental illness becoming at the same time the prevention of delinquency and the encouragement of good

---

thirteen volumes were gone through, with the aid of a fixed questionnaire designed to discover certain things about each book. The books systematically perused are as follows: V. V. Anderson, *Psychiatry in Education*, N.Y., 1932; W. J. Burnham, *The Wholesome Personality*, N.Y., 1932; E. R. Groves and P. Blanchard, *Introduction to Mental Hygiene*, N.Y., 1930; Howard and Patry, *Mental Health*, N.Y., 1935; D. W. La Rue, *Mental Hygiene*, N.Y., 1927; J. J. B. Morgan, *Keeping a Sound Mind*, N.Y., 1934; W. V. Richmond, *Personality: Its Study and Hygiene*, N.Y., 1937; L. F. Shaffer, *The Psychology of Adjustment*, Boston, 1936; G. S. Stevenson and G. Smith, *Child Guidance Clinics*, N.Y., 1934; D. A. Thom, *Everyday Problems of the Everyday Child*, N.Y., 1928; J. E. W. Wallin, *Personality Maladjustments and Mental Hygiene*, N. Y., 1935; F. L. Wells, *Mental Adjustments*, N.Y., 1917; C. B. Zachry, *Personality Adjustments of School Children*, N.Y., 1929. Other literature, especially recent contributions in psychiatry dealing with the relation of mental disorder to social phenomena, was of course read.

[6] Burnham, p. 522: "The democratic ideal in its higher form is based, not on an abstract myth of human equality, made concrete in an equal share of human necessities and social privileges, but based rather on the psychological fact of profound individual differences." "The ideal democratic group today is one where each member of the group has the opportunity to become superior in something according to his special ability."

Howard and Patry consider mobility on the whole a desirable condition, since it offers a goal for effort. But they criticize the mad scramble for money and "material" things. In other words, they condemn some of the particular goals of vertical movement, but they do not condemn (or indeed consciously treat) mobility itself.

La Rue says that me must learn to adapt ourselves to any surroundings. "But that is no reason why we should rest satisfied with all these things, or make no effort to improve our condition."–p. 280. Ambition is assumed all through the book. Self-confidence, a necessary entrepreneurial virtue, is extolled and Emerson is quoted as saying that "Self-trust is the secret of success."

Wells assumes that the aim of life is to get ahead, and that ambition is a prerequisite to a well-functioning mind. P. 11: "The free imagination of wished-for things results well for the mind through painting in more glowing colors the excellence of what is wished for, and firing the ambition to strive for it the more intensely." The success vs. failure motif is apparent.

[7] Morgan, p. 166: "Your birth means that you have been selected as a player in the greatest game ever devised. . . ."

Wells, p. 7: "Yet the worth of existence depends on success in a game infinitely more complicated than that of chess, in which no mistake is ever overlooked and no move ever taken back, and where knowledge from one's own experience often comes too late for use."

sportsmanship.[8] The healthy person is regarded as achieving victory against others only within the rules, by empirico-rational ingenuity and ascetic self-discipline. The maladjusted person must learn to face reality, i.e., the competitive facts.[9] He must not achieve victories in fancy only, or flee the memory of his failures. Parents must not coddle their child and thus make him unfit for the competition of adult life. Yet since to face reality means not only to grasp the fact of competition, but also to estimate correctly one's chances, and since one's chances depend upon capacity and circumstances as well as effort, a safety valve for the competitive drive is provided by the advice that one should not aspire beyond one's ability.[10]

Because competition has for its goal a worldly prize, but a prize not to be won by self-indulgence, the implied existence of competition as a sane way of life is buttressed by the tacit preachment of *worldly asceticism*. Mental hygiene does not frown upon enjoyment for itself, but it does insist that recreation shall be "wholesome." In other words, one should not choose a type of recreation that makes one unfit for the serious business of life,[11] or which violates the canons of Protestant morality. One's behavior should manifest prudence, rationality, and foresight, and material possessions should not be dissipated by whimsical extravagance.[12]

Individualism is tacitly assumed in three ways. (1) The person is held responsible for his own destiny. In case of neurosis his will is the object of treatment. In short he is the entrepreneur.[13] (2) Individual happiness is

[8] Morgan, p. 38: "The fight of the mature adult is thus transformed from the childish attempt to resist all conditions which produce physical discomfort to the battle against any infraction against his self-imposed standards of behavior."

[9] Shaffer states, p. 152, that one symptom of bad adjustment found in the inferiority complex is "a poor reaction to competition."

A literal translation of the phrase "personal efficiency," found so frequently in the literature, would be "competitive ability."

[10] One of the five goals of "progressive" education, as listed by Zachry, p. 271, is: "The cultivation of ambitions which can be attained."

Morgan, p. 151: "Ambition must not be excessive." P. 22: "Facing life squarely is the first principle of mental health."

[11] Groves and Blanchard, p. 302: "The devotion of some leisure time to recreational pursuits is of positive value outside of the enjoyment which it affords, for it enables the individual to return reinvigorated to the more serious routine of study or work."

Another of the five goals of "progressive" education which Zachry lists is "healthful recreation."

[12] Wells, p. 276: "In life, the lubricating function of money to the social machinery is well known. It plays an equally essential part in the smooth operation of one's mental trends."

Shaffer, p. 539: The individual should "employ the scientific method for the solution of his personal problems." P. 382: It is assumed that rationality and insight are possible and desirable.

[13] Shaffer, p. 539: "The chief requirements for hygiene work are freedom and success. Each person must be free to select the kind of task that is most suitable and most satisfying to him. He must have freedom to plan it and to carry it to completion in his own way."

Another of Zachry's five goals of "progressive" education is "personal independence—intellectual and emotional."

the ultimate good. Mental health is interpreted as the satisfaction of individual needs.[14] (3) Human behavior is assumed to be understandable in terms of individuals abstracted from their society. Needs, desires, and mental processes are frequently discussed as if inherent in the organism.[15]

Specialization is implicitly taken for granted in the emphasis upon the value of a particular kind of work adapted to one's talents and identified with one's own personailty.

Utilitarianism is obviously assumed in the action philosophy of mental hygiene. To function, to grow, to do is regarded as the purpose of life. Tangible ends and Progress are regarded as the goals. Human welfare is seen as attainable by the application of rational science.[16]

If the thesis is true that mental hygiene unconsciously incorporates the open-class ethic, it should be further indicated by a study of the movement's personnel. Such a study, constituting a type of circumstantial evidence,[17] was made, and it shows that the persons prominently connected with the movement are of the type one would expect to uphold the Protestant principles. They are mostly upper middle class professionals, predominantly of British ancestry, identified with a Protestant church, and frequently reared and educated in New England. Many of them apparently had well-to-do parents who themselves had risen in life through effort and initiative. Some of them are self-made men of undistinguished parentage in our own or in the old country. In general they seem to have taken to heart the necessity of a calling and have worked, abstained, and striven sufficiently to succeed. It follows from their background and is exemplified in their writings, that they believe in empirical science and have taken the American humanitarian religion seriously enough to apply scientific results zealously to the mental welfare of society. They are (without cavil) idealistic, respectable, and capable, and their sentiments lean on the side of humanitarian individualism.

Aside from the personnel of the movement, there exists for our main thesis still another (and more direct) evidence—derived from examining a central and recurrent concept in the mental hygiene literature, namely,

[14] La Rue, pp. 11–12: "Happiness is, in general, the sign of mental health."

Stevenson and Smith, p. 1: "The child guidance clinic is an attempt to marshal the resources of the community in behalf of children who are in distress because of unsatisfied inner needs. . . ."

[15] Shaffer assumes that individuals possess four types of motives which then come into conflict with the environment.–p. 86.

Zachry says that that child's "instinctive tendencies often conflict with one another. . . ."–p. 45.

[16] Shaffer, p. 539: The individual should "employ the scientific method for the solution of his personal problems." P. 382: Assumes that rationality and insight are possible and desirable.

Another of Zachry's five goals is "purposeful and rational activity."

Morgan, p. 1: Life is ever-changing and demands continuous readjustment. It is "a game with a continual challenge which you must meet if you are to keep alive. Stagnation and death come when you cease to rise to the challenge."

[17] The survey includes data on the lives of 51 persons, leaders of the mental hygiene movement. With no funds for detailed historical or questionnaire research, we could not secure as many facts as we wished. Our conclusions are therefore tentative, but on the information we do have, taken from available bibliographical sources in obituaries, *Who's Who,* etc., they seem quite justified.

"mental health." This concept is usually defined as the "integration," the "balance," the "successful" or "happy functioning" of the personality;[18] but these words are as vague as the initial phrase. Furthermore, no adequate criteria for establishing the presence of this "integration" or "balance" are provided. The only consistent criterion, and in the last analysis the substance of every definition, is normal behavior. Consequently we shall examine what the mental hygiene literature means by "the normal."

Does "normal" refer to the statistical average of actual behavior, or to ideal behavior? It seems that mental hygienists have not seen the issue. In practice they employ the concept in both senses, though ultimately the normative sense prevails. There is in the literature much criticism of *selected* moral rules and attitudes. Sometimes the apparent basis of criticism is that the rules are unrealistic—i.e., that they are too far removed from the average actual behavior. Generally, however, the criticism springs (as it inevitably must) from value-judgments of the author. On the basis of his own conscious or unconscious values, the selected norm may be judged to be "irrational," "unenlightened," and detrimental to mental health. But whence come the author's values? Due to his position in society, and the nature of his work, they must come from the central valuational system of his culture.[19]

[18] Howard and Patry, p. 24: "We have seen that the prime condition of mental health is the integration of the psychophysical and psychosocial organism through the development of stable major circuts of energy or good patterns of behavior." La Rue, p. 13: "Happiness is, in general, the sign of mental health. But it should be lasting happiness; for of course one can be happy for the moment, like the maniac or the drunkard, without having a mind that is really healthy." Richmond: The healthy personality is one which "functions more or less perfectly in its cultural milieu."–p. 248. Shaffer, p. 138: "For a person to satisfy all his motives with regard for their functioning as an interrelated system, is good adjustment. To achieve this requires unified and integrated behavior." Thom, p. 135: "The well-adjusted personality, which characterizes a happy and efficient man or woman, is a harmonious blending of these varied emotions and character traits, resulting in self-control and habits of conformity." Wallin, p. 32: "That individual may be considered to be mentally sound and efficient who is able to react to his physical and social environment in an effective, consistent, and integrated manner. That is, an individual's mental soundness can be judged by the appropriateness and rationality of his behavior patterns on the psychological and social levels."

[19] In the following passage quoted from Howard and Patry, pp. 146–148, we find an illustration of typical reasoning along this line:
"The moralists and theologians who were not able to give sex a rational explanation sought to stamp sex interest out of life. This only tended to dam up its force. [Condemnation of an old moral attitude on ground of its effects.] When psychoanalysis began to disclose it as a factor in mental conflicts, the socalled realists . . . began to play fast and loose with sex themes, with the result . . . a flood of sex liberalism. [Condemnation of current attitude.] . . . There is at present the need of a middle ground between the old attitude of avoidance and the present indiscriminate flaunting of sex themes. [Advocacy of a particular attitude.] Wholesome-minded people are not averse to frank consideration of sex under proper conditions and right motives, but they do not enjoy having it dragged into prominence on every possible pretext and occasion. Dignity and decency are the marks of successful sex adjustment. [Bolstering the proposed attitude with words and phrases of praise and redundant identification of it with health and the right people.] In our approach to the problems and in procedures for the enlightenment of the young these qualities should be our guide and goal." [Assertion that everybody *should* accept the author's goal.] "In our attempts at sex education we have not yet learned to appeal to the highest motive-family formation. . . . Morality for its own sake no longer makes an appeal to young people. All moral codes should be tested by the degree to which

He can and he will criticize particular norms, but he cannot impugn the basic institutions of his society, because it is in terms of these that conduct is ultimately judged to be satisfactory (i.e., adjusted) or unsatisfactory.[20]

The ethical meaning of "normal" is further borne out by the fact that when specific advice is given concerning life problems, the conduct prescribed is ordinarily such as would conform to our ideals, not to be the statistical average. The mental hygienist tends to justify such advice, however, not on moral but on rational or "scientific" grounds. One can best secure mental health, best satisfy one's needs, by conforming. But since for certain selected norms he does not advise conformity, the hygienist violates his own contention. Furthermore, he never brings the question of conformity or non-conformity to a clear issue, because he does not define "individual needs" or "adjustment" apart from moral norms, and because he does not admit that the delinquent may escape detection and hence punishment.[21]

If we are to understand the logic by which mental hygiene identifies mental health with normality, and normality with an unconsciously assumed open-class ethic, we must turn our attention to a central factor in this logic, to what may be called the psychologistic concept of human nature. By the psychologistic approach is meant the explanation of human conduct in terms of traits originating within the individual, as over against traits originating within society. Any explanation is psychologistic, for example, which builds its analysis upon motives, drives, instincts, urges, prepotent reflexes, or what not, ignoring the social genesis of what is called by these names. In mental hygiene these elements are taken as given in the individual, existing prior to social forces and determining concrete actions. Since they are prior to the social, the only other alternative in accounting for them is that they are biologically given. The psychologistic interpretation is individualistic, then, in the sense that it bases its explanation upon that which is purely individual, i.e., the biologically inherited constitution (the purely nonsocial part) of the person.

It is natural that mental hygienists have adopted this conception of human nature. Protestant individualism finds here a scientific rationalization. The philosophy of private initiative, personal responsibility, and individual achievement falls easily into an interpretation of human nature in individualistic terms. Furthermore, for those who are naive in the analysis of social relations and generally unaware of the sociological premises of their own thinking, it is extremely easy to read into the individual, as given in his nature, the characteristics that are really given in his society. By thus reading social traits into original nature a degree of permanence and certainty is given

---

they contribute vital values and call out deeper potentialities." [Justifying the proposed attitude on the basis of its connection with a fundamental institution and hence the central system of values in the culture.]

[20] Here we see an illustration of the conflict between the humanitarian mores (by which certain established practices are criticized) and the more organizational mores (the more basic and unconsciously accepted standards). See W. Waller, "Social Problems and the Mores," *Amer. Soc. Rev.,* i (Dec. 1936): 922–933.

[21] It is often difficult to get behind the emotionality and loquacity of mental hygiene literature to see the essential logic. This paragraph is meant to describe the general features of its main position after all the verbiage has been laboriously sifted.

them which would disappear if they were realized to be merely socially acquired. In other words, psychologism is a means whereby an unconsciously held ethic may be advantageously propagated under the guise of "science." It protects the hygienist from a disconcerting fact—the relativity of normal judgments.

Yet, if applied with logical rigor to matters of conduct, the psychologistic approach would become an incompatible element in mental hygiene doctrine. Since mental hygiene constantly judges life-situations to be wholesome or hygienic according to whether or not they satisfy individual needs, the concept of "individual needs" calls for strict definition. If defined according to a logical application of the psychologistic approach, individual needs would reduce to those that are biologically inherited—namely, the organic. Applying this point of view to conduct, mental hygiene would urge us to satisfy our physiological needs independently of social standards and ideals, and to observe such standards and ideals only in so far as they can be proven to satisfy our needs. Of course, the hygienists do not do this. Instead they inculcate the dominant morality of a mobile society. They do not, then, apply the psychologistic approach with logical rigor, but misinterpret it by including as given in the individual many things which are in reality not genetically but socially determined, such as desires and standards. These social desires and standards construed as inherent in the individual are precisely the Protestant standards that the mental hygienist implicitly follows. It is no wonder, then, that the "scientific" hygiene yields results in striking conformity to the ethical configuration, seeing that the ethical configuration is intrinsically contained in the very definition of the goal to be achieved—namely, satisfaction of individual needs.[22]

We have shown thus far, by its preachments, its personnel, and its conception of mental health and normality, that mental hygiene tacitly assumes the Protestant open-class ethic. Let us now turn to the *results,* rather than the evidences, of the implicit assumptions. We shall argue that the ethical presuppositions, plus the psychologistic approach, necessarily vitiate the scientific validity of much mental hygiene work by limiting and biasing the study of mental disorder and consequently the working conceptions behind mental hygiene practice. Specifically, the presuppositions lead to neglect of the invidious element, and in fact social elements generally, as a determining factor in mental disorder.

[22] Mental hygiene turns out to be not so much a science for the prevention of mental disorder, as a science for the prevention of moral delinquency. Thus an author may state that every individual has a need for some kind of useful work, then draw the conclusion that every individual *must* have useful work to be mentally adjusted, and finally declare that any social customs which do not permit this are irrational and unworthy. The conscious premise, that every individual has the alleged need, is a psychologistic fallacy. The other propositions, avowedly based on the initial premise, are in fact the product of countless unverbalized values which together represent an accepted ethical system.

We are thus able to account for the extraordinary diffuseness of mental hygiene goals. Mental health being defined in terms of conformity to a basic ethic, the pursuit of mental hygiene must be carried on along many fronts. Also, since the fiction of science is maintained, the ethical character of the movement can never be consciously and deliberately stated–hence the goals must be nebulous and obscurantist in character.

An aspect of social relations possessing strong presumptive evidence of responsibility in mental disorders is precisely that which embraces invidious, discriminatory differences. If we suspect already that social forces are implicated, our suspicion becomes doubly certain for this particular branch of social phenomena. Sociological analysis of personality has long stressed the individual's conception of his role in the eyes of others. It has maintained that the self develops through the acquisition and internationalization of the attitudes of others. It has shown that these attitudes, laden with approval or disapproval, not only become in time the foundation of the self but also assume tremendous emotional importance of the individual.[23] Since the attitudes of others are acquired only by symbolic communication, which is social in the strictest sense and necessarily connected with the cultural heritage, it can be seen that the key to the relation between organism and culture lies precisely in the dynamics of the social role. And since the social role is largely a matter of the communicated approval or disapproval of others, involving a constant comparison of one's own position with that of others, the invidious, emulative element is inevitably present. In so far as personality and mentality are socially determined, they are also emulatively determined.

As a slight test of this theory, an analysis of 70 hospitalized cases, reported in the psychiatric literature and mostly with functional disorders, was made.[24] All but four instances showed clear evidence of status involvements. Furthermore, the evidence would seem to bear out Campbell's contention that in the functional disorders the emotional problems are of sufficient intensity and consistency as to indicate a causal relationship.[25]

It follows that in the study of mental disorder, some attention should be devoted to the invidious elements in the social past of the patients. This holds true especially for the functional derangements—those, presumably, with which mental hygiene is most concerned.[26] But in mental hygiene at least, this phase of the subject has been neglected.[27] Much attention has perforce been devoted to guilt feelings, inferiority complexes, anxiety states, and

[23] The works of Cooley, Mead, Faris, and Dewey are here referred to.

[24] This study, though merely a straw in the wind, satisfied us that significant research could be carried on in this direction.

[25] C. M. Campbell, *Destiny and Disease in Mental Disorders,* N. Y., 1935.

[26] In so far as mental disorder results from definite disease processes, its prevention lies within the province of the ordinary public health program, the field of physical hygiene. Only when it is seen as somehow resulting from non-physical forces (Campbell's "personal" as opposed to impersonal factors) does it fall within the province of *mental* hygiene.

[27] Mental hygiene literature sadly neglects to analyze social processes, whether invidious or otherwise. Much is of course written about the importance of "environmental factors," but these so important "factors" are scarcely ever treated so as to discover their specific mode and intensity of operation.

The same criticism applies, though in lesser degree, to psychiatry and abnormal psychology. In them too, even when a school is dealing avowedly with superiority and inferiority, there is a tendency to regard these as individual traits and not explore their social origins. This is true, for example, of Adler's so-called individual school of psychology. The limitation of his point of view has caused him to miss essential features of the very phenomenon he insists is important. Again we may mention the works of Dr. Macfie Campbell, who very skilfully points out the causal importance of what he calls personal factors, but disclaims any attempt to analyze these factors systematically. What he calls "personal" could equally be called socio-genic, and studied sociologically.

emotional conflicts. Yet though these clearly reflect the power of invidious comparison, they are hardly seen to be social at all. The vertical element is merely assumed; it remains unanalyzed while attention is turned to "instincts," "reflexes," "habits," or other bio-individual determinants.

Now if we ask why this neglect, the answer seems obvious. It is a product of the implicit assumption of an open-class philosophy of life. Little attention is paid to the emulative, discriminatory social factors because to analyze them would bring to awareness the unconscious ethical premises. Such analysis would force recognition of the vertical dimension of our society and the axiological judgments associated with it, which have been assumed as premises. Hence it would destroy the myth of scientific objectivity and the myth of the universal individual—myths necessary to the self-confident optimism of the mental hygiene movement.

The logical device by which this blindness to invidious social determinants is made to appear satisfactory to the conscious minds of the mental hygienists, is the psychologistic approach. If human personality is understandable without reference to social reality, then naturally social reality need not be analyzed. The latter can be accepted superficially as something to which the personality must adjust, something which represses or facilitates original wishes; but the more fundamental social forces are not reckoned with. If they are treated at all it is erroneously—the social elements being regarded as inherently given in the individual (i.e., as non-social).

Mental hygiene's neglect of social process springs partly from the fact that mental hygienists are for the most part trained psychologically to look for bio-genetic determinants, rather than sociologically to look for social determinants. But it also arises from the sociologists' own failure to clarify the role of social interaction in the etiology of mental derangement. At any rate mental hygiene seems to be limping along on one foot, because if there *are* social determinants, these are not being discovered and utilized in prevention.

Detailed proof and knowledge of determining social processes will not come until case histories are invented and utilized which give the *significant social past* of the patient. Such histories wait upon two achievements: first, the development of a conceptual scheme which, as a first approximation, indicates what facts in the social past are significant, hence guides the research from the start; and second. the perfection and standardization, and the possible invention of new techniques of social investigation. The first achievement has perhaps been realized in sociological theory, but its application in the gathering of social data about specific patients lags far behind.

While much of our sociological work has not been sufficiently detailed to apply to the etiology of mental disorder, it does point in directions where further investigation may prove fruitful. This is true, for example, of the ecological and comparative approach to the distribution of functional disorders. In other words, though we cannot give an exact description of the operation of social determinants in particular psychoses, we have strong evidence, if not proof, *that* such determinants are there. The *how* need not escape us always. In the last analysis it seems that sociologists could be expected to produce the required knowledge, because they, of all those interested in the problem, are the only ones devoting themselves purely to social relations as such.

Of the two great systems of causation with reference to personality—one the biological (cellular interaction) and the other sociological (communicative interaction) —neither can be ignored by any science of mental disorder. Thus far, however, it seems that far more energy, thought, and money has gone into the investigation of the first. Problems are even stated in such a way as to preclude investigation of the second, and concepts are used which are stop-gaps rather than invitations to a knowledge of it. And yet there exist countless evidences that sociological factors play a significant part in both normal and abnormal behavior.

To show that mental hygiene has neglected genuine factors, and to indicate further why it has done so, it is worth while to reflect upon some possible connections between the class structure and mental disorder.

Be the causes of mental disorder what they may, it is easy to show that the criteria are always social. Sanity lies in the observance of the normative system of the group. This allows wide latitude, of course, and we constantly make allowances for a person's rearing in the specialized culture of his particular groups. But sanity assumes acculturation in some group, and basically it is acculturation in the central mores of the widest society in which the person is an effective social unit. Furthermore, we do not judge by one lapse. We judge, rather, by systematized behavior and ideas in a direction contrary to the accepted motivational complex. Thus a criminal is not regarded as insane because he does something contrary to mores and law. Stealing is an occurrence inherent in our social organization, and we all can see the logic of motives for stealing. But a man who steals because of a motivational complex contrary to the accepted one—say, a kleptomaniac—is judged to be mentally disordered: not because he steals, but because his reasons for stealing are removed from "reality." A man who forgets is not insane. We all forget. But a man who forgets the wrong things, such as his own name, his own city, or the excretory separation of the sexes, is definitely crazy.

In a class society the motivation of one class is understood by the members of other classes, because they each, in conforming to their class standards, are really conforming to the system of standards that constitutes the society. It may be that class ideologies, considered in themselves, vary in the degree of mental health they give their adherents; but this opinion assumes something that we do not possess—namely, a standard of reality by which all ideologies may be judged. In any culture the class ideologies are merely specialized parts of the central ideology, which is not identified simply with the outlook of the dominant class, but with that of all classes.[28] It is not necessarily true, therefore, that the more divergent the class ideology from the cultural standard, the greater the incidence of mental derangement in this class. It is a particular kind of divergence that counts, a divergence in the ultimate norms which unify the entire society and knit together its specialized groups.[29] In case of such divergence other classes will focus attention upon the errant one and will seek to control its thinking and behavior through methods conforming to the sanction of the society. But the important point is that a specialized part is not necessary divergent in this latter sense. The ideological peculiarities of a particular class may be adequately provided for and incorporated in the central ideology.

[28] A class structure presupposes a heirarchy of values. Who possesses the highest values, or possesses these in the greatest degree, is of the highest class. It does not follow, as some would have us believe, that the system of values was instituted for the benefit of the upper class. Rather the system of values sets the framework and determines the goals of competition for position.

[29] This observation seems to be justified by the ecological studies of schizophrenia that have been made. Areas in which conduct violates the norms of the very society of which conduct the persons are a part, are areas of high incidence. Cf. R. E. L. Faris, "Cultural Isolation and the Schizophrenic Personality," *Amer. Jour. of Soc.*, xl (Sept. 1934): 155–164. Also, H. W. Dunham, "The Ecology of the Functional Psychoses in Chicago," *Amer. Soc. Review*, ii (Aug. 1937): 467–479.

This conclusion seems valid in a case as well as an open-class organization, and is partially valid even where class struggle exists. So far as mental disorder is concerned, the significant question is not whether there is a caste or class system, for neither one is inherently destructive of sanity, but whether the system, whatever it is, is unified by a nucleus of common values. When the structure embraces conflicting principles of social organization based on incompatible values, psychic conflicts inevitably result. For example, ends may be presented to one group as possible and desirable, when in fact they are made impossible for that group by a conflicting mode of dominance. A clear illustration appears in the Southern part of the United States, where the avowed morality of equal opportunity to all is categorically denied in practice to Negroes.[30] The behavior of individuals caught in this situation manifests frequent attempts to escape an unbearable reality. Reality seems unbearable, however, only when another reality exists as a *conceivable* alternative; and another is conceivable only when it forms part of the social system and exists as a possibility within the cultural ideology. Mental conflict is engendered, then, not so much by the vertical structure itself as by inconsistency within the structure.

It might seem that a mobile class organization would have deleterious effects upon mental health because of the constant readjustments it requires of its circulating individuals. But the open-class system is protected against this adverse result by the fact that, as distinguished from a caste society, the limits of difference between the mores of different strata are narrow. If the differences were wide, vertical mobility, entailing a shift from one set of mores to a radically different set, would certainly have profound effects upon the person so shifting, and would tend by prohibiting the change. But actually there is a tendency in an open-class system for differences in class modes of thinking to take the form of an infinite number of small gradations, and to reduce themselves to superficial externalities; so that though vertical mobility places the strain of rapid change, responsibility, and adaptation upon the individual,[31] it conpensates for this by the pulverization and externalization of differences. The class variations in mores become one of degree rather than kind. The same fundamental wants and values pervade the whole hierarchy, the only difference being that members of the various classes satisfy these wants and attain these values in different amounts. The climber who moves from the bottom to the top finds that he can still utilize practically all of his old habituations. No fundamental reorganization is required. He merely satisfies the same old wants more readily and in greater abundance. Thus does

30 See W. L. Warner, "American Caste and Class," *Amer. Jour. of Soc.*, xlii (Sept. 1936): 234–237. J. Dollard, *Caste and Class in Southerntown,* New Haven, 1937, especially pp. 72, 89, 182. Also K. Davis, "The American Caste System," unpublished manuscript in possession of the author.

31 Compare P. Sorokin, *Social Mobility,* New York, 1927, Ch. 21. Sorokin concludes that since in a mobile system the individual must adapt himself to changing milieus, mobility increases the incidence of mental disease. He admits increasing superficiality and externalization, however, but he interprets them in terms of the individuals concerned and does not realize that they are even more characteristic of the cultural differences between classes and therefore constitute a compensation for the mental strain. It is only in the initial stages of becoming a mobile system that a class order may engender insanity. But this is a period of social change, and the increased incidence is due to our principle of conflicting values and not to the sheer fact of mobility itself.

the mobile society safeguard the sanity of the mobile person.[32] Basically its members, of whatever class, all share a common set of values—the ethic of an open-class world.

In all this, however, it should be remembered that social class is but the roughest descriptive phrase for the invidious vertical aspect of society. Actually it is not class differences alone that count, but all differences describable in terms of inferiority and superiority. A person's class position offers but the first (though necessary) index of the social determinants in his life. It may be important or unimportant in his particular case, but in either event an indispensable consideration is the sequence of his invidious experiences within limited circles of association—particularly within primary groups. Yet it is precisely these relations, as well as general class factors, that (as already pointed out) have been neglected by mental hygiene.[33]

Our speculations suggest that the vertical structure and mentality are intimately related, and that a neglect of social factors is a vital neglect for the mental hygienist. We have already said that there must be, and is, a reason for such neglect. It is obviously not our view that the mental hygienist is consciously enforcing alien class standards upon unwilling members of a lower stratum. Doubtless there is a tendency to spread the middle class Protestant ethic to classes which are not middle and hence not so mobile, but this could scarcely be interpreted as class "exploitation." We believe, rather, that the mental hygienist is really enforcing, in a secular way and under the guise of science, the standards of the entire society. This leads him beyond the goal of mental health, strictly defined, and to undertake such things as increasing the efficiency of the ordinary individual and readjusting some of our (more superficial) mores. Thus the diffuseness of the mental hygiene goal is integrally related to the hygienist's actual function. Mental hygiene can plunge into evaluation, into fields the social sciences would not touch, because it possesses an implicit ethical system which, since it is that of our society, enables it to pass value judgments, to get public support, and to enjoy an unalloyed optimism. Disguising its valuational system (by means of the psychologistic position) as rational advice based on science, it can conveniently praise and condemn under the aegis of the medico-authoritarian mantle.

Few will doubt that mental hygiene has thus far been less successful in achieving the avowed goal of prevention than has the regular public health movement. Does this represent a lag which will shortly be overcome, or does it represent a circumstance inherent in the nature of the case? The latter view seems more tenable, for the following reasons.

[32] The open-class society is also protected by the fact that the class sieves are never entirely open and hence most people move only a few rungs up or down. For this additional reason the changes required of any individual are usually not overwhelming. It should be remembered too that the open-class ethic places a positive value upon upward movement, and that even in the case of failure it always holds out hopes of recovery and progression. A person's mobility thus fulfills the values.

[33] Psychiatry is waking up to the necessity of studying interpersonal relations. See H. S. Sullivan, "A Note on the Implications of Psychiatry, the Study of Interpersonal Relations, for Investigations in the Social Sciences," *Amer. Jour. of Soc.*, xlii (May 1937): 848–861. Also, Karen Horney, *The Neurotic Personality of Our Time,* New York, 1937; and the works of Macfie Campbell.

Scientific knowledge of mental disorder requires knowledge of social determinants. But there is a social restriction upon the impersonal analysis of personal relations, and especially upon the use of knowledge thus gained. Such knowledge must be employed only for culturally prescribed ends and persons who believe in these ends. Unfortunately, if one serves and believes these cultural ends, one cannot analyze social relations objectively.[34] If this is true of an individual, it is even truer of a movement. The latter, dependent upon public enthusiasm, must inevitably adhere to ethical preconceptions. Mental hygiene hides its adherence behind a scientific façade, but the ethical premises reveal themselves on every hand, partly through a blindness to scientifically relevant facts. It cannot combine the prestige of science with the prestige of the mores, for science and the mores unavoidably conflict at some point, and the point where they most readily conflict is precisely where "mental" (i.e., social) phenomena are concerned. We can say, in other words, that devotion to the mores entails an emotional faith in illusion. Devotion to science, on the other hand, when social illusion constitutes the subject matter of that science, entails the sceptical attitude of an investigator rather than of the believer toward the illusion. In so far as the mental hygienist retains his ethical system, he misses a complete scientific analysis of his subject and hence fails to use the best technological means to his applied-science goal. But if he forswears his ethical beliefs, he is alienated from the movement and suffers the strictures of an outraged society. Actually the mental hygienist will continue to ignore the dilemma. He will continue to be unconscious of his basic preconceptions at the same time that he keeps on professing objective knowledge. He will regard his lack of preventive success as an accident, a lag, and not as an intrinsic destiny. All because his social function is not that of a scientist but that of a practising moralist in a scientific, mobile world.

[34] Psychiatry, as shown by Campbell, Horney, Sullivan, and others, has gradually come to realize the importance of social and cultural factors in the determination of mental derangement. Generally, however, there has been an overestimation of the power this places in the hands of the practitioner. As reported by a sociologist who has spent some time as an observer in a mental hospital, some doctors and psychiatrists assume that with further knowledge of social factors, these can be immediately changed so as to reduce the incidence of mental disorder. But for very profound reasons we cannot plan or alter our culture out of whole cloth. However, there is another type of optimism which is slightly more justified. This involves concentrating upon special or limited social environments as the field of social manipulation. Each of these has been studied in connection with the possible genesis of mental disease, and certain reforms advocated. But often, as in the case of the individual when he was first studied apart from his culture, the possibility of changing these particular social milieus is easily over-estimated. They are parts of our general culture, and resistances to changing them arise which were not at first apparent. Of course one particular individual's relation to one of his special social environments (say the court) can be helpfully altered, but this is casework and does not alter the situation so far as the general population is concerned. (For a detailed consideration of the problem of manipulating limited social milieus, see K. Davis, "The Application of Science to Personal Relations, A Critique of the Family Clinic Idea," *Amer. Sociological Review*, i (April 1936): 236–251.) Some features of society, moreover, are scarcely limited to any particular milieu. One of these is the class structure which, as a phase of the entire social organization, cuts across all special parts of that organization. When speaking of such factors it is difficult to advocate their immediate removal or change without becoming involved in ethical controversies and unseen consequences far transcending the immediate problem in hand.

THOMAS S. SZASZ

The Mental Health Ethic

Let us begin with some definitions. According to *Webster's Third New International Dictionary* (unabridged), ethics is "the discipline dealing with what is good and bad or right and wrong or with moral duty and obligation . . ."; it is also "a group of moral principles or set of values . . ." and "the principles of conduct governing an individual or a profession: standards of behavior. . . ."

Ethics is thus a distinctly human affair. There are "principles of conduct" governing individuals and groups, but there are no such principles governing the behavior of animals, machines, or stars. Indeed, the word "conduct" implies this: only persons *conduct* themselves; animals *behave,* machines *function,* and stars *move.*

Is it too much to say, then, that any human behavior that constitutes conduct—which, in other words, is a product of choice or potential choice, and not simply of a reflex—is, *ipso facto,* moral conduct? In all such conduct, considerations of good and bad, or right and wrong, play a role. Logically, its study belongs in the domain of ethics. The ethicist is a behavioral scientist par excellence.

If we examine the definition and practice of psychiatry, however, we find that in many ways it is a covert redefinition of the nature and scope of ethics. According to Webster's, psychiatry is "a branch of medicine that deals with the science and practice of treating mental, emotional, or behavioral disorders esp. as originating in endogenous causes or resulting from faulty interpersonal relationships"; further, it is "a treatise or text on or theory cf the etiology, recognition, treatment, or prevention of mental, emotional, or behavioral disorder or the application of psychiatric principles to any area of human activity (social psychiatry)"; thirdly, it is "the psychiatric service in a general hospital (this patient should be referred to psychiatry)."

The nominal aim of psychiatry is the study and treatment of mental

Source: Thomas S. Szasz, "The Mental Health Ethic," pp. 25–48 in *Ideology and Insanity* (Garden City, N.Y.: Doubleday & Company, Inc. [Anchor], 1970). Adapted from R. T. De George (ed.), *Ethics and Society* (Doubleday Anchor, 1966). Copyright © 1966 by The Kansas University Endowment Association. Reprinted by permission of the Association and Thomas S. Szasz.

disorders. But what are mental disorders? To accept the existence of a class of phenomena called "mental diseases," rather than to inquire into the conditions under which some persons may designate others as "mentally ill," is the decisive step in the embracing of the mental health ethic.[1] If we take the dictionary definition of this discipline seriously, the study of a large part of human behavior is subtly transferred from ethics to psychiatry. For while the ethicist is supposedly concerned only with normal (moral) behavior, and the psychiatrist only with abnormal (emotionally disordered) behavior, the very distinction between the two rests on ethical grounds. In other words, the assertion that a person is mentally ill involves rendering a moral judgment about him. Moreover, because of the social consequences of such a judgment, both the "mental patient" and those who treat him as one become actors in a morality play, albeit one written in a medical-psychiatric jargon.

Having removed mentally disordered behavior from the purview of the ethicist, the psychiatrist has had to justify his reclassification. He has done so by redefining the quality or nature of the behavior he studies: whereas the ethicist studies moral behavior, the psychiatrist studies biological or mechanical behavior. In Webster's words, the psychiatrist's concern is with behavior "originating in endogenous causes or resulting from faulty interpersonal relationships." We should fasten our attention here on the words "causes" and "resulting." With these words, the transition from ethics to physiology, and hence to medicine and psychiatry, is securely completed.

Ethics is meaningful only in a context of self-governing individuals or groups exercising more or less free, uncoerced choices. Conduct resulting from such choices is said to have reasons and meanings, but no causes. This is the well-known polarity between determinism and voluntarism, causality and free will, natural science and moral science.

Defining psychiatry in the above way leads not only to a reapportionment of disciplines taught in universities, but also promotes a point of view about the nature of some types of human behavior, and about man in general.

By assigning "endogenous causes" to human behavior, such behavior is classified as *happening* rather than as *action*. Diabetes mellitus is a disease caused by an endogenous lack of enzymes necessary to metabolize carbohydrates. In this frame of reference, the endogenous cause of a depression must be either a metabolic defect (that is, an antecedent chemical event) or a defect in "interpersonal relationships" (that is, an antecedent historical event). Future events or expectations are excluded as possible "causes" of a feeling of depression. But is this reasonable? Consider the millionaire who finds himself financially ruined because of business reverses. How shall we explain his "depression" (if we so want to label his feeling of dejection)? By regarding it as the result of the events mentioned, and perhaps of others in his childhood? Or as the expression of his view of himself and of his powers in the world, present and future? To choose the former is to redefine ethical conduct as psychiatric malady.

The healing arts—especially medicine, religion, and psychiatry—operate

---

[1] See Szasz, T. S.: *The Myth of Mental Illness: Foundations of a Theory of Personal Conduct* (New York: Hoeber-Harper, 1961).

within society, not outside it. Indeed, they are an important part of society. It is not surprising, therefore, that these institutions reflect and promote the primary moral values of the community. Moreover, today, as in the past, one or another of these institutions is used to mold society by supporting certain values and opposing others. What is the role of psychiatry in promoting a covert system of ethics in contemporary American society? What are the moral values it espouses and imposes on society? I shall try to suggest some answers by examining the position of certain representative psychiatric works and by making explicit the nature of the mental health ethic. And I shall try to show that in the dialogue between the two major ideologies of our day— individualism and collectivism—the mental health ethic comes down squarely on the side of collectivism.

Men desire freedom and fear it. Karl R. Popper speaks of the "enemies of the open society,"[2] and Erich Fromm of those who "escape from freedom."[3] Craving liberty and self-determination, men desire to stand alone as individuals, but, fearing loneliness and responsibility, they wish also to unite with their fellow men as members of a group.

Theoretically, individualism and collectivism are antagonistic principles: for the former, the supreme values are personal autonomy and individual liberty, for the latter, solidarity with the group and collective security. Practically, the antagonism is only partial: man needs to be both—alone, as a solitary individual, and with his fellow man as a member of a group. Thoreau at Walden Pond and the man in the gray flannel suit in his bureau-cratic organization are two ends of a spectrum: most men seek to steer a course between these extremes. Individualism and collectivism may thus be pictured as the two shores of a fast-moving river, between which we—as moral men—must navigate. The careful, the timid, and perhaps the "wise" will take the middle course: like the practical politician, such a person will seek accommodation to "social reality" by affirming and denying both in-dividualism and collectivism.

Although, in general, an ethical system that values individualism will be hostile to one that values collectivism, and vice versa, an important differ-ence between the two must be noted: In an individualistic society, men are not prevented by force from forming voluntary associations nor are they punished for assuming submissive roles in groups. In contrast, in a collectivis-tic society, men are forced to participate in certain organizational activities, and are punished for pursuing a solitary and independent existence. The reason for this difference is simple: as a social ethic, individualism seeks to minimize coercion and fosters the development of a pluralistic society; whereas collectivism regards coercion as a necessary means for achieving desired ends and fosters the development of a singularistic society.

The collectivist ethic is exemplified in the Soviet Union, as in the case of Iosif Brodsky. A twenty-four-year-old Jewish poet, Brodsky was brought to trial in Leningrad for "pursuing a parasitic way of life." The charge stems

[2] Popper, K. R.: *The Open Society and Its Enemies* (Princeton, N.J.: Princeton University Press, 1950).
[3] Fromm, E.: *Escape from Freedom* (New York: Rinehart, 1941).

from "a Soviet legal concept that was enacted into law in 1961 to permit the exiling of city residents not performing 'socially useful labor.' "[4]

Brodsky had two hearings, the first on February 18 and the second on March 13, 1964. The transcript of the trial was smuggled out of Russia and its translation published in *The New Leader*.[5] In the first hearing Brodsky was vaguely accused of being a poet and of not doing more "productive" work. At its conclusion, the judge ordered Brodsky to be sent "for an official psychiatric examination during which it will be determined whether Brodsky is suffering from some sort of psychological illness or not and whether this illness will prevent Brodsky from being sent to a distant locality for forced labor. Taking into consideration that from the history of his illness it is apparent that Brodsky has evaded hospitalization, it is hereby ordered that division No. 18 of the militia be in charge of bringing him to the official psychiatric examination."[6]

This point of view is characteristic of the collectivist ethic. It is also indistinguishable from that of contemporary American institutional psychiatry. In both systems, a person who has harmed no one but is considered "deviant" is defined as mentally ill; he is ordered to submit to psychiatric examination; if he resists, this is viewed as a further sign of his mental abnormality.[7]

Brodsky was found guilty and sent "to a distant locality for a period of five years of enforced labor."[8] His sentence, it should be noted, was at once therapeutic, in that it sought to promote Brodsky's "personal well-being," and penal, in that it sought to punish him for the harm he had inflicted on the communinty. This, too, is the classic collectivist thesis: what is good for the community is good for the individual. Since the individual is denied any existence apart from the group, this equation of the one with the many is quite logical.

Another Russian man of letters, Valeriy Tarsis, who had published a book in England describing the predicament of writers and intellectuals under the Khrushchev regime, was incarcerated in a mental hospital in Moscow. It may be recalled that the American poet Ezra Pound had been dealt with in the same way: he was incarcerated in a mental hospital in Washington, D.C.[9] In his autobiographical novel, *Ward 7,* Tarsis gives the impression that involuntary mental hospitalization is a widely used Soviet technique for repressing social deviance.[10]

It seems clear that the enemy of the Soviet state is not the capitalist

[4] Quoted in *The New York Times,* August 31, 1964, p. 8.
[5] "The trial of Iosif Brodsky: A transcript." *The New Leader,* 47: 6–17 (August 31), 1964.
[6] Ibid., p. 14.
[7] For a comparison of Soviet criminal law and American mental hygiene law, see Szasz, T. S.: *Law, Liberty, and Psychiatry: An Inquiry into the Social Uses of Mental Health Practices* (New York: Macmillan, 1963), pp. 218–21.
[8] "The trial of Iosif Brodsky," op. cit., p. 14.
[9] See Szasz, *Law, Liberty, and Psychiatry, supra,* Chap. 17.
[10] Tarsis, V.: *Ward 7: An Autobiographical Novel,* transl. by Katya Brown (London and Glasgow: Collins and Harvill, 1965).

entrepreneur, but the lonely worker—not the Rockefellers, but the Thoreaus. In the religion of collectivism, heresy is individualism: the outcast par excellence is the person who refuses to be a member of the team.

I shall argue that the main thrust of contemporary American psychiatry —as exemplified by so-called community psychiatry—is toward the creation of a collectivist society, with all this implies for economic policy, personal liberty, and social conformity.

If by "community psychiatry" we mean mental health care provided by the community through public funds—rather than by the individual or by voluntary groups through private funds—then community psychiatry is as old as American psychiatry. (In most other countries, too, psychiatry began as a community enterprise and never ceased to function in that role.)

Fresh as the term "community psychiatry" is, many psychiatrists freely admit that it is just another slogan in the profession's unremitting campaign to sell itself to the public. At the fourth annual meeting of the Association of Medical Superintendents of Mental Hospitals, the main topic was community psychiatry—"What it is and what it isn't."[11]

"What is community psychiatry?" asked the director of an eastern state hospital. His answer: "I went to two European congresses this summer and I don't know what is meant by the term. . . . When people talk about it, it is rarely clear what it is."[12] To a psychiatrist in a midwestern state, "Community psychiatry . . . means that we collaborate within the framework of existing medical and psychiatric facilities."[13] This view was supported by a psychiatrist from an eastern state hospital who asserted, "In Pennsylvania, the state hospitals are already serving the communities in which they are located. . . . They have been carrying out community psychiatry."[14] Such is the path of progress in psychiatry.

What I found particularly disturbing in this report was that, although many who attended the meeting were uncertain about what community psychiatry is or might be, all declared their firm intention to play a leading role in it. Said a psychiatrist from a midwestern state hospital: What community psychiatry is, whatever it becomes, we'd better have a part in it. We'd better assume leadership or we will get the part relegated to us. We should be functioning as community mental hospitals. If we sit back and say we are not community mental health centers, we will have a great many people telling us what to do."[15] The president of the medical superintendents' organization then called upon the members to "assume a role of leadership." There was general agreement on this: "Unless we participate and take a dominant part, we will be relegated to the bottom of the heap,"[16] warned a psychiatrist from a midwestern state hospital.

[11] "Roche Report: Community psychiatry and mental hospitals." *Frontiers of Hospital Psychiatry,* 1: 1–2 & 9 (November 15), 1964.
[12] Ibid., p. 2.
[13] Ibid.
[14] Ibid.
[15] Ibid., p. 9.
[16] Ibid.

If this is community psychiatry, what is new about it? Why is it praised and recommended as if it were some novel medical advance that promises to revolutionize the "treatment" of the "mentally ill"? To answer these questions would require an historical study of our subject, which I shall not attempt here.[17] Let it suffice to note the specific forces that launched community psychiatry as a discrete movement or discipline. These forces are of two kinds—one political, the other psychiatric.

The social policies of modern interventionist liberalism, launched by Franklin D. Roosevelt in this country, received powerful reinforcement during the presidency of John F. Kennedy. President Kennedy's Message to Congress on "Mental Illness and Mental Retardation" on February 5, 1963, reflects this spirit. Although the care of the hospitalized mentally ill has been traditionally a welfare-state operation—carried out through the facilities of the various state departments of mental hygiene and the Veterans Administration—he advocated an even broader program, supported by public funds. Said the President: "I propose a national mental health program to assist in the inauguration of a wholly new emphasis and approach to care for the mentally ill. . . . Government at every level—federal, state, and local—private foundations and individual citizens must face up to their responsibilities in this area."[18]

Gerald Caplan, whose book Robert Felix called the "Bible . . . of the community mental health worker," hailed this message as "the first official pronouncement on this topic by the head of a government in this or any other country."[19] Henceforward, he added, "the prevention, treatment, and rehabilitation of the mentally ill and the mentally retarded are to be considered a community responsibility and not a private problem to be dealt with by individuals and their families in consultation with ther medical advisers."[20]

Without clearly defining what community psychiatry is, or what it can or will do, the enterprise is proclaimed good merely because it is a team effort, involving the community and the government, and not a personal effort, involving individuals and their voluntary associations. We are told that the promotion of "community mental health" is so complex a problem that it requires the intervention of the government—but that the individual citizen is responsible for its success.

Community psychiatry is barely off the drawing boards; its nature and achievements are but high-flown phrases and utopian promises. Indeed, perhaps the only thing clear about it is its hostility to the psychiatrist in private practice who ministers to the individual patient: he is depicted as one engaged in a nefarious activity. His role has more than a slight similarity to that of Brodsky, the parasite-poet of Leningrad. Michael Gorman, for example,

[17] For further discussion, see Szasz, T. S.: "Whither psychiatry?" This volume, pp. 218–45.

[18] Kennedy, J. F.: *Message from the President of the United States Relative to Mental Illness and Mental Retardation,* February 5, 1963; 88th Cong., First Sess., House of Representatives, Document No. 58; reprinted in *Amer. J. Psychiatry,* 120: 729–37 (Feb.), 1964, p. 730.

[19] Caplan, G.: *Principles of Preventive Psychiatry* (New York: Basic Books, 1964), p. 3.

[20] Ibid.

quotes approvingly Henry Brosin's reflections about the social role of the psychiatrist: "There is no question that the challenge of the role of psychiatry is with us all the time. The interesting thing is what we will be like in the future. Not the stereotypes and strawmen of the old AMA private entrepreneurs."[21]

I have cited the views of some of the propagandists of community psychiatry. But what about the work itself? Its main goal seems to be the dissemination of a collectivistic mental health ethic as a kind of secular religion. I shall support this view by quotations from the leading textbook of community psychiatry, *Principles of Preventive Psychiatry,* by Gerald Caplan.

What Caplan describes is a system of bureaucratic psychiatry in which more and more psychiatrists do less and less actual work with so-called patients. The community psychiatrist's principal role is to be a "mental health consultant"; this means that he talks to people, who talk to other people, and finally someone talks to, or has some sort of contact with, someone who is considered actually or potentially "mentally ill." This scheme works in conformity with Parkinson's Law:[22] the expert at the top of the pyramid is so important and so busy that he needs a huge army of subordinates to help him, and his subordinates need a huge army of second-order subordinates, and so on. In a society faced with large-scale unemployment due to automation and great technological advances, the prospect of a "preventive" mental health industry, ready and able to absorb a vast amount of manpower, should be politically attractive indeed. It is. Let us now look more closely at the actual work of the community psychiatrist.

According to Caplan, a main task of the community psychiatrist is to provide more and better "sociocultural supplies" to people. It is not clear what these supplies are. For example, "the mental health specialist" is described as someone who "offers consultation to legislators and administrators and collaborates with other citizens in influencing governmental agencies to change laws and regulations."[23] In plain English, a lobbyist for the mental health bureaucracy.

The community psychiatrist also helps "the legislators and welfare authorities improve the moral atmosphere in the homes where [illegitimate] children are being brought up and to influence their mothers to marry and provide them with stable fathers."[24] Although Caplan mentions the community psychiatrist's concern with the effects of divorce upon children, there is no comment about advising women who want help in securing divorces, abortions, or contraceptives.

Another function of the mental health specialist is to review "the conditions of life of his target group in the population and then influence[s] those who help to determine these conditions so that their laws, regulations, and policies . . . are modified in an appropriate direction."[25] Caplan emphasizes

[21] Quoted in Gorman, M.: "Psychiatry and public policy." *Amer. J. Psychiatry,* 122: 55–60 (Jan.), 1965, p. 56.

[22] Parkinson, C. N.: *Parkinson's Law and Other Studies in Administration* [1957] (Boston: Houghton Mifflin Co., 1962).

[23] Caplan, op. cit., p. 56.

[24] Ibid., p. 59.

[25] Ibid., pp. 62–63.

that he is not advocating government by psychiatrists; he is aware that the psychiatrist may thus become the agent or spokesman of certain political or social groups. He disposes of the problem by declaring that every psychiatrist must make this decision for himself, and that his book is not addressed to those who wish to provide services for special-interest groups, but rather to "those who direct their efforts primarily to the reduction of mental disorder in our communities."[26] But he admits that the distinction between psychiatrists who exploit their professional knowledge in the service of an organization and "those who work in the organization in order to achieve the goals of their profession" is not that simple in practice. For example, commenting on the role of consulting psychiatrists in the Peace Corps, he blandly observes that their success "is not unassociated with the fact that they were able to whole-heartedly accept the major goals of that organization, and their enthusiasm was quickly perceived by its leaders."[27]

On the psychiatrist's proper role in the medical clinics of his community (specifically in relation to his function in a well-baby clinic, seeing a mother who has a "disturbed" relationship with her child), Caplan writes: "If the preventive psychiatrist can convince the medical authorities in the clinics that his operations are a logical extension of traditional medical practice, his role will be sanctioned by all concerned, including himself. All that remains for him to do is to work out the technical details."[28]

But this is precisely what I regard as the central question: Is so-called mental health work "a logical extension of traditional medical practice," either preventive or curative? I say it is not a logical but a rhetorical extension of it.[29] In other words, the practice of mental health education and community psychiatry is not medical practice, but moral suasion and political coercion.

As was pointed out earlier, mental health and illness are but new words for describing moral values. More generally, the semantics of the mental health movement is but a new vocabulary for promoting a particular kind of secular ethic.

This view may be supported in several ways. Here I shall try to do so by citing the opinions expressed by the Scientific Committee of the World Federation for Mental Health in the monograph, *Mental Health and Value Systems,* edited by Kenneth Soddy.

In the first chapter, the authors candidly acknowledge "that mental health is associated with principles dependent upon the prevailing religion or ideology of the community concerned."[30]

There then follows a review of the various concepts of mental health proposed by different workers. For example, in Soddy's opinion, "A healthy person's response to life is without strain; his ambitions are within the scope

[26] Ibid., p. 65.
[27] Ibid.
[28] Ibid., p. 79.
[29] See Szasz, *The Myth of Mental Illness, supra;* also "The myth of mental illness." This volume, pp. 12–24, and "The rhetoric of rejection." This volume, pp. 49–68.
[30] Soddy, K., ed.: *Cross-Cultural Studies in Mental Health: Identity, Mental Health, and Value Systems* (Chicago: Quadrangle, 1962), p. 70.

of practical realization. . . ."[31] While in the opinion of a colleague whose view he cites, mental health "demands good interpersonal relations with oneself, with others, and with God"[32]—a definition that neatly places all atheists in the class of the mentally sick.

The authors consider the vexing problem of the relation between social adaptation and mental health. They succeed admirably in evading the problem that they claim to be tackling: "[M]ental health and social adaptation are not identical. . . . [This] can be illustrated by the fact that few people would regard a person who had become better adjusted as a result of leaving home and moving into a different society has having thereby become mentally healthy. . . . In the past, and still today in some societies, adaptation to society has tended to be highly valued . . . as a sign of mental health; and failure to adapt has been even more strongly regarded as a sign of mental ill-health. . . . There are occasions and situations in which, from the point of view of mental health, rebellion and non-conformity may be far more important than social adaptation."[33] But no criteria are given for distinguishing, "from the point of view of mental health," the situations to which we ought to conform from those against which we ought to rebel.

There is much more of this kind of sanctimonious foolishness. Thus we are told, "While it is unlikely that agreement could be reached on the proposition that all 'bad' people are mentally unhealthy, it might be possible to agree that no 'bad' person could be said to have the highest possible level of mental health, and that many 'bad' people are mentally unhealthy."[34] The problems of who is to decide who the "bad" people are, and by what criteria they are to decide, are glossed over. This evasion of the reality of conflicting ethics in the world as it exists is the most outstanding feature of this study. Perhaps one of the aims of propounding a fuzzy, yet comprehensive, mental health ethic is to maintain this denial. Indeed, the true goal of the community psychiatrist seems to be to replace a clear political vocabulary with an obscure psychiatric semantic, and a pluralistic system of formal values with a singularistic mental health ethic. Here is an example of the way this is accomplished:

"Our view is that the assumption of an attitude of superiority by one social group towards another is not conducive to the mental health of either group."[35] Some simplistic comments about the Negro problem in America then follow. No doubt, the sentiment here expressed is admirable. But the real problems of psychiatry are bound up not with abstract groups but with concrete individuals. Yet nothing is said about actual relations between people —for example, between adults and children, doctors and patients, experts and clients; and how, in these various situations, the attainment of a relationship that is both egalitarian and functional requires the utmost skill and effort of all concerned (and may, in some cases, be impossible to realize).

Self-revealing as the mental health ethicist is when he discusses mental

31 Ibid., p. 72.
32 Ibid., p. 73.
33 Ibid., pp. 75–76.
34 Ibid., p. 82.
35 Ibid., p. 106.

health and illness, his moral stance is even clearer when he discusses psychiatric treatment. Indeed, the promoter of mental health now emerges as a
social engineer on the grand scale: he will be satisfied with nothing less than
gaining license to export his own ideology to a world market.

The authors begin their discussion of the promotion of mental health by
noting the "resistances" against it: "The principles underlying success in attempts to alter cultural conditions *in the interest of mental health,* and the
hazards of such attempts, are very important considerations for practical mental health work. . . . The introduction of change in a community may be
subject to conditions not unlike those which obtain in the case of *the
child . . ."* (italics added).[36] We recognize here the familiar medical-pscyhiatric
model of human relations: the client is like the ignorant child who must be
"protected," if need be autocratically and without his consent, by the expert,
who is like the omnicompetent parent.

The mental health worker who subscribes to this point of view and
engages in this kind of work adopts a condescending attitude toward his (unwilling) clients: he regards them, at best, as stupid children in need of education, and, at worst, as evil criminals in need of correction. All too often he
seeks to impose value change through fraud and force, rather than through
truth and example. In brief, he does not practice what he preaches. The
egalitarian-loving attitude toward one's fellow man, which the mental health
worker is so eager to export to the "psychiatrically underdeveloped" areas of
the world, seems to be in rather short supply everywhere. Or are we to overlook the relations in the United States between white and black, or psychiatrist and involuntary patient?

The authors are not wholly oblivious of these difficulties. But they seem
to think it sufficient to acknowledge their awareness of such problems. For
example, after commenting on the similarities between Chinese brainwashing
and involuntary psychiatric treatment, they write:

"The term brain-washing has . . . been applied with unfortunate connotations to psychotherapeutic practice *by those who are hostile to it.* We
consider that the lesson of this needs to be taken to heart by all who are
responsible for securing psychiatric treatment of non-volitional patients. The
use of compulsion or deceit will almost certainly *appear, to those who are
unfriendly to or frightened of* the aims of psychotherapy, to be wicked"
(italics added).[37]

The "benevolent" despot, whether political or psychiatric, does not like
to have his benevolence questioned. If it is, he resorts to the classic tactic of
the oppressor: he tries to silence his critic, and, if this fails, he tries to degrade him. The psychiatrist accomplishes this by calling those who disagree
with him "hostile" or "mentally ill." Here we are told that if a person admits
to the similarities between brain-washing and involuntary psychiatric treatment he is, *ipso facto, hostile* to psychotherapy.

The statement about "the lesson . . . to be taken to heart by all who are
responsible for securing psychiatric treatment of nonvolitional patients"
[italics added] requires special comment. The language used implies that

[36] Ibid., p. 173.
[37] Ibid., p. 186.

involuntary mental patients exist in nature—whereas, in fact, they are created, largely by psychiatrists. Thus, after raising the vexing problem of involuntary psychiatric treatment, the authors fail to deal with it in a clear and forthright manner; instead, they impugn the emotional health and moral intentions of those who would dare to look at the problem critically.

This antagonism to a critical examination of his doctrines and methods may be necessary for the mental health woker, just as it is for the missionary or the politician: the aim of each is to conquer souls or minds, not to understand human problems. Let us not forget the dangers of trying to understand another person: the effort invites disproof of one's views and questioning of one's beliefs. The thoughtful person who is content to teach by the example of his own conduct must always be ready to acknowledge error and to change his ways. But this is not what the mental health worker wants: he does not want to change his ways, but those of others.

In an analysis of the mental hygiene movement written nearly thirty years ago, Kingsley Davis has suggested this and more. Commenting on the "family clinic," Davis observed that such agencies offer not medical treatment but moral manipulation: "Before one can cure such patients, one must alter their purpose; in short, one must operate, not on their anatomy, but on their system of values."[38] The trouble is, of course, that people usually do not want to *alter* their goals—they want to *attain* them. As a result, "Only those clients whose ends correspond to socially sanctioned values may be expected to come voluntarily to such a clinic. Other troubled persons, whose wishes are opposed to accepted values, will stay away; they can be brought in only through force or fraud."[39] Nor does Davis shirk from stating what many know but few dare articulate—namely, that ". . . many clients are lured to family clinics by misrepresentation."[40] Similarly, many more are lured to state mental hospitals and community-sponsored clinics. Community psychiatry thus emerges, in my opinion at least, as a fresh attempt to revitalize and expand the old mental hygiene industry.

First, there is a new advertising campaign: mental health education is an effort to lure unsuspecting persons into becoming clients of the community mental health services. Then, having created a demand—or, in this case, perhaps merely the apperance of one—the industry expands: this takes the form of steadily increasing expenditures for existing mental hospitals and clinics and for creating new, more highly automated factories, called "community mental health centers."

Before concluding this review of the ethics of mental health work, I want to comment briefly on the values advocated by the authors of *Mental Health and Value Systems*.

They promote change as such; its direction is often left unspecified. "The success of mental health promotion depends partly upon the creation of a climate favorable to change and a belief that change is desirable and possi-

[38] Davis, K.: "The application of science to personal relations: A critique of the family clinic idea." *Amer. Sociological Rev.*, 1: 236–47 (April), 1936, p. 238.
[39] Ibid., p. 241.
[40] Ibid.

ble."[41] They also emphasize the need to scrutinize certain "unproven assumptions"; none of these, however, pertains to the nature of mental health work. Instead, they list as unproven assumptions such ideas as ". . . the mother is always the best person to have charge of her own child."[42]

I believe that we ought to object to all this on basic logical and moral grounds: if moral values are to be discussed and promoted, they ought to be considered for what they are—moral values, not health values. Why? Because moral values are, and must be, the legitimate concern of everyone and fall under the special competence of no particular group; whereas health values (and especially their technical implementation) are, and must be, the concern mainly of experts on health, especially physicians.

Regardless of what we call it, mental health today is a big business. This is true in every modern society, whatever its political structure. It is impossible, therefore, to comprehend the struggle between individualistic and collectivistic values in psychiatry without a clear understanding of the social organization of mental health care.

Surprising as it may seem, in the United States 98 per cent of the care for the hospitalized mentally ill is provided by federal, state, and county governments.[43] The situation in Great Britain is similar. In the Soviet Union the figure is, of course, 100 per cent.

To be sure, this is not the whole picture for the United States or Great Britain. Private practice is still what the term implies: private. Yet this does not mean that psychiatric inpatient care is paid for by public funds, and psychiatric outpatient care by private funds. Outpatient services are financed both privately and publicly. Including all types of care, it has been estimated that "about 65% of all the treatment of mental patients goes on in tax supported services, and 35% in private and voluntary services."[44]

The implications of the vast and expanding involvement of the government in mental health care have, I think, been insufficiently appreciated. Moreover, whatever problems stem from government control of mental hospital care, these difficulties are connected with a logically antecedent problem: What is the aim of the care provided? It does not help to say that it is to transform the mentally sick into the mentally healthy. We have seen that the terms "mental health" and "mental sickness" designate ethical values and social performances. The mental hospital system thus serves, however covertly, to promote certain values and performances, and to suppress others. Which values are promoted and which suppressed depends, of course, on the nature of the society sponsoring the "health" care.

Again, these points are not new. Similar views have been voiced by others. Davis observed that the prospective clients of family clinics "are told in one way or another, through lectures, newspaper publicity, or discreet

[41] Soddy, op. cit., p. 209.
[42] Ibid., p. 208.
[43] Blain, D.: "Action in mental health: Opportunities and responsibilities of the private sector of society." *Amer. J. Psychiatry,* 121: 422–27 (Nov.), 1964, p. 425.
[44] Ibid.

announcement, that the clinic exists for the purpose of helping individuals out of their troubles; whereas it really exists for the purpose of helping the established social order. Once lured to the clinic, the individual may suffer further deception in the form of propaganda to the effect that his own best interest lies in doing the thing he apparently does not want to do, as if a man's 'best interest' could be judged by anything else than his own desire."[45]

Because of the involuntary character of this kind of clinic or hospital, it follows, according to Davis (and I agree with him), that the service "must find support through subsidy (philanthropic or governmental) rather than through profit from fees. Furthermore, since its purpose is identified with the community at large rather than the person it serves, and since it requires the use of force or misrepresentation to carry out this purpose, it must function as an arm of the law and government. We do not permit the use of force and fraud to individuals in their private capacity. . . . In order, therefore, to settle familial conflicts by enforcing social dictates, a family clinic must in the long run be clothed with the power or at least the mantle of some state-authorized institution for the exercise of systematic deception, such as the church."[46]

Could the community support a clinic devoted to promoting the best interests of the client, rather than of the community? Davis considered this possibility, and concluded that it could not. For, if this kind of clinic is to exist, then, "like the other kind, [it] must use force and deception—not on the client, but on the community. It must lobby in legislative halls, employ political weapons, and above all deny publicly its true purpose."[47] (We have seen organized American psychoanalysis do just this.)[48]

Davis is clear about the basic alternatives that psychiatry must face, but that it refuses to face: "The individualistic clinic would accept the standard of its client. The other kind of clinic would accept the standard of society. In practice only the latter is acceptable, because the state is clothed with the power to use force and fraud."[49] Insofar as family clinics or other kinds of mental health facilities try to render services of both kinds, "they are trying to ride two horses headed in opposite directions."[50]

Comparison of the care provided by mental hospitals in Russia and America supports the contention that the values and performances that psychiatry promotes or suppresses are related to the society sponsoring the psychiatric service. The proportion of physicians and hospital beds to population is about the same in both countries. However, this similarity is misleading. In the Soviet Union, there are about 200,000 psychiatric hospital beds; in the United States, about 750,000. Accordingly, "11.2% of all hospital beds in the

[45] Davis, op. cit., pp. 241–42.
[46] Ibid., pp. 242–43.
[47] Ibid., p. 243.
[48] See Szasz, T. S.: "Psychoanalysis and taxation: A contribution to the rhetoric of the disease concept in psychiatry." *Amer. J. Psychotherapy,* 18: 635–43 (Oct.), 1964; "A note on psychiatric rhetoric." *Amer. J. Psychiatry,* 121: 1192–93 (June), 1965.
[49] Davis, op. cit., p. 244.
[50] Ibid., p. 245.

Soviet Union [are] allocated to psychiatric patients, compared with 46.4% in the USA."[51]

This difference is best accounted for by certain social and psychiatric policies that encourage mental hospitalization in America, but discourage it in Russia, Moreover, the Soviets' main emphasis in psychiatric care is enforced work, whereas ours is enforced idleness; they compel psychiatric patients to produce, whereas we compel them to consume. It seems improbable that these "therapeutic" emphases should be unrelated to the chronic labor shortage in Russia, and the chronic surplus here.

In Russia, "work therapy" differs from plain work in that the former is carried out under the auspices of a psychiatric institution, the latter under the auspices of a factory or farm. Furthermore, as we saw in the case of Iosif Brodsky, the Russian criminal is sentenced to work—not to idleness (or make-work), like his American counterpart. All this stems from two basic sources: first, from the Soviet sociopolitical theory that holds that "productive work" is necessary and good for both society and the individual; second, from the Soviet socioeconomic fact that in a system of mammoth bureaucracies (lacking adequate checks and balances) more and more people are needed to do less and less work. Thus, the Soviets have a chronic labor shortage.

Consistent with these conditions, the Russians try to keep people at their jobs, rather than put them in mental hospitals. If a person is no longer tolerated at his job, he is made to work in "psychiatric outpatient clinics . . . where patients [can] spend the entire day at work. . . ."[52] In the 1930s, during the heyday of Stalinism, there developed an "uncritical infatuation with work therapy," as a result of which "the hospitals came to resemble industrial plants."[53]

It is evident that the distinction, in Russia, between work therapy and plain work is of the same kind as the distinction, in the United States, between confinement in a hospital for the criminally insane and imprisonment in jail. Many of the Soviet hospital shops, we learn, "settle down to operate like regular factory units, keeping their mildly disabled but productive patients there for interminable periods, paying them regular wages while they travel daily back and forth to their homes as if they had permanent jobs. . . . Instances have been reported where the sheltered workshops have been exploited by their managers for private gain. . . ."[54]

In the United States, the government does not usually own or control the means of production. The manufacture of goods and the provision of (most) services is in the hands of private individuals or groups. If the government should have persons under its care produce goods or provide services, it would create a problem of competition with private enterprise. This problem first arose in connection with prisons and now faces us in connection with mental health facilities. The stockholders of General Motors Corporation (or its em-

[51] Wortis, J. and Freundlich, D.: "Psychiatric work therapy in the Soviet Union." *Amer. J. Psychiatry,* 121: 123–25 (Aug.), 1964, p. 123.

[52] Ibid.

[53] Ibid., p. 124.

[54] Ibid., p. 127.

ployees) would be less than happy if the United States Government were to have the inmates of federal prisons manufacture automobiles. Thus, prisoners in America are reduced to making license plates, and mental patients, to mopping floors or working in the kitchen or back ward of the hospital.

The point I wish to make is simple; unlike in Russia, the major socio-economic problem in the United States is an over-abundance, not a scarcity, of consumer goods; likewise, we have an excess, not a shortage, of productive manpower. The result is our well-known chronic unemployment, which rarely dips below 5 per cent of the labor force (without including many elderly persons capable of working). Accordingly, in American mental hospitals, meaningful and productive work is discouraged and, if need be, prevented by force. Instead of defining forced labor as therapy—as do the Soviets —we define forced idleness as therapy. The only work permitted (or encouraged) is labor necessary to maintain the hospital plant and services, and, even in this category, only such work as is considered non-competitive with private enterprise.

As I suggested some time ago,[55] in the United States mental hospitalization serves a twofold socioeconomic function. First, by defining people in mental hospitals as unfit for work (and often preventing them from working even after their discharge), the mental health care system serves to diminish our national pool of unemployment; large numbers of people are classified as mentally ill rather than as socially incompetent or unemployed. Second, by creating a vast organization of psychiatric hospitals and affiliated institutions, the mental health care system helps to provide employment; indeed, the number of psychiatric and parapsychiatric jobs thus created is staggering. As a result, major cutback in the expenditures of the mental health bureaucracy threaten the same kind of economic dislocation as do cutbacks in the expenditures of the defense establishment and are, perhaps, equally "unthinkable."

It seems to me, therefore, that contrary to the oft-repeated propaganda about the high cost of mental illness, we have a subtle economic stake in perpetuating, and even increasing, such "illness." Faced as we are with over-production and underemployment, we can evidently afford the "cost" of caring for hundreds of thousands of "mental patients" and their dependents. But can we afford the "cost" of not caring for them, and thus adding to the ranks of the unemployed not only the so-called mentally ill, but also the people who now "treat" them and do "research" on them?

Whatever the ostensible aims of community psychiatry may be, its actual operations are likely to be influenced by socioeconomic and political considerations and facts such as I have discussed here.

Psychiatry is a moral and social enterprise. The psychiatrist deals with problems of human conduct. He is, therefore, drawn into situations of conflict—often between the individual and the group. If we wish to understand

[55] Szasz, T. S.: "Review of *The Economics of Mental Illness*, by Rashi Fein (New York: Basic Books, 1958)." *AMA Archives of General Psychiatry*, 1: 116–18 (July), 1959.

psychiatry, we cannot avert our eyes from this dilemma: we must know whose side the psychiatrist takes—the individual's or the group's.

Proponents of the mental health ideology describe the problem in different terms. By not emphasizing conflicts between people, they avoid enlisting themselves explicitly as the agents of either the individual or the group. party or moral value, they promote "mental health."

Considerations such as these have led me to conclude that the concept of mental illness is a betrayal of common sense and of an ethical view of man. To be sure, whenever we speak of a concept of man, our initial problem is one of definition and philosophy: What do we mean by man? Following in the tradition of individualism and rationalism, I hold that a human being is a person to the extent that he makes free, uncoerced choices. Anything that increases his freedom, increases his manhood; anything that decreases his freedom, decreases his manhood.

Progressive freedom, independence, and responsibility lead to being a man; progressive enslavement, dependence, and irresponsibility, to being a thing. Today it is inescapably clear that, regardless of its origins and aims, the concept of mental illness serves to enslave man. It does so by permitting—indeed commanding—one man to impose his will on another.

We have seen that the purveyors of mental health care, especially when such care is provided by the government, are actually the purveyors of the moral and socioeconomic interests of the state. This is hardly surprising. What other interests could they represent? Surely not those of the so-called patient, whose interests are often antagonistic to those of the state. In this way, psychiatry—now proudly called "community psychiatry"—becomes largely a means for controlling the individual. In a mass society, this is best accomplished by recognizing his existence only as a member of a group, never as an individual.

The danger is clear, and has been remarked on by others. In America, when the ideology of totalitarianism is promoted as fascism or communism, it is coldly rejected. However, when the same ideology is promoted under the guise of mental health care, it is warmly embraced. It thus seems possible that where fascism and communism have failed to collectivize American society, the mental health ethic may yet succeed.

DAVID J. ROTHMAN

The Challenge of Crime

Eighteenth-century notions of dependency and deviancy did not survive for very long into the nineteenth, nor did its methods of dispensing charity and correction. The social, intellectual, and economic changes that differentiated the states of the new republic from the several colonies prompted a critical reappraisal and revision of the ideas and techniques of social control. Americans felt compelled to rethink inherited procedures and devise new methods to replace old ones. They devoted extraordinary attention to this issue, hoping to establish quickly and effectively alternatives to the colonial system.

Between 1790 and 1890, the nation's population greatly increased and so did the number and density of cities. Even gross figures reveal the dimensions of the change. In these forty years, the population of Massachusetts almost doubled, in Pennsylvania it tripled, and in New York it increased five times; border and midwestern states, practically empty in 1790, now held over three million people. At Washington's inauguration, only two hundred thousand Americans lived in towns with more than twenty-five hundred people; by Jackson's accession, the number exceeded one million. In 1790, no American city had more than fifty thousand residents. By 1830, almost half a million people lived in urban centers larger than that.[1] During these same years factories began to dot the New England and mid-Atlantic rivers. The decade of the 1830's witnessed the first accelerated growth of manufacturing in the

[1] U.S. Bureau of the Census, *Historical Statistics of the United States, Colonial Times to 1957* (Washington, D.C., 1960), 12–14; George Rogers Taylor, *The Transportation Revolution, 1815–1860* (New York, 1951), 6–10, 141–144. The sophisticated studies of geographic mobility take their starting point with 1870, so we have no precise figures for the earlier period. However, gross numbers tell a good deal, and the very transportation revolution that Taylor writes about is another indication of the opportunity for mobility and the frequent use of the facilities. In 1790, the urban population was 5.1 percent of the nation; it rose to 7.3 percent in 1810, declined slightly to 7.1 percent in 1820, and thereafter increased steadily to 1860, reaching 19.8 percent. Some new and important efforts to examine migration patterns in this period may be found in Stephan Thernstrom and Richard Sennett, eds., *Nineteenth-Century Cities* (New Haven, 1969).

Source: David J. Rothman, "The Challenge of Crime," pp. 57–78 in *The Discovery of the Asylum* (Boston: Little, Brown and Company, 1971). Copyright © 1971 by David J. Rothman. Reprinted by permission of Little, Brown and Company.

nation.[2] At the same time, Enlightenment ideas challenged Calvinist doctrines; the prospect of boundless improvement confronted a grim determinism.[3] But these general trends are not sufficient to explain the very specific reactions to the issue of deviant and dependent behavior. To them must be added Americans' understanding of these changes. Under the influence of demographic, economic and intellectual developments, they perceived that the traditional mechanisms of social control were obsolete. The premises upon which the colonial system had been based were no longer valid.

Each change encouraged Americans to question inherited practices and to devise new ones. Inspired by the ideals of the Enlightenment, they considered older punishments to be barbaric and traditional assumptions on the origins of deviant behavior to be misdirected. Movement to cities, in and out of territories, and up and down the social ladder, made it difficult for them to believe that a sense of hierarchy or localism could now stabilize society. When men no longer knew their place or station, self-policing communities seemed a thing of the past. Expanding political loyalties also made colonial mechanisms appear obsolete. Citizens' attachment to state government promoted a broader definition of responsibility, so that a sentence of banishment seemed a parochial response. The welfare of the commonwealth demanded that towns no longer solve their problems in such narrow and exclusive ways.

This awareness provoked at least as much anxiety as celebration. Americans in the Jacksonian period could not believe that geographic and social mobility would promote or allow order and stability. Despite their marked impatience and dissatisfaction with colonial procedures, they had no ready vision of how to order society. They were still trapped in many ways in the rigidities of eighteenth-century social thinking. They knew well that the old system was passing, but not what ought to replace it. What in their day was to prevent society from bursting apart? From where would the elements of cohesion come? More specifically, would the poor now corrupt the society? Would criminals roam out of control? Would chaos be so acute as to drive Americans mad?[4] All of these questions become part of a full, intense, and revealing investigation of the origins of deviant and dependent behavior. To understand why men turned criminal or became insane or were poor would enable reformers to strengthen the social order. To comprehend and control

[2] Douglas North, *The Economic Growth of the United States, 1790–1860* (New York, 1961), 167, 189 ff.; George Rogers Taylor, *Transportation Revolution,* chs. 10–11.
[3] A good starting point for the intellectual history of this period is Perry Miller, *The Life of the Mind in America: From the Revolution to the Civil War* (New York, 1965). See too Charles I. Foster, *An Errand of Mercy* (Chapel Hill, N.C. 1960), for a discussion of the Protestant response to these changing conditions, how they equated movement with a return to barbarism.
[4] One of the best accounts of the tensions that social change created in post-1820 America is Marvin Meyers's *The Jacksonian Persuasion* (Stanford, 1957). Meyers, however, seems to locate all the tensions within the Jackson camp. The materials I discuss in the following chapters show that the anxieties were far more broadly spread through the society. Another account, not as finely drawn as Meyers's, but sensitive to the darker side of the Jackson years is Fred Somkin, *Unquiet Eagle: Memory and Desire in the Idea of American Freedom, 1815–1860* (Ithaca, N.Y., 1967). For an incisive examination of these themes in the world of art see Neil Harris, *The Artist in American Society* (New York, 1966).

abnormal behavior promised to be the first step in establishing a new system for stabilizing the community, for binding citizens together. In this effort, one finds the clearest indications of how large-scale social changes affected thinking and actions of Americans in the Jacksonian period. And here one also finds the crucial elements that led to the discovery of the asylum.

In the immediate aftermath of independence and nationhood, Americans believed that they had uncovered both the prime cause of criminality in their country and an altogether effective antidote. Armed with patriotic fervor, sharing a repugnance for things British and a new familiarity with and faith in Enlightenment doctrines, they posited that the origins and persistence of deviant behavior would be found in the nature of the colonial criminal codes. Established in the days of oppression and ignorance, the laws reflected British insistence on severe and cruel punishments. The case of William Penn seemed typical. He had attempted to introduce mild and humane legislation into his province, drawing up the Great Law of 1682, but the crown, in the person of Queen Anne, had callously disallowed it. "The mild voice of reason and humanity," explained New York Quaker Thomas Eddy, "reached not the thrones of princes or the halls of legislators." The mother country had stifled the colonists' benevolent instincts, compelling them to emulate the crude customs of the old world. The result was the predominance of archaic and punitive laws that only served to perpetuate crime.[5]

A reading of the Enlightenment tract of Cesare Beccaria verified for Americans in the 1970's the link between barbaric laws and deviant behavior. The treatise, *On Crimes and Punishments,* first appeared in 1764, was quickly translated, and was already being quoted by John Adams as early as 1770 in defense of the British soldiers implicated in the Boston Massacre. Beccaria insisted, and American experience seemed to confirm, that "if we glance at the pages of history, we will find that laws, which surely are, or ought to be, compacts of free men, have been, for the most part, a mere tool of the passions of some." They were all too often not only inhumane but self-defeating. "The severity of punishment of itself emboldens men to commit the very wrongs it is supposed to prevent," Beccaria announced. "They are driven to commit additional crimes to avoid the punishment for a single one. The countries and times most notorious for severity of penalties have always been those in which the bloodiest and most inhumane of deeds were committed." Punishment, to be effective, had to be unavoidable. "The certainty of a punishment, even if it be moderate, will always make a stronger impression than the fear of another which is more terrible but combined with the hope of impunity." Beccaria's summary advice was succinct and his program straightforward: "Do you want to prevent crimes? See to it that the laws are clear and simple and that the entire force of a nation is united in their defense."[6]

[5] Thomas Eddy, *An Account of the State Prison or Penitentiary House, in the City of New York* (New York, 1801), 5; this same argument is put forth by William Bradford, *An Enquiry how far the Punishment of Death is Necessary in Pennsylvania* (Philadelphia 1793), 14–20.

[6] See the translation of Henry Paolucci (Indianapolis, 1963), 8, 43–44, 58, 94, for the several quotations.

The young republic quickly took this message to heart, for it fit well with its own history and revolutionary ideals. Americans fully appreciated that the laws could be a tool of the passions of a handful of men. Did this not explain almost every piece of British colonial legislation after 1763? They believed that they had also witnessed the self-defeating quality of cruel punishments. Had not colonial juries often let a prisoner go free rather than condemn him to the gallows for a petty theft? In this way, criminals had escaped all discipline, and the community had allowed, even encouraged, them to persist in their ways. But independence in this new world made the time and place right for reform. The rhetoric of the Revolution had prepared Americans to fulfill a grand mission, and now they would demonstrate how to uplift one part of mankind, the criminal class. With the Revolution, declared Eddy, fitting Beccaria's doctrine into an American context, "the spirit of reform revived . . . strengthened by the general principles of freedom." The criminal codes of New York had to be revised, for the state could not tolerate laws of "barbarous usages, corrupt society, and monarchical principles . . . [so] imperfectly adopted to a new country, simple manners, and a popular form of government."[7]

Independence made citizens increasingly appreciative of conditions in the new world. They were not Englishmen, and their setting was not England's either. In 1793, William Bradford of Philadelphia explained in a widely read pamphlet, *An Enquiry how far the Punishment of Death is Necessary in Pennsylvania,* that the new nation was the ideal place for enacting Beccaria's principles. "It is from ignorance, wretchedness or corrupted manners of a people that crime proceeds," declared Bradford. "In a country where these do not prevail moderate punishments strictly enforced, will be a curb as effectual as the greatest severity." America, a New York reform society declared, was "a land where the theatre of experiment is boundless. The relations of civil society were few and simple, and the complex abuses of long existing systems, in social order, were unknown." Southern states heard the same message. One Virginia legislator urged his colleagues to revise and moderate the criminal laws to make punishments "comport with the principles of our government."[8] And Robert Turnbull, returning from a visit north, counseled the readers of the *Charleston Daily Gazette* that more lenient laws helped to prevent crime, especially here, when "the mind of man is once more accessible to the mild influence of reason and humanity."[9]

[7] Thomas Eddy, *An Account of the State Prison,* 9. Eddy was very familiar with the writings of Beccaria. See too the Philadelphia Society for Alleviating the Miseries of Public Prisons, *Extracts and Remarks on the Subject of Punishment and Reformation of Criminals* (Philadelphia, 1790), 3–4.

[8] William Bradford, *An Enquiry,* 43. The Society for the Prevention of Pauperism in the City of New-York, *Report on the Penitentiary System in the United States* (New York, 1822), 12; for the influence upon them of Beccaria, see 9, 33. To appreciate how widespread these notions were, see E. Bruce Thompson, "Reforms in the Penal System of Tennessee, 1820–1850," *Tennessee Historical Quarterly,* I (1942), 293.

[9] George K. Taylor, *Substance of a Speech . . . on the Bill to Amend the Penal Laws of this Commonwealth* (Richmond, Va., 1796), 23. Robert James Turnbull, *A Visit to the Philadelphia Prison* (Philadelphia, 1796), 3. The Philadelphia pamphlet was a reprint of a newspaper article. See 75–76 for the argument that certainty of punishment was the most critical element in criminal law.

These conceptions had an immediate and widespread appeal. The reform seemed worthy of the new republic, and feasible, so that by the second decade of the nineteenth century, most of the states had amended their criminal codes. The death sentence was either abolished for all offenses save first-degree murder or strictly limited to a handful of the most serious crimes. Instead, the statutes called for incarceration, the offender to serve a term in prison. Construction kept apace with legal stipulations.[10] Pennsylvania led the way, turning the old Philadelphia jail at Walnut Street into a state prison. In 1796, the New York legislature approved funds for building such institutions, and soon opened the Newgate state prison in Greenwich Village. The New Jersey penitentiary was completed in 1797, and so were others in Virginia and Kentucky in 1800. That same year, the Massachusetts legislature made appropriations for a prison at Charlestown, and in short order Vermont, New Hampshire, and Maryland followed suit. Within twenty years of Washington's inaugural, the states had taken the first steps to alter the traditional system of punishment.[11]

In this first burst of enthusiasm, Americans expected that a rational system of correction, which made punishment certain but humane, would dissuade all but a few offenders from a life in crime. They located the roots of deviancy not in the criminal, but in the legal system. Just as colonial codes had encouraged deviant behavior, republican ones would now curtail, or even eliminate it. To pass the proper laws would end the problem. This perspective drew attention away from the prisons themselves. They were necessary adjuncts to the reform, the substitutes for capital punishment, but intrinsically of little interest or importance. A repulsion from the gallows rather than any faith in the penitentiary spurred the late-eighteenth century construction. Few people had any clear idea what these structures should look like or how they should be administered—or even addressed themselves seriously to these questions. To reformers, the advantages of the institutions were external, and they hardly imagined that life inside the prison might rehabilitate the criminal. Incarceration seemed more humane than hanging and less brutal than whipping. Prisons matched punishment to crime precisely: the more heinous the offense, the longer the sentence. Juries, fully understanding these advantages, would never hesitate to convict the guilty, so that correction would be certain. The fact of imprisonment, not its internal routine, was of chief importance.

By the 1820's, however, these ideas had lost persuasiveness. The focus shifted to the deviant and the penitentiary, away from the legal system. Men intently scrutinized the life history of the criminal and methodically arranged

[10] Raymond T. Bye, *Capital Punishment in the United States* (Philadelphia, 1919), 4–9. Ohio, in 1788, was the first to limit the death penalty to murder; Pennsylvania followed suit in 1794. Few states abolished the death penalty altogether; by 1900, only six had done so. See too David B. Davis, "The Movement to Abolish Capital Punishment in America, 1787–1861," *American Historical Review,* 63 (1957), 23–46. A classic nineteenth-century statement is Edward Livingston, *On the Abolition of the Punishment of Death* (Philadelphia, 1831), originally a report to the Louisiana legislature in March 1822.

[11] The first prison structures in the United States are discussed in Orlando F. Lewis, *The Development of American Prisons and Prison Customs, 1776–1845* (Albany, N.Y., 1922), chs. 1–8; less detailed is Blake McKelvey, *American Prisons: A Study in American Social History Prior to 1915* (Chicago, 1936), ch. 1.

the institution to house him. Part of the cause for this change was the obvious failure of the first campaign. The faith of the 1790's now seemed misplaced; more rational codes had not decreased crime. The roots of deviancy went deeper than the certainty of a punishment. Nor were the institutions fulfilling the elementary task of protecting society, since escapes and riots were commonplace occurrences.[12] More important, the second generation of Americans confronted new challenges and shared fresh ideas. Communities had undergone many critical changes between 1790 and 1830, and so had men's thinking. Citizens found cause for deep despair and yet incredible optimism. The safety and security of their social order seemed to them in far greater danger than that of their fathers, yet they hoped to eradicate crime from the new world. The old structure was crumbling, but perhaps they could draw the blueprints for building a far better one.

Americans in the pre-Civil War era intently pondered the origins of deviant behavior. Philanthropists organized themselves into societies to investigate the question, hoping to devise an effective method of punishment. Legislators, no less interested in a theory for crime, prepared to amend the statutes and appropriate the funds for a new system. To judge by the numerous periodical articles, laymen were also concerned with a subject that had a direct and obvious bearing on their daily lives. Traditional answers were no longer satisfactory.[13]

One of the best examples of their effort appeared in the early reports of the inspectors of New York's Auburn penitentiary. These officials, charged with the management of the prison, attempted to understand the causes of deviancy by collecting and appending to their 1829 and 1830 reports to the state legislature biographical sketches of inmates about to be discharged. The purpose of these brief ten- to twenty-line vignettes, the inspectors explained,

[12] The disillusionment with the first experiments appears in many pamphlets; see Thomas Eddy, *An Account of the State Prison*, 15–16, on the disappointment of "many citizens . . . [who] sometimes express a regret at the change . . . and returning to a system of accumulated severity and terror." Other expressions may be found in the Philadelphia Society for Alleviating the Miseries of Public Prisons, *A Statistical View of the Penal Code of Pennsylvania* (Philadelphia, 1817), 35; Stephan White, Sherman Leland, Bradford Sumner, *Report on . . . the State Prison at Charlestown* [Massachusetts], (Boston, 1827), 1. William Tudor, "The Penitentiary System," *North American Review*, 13 (1821), 417–420. Gershom Powers, *A Brief Account of the Construction, Management, and Discipline . . . of the New York State Prison at Auburn* (Auburn, N.Y., 1826), 64–69.

[13] Jacksonian theories on deviancy have received little attention, but see David Brion Davis, *Homicide in American Fiction, 1798–1860* (Ithaca, N.Y., 1957). Davis's analysis is close to mine, but his interests are more in the literary expression of the problem than in the social origins of the ideas and their influence on social policy. There is also a discussion in W. David Lewis, *From Newgate to Dannemora: The Rise of the Penitentiary in New York, 1796–1848* (Ithaca, N.Y., 1965). Lewis argues that 1840 was a turning point, that after that date an environmental concern came to the fore; he finds the influence of phrenology vital to the story. There is, however, as the following discussion will show, much evidence of these ideas in the 1820's, and even more in the 1830's; furthermore, it was not phrenology that accounted for them, I believe, but a peculiar view of American society. For a concise survey of current theories of deviant behavior, see Richard A. Cloward and Lloyd E. Ohlin, *Delinquency and Opportunity* (New York, 1960), chs. 2–4.

was to exhibit "facts which must be interesting, as well to the legislator as to the philanthropist and the Christian." Here, in the life stories of several hundred convicts, they could discover the origins of crime. Impatient with theology and disappointed in the law, they turned to the careers of offenders for the information they wanted.[14]

At first glance, these accounts are curiously naïve. Officials obtained the facts, we are told, in interviews with the convicts just before their release, and obviously made no effort to check the accuracy of the statements. When the sketches recount the events that led up to the prisoner's conviction, each convict emerges as the innocent victim of some misunderstanding. He sold goods he did not know were stolen, or passed bills he did not recognize were counterfeit, or took a horse he did not realize belonged to a neighbor. The investigators, however, did not contradict these assertions or declare their own skepticism. They were not trying to prove that the courts of justice always convicted the right man, that the legal system was infallible. Clearly their concern was different. No record survives of how interrogators conducted the interviews or how they phrased their questions, what kinds of suggestions they openly or covertly made to the convicts. But the finished products follow so set a pattern, and officials were so eager to publicize them, that undoubtedly they heard what they wished to hear, learned what they wished to learn. Their interest was not in the process of conviction, they were quite certain that a collection of criminals stood before them. No, they were preoccupied with the convicts' early years, their growing up in the family, their actions in the community. And of the reliability and pertinence of this information they were certain.

In their search for the roots of deviant behavior, investigators concentrated on the convicts' upbringing, devoting the most space to it in almost every one of these biographies. They focused their questions on the criminals' childhood, recording what they wanted legislators and philanthropists to learn. No matter at what age the deviant committed an offense, the cause could be traced back to his childhood. Prisoner number 315, discharged in 1829, had been convicted for forgery at the age of fifty-five. Until then, he had apparently "maintained a respectable standing in the society." Why had a man of property with no previous record been guilty of such an act? His history provided the answer:

> No. 315.—A.N., born in Massachusetts; father was killed at Quebec when he was very young; family soon after scattered, and he was bound out to a farmer, with whom he lived till of age; was a wild, rude boy, and early addicted to some bad habits, drinking, swearing, etc.

In the early years, if you looked carefully, were the origins of deviancy.

And look carefully they did. The 1829 and 1830 reports of the Auburn penitentiary contained 173 biographies, and in fully two-thirds of them, the

---

[14] "Abstract of Brief Biographical Sketches as Taken From Convicts When Discharged from this Prison," "Annual Report of the Inspectors of the State Prison at Auburn," *N.Y. Senate and Assembly Documents*, 1830, I, no. 38, pp. 37–54. The second group of biographies is found in "Annual Report of Auburn Prison," *N.Y. Senate Docs.*, 1831, I, no. 15, pp. 32–63. All the cases below come from these pages and are identified by their number in sequence. The quotation is from the 1830 report, p. 5.

supervisors selected and presented the data to prove that childhood made the man. Almost always a failure of upbringing—specifically, the collapse of family control—caused deviant behavior. In these sketches, one of three circumstances characterized the failure. First, the children duplicated the parents' corrupt behavior. Prisoner 339 was typical: "Brought up . . . under the influence of a bad example; says his father has been in the New York prison." Or case 317: "Father a very intemperate man, and brought him up to it." Second, the family disintegrated because of death or divorce or desertion, turning an undisciplined child loose on the community. Inevitably, the results were disastrous. H. L., "born in Vermont; after his father's death, when he was a mere boy, worked out for a living and had his own way." And M. R. R.: "His father went off before his remembrance, and never returned . . . his mother married again . . . to a very intemperate bad man, who drove his stepchildren off, and told them he would kill them if they ever came home again." And J. L.: "Parents separated when he was seven on account of his father's going after other women; was then bound out to a farmer . . . ran away from him." Third, the child, through no obvious fault of the parents, left home. M. H., a girl born in Massachusetts, "ran away from her parents at thirteen years of age, and went into Rensselaer county . . . where she . . . soon became a common prostitute."[15]

Investigators had no need to question the truth of these facts. The very presence of the convict at the interview made them self-confirming. They did not doubt that the common whore had run off from her family, that the father of a thief was a drunkard, that a counterfeiter had been on his own from an early age. The moral was clear to them and could not be lost on their readers: deviancy began with the family.

Officials had no difficulty in tracing criminal behavior directly to circumstances of family life. They were certain that children lacking discipline quickly fell victim to the influence of vice at loose in the community. Inadequately prepared to withstand the temptations, they descended into crime. To document this idea, investigators inquired into and reported upon convicts' drinking habits, and those of their companions, and tried to discover other corruptions to which they had succumbed. Once again, they assembled the right facts for the story. In these sketches, the vices permeating the society made the family's failure decisive.

The undisciplined youth typically began to frequent taverns, soon became intemperate, and then turned to crime to support his vice. J. A., a French Canadian, "lost his parents when young, and was thrown friendless upon the world; had troubles which led him to excessive drinking. . . . Convicted of grand larceny." J. T., who had the misfortune to serve an apprenticeship under a drunken master, also "fell into the habit of drinking too much himself; it was in a grocery where he had been drinking too freely, that he committed the crime [theft] that brought him to prison." The temptation

[15] H. L. was case 433; M. R. R., 440; J. L., 319; M. H., 303. Of the 173 cases, 99 were explained directly in terms of parental failures. In 26, the parents set a bad example; in 27, they were absent by reason of death or desertion; in 32 cases, the child left home very young, in 11 he went to an apprentice. Two were at home but "wild," and one was in a "very poor" household.

of liquor was so great that occasionally those properly raised succumbed to it in time of crisis. J. M. "was a steady young man and continued so till after his wife died . . . when he broke up housekeeping and went about from place to place; soon got to drinking too freely, became very intemperate, and at length took to stealing." R. R., "a steady industrious and moral young man . . . has been worth $3000; on account of domestic trouble took to drinking, and followed it up till he came to prison." If the best of sorts might yield to vice, those without rigorous moral training were certain victims.[16]

Persons outside family government often began to wander, falling in with bad company and acquiring the worst habits. Some first became intemperate and then committed crimes, others went directly to theft and burglary. Predictably, M. S., having run away from his apprenticeship at age fourteen, then roamed "about the country, with no other business than stealing." In another common variation, those lacking family counsel took up an occupation that was almost certain to lead to vice and crime. Enlistment in the army was one such step. The authors of these sketches were convinced that military service was a "school for vice." T. L., in their estimation, had proved himself an "apt scholar": while serving with the British forces in Canada, he "gave himself up to drinking, stealing, etc. and was ripe for crime when he came into this state." The American situation was no different: J. L., born in Albany, New York, enlisted after running away from a local farmer. "Had previously been a sober, industrious boy but in the army became very intemperate and vicious; after his discharge, strolled about the country, drinking more and more till he came to prison." Soldiers suffered from too little supervision once they left the barracks. The trouble with the military was that it was not military enough.

The sailor's life also offered an education in immorality. At sea, J. H. "became excessively intemperate, and addicted to all sorts of vice; had no sense of moral obligation; lived without God in the world. When he quit the seas, came into this state . . . through intemperance was led to the commission of a crime." Officials believed it axiomatic that anyone who "has been in almost every seaport in the world," would be "addicted to every bad habit in the world." Some civilian occupations were equally dangerous—for example, digging New York's new canal. J. P., typical of those leaving home without parental consent, "came to work on the [Erie] canal; fell into vicious company, and consequently vicious habits; became intemperate." Soon the courts convicted him for passing counterfeit money. G. J. "had previously been sober and industrious." But on the canal, "he soon got into many bad habits, drinking, gambling, stealing, etc.," till he arrived at the Auburn penitentiary.[17]

These carefully designed, really contrived biographies, undoubtedly

16 J. A., was case 443; J. T., 444; J. M., 493; R. R., 352. Of the 99 cases which defined parental problems as critical, 27 children, according to the biographies, went directly into a life of crime; 13 first succumbed to a vice; 17 wandered and then began committing crimes. Twenty-one followed a corrupting occupation, such as sailor or canal-worker, and 20 ran away or had a bad apprenticeship. One suffered a series of misfortunes.

17 M. S. was case 492; T. L., 480; J. L., 419; J. H., 326; J. P. was case 339; G. J., 340.

strike the modern reader as crude and simplistic versions of later, more sophisticated analyses. Yet when looked at from the vantage point of the eighteenth century, they are in many ways important and different. For one thing, they are highly secular documents. Officials were interested in crime, not sin, and had no inclination to view legal offenses as Lucifer's handiwork or the retributive judgment of an angry God. The accounting system of the colonial period—where crime rates reflected both the community's religiosity and divine judgment on it—was outdated. Officials, in fact, gave surprisingly little attention to the convicts' religious history. Occasionally they noted if someone was raised without family prayer or had never regularly attended church. But even then religious training was an indicator of the quality of his upbringing, and without intrinsic importance. It revealed in one more way how the family had failed to educate and discipline the child.

Nor did these vignettes show the Revolutionary War generation's concern for legal reform. Officials now looked to the life of the criminal, not to the statutes, in attempting to grasp the origins of deviancy. They presented biographical sketches, not analyses of existing codes. They did not bother to gather information about or report upon convicts' previous encounters with the law, what kinds of punishments they had recieved, or their feelings about them. Such questions were for the 1790's, not the 1820's and '30's.

In a still more crucial way the concept of deviant behavior implicit in these sketches signaled a new departure. Although the colonists had blamed inadequate parental and religious training for crime, they were preoccupied with the sinner himself. Convinced that the corrupt nature of man was ultimately at fault, they did not extensively analyze the role of the criminal's family or the church or the general society. Furthermore, they shared a clear understanding of what the well-ordered community *ought to* look like, and this too stifled any inclination to question or scrutinize existing arrangements. Their religious and social certainty covered the discrepancies between ideas and realities, obviating new approaches and theories. Americans in the Jacksonian period stood in a very different position. They learned that men were born innocent, not depraved, that the sources of corruption were external, not internal, to the human condition. Encouraged by such doctrines to examine their society with acute suspicion, they quickly discovered great cause for apprehension and criticism.

But why did they become so anxious in their concern? Why did they so easily discover corruption? They were, it is true, predisposed to this finding, yet it is puzzling that they located all that they looked for. Communities were not overrun with thieves and drunkards, prostitutes and gamblers; the rate of crime, for example, probably did not increase over these years.[18] Rather, Americans conducted this examination with grandiose expectations. Assuming that deviant behavior was symptomatic of a failing in society, they expected to ferret out corruption and eliminate crime. With the stakes so high, they could ignore no possible malfeasance.

[18] Roger Lane, "Crime and Criminal Statistics in Nineteenth-Century Massachusetts," *Journal of Social History,* 2 (1968), 156–163. See also William Nelson, "Emerging Notions of Modern Criminal Law," 461–462; prosecutions for morality practically disappeared in Massachusetts after the Revolution.

Another consideration expanded their list of social evils. Many Americans in the Jacksonian period judged their society with eighteenth-century criteria in mind. As a result, they defined as corrupting the fluidity and mobility that they saw. Thinking that an orderly society had to be a fixed one, they judged the discrepancies between traditional postulates and present reality as promoting deviant behavior. Not having evolved an alternative to the colonial vision of society, they looked back both with envy and discomfort. They were embarrassed about the cruelty and shortsightedness of earlier punishments, and hoped to be humanitarian innovators. Yet they also believed that their predecessors, fixed in their communities and ranks, had enjoyed social order. But how were they now to maintain cohesion in so fluid and open a society? This ambivalence gave a very odd quality to their thinking. On the one hand, they aimed at the heights, about to eliminate crime and corruption. On the other, they doubted the society's survival, fearing it might succumb to chaos. They confronted, it seemed, unprecedented opportunity, and unprecedented peril.

Holding such a position, American students of deviant behavior moved family and community to the center of their analysis. New York officials accumulated and published biographies because this technique allowed them to demonstrate to legislators and philanthropists the crucial role of social organizations. Accordingly, almost every sketch opened with a vivid description of an inadequate family life and then traced the effects of the corruptions in the community. While many a convict may possibly have come from a broken home or been prone to drink, no one ought to take the inspectors' findings as straight facts. They had a prior commitment to gathering and publicizing this type of information to explain the origins of crime. Interviewers probably induced the convicts to describe, whether accurately or not, their early life in grim terms. Sympathetic questioners, letting the criminal know that they thought that much of the blame for his fate rested with his parents, would soon hear him recount his father's drinking habits and the attraction of the tavern around the corner. These sketches reflected the ideas of the questioner, not some objective truth about the criminal. The doctrine was clear: parents who sent their children into the society without a rigorous training in discipline and obedience would find them someday in the prison. The case of W. S. can summarize both the approach and the message: "Lived with his parents who indulged him too much for his good; was a very wild unsteady boy; fond of company and amusements; when he could not get his parents' consent, would go wthout it." The result? "Convicted of an attempt to rape . . . and sentenced to three years."[19]

The pessimism and fear underlying this outlook pointed to the difficulty Americans had in fitting their perception of nineteenth-century society as mobile and fluid into an eighteenth-century definition of a well-ordered community. Their first reaction was not to disregard the inherted concept but to condemn present conditions. Hence, in these biographies a dismal picture emerged of a society field with a myriad of temptations. It was almost as

[19] W. S. was case 301. Note too that poverty as a direct cause of crime did not enter into this story very often. Others, as we will see below, ch. 7, made the link; but here it was a predisposing cause and not in itself a sufficient explanation for deviancy.

if the town, in a nightmarish image, was made up of a number of households, frail and huddled together, facing the sturdy and wide doors of the tavern, the gaudy opening into a house of prostitution or theater filled with dissipated customers; all the while, thieves and drunkards milled the streets, introducing the unwary youngster to vice and corruption. Every family was under seige, surrounded by enemies ready to take advantage of any misstep. The honest citizen was like a vigilant soldier, well trained to guard against temptation. Should he relax for a moment, the results would be disastrous. Once, observers believed, neighbors had disciplined neighbors. Now it seemed that rowdies corrupted rowdies.

Yet for all the desperation in this image, Americans shared an incredible optimism. Since deviant behavior was a product of the environment, the predictable result of readily observable situations, it was not inevitable. Crime was not inherent in the nature of man, as Calvinists had asserted; no theological devils insisted on its perpetuation. Implicit in this outlook was an impulse to reform. If one could alter the conditions breeding crime, then one could reduce it to manageable proportions and bring a new security to society.

One tactic was to advise and warn the family to fulfill its tasks well. By giving advice and demonstrating the awful consequences of an absence of discipline, critics would inspire the family to a better performance. (The biographical sketches, then, were not only investigations but correctives to the problem.) One might also organize societies to shut taverns and houses of prostitution, an effort that was frequently made in the Jacksonian period. But such measures, while important, were slow-working, and by themselves seemed insufficient to meet the pressing needs of this generation. Another alternative then became not only feasible but essential: to construct a special setting for the deviant. Remove him from the family and community and place him in an artificially created and therefore corruption-free environment. Here he could learn all the vital lessons that others had ignored, while protected from the temptations of vice. A model and small-scale society could solve the immediate problem and point the way to broader reforms.

Almost everyone who wrote about deviancy during the Jacksonian era echoed the findings of Auburn's inspectors and many emulated their methodology. Officials at other prisons, conducted similar surveys among convicts, validating the general conclusions reached in New York. Interested laymen, organized into such benevolent societies as the New York Prison Association and the Boston Prison Discipline Society, made their own investigations and then helped to publicize the same ideas among a still broader portion of the population. Well-known reformers, like Dorothea Dix, Francis Lieber, and Samuel Gridley Howe, concerned with a spectrum of causes, paid great attention to the problem of crime and its correction and futher popularized the concepts. Family disorganization and community corruption, an extreme definition of the powers of vice and an acute sense of the threat of disorder were the standard elements in the discussions. A wide consensus formed on the origins of crime.

Prison officials everywhere informed state legislators of the crucial role of the family and community in causing deviant behavior. "The mass of criminals," explained the inspectors of Pennsylvania's Eastern State Penitentiary, "is composed of persons whose childhood and youth were spent in the uncontrolled exercise of vicious instincts." The warden of the Ohio penitentiary listed the breakdown of the household among the leading causes of crime. "Unhappy orphanage," he lamented, "leaves the susceptible youth without those restraints and safeguards which conduct to a life of probity."[20] To buttress this argument one official calculated that of the 235 men committed to the prison in one year, 86 were under twenty-five years of age, a sure sign that the failure of the family was at the root of the problem. Another appropriately conducted interviews and compiled case histories. His most important finding, he believed, was that 221 convicts from a sample of 350 had been "thrown out from under parental influence and restraint," before reaching the age of twenty-one; in fact, 89 of them were without guardians by the time they were twelve. They had "never learned to submit to proper authority," or to understand that "their own safety and happiness are secured by such obedience."

All observers agreed that the forces at work in the community aggravated the family's errors. The future convict, concluded the Pennsylvania group, "social to a fault," took his cues from his surroundings; predictably, "the vices of social life have heralded the ruin of his fortunes and his hopes." Ohio's officials shared this view: "Without the refining and elevating influences of the home, without parental restraint and example, they were thrown upon a cold and selfish world, and often wronged. . . . They have done as might have been expected."[21]

An identical interpretation appeared in the opening pages of the first annual report (1844) of the New York Prison Association. According to one of its founders, the Unitarian minister William H. Channing, the association was formed to aid persons awaiting trial, to help reform convicts, and to assist released prisoners. This commitment, he explained, was not only testimony to a Christian desire to have good triumph over evil and to avoid "the vindictive spirit," but also reflected the community's ultimate responsibility, because of its "neglect and bad usages," for "the sins of its children." The first part of this formulation needed little clarification, but the second did, and so he elaborated on the role of the family and community in the origins of crime.[22]

"The first and most obvious cause," began Channing, "is an evil organization derived from evil parents. Bad germs bear bad fruit." Although his language suggested that a biological process was at work, he did not consider heredity anything more than a predisposing force that could be "cleansed away by a healthful moral influence." A properly organized social system

[20] Inspectors of the Eastern State Penitentiary of Pennsylvania, *Seventeenth Annual Report* (Philadelphia, 1846), 58. *Annual Report of the Ohio Penitentiary for 1850* (Columbus, Ohio, 1851), 12–13.

[21] *Annual Report of the Ohio Penitentiary for 1852* (Columbus, Ohio, 1853), 35; *Annual Report of the Ohio Penitentiary for 1858* (Columbus, Ohio, 1859), 40–41. Inspectors of the Eastern State Penitentiary, *First and Second Annual Report* (Philadelphia, 1831), 10.

[22] New York Prison Association *First Annual Report* (New York, 1845), 30–31. (Hereafter abbreviated N.Y.P.A.)

would "purify away what is bad," and shield its members "from the temptations beneath which they are peculiarly liable to fall." The existence of crime pointed to the community's inability to fulfill its task, not the influence of heredity. Channing went on to link the failure of family training directly to deviant behavior. Of the 156 inmates recently admitted to Pennsylvania's Eastern State Penitentiary, he reported, fourteen had been orphaned by age twelve, thirty-six were missing one parent or another soon thereafter, 143 had received no religious instruction, and 144 never attended Sabbath school. "Such statistics," affirmed the minister, "tell at a glance that early neglect was certainly, in part, probably in great part, the cause of after crime."[23]

Channing too believed that the corruptions pervading the community made early parental neglect so injurious; in fact, he was surprised that the power of vice did not debilitate still more people. "We seldom appreciate," he declared, "how easily, if left alone, unsustained by worthy example . . . we might become lawless and perverse. . . . Slight deviations, uncorrected, hurry the transgressor into a rapid downward course. . . . Tempers ensnare the inexperienced. . . . The spirit of mere adventure entangles the careless into a web of vile associations, from which there is no after escape. . . . How many a young man . . . took, almost without a thought, the first step in that path which ended in the gambler's hell, the plausible deceits of the forger and counterfeiter." Well-baited traps were so pervasive that the slightest miscalculation brought terrible consequences. "The sight of evil, as by contagion, awakens the desire to commit evil." Yet, for all his anxiety about society, Channing, like other Americans in the Jacksonian period, did not succumb to despair. "The study of the *causes* of the crime," he concluded, "may lead us to its *cure*." His environmental theory encouraged rather than stifled action.[24]

Succeeding reports of the New York Prison Association repeated these themes. Continuously stressing the critical role of the family, they reminded parents of the "importance of exercising careful supervision and wholesome discipline." Otherwise the contagion of vice would be irresistible. Intemperance was "the giant whose mighty arm prostrates the greatest numbers, involving them in sin and shame and crime and ruin." And behind it, "never let it be forgotten, lies the want of early parental restraint and instruction." Readers even learned that "the loss of the father more frequently than that of the mother leads to criminal conduct on the part of the children"; for "mothers, as a general thing, are less able than fathers to restrain their sons."

The catalogue of seductions that led hapless youngsters to the penitentiary did not become thinner with time.[25] The 1855 association report devoted a lengthy appendix to the sources of crime, first paying due regard to the position of the family as the "bulwark against temptation," and then spelling out the social evils rampant in the community. There was the tavern and the brothel house—appropriately joined with a quote from Hosea: "whore-

23 *Ibid.*, 31–33.
24 *Ibid.*, 34–35.
25 See, for example, N. Y. P. A., *Nineteenth Annual Report* (New York, 1864), 352. By that date, such views were no longer as popular as they had been in the 1830's, but were still expressed.

dom and wine . . . taketh away the heart"; the theater and the gambling houses were menaces, and so were the men who solid licentious books and pictures at the railroad station and boat landings. Still, no matter how lengthy the list, the organization assured its followers that "energetic and enlightened action of the people in . . . social and individual capacities" would effectively combat crime.[26]

A rival and perhaps more famous association, the Boston Prison Discipline Society, differed on many substantive issues with its New York counterpart, but both agreed on the sources of deviant behavior. Founded in 1825 by Louis Dwight, a onetime agent of the American Bible Society, the Boston group set down a very familiar creed. "This society," announced one of its early reports, "shows the importance of family government. . . . It is the confession of many convicts at Auburn [New York] and Wethersfield [Connecticut] that the course of vice, which brought them to the prison, commenced in disobedience to their parents, or in their parents' neglect." No one was probably surprised to learn that "youth, when unrestrained and neglected by their parents, find their way to the tavern and the grog shop."[27] This was the meaning of member Samuel Gridley Howe's pronouncement: "Thousands of convicts are made so in consequence of a faulty organization of society. . . . They are thrown upon society as a sacred charge; and that society is false to its trust, if it neglects any means for their reformation."[28] Those to blame for this state of affairs had the duty, and seemingly the power to effect reform.

Two of the most important figures in the New York and Boston organizations, Channing and Dwight, had first followed religious careers—the former was actually a minister, the latter had studied for it and then worked for the Bible Society. But one must define very carefully the religious influence in reform societies. The changes in Protestant thinking from the eighteenth to the nineteenth century had certainly increased the clergy's concern and attention to social reform, and because of their insistence that men were to do good by improving the common weal, many Americans participated in benevolent activities. Nevertheless, the prescriptions of what was right action, the definition of the policy that men of goodwill were to enact, revealed more of a secular than a religious foundation. Channing and Dwight echoed prevailing social anxieties; they did not make a uniquely religious perspective relevant. Their vision of the well-ordered society did not indicate the influence of their special training. In this sense, they, unlike their predecessors, followed the pack rather than heading it.[29]

[26] N.Y.P.A., *Tenth Annual Report* (Albany, N.Y., 1855), Appendix A., by James S. Gould, 61–117. Quotations are on pp. 61, 73, 93–94, 108–109, 116–117.

[27] Boston Prison Discipline Society, *Fourth Annual Report* (Boston, 1829), 64. (Hereafter abbreviated B.P.D.S.); B.P.D.S., *Eleventh Annual Report* (Boston, 1835), 35. On Dwight, see William Jenks, *A Memoir of the Reverend Louis Dwight* (Boston, 1856).

[28] Samuel Gridley Howe, *An Essay on Separate and Congregate Systems of Prison Discipline* (Boston, 1846), 79.

[29] John L. Thomas, "Romantic Reform in America, 1815–1865," *American Quarterly,* 17 (1965), 656–681, notes a malaise but attempts to account for it as a crisis in church affairs; the argument here sees the crisis as far broader, touching all the society. So, too, I differ with the stress in Timothy L. Smith, *Revivalism and Social Reform in Mid-Nineteenth Century America* (Nashville, Tenn., 1957). Indeed, the evidence Smith

Noted reformers and pamphleteers in pre-Civil War America were keenly interested in the predicament of the criminal. Francis Lieber was distressed by the treatment of offenders as well as of slaves. "The history of by far the greatest majority of criminals," insisted Lieber, "shows the afflicting fact, that they were led to crime by the bad example of their parents." From this first cause flowed a sequence of events, "a gradual progress in vice, for which society often offers but too many temptations." No effort to assist the deviant should be spared, he argued, for "society takes upon itself an awful responsibility, by exposing a criminal to such moral contagion, that, according to the necessary course of things, he cannot escape its effects."[30] A more celebrated contemporary, Dorothea Dix, wrote about the conviction as well as the insane, publishing an important pamphlet, *Remarks on Prisons and Prison Discipline in the United States*. "It is to the defects of our social organization," declared Dix, "to the multiplied and multiplying temptations to crime that we chiefly owe the increase of evil doers."[31] And like Lieber, she too announced that the community had the responsibility and the resources to confront and eliminate the problem.

The Jacksonians' conception of the causes of crime had an obvious and precise relevance for understanding juvenile delinquency. The child offender, no less than the adult one, was a casualty of his upbringing. The importance of family discipline in a community pervaded with vice characterized practically every statement of philanthropists and reformers on delinquency. Both mature and immature offenders were victims of similar conditions. Not that Americans, insensitive to an idea of childhood, unthinkingly made children into adults. Quite the reverse. They stripped the years away from adults, and turned everyone into a child.

The custodians of juvenile delinquents asked the same questions and drew the same conclusions as wardens in state prisons. No sooner did New York, for reasons we shall soon explore, establish a house of refuge in 1824 to incarcerate minors guilty of criminal offenses, than its managers collected and published case histories. Their inquiries, following a set form, indicated a common perspective on deviant behavior. How long had the youngster been under family government? How often, and how long, had he served as an apprentice? What was the moral character of his parents and his masters? Did the delinquent drink? Or have other vices? What about his companions? What was his first illegal act? His second and his third? The very thoroughness of the examination reflected how much the interrogators valued the information.

Refuge managers located in parental neglect the primary cause of deviant behavior. In typical instances: J. C., at fourteen, ran away from an

brings forward on the actual social welfare work done by religious organizations, as apart from Bible distribution, is not very great.

[30] Lieber's remarks appear in his translator's preface, reprinted in Gustave de Beaumont and Alexis de Tocqueville, *On the Penitentiary System in the United States* (Carbondale, Ill., 1964), 14–15. See too his *Remarks on the Relation between Education and Crime* (Philadelphia, 1835), 13.

[31] (2nd ed., Philadelphia, 1845), 25.

inattentive and corrupt father. He soon returned, to steal six watches; his father helped to sell the loot. R. W., whose parents were intemperate, roamed the streets, and stayed away from home for weeks on end; he pilfered or begged his daily subsistence until arrested. J. L., another inmate caught stealing, recounted that after his father's death, his mother began drinking, "and then we all went to destruction, mother, brothers, sisters, all."[32] Each case was proof that the child who became "his own boss and went in the way that was right in his own eyes," was a prison convict in the making.

The sketches demonstrated the dire consequences of even minor acts of disobedience. The delinquent moved inexorably from petty to major crimes. W. O. first stole one shilling from his father, then some items of clothing from a stranger, later robbed a watch and some broadcloth from a shop, and finally wrecked, burned, and looted a house. E. M. began his career by pilfering small change from drunkards and graduated to highway robbery. J. R. went from pennies to dollars, and C. B. from fruits and cakes in the kitchen cupboard to cash in store registers.[33] What a careless parent dismissed as a comparatively harmless prank was a crucial event. A few pennies and some sweets, as these biographies revealed, were the first symptoms of a criminal life.

The vices at loose in the community invariably brought the unwary and untrained child to the prison gates. Delinquents' careers demonstrated the debilitating influences of the tavern, where they first began to drink, and the noxious quality of theaters and the houses of prostitution, where they learned other corruptions. Temptations seemed so omnipresent that when dedicating a new building at the New York refuge, the presiding minister reminded his audience that, had their parents been less vigorous or their training less thorough, they too might have become delinquent. "Who of us dare to say," he asked, "that if he had been expressed to the same influence, he would have preserved his integrity and come out of the fiery ordeal unscathed? The sight of such a group of children . . . in yonder gallery should fill us with humility and teach us lessons of mercy!"[34]

Thus, Jacksonians located both the origins of crime and delinquency within the society, with the inadequacies of the family and the unchecked spread of vice through the community. The situation appeared bleak, almost desperate. What elements would now stabilize the community? What kind of social order would keep deviancy within bounds? But if the dangers were immense, so were the possibilities. Convinced that crime was the fault of the environment, not a permanent or inevitable phenomenon, and eager to demonstrate the social blessings of republican political arrangements to the world, Americans set out to protect the safety of the society and to achieve unprecedented success in eradicating deviancy. Their analysis of the origin of crime became a rallying cry to action.

[32] Records of the New York House of Refuge, Syracuse University Library; for these biographies, see Case Histories, nos. 78 (December 10, 1825), 800 (September 30, 1830), 2657 (February 24, 1841).

[33] Case no. 11 (January 1, 1825), case 55 (January 15, 1825), 1602 (July 30, 1835), 803 (October 8, 1830). To sample the many volumes of inmates' records, I examined the first 30 cases in the record book volume I, 1824–25, then the first 15 cases in vols. II (1825–27), V (1830–32), VIII (1835–36), XII (1841–42), XX (1851–52).

[34] New York House of Refuge, Thirtieth Annual Report (New York, 1855), 55.

DANIEL J. BOORSTIN

From "Naughtiness" to "Behavior Deviation"

Not until the late nineteenth century was it common in the United States to think of "children" as a distinct class of the nation's population, meriting and requiring special treatment. For most of modern history, the social and psychological meaning of childhood was vague, a child was, for all practical purposes, simply a small adult. The change in American thinking appeared only as "children" became a minority of the population.

As standards of health improved and longevity increased, the absolute number of Americans under twenty years of age rose from 17 million in 1860 to 47.6 million in 1930. At the same time the *proportion* of that youngest segment declined from 51 percent of the population in 1860 to 43 percent by 1900, and down to 38 percent by 1930. This decline in the proportion of "children" from over half to about one third of the population, as Robert Bremmer has observed, made them "more visible and the particular needs of their condition were more easily recognized. So too youth became more self-conscious, more easily identified and more demanding of attention as a separate category in the total population."

While children as a class were beginning to claim special attention simply by becoming a new minority, other forces helped give "children" a new reality. Humanitarian movements of all sorts—to reform prisons, to improve the lot of slaves, to rehabilitate convicts (the movement of which General James Oglethorpe and the founders of Georgia had been part)— gained momentum after the American Revolution. Along with the efforts of Dorothea Dix and others in the early nineteenth century to humanize the treatment of the insane, the blind, the deaf and dumb, came efforts to remove orphan children from almshouses into institutions specifically designed for their welfare and education. Special asylums for deaf children were set up in Philadelphia and New York. A "House of Refuge," the first American institution especially for juvenile delinquents, was founded in New York in 1825 and was followed by others. By the 1840's there were institutions

Source: Daniel J. Boorstin, "From 'Naughtiness' to 'Behavior Deviation'," pp. 227–244 in *The Americans: The Democratic Experience* (New York: Random House, Inc., 1973). Copyright © 1973 by Daniel J. Boorstin. Reprinted by permission of Random House, Inc.

for needy immigrant children, and in 1855 appeared the Children's Hospital of Philadelphia, probably the first hospital in this country designed exclusively for children.

"Reform school," an American expression which implied a special attitude toward young offenders, had come into the language by 1859; and there developed a new branch of criminology, new institutions, and a new literature of "juvenile delinquency." In 1899 Illinois enacted the first "juvenile court" law (incidentally introducing another Americanism), and by 1912 twenty-two states had established juvenile courts.

In 1909 President Theodore Roosevelt convened the first White House Conference on the Care of Dependent and Neglected Children, followed in 1912 by the establishment in the Department of Commerce and Labor of a Children's Bureau, to "investigate and report upon all matters pertaining to the welfare of children and child life." Although federal legislation on child labor was declared unconstitutional (Hammer v. Dagenhart, 1918), state laws on the subject proliferated. More Americans came to see children as a special class with their own peculiar needs and interests.

While these humanitarian movements focused on the children of the poor, on juvenile delinquents, and on criminals, another movement, rooted in the esoteric recesses of philosophy, bore fruit in thousands of schoolrooms and in millions of American households. The "Child Study Movement" in the United States was pioneered by G. Stanley Hall, a brilliant combination of priest, prophet, poet, and experimental scientist. Raised on a farm in western Massachusetts, he was the son of a sternly authoritarian Congregational father, who had determined to cast his son in his own image. To be prepared for the ministry, young Stanley was sent to Williams College. There he and his literary classmates formed a club for mutual uplift in which, as Stanley explained to his parents, "profanity, refreshments, smoking, drinking, impoliteness are contraband." After graduation he spent a brief period at Union Theological Seminary in New York City, where his course included mission work among "fallen" women to acquaint him with the evils of the metropolis. That missionary assignment, as Hall construed it, took him to see scandalous spectacles like "The Black Crook," a "ballet" in which one hundred scantily clad female dancers appeared for the first time on an American stage. After Hall went to see the performance again, he conscientiously reported to his parents that he "sat very near and this time was disgusted."

As Hall's interests moved from theology and philosophy to psychology, he was introduced by Henry Ward Beecher to a wealthy New York merchant who gave him $500 to study for a year in Germany. When Hall arrived in Berlin in 1869, he found German philosophy swirling with neo-Hegelian currents, but his own interests shifted toward science; he witnessed surgical demonstrations, and actually dissected a human body. After returning to the United States, he taught briefly at Antioch College, then went to Harvard, where he met William James, who had just begun to teach his course in physiological psychology. During another stint of study in Germany he was converted to the enticing new science of experimental psychology.

In 1883 Hall was appointed Professor of Psychology at the new Johns Hopkins University. There he jealously refused to make a place for either John Dewey or Charles Sanders Peirce, and he even managed to incur the enmity of the warm and tolerant William James. When Hall left Hopkins to found Clark University at Worcester, Massachusetts, in 1889, the new institution had been especially designed to explore the new frontiers of science. He resolved to make Clark the leader in the new science of psychology and in discovering it uses for education. In this he showed that he had an uncanny prophetic vision of two of the strongest currents of the American future: Psychology (a New Democratic Science of Man) and Education (a New Religion of Democracy).

Hall's experience abroad had suggested to him that reform of education might be the key to a grand spiritual reform of the United States. He saw how after the travail of the Napoleonic Wars a reformed system of education had helped build a new Germany. Perhaps education would be the new American religion, and Hall would be one of the Church Fathers. If so, the theology of this new religion would be scientific. Psychology offered both a scientific faith and a religious science qualified to reshape American institutions and to redefine American morals. The burgeoning sectarian variety—experimental psychology, physiological psychology, behaviorist psychology, psychoanalysis, to mention only a few—would provide dogmas and to spare.

There was something appealingly democratic about Hall's new scientific faith. Christianity had relied on a ministry of the gospel, on sacred authoritative texts, and had enlisted faith in the authority and benevolence of a Fatherly God. But psychology, in Hall's vision, referred man to no Higher Authority (except perhaps the Psychologist). Its sacred text was experience and it made man a rule unto himself. Would you know what man *ought* to be? Discover, for the first time, what man *is*. In place of the "Thou shalt not's" of the Decalogue, psychology would substitute open questions: "What is man?" "How does he behave?" Psychology, the science of uniting the "is" and the "ought," was the supremely democratic science. For it referred all questions of human behavior not to any Higher Authority, nor to some traditional scripture, but to the normal behavior of men.

Psychologists, who were ministers of this new gospel, simply helped man discover what he really was, how he actually behaved. Just as Luther and the new Protestant ministry had striven to liberate men from a priesthood, from a Papal Authority on high, so the psychologists now strove to liberate men from the fears, the taboos, the inhibitions of an authoritarian Protestant morality. For moral rules and regulations, they would substitute *norms*. In this effort to democratize morality, G. Stanley Hall offered a foretaste of new opportunities and new problems to come.

"Child study," of which Hall was the prophet, at first seemed an innocent and obvious enough subject matter. In America, were not schools the most flexible of institutions? If morals were to be democratized, were not the schools a natural place to begin? In American education within a few decades (as the historian Lawrence Cremin has shown) Hall and his followers would accomplish a new Copernican Revolution. The center of the educational universe would shift from the "subject matter" and the teacher to the child. Until his time, Hall explained, education had been *scholiocentric* (centering around the school and its demands), but now it must become *pedocentric* (centering around the child, his needs and desires). Before this revolution could take place, psychologists had to discover what the child himself thought and felt and wanted.

Hall's pioneer exploration, *The Contents of Children's Minds* (1883), attempted to discover what children knew and, also for the first time, what they did *not* know. Since the rise of cities, Hall observed, children were coming to school with an experience different and in many ways more limited than that of their farm-bred grandparents.

As novel as Hall's subject matter was his technique. He used four trained kindergarten teachers to help him draw up and administer 200 questionnaires. By 1894 Hall had devised 15 additional questionnaires, each on a different subject, such as doll playing or children's fears. At the end of that academic year he had collected 20,000 completed returns; the next year he used eight hundred workers to gather 60,000 more. The word "questionnaire" would come into the American language within the next fifteen years from child study and educational psychology, and largely as a result of Hall's work. In place of introspecting, like the great philosophers from Plato to Kant, or debating like the professors and schoolmen, Americans, following Hall, characteristically would advance their knowledge of man by finding new ways of entering into the minds of living men and women, allowing them to speak for themselves. The questionnaire was a kind of ballot, an application of the democratic suffrage to the subject matter of psychology.

Such data provided the raw materials for Hall's "child psychology," or the science of children's minds. The sheer quantity of these facts enticed him to an ever more quantitative and supposedly ever more "scientific" point of view. Hall set out to define "norms" for mental and physical growth. At Clark University he encouraged Franz Boas to gather statistics on the growth of Worcester schoolchildren, hoping in that way to set standards for "normal" growth against which subnormal or diseased children could be identified. These hopes were not quite fulfilled because Boas found such wide variation in rates of growth, but Hall's quest for norms was unabated. He went on in search of standards of performance through tests of children's sight and hearing and their ability to accomplish muscular tasks, and finally sought quantitative standards of "health" and normality. This led some of his opponents to charge that child study was a menace and was fundamentally antidemocratic because it encouraged the view that "certain children are peculiar or abnormal."

With his enthusiasm for statistics, Hall combined an extravagant romanticism. "Childhood as it comes fresh from the hand of God," he preached, "is not corrupt, but illustrates the survival of the most consummate thing in the world." The "guardians of the young," then, "should strive first of all to keep out of nature's way." In his "genetic" psychology, adapted from notions of evolution, Hall described the development of each child as a recapitulation of the development of the human race. From the Darwinian precept that ontogeny recapitulates phylogeny, Hall moved to the practical precept that psychology recapitulates history. The behavior of a "normal" child at any age had a certain sacred appropriateness. Each expression of a child's development was only a step to a higher stage, and so was neither "good" nor "bad."

In his "Children's Lies" (1890), for example, Hall objected to the traditional schoolmaster attitude toward truth telling. Lying, according to Hall, was not simply a vice but a complicated form of behavior, and its significance varied with the stage of the child's development. Most "lying" in children required not punishment but understanding. It commonly expressed the child's undervalued "mythopoetic" faculty, his quest for "easement from a rather tedious sense of the obligation of undiscriminating, universal and rigorously literal veracity." In children, lying was closely related to play, and the child's attitudes embodied the delightful naïveté of earlier stages of man's evolution. As Hall studied the child's fears and his ways of venting anger, he again concluded that they called for respect and understanding. Anger "has its place in normal development."

Hall's "stages" of child development were plainly transforming traditional morality. Parents and teachers were being prepared for a new way of thinking about "naughtiness."

Child study, as Hall prophesied, would also revise the subject matter in schools. "We must overcome the fetishism of the alphabet, of the multiplication table, of grammars, of scales, and of bibliolatry," he preached, "and must reflect that but a few generations ago the ancestors of us all were illiterate . . . that Cornelia, Ophelia, Beatrice, and even the blessed mother of our Lord knew nothing of letters." Foreshadowing the decline of grammar and the rule of the colloquial in twentieth-century America, he predicted, too, that grammar, rhetoric, and syntax would be displaced by the more democratic "language arts" and by public speaking. Language, according to Hall, should never have been taught as a formal discipline. The child should be encouraged to speak, and to speak his true feelings whatever they were, preferably in his own fresh idiom of slang. He must "live in a world of sonorous speech." He should be allowed to fight when he was attacked, as that was only natural. In a word, the child must not be confined in a strait jacket of adult morality.

By 1902, when the free public high school had begun to become a flourishing new American institution, G. Stanley Hall had gone on from child study to the study of adolescence, and he was ready with a new psychology to describe development during the high school years. In "The High School as the People's College" Hall pled for less attention to drill, discipline, skill, or accuracy, and more attention to "freedom and interest." For, he said, "the fundamentals of the soul, which are instinct and intuition, and not pure intellect, are now in season." He founded his view on a newly defined stage in human development which he called "adolescence." This notion, which was to become commonplace by the mid-twentieth century, was essentially (as the historian F. Musgrove has pointed out) a recent American development. The period of physiological change, from the onset of puberty to full maturity as man or woman, was the subject in 1904 of Hall's ponderous two-volume treatise: *Adolescence: Its Psychology and Its Relations to*

Physiology, Anthropology, Sociology, Sex, Crime, Religion and Education.
This, like Hall's earlier works, was an intoxicating concoction of statistics and poetry. Using graphs and charts, drawing on countless questionnaires, measurements, and experiments, Hall defined the varying rates of growth of different parts of the mind and of different faculties at each age up to eighteen or twenty, when growth appeared to stop. "Adolescence begins with the new wave of vitality seen in growth," he rhapsodized, ". . . it is a physiological second birth. The floodgates of heredity seem opened and we hear from our remoter forebears, and receive our life dower of energy." The statistical community of adolescents, then, had to be given the respect and autonomy, the powers of self-development and self-government proper for any other community within the larger republic. "The most plastic, vernal age for seed-sowing, budding, and transplanting from the nursery to the open field . . . this requires an ever longer time during which youth is neither child nor man. . . . To prescribe for these years as if they were simply a continuation of childhood, or as if they were like the college age, minus a few years of rectilinear progress, is the fundamental mistake to which many of the great evils from which we are now suffering are due." The high school, therefore, "should primarily fit for nothing, but should exploit and develop to the uttermost all the powers, for this alone is a liberal education." It had to be a distinct entity, not dominated by the "needs" of college, but instead "the defender of this age against aggression," making its mission "how best to serve one unique age of life, and thereby do the greatest good to the community and to their pupils." Through the high school, the United States could become not merely politically but also psychologically a federal republic: each age and stage (including the neglected states of childhood and adolescence) would be properly respected and allowed to fulfill its peculiar desires.

This "invention of adolescence" in the early twentieth century was the product of American circumstances. Compulsory public education was extended up to age sixteen, for many reasons, including the fact that industry was finding child labor less profitable. Then special institutions for "juvenile delinquency" appeared. Perhaps the nation would never recover from its idealization of adolescence, its new tendency to treat "youth" as a separate right-entitled entity, a new American estate within the Union. In the late 1960's and early 1970's some adolescents themselves, encouraged by their teachers and parents, organized against the very notion of a school. They treated *any* institutionalized education, in fact any institution, as oppressive. Students themselves in unamiable hyperbole called all American schools prisons, and they wrote of "The Student as Nigger." By 1970 there appeared in Washington a bizarre new youth lobby opposing schools, publishing a biweekly newsletter, *FPS* (*the letters don't stand for anything*). And at least a few solemn scholars were suggesting that such movements might be a logical expression of the United Nations Universal Declaration of Human Rights.

The new statistical communities of the young reached beyond the school into the home and elsewhere. Child study, which was reshaping American schools, began to reshape the American family. Before the mid-twentieth century, new democratic notions of the autonomy of the child were intervening in the traditional relations of parents and children.

Arnold L. Gesell, who had become a disciple of Hall at Clark University, was the pioneer. Reaching down to the "preschool years," Gesell would transform the attitudes of parents much as Hall and others had changed the attitudes of teachers. After experience as an elementary school teacher and settlement-house worker, Gesell became interested in the problems of backward children and made a mental-test survey of New Haven elementary schools. (His title of this study, *Exceptional Children and Public School Policy* [1921], was an early American usage of the democratic euphemism "exceptional" to describe the mentally deficient.) In 1911, he founded a psychoclinic for children, the Yale Clinic of Child Development, which he directed until 1948.

Gesell focused his attention on the years when the infant could be neither tested by questionnaire nor interviewed. For the psychologists those years had been a no man's land for which there was little reliable clinical information. But Gesell developed ingenious photographic techniques, using a two-way-mirror arrangement. He and his helpers then devised a novel observation dome; shaped like an astronomical observatory, it was made of finely perforated material painted white on the inside, and it could be rotated while a narrow slot permitted lateral and vertical positions for a Pathé 35-millimeter movie camera. The child inside the dome, under the cool illumination of newly devised Cooper-Hewitt lamps, could not see that he was being observed. In this way each child's behavior could be recorded for close comparison with the behavior of other children of the same age.

Gesell's aim was to record and to analyze the "normative" progress of the infant's development. To supplement the observation dome, Gesell arranged a homelike studio for a more naturalistic photographic survey of the infant's day while the mother was present and caring for the child. Gesell now noted the infant's every move, his sleeping, waking, feeding, bathing, his play, his social behavior and all his other bodily activities. Two years' observation produced his *Atlas of Infant Behavior* (1934), with 3,200 action photographs offering for the first time norms on infant behavior at every hour and every age.

The meaning of all this for the American family began to reach the general public in 1943 when Gesell, with his assistant Frances Ilg, published *The Infant and Child in the Culture of Today: The Guidance of Development in Home and Nursery School*. The phrase "in the Culture of Today" was by no means superfluous. Written during World War II, the book was repetitiously explicit on the relation between democracy and the study of child development. The infant, like all other American citizens, should be preserved from "totalitarian" government and, at long last, should be given his autonomy. "The concept of democracy . . . ," his opening chapter on "The Family in a Democratic Culture" explained, "has far-reaching consequences in the rearing of children. Even in early life the child must be given an opportunity to develop purposes and responsibilities which will strengthen his own personality. Considerate regard for his individual characteristics is the first essential. . . . Only in a democratic climate of opinion is it possible to give full respect to the psychology of child development. Indeed the further evolution of democracy demands a much more refined understanding of infants and preschool children than our civilization has yet attained." The bulk of the book, then, was "a factual statement of the mental growth characteristics of the first five years of life." Facts collected around "age norms" and "nodal ages" (the periods of "relative equilibrium in the progressions toward maturity") from four weeks to five years provided a "Behavior Profile" and a description of a typical "Behavior Day."

Before Gesell, the American parent had no authoritative way of knowing what to expect of his infant. Of course there were rules of thumb about when the infant might be expected to crawl, to walk, to talk. There were grandparents, and there were neighbors' children to compare yours to. But now Gesell gave the parent a catalogue and a calendar of norms: all the kinds of behavior that might be expected, including the hours of waking and sleeping, patterns of crying and eating, and even the moving of fingers and toes.

> Babies pass through similar stages of growth, but not on the same time table. Variations are particularly common in postural behavior. For example, we observed five healthy babies, all of whom are now intelligent school children in their teens. At 40 weeks of age, one of these babies was backward in locomotion; one was advanced. The other three were near average. Baby ONE *"swam"* on his stomach without making headway. Baby TWO *crawled*. Baby THREE *creep-crawled*. Baby FOUR *crept on hands and knees*. Baby FIVE *went on all fours*. There were special reasons why Baby ONE was behind schedule in this particular item. Her general development in language, adaptive and personal-social behavior was quite satisfactory. It would have been regrettable if the mother of Baby ONE had worried unduly over this bit of retardation. Likewise the mother of Baby FIVE had no reason to be unduly elated, since the total behavior picture was near average expectation.
>
> From this example it is clear that age norms and normative character sketches always need critical interpretation. They are useful not only in determining whether a child's behavior is near ordinary expectations, but also whether the behavior is well-balanced in the four major fields (motor, adaptive, language, and personal-social). It is especially desirable that there be no deviations in the field of personal-social behavior. If there are extreme defects or deviations in any field of behavior, the advice of the family physician may be sought and a specialist consulted.

The thrust of Gesell's work was to provide the parent a new kind of standard, distilled from thousands of hours of scientific observation by experts, and from countless precise statistics.

This standard implied a new attitude not only toward behavior, but also toward "misbehavior." What was proper in a child's behavior had, of course, traditionally been governed by moral rules and "Thou shalt not's." "Conceived as a growth mechanism," Gesell warned, "disequilibrium (so often associated with 'naughty' behavior) takes on a less moralistic aspect. This form of disequilibrium is a transitional phase, during which the organism is creating a new ability or achieving a reorientation of some kind. It is a phase of *innovation*." The child whom the grandparent might have called "naughty," the mid-twentieth-century American reader of Gesell would now say was simply showing "behavior deviations." For, Gesell explained, "In a sense all children are problem children, because none can escape the universal problem of development which always presents some difficulties. On the other hand, there are few forms of malbehavior which are not in history and essence a variation or deflection of normal mechanisms."

Gesell was full of good common sense, reminding the parent, as all parents needed reminding, that his baby was not the first infant on earth. Much of what he offered in the solemn jargon of psychology was only the historian's reminder: the world had been going on for some time, and parents had always faced similar problems. But Gesell gave this banal message a new character. He set a different direction for the way parents thought of their relations with their children. Instead of looking to rules of thumb, the old saws and moral exhortations, the parent was now urged to look to scientifically established statistical norms.

Some of the problems of this new world of norms were suggested by Gesell:

> Then there is the story about the very modern boy, not much higher than a table, who wore a pair of horn-rimmed spectacles. A kindly lady leaned over and asked him tactfully, "How old are you, my little boy?" He removed his horn-rimmed spectacles, and reflectively wiped them. "My psychological age, madam, is 12 years; my social age is 8 years; my moral age is 10 years; my anatomical and physiological ages are respectively 6 and 7; but I have not been apprised of my chronological age. It is a matter of relative unimportance." Thereupon he restored his horn-rimmed spectacles.

Gesell's book was not meant for every parent. But it had a remarkable popular success, going through twelve printings in a single year. And these new ways of thinking about child rearing were soon brilliantly translated into everyday language reaching millions. In 1946 Dr. Benjamin Spock, a New Haven-born pediatrician–psychiatrist with a wide practical experience, produced the *Common Sense Book of Baby and Child Care*. In its inexpensive paperback editions it went through some thirty reprintings in ten years, and became Everybody's Guide to Raising a Family. Spock warned against old wives' remedies and urged parents to be guided by their own child's development. Generally following Gesell's notion of a "self-demand" feeding schedule, Spock urged the mother to "be flexible and adjust to the baby's needs and happiness." While the book was by no means revolutionary, reviewers agreed that it "interprets the best in modern thinking." Now every parent had an easy path into the new world of norms.

This world brought its own problems for twentieth-century American parents. Who could forget the Ten Commandments and all that one had been taught about "right" and "wrong"? But once enlightened with "norms" describing how infants or adolescents usually behaved, parents could no longer think by old-fashioned rules. A democratic society was committed to take account of what every person, from Gesell's "quasi-dormant neonate" on up, naturally and spontaneously wanted.

DANIEL J. BOORSTIN

Statistical Morality

In Western Europe the last years of the nineteenth century and the early years of the twentieth century brought new attitudes toward sex among a vanguard few. By 1900 Sigmund Freud had published his basic works in psychoanalysis. In 1909, when G. Stanley Hall brought Freud, who was then still slightly disreputable in European scientific circles, to a conference at Clark University, he caused a stir, but he helped make Freud more respectable in America than he was in his home country. As part of his child study and his discovery of adolescence, Hall himself had described the development of sexuality, and had urged sex education in the schools.

But Hall's discussions of sex were enshrouded in a saccharine polysyllabic mist, which even his fellow psychologists called unctuous. "In the most unitary of all acts," he wrote of sexual intercourse, "which is the epitome and pleroma of life, we have the most intense of all affirmations of the will to live and realize that the only true God is love, and the center of life is worship. Every part of mind and body participates in a true pangenesis. The sacrament is the annunciation hour, with hosannas which the whole world reflects. Communion is fusion and beatitude. It is the supreme hedonic narcosis, a holy intoxication. . . ." At the same time Hall urged that the study of sex must become more objective.

The landmark on the way to a more scientific study of sex was the work of the English man of letters Havelock Ellis, who spent much of his life trying to liberate the English-reading world from its Victorian sexual prejudices. Ellis, like Hall after him, combined science and poetry in his effort to open windows to the wonderful variety of human sexual experience. When the first volume of Ellis' *Studies in the Psychology of Sex* appeared in England in 1897 there was a prosecution for obscenity, and publication was transferred to the United States. By 1910 Ellis had published five more volumes, and a seventh was added in 1928. The work was a wide-ranging collection of examples of human sexual behavior, including numerous phe-

Source: Daniel J. Boorstin, "Statistical Morality," pp. 241–278 in *The Americans: The Democratic Experience* (New York: Random House, Inc., 1973). Copyright © 1973 by Daniel J. Boorstin. Reprinted by permission of Random House, Inc.

nomena (eonism, undinism, kleptolagnia), the very names of which were a mystery. Ellis treated the taboo subject of autoerotism, and compared the sexual experiences of men and women. His books helped make sexual topics discussable in academic and intellectual circles. But the books themselves remained on the shelves of esoterica, and were readily accessible only to doctors and lawyers. Ellis' themes were the unsuspected variety of sexual experience, the subtle variations of sexual experience from person to person, and the wide range of sexual activity (including those generally considered erratic or taboo) among "normal" persons.

The moral, if there was a moral, to Ellis' books was that of all human activities, sex was the least amenable to moral prescriptions or to generalizations about "normality." The motives of Ellis' work remain unclear. All four of his sisters died spinsters and it has been suggested that Ellis' own interest arose from his sexual inadequacy. But the results of his work are less uncertain. He challenged traditional sexual morality by showing how unrealistic were the pious prescriptions and chaste pretensions of teachers, preachers, and doctors, and how naïve it was to be glib about what was "normal."

The contribution of the American pioneer in sexual research turned out to be quite the opposite. The effect, by no means the intention, of the work of Alfred C. Kinsey was to establish new norms of sexual behavior. Kinsey brought quantitative techniques to sexual research and so gave a new, scientifically authenticated prestige to these norms. Only gradually was he recognized as a social scientist of great stature. Like Hall, Kinsey was raised in a strict, moralistic family. Kinsey's Methodist father was so observant of the Sabbath that he would not permit the family to ride to church on Sunday, even with the minister; Sunday milk deliveries were not permitted at the house, and the whole family was required to attend Sunday School, morning services, and evening prayer meeting. After graduating from Bowdoin College in Maine, Kinsey received a Ph.D. in entomology from Harvard in 1920. For his two-volume study of the gall wasp, *Cynips* (1930, 1936), which established him as one of the leading geneticists of the day, Kinsey had gathered some four million specimens, and so had become accustomed to collecting and interpreting statistical data.

During the late 1930's, American colleges were introducing courses in sex education and marriage. This interest had been stirred by Hall's studies of adolescence, by the recently translated works of Freud, by the new profession of psychoanalysis, and by the pioneer clinical studies of Dr. Robert Latou Dickinson. While he practiced gynecology in Brooklyn and Manhattan from 1882 to 1924, Dr. Dickinson had kept careful records of more than five thousand patients, from which he published *A Thousand Marriages* (1932) and *The Single Woman* (1934). These epochal books provided valuable new information on female physiology, fertility, and sterility.

In 1938, when Indiana University decided to move with the times and to offer a noncredit course on marriage, Kinsey was put in charge. As the happily married father of four children and as an eminent biologist of unquestioned personal morality, Kinsey was the ideal choice. The only earlier evidence of Kinsey's attitudes was in 1927 when a special convocation of the male faculty considered disciplinary action against two male student editors of the literary magazine for printing the indecent phrase "phallic worship on campus." The professor of classics had to be called on to explain the meaning of the phrase, and Kinsey had unsuccessfully defended the students.

Kinsey, however, was no reformer but simply a biologist. When meetings were held to plan the course on marriage, Kinsey heard a female faculty member recall what had happened elsewhere in a course on the subject some years before. A woman doctor had given information that was "veiled and garbled, with no real value except to frighten the weak. A regular staff had to be on hand to carry out the ones who fainted each time." Kinsey's course was different. And at the end he asked students to fill out questionnaires about their own experience to guide him for the future.

As a biologist experienced with quantitative data, Kinsey had been appalled at the lack of statistical facts about human sexual behavior. He was encouraged by the pioneer work of a few biologists like Dr. Raymond Pearl of Johns Hopkins (who had made studies of the frequency of sexual intercourse, and of male sexual potency), who came to lecture at Bloomington on "Man and the Animal." But the more Kinsey saw of the vast ignorance about the subject the more determined he became to try to collect a body of useful knowledge. As he turned his scientific focus from the reproductive behavior of gall wasps to the sexual behavior of men and women, he showed the same voracity for facts. "The technique we are using in this study," he insisted, "is definitely the same as the technique in the gall wasp study."

Kinsey spared no trouble in training his interviewers and teaching them to avoid "loading" their questions. His interviewer was instructed to go down an exhaustive list of all kinds of sexual activities and ask each person about all of them. "It is important to look the subject squarely in the eye," Kinsey advised, "while giving only a minimum of attention to the record that is being made. People understand each other when they look directly at each other." Since "evasive terms invite dishonest answers," Kinsey's interviewers never used euphemisms. "We always assume that everyone has engaged in every type of activity. Consequently we always begin by asking *when* they first engaged in such activity. This places a heavier burden on the individual who is inclined to deny his experience; and since it becomes apparent from the form of our question that we would not be surprised if he had had such experience, there seems to be less reason for denying it." Interviews were recorded in a code known only to Kinsey and the interviewer.

Kinsey's goal was to secure 100,000 sex histories. At the time of his death there had been a total of 17,500 interviews, of which Kinsey himself had recorded more than 7,000. That amounted, during the period of his interviewing, to an average of two per day every day in the week for ten years. During the years of his sex research, Kinsey worked more than twelve hours a day and never took a vacation. In 1956, when he was sixty-two, and had had two heart attacks, his doctors warned him to rest. But they could do no more than persuade him to an eight-hour day, and he died that year of overwork.

Sexual Behavior in the Human Male, by Kinsey and his two collaborators, was published in January 1948. A market research firm had given the publishers their "considered scientific opinion," based on an opinion poll, that the book would not sell well. Within three weeks after publication it was on the best-seller list, where it stayed for twenty-seven weeks. By March the book was in its seventh printing, having sold 100,000 copies. Overnight, Kinsey became a celebrity, his name a popular synonym for "startling revelations" about the secret places of American life.

But critics and defenders agreed that this was a pioneer effort to quantify human sexual behavior. "An accumulation of scientific fact completely divorced from questions of moral value and social custom" was the book's avowed purpose. "Practicing physicians find thousands of their patients in need of such objective data. Psychiatrists and analysts find that a majority of their patients need help in resolving sexual conflicts that have arisen in their lives." Earlier scholars, such as Ellis, Freud, Stekel, and Krafft-Ebing, had provided individual sex histories to help the public toward a scientific point of view. At the outset of his book, Kinsey explained:

> But none of the authors of the older studies, in spite of their keen insight into the meanings of certain things, ever had any precise or even approximate knowledge of what average people do sexually. They accumulated great bodies of sexual facts about particular people, but they did not know what people in general did sexually. They never knew what things were common and what things were rare, because their data came from the miscellaneous and usually unrepresentative persons who came to their clinics. . . . The present study is designed as a first step in the accumulation of a body of scientific fact may provide the bases for sounder generalizations about the sexual behavior of certain groups, and, some day, even of our American population as a whole.

The book showed marked differences in sexual behavior patterns between males of different social, educational, and economic levels, between groups born in different decades and those with different degrees of religious belief. Kinsey established the almost universal incidence of masturbation in young males (which pseudoscientific folklore had made the presumed cause of "masturbatory insanity"), and he found the peak of male sexual activity in the late teens. Taboo forms of sexual activity proved to be much more widespread than had been presumed. Instead of simply classifying people as either heterosexual or homosexual, Kinsey had set up a new heterosexual-homosexual rating scale as a continuum on which interviewers placed each individual.

The Commission on Statistical Standards of the American Statistical Association reviewed Kinsey's statistical methods and reported its "overall favorable" impression. Comparing Kinsey and his collaborators with earlier sex researchers, the commission found them "superior to all others in the systematic coverage of their material, in the number of items which they covered, in the composition of their sample . . . in the number and variety of methodological checks which they employed, and in their statistical analyses. . . . their interviewing was of the best."

The public response was much as might have been expected. "It is impossible to estimate the damage this book will do," inveighed a well-known minister, "to the already deteriorating morals of America." College presidents and some gynecologists joined the attack with high emotion. But once the "guilty" facts were out, there was no way of erasing them from the American consciousness. Never again would American thinking about sexual activity be quite the same.

Five years later, in 1953, Kinsey and his staff published *Sexual Behavior in the Human Female*. Within ten days there were 185,000 copies in print, and it, too, was for many weeks on the best-seller list. The techniques in this study were the same, but Kinsey had benefited from some criticisms of his statistical method. The second book offered new facts on the frequency of various kinds of sexual activity, on male-female similarities and on differences in sexual behavior and response, and suggested a surprisingly low rate of frigidity in the female. Again, as might have been expected, Kinsey and the book were attacked, but now with unprecedented vitriol. An Indianapolis minister called Kinsey "a cheap charlatan"; a New York rabbi called the book " a libel on all womankind." With a widely reprinted article by Lionel Trilling, even the avant-garde *Partisan Review* joined the attack. The president of the liberal Union Theological Seminary saw "the current vogue" of Kinsey's work as a symptom of "a prevailing degradation in American morality approximating the worst decadence of the Roman era. The most disturbing thing is the absence of a spontaneous, ethical revulsion from the premises of the study." The Rockefeller Foundation, which had helped finance the research, was widely criticized, and dropped its support. A New York congressman demanded that the Postmaster General ban Kinsey's work from the mails because it was "the insult of the century against our mothers, wives, daughters, and sisters." Catholic publications declared that Kinsey not only was helping the Communists but was helping Americans to "act like Communists." But the president and trustees and students of Indiana University stood fast with Kinsey.

The popular result of Kinsey's work was ironic and unpredicted. His life as a biologist had been devoted to proving the importance of "individuals." According to Kinsey, "The fact of individual variation is one of the fundamentals of biologic reasoning. In its universality it is practically unique among biologic principles. The phenomenon is startling in its magnitude." But Kinsey's intentions were twisted by a public demand for simple norms.

Using the science of statistics, Kinsey had done more than anybody before him to break the taboos on the collecting of objective quantified data on human sexual activity. The next landmark, which showed how far the taboos had been dissolved, was the detailed laboratory study of more than one hundred thousand male and female orgasms. Using a variety of new laboratory devices and electronic recording machines, Dr. William H. Masters and Mrs. Virginia E. Johnson of the Reproductive Biology Research Institute in St. Louis collected statistical data on the sex act directly. They published their results in *Human Sexual Response* (1966). Within a few years, this book had sold a quarter of a million copies at $10 a copy. Masters and Johnson, by producing clinical data on such facts as heartbeat during coitus, removed the mystery from countless details surrounding sexual intercourse. In their preface they declared that their purpose, following Dr. Robert Latou Dickinson, was to help discover "the normal usages and medial standards of mankind." They hoped to join the pioneer scientists by issuing "succinct statistics and physiologic summaries of what we find to be average and believe to be normal."

The Americans' discovery of what was "normal" in sexual behavior took forms which an earlier generation would have considered not only immoral but bizarre. "Group sex"—persons having sexual relations as a couple with at least one other individual—became a publicly noted phenomenon in the mid-1960's. Kinsey's book on the male (1948) had only a single sentence on adult heterosexual group activity, and in his book on the female (1953), "wife-swapping" was dismissed in a paragraph. By the late 1960's the vulgarism "wife-swapping" was being displaced by the euphemism "swinging." By the early 1970's numerous magazines, at least one with a circulation of 50,000, were serving the interests of swingers. A network of swinging clubs reached around the country. Data on 284 swinging couples were collected by Dr. Gilbert D. Bartell, an Illinois anthropologist, and published in 1971, and a growing number of other studies made facts on group sex available to all Americans.

The new data provided convincing, vivid evidence of the widespread "normality" of many of the tendencies recounted in the antiseptic Kinsey statistics. One consequence of the rise of group sex, Dr. Bartell predicted, was "that in the future, men and women will be generally recognized as ambisexual beings, not only in the accepted psychological sense but also in the still 'embarrassing' physiological sense. . . . in swinging this is already beginning to happen, at least to some extent, even among middle-class mid-Americans."

As the new truths took the form of quantitative, scientifically authenticated norms, morality was replaced by normality. Prescriptions were displaced by descriptions. But the new statistical morality carried its own kind of latent prescription. The new knowledge of norms was as "guilty"and as unforgettable as Adam's first bite of the apple in Eden. A man who knew the norms had lost his innocence. Never again could he look on the violations of parental authority, on youthful vices, on extramarital peccadilloes, or on "unnatural" sexual satisfactions with the simple disgust of his grandfathers.

As knowledge proved the infinite variety of personal needs, even the prescription "Thou shalt not be abnormal" became meaningless. Fewer Americans were haunted by pseudoscientific fears or by moral imperatives, Instead they were thrown back on their imperfect knowledge of norms, on their lay interpretation of abstruse scientific data. How did their experience fit with that of other men and women? Americans could discover the rewards and the burdens of having to decide for themselves whether their norms were authentic, and when their deviation from the norm was itself only normal.

JACQUES ELLUL

Technological Morality

A transformation in the lived morality is taking place under our own eyes. We are entering into a new form of morality which could be called technological morality,[1] since it tends to bring human behavior into harmony with the technological world, to set up a new scale of values in terms of technology, and to create new virtues.

Contemporary morality, such as it exists in our society, and which is currently called bourgeois morality, is made up of two quite different elements. One of these is what is left of the Christian morality developed in the Middle Ages and transformed in the sixteenth and seventeenth centuries. It emphasizes the individual virtues and is oriented toward charity. The other is a technological morality, emphasizing collective virtues and oriented toward work. We must remember, moreover, that these two elements are not contradictory. It is Christian morality, in the form which it took from the sixteenth century on, which has been preparing the way for the development of technological morality.

In fact, this "Christian" morality corresponded at that time to the development of the bourgeois world. It emphasized the protection of property (theft becomes an important theme in this morality). It makes work a virtue. It affirms individualism. It dwells on the fact that the world was entrusted by God to man for him to exploit. That justified man in committing himself to the course which the bourgeoisie opened up, that of work to the point of excess, productivity, the priority of economy, etc. For its part, the technological enterprise was the more justified through the emphasis on the ridding of the world of its religious taboos by Jesus Christ. This emphasis came in with the Reformation in the sixteenth century. The world is no longer a place

[1] In this technological morality we include, among others, that morality being developed by human relations agencies in the United States, and that developed in the Soviet Union. This latter is much less dominated by Marxist concepts than by technological principles. Cf., for example, Chambre, *le Marxisme en Union Soviétique,* chap. 6; de Graaf, "Marxismus und Moral in der Sovjetrussischen Literatur," *ZEE,* 1957, No. 5; Delimars, "l'Ethique marxiste et son enseignement en U.S.S.R.," *Cahiers du Bien politique,* 1958.

Source: Jacques Ellul, "Technological Morality," pp. 185–198 in *To Will and to Do* (Philadelphia: United Church Press, 1969), translated by C. Edward Hopkin. Copyright © 1969 by United Church Press. Reprinted by permission.

inhabited by obscure powers, gods or demons, which need to be feared and respected. It is material, and man can do in it what he pleases.

Finally, the Reformation completes the picture by establishing a clear dichotomy between private life, with its personal virtues, salvation, on the one hand, and collective, economic, and political conduct on the other, which latter are free of the control of the church and are outside the "spiritual" domain. There is, then, a sort of spiritual indifferentism in socio-political questions (whereas the Catholic church had always attempted to subject socio-political activity to spiritual direction). Thus this Christian morality favored the spread of moral "values" belonging to technology. The entrance of these values into morality led to the formation of that particular morality, that bourgeois morality, which we shall not describe because it has already been described frequently. In addition, this morality was quite vigorous, for wherever Western society penetrated it tended to impose itself (African countries), and the Soviet Union, which had pretended to eliminate the morality of the bourgeoisie, came back to it even with an accentuation of its characteristics, with an entirely new rigor, at least in the interior of the Soviet Union, and with application to private life as well. Thus we know the severities reserved for adultery, and the fight waged against alcoholism, against youthful depravity, against theft, all according to very bourgeois ideas.

The fact is that this morality was perfectly adapted to the development of the technological society, let us say in its first phase, which we still experience in the West, which is at its height in the Soviet Union and which is just beginning in Africa and Asia. But in the West where we are entering the second phase of the technological society, this morality is no longer sufficient or adapted. That is why we are seeing the formation of a new morality, purely technological, with the progressive elimination of the Christian moral elements contained in the bourgeois morality. This technological morality does not yet exist in its entirety. It is in process of development, but it is certainly the morality of tomorrow.[2]

Technology supposes the creation of a new morality. It informs the whole of public, professional, and private life. One can no longer act except in relation to technical ensembles. Hence there is need to create new patterns of behavior, new ideas, new virtues. At the same time, new choices are set before man which he is in no way prepared to face. Now the more technology is precise, exacting, and efficient, the more it demands that the performer be efficient, precise, prepared. These are not merely questions of competence. They are matters requiring dedication. This man must know how to use the technique, but he must also know how to be its servant. His moral qualities must be at the level of the new world which technology is unveiling. Some moralists have already foreseen this problem, but the idealists have resolved it exactly in reverse, saying that technology puts man's life at stake, that a

[2] Niebuhr's analysis (*Nature and Destiny of Man*) of the characteristics of the new morality of modern man and of its contradiction with Christian ethics is excellent. Belief in the goodness of man, the search, no longer for virtue, but for a reorganization of society or for a plan of education to solve all moral problems, the validation of the reason as a guide to man, faith in salvation through history (or faith in progress), elimination of the concept of fundamental evil in favor of the idea of particular evils, etc., all of that enters into what we are calling technological morality.

new morality must be founded which will permit man to give a meaning to his life once again, to recover the unity of his life, and which will restore the value of freedom.

The project is laudable but inadequate, desirable but inexact. It contradicts reality, for if such a morality were instituted it would make man rebellious toward technology, unavailable for full technological service, reticent in the face of progress, oriented toward a different center of interest from technology, placing the latter at the bottom of the scale of values, all of which is completely inadmissable in a technological society. Hence this project (once again, desirable) has no chance of success. The probability is that a new morality will be created which will put its blessing upon man's subjection to the technological values and will make him a good servant to this new master, in trustfulness and loyalty, in the spirit of a service freely rendered.

Technological morality exhibits two principal characteristics. It is above all a morality of behavior and second, it excludes moral questioning. It is a morality of behavior. That is to say, it is solely interested in man's external conduct. The problems of intention, sentiment, ideals, perplexities of conscience, are none of its concern. Still, it ignores these only as long as they remain inward. If these interior movements were to lay claim to outward expression, then the technological morality would enter into conflict with them, for conduct must always be determined by external and objective motives if man's attitudes are to be consistent with the technological world in which he must live and act. The situation calls for a behavior on man's part which is exact, precise, in harmony with the working of all the categories of techniques which are proliferating in our society. And this behavior should be fixed, not on the basis of moral principles, but in terms of precise technological rules—psychological and sociological. The external act alone has value, and this act should be determined for technological motives. This is one of the principal results of the sciences of man, which—in spite of their proclamations and declarations—are all and always sciences impregnated with morality aimed at adapting man to the technological world.

We well know that the optimum use of techniques of any kind depends upon the user's being psychologically adapted, upon his freedom from scruple and uneasiness (moral or physical), upon his being in tune with the machine, upon his being in sympathy with the operation, upon his being sufficiently motivated, upon his having a scale of values which allows him to find satisfaction and dignity in his own eyes in the very exercise of these techniques. This behavior in harmony with the techniques, which is demanded of man if the techniques are to have their maximum efficiency, must be a behavior which is morally justified. Hence it must not be a behavior which is externally imposed, mechanical, forced, but a behavior to which man gives his adherence for moral motives. Only, this behavior is not itself established for moral motives! It is determined by the organization, by efficiency planning. The more the organization of work, of government, of family life, of living conditions, of traffic, of public health, of recreation, etc.—is perfected, and the more exactly the patterns of behavior are established, the more does efficiency planning tend to displace the moral imperative.

The former moral objective of duties and imperatives, the "closed morality," is progressively eliminated by the organization. It is the latter now, which dictates the true duties, the true social imperatives, and which supplies them with moral value and in this way justifies them. But at the same time this leads to a questioning of the problem of choice between good and evil, a questioning of individual decision, of subjective morality, of open morality. There are fewer and fewer choices to be made (I mean *real* choices), because good behavior is that which is called for by the technique, is described by the technique, is made possible by the technique.

We have already seen that for contemporary moralists morality is the domain of ambiguity, but when they speak that way they are speaking out of their reflections, out of their wishes, out of traditional society. They are not at all talking about a morality which would be of use to a technological society. In such a society, technique excludes ambiguity. The good is clear. The behavior valid for a technical world is dreadfully uniform. It obviously imposes itself upon the individual. There are not a hundred ways of employing a given technique to achieve an end. The technique is itself a way of acting. The conduct demanded of the individual can scarcely be doubted or disputed.

Contemporary man is very generally convinced that the technique is the good, that it concurs in man's good and will bring about his happiness. Should man recoil before this prospect, the proof of the technical good is confirmed, reinforced, and assured by the various pressures at the disposal of the technological civilization: the testimony of its successes, the importance of the necessity for its development, the certainty of progress, the marvelous concordance of the techniques. How can all that fail to convince a man inwardly that he should participate with all his heart in the development of such a good? And if problems still remain, the techniques of psychology will be able to reach into this heart itself, to personalize the objective reasons for the behavior, to obtain through technical procedures loyalty and good will, joy itself in the carrying out of the "duty," which like everything else ceases to be painful and exhausting in the comfortable world of techniques.

On the one hand, in the eyes of contemporary man technical progress is a good in itself, and on the other hand the techniques insure the necessity of a behavior favorable to progress. Technology offers man a fulfillment of the good which is easy, effective, and justified in advance. Man's decision is obtained through adhering to technical progress. There can be no debate, no personal decision involved in the matter. The good is obvious. It goes along with power. There can be no question of escaping it. One will end with a perfected conformism never yet achieved in the moral sphere. In fact, never until now had morality been armed with an unassailable authority. Never before had the good been obvious and beyond dispute. Never had there been a factual identification between the good and happiness. Never had there been a coincidence between individual moral decision for the good and material social development. All this has been realized and achieved by technology. The technological good is irrefutable. It cannot be challenged. Man is moving toward a situation in which he will no longer be able to choose evil. In a certain sense, one can conceive this as putting an end to morality.

In this technological morality there is also set up a scale of values which are truly valid for man and which the individual accepts as such. Without doubt, one of the important facts in this sphere is the transformation of technology itself into a value. For the man of today technology is not only a fact. It is not merely an instrument, a means. It is a criterion of good and evil. It gives meaning to life. It brings promise. It is a reason for acting and it demands our commitment. "A way of dealing with the world and of characterizing it in terms of our continuing and of our momentary requirements." This definition . . . what is it a definition of? of technology? or of value? There could be no better demonstration of the fact that technology has become a value than by pointing out the ambiguity of this definition. Now it is word for word the definition of value given by one of the contemporary representatives of the philosophy of values (Gusdorf). But this is even more exact at the level of the average man. Doubtless for him, in various ways, technology is a value. In various ways, because the meaning which technology has given to his life can as well be comfort, the possession of an appliance, rather than the liberation of the proletariat thanks to technology, or humanity's newfound happiness. This is a criterion of good and evil, for without the slightest doubt everyone today treats technology as a good (a gift of God, etc.), and people cannot avoid talking that way.

Whenever anyone suggests that technology presents certain disadvantages people rush to its defense (it isn't technology, but the fault of man who misuses it . . . but if it is true that the evil here is man's doing, that then means implicitly that technology is the good). And this good is set forth as a thing not to be challenged (it is not possible to call technology into question). One can call everything in our society into question (including God), but not technology. It is seen, then, to be the decisive value. And as a value it is desirable. It indeed merits the dedication of all resources in its behalf. It indeed merits that man sacrifice himself to it—and one finds it normal that there should be martyrs of science, today in reality martyrs of technology. We could easily go on and show that each trait applied by the philosophers to value, in order to characterize it, would exactly apply to modern man's belief in technology, to his judgment of it, and to his behavior toward it.

But we must pass on to a second value of this technological morality, that of the normal. In this technological society the normal tends to replace the moral. Man is no longer asked to act well, but to act normally. The norm is no longer an imperative of the conscience. One gets at it through average behavior, whether this is determined statistically, or by psychological evaluation, or by whatever means. Everything concurs in confirming the predominance of the normal. Increasingly the criminal is treated as a sick, abnormal person, in need of care to help him return to average, normal behavior. Similarly, the highest virtue demanded of man today is adjustment. The worst judgment a man can suffer is to be called maladjusted. (Maladjusted to what? Very exactly, to the technological society. Sociologists and psychologists are agreed in acknowledging that technology is the most frequent cause of maladjustment.) The chief purpose of instruction and education today is to bring along a younger generation which is *adjusted* to this society.

The socially maladjusted exactly corresponds to the immoral of the earlier societies, and the normal exhibits the same characteristics as the older morality. For one thing, it functions as a definition of the good, as a norm, as a requirement to be met imperatively. For another thing, it is a value which makes it possible to judge, to estimate deeds, people, and events. It is a personal, individualized aspiration. Everyone strives today to be normal, and this normal repels the older notion of virtue, of good. Moral judgment is no longer tolerated over against the decision of normalcy. As long as conduct is normal there is no reason to reprove it in the name of morality. It is no longer legitimate to declare good or evil that which is accepted as normal. This is highly characteristic of the Kinsey Report, for example, which rejects traditional sexual morality, not in the name of objective science, but really in the name of the morality of the normal. Now this normal is not exactly the same thing as moral custom.

There is in the concept of the normal a concern for precise knowledge, for the rationale of behavior, for adjustment to the objective conditions of society, for confrontation with the psychological and sociological sciences, since in the final analysis it is the clinical technician who decides what is normal. We see, then, how this value depends upon technology, and is finally subordinated to technological value. It is partly because the normal is established in relation to behavior as registered in a very precise society, the technological society (and it is no mere chance that we see the substitution of the normal for the moral going hand in hand with the setting up of a technological society), and partly because the normal is discovered and developed by techniques, and in no other way.

Finally, we should bear in mind a third value characteristic of this morality; namely, success. In the last analysis, good and evil are synonyms for success and failure. According to the bourgeois formula, stemming from a particular interpretation of the Bible, virtue is always ratified by material success. But with the passage of time (and the temptation was too great for this to be avoided) the conclusion was drawn that success is the clear sign of virtue, since it is virtue's reward. Virtue is invisible. Success is visible. Hence success allows us to presuppose the existence of virtue. The next step is to say that success is, in itself, the good. One is an abbreviation for the other. With this orientation one then seeks to base morality on success, whence the demonstration that "crime doesn't pay." When all is said and done, the reason one should not be a criminal is that it isn't profitable. But if we proceed in this direction we are obliged to admit that strength is one of the essential factors of success, and then we very soon realize that the crucial polarity is not so much that of good and evil as that of strength and weakness—thence, also, the ethical importance of the champion.

The champion is necessarily a representative of the good. In another perspective, that of the Communists, the expression of this identity between success and the good is found in the necessity of adhering to the direction of history. The direction of history is only seen by hindsight at each stage, in the success of a given enterprise. If it did succeed, that *then* means that it was indeed in the direction of history. And since, in the last analysis, it is history which determines what is good, the direction of history manifests the good in the form of success.

As a matter of fact, underneath both the bourgeois and the communist ethical formulae there lies the conviction that one does not argue with results. A successful action is necessarily compelling and is not to be called in question. Now this is essentially linked up with technological operation, since the latter is just what insures effectiveness and results. To be sure, there can be various criteria of success. In the bourgeois society it is money, honors, titles, a higher rung of the social ladder. Under totalitarian regimes one of the essential signs will be membership in the Party. The latter is the content of the good in itself. It is also the guardian of the good. To be outside the Party is not to participate in the good. To be against it is evil. Now the Party is never anything but an instrument for political effectiveness, for the technique of propaganda and of government. Here we find the link between technical procedures and the determination of the good. And likewise, we again find virtue as applied to socio-political action taking precedence over every other virtue.

But we must not forget that the instrument of success in our society is always a technological instrument. Quite consciously it is demonstrated for our benefit that the ultimate goal of technology is not merely a material result, but the fulfillment of the good. Economic abundance will permit man to develop himself spiritually, morally, and culturally. The socialist regime paves the way for a new man, who, freed from alienation and from capitalistic contradictions, will be good. That will come to pass thanks to the technique. But if such is indeed the goal of technology, every technical success participates in the ultimate good, and to oppose this development is to be truly evil and demonic.

Technological morality demands of man a commitment. It calls for the practice of virtues. It cannot be said that it requires new virtues, for these virtues are old, but they are validated, placed in the foreground. Formerly treated as minor, they now become major and exclusive. To a certain extent one may also speak of new virtues—work, for example. Let us not forget that in the traditional societies, in *all* societies, work was looked down upon, treated as animal toil unworthy of man. Every moral, social, and spiritual elevation was translated into an abandonment of work. It was considered a necessity in a pinch, but a damnable necessity. And this is true not only of "primitive" peoples, shepherds, nomads, but of all civilizations—Incas as well as Chinese, Greeks as well as Hindus, Scandinavians as well as Egyptians. They all held work in contempt, and Christian society also. In spite of the two or three biblical texts counseling work, it must not be forgotten that the stream of theological opinion was that work was a mark of condemnation, a sign of our fallen nature, and consequently a necessity which had to be accepted, but in no wise a good or a virtue.

This opinion is changed with the theologians of the Reformation, who for the first time presented the positive aspects of work. But the latter will not become a virtue, and a cardinal virtue, the father of all the virtues, until the bourgeois society of the eighteenth and nineteenth centuries. That is the first time in the history of mankind that work becomes a good, and "worker" a title of nobility. Now let us not forget that that was the time when the power of the bourgeoisie, when its rise to power, was based on work. Having become the ruling class, the bourgeoisie promoted the source of its authority to the status of a value for the whole society. This was the more fitting since the lower classes all worked (as they had never worked before) and one had to grant them a moral satisfaction in exchange for the sacrifices one was demanding of them. "To work is to pray! This work which you are constrained to perform for the glory of the bourgeoisie is a value, both moral and spiritual. You are doing good thereby, and are working your own salvation." Now if all were expected to be mobilized for work in this way, this was, in the final analysis, because of the development of the technique. It was technique which both required and made possible this dedication of man to work. The work which has become the principal virtue in our society is technological work. And the virtues which are elaborated in this morality are all connected with work. Thus, while often of ancient vintage, these virtues now are attached to a new objective.

They are splended disciplinary virtues: the virtues of self-control, of devotion, of trustworthiness in one's work, of responsibility in the performance of tasks, of loyalty, of sacrifice to one's occupation—all are fitted into the central cardinal virtue of "doing good." They all are linked to the employment of techniques. All the virtues by which we see man glorified (and justly glorified) are virtues of work. The performance of superior work is the guage of these virtues, and sacrifice and devotion especially are functions of the creative achievement of technology. All these virtues really have as their aim to facilitate the working and utilization of techniques. This entails three consequences:

1. The gradual elimination of the other moral values: family virtues, good fellowship, humor, play, etc. All that is pushed into the background and counts for less and less. A man may act ignobly toward his comrades or his wife, but if he practices the virtues essential to work all is forgiven him. He is cited as an example. Most of the great heroes of our day, scientists, aviators, etc., are of this type. These virtues are eliminated simply because, in the eyes of modern man, they no longer count, inasmuch as they have nothing to do with the "central motif" of our society.

2. It is constantly being said that technology is nothing without man, that when all is said and done the decision rests with man, and that he is the master of the techniques. But one forgets that, in reality, man is the one who is put into shape to serve the techniques, that the virtues created for him are virtues of work, that the important word is adaptation, and that man has to be "adapted," that consequently morality subordinates man to the techniques.

3. In the technological morality the standard of conduct is objective. A technically well-made combination must function. Whenever it fails to work, if the technical calculation was correct, then there is a human flaw: laziness, dishonesty, or ill will. The evil is of that kind, in a word, sabotage. To be sure, there may be sabotage, objectively considered, whatever might have been the intentions of the individual. What should work doesn't work. That is the fault of the man, whatever his motives might be. The evil is in the sphere of behavior, and like the good is objectively discoverable. In addition,

it is also obvious that this behavior which affects the whole of society should be thoroughly punished. The moral sanction gradually ceases to be a matter of the inward domain of the conscience and becomes political or social.

But there is another very noteworthy virtue in this morality; namely, confidence in the future, an ability to face up to tomorrow, an assurance in hope which is astonishing in troubled times. It is the virtue of "all is possible," which of course expresses in large part the value of the normal. All is possible. Not only is there no predetermined moral or spiritual limit to action, but further, the only acknowledged barrier is that which is not possible today but which will be tomorrow. Nothing is surprising any more, atomic fission, sputnik: that all belongs to the normal course of events. Tomorrow it will be done better. In fact, this virtue especially expresses a morality of the unbounded, of the limitless, to which modern man is perfectly adapted.

The boundlessness of means and of technical success produces a morality of the gigantic and the limitless. The colossal, the "world's biggest," are expressions of this morality. Man no longer recognizes any limits to his conquest When man becomes involved in the process of technical development, at no time does he have occasion to stop and say No. In the conviction that technology leads to the good, and that in the final analysis morality is closely linked to technology, man cannot at any time come to a halt in this march forward (the problem of Oppenheimer and the atomic scientists). From then on, the "more" becomes a criterion in itself. The greater, the higher, the more powerful, that suffices. The new morality justifies automatically that which is "more." It is a close companion to technology in its development and justifies it as it goes along.

The good, then, appears as the surpassing of limits. What one cannot do today he will be able to do tomorrow, and that is good. From the fact that we have to do with a morality of the unlimited, we arrive at a rule of conduct for man which is perfectly adapted to the requirements of modern society, and which is coextensive with his professional activity. Through that aspect, we again see three characteristics of this morality, already indicated in the course of the discussion above. As a whole, it is a morality of occupation, of well-doing, which becomes a total, all-embracing morality for the whole society. It is an essentially total, even totalitarian, collective morality. It is a morality which progressively atrophies the individual virtues of personal morality, and which ends in the disappearance of the individual moral sense in the degree in which it causes the moral problem to disappear.[3] Such are

---

[3] Finally, one should evoke the morality which would arise automatically through biological or chemical manipulations. Let us bear in mind the discourse pronounced by Jean Rostand before the Académie Française in 1962, in which he said this: "It is in the direct line of our progress to learn how to control chemically the deeds of our conduct like the other phenomena of life. It is already possible, through the use of a hormone or a vitamin or an oligo-element, to produce an increase of courage, will-power, maternal love. After the tranquilizers will come the moralizers. We are promised soon to have available drugs to reduce envy and to calm ambition, and how long will it be before we have lozenges for devotion, tablets for gentleness, and pills for self-denial?" This is nothing but an extension of the technological morality, beginning with the moment when it is only a question of securing behavior in conformity with the collective behavior, apart from any individual decision or responsibility.

the characteristics of this technological morality in the course of its development. In the last analysis, it appears as a suppression of morality through the total absorption of the individual into the group.

Concerning all this we are obliged to conclude that an answer to the question of the good does not acquire validity through its being consistent with the social environment, or with the nature of man, nor through its intellectual rigor, nor through the gravity with which it treats man, but through its foundation. "It has no gravity, no depth of rigor, unless it be founded in such a way that man cannot escape it, either by pleading his freedom or his weakness, or again in thinking that he is himself the answer, which only resolves the problem by suppressing it."[4]

---

[4] K. Barth, *Dogm.*, II, 2, 2, p. 57 (cf. *Ch. Dogm.*, II, 2, p. 564).

III

DEVIANT CATEGORIES: COLLECTIVE RULE-MAKING

Introduction

We have seen that, in complex and often subtle ways, society's definitions of deviance are woven into the institutional fabric of time and place. We turn now to the analysis of how this occurs, to the processes of collective rule-making that define deviant categories. These sequences of events have been treated in theoretical terms in Part I and often alluded to in the selections in Part II, but in Part III we focus on concrete norm-creating and norm-changing situations.

Analysis of the emergence or change of norms that define deviance is processual, thus longitudinal, but over a delimited span of time. This period may be as brief as a legislative session or as long as an evolutionary movement requiring decades of struggle. Long or short, the rule-making actions are not isolated episodes but part of a related series of events occurring within a segment of time. Often these events are rendered more meaningful by comparing them with prior periods of related norm-defining, thus affording comparisons with different social conditions and observations on continuities as well as changes.

The selection dealing with the shortest time span of any of the selections in this part is the one by Connor on the Stalinist purge of 1936–1938, although the developments are placed in the context of the history of the U.S.S.R. These events are interpreted as evidence that both deviant categories and large numbers of deviants can be created suddenly by powerful, repressive regimes. Comparisons are made with the official witch-defining and labeling episodes of New England, England, Spain, and other countries. These dramatic happenings may not be so utterly different from the collective defining of deviance in general as it may at first seem. The task is to determine how much is unique and what is generic.

A little longer time span is involved in Sutherland's discussion of the invention and diffusion to several states of sexual psychopath laws. His analysis covers a dozen years or so, beginning in 1937; but he places it against the background of a long-standing Anglo-American stereotype of the sex offender. Bustamante's treatment of the passage and implementation of legislation to control wetbacks emphasizes the most recent decades but also deals with the 1920's, and it reaches back nearly a century for references to the earliest pertinent immigration laws. Matza's analysis of the status of the "disreputable poor" is related to the assimilation of immigrant groups over an unspecified period of decades. He apparently has in mind the typical experiences of American immigrant groups over the past century or more.

In the selection on the changing ideologies of the American Temperance Movement, Gusfield relates shifts in ideas about drinking to social changes from colonial times to the present. This contribution is notable for its effort to specify the social circumstances and the groups involved in the struggle for supporters of particular norms, and for following continuities as well as significant shifts in collective definitions of drinking behavior. Szasz compares the use of medical concepts by psychiatrists to define and control deviant behavior with the use of religious concepts by the inquisitors to define and control witchcraft in the Middle Ages. Chambliss traces changes in the Anglo-American law of vagrancy over several centuries, stressing especially the impact of the decline of serfdom, the breakup of feudalism, and the growth of commerce. He shows how periods of dormancy, when laws are not serving their intended purpose but are unenforced and allowed to stand rather than being repealed, contribute to continuities in legal norms.

With respect to theoretical approaches, conflict perspectives have predominated in analyses of the group processes involved in defining what is normal and what is unacceptably deviant. Conflict approaches are taken in the selections by Matza, Bustamante, and Chambliss. Gusfield's is a status politics analysis, with a pluralistic orientation, portraying efforts to symbolize group status through power struggles to legalize the group's drinking norms. He considers this a symbolic interpretation, treating all group interests other than economic as symbolic. By contrast, Matza emphasizes economic interest groups in an implicitly Marxian depiction of the powerlessness of the poor. Chambliss stresses economic interests, making use of both the concepts of vested-interest group and status group. In his analysis of power in group struggles over conflicting belief, Bustamante uses Becker's concept of "moral entrepreneur."

Connor leans towards conflict analysis but also notes some value in a functionalist interpretation of the Stalinist purge, making use of the view that deviance calls attention to legal norms that define the limits of nonconformity, thus promoting social cohesion (Erikson, 1966: 4–12; Durkheim, 1947: 102). Two other selections also imply Durkheimian themes. One of these is Sutherland's treatment of the arousal of fear by a series of sex crimes and the resulting agitated activity and eventual legislation. The other is the treatment by Szasz of the relation between the rejection of deviant actors and societal fears of dangerous behavior, a discussion oriented implicitly towards Freudian theory. Subconscious motivation, mainly through the mechanism of projection, is suggested in the view that psychiatric labeling of the mentally ill provides society with scapegoats for guilt feelings and fears of ill health.

Collective behavior theory is not utilized explicitly in any of the articles in this section. Sutherland implies such an approach in his treatment of fear and the fact beliefs involved in stereotypes, and he shows that the law-making involved was part of a series of related events. The conceptual categories of panic and of a social movement are suggested but not developed. Gusfield, Chambliss, Szasz, and Bustamante note the appearance of social movements but make little or no use of collective behavior explanations. Connor uses the term "craze" without relating it to collective behavior usage or analysis.

Each of the papers in this section, then, is oriented towards one or more theoretical approaches. In some instances, however, the perspective is implied rather than made explicit. The typical role of theory in these contributions is to provide some concepts and key ideas for organizing and interpreting large amounts of information, much of it historical. The Connor article is more systematically arranged, in terms of testing the applicability to the political purge of Erikson's propositions about legal witch hunts (Erikson, 1966: 19–29).

In several of these selections, particularly those by Chambliss and Sutherland, it is apparent that there is considerable overlap between the sociology of law and the study of the collective defining of deviance. The same is true for political sociology, as seen clearly in the contributions of Gusfield, Connor, Bustamante, and Matza. It is difficult, of course, to draw a nice line between law and politics. The relevance of social stratification is notably apparent in the pieces by Matza, Gusfield, Bustamante, and Chambliss. The overlap with the sociology of organizations will be visible in Part IV, and we have already seen the pertinence of studies of social symbols, urbanization, institutional change, and still other areas of sociological interest. This suggests the importance of the study of the societal definition of deviance for sociology as a whole and the need to relate the study of deviance to general theories of social organization (Winslow, 1970).

References

BECKER, HOWARD S.
    1963   Outsiders: Studies in the Sociology of Deviance. New York: The Free Press.
DURKHEIM, EMILE
    1947   The Division of Labor in Society. New York: The Free Press.
ERIKSON, KAI T.
    1966   Wayward Puritans. New York: John Wiley and Sons, Inc.
SCHUR, EDWIN
    1971   Labeling Deviant Behaviors: Its Sociological Implications. New York: Harper and Row.
WINSLOW, ROBERT W.
    1970   Society in Transition: A Social Approach to Deviancy. New York: The Free Press.

THOMAS S. SZASZ

Society's Internal Enemies
and Protectors

> *I cannot accept your canon that we are to judge*
> *Pope and King unlike other men, with a favourable*
> *presumption that they did no wrong. If there is any*
> *presumption it is the other way against holders of*
> *power, increasing as the power increases. Historic*
> *responsibility has to make up for the want of legal*
> *responsibility.*
>
> —*Lord Acton*[1]

In the past, most people believed in sorcery, sympathetic magic, and witch-craft. Men have a powerful need to perceive the causes of natural disasters, epidemics, personal misfortunes, and death. Magic and witchcraft supply a primitive theory for explaining such occurrences, and appropriate methods for coping with them.

The behavior of persons whose conduct differs from that of their fellows —either by falling below the standards of the group or by surpassing them— constitutes a similar mystery and threat; the notions of demonic possession and madness supply a primitive theory for explaining such occurrences and appropriate methods for coping with them.

These universal beliefs and the practices connected with them are the materials out of which men build social movements and institutions. The beliefs that led to the witch-hunts existed long before the thirteenth century, but it was not until then that European society used them as a foundation for all organized movement. This movement—whose ostensible aim was to protect

[1] John Emerich Edward Dalberg Action, Letter to Bishop Mandell Creighton, in *Essays on Freedom and Power,* p. 335.

Source: Thomas S. Szasz, M.D., "Society's Internal Enemies and Protectors," pp. 3–27 in *The Manufacture of Madness* (New York: Harper & Row, Publishers, Inc., 1970). Copyright © 1970 by Thomas S. Szasz, trustee. Reprinted by permission of Harper & Row, Publishers, Inc.

society from harm—became the Inquisition. The danger was the witch; the protector, the inquisitor. Similarly, although the concept of madness existed long before the seventeenth century, only then did European society begin to organize a movement based on it. This movement—whose ostensible aim was likewise to protect society from harm—was Institutional Psychiatry. The danger was the madman; the protector, the alienist. The persecution of witches lasted for more than four centuries. The persecution of mental patients has lasted for more than three centuries and its popularity is still increasing.

Immediately, two questions arise: If the concept of witchcraft was old and familiar, why, in the thirteenth century, did a persecutory mass-movement crystallize around it? Similarly, if the concept of madness was old and familiar, why, in the seventeenth century, did a persecutory mass-movement crystallize around it?

As a result of a number of historical developments—among them, contacts with alien cultures during the Crusades, the evolution of the "feudal contracts," and the growth of mercantilism and a middle class—people bestirred themselves from their centuries-old stupor and began to seek fresh answers to life's problems. They challenged clerical authority and relied increasingly on observation and experimentation. Modern science was thus born, setting the stage for the protracted conflict between it and theology that was to follow.

Medieval European society was dominated by the Church. In a religious society, deviance is conceptualized in theological terms: the deviant is the witch, the agent of Satan. Thus the sorceress who healed, the heretic who thought for himself, the fornicator who lusted too much, and the Jew who, in the midst of a Christian society, stubbornly rejected the divinity of Jesus—however much they differed from one another—all were categorized as "heretics"; and thus was each, as an enemy of God, persecuted by the Inquisition. The medieval historian Walter Ullman puts it this way: "Publicly to hold opinions which ran counter to or attacked the faith determined and fixed by law was heresy, and the real reason for making heresy a crime was—as Gratian's *Decretum* had explained it—that the heretic showed intellectual arrogance by preferring his own opinions to those who were specially qualified to prounonce upon matters of faith. Consequently, heresy was high treason, committed against the divine majesty, committed through aberration from the faith as laid down by the papacy."[2]

From the medieval point of view; however, as Ullman reminds us, "this suppression of the individual's opinion was not by any means seen as a violation of his rights or of his dignity as a Christian, because a Christian attacking established faith forfeited his dignity. . . . Killing this individual did not violate his dignity, just as killing an animal did not affect anyone's dignity."[3]

In those days, the bond that held men together was not the secular law to which, as citizens, they had given their *consent;* instead, it was the divine law which, as Christians, they unquestioningly obeyed because they had *faith* in God and his vicars on earth. For a millennium, until the latter part of

[2] Walter Ullman, *The Individual and Society in the Middle Ages,* p. 37.
[3] Ibid.

the Middle Ages, the ideal of social relations was not reciprocity but benevolent domination and dutiful submission. The subject's obligations were one-sided: he had no means of enforcing the ostensible duties which his superiors owed him. In the manner of classical Roman writers, the ruler was regarded as "the common father of all." Medieval tracts never tire of emphasizing the royal duty of the king to care for the "feebler members" of society. But this recognition, as Ullman remarks, "was a very long way from ascribing to the subjects . . . any indigenous, autonomous rights with which they could confront the king. If he did not fulfill this duty of his, no power existed on earth to make him do it. The frequency of these hortatory statements stood in inverse proportion to the practical as well as theoretical feasibility of translating them into reality."[4]

For millennia, the hierarchical model of social relations, regarded as the divine blueprint for life on earth as well as in heaven and hell, appeared to men as the only conceivable ordering of human affairs. For obvious psychological reasons, this model has perennial appeal to men. This ideal of a nonreciprocal social relationship began to be undermined, in the twelfth century, by the development of the feudal contract which established a reciprocity of obligations between lord and vassal. *Diffidatio,* or the repudiation of the feudal contract by the vassal if the lord did not fulfill his duties or went beyond the contractual bond, was not based on any sophisticated theories or doctrines, but grew out of feudal practice.[5] Ullman emphasizes that "feudal principles were not imposed upon society 'from above,' but developed gradually by slowly taking into account the actual social exigencies. . . . Historical scholarship has come to recognize that in the West, the turn of the twelfth and thirteenth centuries formed the period in which the seeds for the future constitutional development as well as for the standing of the individual in society were sown. . . . It is easy today to sit back and complacently take for granted the constitutionally fixed position of the individual as a citizen, but one forgets too easily that it was not always so and there was a time spanning the greater part of the Middle Ages, something approaching a millennium, when there was no such thing as a citizen. . . ."[6]

Social transformations of such magnitude do not occur, however, without terrible human sufferings. The rulers, afraid of losing power, redouble their domination; the ruled, afraid of losing protection, redouble their submission. In such an atmosphere of change and uncertainty, rulers and ruled unite in a desperate effort to solve their problems; they find a scapegoat, hold him responsible for all of society's ills, and proceed to cure society by killing the scapegoat.

In 1215, the year King John granted the Magna Carta, Pope Innocent III convened the Fourth Lateran Council. "The assembly was an impressive tribute to his universal power; more than fifteen hundred dignitaries came to Rome from all over the world, to consider the problem of disciplining heretics and Jews. . . ."[7] The Council denounced the Albigensian heresy and

[4] Ibid., p. 25.
[5] Ibid., p. 64.
[6] Ibid., pp. 66, 69, 127.
[7] Abram Leon Sachar, *A History of the Jews,* p. 194.

proclaimed a holy war against it; and it decreed that Jews must wear a yellow badge on their clothing to identify them as Jews.[8]

Beginning in the thirteenth century, all manner of misfortunes—from failing crops to epidemics—were blamed on witches and Jews; their massacre became accepted social practice.[9] "Though the centuries between 1200 and 1600 were four agonizing centuries for the Jews," writes Dimont, "they were equally agonizing centuries for the Christians. Because the charges against the Jews bore such labels as 'ritual murder' and 'Host desecration,' instead of 'witchcraft' and 'heresy,' this should in no way mislead us. The same psychology, the same thinking, the same type of trial, the same type of evidence, the same type of torture went into both. Even as Jews accused of ritual murder were hauled to the stake, Christians accused of witchcraft were burned in adjacent market places."[10]

For more than two centuries, the main brunt of the persecution was borne by the Jews. They were expelled from England and France, converted or killed in vast numbers in the rest of Europe. In one six-month period alone, at the end of the thirteenth century, a hundred thousand Jews were massacred in Franconia, Bavaria, and Austria.[11] The persecution of witches, during this period, was haphazard and sporadic. Their turn came at the end of the fifteenth century.

As the Crusades for the reconquest of the Holy Land were launched by papal bulls, so was this crusade for the reconquest of the spiritual purity of Christian Europe. The decrees of the Fourth Lateran Council were reshaped and redirected by a bull issued by Pope Innocent VIII on December 9, 1484. It read, in part, as follows:

> Desiring with the most heartfelt anxiety, even as Our Apostleship requires, that the Catholic Faith should especially in this Our day increase and flourish everywhere, and that all heretical depravity should be driven far from the frontiers and bournes of the Faithful, We very gladly proclaim and even restate those particular means and methods whereby Our pious desire may obtain its wished effect . . .
>
> It has indeed lately come to Our ears, not without afflicting Us with bitter sorrow, that . . . many persons of both sexes, unmindful of their own salvation and straying from the Catholic Faith, have abandoned themselves to devils, incubi, and succubi. . . .
>
> Wherefore We . . . decree and enjoin that the aforesaid Inquisitors be empowered to proceed to the just correction, imprisonment, and punishment of any persons, without let or hindrance, in every way as if the provinces, townships, dioceses, districts, territories, yes, even the persons and their crimes in this kind were named and particularly designated in Our Letters . . .[12]

[8] Max I. Dimont, *Jews, God, and History*, p. 224.

[9] In this connection, see Norman Cohn, *The Pursuit of the Millennium*, especially pp. 307–319.

[10] Dimont, p. 238.

[11] Sachar, p. 198.

[12] Quoted in Jacob Sprenger and Heinrich Krämer, *Malleus Maleficarum*, pp. xix–xx.

Two years later, in 1486, this papal bull was implemented by the publication of that famous manual for which-hunters, the *Malleus Maleficarum* (*The Hammer of Witches*).[13] There soon followed an epidemic of witchcraft: the incidence of witches increased, as the authorities charged with their suppression covertly demanded that it should; and a corresponding increase of interest in methods aimed at combating witchcraft developed. For centuries the Church struggled to maintain its dominant role in society. For centuries the witch played her appointed role as society's scapegoat.

From the beginning of its labors, the Inquisition recognized the problem of correctly identifying witches. The inquisitors and secular authorities were accordingly provided with criteria of witchcraft, and with specific guidelines for their work. The vast medieval literature on witchcraft is concerned primarily with one or both of these subjects. Among these works, the *Malleus Maleficarum* is recognized as the most important.

Sprenger and Krämer, the Dominican inquisitors who wrote the *Malleus,* begin by asserting that ". . . the belief that there are such beings as witches is so essential a part of the Catholic faith that obstinately to maintain the opposite opinion manifestly savours of heresy."[14] In other words, Satan and his witches are as much a part of the Christian religion as God and his saints; a true believer can no more entertain doubt about the former than about the latter. To question the existence of witches is thus itself a sign of being a heretic (witch).

More precise criteria of witchcraft were soon forthcoming. We are told, for example, that ". . . those who try to induce others to perform . . . evil wonders are called witches. And because infidelity in a person who has been baptized is technically called heresy, therefore such persons are plainly heretics."[15]

The authors of the *Malleus* further narrow the range of suspects when they observe that it is women who are "chiefly addicted to Evil Superstitions." Among women, they assert, "midwives . . . surpass all others in wickedness."[16] The reason why witches are usually women is that "All witchcraft comes from carnal lust, which is in women insatiable."[17] And the reason why men are protected from this heinous crime is that Jesus was a man: ". . . blessed be the Highest who has so far preserved the male sex from so great a crime: for since He was willing to be born and suffer for us, therefore He has granted to men this privilege."[18] In short, the *Malleus* is, among other things, a kind of religious-scientific theory of male superiority, justifying—indeed, demanding—the persecution of women as members of an inferior, sinful, and dangerous class of individuals.

Having thus defined witchcraft, the authors of the *Malleus* offer specific criteria for identifying witches. Several of these pertain to the characteristics

---

13 Sprenger and Krämer.
14 Ibid., p. 1.
15 Ibid., pp. 2–3.
16 Ibid., p. 41.
17 Ibid., p. 47.
18 Ibid.

of diseases. They hold, for example, that the sudden, dramatic onset of illness, or what looks like illness, is a typical sign that the disease is caused by witchcraft: ". . . evil may come so suddenly upon a man that it can only be ascribed to witchcraft";[19] and they cite case histories to substantiate this contention. Here is one:

> A certain well-born citizen of Spires had a wife who was of such an obstinate disposition that, though he tried to please her in every way, yet she refused in nearly every way to comply with his wishes, and was always plaguing him with abusive taunts. It happened that, on going into his house one day, and his wife railing against him as usual with opprobrious words, he wished to go out of the house to escape from quarreling. But she quickly ran before him and locked the door by which he wished to go out; and loudly swore that, unless he beat her, there was no honesty or faithfulness in him. At these heavy words he stretched out his hand, not intending to hurt her, and struck her lightly with his open palm on the buttock; whereupon he suddenly fell to the ground and lost all his sense, and lay in bed for many weeks afflicted with a most grievous illness. Now it is obvious that this was not a natural illness, but was caused by some witchcraft of the woman. And very many similar cases have happened, and been made known to many.[20]

Next Sprenger and Krämer recommend physicians as expert diagnosticians—and as expert witnesses in which trials—upon whose professional judgment inquisitors and laymen are asked to rely in distinguishing diseases due to natural causes from those due to witchcraft.

> And if it is asked how it is possible to distinguish whether an illness is caused by witchcraft or by some natural physical defect, we answer that the first is by means of the judgment of doctors. . . . For example, doctors may perceive from the circumstances, such as the patient's age, healthy complexion, and the reaction of his eyes, that his disease does not result from any defect of the blood or the stomach, or any other infirmity; and they therefore judge that it is not due to any natural defect, but to some extrinsic cause. And since that extrinsic cause cannot be any poisonous infection, which would be accompanied by ill humours in the blood and stomach, they have sufficient reason to judge that it is due to witchcraft.[21]

A third method of distinguishing natural illness from illness caused by witchcraft consisted of interpreting the form assumed by molten lead poured into water. "There are some," say the authors of the *Malleus,* "who can distinguish such illnesses by means of a certain practice, which is as follows. They hold molten lead over the sick man, and pour it into a bowl of water. And if the lead condenses into some image, they judge that the sickness is due to witchcraft."[22, 23]

In the days of the witch-hunts, physicians and priests were thus much

[19] Ibid., p. 87.

[20] Ibid.

[21] Ibid.

[22] Since this was prescribed by the Inquisition and helped its cause, it was not considered magic or sorcery. When individuals employed similar methods in the pursuit of their own interests, they were declared heretics and were severely punished. See, for example, Charles Williams, *Witchcraft,* p. 85.

[23] Ibid.

concerned with the problem of the "differential diagnosis" between natural illness and demonic illness. This distinction seems simple to us only because we disbelieve in supernatural illness; but to our forebears, who believed in it, making this differentiation was a difficult task.[24] Moreover, the doctors and inquisitors engaged in ferreting out witches carried out their work against the backdrop of a closely related problem that was very real indeed: they had to distinguish between persons allegedly guilty of injurious acts, especially prisoners or *veneficae*—and those innocent of any wrong-doing, that is, ordinary persons. By being considered simultaneously a malefactor (as bewitched), like the poisoner, and a victim (as mere instrument of demonic powers), like ordinary all-suffering mankind, the witch helped to obligate the sharp distinction between poisoner and nonpoisoner, guilty and innocent person.

Significantly, the word *witch* comes from a Hebrew word that has been rendered *venefica* in Latin, and *witch* in English. Its original meaning was poisoner, dabbler in magical spells, or fortuneteller. The concept of witch combines occult powers with possibilities of benefaction or malefaction.[25] In Renaissance Europe, poisoning, mainly by means of arsenical compounds, was a common practice. Making and selling poisons became a large and profitable trade, often engaged in by women. "So rooted had [slow poisoning] become in France between the years 1670 and 1680," remarks Mackay, "that Madame de Sévigné, in one of her letters, expresses the fear that Frenchman and poisoner would become synonymous terms."[26] The problem of the correct diagnosis of wtichcraft must be viewed against this background.

Johann Weyer (1515–1588), physician to Duke William of Cleves, was one of the few medical men of his age to speak out against the witch-hunts. Like his contemporaries, Weyer believed in witchcraft and witches;[27] he differed from them only in holding that witch-hunters made the diagnosis of witchcraft too often and too readily. He especially attacked "the uninformed and unskilled physicians [who] relegate all of the incurable diseases, or all of the diseases the remedy for which they overlook, to witchcraft"; and concluded that "they, the physicians themselves are thus the real malefactors."[28] In short, he did not oppose the witch-hunts themselves, but only their "abuses" or "excesses."

Significantly, the full title of Weyer's classic work is *De Praestigiis*

[24] The classification of diseases as either natural or demonic, and of patients as either sick requiring treatment or possessed requiring exorcism, was still popular toward the end of the eighteenth century, and has, indeed, survived to the present. In this connection, see Henri F. Ellenberger. "The Evolution of Depth Psychology," in Iago Galdston (Ed.), *Historic Derivations of Modern Psychiatry;* and also Jean Lhermitte, *True and False Possession.*

[25] For further discussion, see Chapter 6.

[26] Charles Mackay, *Extraordinary Popular Delusions and the Madness of Crowds,* p. 582.

[27] Weyer not only believed in the reality of witches, but claimed to know their exact number and organization. There were, he said, "seven million, four hundred nine thousand, one hundred and twenty-seven, and all of them were controlled by seventy-nine princes." (Quoted in Jerome M. Schneck, *A History of Psychiatry,* p. 41.)

[28] Quoted in Gregory Zilboorg, *The Medical Man and the Witch During the Renaissance,* pg. 140.

Daemonum, et Incantationibus ac Veneficiis—that is, *On the Trickery of Demons and the Prayers of Prisoners.* Beginning with the title and throughout the book Weyer distinguishes between "witches" and "poisoners." He acknowledges that there are evil people who use a variety of poisons to harm and kill their enemies. They are criminals and should be punished. However, the majority of people accused of witchcraft are not of this type. Innocent of any wrongdoing, they are unfortunate, miserable, and perhaps "deluded" individuals. In a letter to his patron, Duke William, explaining the aims of *De Praestigiis* and dedicating it to him, Weyer writes that his "final object" in this work "is legal, in that I speak of punishment, *in another than the accustomed way,* of sorcerers and witches."[29] (Italics added.) And he concluded the letter with an uncompromising rejection of the inquisitorial process and a plea for respect for established judicial procedures. "To you, Prince [he writes], I dedicate the fruit of my thought . . . . You do not, like others, impose heavy penalties on perplexed, poor old women. You demand evidence, and only if they have *actually given poison,* bringing about the death of men or animals, do you allow *the law* to take its course."[30] (Italics added.)

Weyer thus insists that, from a legal point of view, it is necessary to distinguish between two classes of persons: poisoners or persons guilty of criminal acts, and nonpoisoners or persons innocent of criminal acts. But this is precisely the point on which his opponents assail him: because the witches *are* criminals, they maintain, there is no such distincton to be made. Contemporary authorities are quite clear on this. Jean Bodin (1530–1596), a French jurist, leading defender of the Inquisition, and one of Weyer's most impassioned critics, asserts that Weyer is ". . . wrong . . . a witch and a poisoner are one and the same thing. Everything imputed to witches is true."[31] Another critic of Weyer's, a Marburg physician named Scribonius, writing in 1588, objects specifically to Weyer's attempt to prove "that witches only imagine their crimes but that in reality they have done nothing untoward!" To Scribonius, this means that "Weyer does nothing more than to remove the guilt from the shoulders of the witches to free them from the need of any punishment. . . . Yes, I shall say it openly: with Bodin, I believe that Weyer has consecrated himself to the witches, that he is their comrade and companion in crime, that he himself is a wizard and a mixer of poisons who has taken upon himself the defense of other wizards and poison-mixers."[32]

Mystification of the concept of witchcraft and its amalgamation with that of poisoning were useful for the Inquisition; hence, inquisitors opposed attempts to undo this process and punished, as enemies of the established theological order, those who persisted in such efforts. Weyer's critics, as we just saw, objected precisely to his attempts to de-mystify the harmfulness of alleged witches. Doing so was, as the *Malleus* had clearly laid down, a grave and sinful error: "And yet there are some who rashly opposing themselves to all authority publicly proclaim that witches do not exist, or at any rate that they can in no way afflict and hurt mankind. Wherefore, strictly speaking

[29] Quoted in Gregory Zilboorg, *A History of Medical Psychology,* p. 214.
[30] Ibid., p. 215.
[31] Ibid., p. 237.
[32] Zilboorg, *Medical Man and Witch,* pp. 199–200.

those who are convinced of such evil doctrine may . . . be excommunicated, since they are openly and unmistakably to be convicted of false doctrine."[33]

Because it is essential for a clear grasp of our subsequent discussion of witchcraft and its parallels with mental illness, I have tried to show in some detail that the emphasis of Weyer's argument is not where modern psychopathologists claim it is—that is, on a criticism of the concept of witchcraft and on a plea for its replacement by that of mental illness;[34] instead it is on the *procedures* employed by the inquisitors. These methods will be surveyed in the next chapter.

With the decline of the power of the Church and of the religious world view, in the seventeenth century, the inquisitor-witch complex disappeared and in its place there arose the alienist madman complex.

In the new—secular and "scientific" cultural climate, as in any other, there were still the disadvantages, the disaffected, and the men who thought and criticized too much. Conformity was still demanded. The nonconformist, the objector, in short, all who denied or refused to affirm society's dominant values, were still the enemies of society. To be sure, the proper ordering of this new society was no longer conceptualized in terms of Divine Grace; instead, it was viewed in terms of Public Health. Its internal enemies were thus seen as mad; and Institutional Psychiatry came into being, as had the Inquisition earlier, to protect the group from this threat.

The origins of the mental hospital system bear out these generalizations. "The great confinement of the insane," as Michael Foucault aptly calls it, began in the seventeenth century: "A date can serve as a landmark: 1656, the decree that founded, in Paris, the *Hôpital Général.*"[35] The decree founding this establishment, and others throughout France, was issued by the king, Louis XIII: "We choose to be guardian and protector of said *Hôpital Général* as being of royal founding . . . which is to be totally exempt from the direction, visitation, and jurisdiction of the officers of the General Reform . . . and from all others to whom we forbid all knowledge and jurisdiction in any fashion or manner whatsoever."[36]

The original, seventeenth-century, definition of madness—as the condition justifying confinement in the asylum—conformed to the requirements for which it was fashioned. To be considered mad, it was enough to be abandoned, destitute, poor, unwanted by parents or society. The regulations

[33] Sprenger and Krämer, pp. 8–9.

[34] Indeed, since Weyer believed in witchcraft, and since the concept of witchcraft was inextricably intertwined with that of malefaction, he was unable to persuade his critics, or the public, that witches were harmless. Robbins cogently observes that "Weyer was activated by pity rather than by reason. Consequently, his attempted distinction between harmless witches and wicked wizards was easily demolished by his more logical opponents, like Bodin." (Rossell Hope Robbins, *The Encyclopedia of Witchcraft and Demonology*, p. 539.)

Today, the "moderate" critic of the overuse of involuntary psychiatric hospitalization finds himself in the same bind. Since he believes in mental illness, and since the concept of mental illness is inextricably intertwined with malefaction, he, like Weyer before him, is also unable to persuade his critics, or the public, that mental patients are not dangerous.

[35] Michel Foucault, *Madness and Civilization,* p. 39.

[36] Ibid., p. 41.

governing admission to the Bicêtre and the Salpêtrière—the two Parisian mental hospitals destined to become world famous—put into effect on April 20, 1680, provided that "children of artisans and other poor inhabitants of Paris up to the age of twenty-five, who used their parents badly or who refused to work through laziness, or, in the case of girls, who were debauched or in evident danger of being debauched, should be shut up, the boys in the Bicêtre, the girls in the Salpêtrière. This action was to be taken on the complaint of the parents, or, if these were dead, of near relatives, or the parish priest. The wayward children were to be kept as long as the directors deemed wise and were to be released only on written order by four directors."[37] In addition to these persons "prostitutes and women who ran bawdy houses" were to be incarcerated in a special section of the Salpêtrière.[38]

The consequences of these "medical" practices are described by a French observer after the Salpêtrière had been in operation for a century:

> In 1178, the Salpêtrière is the largest hospital in Paris and possibly in Europe: this hospital is both a house for women and a prison. It receives pregnant women and girls, wet nurses and their nurselings; male children from the age of seven or eight months to four or five years of age; young girls of all ages; aged married men and women; raving lunatics, imbeciles, epileptics, paralytics, blind persons, cripples, people suffering from ringworm, incurables of all sorts, children afflicted with scrofula, and so on and so forth. At the center of this hospital is a house of detention for women, comprising four different prisons: *le commun,* for the most dissolute girls; *la correction,* for those who are not considered hopelessly depraved; *la prison,* reserved for persons held by order of the king; and *la grande force,* for women branded by order of the courts.[39]

Surveying this scene, George Rosen bluntly states that "the individual was committed not primarily to receive medical care but rather to protect society and to prevent the disintegration of its institutions."[40]

As recently as 1860, it was not necessary to be mentally ill to be incarcerated in an American mental institution; it was enough to be a married woman. When the celebrated Mrs. Packard was hospitalized in the Jacksonville State Insane Asylum for disagreeing with her minister-husband, the commitment laws of the state of Illinois explicitly proclaimed that "Married women . . . may be entered or detained in the hospital at the request of the husband of the woman or the guardian . . . without the evidence of insanity required in other cases."[41]

In short, it is only a relatively recent rationalization in the history of psychiatry that a person must "suffer" from a "mental disease"—like schizophrenia or senile psychosis—to justify his commitment. Being an unemployed young man, a prostitute, or a destitute old person used to suffice. "We must

[37] George Rosen, Social attitudes to irrationality and madness in 17th and 18th century Europe, *J. Hist. Med. & All. Sc.,* 18: 220–240, 1963; p. 233.
[38] Ibid.
[39] Quoted in Rosen, p. 233.
[40] Ibid., p. 237.
[41] Illinois Statute Book, Sess. Laws 15, Sect. 10, 1852. Quoted in E. P. W. Packard, *The Prisoner's Hidden Life,* p. 37.

not forget," remarks Foucault, "that a few years after its foundation [in 1656], the *Hôpital Général* of Paris alone contained six thousand persons, or around one percent of the population."[42] As a means of social control and of the ritualized affirmation of the dominant social ethic, Institutional Psychiatry immediately showed itself to be a worthy successor ot the Inquisition. Its subsequent record, as we shall see, has been equally distinguished.

The French *hôpital général,* the German *Irrenhaus,* and the English insane asylum thus become the abodes of persons called mad. Are they considered mad, and therefore confined in these institutions? Or are they confined because they are poor, physically ill, or dangerous, and therefore considered mad? For three hundred years, psychiatrists have labored to obscure rather than clarify this simple problem. Perhaps it could not have been otherwise. As happens also in other professions—especially in those pertaining to the regulation of social affairs—psychiatrists have been largely responsible for creating the problems they have ostensibly tried to solve. But then, like other men, psychiatrists cannot be expected to act systematically against their own economic and professional self-interests.

The decree of Louis XIII was not a solitary occurrence. It has been repeated time and again through the history of psychiatry. The German mental hospital system, for example, was inaugurated in 1805 with the following declaration by Prince Karl August von Hardenberg:

> The state must concern itself with all institutions for those with damaged minds, both for the betterment of the unfortunates and for the advancement of science. In this important and difficult field of medicine only unrelenting efforts will enable us to carve out advances for the good of suffering mankind. Perfection can be achieved only in such institutions [state mental hospitals] . . .[43]

The patients upon whose behavior men like Kahlbaum and Kaepelin later erected their systems of psychiatric diagnosis were the inmates of these institutions. During the one hundred years following Prince Hardenberg's declaration, the diversity of mental diseases requiring "diagnosis" and "treatment" multiplied throughout Europe, and so did the number of mental patients requiring confinement.

In our own day—a half millennium after the bull of Innocent VIII, and 150 years after the German declaration of war on insanity—we are exhorted to combat mental illness by no less a personage than a President of the United States of America. On February 5, 1963, President Kennedy declared:

> I propose a national mental health program to assist in the inauguration of a wholly new emphasis and approach to care for the mentally ill. . . . Government at every level—Federal, State, and local—private foundations and individual citizens must all face up to their responsibilities in this area. . . . We need . . . to return mental health care to the mainstream of American medicine.[44]

[42] Foucault, p. 45.
[43] Quoted in Emil Kraepelin, *One Hundred Years of Psychiatry,* p. 152.
[44] John F. Kennedy, Message from the President of the United States relative to mental illness and mental retardation, Feb. 5, 1963, 88th Cong., 1st sess., H. Rep., Doc. No. 58.

It is sobering to contemplate the similarities among these inspirational messages. The good intentions and sincerity of the speakers need not be doubted. Pope, Prince, President—each claims to be trying to help his suffering fellow man. What is chilling is that each ignores the possibility that the alleged sufferer, whether of witchcraft or of mental illness, might prefer to be let alone; that each refuses merely to offer his help and grant his beneficiary the right to accept it or reject it; and, finally, that each denies the painful truth that men upon whom the ministrations of the militant Church and the therapeutic State are imposed by force rightly regard themselves not as beneficiaries and patients but as victims and prisoners.

As we have seen, in the days of the witch-hunts, the methods for identifying a person as a poisoner and as a patient differed radically; the method for identifying him as a witch differed from both, constituting a special procedure. In our day, the methods for identifying a person as a criminal and as a medical patient differ similarly; and the method for identifying him as a mental patient differs from both, again constituting a special procedure. There are good reasons for these distinctions.

We are plagued by some of the same kinds of social problems which plagued people during the declining Middle Ages, and we try to solve them by similar methods. We use the same legal and moral categories: lawbreakers and law-abiding citizens, guilt and innocence; and we, too, use an intermediate category—the madman or mental patient—whom we try to fit into one class or the other. Formerly, the question was: In which class do witches belong? Now it is: In which class do mental patients belong? Institutional psychiatrists and men of enlightened popular opinion hold that, because they are "dangerous to themselves and others," madmen belong in the class of quasi-criminals; this justifies their involuntary incarceration and general mistreatment.

Moreover, to support their ideology and to justify their powers and privileges, institutional psychiatrists combine the notions of mental illness and criminality and resist efforts to separate them. They do this by claiming that mental illness and crime are one and the same thing and that mentally ill persons are dangerous in ways that mentally healthy persons are not. Philip Q. Roche, who received the American Psychiatric Association's Isaac Ray Award for helping to bring law and psychiatry closer together, articulates this view in a characteristic fashion when he asserts that "criminals differ from mentally ill people only in the manner we choose to deal with them. . . . All felons are mental cases . . . crime is a disturbance of communication, hence a form of mental illness."[45] This view—namely, that crime is a product and symptom of mental illness in the same way as, say, jaundice is of hepatitis —held today by most psychiatrists and many lawyers and jurists, is not as novel as its proponents would have us believe. For example, Sir Matthew Hale (1609–1679), Lord Chief Justice of England and, curiously, himself an ardent believer in witchcraft, declared that ". . . doubtless, most persons that

[45] Philip Q. Roche, *The Criminal Mind*, p. 241. For additional examples and a more extended criticism of this view, see Thomas S. Szasz, *Law, Liberty, and Psychiatry*, pp. 91–108.

are felons . . . are under a degree of partial insanity, when they commit these offenses."[46]

We recognize in this view an early manifestation of the change from a religious to a scientific mode of thinking and talking about people and human relations. Instead of saying that "criminals are evil," the authorities say that they are "sick"; in either case, however, the suspects continue to be seen as dangerous to society and hence fit subjects for its sanctions.

It is consistent with this close mental and verbal association between crime and madness[47] that commitment laws are formulated in terms of the individual's supposed "dangerousness" (to himself and others), rather than in terms of his health and illness. Dangerousness, of course, is a characteristic the alleged mental patient shares with the criminal, rather than with the medically ill person.

Mystification of the concept of mental illness and its amalgamation with that of crime are now useful for Institutional Psychiatry, just as mystification of the concept of witchcraft and its amalgamation with poisoning had formerly been useful for the Inquisition. In Weyer's days, the effect of obfuscating the differences between witchcraft and poisoning—theological offense (heresy) and lawbreaking (crime)—was the replacement of accusatorial with inquisitorial procedures. In our day, the effect of obfuscating the differences between madness and dangerousness—psychiatric offense (mental illness) and lawbreaking (crime)—is the replacement of the Bill of Rights with the Bill of Treatments. The upshot in each case is therapeutic tyranny, clerical in the first instance, clinical in the second. The Inquisition thus combined the arbitrariness of theological judgments with the punitiveness of the prevalent penal sanctions. Institutional Psychiatry similarly combines the arbitrariness of psychiatric judgments with the punitiveness of now prevalent penal sanctions. Moreover, institutional psychiatrists now oppose attempts to undo the mystification inherent in the idea of mental illness, and punish, as enemies of the established therapeutic order, those who persist in such efforts[48]—just as formerly the

[46] Quoted in Jonas B. Robitscher, Tests of criminal responsibility: New rules and old problems, *Land & Water Law Rev.*, 3: 153–176, 1968; p. 157.

[47] In actual practice, what does it mean, or can it mean, to assert that crime is a form of mental illness? It can only mean a blurring of the distinctions, which I shall discuss presently, between illness and law-breaking. Suffice it to note here that the judgment of whether a person is sick is made by a physician, typically on the basis of an examination of that person's (called the "patient") body, submitted to the physician voluntarily by the patient himself; regardless of the outcome of this diagnostic process, the decision of whether a therapeutic intervention should be undertaken rests ultimately with the patient. In contrast, the judgment of whether a person is a criminal is made (in Anglo-American Law) by a lay jury, typically on the basis of an examination of information about that person's (called the "defendant") conduct, submitted to the jury, often over the objections of the accused, by the defendant's adversary (called the "prosecutor"); finally, if the outcome of this "diagnostic" process is a finding of guilt, the decision of whether a punitive intervention should be undertaken rests with the jury and the judge (whose choice of actions are, however, prescribed by law).

[48] "The question will inevitably be raised," writes Frederick G. Glaser, "whether sanctions of some form ought to be taken against Dr. Szasz, not only because of the content of his views but because of the manner in which he presents them. He has not chosen to limit his discussion to professional circles, as his magazine article [in

inquisitors opposed attempts to undo the mystification inherent in the idea of witchcraft and persecuted those (like Weyer) who persisted in such efforts.

Nevertheless, we too shall persist in such efforts. Let us begin with the differences between crime and ordinary (bodily) illness. Crime threatens society, not the criminal. When a crime has been committed, the public interest requires the use of broad and vigorous police-diagnostic methods: to protect the public welfare, the criminal must be found and apprehended. Against this, there is a countervailing private interest to carefully limit and supervise such methods: to protect individual liberties, the innocent citizen must be safeguarded against false accusations and imprisonment. Procedures for detecting crime must thus be carefully balanced to satisfy both of these competing interests. These ideas are contained in the legal concept of "due process."[49]

Disease threatens the individual, not society.[50] Since there is no public interest pressing for a diagnosis of illness when an individual suffers pain (as there is for a diagnosis of criminality, when a crime has been committed), the patient is left free to use or avoid whatever medical-diagnostic methods he wishes. If he pursues the diagnosis of his illness too vigorously, or not vigorously enough, his health may suffer, and hence he may suffer. It is therefore reasonable to leave the ultimate power for accepting or rejecting diagnostic procedures for disease in the hands of the patient himself. These ideas are contained in the legal concept of "informed consent."[51]

These two categories, described above in their pure form, coalesce in certain phenomena that exhibit the essential features of both—that is, the dangerousness to self, characteristic of illness, and the dangerousness to others, characteristic of crime. One such phenomenon, all too familiar to medieval and Renaissance man, was contagious illness. When, at last, toward the end of the thirteenth century, Europe was rid of leprosy, it was swept by successive epidemics of bubonic plague which decimated the population. Then, in the sixteenth century, syphilis assumed epidemic proportions.

Like leprosy and the plague, heretical beliefs and practices also spread through populations as if by contagion; and they too were regarded, by those

Harper's], not for the first that he has written, testifies." (Frederick G. Glaser, The dichotomy game: A further consideration of the writings of Dr. Thomas Szasz, _Amer. J. Psychiat._, 121; 1069–1074 [May] 1965; p. 1073.)

This intolerance is understandable. Doubt about the existence or dangerousness of mental patients would limit the methods permitted to institutional psychiatrists in combating mental illness, just as doubt about the existence or dangerousness of witches would have limited the methods permitted to inquisitors in combating witchcraft. The Inquisition thus flourished so long as its agents were entrusted with special powers by the society they served. Institutional Psychiatry now flourishes for the same reason. Only when these powers are curbed does such an institution wither away.

[49] See, generally, Irving Brant, _The Bill of Rights;_ for a critical discussion, see Friedrich A. Hayek, _The Constitution of Liberty,_ especially pp. 188–191.

[50] This is true mainly for noncontagious illness, such as cancer, heart disease, or stroke. Contagious diseases, which I shall discuss presently, resemble both noncontagious illnesses and crimes, inasmuch as they threaten the individual as well as society.

[51] Bernard D. Hirsch, Informed consent to treatment: Medicolegal comment, in Albert Averbach and Melvin M. Belli (Eds.), _Tort and Medical Yearbook,_ Vol. I, pp. 631–638.

who rejected them, as harmful to both self and others. Since contagious illness was understood to be harmful to both the sick person and others, it formed a ready conceptual bridge between ordinary, noncontagious illness (as something harmful to the self) and crime (as something harmful to others). Contagious illness thus became the model for religious heresy, fostering the imagery of witchcraft as a "condition" dangerous for both witch and victim alike. It was therefore considered justified to resort to special measures for controlling the epidemic spread of contagious illnesses and heretical ideas.

In modern society and the modern mind, contagious illness—now symbolized by syphilis and tuberculosis, rather than by leprosy and the plague—has continued to function as a conceptual and logical bridge between illness (as injury to self) and crime (as injury to others); and it became the model for secular heresy (mental illness).

Like syphilis and tuberculosis, nonconforming social beliefs and practices also spread through the population as if by contagion; and they too are regarded, by those who reject them, as harmful to both self and others. It is therefore still considered justified to resort to special measures for controlling contagious diseases (whose social significance has become negligible in industrially advanced nations) and dangerous ideas (whose social significance has skyrocketed in these countries). The result is a pervasive conceptualization of social nonconformity as a contagious disease—that is, the mythology of mental illness; a widespread acceptance of the institution which ostensibly protects the people from this "disease"—that is, Institutional Psychiatry; and popular approval of the characteristic operations of this institution—that is, the systematic use of force and fraud, disguised by the architecture of hospitals and clinics, the rhetoric of healing, and the prestige of the medical profession.

The fundamental parallels between the criteria of witchcraft and mental illness may be thus summarized as follows:

In the Age of Witchcraft, illness was considered either natural or demonic. Since the existence of witches as the analogues of saints[52] could not be doubted (save at the risk of incurring the charge of heresy), the existence of diseases due to the malefaction of witches could also not be doubted. Physicians were thus drawn into the affairs of the Inquisition as experts in the differential diagnosis of these two types of illnesses.

In the Age of Madness, illness is similarly considered either organic or psychogenic. Since the existence of minds as the analogues of bodily organs is not to be doubted (save at the risk of incurring vehement opposition), the existence of diseases due to the malfunction of minds also cannot be doubted.[53] Physicians are thus drawn into the affairs of Institutional Psychiatry

[52] In the theology and folklore of Christianity, saints are the agents of God, responsible for doing some of His good deeds, and witches are the agents of Satan, responsible for doing some of his evil deeds. Of course, good and evil, like beauty and ugliness, lie in the eye of the beholder. Thus, Joan of Arc, burned at the stake as a witch in 1431, was canonized as a saint in 1920. See Joan of Arc, *Encyclopaedia Britannica* (1949), Vol. 13, pp. 72–75.

[53] Illustratives is the following definition of "mind" by Stanley Cobb, the occupant, for more than thirty years, of a distinguished chair in neuropathology at Harvard, and one of America's most honored psychiatrists: "Mind . . . is the relationship of one part of the brain to another. Mind is a function of the grain just as contraction is a function

as experts in the differential diagnosis of these two types of illness. This is why physicians and psychiatrists are so much concerned with the problem of the differential diagnosis between bodily illness and mental illness. This distinction seems simple only if we disbelieve in mental illness; but to most persons, who believe in it, making this differentiation is a difficult task. Moreover, the physicians and psychiatrists engaged in psychiatric "case-finding" carry out their work against a backdrop of a closely related problem that is very real indeed: they must distinguish between persons allegedly guilty of injurious acts, especially acts of violence against family members or famous personages, and those innocent of any wrongdoing, that is, ordinary citizens. By being considered simultaneously a malefactor (as mad), like the criminal, and a victim (as sick), like the sick patient, the mental patient helps to obliterate the sharp distinction between criminal and noncriminal, guilty and innocent person.

Moreover, in each of these situations, the physician must work with the classification imposed on him by his profession and his society. The medical diagnostician had to distinguish persons afflicted with natural diseases from those afflicted with demonic diseases. The contemporary physician must distinguish persons afflicted with bodily diseases from those afflicted with mental diseases.[54] But in making this sort of differential diagnosis, the fifteenth-century physician did not distinguish between two types of diseases; instead he prescribed two types of interventions—one medical, the other theological. In effect, as diagnostician, such a physician was an arbiter deciding who should be treated by means of drugs and other medical methods, and who by a means of exorcism and other inquisitorial methods. *Mutatis mutandis,* the contemporary physician does not distinguish between two types of diseases; instead, he prescribes two types of interventions—one medical, the other psychiatric. In effect, as diagnostician, such a physician is an arbiter deciding who should be treated by means of drugs, surgery, and other medical methods, and who by means of electroshock, commitment, and other psychiatric methods. This is why the method of examination characteristic of Institutional Psychiatry are compulsory: the power of consent is wrested from the "patient" and placed in the hands of medical authorities sitting in judgment on him.

The point we must keep in mind is that in the days of the *Malleus,* if the physician could find no evidence of natural illness, he was expected to find evidence of witchcraft; today, if he cannot diagnose organic illness, he is expected to diagnose mental illness.[55] In both situations, once the subject

---

of muscle or as circulation is a function of the blood-vascular system." (Stanley Cobb, Discussion of "Is the term 'mysterious leap' warranted?" in Felix Deutsch [Ed.], *On the Mysterious Leap from the Mind to the Body,* p. 11.)

[54] My thesis regarding the relations between organic and mental illness thus both resembles and differs from Weyer's regarding the relations between natural and demonic illness. It resembles Weyer's in so far as he maintains that merely because physicians cannot cure a disease, they should not infer from this that the disease is due to witchcraft. It differs from his in so far as he proclaims his belief in witchcraft as a cause of illness and protests only that his colleagues make this diagnosis more often than they should. I hold that, like witchcraft, mental illness is a misconception which can "cause" neither bodily illness nor crime.

[55] In so far as the concept of mental illness functions as a classificatory label justifying the psychiatric denigration of nonconformists, it is logically faulty, not because

comes into the presence of the physician, he becomes a "patient" who cannot be left undiagnosed. The doctor often feels free to choose between two categories only: illness and witchcraft, physical illness and mental illness; he does not feel free—save at the cost of defining himself as professionally inept or socially deviant—to declare that the patient belongs in none of these categories.

In other words, the physician confronted with a person without demonstrable bodily illness is often baffled: Should he consider such a person a "patient"? Should he "treat" him, and if so, for what? In the past, the physician was generally reluctant to conclude that such an individual was neither sick nor possessed, and now he is reluctant to conclude that such a person is neither physically ill nor mentally ill. In the past, the physician tended to believe that such people ought to submit to the ministrations of either medicine or theology. Now he tends to believe that they ought to submit to the ministrations of either medicine or psychiatry. In short, physicians have avoided, and continue to avoid, the conclusion that the foregoing problem falls outside the scope of their expert knowledge and that they should therefore leave the person alone and unclassified—the master of his own fate.[56] These judgments are rendered impossible in principle by two assumptions concerning the therapeutic relationship. The first is that the person facing the medical or theological expert is a helpless, inferior being to whom the physician or priest owes a "responsibility" independent of his (the expert's) knowledge and skill, and which he cannot shirk. The second is that the institutional psychiatrist or inquisitor derives no "selfish" gains from his work with the patient or heretic, and that, were it not for his selfless devotion to healing or saving souls, he would be only too happy to leave the sufferer to his "horrible fate."[57] For these reasons, such messianic therapists feel that they must *do something,* even if what they do is harmful to the sufferer. The unfortunate outcome, until recent times, of most therapeutic interventions for

---

it fails to identify a socially definable characteristic, but because it mislabels it as a disease; and it is morally faulty, not because the physicians and psychologists who use it are badly intentioned, but because it fosters social control of personal conduct without procedural protections of individual liberty. For detailed discussion, see Thomas S. Szasz, *The Myth of Mental Illness.*

[56] What, then, should the physician do when confronted with a "patient" without demonstrable bodily illness? How should he classify and treat him? From the standpoint of a dignified medical ethic—respecting equally the patient's and the physician's rights to self-definition and self-determination—the examiner may satisfy his need for classification by categorizing his professional role or the result of his diagnostic interventions; but he should not impose a categorization on the patient against his will. The physician may thus conclude that he could find no evidence of bodily illness, but not that he found evidence of mental illness; or that he cannot help the client, but not that the client should consult a psychiatrist. In this connection, see Thomas S. Szasz The Psychology of Persistent Pain: A Portrait of L'Homme Douloureux, in A. Soulairac, J. Cahan, and J. Charpentier (Eds.), *Pain,* pp. 93–113.

[57] This is the myth of nonbenefits for coercive therapists; its corollary is the myth of immense benefits for those coercively helped (even if these benefits are temporarily unappreciated by them). Without this imagery, the social inequities of therapeutic exploitations—selfless helpers growing rich at the expense of their selfish victims, so obvious a feature of both the Inquisition and Institutional Psychiatry—could not be maintained; with it, they have been, and continue to be, readily justified.

the patient is therefore hardly surprising. In the first place, before the present century, the healing arts were in an exceedingly primitive state. Moreover, since the therapeutic interventions imposed on patients were prompted largely by the physician's (or priest's) own feelings of self-importance, obligations, guilt, and, of course, possible cravings for power and sadism, they were unrestrained by assessments of their curative value for the client or his informed consent to, or refusal of, the "service." These circumstances still characterize the purveyance of public (and sometimes even of private) psychiatric care, whose quality thus remains similarly unchecked by the free decisions of the ostensible recipients of its services.

It is consistent with this character of the wars on witchcraft and mental illness that vast efforts are made to refine the criteria of witchcraft and mental illness: but these labors only serve to confirm more securely the reality of these threats and the legitimacy of the defenses against them. Herein, as we have seen, lay the fatal weakness of Weyer's against the "excesses" of the witchhunts; and herein too lies the fatal weakness of the "moderate" contemporary opposition against the "excesses" of the Mental Health Movement.

Like Weyer before him, the "moderate" contemporary critic of involuntary mental hospitalization opposes only the "abuses" and "excesses" of Institutional Psychiatry. He wants to improve the system, not abolish it. He too believes in mental illness and in the desirability of committing the insane; his main complaint against involuntary mental hospitalization is that patients are committed too often and too readily—for example, that patients with unrecognized bodily diseases (such as subdural hematoma, brain tumor, cancer of the pancreas, and so forth) are sometimes hastily categorized as psychotic and improperly confined in mental hospitals. This argument only serves to confirm the validity of Institutional Psychiatry's core-concept of mental illness, and the legitimacy of its paradigm intervention, involuntary mental hospitalization.[58]

The foregoing problems of "differential diagnosis" are bound to arise and will persist so long as physicians are entrusted with matters completely unrelated to medicine. A physician may, or may not, be able to ascertain that a patient suffers from bodily illness; but if he thinks the patient does not, he cannot infer from this that his symptoms are due to witchcraft or mental illness—if for no other reason than that there is no such illness.

These problems of "differential diagnosis" would disappear if we regarded the physician as an expert on diseases of the body *only,* and recognized mental illness as a fictitious entity similar to witchcraft. Were we to do this, the physician's evaluative function would be limited to making an organic diagnosis or concluding that he cannot make one; and his therapeutic function, to treating bodily diseases or abstaining from treatment.

The problem of who is a fit subject for commitment would likewise disappear if we regarded involuntary mental hospitalization as a crime against humanity. The question of who was a fit subject for burning at the stake was answered only when witch-hunting was abandoned. I believe that the question

[58] Thomas S. Szasz, Science and public policy: The crime of involuntary mental hospitalization, *Med. Opin. & Rev.,* 4: 24–35 (May), 1968.

of who is a fit subject for commitment will also be answered only when we abandon the practice of involuntary mental hospitalization.[59]

Although the witch-hunts seem to us today an obvious crime, we must be cautious about passing judgment on the men who believed in witchcraft and fought against witches. "Those magistrates who persecuted witches and demoniacs and who lit so many bonfires," asks the noted French historian of psychiatry René Semelaigne, "should they be accused of cruelty, as they frequently are?" He answers: "They too were people of their time and thus had their prejudices, beliefs, and convictions; they thought in their souls and conscience that they were just when they struck the guilty in accordance with the law."[60]

The inquisitors who opposed and persecuted the heretics acted in accordance with their sincere beliefs, just as the psychiatrists who oppose and persecute the insane act in accordance with theirs. In each instance we may disagree with the beliefs and repudiate the methods. But we cannot condemn the inquisitors doubly—first for having certain beliefs, and then for acting upon them. Neither can we condemn the institutional psychiatrists doubly—first for holding that social nonconformity is mental illness, and then for incarcerating the mental patient in a hospital. In so far as a psychiatrist truly believes in the myth of mental illness, he is compelled, by the inner logic of this construct, to treat, with benevolent therapeutic intent, those who suffer from this malady, even though his "patients" cannot help but experience the treatment as a form of persecution.

Although the Inquisition and Institutional Psychiatry developed from different economic, moral, and social conditions, their respective operations are similar. Each institution articulates its oppressive methods in therapeutic terms. The inquisitor saves the heretics's soul and the integrity of his Church; the psychiatrist restores his patient to mental health and protects his society from the dangerously insane. Like the psychiatrist, the inquisitor is an epidemiologist: he is concerned with the prevalence of witchcraft; he is a diagnostician: he establishes who is a witch and who is not; and finally, he is a therapist: he exorcises the devil and thus ensures the salvation of the possessed person's soul. On the other hand, the witch, like the involuntary mental patient, is cast into a degraded and deviant role against her will; is subjected to certain diagnostic procedures to establish whether or not she is a witch; and finally, is deprived of liberty, and often of life, ostensibly for her own benefit.

Finally, as we have noted earlier, once the roles of witch and mental patient become established, occasionally people will seek, for reasons of their own, to occupy these roles voluntarily. For example, Jules Michelet writes that "Not a few [witches] seemed positively to want to go to the stake, and the sooner the better. . . . An English Witch on being led to the stake, tells the crowd not to blame her judges: 'I wanted to die. My family shunned me, my husband repudiated me. If I lived, I should only be a disgrace to my friends. . . . I longed for death, and lied to gain my end.' "[61] Christina Hole

[59] Ibid.
[60] Quoted in Zilboorg, *History of Medical Psychology*, p. 557.
[61] Jules Michelet, *Satanism and Witchcraft*, p. 145.

offers the following interpretation of the motives that led men to incriminate themselves and others as witches: "To accuse an enemy of witchcraft was an easy method of revenge; to declare oneself bewitched was a short cut to that flattering attention so much desired by unbalanced and hysterical individuals. . . . Very often the accuser's main object was to draw attention to himself and to pose as the victim of some witch's peculiar malice. . . . In 1599 Thomas Darling, of Burton-on-Trent, confessed that his story of three years before was quite untrue and his fits a fake. His reason for the deception was one that might have been given by many other lying accusers. 'I did all,' he said, 'either of ignorance, or to get myself glory thereby.' "[62]

Since a desire for "flattering attention" is not confined to "unbalanced and hysterical individuals," but, is, on the contrary, a basic human need, it is easy to see why, under certain circumstances, men will readily assume the roles of witch, criminal, or mental patient.

In sum, what we call modern, dynamic psychiatry is neither a glamorous advance over the superstitions and practices of the witch-hunts, as contemporary psychiatric propagandists would have it, nor a retrogression from the humanism of the Renaissance and the scientific spirit of the Enlightenment, as romantic traditionalists would have it. In actuality, Institutional Psychiatry is a continuation of the Inquisition. All that has really changed is the vocabulary and the social style. The vocabulary conforms to the intellectual expectations of our age: it is a pseudomedical jargon that parodies the concepts of science. The social style conforms to the political expectations of our age: it is a pseudoliberal social movement that parodies the ideals of freedom and rationality.

[62] Christina Hole, *Witchcraft in England*, pp. 94, 101.

DAVID MATZA

The Disreputable Poor

Shifting terms to designate the same entity is a familiar phenomenon in social science. The terms used to refer to backward nations are a notorious example. What used to be called savage societies came to be called primitive, then backward, then preliterate, then nonliterate, then underdeveloped or "so-called underdeveloped" and now, in an optimistic reversion to evolutionary theory, the emerging and even expectant nations. A similar process of word-substitution has occurred with reference to backward and immobilized enclaves within advanced and mobilized societies. I refer to the portion of society currently termed "hard-to-reach."

Though there is no great harm in such an exercise, the names we apply to things do, after all, matter. To say that a rose by any other name is just as sweet is to reckon without the findings of modern social psychology. Calling a rose an onion would under certain very special conditions provoke tears instead of delight. But this startling reversal does not mean that a rose is an onion; it only means that the perceiver can be deceived. Accordingly, word-substitution is consequential, not because the referents of concepts are thereby transformed, but because it is a deception of self and others.

The intellectual price we pay for this deception is more apparent perhaps than the social harm. When terms referring to essentially the same entity shift rapidly, and with so great a sense of orthodoxy, intellectuals and researchers, and the practitioners who depend on them for ideas, remain largely unaware of the historical continuity of the referent to which these shifty concepts apply. Moreover, word-substitution obscures and ultimately suppresses the underlying theories, especially in value-laden or offensive names.

The historical continuity of disreputable poverty has been obscured by the obsessive shifting of terms. One predictable consequence has been the continual rediscovery of the poor—an example of what Sorokin called the Columbus complex. The poor, it seems, are perennially hidden, and the brave explorers of each decade reiterate their previous invisibility and regularly proclaim the distinctive and special qualities of the "new poor." Dr. John Griscom, commenting on the wretchedness of slum life in the 1840's, said, "One-half of the world does not know how the other half lives."[1] Griscom's language and viewpoint were echoed almost a half-century later by Jacob Riis, and now, more than another half-century later, Michael Harrington again rediscovers a heretofore invisible class of submerged poor and again stresses the novelty of their predicament.

Disreputable poverty has gone under many names in the past two centuries. The major thrust and purpose of word-substitution has been to reduce and remove the stigma, and perhaps one reason for its obsessiveness is that the effort is fruitless. The stigma inheres mostly in the referent and not the concept. In five years or so, if not already, the term *hard-to-reach* will be considered stigmatizing and relegated to the dead file of offensive labels. The culmination of this process is not hard to predict since it has already occurred in a discipline even more addicted to word-substitution and mystification than ours—the field of education. There is little doubt that we shall eventually refer to the disreptable poor as "exceptional families."

In referring to the disreputable poor, I mean disreputable in the distinguishing rather than the descriptive sense. Though there is considerable variation, at any given time only a portion of those who can reasonably be considered poor are disreputable. In the term *disreputable* I mean to introduce no personal judgment, but to reckon without the judgments made by other members of society, to ignore the stigma that adheres to this special kind of poverty is to miss one of its key aspects.

The disreputable poor are the people who remain unemployed, or casually and irregularly employed, even during periods approaching full employment and prosperity; for that reason, and others, they live in disrepute. They do not include the majority of those who are unemployed or irregularly employed during a period of mass unemployment such as we are currently experiencing in a relatively mild way. To locate the section of the able-bodied poor that remains unemployed or casually employed during periods of full employment is a difficult task, particularly in the American setting where the number unemployed is subject to frequent and relatively drastic fluctuations. The economist Stanley Lebergott finds that, "No decade [in the twentieth century] has passed without severe unemployment (over 7 percent of the labor force) occurring at least once. And none, except for that of the 1930's, has passed without seeing at least one year of what we may call minimal unemployment (3 percent or less)."[2] Consequently, the line between those who are unemployed only during periods of depression or recession and those who are permanently unoccupied is especially difficult to draw in America.

Despite the difficulties in identifying and locating it, however, one may plausibly assert the existence of a small but persistent section of the poor who

[1] Robert H. Bremner, *From the Depths,* New York: New York University Press, 1956, pp. 5–6.
[2] Stanley Lebergott, "Economic Crises in the United States," in Special Committee on Unemployment Problems, *Readings in Unemployment* (Washington: U.S. Government Printing Office, 1960), pp. 86–87.

differ in a variety of ways from those who are deemed deserving. These disreputable poor cannot be easily reformed or rehabilitated through the simple provision of employment, training or guidance. They are resistant and recalcitrant—from the perspective of the welfare establishment, they are "hard-to-reach."

Conceptions of Disreputable Poverty

Concepts are both instructive and limiting. Each conception of disreputable poverty harbors some measure of wisdom and thus illuminates the referent; each makes us one-eyed and thus obscures it. Thus a sample of conceptions of disreputable poverty may serve to introduce a consideration of its persistent features.

The current conception, "hard-to-reach," considers and defines the disreputable poor from an administrative vantage point. Implicit in the concept is a view of the disreputable poor as human material that can be worked on, helped and hopefully transformed.[3] Reasonably enough, this conception implies that one crucial difficulty is that the material cannot even be got hold of. It is hard-to-reach, at least without great expenditures of time and effort. Only a short step is required to transform the concept from one rooted in administrative perspective to one suggesting an important insight. Surely, they are not hard-to-reach only because the welfare establishment is deficient. Rather, the elusiveness resides at least partially in the stratum itself. The disreputable poor are disaffiliated; they exist in the crevices or at the margins of modern society. Thus, the empirical wisdom inherent in the concept "hard-to-reach," represents a considerable insight. The disreputable poor are probably the only authentic outsiders, for modern democratic industrial life, contrary to romantic opinion, has had a remarkable capacity for integrating increasingly larger proportions of society. For this reason, perhaps, they have been consistently romanticized, glamorized and misunderstood by intellectuals, especially radicals and bohemians who frequently aspire to be outsiders but never quite make it.

Beyond this, the concept "hard-to-reach" tells us little. We should not be discouraged, however, since one insight per concept is doing well. Many concepts are completely nondescript, being the bland and neutral labels best exemplified in the usage of British and American sociologists when they refer as they do to Class 5 or Class E. There is nothing wrong with this. Indeed, from the viewpoint of science it is meritorious. Strictly speaking, concepts should not contain implicit theories since this permits one to smuggle in hypotheses better left to empirical investigation. But concepts that imply specific theories are a boon, providing the theory is empirically sound rather than romantic foolishness. The theory implicit, for instance, in a concept of the "happly poor" is mostly romantic foolishness.

Almost nondescript, but not quite, is the phrase initiated by Warner and

---

[3] For a brief discussion of the administrative-welfare perspective, see Thomas Gladwin, "The Anthropologist's View of Poverty," in *The Social Welfare Forum* (New York: Columbia University Press, 1961), pp. 73–74.

still fashionable among sociologists—the lower-lower class. In repeating the term *lower* and in distinguishing it from the upper-lower class, the concept is suggestive. Since Warner's categories were ostensibly supplied by members of the community, it implies that from *their* perspective, the distinction between two sections of the lower class is meaningful. The difference between lower-lowers and upper-lowers above all pertains to reputation—the one disreputable, the other reputable.

More suggestive is the British term, "problem family." Implicit in this concept are two points. First, to refer to problem families is to observe with typical English understatement that the disreputable poor are a bit of a pain in the neck. They are bothersome, they are disproportionately costly in terms of the amount of care, welfare and policing they elicit. Second, and more important, the term suggests that these families collect problems. They contribute far more than their share to the relief recipients, to crime and delinquency rates, to rates of alcoholism, to the list of unmarried mothers and thus illegitimate children, to divorces, desertions, and to the mentally ill. The idea of plural problems, reinforcing and nurturing each other in the manner of a vicious circle was well stated and developed in the English notion, but the American adaptation, "multiproblem" family, unnecessarily reiterates. Moreover, the American term loses the *double-entendre* implicit in the British formulation.

The remaining concepts, unlike those already discussed, were not attempts to reduce stigma, but, on the contrary, are decidedly offensive terms developed outside the circle of sociologists, social workers and psychiatrists. The first term, *lumpenproletariat,* which despite its wide usage among Marxists was never really clarified or developed systematically, refers to the dirt or scum that inhabits the lower orders, nearby, but not of the working class. The *lumpenproletariat,* according to Burkharin, was one of the "categories of persons outside the outlines of social labor" and bared from being a revolutionary class "chiefly by the circumstance that it performs no productive work."[4] For the Marxist, this stratum was fundamentally reactionary, and in the revolutionary situation, it would either remain apathetic or become mercenary in the service of the bourgeoisie. Bukharin maintains that in the *lumpenproletariat* we find, "shiftlessness, lack of discipline, hatred of the old, but impotence to construct or organize anything new, an individualistic declassed 'personality,' whose actions are based only on foolish caprices."[5]

Frequently, *lumpenproletariat* was used as a derogatory term in the struggles for power among various revolutionaries. If an opponent could be associated with the *lumpenproletariat,* his stature might be lessened. Despite frequent abuse, the term maintained some distinctive meaning. It continued to refer to the disreputable poor, and implicit in the Marxian conception are a number of suggestive insights regarding their character, background and destiny. The description given by Viktor Chernov, a Russian social revolutionary, is typical since it is garbed in highly evaluative language and since he uses the designation to attack an opponent, Lenin.

[4] Nikolai Bukharin, *Historical Materialism* (New York: International, 1925), pp. 284 and 290.
[5] *Ibid.,* p. 290.

Besides the proletarian *"demos"* there exists in all capitalist countries a proletarian *"ochlos,"* the enormous mass of *declasses,* chronic paupers, *Lumpenproletariat,* what may be termed the "capitalistically superfluous industrial reserve army." Like the proletariat, it is a product of capitalist civilization, but it reflects the destructive, not the constructive aspects of capitalism. Exploited and down-trodden, it is full of bitterness and despair, but has none of the traditions and none of the potentialities of organization, of a new consciousness, a new law, and a new culture, which distinguish the genuine "hereditary" proletariat. In Russia the growth of capitalism has been strongest in its destructive, predatory aspects, while its constructive achievements have lagged. It was accompanied by a catastrophic growth of the *"ochlos,"* a tremendous mass of uprooted, drifting humanity. Wrongly idealized at times, as in Gorky's early works, this mob supplied the contingents for those sporadic mass outbursts, pogroms, anti-Jewish and others, for which old Russia was famous. During the war, "the personnel of industry had . . . been completely transformed. . . . The ranks of factory workers, severely depleted by indiscriminate mobilizations, were filled with whatever human material came to hand: peasants, small shopkeepers, clerks, janitors, porters, people of indeterminate trade. . . . The genuine proletariat was submerged in a motley crowd of Lumpenproletarians and Lumpenbourgeois."[6]

What may we infer from this description? First, the *lumpenproletariat* differs in economic function from the proletariat. It is not an industrial working class; instead, it consists of a heterogeneous mass of casual and irregular laborers, farmworkers, artisans, tradesmen, service workers and petty thieves. They work in traditional and increasingly obsolete jobs rather than, in the Marxian phrase, in the technologically advanced sectors of the economy. They are not of stable working-class stock, but include declassed persons of every stratum. Because of its background and character, the *lumpenproletariat* is not easily amenable to organization for political and economic protest. It is apathetic. It has been "hard-to-reach" for agitators as well as for social workers, or at least so thought the Marxists. In point of fact, it has frequently been amenable to political organization, but as soon as it was organized it was no longer *lumpenproletariat,* at least not by Marxian standards.

Another concept worth exploring is one suggested by Thorstein Veblen: the notion of a spurious leisure class. It too was never fully developed. Veblen intimated that at the very bottom of the class system, as at the very top, there developed a stratum that lived in leisure and was given to predatory sentiments and behavior.[7] The resemblance between the genuine and spurious leisure class was also noted by George Dowling in 1893. He wrote in *Scribners,* "The opulent who are not rich by the results of their own industry . . . suffer atrophy of virile and moral powers, and like paupers, live on the world's surplus without adding to it or giving any fair equivalent for their maintenance."[8] The spurious leisure class, like Veblen's pecuniary masters of society, lived in industrial society but temperamentally and functionally were

---

[6] Viktor Chernov, *The Great Russian Revolution* (New Haven: Yale University, 1936), pp. 414–415.

[7] Thorstein Veblen, *The Theory of the Leisure Class* (New York: Huebsch, 1919), Ch. 10.

[8] Bremner, *op. cit.,* p. 22.

not of it. Because they were not dedicated to the spirit of industiral work-manship, they never evinced the matter-of-fact, mechanistic and sober frame of mind so admired by Veblen. Instead, this class, like the genuine leisure class, was parasitic and useless, barbaric and military-minded, and given to wasteful display and frequent excess. The major difference was that its leisure was spurious, bolstered by neither aristocratic right nor financial wherewithal.[9] A spurious leisure class, then, must be peculiarly embittered and resentful. It is dedicated to luxury without the necessary finances, and thus its members are given to pose, pretense and bluster. Veblen's caricature is as harsh as any-thing he had to say about the pecuniary captains of society. Though there is a ring of truth in Veblen's caricature, there is just as surely distortion.

A final conception pertaining to disreputable poverty was that of pauper. The distinction between paupers and the poor, maintained during the 19th and early 20th centuries, is a useful one, and its demise was one of the major casualties of obsessive word-substitution. Harriet Martineau, commenting on England in the early 19th century, observed that "Except for the distinction between sovereign and subject, there is no social difference . . . so wide as that between independent labor and the pauper."[10] Paupers as distinguished from the poor were often characterized as apathetic regarding their condition. While they were not romantically deemed happy, they were considered less miserable or unhappy than the poor. They had adapted to their poverty, and that was their distinctive feature. Robert Hunter said:

> Paupers are not, as a rule, unhappy. They are not ashamed; they are not keen to become independent; they are not bitter or discontented. They have passed over the line which separates poverty from pauperism . . . This distinction between the poor and paupers may be seen everywhere. They are in all large cities in America and abroad, streets and courts and alleys where a class of people live who have lost all self-respect and ambition, who rarely, if ever, work, who are aimless and drifting, who like drink, who have no thought for their children, and who live more or less contentedly on rubbish and alms. Such districts are . . . in all cities everywhere. The lowest level of humanity is reached in these districts . . . This is pauperism. There is no mental agony here; they do not work sore; there is no dread; they live miserably, but they do not care.[11]

Of all the conceptions reviewed, pauperism comes closest to what I wish to convey in the term, disreputable poverty. Though there are differences,[12] many of the features of disreputable poverty are implicit in the conception of pauperism. The concept of pauperism harbored the ideas of disaffiliation and immobilization which, taken together, indicate the outcasting from modern

---

[9] In like manner, Boulding has referred to "poor aristocrats" who pass easily into the criminal and purely exploitative subcultures which survive on "transfer of com-modities and . . . produce very little." See Kenneth Boulding, "Reflections on Poverty," *The Social Welfare Forum* (New York: Columbia University Press, 1961), p. 52.

[10] Cited in Karl Polanyi, *The Great Transformation* (New York: Rinehart, 1944), p. 100.

[11] Robert Hunter, *Poverty* (New York: Macmillan, 1912), pp. 3–4.

[12] For instance, a pauper strictly speaking depends on public or private charity for sustenance while in my conception the disreputable poor are sometimes recipients of welfare. They also work casually or irregularly, and occasionally engage in petty crime.

society suggested by Thomas and Znaniecki. Pauperism, like vice, "declasses a man definitely, puts him outside both the old and new hierarchy. Beggars, tramps, criminals, prostitutes, have no place in the class hierarchy."[13]

Among laymen, the common conception of disreputable poverty has persisted in relatively stable fashion, despite the shifting conceptions held by intellectuals, social scientists and practitioners. This persistence is implicit in a lay conception of pauperism which throughout has insisted on a distinction, radical or measured, between the deserving and undeserving poor. Ordinary members of society still maintain the views expressed in 1851 by Robert Harley, the founder of the New York Association for Improving the Condition of the Poor. The debased poor, he said, "love to clan together in some out-of-the-way place, are content to live in filth and disorder with a bare subsistence, provided they can drink, and smoke, and gossip, and enjoy their balls, and wakes, and frolics, without molestation."[14] One need not concur with Harley's sentiment, still pervasive today, that the debased poor do not deserve sympathy, to concur with the wisdom in the common understanding of the differences between pauper and independent laborer. A distinction between the two, measured instead of radical, refined rather than obtuse, is a preface to understanding the working classes and especially the unemployed among them.

The Situation of Disreputable Poverty

Disreputable poverty has been conceived in many ways. Each conception is illuminating, but also obscuring, since each stresses certain elements of disreputable poverty at the expense of others. To understand disreputable poverty, and to appreciate its complexity, one must distinguish among the various components that constitute its milieu. Disreputable poverty and the tradition it sustains are a compote, blending together the distinctive contribution of each ingredient.

Dregs

The core of disreputable poverty consists of dregs—persons spawned in poverty and belonging to families who have been left behind by otherwise mobile ethnic populations. In these families there is at least the beginning of some tradition of disreputable poverty.[15] In America, the primary examples include immobile descendants of Italian and Polish immigrants and of the remnants of even earlier arrivals—Germans, Irish, and Yankees—and Negroes who have already become habituated to the regions in which disreputable poverty flourishes. The situation of dregs is well described in a

[13] William I. Thomas and Florian Znaniecki, *The Polish Peasant in America* (New York: Dover, reissued 1958), p. 136.
[14] Bremner, *op. cit.,* p. 5.
[15] Boulding suggests that there is perhaps some cause for alarm when "the dependent children who have been aided ask for aid for *their* dependent children," i.e., when a sort of tradition is formed. See Boulding, *op. cit.*

Russell Sage Foundation report on Hell's Kitchen in New York shortly before the First World War.

> The district is like a spider's web. Of those who come to it very few, either by their own efforts or through outside agency, ever leave it. Usually those who come to live here find at first . . . that they cannot get out, and presently that they do not want to . . . It is not [just] that conditions throughout the district are economically extreme, although greater misery and worse poverty cannot be found in other parts of New York. But there is something of the dullness of these West Side streets and the traditional apathy of their tenants that crushes the wish for anything better and kills the hope of change. It is as though decades of lawlessness and neglect have formed an atmospheric monster, beyond the power and understanding of its creators, overwhelming German and Irish alike.[16]

The above statement refers to the dregs of the mid-19th century Irish and German migrations: to those who did not advance along with their ethnic brethren. Only a small proportion of the Irish and Germans living in New York at the time were trapped in the "spider's web" of Hell's Kitchen. Putting Hell's Kitchen in its proper context, Handlin says:

> From 1870 onward the Irish and Germans were dynamically moving groups . . . [However] Some remained unskilled laborers. They stayed either downtown or in the middle West Side, beyond Eighth Avenue and between 23rd and 59th streets, where the other shanty towns were transformed into Hell's Kitchen, a teeming neighborhood that housed laborers from the docks and from the nearby . . . factories, and also a good portion of the city's vice and crime.[17]

Rural immigrants to urban areas in the United States and other nations usually entered the system at the very bottom, but in the course of a few generations—depending on the availability of new ethnic or regional replacements and numerous other factors—their descendants achieved conventional, reputable positions in society. But some proportion of each cohort, the majority of which advances to the reputable working class or the lower rungs of the middle class, remains behind. Each experience of ethnic mobility leaves a sediment which appears to be trapped in slum life, whether as a result of insistence on maintaining traditional peasant values, family disorganization, relatively lower intelligence, more emotional problems, or just plain misfortune. These are the dregs who settle into the milieu of disreputable poverty and maintain and perpetuate its distinctive style. Neighborhoods in which this style flourishes possess diversified populations which, like the layers of a geological specimen, reflect its dim history. Handlin describes a single tenement in such an area.

> The poor and the unsuccessful [of each ethnic group] were generally lost in the characterless enclaves scattered throughout the city, in part of the West Side, in Greenwich Village, in Brooklyn, and later in Queens where

---

[16] *West Side Studies,* Vol. 1 (New York: Russell Sage Foundation, 1914), pp. 8–9; also see Richard O'Connor, *Hell's Kitchen* (Philadelphia Lippincott, 1958), p. 176.

[17] Oscar Handlin, *The Newcomers* (Cambridge: Harvard University Press), 1959, p. 31.

they were surrounded by communities of the foreign-born. The very poorest were left behind, immobilized by their failure, and swamped by successive waves of immigrants. In the notorious "Big Flat" tenement on Mott Street, for instance, lived 478 residents, of whom 368 were Jews and 31 Italians, who were just entering the neighborhood. But there were also 31 Irish, 30 Germans, and 4 natives, a kind of sediment left behind when their groups departed.[18]

Dregs are the key component of the milieu of disreputable poverty, because they link new cohorts entering the lowest level of society and the old cohorts leaving it. In the conflict between new and old ethnic arrivals, the unseemly traditions of disreputable poverty are transmitted. These traditions are manifested in a style of life distinctive to disreputable poverty, and apparently similar in different parts of the world. What are the main features of this style?

Income in this stratum is obviously low, but "more important even than the size of income is its regularity."[19] Unemployment and underemployment are common. When work can be found it is typically unskilled or at best semi-skilled. Job duration is relatively short; hiring is frequently on a day-to-day basis. Child labor lingers on,[20] and in many of these families, the wage earner, if there is one, suffers from frequent ill health resulting in intermittent employment. Savings even over a very short time are virtually unknown and as a result, small quantities of food may be bought many times a day, as the need arises. Also evident is "the pawning of personal possessions, borrowing from local money lenders at usurious rates, and the use of second-hand clothing and furniture."[21] The Brock Committee in England indignantly observed that "an important feature of this group is misspending." "Misspending," the committee asserts, "is the visible expression of thriftlessness and improvidence." The Brock Committee was impressed with the frequency with which "money is squandered on gambling, drinking, cigarettes, and unnecessary household luxuries when bare necessities are lacking."[22] Available resources are frequently mismanaged. "Rent is typically in arrears . . . and similar irresponsibility is shown towards bills and debts."[23]

To British investigators, the most obvious common feature of these families is the disorder of family life.[24] People frequently resort to violence training children and in settling quarrels; wifebeating, early initiation into sex and free unions or consensual marriage are common, and the incidence of abandoned mothers and children is high.[25] "The children play outside until late in the evening . . . and are sent to bed, all ages at the same time, when the parents are tired . . ." in many of these homes there is no clock,

[18] Handlin, *op. cit.,* p. 29.

[19] Tom Stephens (ed.), *Problem Families* (London: Victor Gollancz, 1946), p. 3.

[20] Oscar Lewis, *The Children of Sanchez* (New York, Random House, 1961), p. xxvi.

[21] *Ibid.*

[22] Cited in C. P. Blacker, ed., *Problem Families: Five Inquiries* (London: Eugenics Society, 1952), p. 3.

[23] Stephens, *op. cit.,* p. 3.

[24] *Ibid.,* p. 4.

[25] Lewis, *op. cit.,* p. xxvi.

and "one may visit at ten in the morning to find the entire household asleep."[26] Relations between parents are often characterized by constant dissension and an absence of affection and mutual trust.[27] As a result, family dissolution is frequent and there is a distinct pressure towards a mother-centered family—a rather disorganized version of what anthropologists call serial monogamy with a female-based household.[28] Though family solidarity is emphasized, it is an ideal that is rarely even approximated.[29] The disposition to paternal authoritarianism is strong, but since paternal authority is frequently challenged, its implementing frequently requires a show of power or force. The discipline of children has been described "as a mixture of spoiling affection and impatient chastisement or mental and physical cruelty."[30] Moreover, the household is extremely complex. It may contain "in addition to the joint off-spring, . . . children of diverse parentage. There may be children from previous marriages, illegitimate children, and children of near-relatives and friends who have deserted, died, or been imprisoned."[31] Thus, the normal manifestations of sibling rivalry are perhaps heightened.

The disreputable poor are "the least educated group in the population and the least interested in education."[32] Returning to the Brock Committee, we learn that this group suffers from "an intractable ineducability which expresses itself in a refusal, or else an incapacity to make effective use of the technical advice available."[33] To the uncritical and the indignant these families seem content with squalor,[34] a misunderstanding that obviously arises from failure to distinguish between satisfaction and apathy.

The disreputable poor "react to their economic situation and to their degradation in the eyes of respectable people by becoming fatalistic; they feel that they are down and out, and that there is no point in trying to improve . . ."[35] Their life is provincial and locally oriented. "Its members are only partly integrated into national institutions and are a marginal people even when they live in the heart of a great city."[36] Typically, they neither belong to trade unions nor support any political party.[37] They are immobilized in that they do not participate in the two responses to discontent characteristic of Western working classes—collective mobilization culminating in trade unions, ethnic federations or political action, and familial mobilization cul-

[26] Stephens, *op. cit.*, p. 4.
[27] *Ibid.*, p. 5.
[28] Some, like Walter Miller, are so taken by the durability of this style that, straight-faced, they hold the adjective "disorganized" to be an unwarranted ethnocentric imputation. See *Delinquent Behavior: Culture and the Individual* (Washington: National Education Association, 1959), pp. 94–97.
[29] Lewis, *op. cit.*, p. xxvi.
[30] Stephens, *op. cit.*, p. 5.
[31] Blacker, *op. cit.*, p. 32, and for a perceptive documentation, Lewis, *op. cit.*, in its entirety.
[32] Joseph A. Kahl, *The American Class Structure*, New York: Rhinehart, 1953, p. 211.
[33] Blacker, *op. cit.*, p. 16.
[34] Hunter, *op. cit.*, pp. 3–4.
[35] Kahl, *op. cit.*, p. 211.
[36] Lewis, *op. cit.*, p. xxvi.
[37] Genevieve Knupfer, "Portrait of the Underdog," *Public Opinion Quarterly*, Spring 1947, pp. 103–114.

minating in individual mobility. Members of this group are attracted episodically to revolutionary incidents[38] or at the individual level to criminal behavior in the form of a quick score or hustle.[39] Both are best viewed as forms of quasi-protest, however, since they contemplate quick and easy remedy without recognizing the onerous necessities of sustained and conscientious effort. Except for episodic manifestations of quasi-protest, the characteristic response of the disreputable poor, especially the dregs, is apathy.

Thus, the style of disreputable poverty apparently transcends national boundaries. Transmission of this style from one cohort to the next is a major contribution of dregs, but it is not the only mark they make on the texture of disreputable poverty. Just as important, perhaps, is the unmistakable tone of embittered resentment emanating from their immobility. Dregs are immobile within a context of considerable mobility in their ethnic reference groups, consequently, they are apt to see the good fortunes of ethnic brethren as desertion and obsequious ambition. Their view of those who have been successfully mobile is likely to be jaundiced and defensive. How else explain their own failure? What the reputable applaud as sobriety and effort must seem to those left behind an implicit, if not explicit, rejection of their way of life, and thus a rejection of themselves as persons.

From their resentful assessment of successful ethnic brethren, and also from the peculiarly seamy view of law enforcement agencies afforded slum denizens, another distinctive element emerges. A cynical sense of superiority appears, based on the partially accurate belief that they are privy to guilty knowledge shared only with influential insiders. In a word, they are "hip," free of the delusions regarding ethics and propriety that guide the "square" citizenry. Thus, for instance, "hip" slum-dwellers in New York knew or claimed to know of the incidents underlying the famous basketball scandals years before the public was shocked by the exposés, just as "hip" slum-dwellers in Chicago knew or claimed to know of the incidents underlying the police scandals there a few years ago.

Newcomers

Recent arrival is the second component of disreputable poverty. Not all newcomers gravitate to these regions—mostly those without marketable skills or financial resources. Irish newcomers escaping to America even before the great famine settled in neighborhoods already infamous and in disrepute. Ernst describes one of the most notorious of these neighborhoods in New York.

> To live in the lower wards required some money. The penniless stranger, wholly without means, could not afford the relative luxury of a boarding-house. His search for shelter led him to the sparsely populated sections north of the settled part of town. In the twenties and thirties Irish immigrants clustered around the "five points," a depressed and unhealthy area on the site of the filled-in Collect swamp in the old Sixth ward. Here, at little or no cost, the poorest of the Irish occupied dilapidated old dwellings and

[38] E. J. Hobsbawm, *Social Bandits and Primitive Rebels,* New York: Free Press, 1960.
[39] Walter Miller, "Lower Class Culture as a Generating Milieu of Gang Delinquency," *Journal of Social Issues,* 14 (1958), pp. 5–19.

built flimsy shanties. . . . In the heart of the Five Points was the old brewery, erected in 1792. . . . Transformed into a dwelling in 1837, the Old Brewery came to house several hundred men, women, and children, almost equally divided between Irish and Negroes, including an assortment of "thieves, murderers, pickpockets, beggars, harlots, and degenerates of every type" . . . As early as 1830 the Sixth ward, and the Five Points in particular, had become notorious as a center of crime. . . . The criminality of the area was usually overemphasized, but poverty was widespread, and thousands of law-abiding inhabitants led wretched lives in cellars and garrets.[40]

Numerically, newcomers are probably the largest component of the disreputable poor, but it is important to recall that except for a small proportion their collective destiny is eventually to enter reputable society. Thus, the new ethnics do not fully exhibit the features of disreputable poverty described above nor do they manifest the embittered sense of defeat and resignation characteristic of dregs. They are more apt to express a sort of naïve optimism, especially since their new urban standard of life is, if anything, higher than standards previously experienced.

Newcomers contribute an exotic element, whether they are European, Latin American, or indigenously American as in the case of southern Negroes and whites. Typically backward peoples, they season the streets of the metropolis with peasant traditions. It is this element of exotic and strange customs that has excited the imagination of bohemians and other intellectuals and led to the persistent romanticizing of life among the disreputable poor. Unfortunately, however, this exotic quality is double-edged, and one of the edges is considerably sharper than the other. Admiration from intellectuals was of little consequence for newly-arrived ethnics, especially compared with their persistent humiliation and degradation by resident ethnics.

The style of disreputable poverty was transmitted in the context of humiliation and victimization. The newcomers are, in the folklore of slum traditions and, to a considerable degree in reality, untutored in the ways of slum sophistication. "Greenhorns," "banana-boaters," whatever they were called, they learn the style of disreputable poverty primarily through being victims of it. They learn not by doing but, initially, by being had. This traditional pattern is neatly summarized in an older description of the environment of newcomers in American slums, a description refreshingly free of the contrived relativism that currently misleads some anthropologists and sociologists.

> The moral surroundings are . . . bad for them. In tenement districts the unsophisticated Italian peasants or the quiet, inoffensive Hebrew is thrown into contact with the degenerate remnants of former immigrant populations, who bring influence to bear to rob, persecute, and corrupt the newcomers.[41]

Transmission of the style of disreputable poverty in the context of humiliation and victimization helped to dampen the optimism with which newcomers frequently arrived, and thus facilitated its adoption by a segment of them. Optimism and other cultural resistances were never completely obliterated,

[40] Robert Ernst, *Immigrant Life in New York City, 1825–1863,* New York: King's Crown Press, 1949, p. 39.
[41] *United States Industrial Commission on Immigration,* Volume XV of the Commission's Report, Washington: Government Printing Office, 1901, p. xlvii.

however, and only a small though variable proportion succumbed to the temptations of disreputable poverty. Ethnic groups entering America and other nations have varied considerably in their vulnerability,[42] but in each one at least a few families became dregs.

Why have the newly arrived ethnics been so persistently humiliated and degraded by the old ethnic remnants? At one level, the answer seems simple. Despite all their failings, those who were left behind could lord it over the new arrivals for they at least were Americanized, though not sufficiently Americanized to be confident. Embittered and resentful on the one hand, and anxious and uncertain about their Americanism on the other, the ethnic dregs suffered from the classic conditions under which groups seek out scapegoats.

Skidders

Skidders are a third component in the milieu of disreputable poverty. These are men and women who have fallen from higher social standing. They include alcoholics, addicts, perverts and otherwise disturbed individuals who come, after a long history of skidding, to live in the run-down sections of the metropolis. To a slight extent low-cost public housing has concealed skidders from immediate view, but it still serves only a small proportion of the poor, and at any rate tends to be reserved for the deserving poor. Among the disreputable poor, the visibility of skidders remains high.

Occasionally, with the skidders, one finds some especially hardy bohemians who take their ideology seriously enough to live among their folk. But it is the skidders rather than bohemians who contribute importantly to the culture of disreputable poverty. Even when they live in sections of this sort, bohemians tend to be insulated partially by their clannishness but primarily because they are ungratefully rejected by the authentic outsiders they romanticize.

Skidders contribute a tone of neuroticism and flagrant degradation. They are pathetic and dramatic symbols of the ultimate in disreputable poverty. Perhaps more important, they are visible evidence of the flimsy foundations of success and standing in society and as such furnish yet another argument against sustained and conscientious effort. These are the fallen; they have achieved success and found it somehow lacking in worth. Skidders are important not because they are very numerous among the disreputable poor but rather because they dramatically exemplify the worthlessness of effort. While their degradation may sometimes goad others, particularly the new ethnics, to conscientious efforts to escape a similar fate, the old ethnic dregs take the skidders's fall as additional evidence of the meanness of social life, and the whimsy of destiny.

The Infirm

The infirm are the final element in the milieu of disreputable poverty. Before age, injury or illness made them infirm, these people belonged to other

---

[42] The reasons for this variability are complicated; some of them will be suggested in the final section on "The Process of Pauperization."

strata—especially in the reputable sections of the working class. Their downward shift may take the form of physically moving from a reputable to a disreputable neighborhood, but more frequently, perhaps, the infirm stay put and the neighborhood moves out from under them. Frequently, they belong to old ethnic groups, but not to the dregs since they have achieved or maintained reputable status. They slip because of some misfortune, aging being the most common. Their contribution is in part similar to the skidders', but without the blatant elements of neuroticism and degradation. Like the skidders, they testify to the flimsy foundations of respectability, the worthlessness of sustained effort, and the whimsical nature of fate or destiny. Like the skidders—even more so because they have done less to provoke their fate— they symbolize the beat (and not in the sense of beatific) aspects of life among the disreputable poor.

But the infirm have a distinctive contribution of their own to make. In a completely ineffective way, the infirm oppose the tradition of disreputable poverty. Their cantankerous complaints and what is surely perceived as their nosy interference frequently precipitate a flagrant and vengeful show of license and sin; the infirm become a captive and powerless audience before whom the flaunting and mischievous youth who inhabit this world can perform. Intruders in this world because they are of different stock, because they claim reputability, or both, they are simultaneously powerless and rejected. Those who claim reputability in a disreputable milieu inevitably give the appearance of taking on airs, and are thus vulnerable to ridicule and sarcasm —the typical sanctions for that minor vice. Furthermore, their opposition is weakened because before long the law enforcement agencies begin viewing them as pests, for the police cannot, after all, bother with their complaints if they are to attend to the serious violations that abound in these areas. The infirm are the one indigenous source of opposition but their marginal status makes them powerless to effect change. Thus, their distinctive contribution is to demonstrate the pettiness of character and the incredible impotence of those who oppose disreputable poverty.

In the situation of disreputable poverty, the various elements that coincidentally inhabit its regions conspire to perpetuate immobilization. Thus, part of the explanation for its anachronistic persistence lies in the relations among its components. But at best this is a partial explanation only; at worst it begs the more basic questions. To understand how disreputable poverty is produced and maintained, we must turn to the process of pauperization.

The Process of Pauperization

Although disreputable poverty has always existed, we do not yet know how the ranks of the disreputable poor are periodically replenished, on something approximating a mass basis, or how fractions of newcomers are selected to join them. These two related questions make up the topic of pauperization. My answers are intended only to illustrate certain facets of the process, not to present a general theory of pauperization.

Pauperization is the process that results in disreputable poverty. That aspect of it by which the population is periodically replenished may be termed *massive generation;* that by which newcomers pass into the ranks of disreputable poverty may be termed *fractional selection.*

Massive Generation

Let us begin cautiously by guarding against two antithetical beliefs, both common—one connected with that hardy variety of humanitarian conservatism we now call "liberalism," the other associated with that harsh variety of economic liberalism we now call "conservatism." The first view all but denies the possibility of pauperization, claiming that the very category of disreputable poverty is a prejudice with no substantive foundation and that pauperization is merely an unwarranted imputation. The second view makes rather different assumptions, claiming that pauperization occurs whenever the compulsion to work is relieved. According to this latter view, the poor are readily susceptible to the immobilization and demoralization implicit in disreputable poverty and will succumb whenever they are given the slightest opportunity. My own view is intermediate, pauperization, in the form of massive generation, is always a possibility, and occasionally occurs, but it requires extreme and special conditions. Pauperizing a significant part of a population is possible, but relatively difficult to accomplish. It must be worked at conscientiously even if unwittingly.

The circumstances attending the early phases of industrialization in England offer a classic illustration of massive pauperization. As far as can be told, mass pauperization is not, and never has been, a necessary or even a normal feature or by-product of industrialization or, more specifically, of primitive accumulation. Instead, it was probably an unanticipated consequence of purposive social action regarding the poor during the early phases of English industrialization. Mass pauperization was implicit in the sequence of Poor Laws by which the harsh reform of 1834 was built on the indulgent and slovenly base provided by Speenhamland. Neither the reform of Izy nor Speenhamland alone, I suggest, was sufficient to accomplish a massive generation of disreputable poverty. But together, they achieved a major replenishing.

The principal consequence of Speenhamland was to enlarge the ranks of the potential disreputable poor. This was accomplished through the moral confusion associated with a policy which in essence violated normal expectations regarding the relation between conscientious effort and economic reward.[43] Under Elizabethan law, which prevailed before Speenhamland, "the poor were forced to work at whatever wages they could get and only those who could obtain no work were entitled to relief."[44] In the 1790's, England experienced a series of bad harvests. Combined with a rise in prices connected with the war with France, in the wider context of enclosures, this caused distress and led to a number of disturbances, "an alarming combination in view of the horror with which the revolutionary aims of the French were re-

[43] This interpretation is based on, but departs somewhat from that suggested in Polanyi, *op. cit.*
[44] *Ibid.,* p. 79.

garded."[45] The reaction to this potential crisis was Speenhamland. Maurice Bruce describes the conditions attending the adoption of this plan:

> Numerous were the remedies proposed, though any increase of wages was keenly deprecated lest it should prove impossible to lower them when prices fell again . . . The influential and operative remedy, the spontaneous reaction to England's first wartime inflation, was the decision of the Berkshire Justices at Speenhamland in 1795 to supplement wages from the (poor) rates on a sliding scale in accordance with the price of bread and the size of families concerned. This historic "Speenhamland system" was given legislative sanction in the following year.[46]

Thus, one major aspect of Speenhamland was a peculiar system of outdoor relief in which "aid-in-wages" was regularly endorsed in such a way as to make indistinguishable independent laborers and paupers. The wages of the former were depressed,[47] while the lot of the latter was obviously improved. "The poor-rate had become public spoil . . . To obtain their share the brutal bullied the administrators, the profligate exhibited their bastards which must be fed, the idle folded their arms and waited till they got it; ignorant boys and girls married upon it; poachers, thieves and prostitutes extorted it by intimidation; country justices lavished it for popularity and Guardians for convenience. This was the way the fund went."[48]

Consequently, Speenhamland enlarged the ranks of potential disreputable poverty by obscuring the time-honored distinction between the independent laborer and the pauper. As Harriet Martineau observed, "Except for the distinction between sovereign and subject there is no social difference in England so wide as that between independent laborer and the pauper; and it is equally ignorant, immoral and impolite to confound the two."[49] Describing some of the ways in which this confounding occurred, Karl Polanyi has suggested the effect of this confounding on the productivity of the labor force so indiscriminately subsidized:

> Under Speenhamland . . . a man was relieved even if he was in employment, as long as his wages amounted to less than the family income granted him by the scale. Hence, no laborer had any material interest in satisfying his employer, his income being the same whatever wages he earned . . . The employer could obtain labor at almost any wages; however little he paid, the subsidy from the rates brought the worker's income up to scale. Within a few years the productivity of labor began to sink to that of pauper labor, thus providing an added reason for employers not to raise wages above the scale. For once the intensity of labor, the care and efficiency with which it was performed, dropped below a definite level, it became indistinguishable from "boondoggling," or the semblance of work maintained for the sake of appearance.[50]

[45] Maurice Bruce, *The Coming of the Welfare State*, London: Batsford, 1961, pp. 41–42.

[46] *Ibid.*

[47] Polanyi, *op. cit.*, p. 280.

[48] *Ibid.*, p. 99.

[49] Cited in *ibid.*, p. 100.

[50] *Ibid.*, p. 79; also see Marcus Lee Hansen, *The Atlantic Migration, 1607–1860*, Cambridge: Harvard University, 1940, p. 128.

Though boondoggling and other forms of demotivation were implicit in Speenhamland's peculiarly indiscriminate system of outdoor relief, that in itself was probably not sufficient for the massive generation of paupers. Pauperization implies more than demotivation of effort; it also implies a more general demoralization, the emergence of a view in which work is taken as punishment or penalty. These features of pauperization both appeared in substantial, though obviously limited, sections of the amorphous mass in which laborers and paupers were confounded, and both may perhaps be traced to an institution which was already apparent under Speenhamland but came to full fruition in the subsequent policies enacted in the Poor Law reforms of 1834. Pauperization awaited an institution in which persistent poverty was *penalized,* and in which the form taken by penalization was *coerced labor* administered on an *indoor* basis.

Under Speenhamland, the penalizing of poverty in the workhouse was a minor appendage to its major feature, indiscriminate outdoor relief. Under the reform of 1834 poverty was penalized on an indoor basis as the major governmental policy in regulating the poor. Since this policy of penalization was pursued, first side by side with, and subsequently in the wake of a policy that confounded laborers with paupers, it was well suited to realize the enormous potential for massive pauperization implicit in that confounding. Penalizing poverty through the workhouse reinforced and established, inadvertently but effectively, whatever mere propensities resulted from the indiscriminate use of outdoor relief under Speenhamland. The indolence and boondoggling occasioned by Speenhamland created the propensity for mass pauperization, but to be transformed into true paupers, those exhibiting indolence had to be stigmatized or defamed, work had to be reconstituted as penal sanction, and demoralization centralized under the roof of a facilitating institution. All of this was accomplished by the workhouse system.

Under Speenhamland, a man and his family would be put in the poorhouse if they had been on the rates for an extended period of time.[51] Once there, suggests Polanyi, "the decencies and self-respect of centuries of settled life wore off quickly in the promiscuity of the poorhouse where a man had to be cautious not to be thought better off than his neighbor, lest he be forced to start out on the hunt for work, instead of boondoggling in the familiar fold."[52] In the poorhouse the ancient culture of paupers could now be disseminated to those who had been thrown together with them, and the potential for massive generation of disreputable poverty could be realized. Moreover, the confusion regarding the moral value of work could be compounded and finally resolved by the unmistakable lesson of the workhouse—work is a penalty, to be avoided and viewed with resentment.[53]

Collecting the indolents in an indoor setting was important for another reason. Persons receiving poor relief during Speenhamland were not yet overwhelmingly concentrated in the urban slums we have come to associate with a tradition of disreputable poverty. Most were still distributed over chiefly

[51] Polanyi, *op. cit.*, p. 99.

[52] *Ibid.*

[53] The moral confusion regarding the status of work occasioned by this dual aspect of Speenhamland is discussed by Reinhard Bendix, *Work and Authority in Industry,* New York: Harper Torchbooks, 1963, pp. 40–42.

agricultural areas.[54] Thus, the concentration that facilitates the formation of a subculture was aided by the poorhouse system. The poorhouses and work-houses served the same function for the disreputable poor that Marx assigned the factories in the development of an industrial proletariat and the same func-tion assigned by criminologists to prisons in disseminating the standards and techniques of criminality. Each is a center for the collection of traits which can then be conveniently disseminated.

The defamation of character implicit in commitment to a workhouse is clearest after the Poor Law Reform of 1834. This reform was a direct reaction to Speenhamland. It was calculated to avoid the indulgence of indolence ap-parent in the previous system. The Webbs summarize the reformers' motives:

> The decisive element [in the Poor Law Reform amendments of 1834] was undoubtedly a recognition of the bad behavior induced alike among employers and employed by the various devices for maintaining the able-bodied, wholly or partially, out of the Poor Rate. When, under the allowance system, the farmers and manufacturers became aware that they could reduce wages indefinitely, and the manual workers felt secure of subsistence without the need for exerting themselves to retain any particular employment, the standard of skill and conduct of all concerned rapidly declined. To single out the full-whitted employer and the lazy workman for special grants out of public funds, to the detriment of the keen organizer and the zealous worker, was obviously bad psychology as well as bad economics. When adding to the number of children automatically increased the family income, young persons hastened to get married, as it was, indeed, intended they should do by the Justices of the Peace who adopted the Speenhamland Scale . . . The Eliza-bethan Poor Law had become, by the beginning of the nineteenth century, a systematic provision, not so much for the unfortunate as for the less com-petent and the less provident, whom the humanity or carelessness of the Justices and the Overseers had combined specially to endow out of public funds.[55]

The reform of 1834 was an extreme reaction to Speenhamland, but instead of undoing the effects of Speenhamland, it compounded them, for penalizing poverty completed the historic process of pauperization begun by the moral confusion occasioned by Speenhamland. The abolition of Speen-hamland was in some respects, as Polanyi suggests, "the true birthday of the modern working-classes" because it forced them to mobilize on their own behalf. But just as surely, the same abolition and the same enactment of the Reform Act was the "true birthday of the modern disreputable poor," for it signalled the last phase of the pauperization process. If "Speenhamland was an automaton for demolishing the standards on which any kind of society could be based," then the reform was an instrument for institutionalizing the standards which replaced those "on which any kind of society could be based."

The reform of 1834 was designed in the hope that the poor would be

54 Neil J. Smelser, *Social Change in the Industrial Revolution,* Chicago: University of Chicago Press, 1959, p. 350.

55 Sidney and Beatrice Webb, *English Poor Law History,* Vol. 8 of *English Local Government,* London: Longmans, Green, 1929, pp. 14–15.

severely discouraged from going on the rates by the stigma now attached to the workhouse and the conditions characterizing it.

> The new law provided that in the future no outdoor relief should be given . . . Aid-in-wages was . . . discontinued . . . It was now left to the applicant to decide whether he was so utterly destitute of all means that he would voluntarily repair to a shelter which was deliberately made a place of horror. The workhouse was invested with a stigma; and staying in it was made a psychological and moral torture . . . The very burial of a pauper was made an act by which his fellow men renounced solidarity with him even in death.[56]

Surely, this was to reinstitute the distinction between independent laborer and pauper, but only after forty years of confounding precisely that issue. Together the two policies comprised the classic way to generate a mass population of paupers.

Doubtless, pauperization is easier to accomplish when the population in question is a subjugated national or ethnic group rather than an indigenous group of subjects or citizens. Subjugated people are regarded as moral inferiors to begin with, capable of a variety of vices which typically include indolence and immorality. Pauperizing an indigenous population is more difficult in the measure that national affinities limit, though without necessarily precluding, the possibilities of imputing subhuman stature. The English case is classic precisely because pauperizing some parts of an indigenous population is difficult, but in that case too, the extent of indigenous pauperization is easily exaggerated, for many who were caught in the curious combination of Speenhamland indulgence and Reform penalization were in fact not English but Irish. Some of the Irish in England were pauperized by the same circumstances that affected indigenous Englishmen, but many more were pauperized by a separate process, one that illustrates the pattern of extreme subjugation by which the poor among captive or conquered peoples are commonly pauperized. This second pattern of massive pauperization is of paramount importance in the United States because it perhaps produced the two major ethnic contributors to the tradition of disreputable poverty—the Irish and the Negro.[57]

The great Irish famine was only the culmination of a long period of subjugated poverty which drove the Irish eastward across the channel to England and westward to America. Both before and during the famine it is very likely that England rather than America received the most profoundly pauperized sections of the Irish poor,[58] if only because migration to nearby England was economically more feasible.[59] Ireland was an impoverished colony, be-

---

[56] Polanyi, *op. cit.,* pp. 101–102.

[57] For a general sense in which Irish and Negroes were at least somewhat different from other immigrant groups in America, see Nathan Glazer and Daniel P. Moynihan, *Beyond the Melting Pot,* Cambridge: The M.I.T. Press and Harvard University Press, 1963.

[58] John A. Jackson, *The Irish in Britain,* London: Routledge and Kegan Paul, 1963, p. 9; also see Cecil Woodham-Smith, *The Great Hunger,* London: Hamish Hamilton, 1962, p. 270.

[59] One cannot help observing that there was a certain poetic justice in this preference for nearby England. The paupers came home to roost, sponging, as it were, on the very regime that had so ingeniously pauperized them. There is no evidence that the

fore, during, and after its great famine, and perhaps, as travelers during the period suggested, impoverished to an extent unrivaled in the rest of Europe.[60] Impoverishment, however, is not the same as pauperization. In the Irish experience, extreme economic impoverishment was combined with profound political subjugation. Just as penalization pauperizes an indigenous population, political subjugation of a captive or colonized people may transform the merely poor into paupers through the agency of oppression and degradation. The political subjugation experienced by the Irish was tantamount to the penalization of the entire island.

Beginning in 1695, the Irish were subjected to the infamous Penal Laws which Edmund Burke aptly described as "a machine of wise and elaborate contrivance, and as well fitted for the oppression, impoverishment and degradation of a people and the debasement in them of human nature itself, as ever proceeded from the perverted ingenuity of man." The Penal Laws were long, elaborate and developed over a number of generations.[61] Their character is perhaps conveyed by the fact that on two occasions it is stated that the law "does not suppose any such person to exist as a Roman Catholic."[62] Some provisions were potentially subversive of family life: "If the eldest son of a landholder apostatized and renounced the Catholic religion, he became sole owner of the property and immediately his father was inhibited from placing impediments on it . . . The son could disinherit the father,"[63] and in the process dispossess all of his younger brothers, who were otherwise entitled to an equal share.

The effects of the Penal Laws are suggested by Woodham-Smith. She says:

> The material damage suffered through the Penal Laws was great; ruin was widespread, old families disappeared and old estates were broken up; but the most disastrous effects were moral. The Penal Laws brought lawlessness, dissimilation and revenge in their train, and the Irish character, above all the character of the peasantry did become, in Burke's words degraded and debased. The upper classes were able to leave the country and many middle-class merchants contrived with guile, to survive, but the poor Catholic peasant bore the full hardship. His religion made him an outlaw; in the Irish House of Commons he was described as "the common enemy," and whatever was inflicted on him, he must bear, for where could he look for redress? To his landlord? Almost invariably an alien conqueror. To the law? Not when every person connected with the law, from the jailer to the judge, was a Protestant who regarded him as "the common enemy."[64]

Irish paupers were prompted by so frivolous a motive, however; only the gypsies among the disreputable poor are regularly guided by such considerations. For a discussion of the peculiar gypsy version of disreputable povery see my "Gypsies: Deviant Exemplars," in *Deviant Phenomena*, Prentice-Hall, forthcoming.

[60] Woodham-Smith, *op. cit.,* pp. 19–20.
[61] For a brief summary of the Penal Laws, see George Potter, *To the Golden Door,* Boston: Little, Brown 1960, pp. 26–28.
[62] *Ibid.*
[63] *Ibid.*
[64] Woodham-Smith, 27–28.

The lingering effects of the Penal Laws were instrumental in creating the two traditions for which the Irish later became noted, terrorist rebellion and disreputable poverty.

The pauperization of the Irish peasantry was not simply a consequence of the Penal Laws. It was also facilitated by the Irish system of land tenure headed by absentee landlords and managed largely by local agents. Under the policy of surrender and regrant of land, most Irish farmers had become rent-paying tenants.[65] Moreover, the land system, and especially the institution of "cant," seemed almost calculated to punish conscientious effort and reward slovenliness.

> The most calloused abuse by the landlord of his ownership was the practice of putting up farms for "cant" [or public auction] when leases expired. No matter how faithfully a tenant paid his rent, how dutifully he had observed regulations, or how well he had improved the property by his own labors, he was in constant danger of being outbid for his farm by the "grabber" upon the expiration of the lease . . . Moreover, in the Catholic parts of Ireland . . . the tenant was not entitled to compensation for improvements brought by himself . . . Hard experience had taught the tenant the penalties of improving the property he leased or hired and the self-interest of slovenliness. If he improved the property, his rent was raised! . . . Progress and improvement, instead of being encouraged by the landlord for his own interests, were penalized. This upside-down system withered the character, destroyed the initiative, and squelched the ambition of the Irish tenant.[66]

A key factor in pauperization, as in the English Poor Law policy, was the negative association of work with sanction. In one instance, conscientious effort was punished, whereas in the other it was used as a punishment. Either form of association of work with a negative sanction facilitates pauperization. Mere indolence is converted to an active antagonism to work. By the time the Irish began to emigrate to America, the policy of political subjugation along with the economic impoverishment of the island had had its effect. A substantial proportion of the population had been pauperized though, almost certainly, it was nothing approaching a majority. So difficult is the process of pauperization that no more than a substantial minority are likely to succumb to it. Counteracting the forces for degradation and demoralization are always the stabilizing and moralizing forces of family, religion, and primary group solidarity; these are weakened but never obliterated. Beaumont, a French observer, put the practical effects of pauperization nicely: "All the faculties of his soul that despotism has touched are blighted; the wounds there are large and deep. All this part of him is vice, whether it be cowardice, indolence, knavery or cruelty; half of the Irishman is a slave."

In the years just before the famine and great emigration, the Irish poor were subjected to the workhouse system, which was instituted in the English parliament as part of the Irish Poor Law act of 1838. Thus, in Ireland, the penalizing of poverty in a workhouse system came in the wake of the political subjugation epitomized by the Penal Laws, whereas in the English case, the penalizing of poverty follows the indulgence of Speenhamland.

[65] Ernst, *op. cit.*, p. 5.
[66] Potter, *op. cit.*, p. 44.

By the 1820's the poor rates in England had reached unprecedented heights. Whereas the total rate in 1696 was 400,000 pounds, in 1776 it was about one and a half million, in 1796 it passed two million, in 1802 it had risen to four and a quarter million, by 1818 close to eight million and still in 1832 seven million.[67] This represented only a small part of the national income, "probably no more than two percent," but "it amounted to one-fifth of the national expenditure and to people who had no means of assessing the national income it loomed appallingly large and seemed to threaten the economic foundations of society."[68] The rate seemed especially high since a large number of able-bodied workers were being supported by it. Not surprisingly, many of the English rate-payers "blamed the Irish pauper in England and demanded a Poor Law for Ireland."[69] Irish emigration to England and Scotland was heavy, throughout the 18th and earth 19th centuries, first as seasonal agricultural labor and increasingly as more or less settled industrial workers. "By 1841, shortly before the great famine, fully 419,256 Irish-born persons were living permanently in England and Scotland."[70] Given the English knowledge of the pauperized state of the Irish, it was to be expected that the Irish would be blamed for what were conceived as staggeringly high poor rates. The enactment by the English of an Irish Poor Law in 1838 was promoted by the desire to make Irish property responsible for its own poverty, and thus to slow the emigration of the Irish poor to England. But Irish landlords were simply not up to the task, and the major effect of the Act was to spur "Assisted Emigration" from Ireland, mostly to America via Quebec. Under the Irish Poor Law of 1838 the workhouse became an intermediate step—a halfway house between eviction from the land and emigration to America. The law taxed Irish landlords so highly that they showed "a sudden zeal to promote emigration. The new law integrated emigration with evictions by setting up workhouses for the dispossessed, and since the same act provided for assisted emigration, the workhouse became the intermediate step between eviction and departure from Ireland."[71] This sequence of eviction, sentence to the poorhouse and assisted emigration achieved special importance with the onset of the Irish famine in 1845.

The penalization of poverty was the last phase in a long history of the English pauperization of the Irish poor. By coincidence, it occurred shortly before the great emigration to America. Thus, a substantial proportion of emigrants to America had experienced *both* the punishing of conscientious effort, as a result of the cant system, and the use of conscientious effort as punishment in the workhouse, along with political subjugation under the English. The disreputable poverty of the Irish immigrant in America is best understood in the context of this dubious legacy, and the subsequent tradition of disreputable poverty in urban America is best understood by stressing that

[67] These figures are from Bruce, *op. cit.*, pp. 76–77, and Polanyi, *op. cit.*, p. 110.
[68] Bruce, *op. cit.*, pp. 76–77.
[69] Ernst, *op. cit.*, p. 5.
[70] *Ibid.*
[71] *Ibid.*

our first massive immigration of the very poor was that of already pauperized Irish fleeing in "assisted" fashion from the great famine.[72]

In America, the Irish were almost immediately considered worthless paupers. This stigma was applied not only to those who were already truly pauperized but also to those who had somehow remained simply poor. Since the worthy poor too were frequently out of work, they were lumped together with their more disreputable brethern. Potter summarizes their predicament:

> The "indolent Irish" had been a characterization fixed on the race by the English in Ireland that American inherited. Superficial observation gave it currency in America for two major reasons. One was the frequent spells of unemployment the Irishman suffered from the nature of his manual work— inclement weather, cyclical depressions, and job competition. On this score the description was unjust because of the elements beyond the individual Irishman's control. The other [reason] was the shiftlessness of a ragtag and bobtail minority, noisy, dissolute, troublesome, gravitating to public relief, which unfairly settled a distorted reputation on the race in the minds of people often initially prejudiced.[73]

Given the disreputability of the Irish, they probably encountered greater discrimination than other minorities in America. "Potential employers disliked and even feared their religion, shuddered at 'Irish impulsiveness' and turbulence, and were disgusted and morally shocked at the Irish propensity for strong drink." In all likelihood, "no other immigrant nationality was proscribed as the Catholic Irish were."[74]

Fractional Selection

Fractional selection is the process whereby some fraction of newcomers pass into the ranks of disreputable poverty. It is the more normal, less dramatic, process of pauperization, depending on existing traditions of disreputable poverty, which are only occasionally replenished on a massive scale by newly generated cohorts. Given the relative absence of massive generation, the process of fractional selection is the major hindrance to the gradual attrition of disreputable poverty. The conversion of newcomers to dregs provides for the partial replacement of the pauperized individuals who somehow transcend their circumstance, and pass into the reputable sections of society. Consequently, the survival of disreputable poverty has partly depended on barring newcomers from the normal routes of social mobility. Thus, the general conditions underlying fractional selection into the ranks of disreputable poverty are for the most part simply the reverse of those favoring social mobility. These general conditions need no special restatement. Instead, I want to stress the temporal context of the circumstances favoring mobility.

[72] The other important stream feeding this tradition in America, and massively replendishing the population of the disreputable poor, will be discussed in a later publication. It consists, of course, of Negroes, many of whom were pauperized as a result of enslavement and continued political subjugation after formal emancipation.

[73] Potter, *op. cit.*, pp. 84–85.

[74] Ernst, *op. cit.*, pp. 66–67.

Strong family organization, a cultural heritage stressing achievement, an expanding economy, an upgraded labor force, a facilitating demographic context and other conditions generally favoring mobility, have their effect within a temporal context. Once a period, the length of which will be suggested, is over, these general circumstances favoring advancement are hampered by demoralization, first in the form of being severe discouragement or immobilization, and subsequently in the form of relaxed moral standards. Demoralization signals the culmination of the process by which some proportion of newcomers are selected for disreputable poverty.

The period during which newcomers enjoy relatively high morale is the temporal context within which the general factors favoring social mobility flourish. Its length varies, but the limits may be suggested. Demoralization may be avoided, until newcomers are reduced to dregs, and the reduction of newcomers to dregs occurs when the steady desertion of mobile ethnic brethren is dramatically climaxed by an ecological invasion of new bands of ethnic or regional newcomers. When newcomers to the milieu of disreputable poverty predominate as neighbors and workmates, the remnants of earlier cohorts resentfully begin to notice what they have finally come to. They must now live and work with "them," and suddenly the previously obscure relation between their lot and that of their more fortunate or successful brethren from the original cohort is clear. They have become dregs, reduced to actually living and working with "niggers," or other newcomers in the milieu of disreputable poverty. Pauperization through fractional selection occurs, then, when newcomers take over the neighborhood and workplace. This kind of pauperization becomes more pronounced when the newcomers who have overtaken the dregs are themselves replaced by yet another cohort of newcomers. Thus, the milieu of disreputable poverty is temporally stratified; the older the vintage, the more thorough the pauperization.

The spiteful and condescending clucking of the now reputable segments of the original ethnic cohort is the main agency in demoralizing those who still live in a disreputable milieu. The attitudes of the reputable are illustrated by the comments of upper-lower class Irish, reported by Warner and Srole:[75]

> "Maybe we haven't made a million dollars, but our house is paid for and out of honest wages, too," said Tim.
> "Still, Tim, we haven't done so bad. The Flanagans came here when we did and what's happened to them? None of them is any good. Not one of them has moved out of the clam flats."
> "You're right, Annie, we are a lot better than some. Old Pat Flanagan, what is he? He is worse than the clam diggers themselves. He has got ten or twelve kids—some of them born in wedlock and with the blessings of the church, but some of them are from those women in the clam flats. He has no shame."
> "His children," said Annie, "are growing into heathens. Two of them are in the reform school, and that oldest girl of his has had two or three babies without nobody admitting he was the father."

[75] W. Lloyd Warner and Leo Srole, *The Social Systems of American Ethnic Groups,* New Haven: Yale University Press, 1945, pp. 12–13.

When they are forced to live and work with newcomers, the remnants need no longer overhear the disparaging comments of the reputable members of their ethnic cohort. They disparage themselves. They know what they have come to, for they share the wider social view that the newcomers are profoundly inferior and detestable. The irony here is that the demoralization of old ethnics and their subsequent transformation to dregs results from the provincialism that simultaneously maintains ethnic identity long after it has been partially obscured in other parts of society, and manifests itself in pervasive prejudices perhaps unmatched elsewhere.[76] Thus, the measure in which the old cohorts are reduced to dregs depends partly on the extent to which they themselves denigrate newcomers. For now they become in the eyes of significant others, and in that measure to themselves, "just like them."[77]

I have suggested that the general conditions facilitating social mobility, and, thus, the departure of newcomers from the milieu of disreputable poverty, are rendered ineffective by the demoralizing encounter with a new contingent of ethnic or regional poor. Thereafter, though the conditions normally favoring social mobility persist, they are dampened by the pauperization of the remnant ethnic stock.

Conclusion

The disreputable poor are an immobilized segment of society located at a point in the social structure where poverty intersects with illicit pursuits. They are, in the evocative words of Charles Brace, "the dangerous classes" who live in "regions of squalid want and wicked woe."[78] This stratum is replenished only rarely through massive generation, and there is little evidence that anything in the current American political ecomony fosters this sort of pauperization. Still, the tradition of disreputable poverty persists, partly because the legacy of the pauperized Irish immigrants has been continued in some measure by the fractional selection of subsequent immigrants, and partly because the internal situation of disreputable poverty conspires toward that end. Additionally, however, it persists for a reason that I have hardly touched in this essay: it persists because the other main carrier of the tradition of disreputable poverty in America has only now begun to mobilize, and, thus, to undo the effects of its enduring pauperization. When the Negro mobilization has run its course, and if no other massive pauperization occurs, the tradition of disreputable poverty will have used up its main capital and be reduced to squandering the interest drawn from fractional selection and its own internal situation—a fitting fate for so improvident a tradition.

[76] See S. M. Lipset, "Working-Class Authoritarianism," in *Political Man,* Garden City, N.Y.: Doubleday, 1960, Ch. 4.

[77] The viciousness and bigotry with which the previous ethnic cohort treats newcomers is not just a consequence of their higher levels of provincialism and prejudice; what we regard as residential and occupational desegregation is to ethnic remnants a visible social indication of pauperization.

[78] Bremner, *op. cit.,* p. 6.

JOSEPH R. GUSFIELD

Status Conflicts and the Changing Ideologies of the American Temperance Movement

Studies of American social movements have devoted most attention to organized attempts to improve or maintain the economic or political position of specific parts of the social structure. The temperance movement, however, has often seemed on the periphery of major political events. Despite its 130-year record of vitality and significance, and despite the achievement of a Constitutional amendment, the temperance movement has been little studied by American scholars (26, 29). Not clearly related to economic or political aims of classes in the economy, it has been difficult to subsume under the traditional views of political life.

Recently, Richard Hofstadter has proposed a useful distinction between "interest politics" and "status politics" (21, p. 43 ff.). Groups which use political agencies to achieve concrete economic aims are engaged in "interest politics." Such interest-oriented activities have formed the bulk of historical analyses in the United States. Sometimes, however, movements arise which display no clear-cut economic goals. The adherents are concerned with improving or maintaining their deference or prestige in the society. Such movements are likely to pursue symbolic goals, not readily explainable by a theory of group interests. The economic position of the adherents is not touched by the movement. At stake is the place of the group in the status order, in the distribution of honor or prestige.

This chapter is based upon the author's Middle Class Reform: A Study in the American Temperance Movement (*a monograph*). *The project was partially supported by a Summer Faculty Fellowship granted by the University of Illinois Graduate Research Board.*

Source: Joseph R. Gusfield, "Status Conflicts and the Changing Ideologies of the American Temperance Movement," pp. 101–118 in David J. Pittman and Charles R. Snyder (eds.), *Society, Culture and Drinking Patterns* (New York: John Wiley & Sons, Inc., Publishers, 1962). Copyright © 1962 by John Wiley & Sons, Inc., Publishers. Reprinted by permission of John Wiley & Sons, Inc.

The American temperance movement may best be understood as an example of a status movement. Through its social base and through its central concern, drinking, the movement has been linked to major distinctions in the American status order. Both as a means to consolidate new status and as a means to defend positions now threatened, the temperance movement has reflected status struggles of the nineteenth and twentieth centuries. As these changed, the commanding doctrines and images of the movement and its ideological structure have correspondingly changed.

Temperance and the American Middle Class

The Status Significance of Alcohol Consumption

Organized efforts to control and limit drinking or the sale of alcoholic beverages have been persistent in the United States since the early nineteenth century. Although alcohol has not been the only item of consumption with which reformers have been concerned, it has been the one most provocative of controversy. The prohibition of narcotics has met little organized opposition. The prohibition of cigarettes, coffee, or cola beverages has not aroused a strong or vibrant movement. Why has alcohol been so significant an issue?

Drinking (we use this word to include alcoholic consumption, including liquors, wines, beer, and hard cider) performs several functions at an individual and societal level. We shall focus our attention on its use as a symbol of status in American life. The use, or the abstinence from, alcohol has appeared in American life as one means for the validation of the social position of its users or non-users. In prescribed forms or in conspicuous nonconsumption, it is one of the ways by which people indicate to others the "place" they hold in the status order. Proper drinking habits are one of the necessary behavior patterns for maintaining membership in specific status-bearing groups.

In American society, drinking is often one important sign which differentiates age groups and sexes. In many groups, the young man symbolizes his entry into adulthood by being permitted to use alcohol. One of the legal privileges of adulthood in American communities is that of buying liquor in taverns. Although there has been much change, the American male still defines the use and abuse of alcohol as a male privilege, a symbol of his power and prestige when compared to the female. The disapproval of female drunkenness is greater than the disapproval of male drunkenness.

The kinds of beverages used, the amount and frequency of drinking and the permissiveness shown toward insobriety vary among human cultures (23). Recent studies of American life (many of which are summarized or presented in this volume) have examined the drinking patterns of ethnic groups and social classes. Similar variation has been found. An example of this variation is the finding that upper socio-economic groups are more permissive in their acceptance of drinking than are the lower middle classes (1, 10, 33).

Alcohol consumption has often appeared as a negative status symbol in American life. Sobriety and abstinence have often been part of the style of

life necessary for members of the middle class. The opposite has often been
seen as the mark of lower class life. Drinking has been part of the negative
reference group—the group whose behavior patterns are to be avoided (28).
Whatever the rejected behavior is, the fact that it is associated with negative
reference models heightens the avoidance of it and makes it a fit symbol of
status. It becomes a clearer sign of membership in one group and of exclusion
from the other. We can see an example of this in religious sects which have
split off from some parent church. Frequently, such sects enjoin areas of
behavior which have become associated with the parent. Prohibitions against
dancing, gambling, wearing of ties, drinking, or engaging in sports serve to
distinguish the life style of the sect from that of the parent (14, 17, 32).

Temperance and Middle Class Ethics

While most symbols of group differentiation have some moral connotation, temperance has carried a heavy load of ethical content. Its role as a
status symbol has been especially important because it has been related to
styles of ethical behavior obligatory in the value system of American middle
classes of the nineteenth century. A moral quality has adhered to abstinence
and sobriety. One of the early temperance tracts (35) put it this way:

> The Holy Spirit will not visit, much less will He dwell with him who is under
> the polluting, debasing effects of intoxicating drink. The state of heart and
> mind which this occasions is to Him loathsome and an abomination.

In the complex of values which has characterized the American middle
classes, self-mastery, industry, thrift, and moral conduct have been signs of
attainment of prized character traits. Adherence to self-denial has been
viewed as a necessary step to the achievement of social and economic success.
Recreation, sermonized a Protestant minister of the 1850's, makes us fit for
the work of the world. Amusement is pleasure for its own sake and is rejected
because it has no utility for the economic and industrial life (9). Drunkenness and indulgence are signs of the value-orientation of the person and
hence possess status meaning.

The ethic which supported temperance and the temperance movement
was associated with the rise to dominance of the middle classes in American
life. Temperance became obligatory behavior for all who sought to operate
within the major social institutions. If sobriety in all areas of life is demanded
by family, employer, and friend, then the young man should at least preserve
his reputation if he wishes to "strive and succeed." The character valued by
a dominant class is supported by the rewards which it obtains and the punishment which its presence entails.

As social classes rise and fall, as new classes emerge and contend for
power and status, the status value of styles of life are called into question.
Because it has been a significant status symbol, drinking has been an issue
through which status struggles have been manifested. As the fortunes and
the honor of the old middle class have risen and fallen, the temperance
movement has shifted and changed its characteristics.

Temperance: Federalist Aristocracy and Jacksonian Common Man

In postcolonial America political and social power were largely in the hands of an aristocracy of wealth, based on the commercial capitalism of the East and the semi-feudal plantations of the South. American social structure was deeply and rigidly divided into discrete classes. " . . . Democracy was new; men were still described as gentlemen and simplemen . . . disparities of rank were still sustained by those of property" (13, p. v). As this social system gave way to equalitarian attack, the temperance movement emerged. At first, it was an attempt to control the new upsurge of democracy by defenders of the old order. Later it changed into an expression of the growing and now dominant middle classes in their efforts to reform and control their communities.

Drinking in Colonial America

In the colonial period, drinking took place within a social system in which it was limited and controlled. Drunkenness occurred and was punished, but it was seldom frequent or widespread. Taverns were licensed, less to reform the habits of customers than to regulate inns for the benefit of the traveler. Beers and wines were often used with meals and innkeepers were respected members of the community. The moderate use of alcohol was approved and the tavern was one of the major social centers. Even though drunkenness increased with the development of towns in the eighteenth century, conditions were well confined within the boundaries of propriety (26).

The Break-up of the Old Order

The appearance of a "drinking problem" was symptomatic of the breakdown in the system of social controls which had characterized colonial America. After the Revolution, the United States entered a period in which the small farmer and the artisan pressed for a greater degree of participation in the affairs of the nation. Clearly, the old order of status and political power based on wealth and breeding was under attack. This change in the social atmosphere was paralleled by a decline in religious devotion and a great upsurge in drinking. During the late eighteenth century, religious controls were less effective as instruments of social control over the farmer and the townsman. Drinking was far more common and drunkenness more acceptable. Apparently the experience of camp and battlefield had been carried over into civilian life.

In New England, the political leadership of the aristocracy of wealth and the moral leadership of the established churches worked hand in hand. A threat to one was also a threat to the other. Both the clergy and the judiciary were viewed as stabilizing influences in society. Coming in a period of political conflict, the increase in drinking and in religious infidelity had a special meaning for those who were committed to the old order.

The Temperance Movement Before 1840: Outer-Directed Reform

In its earliest phase, from the late eighteenth century to about 1840, the temperance movement was dominated by the effort of the old order to maintain the status of the New England aristocracy through reform of the now advancing "common man." In the programs of the earliest known local temperance organization, the reform of the employee by the employer is given an important position (11). The Litchfield, Connecticut, organization in 1789 pledged discontinuance of distilled spirits for both members and their employees (26). The Moreau, New York, Temperance Society (founded in 1808), made the increased efficiency of labor the central point in its argument for limited drinking (24, 26).

While both of these organizations proved to have a short life, they revealed the tone of the more stable associations which developed later. These were political Federalist and religious orthodox Calvinist in composition. In their doctrines and principles they expressed fear of the common man as an underlying source of concern with drinking. In their efforts at reform they were oriented to reforming others—the classes below them and outside the movement. While they included themselves, their major orientation was outer-directed.

This is seen in the career of the Reverend Lyman Beecher, the leading voice of the early temperance movement, as well as the leader of Neo-orthodoxy in New England. In religion, he inherited the leadership of the moral regeneration movement among the New England Calvinists. In politics he was a staunch Federalist. It was Beecher who headed the attack on republicanism and infidelity. In 1811 he surprised the faithful by a demand for prohibitions against ministerial drinking. In 1813 he was responsible for the development of the Connecticut Society for the Reformation of Morals. In a speech at Yale College in 1812, he revealed the relationship between Federalism, orthodox religion, and temperance:

> Our institutions, civil and religious, have outlived that domestic discipline and official vigilance in magistrates which rendered obedience easy and habitual. The laws are now beginning to operate extensively on necks unaccustomed to the yoke, and when they shall become irksome to the majority, their execution will become impracticable. . . . To this situation we are already reduced in some districts of the land. Drunkards reel through the streets day after day . . . with entire impunity. Profane swearing is heard . . . (2, Vol. 1, pp. 255–256).

During the 1820's and the early 1830's the temperance movement developed as a well-organized force. Its prevalent tone was anti-Jacksonian and its officers generally men of wealth, prominence, and Federalist persuasion. This was true of the Massachusetts Society for the Suppression of Intemperance, founded in 1813. It was also true of the early period of the first temperance association (1826), the American Temperance Society. Congregational and Presbyterian ministers formed a very large portion of the leadership. The same religions predominated among the secular leadership. New England, and especially eastern Massachusetts, was the major source of members of the executive community (4, 6). In its use of persuasive materials, the temperance movement made Beecher's *Six Sermons on Intemperance* the leading statement of the temperance cause. These sermons, written in 1826, presented the same tone of a defense of the old order already exemplified above. Despite the fact that the Methodists had strongly endorsed temperance positions, they had almost no representation in the organized movement during this period. In western Massachusetts, where the Methodists were strong, they were also fiercely pro-Jackson. The dividing lines, it is clear, were those of class and status.

The Entry of the Common Man: Self-Directed Reform

As aristocratic dominance gave way, so did the power of the orthodox churches. Religion was not shoved aside in a wave of equalitarian secularism, somewhat as the French Revolution developed anticlericalism. Instead, evangelical and revivalistic religions emerged as new sources of social control and as effective agencies in promoting the temperance ethic. The Methodists had condemned the sale of liquor as early as John Wesley's visit to the United States in the late eighteenth century. Frontier communities depended on the church as a major source of order and morality. The revivalism of the Great Awakening in 1815 and the many similar events afterwards were partly responsible for the spread of temperance attitudes among the mass of middle- and lower-class citizens. Their appearance in the organized temperance movement changed its character, doctrines, and composition.

The loss of control by the "rich, the well-born and the able" (26, p. 92) is evident in the appearance of new movements, tactics, and organizations. These newer aspects of the temperance movement made an appeal to the average man through emotional and dramatic means. Unlike the earlier movement, they were usually led by secular persons.

Within the temperance movement of the 1830's the chief issues were those of the scope and the method of temperance. New demands had arisen for a more direct political attack on the sale of liquor. Demands had emerged for a position of total abstinence rather than the previous positions of limited and moderate drinking. The social basis of the abstinence issue is suggested by the heavier strength of total abstinence supporters in the West than in the East. Endorsement of total abstinence lost wealthy supporters in New York State. Two changes occurred to the movement in this period: It became more extremist as it became more equalitarian, and it was more directly drawn into political controversies.

The increased extremism of the movement may be due to the fact that it was increasingly oriented toward the same group that constituted its membership. It was more and more self-oriented, seeking to develop and maintain the reform of its membership and the social classes in which they were affiliated. By 1840, the development of temperance as a sign of religious and social acceptance had been accomplished. The new temperance organizations made their appeal to reformed drunkards, to artisans, and to a social segment with experience in the revivalistic meetings of the time. Temperance programs were conducted with the style and the techniques of Methodist, Baptist, and non-orthodox Presbyterian camp meetings. Emphasis in meetings was on the confession, the pledge, and the flamboyant oratory of a secular leadership, often composed of reformed drunkards. Often, the temperance organization also functioned as insurance society and lodge for the city or town workers. Such groups had a popularity which the more staid and conservative organizations could not capture. To the vivid appeals of the newer associations there were added the highly emotional and dramatic qualities of the temperance story, such as *Ten Nights in a Barroom* or *The Drunkard*.

Abstinence was thus becoming a potent sign of middle-class status, distinguishing the abstainer from the lower levels of the ne'er-do-wells, the unambitious and the irreligious. Abstinence displayed one's religious adherence and showed that the abstainer had the character which both sought and merited the fruits of ambition. Temperance fiction repeatedly told a story in which the fruit of the vine is laziness, poverty and disgrace. The convert to abstinence achieves prosperity through his industriousness. In L. M. Sargent's *Wild Dick and Good Little Robin* we find the typical denouement:

> Richard (having reformed) continued to grow in favor with God and man. He gave Farmer Little complete satisfaction by his obedience, industry and sobriety. He was permitted to cultivate a small patch of ground, on his own account . . . (34, p. 33).

Two other social conflicts contributed to the new context of the temperance movement. The first of these was the clash between native and immigrant which emerged during the 1840's and 1850's. Immigrants from Ireland and Germany were heavy additions to the American labor force in this period. There was little institutionalized opposition to drinking among either the Irish or the Germans. Catholic or Lutheran, they brought a non-Calvinist culture into puritan America. Generally at the bottom of the American social and economic scale, they enhanced the negative reference of alcohol consumption (19). One important source of the Know-Nothing vote was in temperance adherents. The area and period of greatest legislative triumphs for the temperance movement was also the area and period of greatest Know-Nothing dominance (3, 18).

The second social conflict united classes in the North against the South. By 1840 the struggle between Federalist and Republican was over. Early in its career temperance had found political allies in the struggles for religious reforms, such as the Sabbatarian movement and the promotion of foreign missions. After 1840 it was part of the complex of antislavery, nativism, and political Republicanism. Both the prairies and the East were attracted to temperance. So strong was the alliance between Abolition and temperance that the temperance movement was unable to develop in the South. Despite a promising beginning in the 1820's the South remained virtually closed to temperance organizations until after 1900.

The life of Neal Dow, temperance leader and founder of the Maine prohibition law, illustrates the complex of alliances which came to provide the foundations of the temperance movement before the Civil War. He was intensely anti-Jackson in the 1820's. In 1932 he found a place in the nativist anti-Masonry movement. In 1848 he became a Free Soiler and in 1856 staunchly supported the new Republican ticket. At all times he was a devout adherent of the antislavery cause. His political life expresses the changing national issues manifested in the temperance movement (12).

By the outbreak of the Civil War, temperance was dominant in the moral code of American drinking. The middle class had come to supremacy in American values and politics. This class consisted of the small retailer, the independent farmer, the local professional and the owner of the small factory. During much of the nineteenth century, American education, politics, religion, economic virtues, and social movements reflected the characteristic perspectives of this class. In experience they were rural; in religion they were Protestant. Whether they lived in small town, city or farm their background reflected the virtues of agricultural life. Common experiences in a world of economic expansion based on individual mastery supported a value system. Industry, thrift, self-discipline, foresight, and sobriety were clearly understood to be the virtues of the good and the successful.

Temperance: The Unity of Progressivism

The temperance movement before the Civil War had been a movement to reform the middle classes. From the post-Civil War period to about 1900, two streams are found in temperance: an ameliorative movement to convert the urban lower class to the virtues of American middle-class life and a movement against the sophisticated easterner and the urban upper classes. Each stream was related to larger movements in American politics. Dual streams of urban Progressivism and rural Populism coursed through the riverbeds of temperance.

Progressive Social Christianity: Response to the Urban Challenge

The bundle of social problems wrapped up in the terms urbanization and industrialization took form in the last 25 years of the nineteenth century. In the wake of an industrial and immigrant proletariat, many reform movements emerged, attempting to reconcile the realities of the city with the ideals of middle class small town society. Religion was one major source of the impulse to improve man's lot and to enable him to reach perfection, or the closest to perfection—middle-class respectability and success.

Henry May (27) has distinguished three forms of the movement called Social Christianity: (*a*) a conservative form, accepting the principle of a laissez-faire individualism in economic affairs but seekng to soften its harsher consequences through individualistic, voluntary, and philanthropic means; (*b*) a Progressive Christianity, searching to improve the form of present institutions but accepting the general outlines of the political and economic order; (*c*) a radical Christianity which rejected the capitalist framework and sought to fashion a new order. All three forms are discoverable in the temperance movement of this period, often in the same organization. Of the three forms, however, it was the Progressivist which exerted the most influence. The Social Gospel, an essentially Progressivist movement, had its source in the educated and pious middle classes, not in the ranks of the urban disinherited or the rural disaffetced.

The activities of the Woman's Christian Temperance Union can be used to illustrate the reformist and Progressivist temper during the 1880's and 1890's. Its actions manifested the concerns of a dominant social group for the urban problems arising in an industrial society.

One response of this temperance organization was an orientation which viewed temperance as a solution to the problems of the urban worker. As in the early period of temperance history, the movement was not addressed to its members or to their social groups. Instead it was addressed to the outsider, the urban lower classes. Committees existed to carry the temperance message to miners, railroad men, lumbermen, and to the newly arrived immigrants. The object of reform is in the status level below the membership. To the workingman the message was clear: sober workers are the answer to problems of mass poverty. Abstinence is the route to success and acceptance in the middle class. An assimilationist solution is offered: embrace the character traits of the middle class. The use of abstinence as a symbol and a price is central to this appeal.

A second response to the W.C.T.U. was support of movements aimed at amelioration of the inequities suffered by the urban poor. The "temptations" of the working girl in the city, the intemperance of the working classes, the effort to reform prison life, the fight for limits on child labor—all these were objects of W.C.T.U. support. Despite their view of temperance as a solution to problems of the business cycle, the W.C.T.U. showed great sympathy with the struggles of labor during the 1890's. They applauded the Supreme Court decisions favoring a right to strike and chided employers to refrain from "kindling the spirit of animosity among those struggling under the iron heel of oppression" (36, p. 447).

The Progressivist motif in the temperance movement was not the ideology of a group under threat of the deprivation of power or status. They did not fear the underprivileged. They could afford a reformist and ameliorative spirit. While an aggressive nativist strain certainly appears in early W.C.T.U. documents (the 1870's), during the 1880's and 1890's the dominant attitude toward the immigrant was that of an effort to Americanize and "Christianize" the stranger. In the descriptions of immigrants and in the work of W.C.T.U. committees emphasis is placed on missionizing rather than on rejection. Despite the existence of an intensive and aggressive nativist movement in the United States during the 1890's, the W.C.T.U. formed no linkage with any organized aggressive nativist groups. As in its temperance ideology, it looked downward at the urban poor and upward to their ascendance into the middle class under the sponsorship of the native, rural Protestant.

Temperance and Populism

The Populist strain in the temperance movement was a decidedly different motivational force from that of Progressivism. Nineteenth century Populism was the political movement of the social segment, the American farmer, under strong threat of loss of power, status, and income. It did not seek to uplift the downtrodden. Its adherents were one form of the downtrodden. Temperance played a role within the movement. It was manifested in the development and growth of the Prohibitionist party and in the protemperance positions of such Populist organizations as the Grangers, the Greenbackers, the Non-Partisan League and the People's party, in its earlier stage.

The affinity between Populism and temperance was more historical than meaningful and logical. Agrarian radicalism was rife in the areas in which temperance had become dominant. The roots of the radicalism lay in the nature of crops and in the economic relationships between farmer, small town, and city. Temperance came along for the ride. Nevertheless, one stream of the temperance movement was accordingly couched in the language and in the perspective of the Populists. In their effort to gain adherents, each appealed to the aims of the other.

The Prohibitionist party platforms of the 1870's and 1880's are one source of evidence for a Populist stream in the temperance movement. Along with prohibition, female suffrage, and an antipolygamy amendment, these platforms recommended such Populist items as the graduated income tax, direct election of senators, abolition of stock exchanges, and governmental control of railroads (7). The Prohibitionist party found its strongest support in the areas of Populist sympathies, in the midwestern states of Iowa, Kansas, Nebraska, Indiana, and North Dakota.

Where Progressivists aimed at converting sinners, the Populists aimed at controlling power. Prohibition was congruent with the political emphasis of the Populists. Further, the perspective of the Populist saw big business as arch-villain. Involved in the opposition to Eastern financial and industrial capitalism, the Populist was quick to emphasize the liquor industry as the source of intemperance. While all wings of the temperance movement opposed the sale of liquor, the Prohibitionist party made this the central plank. The title of the collected addresses of the Prohibitionist orator, John B. Finch, suggests the Populist strain in temperance. It was called *The People versus the Liquor Traffic.*

The relation of temperance to Populism further enhanced the antiurban and nativistic strains in temperance circles. Among the agrarian circles, where temperance was a widely held norm. Populism and temperance formed a single unit. One delegate to the People's party convention of 1892 remarked that a "logical Populist" was one who had been first a Granger, then a Greenbacker, then a Prohibitionist, and then a Populist (20, p. 305). The agrarianism of the Populist was one important source of temperance strength and represented a fear of urban life in contrast to the urban reformism of the W.C.T.U.

The Unity of the Temperance Movement

There were decided limits to the influence of the Populist spirit in the temperance movement of the nineteenth century. Temperance was only one string on the Populist fiddle and Populism only one stop on the temperance flute. When the People's party drew up their platform of 1892, they refused to endorse prohibition. The fear of antagonizing the German vote was too strong. Although Frances Willard, then president of the W.C.T.U., chaired that convention and was a leading spokesman of the Populists, she was unable to enlist the state W.C.T.U. organization to support them. These movements touched and influenced each other. They did not absorb each other.

It is the breadth of the temperance movement in the late nineteenth century which is so impressive. Almost every progressive, radical, or conservative movement had some alliance with it. Populists and Progressives, labor and farmer, urban and rural, male and female, Christian and secularist had for some reason or opportunity to be an adherent or a sympathizer in the temperance movement. To belong to one was not to be disloyal to the other. The overlapping of conservative, progressive, and radical is the outstanding quality of the movement in this period of history.

Nowhere can the unifying character of the temperance movement be better observed than in the career of the famous National W.C.T.U. president, Frances Willard. She was one of those Reformers with a capital "R" who fill the pages of nineteenth century American history. Her motto might well have been, "Nothing new shall be alien unto me." She threw herself into the suffrage movement, the dress reform crusade, the spread of cremation, the vegetarian cause, the kindergarten campaigns, and a multitude of other reform interests. After 1890 she added Populism, Fabianism and Christian Socialism to her major concerns. Sparking the campaign for equal rights for women, she learned to ride a bicycle in order to popularize the freer and healthier costume which permitted this form of exercise. Willard attempted to unite the C.W.T.U., the Populist, and the Prohibitionist party. She used her influence to throw W.C.T.U. support behind female suffrage and the labor movement.

The attempt of Frances Willard to convert a humanitarian, middle-class organization into an arm of political and economic radicalism was not successful. Yet the fact that she was able to forge links of understanding and aid between conservative and radical social Christianity, between urban and rural interests, and between the needs and aims of immigrant labor and native middle class demonstrates the unifying impact of the temperance movement in its Progressive phase. While church circles condemned the strikes of the 1890's, the W.C.T.U. defended the rights of labor unions. When Populism was viewed as a political terror by respectable members of the middle class, at least the W.C.T.U. listened to criticism of the social order.

The Polarization of Forces

With the tremendous increase in immigration after 1890, large numbers of Catholics and Jews entered the American population. With the development of industry and the growth of cities, the dominance of the rural, agricultural segments of the society appeared to be waning. As America entered the twentieth century, the bonds of unity were again under great strain. During a 20-year period of relative prosperity, the struggle for status was marked. While the temperance issue had been peripheral to political concerns in the past, in the twentieth century it became a dominant political question. One consequence of this dominance was the decrease in the unifying functions the temperance movement had performed in the past.

The Populist strain in temperance had been aggressively antiurban and antialien. It had seen the goal of the movement to lie in the abolition of the liquor industry. Humanitarian aims of reform and conversation were decidedly secondary concerns. After 1900, this strain in the movement increased and spread to the church-going, middle-class citizens. The humanitarian strain which sparked Progressive Christianity lessened, although it remained as one source of temperance activity.

After 1900, leadership of the temperance movement shifted to the Anti-Saloon League and the Methodist Board of Temperance and Morality. Both of these organizations gave supreme importance to the political aim of state, local and national prohibition. While the W.C.T.U. continued its humanitarian and conversionary activities they were decidedly secondary to its support of prohibition. Thus the movement underwent two radical changes:

In the first place, actions were oriented to a specific concern with temperance legislation. The Protestant churches were mobilized as political pressure groups (29). With the work of the League and the Board, the South became a vital part of the temperance movement, adding to the Populist strain in temperance. Unlike the Prohibitionist party, no alliance between temperance and other organized movements was formed or desired. Temperance became an issue divorced from other political programs and ideologies.

Secondly, the Social Gospel ceased to be a source of temperance sentiment. Despite the fact that the Social Gospel increased its influence in American churches after 1900, in the temperance movement the opposite was the case. Even the movement for female suffrage was less actively sponsored by the W.C.T.U. after 1900 than it had been in earlier years. Within the W.C.T.U., the urban worker is less often viewed as an object of reform and more often approached as a possible voter in the Prohibitionist cause. Work of W.C.T.U. committees indicated decline in general reformist interests.

The segregation of temperance from other movements, at the same time as it became a dominant issue in politics, fostered the polarization of status groups in American life. That segregation was both a manifestation and an enhancing force in pitting the urban, secular, immigrant groups against the rural, Protestant, and native middle classes. As the power of the church member led to victory after victory for prohibition in state and local campaigns, the wets were pushed into greater organization. After the Eighteenth Amendment was passed, the status struggle was in full force. The dominance of the middle-class style of life was symbolized in Prohibition. It became the focal point for the political and social ambitions of American status groups.

The polarization of forces and the central position of the temperance issue helped explain why the temperance movement in the 1920's became linked to aggressive nativism, agrarian defense, and a conservative economic order. The very success of political pressure made the temperance movement wary of change. The prosperity of the 1920's was attributed to Prohibition. The Ku Klux Klan and aggressive nativism were one strong source of temperance support .The humanitarian impulse was still there, as in the W.C.T.U., but it was enfeebled beside the louder voices.

The nomination of Al Smith was the climax. Seldom has there been an

American election in which economic issues were less important. Smith forced the commitments and loyalties of the American public to the status groups ranged against each other. Catholic and Protestant, urban and rural, agriculture and industry, wet and dry—in these dichotomies, the Progressivist strain was lost. The urban, northern middle class, once a strong temperance support, was weakened in the struggle.

Middle Class Decline and Moral Indignation

The Post-Repeal Change in Drinking Habits

Two quotations sum up much of the shift in American drinking habits since the repeal of the Eighteenth Amendment. The first is from the W.C.T.U. journal, *The Union Signal,* and was written in 1889:

> The class least touched by the evil thus far is that which here, as elsewhere in the land, forms its bone and sinew—the self-respecting and self-supporting class whose chief pleasures in life center in and about the home (37, p. 3).

The second quotation is from an interview with a member of the National W.C.T.U. staff in 1953:

> There has been a breakdown in the middle classes. The upper classes have always used liquor. The lower classes have always used liquor. Now the middle class has taken it over. The thing is slopping over from both sides.

After Repeal, total abstinence became less acceptable than it had been before Prohibition. Added to the upsurge of the non-Protestant and secular group was an increased permissiveness toward drinking among the middle classes. The change in drinking norms is itself a reflection of deeper shifts in life styles and social structure. Many observers have called attention to the development of a new segment in the middle class. With the rise of a corporate economy of large-scale organizations, a new middle class of salaried white-collar workers, managerial employees, and professionals has developed. The styles of life of such groups contrast with those of the old middle class of small enterprises, independent farmers, and free professionals. The new middle class is less likely to adhere to old middle class values. In an economy of surplus and in an atmosphere of organizations, mastery over other men supplants mastery over things and over the self as character virtues. Ability to "get along with others," to be tolerant, and to express solidarity are prized to the detriment of the complex of old middle class virtues. As the new class increases in size, a split has occurred within the middle classes between the old and the new sectors.

The cosmopolitanism of the new middle class supports the norms of permissive drinking. Unlike earlier periods, the aspirant to middle class status may now find that abstinence has become a negative symbol. The advocacy of moderate drinking has become widely held among church-going, respectable members of the middle classes in America. As one temperance writer has put it:

Cocktails or Scotch and soda have become a badge of membership in the upper middle class to which every college student aspires (25, p. 864).

The Alienation of the Temperance Movement

One result of the change in middle class drinking habits has been the development of a posture of alienation within the temperance movement. This has arisen as church, school, community, and government have assumed a more hostile attitude toward temperance and toward the temperance adherent.

An area in which the change has been most crucial is that of the church. The Protestant church-goer and the Protestant clergy are less likely today to support a policy of total abstinence than before Repeal. The churches are reluctant to aid temperance organizations, in many cases. Ministers are less willing to preach and teach temperance doctrines. A neutral or moderationist stand has greater acceptance in church circles than it had in the earlier period.

Faced with a hostile environment, the temperance adherent feels ostricized, shunned, and ridiculed even among the circles in which he or she was formerly welcomed. One W.C.T.U. member in a rural town expressed this common sentiment in the following interview excerpt:

> Well, as you have probably learned, this isn't the organization it used to be. It isn't popular you know. The public thinks of us—let's face it—as a bunch of old women, as frowzy fanatics. I've been viewed as queer, as an old fogey for belonging to the W.C.T.U. . . . This attitude was not true thirty years ago.

Temperance and the Middle-Class Status Struggle

In its contemporary form, the temperance movement is embedded in the struggle between old and new segments of the middle classes to enunciate the dominant life styles in America. Temperance has emerged as a symbol of the defense of an old status order against the rise of a new one. The negative reference symbol is no longer the urban underprivileged. The Populist element has widened to include the middle class as well as the upper class as objects of reform and opposition. The linkage between temperance and other movements appears in the complex of social, political, and economic programs expressing the defense of traditionalist values.

The figure now appearing as a central target of both reform effort and righteous disapproval is that of the moderate drinker. This doctrine of moderate drinking is most likely to be found in the upper-middle-class circles where temperance was formerly accepted. The resentment and indignation of the temperance movement has been directed toward this group. A A.C.T.U. journal editorial presents a typical attitude:

> Once the drinker and the drunkard were frowned upon. One who was drinking was not welcome at a party; he was not entrusted with an office in his or her church. . . . Drinking has now become so prevalent that one who would cry out against it is regarded as a fanatic. Even the preacher who dares to speak out boldly is sometimes regarded as exceedingly narrow and

such narrowness would make that preacher unacceptable to some churches (38, p. 9).

In editorials, articles, and fiction, temperance organizations reflect the belief that total abstinence is now a negative reference symbol among the upper-middle classes. The argument of social pressure—everybody drinks and drinking is socially necessary—is constantly attacked in temperance literature. The context of the drinker is now set in respectable, church-going, middle-class circles. The conflict is posed as one between moderate drinkers as prestige figures and the old-fashioned total abstainer. In one fiction story in the W.C.T.U. journal, the heroine, Jane, reveres her "old-fashioned Christian grandmother." Jane's mother ridicules the daughter's temperance pledge as prudishness and as a hindrance to her social position (39).

This defection of the upper-middle class from the temperance movement is further indicated by shifts in the social composition of local leaders in the W.C.T.U. In a previous study (15) we have shown that wives with husbands in upper-middle class and upper class occupations are less often found in local officer positions in the W.C.T.U. since Repeal than they were in the previous periods. The local professional and the businessman is less likely to support temperance today than he was in an earlier era.

The Fundamentalist Response

As temperance is a symbol of the status conflict between old and new middle classes, it is embedded in a general defense of traditional values. This more general clash is a source of temperance enthusiasm and a possible area for alliances between the temperance movement and other organizations.

We refer to this more generalized defense movement as the "fundamentalist response." It involves an intense and positive affirmation of traditional values and an intense rejection of values associated with modernism (30, 31). Forces of science, secularism, urbanization, and political change are viewed as detrimental to the value system embodied in traditional nineteenth century ideals. The clash is then defined as that of old against new.

The prime motive for this general movement is indignation at lost status —the decline in power and prestige attendant upon transitions in the American economy, government, and social structure. As a general movement it is identified as one element in right-wing conservatism—fundamentalist in religion, nativist in domestic issues, nationalist in foreign policy, and right-wing in politics.

Evidence for sentiments of fundamentalism appear in shifting concerns of the W.C.T.U., in committee activities, toward greater emphasis on the re-establishment of religious ritual in families, in traditionalist systems of character training for children, in a rejection of past internationalist foreign policy positions and in the espousal of opposition to the United Nations. In speeches during the 1930's, W.C.T.U. officials displayed a defensive conservatism on political and economic questions.

The central concept in this conservatism is that of "character." We have seen that this was also central in the value system supporting temperance. The argument is now set forth that the evils of the present day are the result of the decline in positive supports to the development of adequate character traits. The ills of society are then the consequence of intemperance produced through the decline in religious values:

> A good *old-fashioned* revival would greatly correct what ails us by getting people out of such things as saloons, race-tracks and gambling places and into the churches. People have changed, not God. . . . More parents than children are delinquent. Religion, in terms of sincerity, weekly church-going and grace before meals is the best form of juvenile protection (8).

This form of middle-class conservatism is not based on direct economic interest. In religion and politics, change is rejected where it threatens the status of the old values around which the life style of the old middle class had been organized. It is the decline in importance of these symbols and the values they symbolize which is experienced as deprivation. It is the supplanting symbols which are objects of indignation.

The Dilemma of the Temperance Movement

Efforts to link the temperance movement to extremist forms of neo-Populist indignation have not been successful. There are many instances of the existence of such sentiments in temperance adherents. Statements of officers on political issues, testimony before congressional committees, and interviews reveal a strain of aggressive nativism, of right-wing political positions, and of nationalistic xenophobia. During the nineteenth century the temperance movement gained much zeal and enthusiastic support from the linkage to major social movements in other spheres. The possibility does exist today of moving the temperance effort even closer to the fundamentalist response. In general, temperance organizations have not done so. They have sought to temper neo-Populism with the sweeter waters of a humanitarian Progressivism. The dilemma of the movement lies in the difficulties this entails in the current society.

The problem of current temperance ideology has been sketched in the section above. That problem arises from the changed status of total abstinence as a symbol of social position. Drinking is more acceptable within middle-class circles than it was in earlier periods. This change has converted temperance adherence into a rejected and minority position in American life. Especially significant both for prestige and for organizational effectiveness, this change has undermined the role of the churches and the schools as active agents in the training and mobilization of temperance support. The temperance movement can no longer depend on school, church, and family to produce a generation of adherents and sympathizers.

The issue is thus posed as one of choice between alternative social bases. Sentiments supporting temperance are an element in the neo-Populist and aggressive extremism of some forces in the fundamentalist response. However, this movement, with its xenophobia, nativism, and ultraconservative politics, is a minority position unacceptable within the mainstream of contemporary middle-class respectability. "Somewhere along the way the Populist-Progressive tradition has become sour, become ill-liberal and ill-tempered" (22, p. 19). The churches will no longer support the polarization of social forces which they were willing to support in the prohibition conflict of the early twentieth century. To secure this social base of prestige the temperance movement finds it necessary to link its ideology to a humanitarian progressivism, emphasizing the prevention of chronic alcoholism, as well as subsidiary concerns such as juvenile delinquency and drug addiction. Political and social issues beyond this narrowed approach run the risk of alienating the movement by identifying it with the social base of the extremist, the "right-wing radical."

The sources of zeal and enthusisam lie in the sentiments of indignation nourished by loss of old middle-class status. The sources of prestige and acceptance lie in the middle-class groups now heavily exposed to doctrines of moderation in drinking and less moved by the fundamentalist response. To win support here the movement must blunt the edges of sharper conflicts, raging around the status split in the middle classes. Concern with the chronic alcoholic and other popular social problems may greatly change the character of the movement.

In the past the temperance movement has been an attack upon immorality. For the old middle class in American life, drinking has been pre-eminently a moral issue and a status divider. It was a threat to the character and values which they prized. Abstinence was a ticket of admission into respectability. As the guardians of the dominant values, the old middle class could function as prize specimens of the efficacy of those values. This moral and valuational base is no longer the root of humanitarian sentiment in alcohol problems. When temperance becomes linked to movements of health, then the professionals—the doctors, psychiatrists, sociologists, and other scientific personnel—lay greater claim to a public hearing than can the temperance movement.

A cloud of alienation and rejection hangs over the American temperance movement. Whether to seek its removal or to use a source of organized zeal is the basic dilemma of the contemporary movement. Through much of its history the temperance movement has remained a remarkably diffuse movement. It has been open to adherents of many other organized movements, many of which opposed and contradicted each other. While events of the past 40 years have diminished its diffuse quality, the movement has not yet embraced a highly polarized position. In the past it was a meeting point for seemingly diverse elements in the American society. Each successive wave of conflict, defeat, and rejection accentuated the alienation of the movement from its past base in a dominant middle class. During the twentieth century the middle-class ideology of Progressivist welfare for the downtrodden has played less and less of a role. Many forces, however, pull the movement back toward less extreme and more accommodative functions. There are important aspects of the temperance movement which function as mechanisms of social cohesion, stressing common interests and sentiments in American life. The more diffuse the movement, the more it is capable of gaining a less zealous but higher status base, closer to centers of institutional control. It is when social movements are ideologically closed to all but the most deeply committed that they most accentuate the schisms and conflicts of the society.

References

1. Bacon, Selden D., and Robert Straus, *Drinking in College,* New Haven: Yale University Press, 1953.
2. Beecher, Charles (Ed.), *Autobiography of Lyman Beecher,* New York: Harper and Brothers, 1864.
3. Billington, Ray, *The Protestant Crusade, 1800–1860,* New York: The Mac-Millan Company, 1938.
4. Bodo, J. R., *The Protestant Clergy and Public Issues,* Princeton, N.J.: Princeton University Press, 1954.
5. Bridenbaugh, C., *Cities in the Wilderness,* New York: Ronald Press, 1938.
6. Clark, George, *History of Temperance Reform in Massachusetts, 1813–1883,* Boston: Clarke and Carruth, 1888.
7. Colvin, D. L., *Prohibition in the United States,* New York: George H. Doran Company, 1926.
8. Colvin, Mrs. D. L., Address by the President of the National W.C.T.U., quoted in *The Chicago Daily News,* Sept. 10, 1951.
9. Cuyler, T. L., "Christian Recreation and Unchristian Amusements," sermon delivered at Cooper Institute, New York, Oct. 24, 1858. Reprinted in pamphlet form and contained in the Fahnstock Collection of pre-Civil War pamphlets, Vol. 6, Champaign, Ill.: University of Illinois Library.
10. Dollard, John, "Drinking Mores of the Social Classes," in *Alcohol, Science and Society,* New Haven, Conn.: Journal of Studies on Alcohol, 1945.
11. Dorchester, D., *The Liquor Problem in All Ages,* New York: Phillips and Hunt, 1887.
12. Dow, Neal, *Reminiscences,* Portland, Me.: Express Publishing Company, 1898.
13. Fox, D. R., *The Decline of Aristocracy in the Politics of New York,* New York: Columbia University Press, 1919.
14. Goldschmidt, Walter, "Class Denominationalism in Rural California Churches," *Amer. J. Sociol.,* 49: 348–355, 1944.
15. Gusfield, Joseph R., "Social Structure and Moral Reform: A Study of the Women's Christian Temperance Union," *Amer. J. Sociol.,* 61: 221–232, 1955.
16. ———, "The Problem of Generations in an Organizational Structure," *Social Forces,* 35: 323–330, 1957.
17. Hall, Thomas, *The Religious Background of American Culture,* Boston: Little, Brown and Company, 1940.
18. Handlin, Oscar, *Boston's Immigrants,* Cambridge, Mass.: Harvard University Press, 1941.
19. Hansen, Marcus, *The Immigrant in American History,* Cambridge, Mass.: Harvard University Press, 1940.
20. Haynes, F., *Third Party Movements,* Iowa City: State Historical Society of Iowa, 1916.
21. Hofstadter, R., "The Pseudo-Conservative Revolt," in D. Bell (Ed.), *The New American Right,* New York: Criterion Press, 1955.
22. ———, *The Age of Reform,* New York: Alfred A. Knopf, 1955.
23. Horton, Donald, "The Functions of Alcohol in Primitive Societies," *Quart. J. Stud. Alc.,* 4: 199–319, 1943.
24. Ingraham, W., "The Birth at Moreau of the Temperance Reformation," *Proceedings,* VI, 115–133, New York State Historical Association.
25. King, Albion Roy, "Drinking and College Discipline," *Christian Century,* July 25, 1951, 864–866.
26. Krout, John Allen, *The Origins of Prohibition,* New York: Alfert A. Knopf, 1925.

27. May, Henry, *Protestant Churches and Industrial America,* New York: Harper and Brothers, 1949.
28. Merton, Robert, "Continuities in Reference Group Theory," in Robert Merton, *Social Theory and Social Structure,* Glencoe, Ill.: The Free Press, 1957.
29. Odegard, P., *Pressure Politics,* New York: Columbia University Press, 1928.
30. Parsons, Talcott, "Certain Primary Sources and Patterns of Aggression in the Social Structure of the Western World," *Psychiatry,* 10: 167–182, 1947.
31. ———, "Some Sociological Aspects of Fascist Movements," *Social Forces,* 21: 138–147, 1942–43.
32. Pope, Liston, *Millhands and Preachers,* New Haven, Conn.: Yale University Press, 1943.
33. Riley, John W. Jr., and Charles F. Marden, "The Social Pattern of Alcoholic Drinking," *Quart. J. Stud. Alc.,* 8: 265–273, 1947.
34. Sargent, L. M., "Wild Dick and Good Little Robin," in *Temperance Tales,* Boston: Whipple and Damrell, 1836.
35. *Temperance Manual,* no publisher, 1836.
36. Woman's Christian Temperance Union, *Annual Report,* 1894.
37. ———, *The Union Signal,* May 16, 1889.
38. ———, *The Union Signal,* Feb. 21, 1953.
39. ———, *The Union Signal,* June 3–July 29, 1939.

WALTER D. CONNOR

The Manufacture of Deviance: The Case of the Soviet Purge, 1936-1938

Recent sociological and historical studies of forms of religious deviance (notably witchcraft) endemic in many areas in the sixteenth and seventeenth centuries (Erikson, 1966; Trevor-Roper, 1967; Currie, 1968) illustrate instances in which social control agencies largely shaped and sustained the epidemics of deviance they purportedly strove to suppress. The specific deviant acts they deal with—pacts with the devil, bewitching, and others—are frequently bizarre, and most often the inventions of popular beliefs and of the control agencies themselves. While some of the accused probably did believe themselves to be witches, most of this deviance was manufactured.

This study concerns itself with a modern instance of the manufacture of deviance—the Stalinist purge, the Soviet "Great Terror" of 1936–1938. The lessons derived from it may point to a need to rethink some contemporary ideas about deviance. Centuries, and deep historical, cultural and ideological differences separate the purge from the campaigns against witches and heretics in England, Europe and Puritan Massachusetts; yet important similarities argue the value of examining the purge, its mechanics and outcome, within a comparative framework which includes the earlier anti-deviance campaigns. Each of these campaigns recruited masses of persons to deviant status, the majority of whom were in fact innocent of the acts with which they were charged. And in each, deviance-invention had more or less traumatic effects on the society in which it took place.

The purge has hitherto been of interest mainly to political scientists and historians (Conquest, 1968; Beck and Godin, 1951; Brzezinski, 1956) and to those of its victims who survived to write their memoirs. On the surface, perhaps, it appears too much a political move, too planned and orchestrated, to fit readily into that class of events which may profitably be examined by the

Source: Walter D. Connor, "The Manufacture of Deviance: The Case of the Soviet Purge, 1936–1938," American Sociological Review, 37 (August, 1972), pp. 403–413. Copyright © 1972 by The American Sociological Association. Reprinted by permission.

sociology of deviance. Yet, as sociological attention increasingly encompasses control as something other than simple reaction to deviance, questions about planning and orchestration in detecting and prosecuting deviance are of growing significance. Deviance, as manifested in defining certain acts as deviant, and identifying persons as deviant by connecting them with deviant acts, comes to be seen at least partially an effect of control. However the purge has been viewed in the past, as an example of a case in which control produced deviance on an enormous scale it is a topic worthy of sociological investigation.

More directly, studies of witch-crazes and religious controversies have suggested generalizations about processes of large-scale deviance whose fit to the facts of the purge remains to be tested. As we shall see, the fit is quite good at some points; at others, however, the case of the purge suggests a need for reformulation.

Erikson develops three theoretical themes on the basis of three deviance epidemics in Puritan society—the Antinomian religious controversy, the "invasion" of Massachusetts Bay by the Quakers, and the Salem witchcraft episode. The three themes concern the style or type of deviance characteristic of a community, the volume of deviance a community can recognize, and the way a community handles the problem of the deviants within it—its deployment pattern (1966: 19–29).

The first suggests that "every community . . . has its own characteristic styles of deviant behavior," styles conditioned by the community's emphasis on particular types of values—political, economic, religious etc. Thus, deviance seems to appear "at exactly those points where it is most feared" (see Erikson, 1966: 19–21). The dominant values of the Puritan community were religious: around the orthodoxy they formed, the group's identity was built. Hence, the deviance that appeared was of a religious variety. This proposition can easily be demonstrated in the Soviet case. The U.S.S.R. has been, and is, a politicized society, attaching political relevance to a whole range of behaviors not so regarded in many other nations, placing a high premium on political orthodoxy, and fearing subversion and disloyalty. As such, it has tended to beget political deviance.

The second of these themes, which concerns the volume of deviance, is of greater interest here, since it is one that the purge calls in question. Erikson suggests that "the amount of deviation a community encounters is apt to remain fairly constant over time" (1966: 23). Encountering (perceiving, recognizing) deviance takes place within limits imposed by enforcement capacities. Generally, communities are limited to recognizing the number of deviants that can be handled in jails, hospitals, etc.

> When the community tries to assess the size of its deviant population, then, it is usually measuring the capacity of its own social control apparatus and not the inclinations toward deviance found among its members (1966:25).

To some degree, then, constancy over time in the amount of deviance encountered is a function of stability in the capacity of the social control apparatus. Beyond noting that generally "we invoke emergency measures when the volume of deviance threatens to grow beyond some level we have learned to consider "normal" 1966: 24), Erikson does not discuss factors that might effect change in the capacity of the social control apparatus.

The constancy proposition receives empirical support from Essex County crime statistics during the "Quaker invasion." While the rate of recorded offenses climbed sharply, the number of convicted persons rose scarcely at all during this period.

> A crime wave lashed across Essex County which almost doubled the number of offenses handled by the local court, yet the size of the deviant population itself did not increase to any appreciable degree (1966: 179).

The rise of deviance without a concomitant increase in deviants suggests that during the thirty-year period, other, non-Quaker, non-religious deviants, were displaced from judicial attention and that displacement was a product of Essex County's relatively "fixed" capacities for handling deviants.

From this capsule summary of a complex argument one point emerges clearly: in the period of the "Quaker invasion," a major "crime wave," the number of recognized deviants remained roughly the same as in the period before its onset. Erikson's constancy notion fits the experience of Essex County: as we shall see, it does not fit a modern instance of a "crime wave" on a larger scale—the Soviet purge of 1936–1938. Those years saw the recognition of massive numbers of new deviants, and there is little evidence that the old were displaced.

Critical to any analysis of the handling of "deviance epidemics" is an examination of control systems, their differences, and the impact of these differences on deviance itself. Currie (1968: 28–39) distinguishes two types of control systems—"repressive" and "restrained." He examines the difference between the nature and scale of witch-control activities in Europe under the Inquisition and in England, (where the Inquisition did not exist), and attributes the differences in scope between the English control effort ("witchcraft as racket") and the continental operations ("witchcraft as industry") to differences in the control systems. The Inquisition approximated, in its structure and operations, a repressive control system, whose marks were "invulnerability to restraint from other social institutions," "systematically established extraordinary powers for suppressing deviance and a lack of internal restraints," and "a high degree of structured interest in the apprehension and processing of deviants" (1968: 16). The legal restraints of continental trial procedure (weaker in any case, given the inquisitorial nature of that procedure, than those in English accusatorial proceedings) bound the Inquisitors little, if at all. Torture, indefinite imprisonment and other special powers were at their disposal, and motive for recruiting as many, and as prosperous, witches as possible was supplied by the practice of the Inquisition's confiscating the accused witches' property.

Witchcraft in England assumed very different dimensions, given the English control system's closer approximation of a restrained system, distinguished by accountability and restraint, a lack of extraordinary powers, and a low degree of interest in deviant-apprehension. Procedural safeguards were greater, and the confiscation of witches' property never became the rule (Currie, 1968: 20). The markedly smaller number of witches detected tended, *contra* continental experience, to be drawn from socially marginal populations, rather than the wealthy and important. If processing witches in Europe assumed the face of industrial bureaucracy, in England it had the look of petty entrepreneurship. The control system of Massachusetts Bay, while open to abuses, was for obvious historical and cultural reasons closer to the restrained English system than to the continental Inquisition (1968: 8, n.3), and behaved, within limits, as a restrained system would be predicted to. That the Soviet control system of the purge years approximated the ideal of a repressive system, as we shall argue below, is crucial in explaining why the purge does not fit Erikson's proposition regarding "constancy over time" in the amount of deviance detected.

(Erikson's third theme, concerning "deployment patterns" and their cultural conditioning (1966: 27–29, 185–205), is an attempt to explain aspects of the American experience. Some of the issues raised are, however, relevant to the Soviet case, and shall be considered in the concluding sections.)

The remaining sections of this paper will describe and analyze a single case of "epidemic deviance"—the purge—in an attempt to support the following propositions:

> (1) that the limits on the amount of deviance a society can "afford to recognize" rather than being constant over time are, in fact, quite elastic under certain circumstances, and allow for rapid increase in the number of deviants recognized;
> (2) that the critical circumstance under (1) is the existence of a repressive control system, as exemplified by the Inquisition and the Soviet system in the 1930's (Erikson focuses on a set of cases involving a relatively restrained control system—a focus which precludes examining the behavior of repressive systems.);
> (3) that the elasticity of a repressive control system may be (as in the Soviet case) amplified by a deployment pattern which appears to reduce the costs of recruiting and maintaining a deviant population, through setting up camps rather than prisons, removing deviants to geographically remote areas, and trying to maintain their contribution to the economy through forced labor, all of which allow rapid expansion in the intake of deviants.

Finally, two additional themes run through what is to follow: first, the tendency of the deviant-detection activities of repressive control systems to snowball, almost randomly recruiting deviants, and second, the irrelevance, under certain circumstances, of prior community support, or the lack thereof, for the progress of the purge. As we shall see, even its victims, once in the interrogation phase, often found it in their interest, as they saw it, to cooperate in expanding the purge.

The Victims

Many authors have tried to estimate the scope of the purge, to number its victims. Their figures—admittedly loose and tentative approximations—have one thing in common: they reflect a social upheaval probably unmatched in modern peacetime history.[1]

Since this study is a discussion of sociological questions raised by the purge (and since space constraints preclude it), no lengthy description of the victim population is offered here. Extended treatments of it are available in other sources (Beck and Godin, 1951: 86–170; Conquest, 1968: 276 ff.). For present purposes, it may suffice to note that the victim population was diverse, reflecting many subgroups in Soviet society, and at the same time, special. Beyond the most visible victims—the high party and state officials who appeared in the dock at the Moscow trials—party and state bureaucrats at the provincial and district levels were hard hit. Rank-and-file old Bolsheviks, as well as members of other defunct revolutionary parties, perished in large numbers. Industrial managers, engineers, transport officials and others with resopnsible posts in large organizations contributed to the victim group in numbers greatly disproportionate to their share of the population, as did the Soviet officer corps, from marshals on down. Citizens with relatives abroad, or other foreign contacts (many if not most of them legal, in trade, tourist, or cultural organizations), as well as foreign Communists who had emigrated to the USSR, were arrested in large numbers. Other target groups included relatives of those arrested, and members of Soviet ethnic minorities residing in cities outside their own areas.

While diverse, this population, heavily composed of better-educated urban groups, was less diverse than Soviet society itself. It included in large numbers members of the new Soviet elite, persons whose careers had been made primarily in the years since the revolution. The purge fell less heavily on those at the bottom of Soviet society—the lower working strata, the collective farm peasantry. All victims were, however, united in facing situations of presumed and nonrebuttable guilt after their arrest.

Processing and Confession

Where offenses do not lend themselves easily to proof by eyewitness testimony (as in the witch's pact with the devil, the conspiracies of counterrevolutionaries, and any offense which has not actually been committed), confession must play a major role in establishing guilt. Victims of the Soviet purge were in fact required to confess not only their own guilt, but also the guilt of others, to their interrogators. Confessions were critical to the purge, for many reasons.

First, the Stalin regime encountered a large public relations problem in the purge. The Soviet Union was, by the mid-1930's, held to have left behind the Red terror, the "class justice" of its ealier years. Thus, to admit that a prophylactic purge, and not the uncovering of a vast network of political

[1] Relatively thorough reviews of the available data and discussions of earlier estimates of the number of victims, are presented in two recent sources (Conquest, 1968: 525–535; Swianiewicz, 1965: 25–40). Conquest, for example, estimates that seven million persons were arrested in 1937–1938. Any discussion of these matters here would require many pages; the interested reader is therefore referred to the sources above.

deviants, was taking place would have compromised the Soviet Union too much in the eyes of both enemies and admirers. Confessions at the Moscow trials convinced many foreigners and Soviet citizens that, however implausible, old Bolsheviks were in truth selling out the nation, and that the Soviet Union was indeed infested with active plotters and saboteurs. The accusations were untrue, but given the commitment made to ferreting out deviants, they had to be proven nonetheless. Where evidence cannot be convincing (since it does not exist), confessions may fill the gap.

Second, the success of individual interrogators of the NKVD in extracting confessions indicated their vigilance, and in part guaranteed their own safety. Accusations of insufficient vigilance changed many an interrogator into an accused, while a high "productivity index" was some disproof of leniency. As the purge intensified, the spectacle of interrogators following those they processed to the camps was not uncommon. (see Beck and Godin, 1951: 238; Ginzburg, 1967: 139, 388–390; Weissberg, 1951: 298).

Third, each confessing deviant, in naming his recruiters, and those whom he had recruited to anti-state activity, supplied an important input. The more persons, and the more important the persons, who could thus be detected, the more credible the vigilance and effectiveness of the entire NKVD.

Many accused, reluctant to implicate other innocents, filled their recruit quota with those beyond reach. Experienced prisoners often provided new arrivals with names of the dead or arrested who could be recruited with impunity. But others were convinced that the key to ending the purge, and to their own release, lay in reducing the process to complete absurdity. These sought to drive the purge to its limits by implicating all those in responsible positions still at large. Military officers implicated their whole units, officials denounced everyone in their organizations, academics their colleagues (see Weissberg, 1951:314–317; Beck and Godin, 1951:188, 194–200).

Confessions, of course, were seldom voluntary. They were the product of interrogation, and the speed and fullness of confession depended on the mechanics of the interrogation process. Except in the cases of some special victims such as military and NKVD officers, early in the purge little physical violence seems to have been used on the accused. More often, the first stage of interrogation was to persuade the prisoner that the NKVD already knew everything, that only one's official confession, identification of recruits, and minor details were lacking.[2] In return for cooperation, light sentences were often promised. Persistence in denying guilt lead to threats of heavier sentences or death penalties as well as arrest or exile for relatives still at large.

Those who refused to cooperate, were subjected to the "conveyor"—a lengthy, sleepless interrogation by a succession of well-rested interrogators (see, e.g. Beck and Godin, 1951: 53–54; Weissberg, 1951: 53–54, 238 ff.; Ginzberg, 1967: 83 ff.).

But the conveyor was time-consuming. A speedier, more efficient method of processing was needed. (The amount of time between arrest and formal

---

[2] However, one was often not told what one's offense was. This had to be invented by the accused himself. As the prison culture became more aware of what the interrogators sought, experienced prisoners could often help newcomers with inventing their legends. (See Conquest, 1968: 304–305.)

dispatch to a camp varied. For workers and peasants, whose confessions were expected to be simple, only a few months generally elapsed. Members of the intelligensia typically took longer) (see Beck and Godin, 1951: 75). The "breakthrough" for permission to use systematic beatings and other torture, came in August, 1937 (Conquest, 1968: 307). Thereafter, the purge moved toward its peak.

In essence, then, one became a deviant upon arrest. Practically speaking, one could not prove his innocense.

> [A] person whose work had always been above reproach was undoubtedly covering up counterrevolutionary activities. But should there have been any instance of trouble or any accident in the defendant's place of work, that was proof of his sabotaging activities. If the defendent admitted having observed anything suspicious in the private or professional life of a superior who was also under indictment, he was guilty of a lack of revolutionary alertness. If a woman repudiated her husband once he was arrested, she thereby admitted that she thought him a counterrevolutionary and was therefore guilty for having lived with him. If she did not renounce him, she was guilty of questioning the infallibility of the NKVD. (Lipper, 1951: 38.)

Such guides for behavior interpretation are strikingly similar to those used to detect witches centuries earlier.

> If the accused was found to be in good repute among the populace, he or she was clearly a witch, since witches invariably sought to be highly thought of; if in bad repute, then he or she was also clearly a witch, since no one approves of witches. If the accused was especially regular in worship or morals, it was argued that the worst witches made the greatest show of piety. (Currie, 1968: 15.)

The Vigilance Industry

Explaining the growth and acceleration of the purge involves examining the purge machinery—the Soviet secret police or NKVD—which, in the period that concerns us, amply satisfied Currie's three criteria of repressive control systems.

Invulnerability to Restraint

As a practical matter, the NKVD was invulnerable to all external restraints, save those imposed by the top leadership: essentially, Stalin himself.[3] Beyond this, the NKVD was unrestrained, as the toll of victims among the top Party, government, economic and military leadership shows. By and large, the leadership of other social institutions found cooperation with the NKVD in rooting out deviants in their midst the only course that offered a modicum of safety. Attempts at restraint were *prima facie* evidence of counterrevolutionary or subversive intent.

---

[3] Indeed, in running its course, the purge consumed the two chief purgers—NKVD heads Yagoda and Yezhov.

Extraordinary Powers

The powers granted the NKVD in coping with deviants vastly exceeded the normal Soviet criminal law, substantive and procedural. First, a contamination principle operated, whereby not only the presumptive deviant, but his friends and acquaintances, and *their* friends, might also be arrested on an assumption of, at worst, their complicity and at best, their "lack of vigilance" (see Conquest, 1968: 260, 300). Second, physical beating, while probably used in many criminal interrogations, was not officially sanctioned: after August, 1937, its application to "politicals" received official sanction. Third, the trial mode of political deviants diverged markedly from that of regular criminals: trials *in absentia,* trials by special three-man boards rather than people's courts, the lack of any provisions for a defense—all these gave the NKVD extraordinary processing powers over those marked for removal.

Structured Interests

The Soviet seige mentality of the 1920's and 1930's, coupled with the impact of Stalin's own personality, gave the secret police a large role to play, and conferred a privileged status on its members. As a control institution, the NKVD had interests in maintaining itself and acquiring powers and resources —interest it could promote by detecting (or inventing) growing members of deviants. In this sense, at least, there were positive rewards to be gained.

Yet such a view minimizes the degree to which, in 1937–1938, the NKVD was a mechanism whose motive force Stalin largely supplied. Within this mechanism, individual workers had another sort of interest: sparing themselves from the fate of deviants. Some, of course, pursued promotion, etc., within the NKVD. But it seems doubtful that such rewards offered as much stimulus as enrichment from confiscating witches' property offered the Renaissance inquisitors (Currie, 1968: 21–24).

The NKVD was, simultaneously, both a source and target of the pressures for ever-increasing vigilance, pressures with which early in the purge many officers over-complied, creating the momentum that would characterize it at its peak. Thus, it appears, the terror extended beyond any targets Stalin himself might have seen as "rational." As an organization, the NKVD could not pull back from its activities. While many interrogators may have doubted the deviants' guilt, "they were caught in their own system. It was impossible for them not to arrest a man who had been denounced as an agent of Hitler" (Conquest, 1968–465). Nor could NKVD administrations at the provincial and district level safely restrict their output of arrests: many, indeed, received orders from Moscow specifying "target figures," indicating that so many nameless thousands of wreckers or saboteurs lived in their jurisdictions who should be identified and apprehended (see Petrov and Petrov, 1956: 73; Medvedev, 1971:284).

Opportunities arose for self-aggrandizement by the unscrupulous, who denounced others out of enmity, ambition, or covetousness. Some sought their superior's job, others more room in a crowded communal apartment. For some, denunciations became a quasi-racket. Two men in Kiev denounced over 169 people. A party member in Odessa denounced 230, and another in

Poltava his entire party organization. One industrious denouncer applied for a free vacation, claiming he had spent his strength struggling with the enemy (Conquest, 1969: 280).

Added to these amateurs were the "secret collaborators" of the NKVD, or *seksots*. *Seksots* were both voluntary and involuntary. The voluntary were those who enjoyed the work of denunciation, or felt they were serving the cause. The latter delivered denunciations for fear of their own arrest or in hopes of improving the lot of arrested relatives. These soon found themselves entangled in a system interested only in incriminating information. When none existed, self-interest dictated its manufacture: "the *seksot* who failed to produce information was himself automatically suspect" (Conquest, 1968: 281; see also Beck and Godin, 1951: 164–166).

The Purge in Review

Many questions about the purge are, and will probably remain unanswered. As Dallin and Breslauer (1970: 5) note, both "the purposes and the functions of political terror are many." The latter may be, however, somewhat clearer than the former. The purge's results, at least, are observable. As to the purposes of the purge as a species of political terror, the present author agrees with Dallin and Breslauer that "we can do little more than guess." Purpose, however clear it may have been in Stalin's mind initially, cannot well account for the purge's scale, cannot easily explain its reaching a point at which the "NKVD . . . had files proving that almost every leading official everywhere was a spy" (Conquest, 1968: 316). As the purge developed from an operationally rational desire by Stalin to eliminate all potential sources of opposition and potential support for that opposition, it reached a point where a "spillover of victimization" occurred (see Dallin and Breslauer, 1970: 27–28). Arrests by quota, even when ordered from Moscow, probably partly resulted from NKVD over-compliance, rather than clear political purpose. But arrests by quota, and other elements contributing to the spillover, did reflect the repressive character of the NKVD—a system whose very characteristics made for constant growth in the volume of deviance it encountered. Eventually, the purge reached its limits, but they were the limits characteristic of a repressive, rather than a restrained control system.

> The first substantial question an interrogator asked was "Who are your accomplices?" So from each arrest several other arrests more or less automatically followed. But if this had gone on for a few more months and each new victim named only two or three accomplices, the next wave would have struck at 10 to 15 percent of the population, and soon after that at 30 to 45 percent . . . we can see that the extreme limits had been reached. To have gone on would have been impossible economically, politically—and even physically, in that interrogators, prisons and camps, already grotesquely overloaded, could not have managed it. (See Conquest, 1968: 316–317.)

Though it had reached its limits, the purge did not "collapse under its own weight." It came to an end by a decision which reflected the realities: not a formal decree, but a decision communicated in cues too obvious to be ignored. In a late 1938, selective prosecutions of regional NKVD heads (See Conquest, 1968: 466–467) for "abuse of authority," "unjustified arrest" and similar charges, signalled the change, and were further confirmed by the dismissal of the national NKVD head, Yezhov, in December, 1938. He disappeared in February, 1939. The purge had run its course.

The Elasticity of Limits

The purge, as we have seen, was marked by rapid growth, rather than stability, in the number of deviants detected. That such rapid growth occurred, a product of the repetitive cycle of arrests, confessions and denunciations, does not refute the claim that such processes have limits, nor contravene the observation that societies can afford to recognize only so much deviance: rather, the purge illustrates how far such processes may go, how many can be removed from society before the costs are recognized, the limits reached. The rapid growth indicates an elasticity, rather than constancy, in the amount of deviance that can be afforded over the short term at least.[4]

To return to the issues raised earlier: what factors present in the purge could account for the elasticity of its limits? First, the very nature of repressive control systems involves a strain toward detecting and processing deviants in increasing numbers, including a broadening of the definition of deviance, and the recruitment of even the innocent to the status of "deviants." The concern of the NKVD rank and file for their safety guaranteed their vigilance. At higher levels, the NKVD leadership could well understand that its place in the system depended on continuing combat against the opposition: the more dangerous the opposition, the more secure the place of the secret police, and hence the strain toward exaggerating (and inventing) that opposition (see Brzezinski, 1956: 20–23). In its demand for more and more evidence of political deviation the NKVD was open to exploitation by those who sought job advancement, more living space or other goods through denunciations. The NKVD's mode of operation was supported by the top and bottom of Soviet society: Stalin's suspicion, which gave the initial push, was borne out by the deviance the NKVD uncovered, and encouraged an intensified hunt, while at the bottom *seksots* and racketeering denouncers responded to the atmosphere, supplying more denunciations. Finally, those already arrested, who sensed that the purge could be pushed to its limits and hopefully reversed thereby, contributed still more denunciations.

Of interest is the rapid growth of the purge in the absence of any substantial prior community support for an operation of the scope it was to assume. While the mobilization of previously-weak anti-deviance sentiments

[4] In support of his constancy argument, Erikson reviews data from the "Quaker invasion" (1966: 107–136, 163–181). The Salem witchcraft episode, however, would seem to suggest a certain elasticity (though only suggest, since comparable statistics for the short time-span involved are not available) even in a relatively restrained control system. The Witchcraft hysteria spread, multiplying accusations and filling the jails (*Ibid:* 145–153) until, when it could no longer be afforded, its growth was checked. Whether, during the period, common criminals who might otherwise have inhabited the jails were displaced from judicial attention, one can only speculate.

among the broader public by interested parties may be observed in many types of societies, and millions of Soviet citizens may have come to believe that the victims were, indeed, "enemies of the people" (Medvedev, 1971: 365–367), the purge case seems extreme in this regard. Here we may be dealing with a corollary of those modern social systems in which repressive control can flourish: a radical asymmetry of power, and, by implication, an extremely narrow monopoly on decisions about what constitutes deviance, its proofs, and how society will proceed against it. The idea that societies do not define deviance, but that groups or persons with specific interests and the requisite resources do construct such definitions and make them stick, is not new (Becker, 1963: 15, 17 and ff.; Merton, 1966: 784–785). Characteristic of the Soviet Union was a radical monopoly of such powers—their concentration in the hands of Stalin and a handful close to him. His own personality, rather than the collective interests and apprehensions of the Soviet upper elite (many of whom were purge victims), shaped the purge to a large degree. In such situations, over the short run at least, community sentiment counts little, and leadership decisions more.

Continental witch persecutions likewise seem to have halted only when monarchs or officials who were well-insulated themselves from charges of witchcraft applied restrictions on torture and confiscation of property (Currie, 1968: 22, 24). As Dallin and Breslauer (1970: 83) argue, "terror as an instrument of purposive policy does not erode or wither 'on its own' . . . The decline in its use requires active or passive, explicit or tacit, decision-making."[5] One might add that, as the purge demonstrates, even when the terror launched by a repressive control system *outgrows* purposive policy, its halt still seems to require such decision-making. The purge went beyond any limits community sentiment could have imposed. As Brzezinski (1956: 31), observes, the ability to recruit deviants on the scale of the purge already demonstrates a radical monopoly of power. "The purge is an expression of the regime's power, not an effort to achieve it."

Much like the Inquisition, which shared its characteristics of repressive control, the NKVD created its own opportunities, invented the deviance it was to repress. In a relatively short period, it "recognized" millions of previously-hidden political deviants. The total number of deviants increased, with no evident displacement of non-political deviants.[6] The degree of elasticity in the limits, then, seems strongly related to the nature of the control system: restrained and repressive systems behave differently, with different results. The distinction is critical, and one cannot generalize to the behavior of all control systems by investigating the behavior of one type.

[5] The Puritan control system, in its most extreme crisis—the Salem witch hysteria— wound down due to the incredulousness of the leading men which emerged rapidly as community leaders themselves came to be numbered among the accused. (Erikson, 1966: 149–153). While a decision thus curtailed the terror here as well, it is interesting to note that, in the purge, leading men were among the foremost victims.

[6] In fact, some persons apparently sought definition as non-political deviants (through commission of, and jailing for, minor criminal offenses) in order to preempt identification as "politicals" (see, *e.g.,* Beck and Godin, 1951: 96–97). Residence in a local jail on a nonpolitical charge was one way of sitting out the peak of the purge.

A final factor—the Soviet deployment pattern[7]—seems critical in two ways: first, it amplified the recruitment and containment capabilities of an already repressive control system, and second, it represents an alternative to the model of a relatively fixed-capacity containment system, on which the notion of limits on the recognizable quantity of deviance seems to depend.

The Soviet deployment pattern was one in which some of the problems of expense in controlling and containing deviant populations—recruiting personnel, constructing detention facilities, losing the labor capacities of the confined—all seemed, at least, less pressing than in other systems.

The secret police were, despite (or perhaps because of) the nature of their work, a favored group in Soviet society. The privileges and high salary of an NKVD officer were, for some, enough incentive to minimize recruitment problems. Even before the purge, the NKVD was a large, quasi-military body, with thousands of troops—a pool from which convoy detachments, guards, etc, could be drawn (see Medvedev, 971: 392).

Perhaps more important was the question of "brick and mortar"; for while these are expensive, little of either was used for long-term containment of purge victims. The prisons of the large cities were grotesquely crowded in 1938, cells holding ten times the number for which they had been intended. To construct new stone or brick prisons to hold the millions arrested would, indeed, have been a task awesome enough to create new limits. Such limits were not inherent in the course actually taken: recommissioning disused buildings—churches, monasteries, hotels, etc.—as prisons, and, more important, containing prisoners in camps—wood buildings, barbed wire "walls." Such a solution was less capital-intensive by far than the alternatives. When, as was often the case, a train containing thousands of prisoners ended its eastward journey in a desolate area of Siberia or Central Asia, and the prisoners, under armed guard, constructed most of the camp facilities themselves, considerable short-term savings resulted. It was in such camps that the vast majority of prisoners were held: the simplicity of construction and materials, the ready labor supply guaranteed, for a considerable time, that the containment capacity of the Soviet system was not fixed, but indefinitely expandable. Sending the prisoners to remote, relatively unpopulated areas enabled the regime to avoid the problems that might arise from containing massive numbers of convicts in or near population centers.

Another critical element of the Soviet deployment pattern (and one which distinguishes it from the other historical examples noted here) was convict involvement in forced labor. This is not the place for a full discussion of the forced labor theory,[8] but the opportunities inherent in convict

[7] This term is used here in a somewhat different sense than that employed by Erikson (1966: 27–29). At issue here are the physical, geographical, and economic aspects of deployment.

[8] Essentially, this theory saw the *raison d' être* for the purge in the need to supply cheap labor to arduous and remote industries. It was popular with the prisoners themselves (Beck and Godin, 1951: 225–226), though some raised the obvious objection that recruiting trained bureaucrats, technicians and managers to such unskilled work made no sense (Weissberg, 1951: 292–293). The most comprehensive and sophisticated treatment of the theory (and also of pre-purge forced labor policies in the USSR) is by an economist who himself was a forced laborer. See Swianiewicz, 1965.

labor perhaps contributed to the scope of the purges. The costs of maintaining large numbers in confinement can be reduced by retaining the confined as part of the active labor force. Even in the pre-Soviet period, Russia had a tradition of using convict labor in jobs unattractive to free labor. In the earlier Soviet period, forced labor was used heavily in construction, lumbering, and extractive industries. Such was the fate of purge victims. They were not retired from economic production, nor was their labor "make-work."

This does not mean that it was economically rational. Removing millions of citizens, many highly skilled and educated, from their normal work clearly bespeaks irrationality. But using their labor power may, given deviant recruitment, have been seen as more economical than confining them in prisons (see Medvedev, 1971: 394). In any case, to many the whole enterprise probably appeared rational. In retrospect the purges make little economic sense. The critical break-through in industrialization had been reached by 1935; the extractive industries in remote sections of the country could probably have been maintained by positive incentives; the arrest and disappearance of skilled technicians and managers harmed the economy. Whether all this was understood in the 1930's, we cannot tell. But to some, at least, forced labor in unattractive industries in remote areas seemed a rational way to deploy the millions of deviants arrested in 1936–1938.

Thus, it seems that the idea that all societies experience a relative stability in the number of deviants they encounter, a stability rooted in relatively stable containment and control capacities, needs modifying. As with all single cases, the Soviet experience is, presumably, not to be duplicated completely. But some of its elements may be (or may have been), and thereby deserve consideration when one examines the generalizations about social control activities discussed here. The experience of the purge suggests that the limits on deviant-recruitment vary greatly in elasticity with the type of control system involved, and that they can be broad indeed. It also indicates the sort of economic, physical and geographic circumstances under which repressive control systems can recruit rapidly increasing numbers of deviants to permanent service at the borders of society, without assessing the effects as too expensive to be borne.

Beyond these issues, the purge is of more general interest to students who view deviance through "conflict" or "functionalist" perspectives. Many purge characteristics support a conflict interpretation. The mode of securing confessions and denunciations, the quotas, the size of the enterprise, all point to the importance of the radical disparity in power between rulers and ruled (the latter including most of the elite itself) in the Soviet case. It is hard to argue the validity of a functionalist interpretation, in a strict sense: that the purge showed the Soviet social order generating the deviance it needed to define its boundaries. Neither Soviet society, nor the Soviet elite, needed the purge. The deviance was "generated," but for the most part in a very special sense: it was invented. The victims' crimes were not acts engaged in, *then* defined as deviance: they were acts that had not taken place. The purge, in its general traumatic impact on Soviet life (especially among the military) was, in fact, more evidently dysfunctional in light of the next large challenge the Soviet system would face—the German invasion of 1941. Indeed, as the record of wartime collaboration between some nationalities and the Nazis demonstrates, it had not managed, despite its massive intake, to remove all potential "traitors" from circulation.

Yet, viewed from another angle, the functionalist perspective may be useful. It is arguable, at least, that the purge in fact resulted in a redefinition of Soviet society's behavioral boundaries (though not a necessary one), by making clear to those who remained the degree of political dissent that would be regarded as tolerable (nil), and the degree of personal security one might expect (relatively little) even if one were performing a responsible job to the best of one's abilities. The purge defined boundaries which held to the end of the Stalin era. In retrospect, they seem unnecessary, indeed inimical, to societal integration and the adaptive capabilities of Soviet society; but they were real, and characteristically Soviet. In light of Stalin's radical monopoly of power, one wonders if he, and those close to him did not, at least early in the purge, have some notion that boundary-defining, as well as preemptively crushing potential opposition, was what they were about. Given the (probably permanent) poverty of the historical record here, all one can do is wonder.

References

BECK, F. and W. GODIN (pseuds.)
    1951   Russian Purge and the Extraction of Confession. New York: The Viking Press.
BECKER, HOWARD S.
    1963   Outsiders: Studies in the Sociology of Deviance, New York: Free Press.
BRZEZINSKI, ZBIGNIEW K.
    1956   The Permanent Purge: Politics in Soviet Totalitarianism. Cambridge: Harvard University Press.
BUBER-NEUMANN, MARGARETE
    1950   Under Two Dictators. New York: Dodd, Mead.
CONQUEST, ROBERT
    1968   The Great Terror: Stalin's Purge of the Thirties. New York: The Macmillan Company.
CURRIE, ELLIOTT P.
    1968   "Crime without criminals: witchcraft and its control in Renaissance Europe." Law and Society Review 3 (October):7–32.
DALLIN, ALEXANDER, and GEORGE W. BRESLAUER
    1970   Political Terror in Communist Systems. Stanford: Stanford University Press.
ERIKSON, KAI T.
    1966   Wayward Puritans: A Study in the Sociology of Deviance. New York: John Wiley and Sons.
GINSBURG, EVGENIIA SEMENOVNA
    1967   Journey into the Whirlwind. New York: Harcourt, Brace & World.
LIPPER, ELINOR
    1951   Eleven Years in Soviet Prison Camps. Chicago: Regnery.
MEDVEDEV, ROY

1971 Let History Judge: The Origins and Consequences of Stalinism. New York: Knopf.

MERTON, ROBERT K.
1966 "Social problems and sociological theory." Pp. 775–823 in Robert K. Merton and Robert A. Nisbet (eds.), Contemporary Social Problems. (2nd edition) New York: Harcourt, Brace & World.

PETROV, VLADIMIR, and EVDOKIA PETROV
1956 Empire of Fear. New York: Praeger.

SWIANIEWICZ, S.
1965 Forced Labour and Economic Development. London: Oxford University Press.

TREVOR-ROPER
1967 Religion, the Reformation and Social Change. London: Macmillan.

WEISSBERG, ALEXANDER
1951 The Accused. New York: Simon and Schuster.

JORGE A. BUSTAMANTE

The "Wetback" as Deviant:
An Application of
Labeling Theory

Introduction

Those who illegally stream across the Mexico-U.S. border are called "wet-backs" because they cross the Rio Grande without the benefit of a bridge. All other illegal migrants from Mexico are referred to by the same term. Thus, wetback characterizes anyone who enters illegally from Mexico. The term, then, carries an unavoidable connotation—one who has broken the law. This paper will deal with some of the questions that arise from that connotation. In the first part, we describe the historical emergence of the wetback, discussing the roles of the persons involved in the violation of the immigration law and some of the socioeconomic consequences of the wetback as a deviant. In the second part, we examine the wetback as a case of deviance through labeling theory. In this approach the deviant character of the wetback is analyzed as a process of interaction. Each role in this process will be discussed in terms of its interests, power, and consequences with respect to those of the roles of the other participants. Finally, the concept of "antilaw entrepreneur" is introduced, and its explanatory potential is indicated.

This paper is a theoretical elaboration of a research project on wetbacks. The larger project (U.S. Mexico Border Studies) was directed by Dr. Julian Samora of the University of Notre Dame, to whom I am grateful. The research project was supported by a grant from the Ford Foundation. The opinions expressed in the report do not necessarily represent the views of the Foundation. I am also in debt to Professors Richard Schwartz, Fabio Barbosa-Dasilva, Hernan Vera, Robert Antonio, and Dennis Terzola for the valuable comments on an earlier version of this paper. An early version of this paper was presented at the Annual Meetings of the American Sociological Association in Washington, D.C., and at the 7th World Congress of Sociology in Varna, Bulgaria, in 1970.

Historical Background

In 1882, during President Arthur's administration, the first immigration law was passed following a strong nativist movement. The same year the first "Chinese exclusion act" established significant limits to what was considered an "invasion of Orientals" who had been a preferred source of cheap labor for West Coast employers (Wittke 1949, p. 13). The search for cheap labor turned to Japanese and Filipino immigrants, who then became the target of "exclusionists." Campaigns like the "swat the Jap" campaign in Los Angeles and those inspired by the writings of Madison Grant and Lothrop Stoddard led to further restrictions of immigration from the Orient. The "Asian barred zone" provisions excluded immigration from Oriental countries as a source for cheap labor (Daniels and Kitano 1970, p. 53).

In the first decade of the century, eastern and southern European immigration became the focus of nativist and exclusionist crusades. Pressure generated by those movements crystallized in the appointment of a commission by the U.S. Congress to study immigration; the result of that study is known as the Dillingham Commission Report (1907–10). Throughout this voluminous report a long-debated distinction between the "old" and "new" immigration was made. It was argued that the values and occupations of the "old immigrants" (Anglo-Saxons and Nordics) were threatened by the "newer immigrants," southern and eastern Europeans and Asians (Hourwich 1912, p. 19). The distinction between new and old immigration created a dichotomy about which many pages of "scientific" reports were written in support of the undesirability of the new immigration.

Campaigns demanding restriction of the new immigration finally crystallized in the immigration laws of 1921 and 1924, which established quotas restricting immigration from all countries except those in the western hemisphere.

In the meantime, social scientists conducted research on the immigration phenomenon; they found empirical evidence showing that immigration to the United States has consistently supplied cheap labor (Eckler and Zoltnick 1949, p. 16; Hourwich 1912, pp. 167–72).

All countries which provided cheap labor for the United States were affected by the quota system established by the Immigration Act of 1921. Thus, the search for cheap labor turned to the western hemisphere, to which the quota system did not apply (Marden and Meyer 1968, p. 104); Mexican immigrants were found to be the most suitable replacement (Samora and Bustamante 1971). The suitability of Mexican labor rested on (1) geographical proximity; (2) the uninterrupted tradition of immigration, which was internal when most of southwestern United States was still part of Mexico (McWilliams 1968, pp. 162–69); and (3) unemployment and unrest in Mexico, created by several years of revolution (Bustamante, in press).

A tremendous increase in Mexican immigration during the first quarter of the century (Grebler 1966, p. 20) corresponded to the increased demand for unskilled labor in the economic expansion of the Southwest. Mexicans crossed 1,870 miles of an almost completely open border (Gamio 1930, p. 10) to reach the steel industry in East Chicago (Samora and Lamanna

1970), railroad construction, and, most significantly, agricultural expansion in the Southwest (Samora 1971).

In this period the Mexican who wanted to legally cross the border had to go through a complicated procedure to be admitted into the United States. Those procedures included, in particular, a literacy test, "a condition which many immigrants cannot fulfill" (Gamio 1930, p. 11). Therefore, many took advantage of the "open" border policy toward Mexican laborers.

Moreover, the illegal immigrant could stay in the United States untroubled as long as he avoided the authorities who might disclose his status. Since no specific authorities were entrusted with apprehending illegal immigrants, the dangers of being caught were further minimized (Jones 1965, p. 13). Thus, the illegal immigrant's status was not visibly distinct from the legal immigrant's. The illegal entrant was able to maintain his violation in a state of "primary deviance" (Lemert 1951, pp. 70–78).

The appearance of the Border Patrol in 1924 altered the primary deviance of the illegal entrant by crystallizing a new social reaction to the violation of immigration laws. The new police force was to reveal those primary deviants, violators of immigration laws. In this process, the term "wetback," previously purely descriptive, acquired a new meaning. It became the "label" or "stigma" by which the illegal immigrant was made visible. At the same time, the label "wetback" also became the symbol by which the illegal immigrant was able to identify a new "me" for himself (Mead 1918, pp. 577–602), and a new role which better equipped him to meet the social reaction to his behavior (illegal entrance) (Lemert 1967, pp. 42–51).

The establishment of the Border Patrol in 1924 not only made the wetback more visible as a law breaker; it also brought changes in the patterns of behavior of the illegal immigrants. The freedom of interaction the illegal immigrant had had before 1924 was considerably reduced. He now had to walk, to speak, and to bear any treatment with the fear of being caught by or "turned in" to the Border Patrol.

The interaction most significantly changed was between illegal migrant worker and employer. Before 1924 labor conditions resulted from differential access to mechanisms of power and from the interplay of labor-force supply and demand. The organization of the Border Patrol brought a new factor: the illegal migrant could always be caught and sent back to Mexico. To be "turned in" became a threat always present in the migrant's mind that interfered with his social contacts. Social contacts, except for those with an employer or prospective employer, could be avoided for self-protection. The explicit or implicit threat of being denounced by the employer became a new significant element in the settlement of work contracts. It could be used to impose oppressive salaries and working conditions. In his search for a job he could no longer freely accept or reject a given offer; he always had to consider the alternative of being denounced to the Border Patrol.[1]

[1] Data from 493 interviews that I conducted with wetbacks in 1969 show that 8% of the interviewees were "turned in" by their employers without being paid for their work. A year later, similar situations were encountered by the author during a participant observation as a "wetback" conceived to validate previous findings (a report of these experiences and the larger research project appears in Samora 1971). Further evidence of these and other kinds of exploitation of the "wetback" are reported by Saunders and Leonard 1951, p. 72; Hadley 1956, p. 352; and Jones 1965, pp. 14–20.

The importance of the "wetback problem" gains further emphasis in its numerical proportions. Although no reliable statistics exist on the actual number of wetbacks who have entered the United States, an approximate idea can be inferred from the records of expatriated wetbacks. Records for the period 1930–69 indicate that 7,486,470 apprehensions of wetbacks were made by the U.S. Immigration Authority (U.S. Immigration and Naturalization Service 1966, 1967–68). The highest rates were concentrated in the decades 1941–60, during which 5,953,210 expulsions of wetbacks were made. The size of the population involved clearly defines the importance of the problem.

When we look at the sociocultural characteristics of the persons involved, we see that the problem is much larger. Most are poor peasants from central and northern states in Mexico who come to the United States only to find work to survive (Samora 1971, p. 102). They are willing to accept anything—good or bad treatment, illness, starvation, low wages, poor living conditions; all are taken philosophically and accepted without struggle. Their struggle is concentrated on pure survival (Saunders and Leonard 1951, p. 6).

The Network of Social Relations of Wetbacks

Various groups of people come in contact with the wetback in the United States. In this section we will review four major groups: (1) the employer who benefits from a cheap labor pool, (2) the southwestern Mexican-American farm worker who suffers from the competition of these low-paid workers, (3) the lawmaker who is in the ambiguous position of defender of the law and protector of the "illegal" interests of farm entrepreneurs, and (4) the law enforcer who is directly responsible for enforcing the laws.

The Employer

In all economic enterprises, and in particular agricultural enterprises, labor constitutes a major segment of production costs. Rational manipulation of all instruments of production in pure economic terms requires the minimization of costs in all areas to achieve the highest possible economic return. Workers willing to accept labor contracts below going wages clearly become a positive asset in that they assure higher returns for the entrepreneur. Moreover, other economic advantages besides low wages accrue from the employment of wetback labor. First, in some kinds of employment no strict accounting of working hours is kept, since work contracts based on daily labor may involve as many as twelve hours (Hadley 1956, p. 347). Second, little or no responsibility for disability occurs, since the wetback must assume responsibility for his own injuries and accidents. Third, the employer is under no obligation, legal or otherwise, to provide health and medical services, sanitary facilities, or even decent housing (American G.I. Forum of Texas and Texas State Federation of Labor 1953, pp. 17–27). As a result, what the wetback receives as wages and other standard "fringe benefits" is determined only by the employer's conscience and the current standards of neighbors and friends (Hadley 1956, p. 347). Even in pure economic terms, then, the position of the rural entrepreneur vis-à-vis the wetback is highly advantageous; by using wetbacks as workers, farmers can maximize possible economic gains in labor costs (Samora 1971, pp. 98–103).

The Mexican-American Farm Worker

Whereas the rural entrepreneur gains by the presence of wetbacks, the Mexican-American rural workers lose in competition for jobs. They feel that wetbacks push work contract conditions to the lowest possible level, a "charity" level out of step with living requirements in the United States. Their personal suffering from such competition is unjust, since, while being penalized by this competition, they have to pay the costs of citizenship (e.g., income and other taxes) and receive little or no benefit from such required contributions. Further, wetbacks break the possible cohesion of the rural labor force, and so they lose bargaining power with rural entrepreneurs. Finally, the manipulation of the mass media and urban lobbying groups by the rural entrepreneur creates an artificial shortage of labor which serves to ensure the permanence of wetbacks. At the same time, Mexican-American workers are prevented from speaking in the mass media to unmask the artificial labor shortage (Hadley 1956, p. 345).

The Lawmaker

The lawmaker should be the one to bridge the gap between the conflicting demands of the entrepreneur and the Mexican-American. Nevertheless, the most general pattern followed by lawmakers is to consider the wetback problem and the working situation on the border as something unavoidable or expected. Legal attempts to effectively prevent the wetback from crossing the border are stricken from proposed codes by the lawmakers on the rationale that the farmer along the border wants wetback labor (U.S., Congress, Senate 1953, p. 10). The "realistic" attitude of these lawmakers seems to be either that it is convenient to conform or worthless to struggle against the situation. Thus, the U.S. immigration law is broken in order to maintain a supply of wetbacks. For many southern, and in particuar Texas, legislators, there is no evil in maintaining the influx of wetbacks.

Protection of the interests of wetback employers by lawmakers is best illustrated by a law (U.S. Congress, 8 U.S.C., section 1324, 1952) which makes it a felony to be a wetback but not to hire one.[2] This is a paradoxical situation which legitimizes the hiring of wetbacks in spite of the general recognition that it is the possibility of being hired that attracts Mexican work-

[2] That law provides that "any person who willfully or knowingly conceals, harbors, or shields from detection, in any place including any building or by any means of transportation, or who encourages or induces, or attempts to encourage or induce, either directly or indirectly, the entry into the United States of any alien shall be guilty of a felony. Upon conviction he shall be punished by a fine not exceeding $2,000 or by imprisonment for a term not exceeding five years, or both, for each alien in respect to whom the violation occurs. *Provided, however, that for the purposes of this section, employment, including the usual and normal practices incident to employment, shall not be deemed to consitute harboring*" (italics added; Samora 1971, p. 139).

ers to cross illegally to the United States. This situation was pointed out by Ruben Salazar (recently killed in the Chicago Moratorium in Los Angeles) in an article published in the *Los Angeles Times* (April 27, 1970): "There is no law against hiring wetbacks. There is only a law against being a wetback" (Samora 1971, p. 139).

The Law Enforcer

The border patrol is directly responsible for the prevention of wetback crossings and for the apprehension of wetbacks already in the United States. Theoretically, such a role would place the patrol in direct confrontation with the rural entrepreneurs using wetback labor, inasmuch as they enforce laws made in the interests of the total society. Their activities would, in part, protect the immediate interests of the legal rural workers.

Nevertheless, evidence suggests that such relationships of reciprocity are not realized (Saunders and Leonard 1951, p. 68); instead, the conflict between the Border Patrol and entrepreneurs is somehow transformed into covert cooperation through a "pattern of evasion" of the law (see Williams 1951). This transformation involves the following: first, the entrepreneurs offer little resistance to the apprehension of wetbacks, in exchange for the patrol's overlooking the wetbacks when work needs to be done. Second, wetbacks openly at work may informally legitimate their status as workers and thus remain unharassed. Third, complete enforcement of the law by state and national authorities, and with minimum cooperation from local people, is theoretically possible (Saunders and Leonard 1951, p. 68).

The Labeling Approach to Deviant Behavior

Theories which view deviance as a quality of the deviant act or the actor cannot help us understand the wetback as deviant. "Wetback" became the label for a deviant after the appearance of the Border Patrol, and various social groups came to *react* differently to the presence of wetbacks. It is singularly characteristic of this deviant type that it occurs in a cross-cultural context; as a Mexican, the wetback breaks an American law and receives negative legal sanction while, at the same time, he positively fulfills the needs of specific American groups. This context of deviance fits well into the framework of labeling theory. According to Becker (1963, p. 91), deviance cannot be viewed as homogeneous because it results from interaction and consists of particular responses by various social groups to a particular behavior of the prospective deviant or outsider.

In this context, we must analyze the wetback in interaction, singling out the responses of the various groups making up the network which lables his behavior as deviant. The deviant character of the wetback, then, lies not in him nor in his behavior but in the superimposition of the deviant label on him.

Becker's use of labeling theory in deviance is of particular interest to us because of his stress on the political dimensions of the labeling processes. He emphasizes the fact that the legal norms and the behavior classified as deviant must be viewed as part of a political process in which group A, *in conflict* with group B, defines the rules for group B. The degree of group A's success in imposing such rules and in enforcing them depends primarily upon the political and economic power of group A. Furthermore, the will of group A is often an expression of a class interest rather than solely of individual members of group A. In such a case, enforcement of the rules becomes applicable to all members of that class, excluding members of group B whose class interests are the same as group A's.

Becker further indicates that labeling always begins with the initiative of a "moral entrepreneur" (Becker 1963, pp. 147–63), a leader (individual or group) who crusades for new rules to stop something that he views as wrong. Moral entrepreneurs are interested in the content of rules and are very often involved in what they view as humanitarian or moral reformism. In their crusades, they typically say they want to help those beneath them to achieve a better status, and in the process "they add to the power they derive from the legitimacy of their moral position the power they derive from their superior position in society" (Becker 1963, p. 149). The outcome of a successful moral crusade is the establishment of a new set of rules (i.e., the immigration laws of 1921 and 1924) and corresponding enforcement agencies and officials (i.e., the U.S. Border Patrol). The new law enforcers justify their existence by attempting to fulfill the new activities, and, in their performance, they try to win the respect of prominent persons.

Once a law and its enforcers come into existence the process of labeling becomes independent of the moral entrepreneur. The enforcer becomes the most important actor, and while enforcing the law he stigmatizes or labels certain individuals as deviants. Thus, there is a process of interaction in which some actors will enforce rules "in the service of their own interest," whereas others, also "in the service of their own interest," commit acts labeled as deviant (Becker 1963, p. 162).

The Wetback Labeling Process

The labeling process started with a moral crusade under the leadership of moral entrepreneurs representing the moral spirit of the American legal system. The results of the crusade were new legal codes (the immigration laws of 1921 and 1924) and the establishment of organizations and specialized personnel (e.g., the Border Patrol) to implement the new codes. The moral component of the legitimization of the new codes rests on the righteousness of the law, inasmuch as it protects the interests of nationals who otherwise would be defenseless against the threat of foreign competitors.

This organizational superstructure, whose purpose was to carry out the moral imperatives, resulted in a radical transformation of the previous interactions of foreign laborers. Of immediate concern was the reinforcement of the illegal status of immigrant workers under the deviant label of wetback. Nevertheless, moral imperatives, even those incorporated legally and implemented by specialized personnel, are not the only basis of motivation and rationalization of action. Others, especially political and economic interests, can be at variance with these new moral imperatives and influence behavior. When we examine such conflicting motivations we see that they may be selectively used, depending on the context of the action and the character of the actor—in particular his power. Thus, the rural entrepreneur in certain situations (e.g., harvest time) uses economic motivation to hire wetbacks with contracts calling for long hours of work and the lowest possible pay. In other situations (say, when he has unwanted workers) he uses the moral imperative to denounce wetbacks to the Border Patrol. A similar differential use of motivation occurs with other groups. It is necessary to specify the nature of motivations at play in the wetback case.

Looking at interests as a source of motivations, we shall focus on them at the juncture where they shape action; that is, at the point of interaction between wetbacks and the groups of actors discussed in this paper. A distinction will be made between group interests related to the presence of the wetback and group interests related only to each actor's role independent of the presence of the wetback. The latter would be those interests pertaining to the maintenance of the role played by actors of each group, that is, (1) the Mexican-American farm worker's role interest would be to maximize wages, (2) the farmer's (wetback employer's) role interest would be to maximize profit, (3) the lawmaker's role interest would be to provide legislation that meets the necessities of his constituencies and the country, (4) the law enforcer's (Border Patrol's) role interest would be to enforce immigration laws, (5) the moral entrepreneur's role interest would be to define good and evil for society. On the other hand, group interest related to the presence of the wetback seems to indicate a different dimension of each actor's role, as, respectively, (1) to stop the influx of wetbacks in order to avoid their competition for jobs and to increase bargaining power vis-à-vis the farmer, (2) to maximize profits by the use of the wetback cheap labor, (3) to gain political support from the farmers by protecting their interests, (4) to enforce immigration laws selectively, (5) to define protection of nationals against foreign competition as good and entrance to the United States without inspection as immoral.

This distinction of interests seems to promote understanding of some contradictions in the wetback phenomenon, such as (1) condemning the wetback by defining him as a deviant and, at the same time, maintaining a demand for his labor force which is reflected in a steadily increasing influx of wetbacks each year (Samora 1971, pp. 195–96); (2) penalizing a person for being a wetback, but not a farmer for hiring one (U.S. Congress, 8 U.S.C., section 1324, 1952); (3) maintaining an agency for the enforcement of immigration laws and at the same time exerting budget limitations and/or political pressures to prevent successful enforcement of the law (Hadley 1956, p. 348).

These are some of the contradictions that become apparent in the wetback case, but they are nothing less than reflections of contradictions in society at large. This is particularly obvious to us when we see the conflict of interests between the farmer and Mexican-American farm worker (each tries to maximize his economical gains at the expense of the other) and when we see the presence of the wetback kept undercover as a veil hiding deeper conflict. Indeed, when the role of the wetback is introduced in agricultural production, we see a different conflict of interests taking place—namely, that between the Mexican-American worker and the wetback. The former blames the latter for lowering working conditions and standards of living.

The nature of the two conflicts should be differentiated. Whereas the conflict of interests between the Mexican-American farm worker and the farmer is determined by the position each plays in a particular mode of agricultural production, the conflict between the Mexican-American worker and the wetback is determined primarily by a set of beliefs that are not necessarily grounded in reality, namely, that wages and working conditions are determined by external laws of supply and demand independent of the employers; that the wetback *causes* low wages and low standards of living for the farm worker, etc. It is important to note the point here that the conflicts "created" by the wetback would disappear with an unrestricted enforcement of immigration laws.

Another aspect of our discussion of group interest is the power that supports each specified interest and respective action. Since the groups themselves reflect status differentials, it is the differences in power (and possible collisions of power) that give form to the interaction. Furthermore, the power legitimization of these actions sustains the existing form against any possible transformation.

Power differences among the various actors result from their ability to manipulate or influence interaction in the direction of their interests (see Gamson 1968). In this interpretation, the wetback employer is clearly the most powerful category, since he is able to influence all other actors. On the other extreme is the wetback. He clearly appears at a disadvantage. As an outsider he has no legitimacy. He is not eligible for public assistance or for the benefits of an eventual "moral entrepreneur," since he is not eligible to stay in the country, unless he is in jail. He is also not eligible for other benefits because of the stigma of having once broken the immigration laws. This might, technically, prevent him from acquiring legal residence or citizenship in the United States. The wetback only has the original motivation which made him cross the border (survival) and a new one resulting from the deviant label (not to be caught) which becomes another element of pure survival. As an outsider with such elemental interests he dares not complain—the only possible protest comes when his survival is in jeopardy and his only course of action is to return to Mexico.

A Conceptual Addendum to Becker's Schema

Labeling theory provides us with the concept of moral entrepreneur. Applying the elements of this type to the case under analysis, we find a new type in the role of the wetback employer. His crusade is directed toward the self-serving enforcement of existing laws. The source of his crusade is the threat of the loss of cheap labor that would occur if the laws were enforced. Evidently the characteristics of this second type are the polar opposites of those of the moral entrepreneur. The imperative he singles out as a banner is economic rather than moral. The crusade he leads is supported by power and economic interest rather than moral righteousness. This type can perhaps be characterized as an *antilaw entrepreneur*. In order to be successful he associates the law enforcer and the lawmaker in his enterprise and becomes able to manipulate the law in two ways: first, by preventing its enforcement whenever he needs cheap labor; second, by stimulating its enforcement when he needs to dispose of a complaining or useless wetback.

A view of the contradictions of society apparent in the wetback case has allowed us to introduce the antilaw entrepreneur. Such a concept is useful for the understanding of deviance because it shows that violation of a law can also become the goal of an enterprise in the same sense that the creation of a law may be the goal of an enterprise. Both crusades, to be successful, require leaders holding legitimate power, although in one case they have the added legitimization of answering to a moral imperative, whereas in the other they answer to the economic interests of a specialized group. The law enforcer, the lawmaker, and a powerful group of rural entrepreneurs can launch such a crusade against the law and yet not be "labeled" as deviants.

If a Border Patrol man states firmly that to enforce the law would "ruin the fields" (Saunders and Leonard 1951, p. 68), and a lawmaker refers to specific measures in the Senate to allow the influx of wetbacks (U.S., Congress, Senate 1953), and a former vice president of the United States (John Nance Garner) says, "If they [wetback employers] get the Mexican labor it enables them to make a profit" (Jones 1965, p. 17), then the essential objectives of the enterprise are spelled out. The continuing presence of wetbacks is in no little measure an indication of the success of the antilaw entrepreneur.

Conclusion

The preceding analysis leads us to see—

(1) the wetback as one who crosses the U.S.–Mexican border illegally, taking advantage of the limited enforcement of the U.S. immigration laws;
(2) the interaction process in which such a man is labeled as deviant, a label that will constitute a central element of a process of exploitation;
(3) the deviant label making the wetback more attractive as a worker than the Mexican-American (at the same time, paradoxically, such a label—an element of destitution—becomes what the wetback exchanges for an unstable taste of survival);
(4) the labeling process in which the wetback is "created," in which interests and power are arranged in an action that we have typified as an antilaw enterprise.

And finally, a human being with the alternatives of being exploited by a country forcing him to become a deviant or of facing misery in his own country by not doing so.

References

American G.I. Forum of Texas and Texas State Federation of Labor. 1953. *What Price Wetbacks?* Austin: American G.I. Forum of Texas and Texas State Federation of Labor (AFL).

Becker, Howard S. 1963. *Outsiders: Studies in the Sociology of Deviance.* New York: Free Press.

Bustamante, Jorge A. In press. *Don Chano: Autobiografía de un Emigrante Mexicano.* Mexico City: Instituto de Investigaciones Sociales of the National University of Mexico.

Daniels, Roger, and Harry H. L. Kitano. 1970. *American Racism: Exploration of the Nature of Prejudice.* Englewood Cliffs, N.J.: Prentice-Hall.

Eckler, Ross A., and Jack Zlotnick. 1949. "Immigration and Labor Force." In *The Annals,* edited by Thorsten Sellin. Philadelphia: American Academy of Political and Social Sciences.

Gamio, Manuel. 1930. *Mexican Immigration to the United States.* Chicago: University of Chicago Press.

Gamson, William. 1968. *Power and Discontent.* Homewood, Ill.: Dorsey.

Grebler, Leo. 1966. "Mexican Immigration to the United States." Mexican American Study Project, Advanced Report no. 2. Los Angeles: University of California.

Hadley, Eleanor M. 1956. "A Critical Analysis of the Wetback Problem." *Law and Contemporary Problems* 21 (Spring): 334–57.

Hourwich, Isaac A. 1912. *Immigration and Labor.* New York: Putnam.

Jones, Lamar B. 1965. "Mexican American Labor Problems in Texas." Ph.D. dissertation, University of Texas.

Lemert, Edwin M. 1951. *Social Pathology.* New York: McGraw-Hill.

————. 1967. *Human Deviance, Social Problems, and Social Control.* Englewood Cliffs, N.J.: Prentice-Hall.

McWilliams, Carey. 1968. *North from Mexico.* Westport, Conn.: Greenwood.

Marden, Charles F., and Gladys Meyer. 1968. *Minorities in American Society.* New York: American Book Co.

Mead, George H. 1918. "The Psychology of Punitive Justice." *American Journal of Sociology* 23 (March): 577–602.

Samora, Julian, assisted by Jorge A. Bustamante and Gilbert Cardenas. 1971. *Los Mojados, the Wetback Story.* Notre Dame, Ind.: University of Notre Dame Press.

Samora, Julian, and Jorge A. Bustamante. 1971. "Mexican Immigration and American Labor Demands." In *Migrant and Seasonal Farmworker Powerlessness.* Pt. 7B. Hearings, U.S. Senate, Committee on Labor and Public Welfare. Washington, D.C.: Government Printing Office.

Samora, Julian, and Richard A. Lamanna. 1970. "Mexican American in a Midwest Metropolis: A Study of East Chicago." In *The Mexican American People: The Nation's Second Largest Minority,* edited by V. Webb. New York: Free Press.

Saunders, Lyle, and Olen F. Leonard. 1951. *The Wetback in the Lower Rio Grande Valley of Texas.* Inter-American Education Occasional Papers, no. 7. Austin: University of Texas.

U.S. Immigration and Naturalization Service. 1966. *Annual Report of the United States Immigration and Naturalization Service.* Washington, D.C.: Government Printing Office.

————. 1967–68. *Report of Field Operations of the Immigration and Naturalization Service.* Washington, D.C.: Government Printing Office.

U.S., Congress, Senate. 1953. Appropriation Hearings on S. 1917 before the Subcommittee of the Senate Committee of the Judiciary 83rd Cong., 1st sess., p. 123 (Senator McCarran).

Williams, Robin, Jr. 1951. *American Society: A Sociological Interpretation.* New York: Knopf.

Wittke, Carl, 1949. "Immigration Policy prior to World War I." In *The Annals,* edited by Thorsten Sellin. Philadelphia: American Academy of Political and Social Science.

WILLIAM J. CHAMBLISS

A Sociological Analysis
of the Law of Vagrancy

With the outstanding exception of Jerome Hall's analysis of theft[1] there
has been a severe shortage of sociologically relevant analyses of the relationship between particular laws and the social setting in which these laws emerge,
are interpreted, and take form. The paucity of such studies is somewhat
surprising in view of widespread agreement that such studies are not only
desirable but absolutely essential to the development of a mature sociology
of law.[2] A fruitful method of establishing the direction and pattern of this
mutual influence is to systematically analyze particular legal categories, to
observe the changes which take place in the categories and to explain how
these changes are themselves related to and stimulate changes in the society.
This chapter is an attempt to provide such an analysis of the law of vagrancy
in Anglo-American Law.

Legal Innovation: The Emergence of
the Law of Vagrancy in England

There is general agreement among legal scholars that the first full fledged
vagrancy statute was passed in England in 1349. As is generally the case with

[1] Hall, J., *Theft, Law and Society* (Bobbs-Merrill, 1939). See also, Alfred R.
Lindesmith, "Federal Law and Drug Addiction," *Social Problems,* Vol. 7, No. 1, 1959,
p. 48.

[2] See, for examples, Rose, A., "Some Suggestions for Research in the Sociology of
Law," *Social Problems,* Vol. 9, No. 3, 1962, pp. 281–283, and Geis, G., "Sociology,
Criminology, and Criminal Law," *Social Problems,* Vol. 7, No. 1, 1959, pp. 40–47.
*For a more complete listing of most of the statutes dealt with in this report the reader
is referred to Burn,* The History of the Poor Laws. *Citations of English statutes should
be read as follows: 3 Ed. 1. c. 1. refers to the third act of Edward the first, chapter one,
etc.*

Source: William J. Chambliss, "A Sociological Analysis of the Law of Vagrancy,"
Social Problems, 12, I (Fall, 1964) pp. 67–77. Copyright © 1967 by The Society for
the Study of Social Problems. Reprinted by permission of The Society and William J.
Chambliss.

legislative innovations, however, this statute was preceded by earlier laws which established a climate favorable to such change. The most significant forerunner to the 1349 vagrancy statute was in 1274 when it was provided:

> Because that abbies and houses of religion have been overcharged and sore grieved, by the resort of great men and other, so that their goods have not been sufficient for themselves, whereby they have been greatly hindered and impoverished, that they cannot maintain themselves, nor such charity as they have been accustomed to do; it is provided, that none shall come to eat or lodge in any house of religion, or any other's foundation than of his own, at the costs of the house, unless he be required by the governor of the house before his coming hither.[3]

Unlike the vagrancy statutes this statute does not intend to curtail the movement of persons from one place to another, but is solely designed to provide the religious houses with some financial relief from the burden of providing food and shelter to travelers.

The philosophy that the religious houses were to give alms to the poor and to the sick and feeble was, however, to undergo drastic change in the next fifty years. The result of this changed attitude was the establishment of the first vagrancy statute in 1349 which made it a crime to give alms to any who were unemployed while being of sound mind and body. To wit:

> Because that many valiant beggars, as long as they may live of begging, do refuse to labor, giving themselves to idleness and vice, and sometimes to theft and other abominations; it is ordained, that none, upon pain of imprisonment shall, under the colour of pity or alms, give anything to such which may labour, or presume to favour them towards their desires; so that thereby they may be compelled to labour for their necessary living.[4]

It was further provided by this statute that:

> . . . every man and woman, of what condition he be, free or bond, able in body, and within the age of threescore years, not living in merchandize nor exercising any craft, nor having of his own whereon to live, nor proper land whereon to occupy himself, and not serving any other, if he in convenient service (his estate considered) be required to serve, shall be bounded to serve him which shall him require. . . . And if any refuse, he shall on conviction by two true men, . . . be commited to gaol till he find surety to serve.
>
> And if any workman or servant, of what estate or condition he be, retained in any man's service, do depart from the said service without reasonable cause or license, before the term agreed on, he shall have pain of imprisonment.[5]

There was also in this statute the stipulation that the workers should receive a standard wage. In 1351 this statute was strengthened by the stipulation:

> And none shall go out of the town where he dwelled in winter, to serve the summer, if he may serve in the same town.[6]

[3] 3 Ed. 1. c. 1.
[4] 35 Ed. 1. c. 1.
[5] 23 Ed. 3.
[6] 25 Ed. 3 (1351).

By 34 Ed. 3 (1360) the punishment for these acts became imprisonment for fifteen days and if they "do not justify themselves by the end of that time, to be sent to gaol till they do."

A change in official policy so drastic as this did not, of course, occur simply as a matter of whim. The vagrancy statutes emerged as a result of changes in other parts of the social structure. The prime-mover for this legislative innovation was the Black Death which struck England about 1348. Among the many disastrous consequences this had upon the social structure was the fact that it decimated the labor force. It is estimated that by the time the pestilence had run its course at least fifty per cent of the population of England had died from the plague. This decimation of the labor force would necessitate rather drastic innovations in any society but its impact was heightened in England where, at this time, the economy was highly dependent upon a steady supply of cheap labor.

Even before the pestilence, however, the availability of an adequate supply of cheap labor was becoming a problem for the landowners. The crusades and various wars had made money necessary to the lords and, as a result, the lord frequently agreed to sell the serfs their freedom in order to obtain the needed funds. The serfs, for their part, were desirous of obtaining their freedom (by "fair means" or "foul") because the larger towns which were becoming more industrialized during this period could offer the serf greater personal freedom as well as a higher standard of living. This process is nicely summarized by Bradshaw:

> By the middle of the 14th century the outward uniformity of the manorial system had become in practice considerably varied . . . for the peasant had begun to drift to the towns and it was unlikely that the old village life in its unpleasant aspects should not be resented. Moreover the constant wars against France and Scotland were fought mainly with mercenaries after Henry III's time and most villages contributed to the new armies. The bolder serfs either joined the armies or fled to the towns, and even in the villages the free men who held by villein tenure were as eager to commute their services as the serfs were to escape. Only the amount of "free" labor available enabled the lord to work his demesne in many places.[7]

And he says regarding the effect of the Black Death:

> . . . in 1348 the Black Death reached England and the vast mortality that ensued destroyed that reserve to labor which alone had made the manorial system even nominally possible.[8]

The immediate result of these events was of course no surprise: Wages for the "free" man rose considerably and this increased, on the one hand, the landowner's problems and, on the other hand, the plight of the unfree tenant. For although wages increased for the personally free laborers, it of course did not necessarily add to the standard of living of the serf, if anything it made his position worse because the landowner would be hard pressed to pay for the personally free labor which he needed and would thus find it more and

[7] Bradshaw, F., *A Social History of England*, p. 54.
[8] *Ibid.*

more difficult to maintain the standard of living for the serf which he had heretofore supplied. Thus the serf had no alternative but flight if he chose to better his position. Furthermore, flight generally meant both freedom and better conditions since the possibility of work in the new weaving industry was great and the chance of being caught small.[9]

It was under these conditions that we find the first vagrancy statutes emerging. There is little question but that these statutes were designed for one express purpose: to force laborers (whether personally free or unfree) to accept employment at a low wage in order to insure the landowner an adequate supply of labor at a price he could afford to pay. Caleb Foote concurs with this interpretation when he notes:

> The anti-migratory policy behind vagrancy legislation began as an essential complement of the wage stabilization legislation which accompanied the breakup of feudalism and the depopulation caused by the Black Death. By the Statutes of Labourers in 1349–1351, every able-bodied person without other means of support was required to work for wages fixed at the level preceding the Black Death; it was unlawful to accept more, or to refuse an offer to work, or to flee from one county to another to avoid offers of work or to seek higher wages, or go give alms to able-bodied beggars who refused to work.[10]

In short, as Foote says in another place, this was an "attempt to make the vagrancy statutes a substitute for serfdom."[11] This same conclusion is equally apparent from the wording of the statute where it is stated:

> Because great part of the people, and especially of workmen and servants, late died in pestilence; many seeing the necessity of masters, and great scarcity of servants, will not serve without excessive wages, and some rather willing to beg in idleness than by labour to get their living: it is ordained, that every man and woman, of what condition he be, free or bond, able in body and within the age of threescore years, not living in merchandize, (etc.) be required to serve. . . .

The innovation in the law, then, was a direct result of the aforementioned changes which had occurred in the social setting. In this case these changes were located for the most part in the economic institution of the society. The vagrancy laws were designed to alleviate a condition defined by the lawmakers as undesirable. The solution was to attempt to force a reversal, as it were, of a social process which was well underway; that is, to curtail mobility of laborers in such a way that labor would not become a commodity for which the landowners would have to compete.

Statutory Dormancy: A Legal Vestige

In time, of course, the curtailment of the geographical mobility of laborers was no longer requisite. One might well expect that when the function

[9] *Ibid.,* p. 57.
[10] Foote, C., "Vagrancy Type Law and Its Administration," *Univ. of Pennsylvania Law Review* (104), 1956, p. 615.
[11] *Ibid.*

served by the statute was no longer an important one for society, the statutes would be eliminated from the law. In fact, this has not occurred. The vagrancy statutes have remained in effect since 1349. Furthermore, as we shall see in some detail later, they were taken over by the colonies and have remained in effect in the United States as well.

The substance of the vagrancy statutes changed very little for some time after the first ones in 1349–1351 although there was a tendency to make punishments more harsh than originally. For example, in 1360 it was provided that violators of the statute should be imprisoned for fifteen days.[12] and in 1388 the punishment was to put the offender in the stocks and to keep him there until "he find surety to return to his service."[13] That there was still, at this time, the intention of providing the landowner with labor is apparent from the fact this this statute provides:

> . . . and he or she which use to labour at the plough and cart, or other labour and service of husbandry, till they be of the age of 12 years, from thenceforth shall abide at the same labour without being put to any mistery or handicraft: and any covenant of apprenticeship to the contrary shall be void.[14]

The next alteration in the statutes occurs in 1495 and is restricted to an increase in punishment. Here it is provided that vagrants shall be "set in stocks, there to remain by the space of three days and three nights, and there to have none other sustenance but bread and water; and after the said three days and nights, to be had out and set at large, and then to be commanded to avoid the town."[15]

The tendency to increase the severity of punishment during this period seems to be the result of a general tendency to make finer distinctions in the criminal law. During this period the vagrancy statutes appear to have been fairly inconsequential in either their effect as a control mechanism or as a generally enforced statute.[16] The processes of social change in the culture generally and the trend away from serfdom and into a "free" economy obviated the utility of these statutes. The result was not unexpected. The judiciary did not apply the law and the legislators did not take it upon themselves to change the law. In short, we have here a period of dormancy in which the statute is neither applied nor altered significantly.

A Shift in Focal Concern

Following the squelching of the Peasant's Revolt in 1381, the services of the serfs to the lord " . . . tended to become less and less exacted, although in certain forms they lingered on till the seventeenth century. . . . By the six-

---

12 34 Ed. 3 (1360).
13 12 R. 2 (1388).
14 *Ibid.*
15 11 H. & C. 2 (1495).
16 As evidenced for this note the expectation that " . . . the common gaols of every shire are likely to be greatly pestered with more numbers of prisoners than heretofore . . . " when the stautes were changed by the statute of 14 Ed. c. 5 (1571).

teenth century few knew there were any bondmen in England . . . and in 1575 Queen Elizabeth listened to the prayers of almost the last serfs in England . . . and granted them manumission."[17]

In view of this change we would expect corresponding changes in the vagrancy laws. Beginning with the lessening of punishment in the statute of 1503 we find these changes. However, instead of remaining dormant (or becoming more so) or being negated altogether, the vagrancy statutes experienced a shift in focal concern. With this shift the statutes served a new and equally important function for the social order of England. The first statute which indicates this change was in 1530. In this statute (22 H. 8. c. 12 1530) it was stated:

> If any person, being whole and mighty in body, and able to labour, be taken in begging, or be vagrant and can give no reckoning how he lawfully gets his living; . . . and all other idle persons going about, some of them using divers and subtle crafty and unlawful games and plays, and some of them feigning themselves to have knowledge of . . . crafty sciences . . . shall be punished as provided.

What is most significant about this statute is the shift from an earlier concern with laborers to a concern with *criminal* activities. To be sure, the stipulation of persons "being whole and mighty in body, and able to labour, be taken in begging, or be vagrant" sounds very much like the concerns of the earlier statutes. Some important differences are apparent however when the rest of the statute includes those who " . . . can give no reckoning how he lawfully gets his living"; "some of them using divers subtil and unlawful games and plays." This is the first statute which specifically focuses upon these kinds of criteria for adjudging someone a vagrant.

It is significant that in this statute the severity of punishment is increased so as to be greater not only than provided by the 1503 statute but the punishment is more severe than that which had been provided by *any* of the pre-1503 statutes as well. For someone who is merely idle and gives no reckoning of how he makes his living the offender shall be:

> . . . had to the next market town, or other place where they [the constables] shall think most convenient, and there to be tied to the end of a cart naked, and to be beaten with whips throughout the same market town or other place, till his body be bloody by reason of such whipping.[18]

But, for those who use "divers and subtil crafty and unlawful games and plays," etc., the punishment is " . . . whipping at two days together in manner aforesaid."[19] For the second offense, such persons are:

> . . . scourged two days, and the third day to be put upon the pillory from nine of the clock till eleven before noon of the same day and to have one of his ears cut off.[20]

[17] Bradshaw, *op. cit.*, p. 61.
[18] 22 H. 8. c. 12 (1530).
[19] *Ibid.*
[20] *Ibid.*

And if he offend the third time " . . . to have like punishment with whipping, standing on the pillory and to have his other ear cut off."

This statute (1) makes a distinction between types of offenders and applies the more severe punishment to those who are clearly engaged in "criminal" activities, (2) mentions a specific concern with categories of "unlawful" behavior, and (3) applies a type of punishment (cutting off the ear) which is generally reserved for offenders who are defined as likely to be a fairly serious criminal.

Only five years later we find for the first time that the punishment of death is applied to the crime of vagrancy. We also note a change in terminology in the statute:

> and if any ruffians . . . after having been once apprehended . . . shall wander, loiter, or idle use themselves and play the vagabonds . . . shall be eftfoons not only whipped again, but shall have the gristle of his right ear clean cut off. And if he shall again offend, he shall be committed to gaol till the next sessions; and being there convicted upon indictment, he shall have judgments to suffer pains and execution of death, as a felon, as an enemy of the commonwealth.[21]

It is significant that the statute now makes persons who repeat the crime of vagrancy a felon. During this period then, the focal concern of the vagrancy statutes becomes a concern for the control of felons and is no longer primarily concerned with the movement of laborers.

These statutory changes were a direct response to changes taking place in England's social structure during this period. We have already pointed out that feudalism was decaying rapidly. Concomitant with the breakup of feudalism was an increased emphasis upon commerce and industry. The commercial emphasis in England at the turn of the sixteenth century is of particular importance in the development of vagrancy laws. With commercialism came considerable traffic bearing valuable items. Where there were 169 important merchants in the middle of the fourteenth century there were 3,000 merchants engaged in foreign trade alone at the beginning of the sixteenth century.[22] England became highly dependent upon commerce for its economic support. Italians conducted a great deal of the commerce of England during this early period and were held in low repute by the populace. As a result, they were subject to attacks by citizens and, more important, were frequently robbed of their goods while transporting them. "The general insecurity of the times made any transportation hazardous. The special risks to which the alien merchant was subjected gave rise to the royal practice of issuing formally executed covenants of safe conduct through the realm."[23]

Such a situation not only called for the enforcement of existing laws but also called for the creation of new laws which would facilitate the control of persons preying upon merchants transporting goods. The vagrancy statutes were revived in order to fulfill just such a purpose. Persons who had committed no serious felony but who were suspected of being capable of doing so

21 27 H. 8. c. 25 (1535).
22 Hall, *op. cit.,* p. 21.
23 *Ibid.,* p. 23.

could be apprehended and incapacitated through the application of vagrancy laws once these laws were refocused so as to include " . . . any ruffians . . . [who] shall wander, loiter, or idle use themselves and play the vagabonds. . . ."[24]

The new focal concern is continued in 1 Ed. 6. c. 3 (1547) and in fact is made more general so as to include:

> Whoever man or woman, being not lame, impotent, or so aged or diseased that he or she cannot work, not having whereon to live, shall be lurking in any house, or loitering or idle wandering by the highway side, or in streets, cities, towns, or villages, not applying themselves to some honest labour, and so continuing for three days; or running away from their work; every such person shall be taken for a vagabond. And . . . upon conviction of two witnesses . . . the same loiterer (shall) be marked with a hot iron in the breast with the letter V, and adjudged him to the person bringing him, to be his slave for two years. . . .

Should the vagabond run away, upon conviction, he was to be branded by a hot iron with the letter S on the forehead and to be thenceforth declared a slave forever. And in 1571 there is modification of the punishment to be inflicted, whereby the offender is to be "branded on the chest with the letter V" (for vagabond). And, if he is convicted the second time, the brand is to be made on the forehead. It is worth noting here that this method of punishment, which first appeared in 1530 and is repeated here with somewhat more force, is also an indication of a change in the type of person to whom the law is intended to apply. For it is likely that nothing so permanent as branding would be applied to someone who was wandering but looking for work, or at worst merely idle and not particularly dangerous *per se*. On the other hand, it could well be applied to someone who was likely to be engaged in other criminal activities in connection with being "vagrant."

By 1571 in the statute of 14 Ed. c. 5 the shift in focal concern is fully developed:

> All rogues, vagabonds, and sturdy beggars shall . . . be committed to the common goal . . . he shall be grievously whipped, and burnt thro' the gristle of the right ear with a hot iron of the compass of an inch about. . . . And for the second offense, he shall be adjudged a felon, unless some person will take him for two years in to his service. And for the third offense, he shall be adjudged guilty of felony without benefit of clergy.

And there is included a long list of persons who fall within the statute: "proctors, procurators, idle persons going about using subtil, crafty and unlawful games or plays; and some of them feigning themselves to have knowledge of . . . absurd sciences . . . and all fencers, bearwards, common players in interludes, and minstrels . . . all juglers, pedlars, tinkers, petty chapmen . . . and all counterfeiters of licenses, passports and users of the same." The major significance of this statute is that it includes all the previously defined offenders and adds some more. Significantly, those added are more clearly criminal types, counterfeiters, for example. It is also significant that there is the following qualification of this statute: "Provided also, that this act shall not

[24] 27 H. 8. c. 25 (1535).

extend to cookers, or harvest folks, that travel for harvest work, corn or hay."

That the changes in this statute were seen as significant is indicated by the following statement which appears in the statute:

> And whereas by reason of this act, the common goals of every shire are like to be greatly pestered with more number of prisoners than heretofore hath been, for that the said vagabonds and other lewd persons before recited shall upon their apprehension be committed to the said goals; it is enacted. . . .[25]

And a provision is made for giving more money for maintaining the gaols. This seems to add credence to the notion that this statute was seen as being significantly more general than those previously.

It is also of importance to note that this is the first time the term *rogue* has been used to refer to persons included in the vagrancy statutes. It seems, *a priori,* that a "rogue" is a different social type than is a "vagrant" or a "vagabond"; the latter terms implying something more equivalent to the idea of a "tramp" whereas the former (rogue) seems to imply a more disorderly and potentially dangerous person.

The emphasis upon the criminalistic aspect of vagrants continues in Chapter 17 of the same statute:

> Whereas divers *licentious* persons wander up and down in all parts of the realm, to countenance their *wicked behavior;* and do continually assemble themselves armed in the highways, and elsewhere in troops, *to the great terror* of her majesty's true subjects, *the impeachment of her laws,* and the disturbance of the peace and tranquility of the realm; and whereas many outrages are daily committed by these dissolute persons, and more are likely to ensue if speedy remedy be not provided. (Italics added.)

With minor variations (*e.g.,* offering a reward for the capture of a vagrant) the statutes remain essentially of this nature until 1743. In 1743 there was once more an expansion of the types of persons included such that "all persons going about as patent gatherers, or gatherers of alms, under pretense of loss by fire or other casualty; or going about as collectors for prisons, gaols, or hospitals; all persons playing of betting at any unlawful games; and all persons who run away and leave their wives or children . . . all persons wandering abroad, and lodging in alehouses, barns, outhouses, or in the open air, not giving good account of themselves," were types of offenders added to those already included.

By 1743 the vagrancy statutes had apparently been sufficiently reconstructed by the shifts of concern so as to be once more a useful instrument in the creation of social solidarity. This function has apparently continued down to the present day in England and the changes from 1743 to the present have been all in the direction of clarifying or expanding the categories covered but little has been introduced to change either the meaning or the impact of this branch of the law.

We can summarize this shift in focal concern by quoting from Halsbury. He has noted that in the vagrancy statutes:

[25] 14 E., c. 5. (1571).

. . . elaborate provision is made for the relief and incidental control of destitute wayfarers. These latter, however, form but a small portion of the offenders aimed at by what are known as the Vagrancy Laws, . . . many offenders
who are in no ordinary sense of the word vagrants, have been brought under
the laws relating to vagrancy, and the great number of the offenses coming
within the operation of these laws have little or no relation to the subject of
poor relief, but are more properly directed towards the prevention of crime,
the preservation of good order, and the promotion of social economy.[26]

Before leaving this section it is perhaps pertinent to make a qualifying
remark. We have emphasized throughout this section how the vagrancy statutes underwent a shift in focal concern as the social setting changed. The
shift in focal concern is not meant to imply that the later focus of the statutes represents a completely new law. It will be recalled that even in the first
vagrancy statute there was reference to those who "do refuse labor, giving
themselves to idleness and vice and sometimes to theft and other abomina-
tions." Thus the possibility of criminal activities resulting from persons who
refuse to labor was recognized even in the earliest statute. The fact remains,
however, that the major emphasis in this statute and in the statutes which
followed the first one was always upon the "refusal to labor" or "begging."
The "criminalistic" aspect of such persons was relatively unimportant. Later,
as we have shown, the criminalistic potential becomes of paramount importance. The thread runs back to the earliest statute but the reason for the
statutes' existence as well as the focal concern of the statutes is quite different in 1743 than it was in 1349.

Vagrancy Laws in the United States

In general, the vagrancy laws of England, as they stood in the middle
eighteenth century, were simply adopted by the states. There were some exceptions to this general trend. For example, Maryland restricted the application of vagrancy laws to "free" Negroes. In addition, for *all* states the vagrancy
laws were even more explicitly concerned with the control of criminals and
undesirables than had been the case in England. New York, for example,
explicitly defines prostitutes as being a category of vagrants during this
period. These exceptions do not, however, change the general picture significantly and it is quite appropriate to consider the U.S. vagrancy laws as
following from England's of the middle eighteenth century with relatively
minor changes. The control of criminals and undesirables was the *raison d'être*
of the vagrancy laws in the U.S. This is as true today as it was in 1750. As
Caleb Foote's analysis of the application of vagrancy statutes in the Philadelphia court shows, these laws are presently applied indiscriminately to
persons considered a "nuisance." Foote suggests that ". . . the chief significance of this branch of the criminal law lies in its quantitative impact and
administration usefulness."[27] Thus it appears that in America the trend begun

[26] Earl of Halsbury, *The Laws of England* (Butterworth & Co., Bell Yard, Temple
Bar, 1912), pp. 606–607.
[27] Foote, *op. cit.*, p. 613. Also see in this connection, Irwin Deutscher; "The Petty
Offender," *Federal Probation*, XIX, June, 1955.

in England in the sixteenth, seventeenth and eighteenth centuries has been carried to its logical extreme and the laws are now used principally as a mechanism for "clearing the streets" of the derelicts who inhabit the "skid roads" and "Bowerys" of our large urban areas.

Since the 1800's there has been an abundant source of prospects to which the vagrancy laws have been applied. These have been primarily those persons deemed by the police and the courts to be either actively involved in criminal activities or at least peripherally involved. In this context, then, the statutes have changed very little. The functions served by the statutes in England of the late eighteenth century are still being served today in both England and the United States. The locale has changed somewhat and it appears that the present day application of vagrancy statutes is focused upon the arrest and confinement of the "down and outers" who inhabit certain sections of our larger cities but the impact has remained constant. The lack of change in the vagrancy statutes, then, can be seen as a reflection of the society's perception of a continuing need to control some of its "suspicious" or "undesirable" members.[28]

A word of caution is in order lest we leave the impression that this administrative purpose is the sole function of vagrancy laws in the U.S. today. Although it is our contention that this is generally true it is worth remembering that during certain periods of our recent history, and to some extent today, these laws have also been used to control the movement of workers. This was particularly the case during the depression years and California is of course infamous for its use of vagrancy laws to restrict the admission of migrants from other states.[29] The vagrancy statutes, because of their history, still contain germs within them which make such effects possible. Their main purpose, however, is clearly no longer the control of laborers but rather the control of the undesirable, the criminal and the "nuisance."

Discussion

The foregoing analysis of the vagrancy laws has demonstrated that these laws were a legislative innovation which reflected the socially perceived necessity of providing an abundance of cheap labor to landowners during a period when serfdom was breaking down and when the pool of available labor was depleted. With the eventual breakup of feudalism the need for such laws eventually disappeared and the increased dependence of the economy upon industry and commerce rendered the former use of the vagrancy statutes unnecessary. As a result, for a substantial period the vagrancy statutes were dormant, undergoing only minor changes and, presumably, being applied infrequently. Finally, the vagrancy laws were subjected to considerable alteration through a shift in the focal concern of the statutes. Whereas in their inception the laws focused upon the "idle" and "those refusing to

[28] It is on this point that the vagrancy statutes have been subject to criticism. See for example, Lacey, Forrest W., "Vagrancy and Other Crimes of Personal Condition," *Harvard Law Review* (66), p. 1203.

[29] *Edwards v. California,* 314 S. 160 (1941).

labor" after the turn of the sixteenth century and emphasis came to be upon "rogues," "vagabonds," and others who were suspected of being engaged in criminal activities. During this period the focus was particularly upon "road-men" who preyed upon citizens who transported goods from one place to another. The increased importance of commerce to England during this period made it necessary that some protection be given persons engaged in this enter-prise and the vagrancy statutes provided one source for such protection by re-focusing the acts to be included under these statutes.

Comparing the results of this analysis with the findings of Hall's study of theft we see a good deal of correspondence. Of major importance is the fact that both analyses demonstrate the truth of Hall's assertion that "The functioning of courts is significantly related to concomitant cultural needs, and this applies to the law of procedure as well as to substantive law."[30]

Our analysis of the vagrancy laws also indicates that when changed social conditions create a perceived need for legal changes that these altera-tions will be effected through the revision and refocusing of existing statutes. This process was demonstrated in Hall's analysis of theft as well as in our analysis of vagrancy. In the case of vagrancy, the laws were dormant when the focal concern of the laws was shifted so as to provide control over potential criminals. In the case of theft the laws were re-interpreted (interestingly, by the courts and not by the legislature) so as to include persons who were trans-porting goods for a merchant but who absconded with the contents of the packages transported.

It also seems probable that when the social conditions change and previ-ously useful laws are no longer useful there will be long periods when these laws will remain dormant. It is less likely that they will be officially negated. During this period of dormancy it is the judiciary which has principal re-sponsibility for *not* applying the statutes. It is possible that one finds statutes being negated only when the judiciary stubbornly applies laws which do not have substantial public support. An example of such laws in contemporary times would be the "Blue Laws." Most states still have laws prohibiting the sale of retail goods on Sunday yet these laws are rarely applied. The laws are very likely to remain but to be dormant unless a recalcitrant judge or a vocal minority of the population insist that the laws be applied. When this happens we can anticipate that the statutes will be negated.[31] Should there arise a perceived need to curtail retail selling under some special circum-stances, then it is likely that these laws will undergo a shift in focal concern much like the shift which characterized the vagrancy laws. Lacking such application the laws will simply remain dormant except for rare instances where they will be negated.

This analysis of the vagrancy statutes (and Hall's analysis of theft as well) has demonstrated the importance of "vested interest" groups in the

---

[30] Hall, *op. cit.*, p. XII.

[31] Negation, in this instance, is most likely to come about by the repeal of the statute. More generally, however, negation may occur in several ways including the declaration of a statute as unconstitutional. This later mechanism has been used even for laws which have been "on the books" for long periods of time. Repeal is probably the most common, although not the only, procedure by which a law is negated.

emergence and/or alteration of laws. The vagrancy laws emerged in order to provide the powerful landowners with a ready supply of cheap labor. When this was no longer seen as necessary and particularly when the landowners were no longer dependent upon cheap labor nor were they a powerful interest group in the society the laws became dormant. Finally a new interest group emerged and was seen as being of great importance to the society and the laws were then altered so as to afford some protection to this group. These findings are thus in agreement with Weber's contention that "status groups" determine the content of the law.[32] The findings are inconsistent, on the other hand, with the perception of the law as simply a reflection of "public opinion" as is sometimes found in the literature.[33] We should be cautious in concluding, however, that either of these positions are necessarily correct. The careful analysis of other laws, and especially of laws which do not focus so specifically upon the "criminal," are necessary before this question can be finally answered.

In conclusion, it is hoped that future analyses of changes within the legal structure will be able to benefit from this study by virtue of (1) the data provided and (2) the utilization of a set of concepts (innovation, dormancy, concern and negation) which have proved useful in the analysis of the vagrancy law. Such analyses should provide us with more substantial grounds for rejecting or accepting as generally valid the description of some of the processes which appear to characterize changes in the legal system.

[32] M. Rheinstein, *Max Weber on Law in Economy and Society* (Harvard University Press, 1954).

[33] Friedman, N., *Law in a Changing Society* (Berkeley and Los Angeles: University of California Press, 1959).

EDWIN H. SUTHERLAND

The Diffusion of
Sexual Psychopath Laws

This paper is an analysis of the diffusion of sexual psychopath laws from the
point of view of collective behavior. Since 1937 twelve states and the District
of Columbia have enacted sexual psychopath laws. With minor variations they
provide that a person who is diagnosed as a sexual psychopath may be confined for an indefinite period in a state hospital for the insane. This confinement is not ordered by a criminal court as a punishment for crime but by a
probate court for the protection of society against persons who are believed to
have irresistible sexual impulses.[1]

Implicit in these laws is a series of propositions which have been made
explicit in an extensive popular literature, namely, that the present danger
to women and children from serious sex crimes is very great, for the number
of sex crimes is large and is increasing more rapidly than any other crime; that
most sex crimes are committed by "sexual degenerates," "sex fiends," or "sexual
psychopaths" and that these persons persist in their sexual crimes throughout life; that they always give warning that they are dangerous by first committing minor offenses; that any psychiatrist can diagnose them with a high
degree of precision at an early age, before they have committed serious sex
crimes; and that sexual psychopaths who are diagnosed and identified should
be confined as iresponsible persons until they are pronounced by psychiatrists
to be completely and permanently cured of their malady.[2]

[1] In some states conviction of a sex crime is a prerequisite to the operation of this
law. Even in this case the significant characteristic of the law is that it takes the
criminal out of the realm of ordinary punishment and treats him as a patient with a
mental malady.

[2] J. Edgar Hoover, "How Safe Is Your Daughter?" *American Magazine*, CXLIV
(July, 1947), 32–33; David G. Wittels, "What Can We Do about Sex Crimes?" *Satur-
day Evening Post*, CCXXI (December 11, 1948), 30 ff.; C. J. Dutton, "Can We End
Sex Crimes?" *Christian Century*, XLIV (December 22, 1937), 1594–95; F. C. Wald-
rup, "Murder as a Sex Practice," *American Mercury* (February, 1948), 144–58; Charles

Source: Edwin H. Sutherland, "The Diffusion of Sexual Psychopath Laws," *American
Journal of Sociology*, 56 (September, 1950), pp. 142–148. Copyright © 1950 by The
University of Chicago Press. Reprinted by permission.

Most of these propositions can be demonstrated to be false and the others questionable. More particularly, the concept of the "sexual psychopath" is so vague that it cannot be used for judicial and administrative purposes without the danger that the law may injure the socitey more than do the sex crimes which it is designed to correct. Moreover, the states which have enacted such laws make little or no use of them. And there is no difference in the trend in rates of serious sex crimes, so far as it can be determined, between the states which enact such laws and adjoining states which do not.[3]

These dangerous and futile laws are being diffused with considerable rapidity in the United States. Michigan first enacted such a law in 1937.[4] Illinois followed in 1938, and California and Minnesota in 1939. Thus four states have had these laws for ten years. In 1943 Vermont passed a sexual psychopath law; in 1945 Ohio; in 1947 Massachusetts, Washington, and Wisconsin; in 1948 the District of Columbia; and in 1949 Indiana, New Hampshire, and New Jersey. They continue to spread, with no indication of abatement. What is the explanation of this diffusion of laws which have little or no merit?

First, these laws are customarily enacted after a state of fear has been aroused in a community by a few serious sex crimes committed in quick succession. This is illustrated in Indiana, where a law was passed following three or four sexual attacks in Indianapolis, with murder in two. Heads of families bought guns and watchdogs, and the supply of locks and chains in the hardware stores of the city was completely exhausted.[5]

The sex murders of children are most effective in producing hysteria. Speaking of New York City in 1937, after four girls had been murdered in connection with sexual attacks, Austin H. MacCormick says:

> For a while it was utterly unsafe to speak to a child on the street unless one was well-dressed and well-known in the neighborhood. To try to help a lost child, with tears streaming down its face, to find its way home would in some neighborhoods cause a mob to form and violence to be threatened.[6]

The hysteria produced by child murders is due in part to the fact that the ordinary citizen cannot understand a sex attack on a child. The ordinary citizen can understand fornication or even forcible rape of a woman, but he concludes that a sexual attack on an infant or a girl of six years must be the act of a fiend or maniac. Fear is the greater because the behavior is so incomprehensive.

A protracted man-hunt following a sex attack arouses additional fear. The newspapers report daily on the progress of the chase, and every real or imagined sex attack, from near and far, is given prominence. In the case of

---

Harris, "A New Report on Sex Crimes," *Coronet* (October, 1947), 3–9; Howard Whitman, "Terror in Our Cities: No. I, Detroit," *Collier's,* November 19, 1949, pp. 13–15, 64–66.

[3] These appraisals of the sexual psychopath laws have been elaborated in my paper in the *Journal of Criminal Law and Criminology,* XL (January–February, 1950), 534–54.

[4] This law was declared unconstitutional, but a revised law was enacted in 1939.

[5] *Time,* November 24, 1947, pp. 29–30.

[6] "New York's Present Problem," *Mental Hygiene,* XX (January, 1938), 4–5.

Fred Stroble in Los Angeles in November, 1949, three days elapsed between the discovery of the mutilated body of his victim and his capture. A description of the crime and of the suspected criminal was sent to all adjoining cities and counties, and blockades were set up along the Mexican border. Watches were set in hotels, motels, bus stations, railway stations, and saloons. Hundreds of reports came to the police from Los Angeles and from other cities. Timid old men were pulled off streetcars and taken to police stations for identification, and every grandfather was subject to suspicion. The body of a drowned man, recovered from the ocean, was at first reported to be Stroble. The history of Stroble's molestations of other girls was reported. A detailed description of seven other cases of sexual murders of girls in Los Angeles since 1924 was published. At the end of the week, twenty-five other cases of molestations of girls in Los Angeles had been reported to the Los Angeles police.[7] After three days it appeared that Stroble had gone to Ocean Park, on the edge of Los Angeles, and had stayed in hotels there. He then returned to Los Angeles with the intention of surrendering to the police. He went into a bar after alighting from a bus and was recognized and pointed out to a policeman. The picture of the policeman who made the arrest was published in scores of newspapers over the United States as the "capturer of the sex fiend." After his capture, other details of the case and of related cases kept the community in a state of tension. As soon as the district attorney secured from Stroble an account of the manner of the murder, he went to the assembled reporters and repeated the story, "with beads of sweat standing on his face and neck." The psychiatrist's diagnosis of Stroble was published: he loved this little girl because he was a timid and weak old man, insufficiently aggressive to approach grown women; the murder of the girl was merely an incident due to fear of being caught and punished.

Fear is seldom or never related to statistical trends in sex crimes. New York City's terror in 1937 was at its height in August, although that was not the month when sex crimes reached their peak. The number of sex crimes known to the police of New York City was 175 in April, 211 in May, 159 in August, and 177 in September.[8] Ordinarily, from two to four spectacular sex crimes in a few weeks are sufficient to evoke the phrase "sex crime wave."

Fear is produced more readily in the modern community than it was earlier in our history because of the increased publicity regarding sex crimes. Any spectacular sex crime is picked up by the press associations and is distributed to practically all the newspapers in the nation; in addition, it is often described in news broadcasts. Then weekly and monthly journals published general articles on sex crimes. All this produces a widespread uneasiness which, given a few local incidents, readily bursts into hysteria.

Although this condition of fear has been found in all the states prior to the enactment of their sexual psychopath laws, it is not a sufficient explanation of the laws. For generations communities have been frightened by sex crimes

[7] "Molestation" is a weasel word and can refer to anything from rape to whistling at a girl.

[8] Citizens' Committee for the Control of Crime in New York, "Sex Crimes in New York City," quoted in *Journal of Criminal Law and Criminology*, XXIX (May, 1938), 143–44.

and have not enacted sexual psychopath laws. In the present generation the states which have not enacted sexual psychopath laws have had similar fears.

A second element in the process of developing sexual psychopath laws is the agitated activity of the community in connection with the fear. The attention of the community is focused on sex crimes, and people in the most varied situations envisage dangers and see the need of and possibility for their control. When a news broadcaster, in connection with the Stroble case, expressed the belief over the radio that something should be done, he received more than two hundred telegrams agreeing with him. The mother of the murdered girl demanded punishment for the daughter of Stroble, who had harbored him without notifying the parents of girls in the neighborhood that he was a dangerous criminal. A woman spoke in condemnation of strip-tease and other lewd shows as stimulating sex fiends and demanded that they be closed. Letters to the editors demanded that sex criminals be castrated; others recommended whipping. The City Council of Los Angeles adopted a resolution demanding that the legislature of the state be called in special session to enact laws which would punish sex crimes more severely and would make sex criminals ineligible for parole. The attorney-general of the state sent a bulletin to all sheriffs and police chiefs urging them to enforce strictly the laws which required registration of all sex criminals. The judiciary committee of the state legislature appointed a subcommittee to study the problem of sex crimes and to make recommendations to a special session of the legislature. The superintendent of city schools urged, among other things, that sex offenders who loitered around the schools should be prosecuted. The grand jury met and started a general investigation of sex crimes. The Juvenile Protective Committee urged an appropriation of $50,000 for medical and clinical treatment of sex offenders, and the County Probation Department energetically requested the authorizing of a psychiatric clinic for the study and supervision of sex offenders. It was reported that some psychiatrists in the city opposed these suggestions for psychiatric clinics as "socialized medicine" and "statism."

In the meantime, organization developed in other directions. The sheriff's office set up a special detail on sex offenses, with a staff to co-ordinate all police activities on sex offenses in the county. The Parent-Teacher Association sponsored mass meetings, with blanks on which interested persons could enroll as members of an organization which would continue its efforts until effective action for control of sex crimes was taken. At the first mass meeting, attended by about eight hundred people, speakers were scheduled to explain the existing laws and procedures and to suggest programs for improvement. The news of the Stroble crime and of subsequent events was carried over the nation by the press associations and produced national reactions. J. Edgar Hoover was quoted as calling for an all-out war against sex criminals. The Associated Press's science editor wrote a syndicated column on the views of leaders in the nation regarding methods of controlling sex crimes.

The third phase in the development of these sexual psychopath laws has been the appointment of a committee. The committee gathers by the many conflicting recommendations of persons and groups of persons, attempts to determine "facts," studies procedures in other states, and makes recommendations, which generally include bills for the legislature. Although the general fear usually subsides within a few days, a committee has the formal duty of following through until positive action is taken. Terror which does not result in a committee is much less likely to result in a law. The appointment of a committee is a conventional method of dealing with any problem. Even during the recent agitations in California and Michigan, which have had sexual psychopath laws for ten years, committees have been appointed to study sex crimes and to make recommendations.

These committees deal with emergencies, and their investigations are relatively superficial. Even so, the community sometimes becomes impatient. Before a committee appointed by the Massachusetts legislature had had time for even a superficial investigation, the impatient legislature enacted a sexual psychopath law. The committee report several months later recommended that the statute which had just been enacted should be repealed on the ground that sex crimes should not be considered apart from the general correctional system of the state.[9] Similarly, the legislature of New Jersey enacted a sexual psychopath law in 1949 and also appointed a committee to investigate sex crimes and to suggest a policy. In New York City, on the other hand, the mayor took certain emergency actions in 1937 and did not appoint a committee until several months after the crisis. This committee made a very thorough study of all sex crimes in New York City in the decade 1930–39 and did not report for two or three years. The result was that New York State did not enact a sexual psychopath law; and, in fact, the committee was divided in its recommendation that such a law should be enacted.

In some states, at the committee stage of the development of a sexual psychopath law, psychiatrists have played an important part. The psychiatrists, more than any others, have been the interest group back of the laws. A committee of psychiatrists and neurologists in Chicago wrote the bill which became the sexual psychopath law of Illinois; the bill was sponsored by the Chicago Bar Association and by the state's attorney of Cook County and was enacted with little opposition in the next session of the state legislature.[10] In Minnesota all of the members of the governor's committee except one were psychiatrists. In Wisconsin the Milwaukee Neuropsychiatric Society shared in pressing the Milwaukee Crime Commission for the enactment of a law. In Indiana the attorney-general committee received from the American Psychiatric Association copies of all of the sexual psychopath laws which had been enacted in other states.

Such actions by psychiatrists are consistent in some respects with their general views. Most psychiatrists assert that serious sex crimes are the result of mental pathology, although few of them would make such unqualified statements as that attributed to Dr. A. A. Brill at the time of the panic in

---

[9] Massachusetts, "Report of the Commission for Investigation of the Prevalence of Sex Crimes," *House Reports*, Nos. 1169 and 2169, 1948.

[10] W. S. Stewart, "Concerning Proposed Legislation for the Commitment of Sex Offenders," *John Marshall Law Quarterly*, III (March, 1938), 407–21; W. H. Haines, H. R. Hoffman, and H. A. Esser, "Commitments under the Criminal Sexual Psychopath Law in the Criminal Court of Cook County, Illinois," *American Journal of Psychiatry*, CV (November, 1948), 422.

New York City in 1937: "Sex crimes are committed only by people of defective mentality. All mental defectives have either actual or potential sex abnormalities."[1] Also, psychiatrists almost without exception favor the view that criminals should be treated as patients. Moreover, since the sexual psychopath laws usually specify that the diagnosis for the court shall be made by psychiatrists, they have an economic interest in the extension of this procedure.

While psychiatrists have often played an important part in the promotion of sexual psychopath laws, many prominent psychiatrists have been forthright in their opposition to them. They know that the sexual psychopath cannot be defined or identified. Probably most of the psychiatrists in the nation have been indifferent to legislation; they have exerted themselves neither to promote nor to oppose enactment.

The function of the committee is to organize information. The committee, dealing with emergency conditions, customarily takes the information which is available. Much of this has been distributed through popular literature, which contains the series of propositions outlined above. The latter are customarily accepted without firsthand investigation by the committee and are presented to the legislature and the public as "science." Although these propositions are all false or questionable, they have nevertheless been very effective in the diffusion of the laws. Bills are presented to the legislature with the explanation that these are the most enlightened and effective methods of dealing with the problem of sex crimes and that the states which have sexual psychopath laws have found them effective. Very little discussion occurs in the legislature. When the bill for the District of Columbia was presented in Congress, the only question asked was whether this bill, if enacted, would weaken or strengthen the sex laws; the questioner was satisfied with a categorical reply that the bill would strengthen them.[12]

The law is similarly presented to the public as the most enlightened and effective method of dealing with sex offenders. After the sexual psychopath bill had been drafted in Indiana, the *Indianapolis Star* had the following editorial:

> Indiana today is one step nearer an enlightened approach to the growing menace of sex crimes. A proposed new law to institutionalize sexual psychopathics until pronounced permanently recovered has been drafted by a special state citizens' committee which helped the attorney general's office to study the problem. . . . Such a law should become a realistic, practical answer to the sex crime problem. This type of legislation has succeeded elsewhere and is long overdue in Indiana.[13]

The diffusion of sexual psychopath laws, consequently, has occurred under the following conditions: a state of fear developed, to some extent, by a general, nation-wide popular literature and made explicit by a few spectacular sex crimes: a series of scattered and conflicting reactions by many individ-

---

[11] Quoted in *Time*, August 23, 1937, pp. 42–44. If the Kinsey Report is trustworthy, all males, whether defective or not, "have either actual or potential sex abnormalities."

[12] *Congressional Record*, XCIV (April 26, 1948), 4886.

[13] December 8, 1948.

uals and groups within the community; the appointment of a committee, which in some cases has been guided by psychiatrists, which organizes existing information regarding sex crimes and the precedents for their control and which presents a sexual psychopath law to the legislature and to the public as the most scientific and enlightened method of protecting society against dangerous sex criminals. The organization of information in the name of science and without critical appraisal seems to be more invariably related to the emergence of a sexual psychopath law than is any other part of this genetic process.

The most significant reason for the specific content of the proposals of these committees—treatment of the sex criminal as a patient—is that it is consistent with a general social movement.[14] For a century or more two rival policies have been used in criminal justice. One is the punitive policy; the other is the treatment policy. The treatment policy is evidenced by probation, parole, the indeterminate sentence, the juvenile court, the court clinic, and the facilities in correctional institutions for education, recreation, and religion. The treatment policy has been gaining, and the punitive policy has been losing, ground.

The trend toward treatment and away from punishment is based on cultural changes in the society. The trend away from punishment in criminal justice is consistent with the trend away from punishment in the home, the school, and the church. The trend toward treatment is consistent with a general trend toward scientific procedures in other fields, as illustrated by medicine, with its techniques of diagnosis and with treatment and prevention based on scientific knowledge of the causes of disease. The trend away from punishment toward treatment is not, however, based on a demonstration that treatment is more effective than punishment in protecting society against crime, for no such demonstration is available. Also, the fact that the trend in punishment is consistent with trends in other aspects of culture is not an adequate explanation of the trend in punishment. A general theory of social change must include more than a showing that one part of a culture changes consistently with other parts of a culture.

Not only has there been a trend toward individualization in treatment of offenders, but there has been a trend also toward psychiatric policies. Treatment tends to be organized on the assumption that the criminal is a socially sick person; deviant traits of personality, regarded as relatively permanent and generic, are regarded as the causes of crime. Since the time of Lombroso, at least, the logic of the typological schools of criminology has remained constant, while the specific trait used as the explanation of criminal behavior has changed from time to time. The first school held that criminals constitute a physical type, either epileptoid or degenerate in character; the second, that they are feeble-minded; the third, and current, school holds that criminals are emotionally unstable. All hold that crime can be caused only by a mental pathology of some type. The professionally trained persons other than lawyers who are employed in the field of criminal justice, whether as social workers,

[14] See Herbert Blumer, "Social Movements," chap. xxiii in *New Outline of the Principles of Sociology,* edited by A. M. Lee (New York: Barnes & Noble, 1946).

psychologists, psychiatrists, or sociologists, tend toward the belief that emotional traits are the explanation of crime. This conclusion likewise has not been demonstrated, and the body of evidence in conflict with the conclusion is increasing.

A specific aspect of this trend toward treatment of offenders as patients is the provision for psychotic and feeble-minded criminals. When such persons do the things prohibited by criminal law, they may be held to be irresponsible from the legal point of view and may still be ordered to confinement in institutions for the protection of society. All the states have some provision for psychotic criminals, and several have provisions for feeble-minded criminals. In some European nations the provisions for psychotic and feeble-minded criminals have been expanded and generalized under the name of "social security" laws: some have included sexual criminals under their social security measures, and the latter are the direct precedents for the sexual psychopath laws of the United States.

One of the questions in criminal law has been the criterion of responsibility. The courts have generally held that "knowledge of right and wrong" is the most satisfactory criterion. The psychiatrists have generally opposed this; they have argued that 90 percent of the inmates of state hospitals for the insane can distinguish right from wrong but are, nevertheless, legally irresponsible. The important consideration, they argue, is that the psychotic person has impulses which he cannot control and that "irresistible impulse" should be substituted for "knowledge of right and wrong" as the criterion. The psychiatrists, however, have not been able to make their criterion clear cut for practical purposes.

The trend away from punishment and toward treatment of criminals as patients is to some extent a "paper" trend'. Laws are enacted which provide for treatment rather than punishment; but the treatment goes on within a framework of punishment, and in many respects the punitive policies continue, despite changes in legislation. Probation, for instance, is upheld from the constitutional point of view as a suspension of punishment rather than as a method co-ordinate with punishment and is regarded by some persons as effective primarily because of the threat implied in it that punishment will follow violation of probation.

The sexual psychopath laws are consistent with this general social movement toward treatment of criminals as patients. Some laws define sexual psychopaths as "patients"; they provide for institutional care similar to that already provided for psychotic and feeble-minded criminals; they substitute the criterion of "irresistible impulse" for the criterion of "knowledge of right and wrong"; and they reflect the belief that sex criminals are psychopathic. The consistency with a general social movement provides a part of the explanation of the diffusion of sexual psychopath laws.

In the United States the connection between the enactment of sexual psychopath laws and the development of treatment policies is, at best, vague and loose. This is obvious from a consideration of the distribution of the laws. Three New England states, one Middle Atlantic state, and two Pacific Coast states have passed such laws; but the remainder—half of all the states with sexual psychopath laws—are in the North Central region. These laws, in fact, have been enacted in a solid block of North Central states: Ohio, Indiana, Illinois, Michigan, Wisconsin, and Minnesota. On the other hand, no state in the southern, South Central, or Mountain regions has a sexual psychopath law. These regions also are less committed to treatment policies than are the regions which have sexual psychopath laws. While this association may be found when large regions are compared, it is not found when specific states are compared; New York State, for instance, has had an extensive development of treatment policies but no sexual psychopath law. Similarly, the states which have sexual psychopath laws are not differentiated clearly from states which do not have such laws by any statistical variable which has been discovered: they are not differentiated by the rate of rape, by the racial composition of the population, by the proportion of immigrants in the population, by the sex ratio in the population, or by the extent of industrialization or urbanization.

IV

ORGANIZATIONAL HANDLING AND DEVIANT CATEGORIES

Introduction

Suggestions concerning the effects of deviance-controlling organizations on the collective definition of deviant categories have appeared in the previous parts of this book. In this section we concentrate on these effects, on the ways in which societal definitions are reinforced and altered. Becker called attention to the rule enforcer, his second type of "moral entrepreneur," suggesting that the enforcer exercises discretion, sets priorities, and spends much time legitimizing his role activities and in "coercing" respect (Becker, 1963: 155–163). In performing the tasks of identifying and processing deviants, rule enforcers act as occupants of positions in formal organizations. So also do occupants of rehabilitative roles, whether the agencies are voluntary or involuntary, public or private.

In deviance-controlling organizations it is difficult to separate the rehabilitators neatly from the rule enforcers. Probation and parole are examples of rehabilitative effort, or at least rhetoric, within the framework of criminal law controls. In prior parts of the book we have noted the view of Thomas Szasz that psychiatry is a medical mask for the social control of deviant behavior, as seen most clearly in involuntary commitments. We are concerned here with both enforcement and rehabilitative roles, and with mixed roles, and with the overall effects on collective definitions of both involuntary and voluntary control organizations.

Variables affecting the decisions and actions of deviance-controlling organizations and their effects on officially labeled persons are stressed in much of the literature on deviance. The effects of officially held stereotypes of deviants (Piliavin and Briar, 1964; Sudnow, 1965; Scheff, 1964), of etiological assumptions or other cognitive beliefs in organizational ideologies (Stoll, 1968), of methods of keeping agency records (Kitsuse and Cicourel, 1963; Skolnick, 1966), of different clinical models and diagnostic procedures (Mercer, 1973; Seeley, 1962), of the behavior of potential clients towards the rule enforcers (Bittner, 1967; Miller and Schwartz, 1966; Petersen, 1972), and of official actions that coerce deviants to conform to public images of them (Scott, 1967, 1969; Spradley, 1970) have all received attention. In many such studies there are suggestions of possible agency influences on the collective definition of deviant categories, but direct evidence of such effects is not plentiful.

The selection by Currie on the control of witchcraft in Renaissance Europe stresses the different effects of repressive and restrained regimes and how effectively deviance can be invented by control systems. It is helpful to compare this with the selection by Connor on the Soviet purge in Part III and with the suggestions by Erikson in Part I concerning organizational processing and the manufacture of deviance. Such instances, while extreme, raise such questions as: Can repression of deviants not become extreme by democratic consensus as well as by authoritarian decree? Is repression-restraint not a continuous rather than a dichotomous variable? At a given time do controls that seem reasonable to some people not often seem repressive to others? And do major shifts in predominant sentiment not occur, so that the restraint of one time appears in retrospect to have been repression?

Scheff's evidence that rural courts make a more rational effort to adjudicate allegations of mental illness than urban courts do has major implications. If it is generally more common in urban courts to act on the presumption of insanity, perhaps urbanites are less willing to tolerate and live with emotional problems or less able to hide them. The selection from Goffman contrasts the mental patient's willful deviance with the involuntary and thus nonthreatening deviance of the physically ill person. Let us add the suggestion that the willful intention to violate certain kinds of norms is more threatening in urban settings than in rural and that courts, clinics, and hospitals assist the family in meeting this threat. Quite possibly the rural-urban differences in statistics on mental illness reflect this social control response rather than actual differences in the incidence of emotional problems. Very likely the higher rates reflect the greater proportion of rule enforcers and therapists, but why do urban areas feel the need of more such specialists? Because of more education and more humaneness or because of less tolerance for willful deviance?

Bureaucratic self-preservation is the emphasis in Dickson's paper on the crusading role of the Narcotics Bureau in the passage of the federal Marihuana Tax Act, which broadened the definition of criminal drug possession by bringing a nonnarcotic drug under Bureau control. Whether bureaucrats act in such instances out of sheer self-interest or out of genuine conviction about the fact beliefs and the values concerned, deviance-controlling organizations evidently can have a major impact on the scope of their own authority. Berry's contribution shows how organizational variables may be involved in broadening the definition of juvenile delinquency, the target population, and the services rendered and in lowering the level of seriousness required for agency intervention.

Voluntary organizations devoted to rehabilitating deviants may also facilitate social control. Why do some of these voluntary agencies fail to gain public support while others are lionized? Can the popular ones influence public definitions of deviance, or do they merely conform to them? The selection by Trice and Roman accounts for both the popularity and rehabilitative success of Alcoholics Anonymous in terms of the adoption of the repentent role, by means of which hedonism is rejected and middle class ideals of personal responsibility are embraced. They believe this approach has influenced the public's perception of drinking. Synanon, a popular voluntary organization for rehabilitating drug addicts with an approach adapted from Alcoholics Anonymous, also has perhaps influenced public perception by dramatizing the repentent role (Yablonsky, 1965). In the selection from Goffman the general process involved here is called "apology," the ritual expression that the offense is not an accurate indication of the person's attitude towards social norms.

Both conflict and consensus themes may be found in these studies, and perhaps some pluralism, but not in systematic form. There is also some implicit use of interactionist perspectives. Little use is made of organizational theory, although Berry deals with three organizational variables and he and Dickson imply some propositions about bureaucratic self-preservation and growth. These and some other materials show organizational effects on the collective definition of deviance, but we stand in need of more carefully designed and theoretically guided studies of these relationships.

References

BECKER, HOWARD S.
> 1963   Outsiders. New York: The Free Press.

BITTNER, EGON
> 1967   "The Police on Skid Row: A Study of Peace Keeping." American Sociological Review 32 (October): 699–715.

KITSUSE, JOHN I., and AARON V. CICOUREL
> 1963   "A Note on the Use of Official Statistics." Social Problems 12 (Fall): 131–139.

MERCER, JANE R.
> 1973   Labeling the Mentally Retarded. Berkeley: University of California Press.

MILLER, DOROTHY, and MICHAEL SCHWARTZ
> 1966   "County Lunacy Commission Hearings: Some Observations on Commitments to a State Mental Hospital." Social Problems 14 (Summer): 26–35.

PETERSEN, DAVID M.
> 1972   "Police Disposition of the Petty Offender." Sociology and Social Research 56, (April): 320–330.

PILIAVIN, IRVING, and SCOTT BRIAR
> 1964   "Police Encounters with Juveniles." American Journal of Sociology 69 (September): 206–214.

SCHEFF, THOMAS J.
> 1964   "Typification in the Diagnostic Practices of Rehabilitation Agenies." In Marvin B. Sussman (ed.), Sociology and Rehabilitation. Washington, D.C.: American Sociological Association.

SCOTT, ROBERT A.
> 1967   "The Selection of Clients by Social Welfare Agencies: The Case of the Blind." Social Problems 14 (Winter): 248–257.
> 1969   The Making of Blind Men. New York: Russell Sage.

SEELEY, JOHN R.
> 1962   "Alcoholism is a Disease: Implications for Social Policy." In David J. Pittman and Charles R. Snyder (eds.), Alcohol, Culture and Drinking Patterns. New York: John Wiley & Sons.

SKOLNICK, JEROME H.
> 1966   Justice Without Trial. New York: John Wiley & Sons.

SPRADLEY, JAMES P.
    1970   You Owe Yourself a Drunk. Boston: Little, Brown and Co.
STOLL, CLARICE S.
    1968   "Images of Man and Social Control." Social Forces 47 (December):
           119–127.
SUDNOW, DAVID
    1965   "Normal Crimes: Sociological Features of the Penal Code in a Public
           Defender Office." Social Problems 12 (Winter): 255–276.
YABLONSKY, LEWIS
    1965   The Tunnel Back: Synanon. New York: The Macmillan Co.

ELLIOTT P. CURRIE

Crimes Without Criminals: Witchcraft and Its Control in Renaissance Europe

The sociological study of deviant behavior has begun to focus less on the deviant and more on society's response to him.[1] One of several implications of this perspective is that a major concern of the sociology of deviance should be the identification and analysis of different kinds of systems of social control. Particularly important is the analysis of the impact of different kinds of control systems on the way deviant behavior is perceived and expressed in societies.

By playing down the importance of intrinsic differences between deviants and conventional people, and between the social situation of deviants and that of nondeviants, the focus on social response implies much more than the commonplace idea that society defines the kinds of behavior that will be considered odd, disgusting, or criminal. It implies that many elements of the behavior system of a given kind of deviance, including such things as the rate of deviance and the kinds of people who are identified as a deviant, will be significantly affected by the kind of control system through which the behavior is defined and managed.

[1] This approach is presented in the following works, among others; H. S. Becker, *Outsiders* (1963); K. T. Erikson, *Wayward Puritans* (1966); J. I. Kitsuse. "Societal Response to Deviance. Some Problems of Theory and Method," 9 *Social Problems* 247–56 (Winter 1962); E. Goffman, *Stigma* (1963); and *Asylums* (1962). Earlier general statements in a similar vein can be found in E. M. Lemert, *Social Pathology* (1951); and F. Tannenbaum, *Crime and the Community* (1951).

The research on which this chapter is based was partially supported by a grant from the Ford Foundation, administered by the Center for the Study of Law and Society. I thank Howard S. Becker, Egon Bittner, Fred Dubow, David Matza, Sheldon L. Messinger and Philip Selznick for their comments on earlier versions, though they are not to be held responsible for the outcome.

In this paper, I attempt to add to the rather small body of research on kinds of social control systems and their impact.[2] The subject is witchcraft in Renaissance Europe, and in particular, the way in which the phenomenon of witchcraft differed in England and in continental Europe,[3] as a result of differences in their legal systems. I will show that the English and the continental legal systems during this period represented the two ends of a continuum along which different social control systems may be placed, and I will suggest some general ways in which each kind of control system affects the deviant behavior systems in which it is involved. Along the way, however, I will also suggest that the *degree* to which a social control system can influence the character of a deviant behavior system is variable and depends in part on the *kind* of behavior involved and the particular way it is socially defined.

Witchcraft as Deviance

Something labeled witchcraft can be found in many societies, but the particular definition of the crime of witchcraft which emerged in Renaissance Europe was unique. It consisted of the individual's making, for whatever reason and to whatever end, a pact or covenant with the Devil, thereby gaining the power to manipulate supernatural forces for anti-social and un-Christian ends. What was critical was the pact itself; not the assumption or use of the powers which it supposedly conferred, but the willful renunciation of the Faith implied by the act of Covenant with the Devil. Thus, on the Continent, witchcraft was usually prosecuted as a form of heresy, and in England as a felony whose essence was primarily mental.[4] Witchcraft, then, came to be defined as a sort of thought-crime. It was not necessarily related to the practice of magic, which was widespread and had many legitimate forms. There were statutes forbidding witchcraft before the Renaissance, but the new conception of witchcraft involved important changes in both the nature and the seriousness of the crime. Early legislation, throughout Europe, had tended to lump witchcraft and magic in the same category, and to deal with them as minor offenses. In ninth-century England, the Law of the Northumbrian Priests held that if anyone ". . . in any way love witchcraft, or worship idols, if he be a king's thane, let him pay X half-marks; half to Christ, half to the king. We are all

---

[2] One interesting study along these lines is E. M. Schur, Narcotic Addiction in England and America; The Impact of Public Policy (1963).

[3] Erikson, *supra* note 1, discusses some aspects of witchcraft in America, which unfortunately cannot be discussed here without unduly lengthening the paper. For the curious, though, it should be noted that the American experience was in general much closer to the English than to the continental experience, particularly in terms of the small number of witches executed. For anyone interested in American witchcraft, Erikson's discussion and bibliography is a good place to start.

[4] Elizabeth's statute of 1563 made witchcraft punishable by death only if it resulted in the death of the bewitched; witchcraft unconnected with death was a lesser offense. However, in 1604 James I revised the statute to invoke the death penalty for witchcraft regardless of result. On this point see R. T. Davies, *Four Centuries of Witch Beliefs* 15, 41–42 (1947).

to love and worship one God, and strictly hold one Christianity, and renounce all heathenship."[5]

Similar mildness is characteristic of other early English legislation, while the Catholic Church itself, in the 13th century, explicitly took the position that the belief in witchcraft was an illusion.[6] In no sense were witches considered by ecclesiastical or secular authorities to be a serious problem, until the 15th century.

I cannot speculate here on the process through which the early conception of witchcraft as, essentially, the witch's delusion evolved to the point where the witch was believed to have actual powers. Suffice it to say that such a shift in definition did take place,[7] that during the 15th and 16th centuries a new theological and legal conception of witchcraft emerged, which amounted to an official recognition of a hitherto unknown form of deviance. In 1484, Pope Innocent IV issued a Bull recognizing the seriousness of the crime of witchcraft, affirming its reality, and authorizing the use of the Holy Inquisition to prosecute it with full force. As an indication of the state of thinking on witchcraft at this time, this document serves admirably.

> It has recently come to our attention, not without bitter sorrow, that . . . many persons of both sexes, unmindful of their own salvation and straying from the Catholic Faith, have abandoned themselves to devils . . . and by their . . . accused charms and crafts, enormities and horrid offenses, have slain unborn infants and the offspring of cattle, have blasted the produce of the earth . . . these wretches furthermore afflict and torment men and women . . . with terrible and piteous pains. . . . Over and above this they blasphemously renounce the Faith which is theirs by the Sacrament of Baptism, and do not shrink from committing and perpetrating the foulest abominations and filthiest excesses . . .[8]

A few years later, the new conception of witchcraft was given practical impetus with the publication of a manual known as the *Malleus Maleficarum,* or Witch-Hammer, written by two German Inquistors under Papal authorization, which set forth in systematic form the heretofore diffuse beliefs on the

[5] Quoted in M. Murray, *The Witch-Cult in Western Europe* 22 (1962). Other early legislation is also quoted by Murray, and can also be found in C. L'Estrange Ewen, *Witch Hunting and Witch Trials* 1–5 (1929).

[6] This position was formulated in a document known as the *Capitulum Episcopi,* apparently written in 1215, which molded Church policy for over 200 years. It reads in part as follows:

> Some wicked women . . . seduced by the illusions and phantasms of demons, believe and profess that they ride at night with Diana on certain beasts with an innumerable company of women, passing over immense distances . . . priests everywhere should preach that they know this to be false, and that such phantasms are sent by the Evil Spirit, who deludes them in dreams. . . .

Quoted in 3 H. C. Lea, *A History of the Inquisition in the Middle Ages 493* (1888), and in Murray, *supra* note 5, at 22.

[7] The shift, however, did not take place all at once, nor did it take place without important ideological struggles both within and beyond the Church; a number of important figures remained skeptical throughout. Interesting materials on this process can be found in 1 H. C. Lea, *Materials Toward a History of Witchcraft* (1939).

[8] Quoted in Davies, *supra* note 4, at 4.

nature and habits of witches, means for their discovery, and guidelines for their trial and execution.[9] At this point, the witch persecutions in continental Europe entered a peak phase which lasted into the 18th century. Estimates of the number of witches executed in Western Europe vary, but half a million is an average count.[10] Although there were consistently dissident voices both within and outside of the Church, the prevalence of witches was a fact widely accepted by the majority, including a number of the most powerful intellects of the time. Luther and Calvin were believers, as was Jean Bodin, who wrote an extremely influential book on witches in which he argued, among other things, that those who scoffed at the reality of witches were usually witches themselves.[11] Witchcraft was used as an explanation for virtually everything drastic or unpleasant that occurred; leading one Jesuit critic of the persecutions to declare: "God and Nature no longer do anything; witches, everything."[12] In the 15th century, a delayed winter in the province of Treves brought over a hundred people to the stake as witches.[13]

Once officially recognized, the crime of witchcraft presented serious problems for those systems of control through which it was to be hunted down and suppressed. The fact that no one had ever been seen making a pact with the Devil made ordinary sources of evidence rather worthless. Ordinary people, indeed, were in theory unable to see the Devil at all; as an eminent jurist, Sinistrari, phrased the problem. "There can be no witness of that crime, since the Devil, visible to the witch, escapes the sight of all beside."[14] The attendant acts—flying by night, attending witches' Sabbaths, and so on—were of such nature that little reliable evidence of their occurrence could be gathered through normal procedures. The difficulty of proving that the crime had ever taken place severely taxed the competence of European legal institutions, and two different responses emerged. In England, the response to witchcraft took place within a framework of effective limitations on the suppressive power of the legal order and a relatively advanced conception of due process of law; on the Continent, the response took place within a framework of minimal limitations on the activity of the legal system, in which due process and legal restraint tended to go by the board.

Continental Europe: Repressive Control

In continental Europe, people accused of witchcraft were brought before the elaborate machinery of a specialized bureaucratic agency with unusual powers and what amounted to a nearly complete absence of institutional restraints on its activity. Originally, the control of witchcraft was the re-

[9] This remarkable work has been translated. J. Sprenger & H. Kramer, *Malleus Maleficarum* (M. Summers transl. 1948).

[10] This estimate is from G. L. Kittredge, *Notes on Witchcraft* 59 (1907).

[11] Davies, *supra* note 4, at 25, 5–9.

[12] Father Friedrich Spee, quoted in Kittredge, *supra* note 10, at 47.

[13] Lea, *supra* note 6, at 549.

[14] Quoted in G. Parrinder, *Witchcraft: European and African* 76 (1958).

sponsibility of the Inquisition. After the disappearance, for practical purposes, of the Inquisition in most of Western Europe in the 16th century, witches were tried before secular courts which retained for the most part the methods which the Inquisition had pioneered.[15] This was as true of the Protestant sectors of Europe—England excepted—as it was of those which remained Catholic.[16] The methods were effective and extreme.

Ordinary continental criminal procedure approximated the "inquisitorial" process, in which accusation, detection, prosecution and judgment are all in the hands of the official control system, rather than in those of private persons; and all of these functions reside basically in one individual.[17] The trial was not, as it was in the "accusatorial" procedure of English law, a confrontative combat between the accuser and the accused, but an attack by the judge and his staff upon the suspect, who carried with him a heavy presumption of guilt. Litigation was played down or rejected.[18]

> The system of procedure called inquisitorial is more scientific and more complex than the accusatory system. It is better adapted to the needs of social repression. Its two predominant features are the secret inquiry to discover the culprit, and the employment of torture to obtain his confession.[19]

Above and beyond the tendencies to repressive control visible in the inquisitorial process generally, the establishment of the Holy Inquisition in the 13th century as a weapon against heresy ushered in a broadening of the powers of the control system vis-à-vis the accused. Ecclesiastical criminal procedure had always been willing to invoke extraordinary methods in particularly heinous crimes, especially those committed in secret.[20] With the coming of the Inquisition a good many procedural safeguards were systematically cast aside, on the ground that the Inquisition was to be seen as "an impartial spiritual father, whose functions in the salvation of souls should be fettered by no rules."[21] Thus, in the interest of maintaining the ideological purity of Christendom, the legal process became conceived as a tool of the moral order, whose use and limits were almost entirely contingent on the needs of that order.

Nevertheless, certain powerful safeguards existed, in theory, for the accused. Chief among these was a rigorous conception of proof, especially in the case of capital crimes. In general, continental criminal procedure, at least from the 15th century onward, demanded, a "complete proof" as warrant for capital punishment. "Complete proof" generally implied evidence on the order of testimony of two eyewitnesses to the criminal act or, in the case of certain crimes which otherwise would be difficult to establish, like heresy or conspiracy against the Prince, written proofs bound by rigorous standards of authenticity.[22] In most cases of heresy and of witchcraft generally, proof

[15] Lea, *supra* note 7, at 244.
[16] G. L. Burr, *The Fate of Dietrich Flade, Papers of the American Historical Association*, pt. 3, 11 (July 1891).
[17] *See* A. Esmein, *A History of Continental Criminal Procedure* 8 *passim* (1913).
[18] *Ibid*. at 9.
[19] *Ibid*. at 8.
[20] *Ibid*. at 128.
[21] H. C. Lea, *History of the Inquisition in the Middle Ages* 405 (1958).
[22] Esmein, *supra* note 17, at 622–23.

of this order was hard, if not impossible, to come by, for obvious reasons. As a result, it was necessary to form a complete proof through combining confession, which was strong but not complete evidence, with another indication, such as testimony by one witness.[23] The result was tremendous pressure for confession at all costs, as well as a pressure for the relaxation of standards for witnesses and other sources of lesser evidence. The pressure for confession put a premium on the regular and systematic use of torture. In this manner, the procedural safeguard of rigorous proof broke down in practice through the allowance of extraordinary procedures which became necessary to circumvent it.[24]

In theory, there were some restraints on the use of torture, but not many. One 16th century German jurist argued that it could not be used without sufficient indication of guilt, that it could not be used "immoderately," and that it should be tempered according to the strength, age, sex and condition of the offender. German officials, when approving the use of torture, usually added the phrase *Doch Mensch-oder-Christlicher Weise,*—roughly, "In humane or Christian fashion."[25] In theory, confessions under torture had to be reaffirmed afterward by the accused; but torture, though it could not lawfully be repeated, could be "continued" indefinitely after interruption, and few accused witches could maintain a denial of their confession after several sessions.[26]

Besides being virtually required for the death penalty, confession was useful in two other important ways, which consequently increased the usefulness of torture. First, confession involved the denunciation of accomplices, which assured a steady flow of accused witches into the courts.[27] Secondly, confessions were publicly read at executions, and distributed to the populace at large, which reinforced the legitimacy of the trials themselves and re-created in the public mind the reality of witchcraft itself. If people *said* they flew by night to dance with the devil, then surely there was evil in the land, and the authorities were more than justified in their zeal to root it out. In extorting confessions from accused witches, the court also made use of means

[23] *Ibid.* at 625. It would still, of course, have been difficult to get even one reliable witness to an act of witchcraft; in practice, the testimony of one accused, under torture, was used for this purpose.

[24] *See* Esmein, *supra* note 17, at 625. In a study of the criminal process in China, Cohen relates, in a similar vein, that the requirement of confession for conviction in Manchu China reinforced the temptation to use torture on the accused. *See* J. A. Cohen, "The Criminal Process in the People's Republic of China; an Introduction," 79 *Harv. L. Rev.* 473 (1966). It should be noted that the employment of torture by the Inquisition was a retrograde step in continental criminal procedure. The Church explicitly condemned torture; after it had been used by the Romans, torture was not again a standard procedure in Western Europe until it was reactivated in the 1200s in the offensive against heresy. *See* Esmein, *supra* note 17, at 9. It was early laid down as an accepted rule of Canon Law that no confession should be extracted by torment; but the elimination of trials by ordeal in the 13th century, coupled with the rise of powerful heretical movements, put strong pressure on the Church to modify its approach. Originally, torture was left to the secular authorities to carry out, but a Bull of Pope Alexander IV in 1256 authorized Inquisitors to absolve each other for using it directly, and to grant each other dispensation for irregularities in its use. *See* Lea, *supra* note 1, at 421.

[25] 2 Lea, *supra* note 7, at 854–55.

[26] Lea, *supra* note 1, at 427–28; Esmein, *supra* note 17, at 113–14.

[27] 2 Lea, *supra* note 7, at 885.

other than torture. Confession was usually required if the accused were to receive the last sacraments and avoid damnation,[28] and the accused, further, were frequently promised pardon if they confessed, a promise which was rarely kept.[29]

In line with the tendency to relax other standards of evidence, there was a considerable weakening of safeguards regarding testimony of witnesses. Heretics could testify, which went against established ecclesiastical policy; so could excommunicates, perjurors, harlots, children and others who ordinarily were not allowed to bear witness. Witnesses themselves were liable to torture if they equivocated or appeared unwilling to testify; and, contrary to established procedure in ordinary continental courts, names of witnesses were withheld from the accused.[30]

In general, prisoners were not provided with information on their case.[31] Most of the proceedings were held in secret.[32] The stubborn prisoner who managed to hold to a denial of guilt was almost never released from custody[33] and frequently spent years in prison.[34] Acquittal, in witchcraft and heresy cases, was virtually impossible. Lacking enough evidence for conviction, the court could hold an accused in prison indefinitely at its discretion. In general, innocence was virtually never the verdict in such cases; the best one could hope for was "not proven."[35]

Legal counsel for the accused under the Inquisition was often prohibited, again contrary to ordinary continental procedure.[36] Where counsel was allowed, it was with the disturbing understanding that successful or overly eager defense laid the counsel himself open to charges of heresy or of conspiracy to aid heretics.[37] Moreover, counsel was appointed by the court, was warned not to assume a defense he "knew to be unjust," and could be sum-

---

[28] 3 Lea, *supra* note 6, at 506.

[29] *Ibid.* at 514; 2 Lea, *supra* note 7, at 895. Deception by the court in witchcraft cases was widely approved. Bodin argued that the court should use lying and deception of the accused whenever possible; the authors of the *Malleus Maleficarum* felt that it was a good idea for the courts to promise life to the accused, since the fear of execution often prevented confession.

[30] Esmein, *supra* note 17, at 91–94; Lea, *supra* note 21, at 434–37.

[31] Esmein, *supra* note 17, at 129.

[32] Lea, *supra* note 21, at 406.

[33] *Ibid.* at 419.

[34] *Ibid.* at 419.

[35] *Ibid.* at 453. The following quote from the period shows one important motive behind the absence of outright release:

If by torture he will say nothing nor confess, and is not convicted by witnesses . . . he should be released at the discretion of the judge on pain of being attained and convicted of the matters with which he is charged and of which he is presumed guilty . . . for if he be freed absolutely, *it would seem that he had been held prisoner without charge.*

Quoted in Esmein, *supra* note 17, at 130 (emphasis added).

[36] Esmein, *supra* note 17, at 91–94. This was particularly critical in continental procedure, where presumption of guilt made the defense difficult in any case; it was less critical in England, where the burden of proof was on the court. The Church well knew the vital importance of counsel in criminal trials; *free* counsel was provided, in many kinds of ordinary cases, to those unable to afford it. *See* Lea, *supra* note 21, at 444–45.

[37] Sprenger & Kramer, *supra* note 9, at 218; Lea, *supra* note 21, at 444–45.

moned by the court as a witness and made to turn over all his information to the court.[38]

Lesser indications of guilt were supplied through the court's use of impossible dilemmas. If the accused was found to be in good repute among the populace, he or she was clearly a witch, since witches invariably sought to be highly thought of; if in bad repute, then he or she was also clearly a witch, since no one approves of witches. If the accused was especially regular in worship or morals, it was argued that the worst witches made the greatest show of piety.[39] Stubbornness in refusing to confess was considered a sure sign of alliance with the Devil, who was known to be taciturn.[40] Virtually the only defense available to accused witches was in disabling hostile witnesses on the grounds of violent enmity; this provision was rendered almost useless through the assumption that witches were naturally odious to everyone, so that an exceptionally great degree of enmity was required.[41]

A final and highly significant characteristic of the continental witch trial was the power of the court to confiscate the property of the accused, whether or not he was led to confess.[42] The chief consequence of this practice was to join to a system of virtually unlimited power a powerful motive for persecution. This coincidence of power and vested interest put an indelible stamp on every aspect of witchcraft in continental Europe.

All things considered, the continental procedure in the witch trials was an enormously effective machine for the systematic and massive production of confessed deviants. As such, it approximates a type of deviance-management which may be called repressive control. Three main characteristics of such a system may be noted, all of which were present in the continental legal order's handling of the witch trials:

1. Invulnerability to restraint from other social institutions
2. Systematic establishment of extraordinary powers for suppressing deviance, with a concomitant lack of internal restraints
3. A high degree of structured interest in the apprehension and processing of deviants

The question at hand is what the effects of this type of control structure are on the rate of deviance, the kinds of people who become defined as deviant, and other aspects of the system of behavior that it is designed to control. This will be considered after a description of the English approach to the control of witchcraft, which, having a very different character, led to very different results.

England: Restrained Control

There was no Inquisition in Renaissance England, and the common law tradition provided a variety of institutional restraints on the conduct of the witch trials. As a consequence, there were fewer witches in England, vastly

38 2 Lea, *supra* note 21, at 517–18.
39 2 Lea, *supra* note 7, at 858.
40 Lea, *supra* note 6, at 509.
41 *Ibid.* at 517.
42 2 Lea, *supra* note 7, at 808–11; Lea, *supra* note 21, at 529.

fewer executions, and the rise of a fundamentally different set of activities around the control of witchcraft.

Witchcraft was apparently never prosecuted as a heresy in England, but after a statute of Elizabeth in 1563 it was prosecuted as a felony in secular courts.[43] The relatively monolithic ecclesiastical apparatus, so crucial in the determination of the shape of witch trials on the Continent, did not exist in England; the new definition of witchcraft came to England late and under rather different circumstances.[44] English laws making witchcraft a capital crime, however, were on the books until 1736 although executions for witchcraft ceased around the end of the 17th century.[45] Nevertheless, the English laws were enforced in a relatively restrained fashion through a system of primarily local courts of limited power, accountable to higher courts and characterized by a high degree of internal restraint.

With a few exceptions, notably the Star Chamber, English courts operated primarily on the accusatory principle, stressing above all the separation of the functions of prosecution and judgment, trial by jury, and the presumption of the innocence of the accused.[46] Accuser and accused assumed the role of equal combatants before the judge and jury; prosecution of offenses generally required a private accuser.[47] The English trial was confrontative and public, and the English judge did not take the initiative in investigation or prosecution of the case.[48] Again unlike the situation on the Continent, the accused witch could appeal to higher authority from a lower court, and could

[43] The statute is 5 Eliz., c. 16 (1563); see Davies, *supra* note 4, at 15, for a partial quote of this statute; and p. 42, for a quote from James I's 1604 statute making witchcraft per se, without involving the death of another person, a capital offense.

An earlier statute (33 Hen. 8, c. 8 [1541] made witchcraft a felony, but was repealed in 1547 and probably used only sporadically and for largely political purposes. Before that, too, there were occasional trials for witchcraft or sorcery, and witchcraft of a sort, as I have shown, appears in the earliest English law. But this was the older conception of witchcraft, blurring into that of magic; and it was not until Elizabeth's statute that witch trials began in earnest. *See* W. Notestein, *A History of Witchcraft in England* ch. 1 (1911).

[44] Two of these circumstances may be mentioned. One was the general atmosphere of social and political turmoil surrounding the accession of Elizabeth to the throne; another was the return to England, with Elizabeth's crowning, of a number of exiled Protestant leaders who had been exposed to the witch trials in Geneva and elsewhere and had absorbed the continental attitudes toward witchcraft. One of these, Bishop John Jewel of Salisbury, argued before the Queen that

> This kind of people (I mean witches and sorcerers) within the last few years are marvelously increased within your Grace's realm. These eyes have seen the most evident and manifest marks of their wickedness. Your Grace's subjects pine away even unto death, their color fadeth, their speech is benumbed, their senses are bereft. Wherefore your poor subject's most humble petition to your Highness is, that the laws touching such malefactors may be put in due execution. Davies, *supra* note 4, at 17; *cf.* Notestein, *supra* note 43.

[45] *See* Ewen, *supra* note 5, at 43. On the repeal of the witch laws, *see* 2 Sir J. F. Stephen, *History of the Criminal Law in England* 436 (1883).

[46] *See* Esmein, *supra* note 17, at Introduction. Esmein notes the similarity between the politically-oriented Star Chamber and the typical continental court. A few cases of witchcraft, notably those with political overtones, were processed there; *see* C. L'Estrange Ewen, *Witchcraft in the Star Chamber* esp. 11 (1938).

[47] Esmein, *supra* note 17, at 107, 336.

[48] *Ibid.* at 3, 6.

sue an accuser for defamation; such actions frequently took place in the Star Chamber.[49] Reprieves were often granted.[50] From the middle of the 17th century, the accused in capital cases could call witnesses in their defense.[51] In general, the English courts managed to remain relatively autonomous and to avoid degeneration into a tool of ideological or moral interests: Voltaire was to remark, in the 18th century, that "In France the Criminal Code seems framed purposely for the destruction of the people; in England it is their safeguard."[52]

There were, nevertheless, important limitations to this picture of the English courts as defenders of the accused. Accusatory ideals were not always met in practice, and many elements of a developed adversary system were only latent. Defendants were not allowed counsel until 1836.[53] In general, since the defendant entered court with a presumption of innocence, the English courts did not demand such rigorous proofs for conviction as did the continental courts. Testimony of one witness was usually sufficient for conviction in felony cases; children were frequently allowed to testify.[54] In practice, however, this worked out differently than might be expected. The lack of complex, rigid standards of proof in English courts meant that there was little pressure to subvert the series of safeguards surrounding the accused through granting the court extraordinary powers of interrogation, and it went hand-in-hand with a certain care on the part of the courts for the rights of the defendant. Torture, except in highly limited circumstances as an act of Royal prerogative, was illegal in England, and was never lawfully or systematically used on accused witches in the lower courts.[55]

Given the nature of the crime of witchcraft, witnesses were not always easily found; given the illegality of torture, confessions were also relatively rare. In this difficult situation, alternative methods of obtaining evidence were required. As a consequence, a variety of external evidence emerged.

Three sources of external evidence became especially significant in English witch trials. These are pricking, swimming, and watching.[56] Pricking was based on the theory that witches invariably possessed a "Devil's Mark," which was insensitive to pain. Hence, the discovery of witches involved searching the accused for unusual marks on the skin and pricking such marks with an instrument designed for that purpose. If the accused did not feel pain,

[49] *Cf.* Ewen, *supra* note 46.
[50] Ewen, *supra* note 5, at 32.
[51] Esmein, *supra* note 17, at 342.
[52] Quoted in Esmein, *supra* note 17, at 361.
[53] *Ibid.* at 342.
[54] Ewen, *supra* note 5, at 58.
[55] Torture may have been used on some witches in the Star Chamber. Notestein, *supra* note 43, at 167, 204 suggests that it may have been used illegally in a number of cases; nevertheless, torture was not an established part of English criminal procedure, except in the limited sense noted above. *See* Stephen, *supra* note 45, at 434; Ewen, *supra* note 5, at 65. It was allowed in Scotland, where, predictably, there were more executions; several thousand witches were burned there during this period. *See* G. F. Black, *A Calendar of Cases of Witchcraft in Scotland, 1510–1727,* 13–18 (1938); Notestein, *supra* note 43, at 95–96.
[56] This discussion is taken from Ewen, *supra* note 5, at 60–71, and from remarks at various places in Notestein, *supra* note 43.

guilt was indicated. Often, pricking alone was considered sufficient evidence for conviction.

Swimming was based on the notion that the Devil's agents could not sink in water, and was related to the "ordeal by water" common in early European law.[57]

> The victim was stripped naked and bound with her right thumb to her right toe, and her left thumb to her right toe, and was then cast into the pond or river. If she sank, she was frequently drowned; if she swam she was declared guilty without any further evidence being required.[58]

The third source of evidence, watching, reflected the theory that the Devil provided witches with imps or familiars which performed useful services, and which the witch was charged with suckling. The familiars could therefore be expected to appear at some point during the detention of the suspected witch, who was therefore placed in a cell, usually on a stool, and watched for a number of hours or days, until the appointed watchers' observed familiars in the room.

A number of other kinds of evidence were accepted in the English trials. Besides the testimony of witnesses, especially those who claimed to have been bewitched, these included the discovery of familiars, waxen or clay images, or other implements in the suspect's home, and of extra teats on the body, presumably used for suckling familiars.[59]

These methods were called for by the lack of more coercive techniques of obtaining evidence within the ambit of English law. In general, the discovery and trial of English witches was an unsystematic and inefficient process, resembling the well-oiled machinery of the continental trial only remotely. The English trial tended to have an ad hoc aspect in which new practices, techniques and theories were continually being evolved or sought out.

Finally, the confiscation of the property of suspected witches did not occur in England, although forfeiture for felony was part of English law until 1870.[60] As a consequence, unlike the continental authorities, the English officials had no continuous vested interest in the discovery and conviction of witches. Thus, they had neither the power nor the motive for large-scale persecution. The English control system, then, was of a "restrained" type, involving the following main characteristics:

1. Accountability to, and restraint by, other social institutions
2. A high degree of internal restraint, precluding the assumption of extraordinary powers

[57] See M. Hopkins, *The Discovery of Witches* 38 (1928).
[58] Quoted in Ewen, *supra* note 5, at 68; Ewen argues, though, that swimming alone was probably not usually sufficient evidence for the death penalty.
[59] *Ibid.* at 68.
[60] Forfeiture grew out of the feudal relation between tenant and lord. A felon's lands escheated to the lord, and his property also was forfeited to the lord. A later development made the King the recipient of forfeited goods in the special case of treason; this was struck down in the Forfeiture Act of 1870. *See* 1 F. Pollack & W. Maitland, *A History of English Law Before the Time of Edward I* 332 (1895). This is, of course, a very different matter from the direct confiscation of property for the court treasury which was characteristic of the Continent.

3. A low degree of structured interests in the apprehension and processing of deviants

The English and continental systems, then, were located at nearby opposite ends of a continuum from restrained to repressive control of deviance. We may now look at the effects of these differing control systems on the character of witchcraft in the two regions.

Witchcraft Control as Industry: The Continent

On the Continent, the convergence of a repressive control system with a powerful economic motive created something very much like a largescale industry based on the mass stigmatization of witches and the confiscation of their property. This gave distinct character to the *rate* of witchcraft in Europe, the kinds of people who were convicted as witches, and the entire complex of activities which grew up around witchcraft.

The Inquisition, as well as the secular courts, were largely self-sustaining; each convicted witch, therefore, was a source of financial benefit through confiscation.[61] "Persecution," writes an historian of the Inquisition, "as a steady and continuous policy, rested, after all, upon confiscation. It was this which supplied the fuel to keep up the fires of zeal, and when it was lacking the business of defending the faith languished lamentably."[62]

The witchcraft industry in continental Europe was a large and complex business which created and sustained the livelihoods of a sizable number of people. As such, it required a substantial income to keep it going at all. As a rule, prisoners were required to pay for trial expenses and even for the use of instruments of torture.[63] Watchmen, executioners, torturers and others, as well as priests and judges, were paid high wages and generally lived well.[64] A witch-judge in 17th-century Germany boasted of having caused 700 executions in three years, and earning over 5,000 gulden on a per-capita basis.[65] A partial account of costs for a single trial in Germany reads as follows:[66]

	Florins	Batzen	Pfennige
For the Executioner	14	7	10
For the Entertainment and Banquet of the Judges, Priests and Advocate	32	6	3
For Maintenance of the Convicts and Watchmen	33	6	6

[61] Self-sustaining control systems often view presumptive deviants as a source of profit. On a smaller scale, it has been noted that some jurisdictions in the American south have been known to make a practice of arresting Negroes en masse in order to collect fees. *See* G. B. Johnson, "The Negro and Crime," in *The Sociology of Crime and Delinquency* (M. Wolfgang, L. Savitz, & N. Johnston, 1962).

[62] Lea, *supra* note 21, at 529.

[63] Lea, *supra* note 6, at 524; 3 Lea, *supra* note 7, at 1080.

[64] Lea, *supra* note 7, at 1080.

[65] *Ibid.* at 1075.

[66] *Ibid.* at 1162.

A total of 720,000 florins were taken from accused witches in Bamberg, Germany, in a single year.[67] Usually, the goods of suspected witches were sold after confiscation to secular and ecclesiastical officials at low prices.[68] Of the prosecutions at Trier, a witness wrote that: "Notaries, copyists, and inn-keepers grew rich. The executioner rode on a blooded horse, like a courtier, clad in gold and silver; his wife vied with noble dames in the richness of her array . . . not till suddenly, as in war, the money gave out, did the zeal of the Inquisitors flag."[69] During a period of intense witch-burning activity at Trier, secular officials were forced to issue an edict to prevent impoverishment of local subjects through the activities of the Inquisitors.[70]

Like any large enterprise, the witchcraft industry was subject to the need for continual expansion in order to maintain its level of gain. A mechanism for increasing profit was built into the structure of the trials, whereby, through the use of torture to extract names of accomplices from the accused, legitimate new suspects became available.

The creation of a new kind of deviant behavior was the basis for the emergence of a profit-making industry run on bureaucratic lines, which combined nearly unlimited power with pecuniary motive and which gave distinct form to the deviant behavior system in which it was involved.

Its effect on the scope or rate of the deviance is the most striking at first glance. Several hundred thousand witches were burned in continental Europe during the main period of activity, creating a picture of the tremendous extent of witchcraft in Europe. The large number of witches frightened the population and legitimized ever more stringent suppression. Thus, a cycle developed in which rigorous control brought about the appearance of high rates of deviance, which were the basis for more extreme control, which in turn sent the rates even higher, and so on.

A second major effect was the selection of particular categories of people for accusation and conviction. A significant proportion of continental witches were men, and an even more significant proportion of men and women were people of wealth and/or property. This is not surprising, given the material advantages to the official control apparatus of attributing the crime to heads of prosperous households.

In trials of Offenburg, Germany, in 1628, witnesses noted that care was taken to select for accusation "women of property."[71] A document from Bamberg at about the same time lists the names and estimated wealth of twenty-two prisoners, nearly all of whom are propertied, most male, and one a burgher worth 100,000 florins.[72] In early French trials, a pattern developed which began with the conviction of a group of ordinary people, and then moved into a second stage in which the wealthy were especially singled out for prosecution.[73] In German trials, the search for accomplices was directed

[67] *Ibid.* at 1177–78.
[68] *Ibid.* at 1080.
[69] Burr, *supra* note 16, at 55.
[70] *Ibid.* at 55, fn.
[71] 3 Lea, *supra* note 7, at 1163.
[72] *Ibid.* at 1177–78.
[73] Lea, *supra* note 21, at 523–27.

against the wealthy, with names of wealthy individuals often supplied to the accused under torture.[74] At Trier, a number of burgomasters, officials, and managers of large farms were executed as witches.[75] An eyewitness to the trials there in the late 16th century was moved to lament the fact that "[b]oth rich and poor, of every rank, age and sex, sought a share in the accursed crime."[76] Apparently, resistance or dissent, or even insufficient zeal, could open powerful officials to accusation and almost certain conviction.[77]

Thus, though it was not the case that all continental witches were well-to-do or male, a substantial number were. The witch population in England, to be considered shortly, was strikingly different.

The mass nature of the witchcraft industry, the high number of witches in Europe, and the upper-income character of a sufficient proportion of them,[78] were all due to the lack of restraints on court procedure—especially, of the systematic use of torture—coupled with the legal authority to confiscate property, which added material interest to unrestrained control. That the prevalence of witches in continental Europe was a reflection of the peculiar structure of legal control is further implied by the fact that when torture and/or confiscation became from time to time unlawful, the number of witches decreased drastically or disappeared altogether. In Hesse, Phillip the Magnificent forbade torture in 1526 and, according to one witness, "nothing more was heard of witchcraft till the half-century was passed."[79] In Bamberg, pressure from the Holy Roman Emperor to abandon confiscation resulted in the disappearance of witchcraft arrests in 1630.[80] The Spanish Inquisitor Salazar Frias issued instructions in 1614 requiring external evidence and forbidding confiscation; this move marked the virtual end of witchcraft in Spain.[81] It was not until criminal law reform began in earnest in the 18th century that witches disappeared, for official purposes, from continental Europe.

A form of deviance had been created and sustained largely through the efforts of a self-sustaining bureaucratic organization dedicated to its discovery and punishment, and granted unusual powers which, when removed, dealt a final blow to that entire conception of deviant behavior. In England too, witches existed through the efforts of interested parties.[82] but the parties were of a different sort.

[74] Lea, *supra* note 7, at 235.

[75] Burr, *supra* note 16, at 29, 34.

[76] *Ibid.* at 19.

[77] This fact is graphically presented in Burr's chronicle of Dietrich Flade, a powerful court official at Trier whose ultimate execution for witchcraft was apparently in part the result of his failure to zealously prosecute witches in his district.

[78] That a greater percentage of wealthy witches did not appear is due in part to the fact that wealthy families often paid a kind of "protection" to local officials to insure that they would not be arrested. *See* 3 Lea, *supra* note 7, at 1080.

[79] *Ibid.* at 1081.

[80] *Ibid.* at 1173–79. In part, also, the decrease in arrests was due to the occupation of the area by an invasion of the somewhat less zealous Swedes.

[81] Parrinder, *supra* note 14, at 79.

[82] It should be stressed that quite probably, a number of people, both in England and on the Continent, did in fact believe themselves to be witches, capable of doing all the things witches were supposed to be able to do. Some of them, probably, had the intent to inflict injury or unpleasantness on their fellows, and probably some of these

Witchcraft Control as Racket: England

The restrained nature of the English legal system precluded the rise of the kind of mass witchcraft industry which grew up on the Continent. What the structure of that system did provide was a context in which individual entrepreneurs, acting from below, were able to profit through the discovery of witches. Hence, in England, there developed a series of rackets through which individuals manipulated the general climate of distrust, within the framework of a control structure which was frequently reluctant to approve of their activities. Because of its accusatorial character, the English court could not systematically initiate the prosecution of witches; because of its limited character generally, it could not have processed masses of presumed witches even had it had the power to initiate such prosecutions; and because of the absence of authority to confiscate witches' property, it had no interest in doing so even had it been able to. Witch prosecutions in England were initiated by private persons who stood to make a small profit in a rather precarious enterprise. As a result, there were fewer witches in England than on the Continent, and their sex and status tended to be different as well.

Given the lack of torture and the consequent need to circumvent the difficulty of obtaining confessions, a number of kinds of external evidence, some of which were noted above, became recognized. Around these sources of evidence there grew up a number of trades, in which men who claimed to be expert in the various arts of witchfinding—pricking, watching, and so on—found a ready field of profit. They were paid by a credulous populace, and often credulous officials, for their expertise in ferreting out witches. In the 17th century, the best-known of the witchfinders was one Matthew Hopkins, who became so successful that he was able to hire several assistants.[83] Hopkins, and many others, were generalists at the witchfinding art; others were specialists in one or another technique. Professional prickers flourished. A Scottish expert who regularly advertised his skill was called to Newcastle-upon-Tyne in 1649 to deal with the local witch problem, with payment guaranteed at twenty shillings per convicted witch. His technique of selecting potential witches was ingenious and rather efficient, and indicates how the general climate of fear and mistrust could be manipulated for profit. He sent bell-ringers through the streets of Newcastle to inquire if anyone had a complaint to enter against someone they suspected of witchcraft. This provided a legitimate outlet for grievances, both public and private, against the socially marginal, disapproved, or simply disliked, and was predictably suc-

---

were included in the executions. This does not alter the fact that the designation of witches proceeded independently of such beliefs, according to the interests of the control systems. Some students of witchcraft have suggested that the promotion of witch beliefs by the official control systems provided a kind of readymade identity, or role, into which some already disturbed people could fit themselves. This is a more subtle aspect of the creation of deviance by control structures, and has, I think, applicability to certain contemporary phenomena. The images of deviance provided by newspapers and police may provide a structured pattern of behavior and an organized system of deviant attitudes which can serve as an orienting principle for the otherwise diffusely dissatisfied.

[83] See Hopkins, *supra* note 57. This is a reproduction of Matthew Hopkins' own manual for the discovery of witches.

cessful; thirty witches were discovered, most of whom were convicted.[84] Several devices were used by prickers to increase the probability of discovery and conviction. One was the use of pricking knives with retractable blades and hollow handles, which could be counted on to produce no pain while appearing to be embodied in the flesh—thus demonstrating the presence of an insensible "Devil's Mark."[85]

Professional "watchers," too, thrived in this climate. A voucher from a Scottish trial in 1649 is indicative:[86]

	Pounds	Shillings
Item: In the first, to Wm. Currie and Andrew Gray, for the watching of her the space of 30 days, each day 30 shillings—	45	0
Item: More to John Kincaid for brodding (pricking) of her—	6	0
More for meat and drink and wine for him and his men	4	0

An essential characteristic of all these rackets was their precariousness. To profess special knowledge of the demonic and its agents opened the entrepreneur to charges of fraud or witchcraft; money could be made, but one could also be hanged, depending on the prevailing climate of opinion. The Scottish pricker of Newcastle was hanged, and many other prickers were imprisoned;[87] the witchfinder Hopkins continually had to defend himself against charges of wizardry and/or fraud, and may have been drowned while undergoing the "swimming" test.[88] People who professed to be able to practice magic—often known as "cunning folk"—frequently doubled as witchfinders, and were especially open to the charge of witchcraft.[89]

The peculiar and restrained character of the English control of witches led to characteristic features of the behavior system of English witchcraft. The lack of vested interest from above, coupled with the absence of torture and other extraordinary procedures, was largely responsible for the small number of witches executed in England from 1563 to 1736.[90] Of those indicted for witchcraft, a relatively small percentage was actually executed—again in contrast to the inexorable machinery of prosecution in continental Europe. In the courts of the Home Circuit, from 1558 to 1736, only 513 indictments were brought for witchcraft; of these, only 112, or about 22 per cent, resulted in execution.[91]

[84] Ewen, *supra* note 5, at 62.

[85] *Ibid.* at 62.

[86] Quoted in Black, *supra* note 55, at 59, This is apparently unusual for a Scottish trial, since these methods of evidence were less crucial, given the frequent use of torture.

[87] Ewen, *supra* note 5, at 63.

[88] Hopkins, *supra* note 57, at 45. Summers, the editor of Hopkins' work, denies that Hopkins was drowned in this fashion. Hopkins' pamphlet includes a lengthy question-and-answer defense of his trade, part of which reads as follows: "Certaine queries answered, which have been and are likely to be objected against Matthew Hopkins, in his way of finding out Witches. Querie 1. That hee must needs be the greatest Witch, Sorcerer, and Wizzard himselfe, else hee could not doe it. Answer: If Satan's Kingdome be divided against itselfe, how shall it stand?" *Ibid.* at 49.

[89] On "cunning folk" generally, *see* Notestein, *supra* note 43, at ch. 1.

[90] *Cf.* Ewen, *supra* note 5, at 112; Kittredge, *supra* note 10, at 59.

[91] Ewen, *sura* note 5, at 100.

Further, English witches were usually women and usually lower class. Again, this was a consequence of the nature of the control structure. English courts did not have the power or the motive to systematically stigmatize the wealthy and propertied; the accusations came from below, specifically from the lower and more credulous strata or those who manipulated them, and were directed against socially marginal and undesirable individuals who were powerless to defend themselves. The process through which the witch was brought to justice involved the often reluctant capitulation of the courts to popular sentiment fueled by the activities of the witchfinders; the witches were usually borderline deviants already in disfavor with their neighbors. Household servants, poor tenants, and others of lower status predominated. Women who worked as midwives were especially singled out, particularly when it became necessary to explain stillbirths. Women who lived by the practice of magic—cunning women—were extremely susceptible to accusation. Not infrequently, the accused witch was a "cunning woman" whose accusation was the combined work of a witchfinder and a rival "cunning woman." In the prevailing atmosphere, there was little defense against such internecine combat, and the "cunning" trade developed a heavy turnover.[92] In general, of convicted witches in the Home Circuit from 1564–1663, only 16 of a total of 204 were men,[93] and there is no indication that any of these were wealthy or solid citizens.

The decline of witchcraft in England, too, was the result of a different process from that on the Continent, where the decline of witchcraft was closely related to the imposition of restraints on court procedure. In England, the decline was related to a general shift of opinion, in which the belief in witchcraft itself waned, particularly in the upper strata, as a result of which the courts began to treat witchcraft as illusory or at best unprovable. English judges began refusing to execute witches well before the witch laws were repealed in 1736; and although there were occasional popular lynchings of witches into the 18th century, the legal system had effectively relinquished the attempt to control witchcraft.[94] With this shift of opinion, the entire structure of witchcraft collapsed, for all practical purposes, at the end of the 17th century.[95]

Conclusion

If one broad conclusion emerges from this discussion, it is that the phenomenon of witchcraft in Renaissance Europe strongly reinforces on one level the argument that deviance is what officials say it is, and deviants are those

[92] Notestein, *supra* note 43, at 82.

[93] Ewen, *supra* note 5, at 102–108. Also, *cf.* the list of English witches in Murray, *supra* note 5, at 255–70.

[94] *See* Davies, *supra* note 4, at 182–203.

[95] An incident supposedly involving the anatomist William Harvey is indicative of this change of opinion. Harvey, on hearing that a local woman was reputed to be a witch, took it upon himself to dissect one of her familiars, which took the shape of a toad; he found it to be exactly like any other toad, and a minor blow was struck for the Enlightenment. *See* Notestein, *supra* note 43, at 111.

so designated by officials. Where the deviant act is nonexistent, it is necessarily true that the criteria for designating people as deviant do not lie in the deviant act itself, but in the interests, needs, and capacities of the relevant official and unofficial agencies of control, and their relation to extraneous characteristics of the presumptive deviant. Witchcraft was invented in continental Europe, and it was sustained there through the vigorous efforts of a system of repressive control; in England it was sustained, far less effectively, through the semi-official efforts of relatively small-time entrepreneurs. In both cases, witchcraft as a deviant behavior system took its character directly from the nature of the respective systems of legal control. On the Continent, the system found itself both capable of and interested in defining large numbers of people, many of whom were well-to-do, as witches; therefore, there *were* many witches on the Continent and many of these were wealthy and/or powerful. In England, the control system had little interest in defining anyone as a witch, and consequently the English witches were those few individuals who were powerless to fend off the definition supplied by witchfinders on a base of popular credulity. Witches were, then, what the control system defined them to be, and variation in the behavior system of witchcraft in the two regions may be traced directly to the different legal systems through which that definition was implemented.

Witchcraft, however, is an extreme case. It is made extreme by virtue of the extent to which it is an *invented* form of deviance, whose definition lacks roots in concrete behavior. While it could be argued that all definitions of deviance, referring to whatever kinds of acts, contain a degree, however slight, of this element of invention, it is certainly true that the degree to which it is present is highly variable. There may be a large element of invention in current American definitions of mental illness, and perhaps drug addiction;[96] there is less in the definition of murder or battery. This means that variations in the behavior system of mental illness or drug addiction are more likely to result from differences in the control system through which they are managed than are variations in the behavior system of murder or battery. This is not to say that the definitions of the latter kinds of deviance are somehow fixed or inherent in the acts to which they refer, rather than being socially derived. Eskimos define murder differently from Englishmen, and present-day Englishmen define it differently from medieval Englishmen.[97] But the fact that the definition of murder is closely connected to a tangible, concrete and potentially highly visible act[98] means that its social derivation has minimal consequences,

[96] On mental illness, see the various works of, among others, T. Szasz. In the case of drugs it may be argued that the discrepancy between the legal and medical definitions of marijuana use bespeaks the existence of a sizeable element of official invention.

[97] Strictly speaking, this discussion would have to be backed up by data throwing light on the treatment of murder under different control systems; it is therefore to be considered speculative. Common sense, though, suggests that there is something peculiar about crimes like witchcraft which probably makes for a profound impact on the character of social control.

[98] By visibility I refer to consequences primarily, rather than commission. Proof of homicide generally requires a body, which is a highly visible thing. Offenses which, unlike witchcraft, have reference to an act which is real but of low visibility—such as heresy or thought—crimes generally, and some of the "victimless" crimes—create many of the same consequences for control systems as do invented offenses. Again, this is

especially for variation in the behavior system of murder under different systems of legal control. Systems of control create the character of the deviance which they define and manage only to the extent that a gap between deviant definition and deviant act gives them the latitude to do so. Anyone could be called a witch in Renaissance Europe, given the fact that witchery could be neither proved nor disproved; and witches were therefore created according to the capacity of the relevant control systems to create them, and were created in the image of the interests of these systems. It is more difficult, however, to create murderers, and especially difficult to create more murderers than there are victims. Hence, the element of potential creativity of the control system and thus a variation in the deviant behavior system under different control systems is reduced.

This has more than academic relevance, for it speaks directly to the problem of the abuse of the function of social control by the officials and institutions charged with it. To the extent that the element of invention enters into a society's definition of deviance, there is an open invitation to potentially abusive creativity on the part of systems of controls or, particularly in the case of societies with limited systems of control, on the part of individuals or groups peripheral to the control system.[99] The case of witchcraft in England shows that virtually no amount of limitation on the power of a control system can consistently and effectively protect individuals against such abuse, once an invented definition of deviance has become officially established. Beyond this, invented deviance undermines the ability of control agencies to maintain procedural integrity. The inevitable inability of both continental and English legal systems to deal with witchcraft without straining normal standards of procedure illustrates this. It could be argued that a number of such definitions which contain at least a large element of invention—currently exist in this country, with the consequence of severely straining standards of due process of law in the institutions charged with controlling them.[100] It would be profitable to study some of these with an eye to establishing relations between degree of "invention" and degree of strain on established standards of legal procedure.

Different kinds of deviance, then, vary in the degree to which they can be creatively imputed to people, and hence in the degree of variability in their behavior systems which may occur across different control systems. Keeping this in mind, some generalizations can be suggested about the effects of the two kinds of control systems—repressive and restrained—which have been defined above.

---

largely because their commission is so difficult to establish through ordinary means that extraordinary means may need to be invoked, and if that is done, not only does the character of the control system change, but the offense now become virtually impossible to *disprove*. As a consequence, the official incidence of the offense can vary greatly depending on the interests of the control system.

[99] The remarks above apply here as well. This, of course, is an important factor in the rejection of legal control of mental acts by democratically inclined people.

[100] As indicated above, I believe this may be at least partially true of definitions of mental illness and of drug addiction. It is also perhaps relevant to certain kinds of political offenses built on the notion of "subversion," and on certain peculiar categories of juvenile justice, such as the notion of "incorrigibility," among others.

Repressive control systems, by virtue of their superior power to accuse, convict, and certify deviants, tend to create a higher official incidence of a given kind of deviance than do systems of restrained control.[101] This is reflected both in a higher rate of accusation or stigmatization and in a higher ratio of conviction to accusation. A system of repressive control will uncover and successfully prosecute an exceptionally high amount of deviance; further, it may do so more or less independently of the actual incidence of the deviance —through, among other things, its ability to systematically produce confessions from, if necessary, the innocent. A system of restrained control, on the other hand, produces a relatively low rate of official deviance and is restricted in its ability to creat deviance independently of its actual incidence. Restrained systems may, and generally do, process *less* deviance than actually exists; rarely, however, can they successfully or consistently process *more*.

Systems of repressive control, in the nature of things, tend to develop a greater vested interest in the successful prosecution of deviants than do restrained systems. This tends to increase the effect of creating an exceptionally large deviant population under systems of repressive control. Repressive systterms combine the power to successfully prosecute masses of deviants with a structured motive for doing so, both of which are lacking in the restrained system. The ability of continental witchcourts to confiscate the property of witches is but one example of this kind of vested interest. Similarly, vested interests in deviance may be political, religious, or psychic, rather than economic; in any case, even lacking such specific interests, systems of repressive control tend to foster the growth of an "industry" geared to the official creation of deviance, with a complex organizational structure which strains toward self-perpetuation.[102] They support a division of labor whose personnel depend for their livelihood on the continued supply of confirmed deviants. Even at best, therefore, there is a degree of tension between organizational interests and the security of individuals which is not found in the restrained system, and a powerful strain toward arbitrariness and the relaxation of procedural standards.

Restrained systems, on the other hand, may be vulnerable to abuse from below. This is particularly true where the community generates definitions of deviance which include a large amount of invention, putting a strain on the ability of the system to handle deviance while keeping its procedural standards intact. Under these circumstances especially, restrained systems tend to foster the development of a system of "rackets" around the deviant activity, involving officials, deviants themselves, and private or semi-official entrepreneurs operating on the precarious borderline between licit and illicit behavior.

Because of their combination of power and interest, repressive control systems tend to concentrate most heavily on stigmatizing people whose suc-

[101] Under the system of expanded control during the politically harsh years 1949–1953 in Communist China, approximately 800,000 political deviants—"counterrevolutionaries," "class enemies," and so on—were liquidated. *See* Cohen, *supra* note 24, at 477–78.

[102] Special agencies of enforcement or prosecution within the context of a generally restrained system may, of course, develop vested interests of this kind, but their effect is limited by the nature of the larger system. For an example of this, see discussion of the enforcement of marijuana laws, in Becker, *supra* note, 1, at 121–46.

cessful prosecution will be most useful in terms of the system's own needs and goals. This is true whether the goal is economic profit or the elimination of sources of moral or political dissent, or a combination of these. Consequently, the deviant population under a system of repressive control will contain an unusually large number of relatively wealthy and/or powerful people, and of solid citizens generally. Under a restrained control system, on the other hand, the typical deviant will be lower-class; the deviant population will be most heavily represented by the relatively powerless, who lack the resources necessary to make successful use of those safeguards which the restrained system provides, and who are particularly vulnerable to abuse.

THOMAS J. SCHEFF

Social Conditions for Rationality: How Urban and Rural Courts Deal with the Mentally Ill

Formal legal procedure is a highly developed instrument for arriving at rational decisions concerning complex and uncertain situations. Legal procedures are institutionalized means for substantial rationality, i.e., for obtaining "intelligent insight into the inter-relations of events in a given situation."[1] Like scientific method, trial procedures and due process serve to control and reduce, though not to eliminate, bias in situations of uncertainty.

One of the central concerns in the sociology of knowledge has been the attempt to determine the social conditions under which substantial rationality occurs. This paper pursues the question by discussing some of the variation in the procedures for hospitalizing and committing persons alleged to be mentally ill, in metropolitan and non-metropolitan jurisdictions in a Midwestern state. My sources of information were interviews with judges, psychiatrists, and other officials in 20 of its counties and observations of judicial hearings, psychiatric interviews, and other procedures in four of the jurisdictions, those courts with the largest number of mental hearings.[2]

[1] Karl Mannheim, *Man and Society in an Age of Reconstruction* (London: Routledge, 1935), 52–54.

[2] The larger study on which this paper is based is described in "Legal and Medical Decision-making in the Hospitalization of the Mentally Ill: A Field Study." (in press). For a detailed description of the psychiatric screening procedures, see the author's "The Societal Reaction to Deviance: Ascriptive Elements in the Psychiatric Screening of Mental Patients," *Social Problems* 11 (1964) 401–413.

Source: Thomas J. Scheff, "Social Conditions for Rationality: How Urban and Rural Courts Deal with the Mentally Ill," *American Behavioral Scientist,* 7, VII (March, 1964), pp. 21–24. Copyright © 1964 by Sage Publications, Inc. Reprinted by permission of Sage Publications, Inc., and Thomas J. Scheff.

Non-Rational Procedures and Urban Courts

The major result of our study was the conclusion that in three of the four metropolitan courts, the civil procedures for hospitalizing and committing the mentally ill had no serious investigatory purpose, but were ceremonial in character. Although all four of the courts carried through various procedures required by statute, the psychiatric examination, the judicial hearing, and other steps, hospitalization and treatment appeared to be virtually automatic after the patient had been brought to the attenion of the courts.[3]

In nine of the 16 other counties, however, these civil procedures appeared to serve at least some investigatory purpose. At one or more points in the screening process (the application for judicial inquiry, the psychiatric examination, the judicial hearing) detailed investigation was conducted and patients were released or their release was seriously considered.

These observations suggest that for civil procedures concerning mental illness, rationality is associated with a nonmetropolitan setting, and bias and the presumption of illness with metropolitan jurisdictions. Before exploring some of the reasons for this relationship, it is necessary to justify the contention that the procedures used in the metropolitan jurisdictions are not rational.

Most of the officials whom we interviewed did not disagree with our description of the typical events in these procedures, but argued that the procedures were justified by larger considerations of a medical and humanitarian character. Their arguments can be summarized in the following five statements:

1. The condition of mentally ill persons deteriorates rapidly without psychiatric assistance.
2. Effective psychiatric treatments exist for most mental illnesses.
3. Unlike surgery, there are no risks involved in involuntary psychiatric treatment: it either helps or is neutral, it can't hurt.
4. Exposing a prospective mental patient to questioning, cross-examination, and other screening procedures exposes him to the unnecessary stigma of trial-like procedures, and may do further damage to his mental condition.
5. There is an element of danger to self or others in mental illness. It is better to risk unnecessary hospitalization than the harm the patient might do himself or others.

Although these statements appear to be plausible, statements rebutting each of them are equally plausible.

[3] Similar findings are reported in Herbert J. Jaffe, "Civil Commitment of the Mentally Ill," *Pennsylvania Law Review,* 107 (March 1959), 668–85; John H. Hess and Herbert E. Thomas, "Incompetency to Stand Trial; Procedures, Results and Problems," paper presented at the 1962 convention of the American Psychiatric Association; Kutner, "The Illusion of Due Process" . . . reprinted in this volume; Mechanic, "Some Factors in Identifying and Defining Mental Illness," reprinted in this volume; Robert Ross Mezer and Paul D. Rheingold, "Mental Incapacity and Incompetency: A Psycho-Legal Problem," *American Journal of Psychiatry,* 118 (1962), 827–31 (note particularly the comment on p. 829 regarding the presumption of incapacity).

1. The assumption that psychiatric disorders usually get worse without treatment rests on very little other than evidence of an anecdotal character. There is just as much evidence that most acute psychological and emotional upsets are self-terminating.[4]
2. It is still not clear, according to systematic studies evaluating psychotherapy, drugs, etc., that most psychiatric interventions are any more effective, on the average, than no treatment at all.[5]
3. There is very good evidence that involuntary hospitalization may affect the patient's life—his job his family affairs, etc. There is some evidence that too hasty exposure to psychiatric treatment may convince the patient that he is "sick," prolonging what might have been an otherwise transitory episode.[6]
4. This assumption is correct, as far as it goes. But it is misleading because it fails to consider what occurs when the patient who does not wish to be hospitalized is forcibly treated. Such patients often become extremely indignant and angry, particularly in the event, which is common, that they are deceived into coming to the hospital on a pretext.
5. The element of danger is usually exaggerated both in amount and degree. In the psychiatric survey of new patients in state mental hospitals, conducted as part of the present study, danger to self or others was mentioned in less than a fourth of the cases. Furthermore, in those cases where danger is mentioned, it is not always clear that the risks involved are greater than those encountered in ordinary social life. This issue has been discussed by Ross, an attorney: A truck driver with a mild neurosis who is "accident prone" is probably a greater danger to society than most psychotics; yet, he will not be committed for treatment, even if he would be benefited. The community expects a certain amount of dangerous activity. I suspect that as a class, drinking drivers are a greater danger than the mentally ill, and yet the drivers are tolerated or punished with small fines rather than indeterminate imprisonment.[7]

These latter five statements indicate that arriving at a rational decision concerning hospitalization is not usually a simple and expedient matter. In marginal cases, which frequently arise, a rational disposition would require

[4] For a review of epidemiological studies of mental disorder see Richard J. Plunkett and John E. Gordon, *Epidemiology and Mental Illness.* Most of these studies suggest that at any given point in time, psychiatrists find a substantial proportion of persons in normal populations to be "mentally ill." One interpretation of this finding is that much of the deviance detected in these studies is of short duration. For a further discussion of this question, see Thomas J. Scheff, "The Role of the Mentally Ill and the Dynamics of Mental Disorder: A Research Framework," *Sociometry* 26 (December 1963), 436–53.

[5] For an assessment of the evidence regarding the effectiveness of electroshock, drugs, psychotherapy, and other psychiatric treatments, see H. J. Eysenck, *Handbook of Abnormal Psychology,* Basic Books, New York, 1961, Part III.

[6] For examples from military psychiatry, *see* Albert J. Glass, "Psychotherapy in the Combat Zone," in *Symposium on Stress* (Washington, D.C.: Army Medical Service Graduate School, 1953), and B. L. Bushard, "The U.S. Army's Mental Hygiene Consultation Service," in Symposium on Preventive and Social Psychiatry, 15–17 (April 1957) Walter Reed Army Institute of Research, Washington, D.C., pp. 431–43. For a discussion of essentially the same problem in the context of a civilian mental hospital, cf. Erikson, "Patient Role and Social Uncertainty."

[7] Hugh Allen Ross, "Commitment of the Mentally Ill: Problems of Law and Policy," *Michigan Law Review,* 57 (1959), 145–1018, p. 962.

careful investigation and assessment. Yet in many of the marginal cases we observed, investigation and assessment were quite limited or absent entirely. Some examples of the attitudes and action of the officials illustrate this point.

Examination and Hearing

The examination by the psychiatrists in the urban courts virtually never led to extensive knowledge of the facts. These examinations appeared to be short (about 10 minutes on the average), hurried, and largely routine. Yet the psychiatrists we interviewed uniformly stated that such a short interview was almost worthless with all but the most extreme cases.

One of the examiners, after stating in an interview (before we observed his examinations) that he usually took about thirty minutes, stated: "It's not remunerative. I'm taking a hell of a cut. I can't spend 45 minutes with a patient. I don't have the time, it doesn't pay." In the examinations that we observed, this physician actually spent 8, 10, 5, 8, 8, 7, 17, and 11 minutes with the patients, or an average of 9.2 minutes.

The key step in the entire sequence is the judical hearing. Yet these hearings were usually limited to the minimum act required by statute. In one urban court (the court with the largest number of cases) the only contact between the judge and the patient was in a preliminary hearing. This hearing was held with such lightning rapidity (1.6 minutes average) and followed such a standard and unvarying format that it was obvious that the judge made no attempt to use the hearing results in arriving at a decision. He asked three questions uniformly: "How are you feeling?" "How are you being treated?", and "If the doctors recommend that you stay here a while, would you co-operate?" No matter how the patient responded, the judge immediately signified that the hearing was over, cutting off some of the patients in the middle of a sentence.

Even in those courts where some attempt was made to ascertain the circumstances surrounding the case, the judge did not appear to assess the meaning of the circumstances in order to make a rational disposition. For example, in another urban court, the judge seemed to use the hearing to gather information. He attempted to relax the patient, reassure him, get his point of view, and test his orientation. (Of the four courts, the hearings in this court lasted longest: 12 minutes average, as against 1.6, 6, and 9 minutes in the other three courts.) Yet in all the hearing we observed (43), including those in which the judge himself demonstrated that the patient's behavior and orientation were unexceptionable, the judge went on to commit to or continue hospitalization.

The way in which this same judge reacted to a difficult case can be used to illustrate another facet of the concept of substantial rationality. The examining psychiatrists had recommended commitment for the patient, a police-man, whom they had diagnosed as severely depressed. Another psychiatrist (not one of the examiners) had once told the judge that there was always the risk of suicide in severe depression. The patient, however, had no history of suicide attempts, and strenuously denied any suicidal intention. The patient had retained his own attorney (which is unusual) who pleaded at the hearing that the patient be released to the care of a private physician, because if he were committed he would almost certainly lose his job. The judge refused to consider the plea stating that if there were *any* risk of suicide, he did not want to be responsible for having released the patient.

Reaching a decision in this case could never be a simple matter, since it requires the evaluation and comparison of a number of disparate considerations: what is the likelihood that the patient would commit suicide if released? Is this likelihood greater than those which are or should be tolerated in the community? What is the likelihood that the patient would lose his job if committed? How should this likelihood be weighed relative to the likelihood of suicide? This latter question particularly is a complex question, involving joint consideration of likelihoods and "costs" of seemingly incommensurate events. Decisions which meet the criteria of substantial rationality thus require consideration of diverse kinds of information, and equally important, the judicious comparison and weighing of the information.

The Attempt at Rationality in Rural Courts

In some of the non-metropolitan counties we investigated, these kinds of questions were addressed to some degree. In the application for judicial inquiry or in the judicial hearing, or, in two jurisdictions, in the psychiatric screening, serious investigation and assessment were undertaken. In three of the less populated counties, the judge himself heard the testimony before the application for judicial inquiry, and in some cases had the county sheriff or other officer investigate the situation even before issuing an application. In the hearing, several of the judges required that the relatives and the examining psychiatrists be present, allowing for the possibility of confrontation and cross-examination.

It is also true, however, that the procedures in three of the non-metropolitan counties were even more peremptory than in the metropolitan courts. In these three courts, the person alleged to be mentally ill was simply conveyed to the distant state mental hospital, after the application for judicial inquiry had been accepted, without examination or hearing. This occurred even though the Attorney General had issued the opinion that this procedure was illegal.

Allowing for a number of such exceptions, the findings discussed above point to the absence of substantial rationality in the metropolitan courts, and the presence of a degree of rationality in the non-metropolitan courts. On the basis of this relationship, we can now consider some of the conditions which facilitate and impede substantial rationality.

Conditions Favoring Substantial Rationality

Although we ordinarily think of the metropolitan court as being richer in resources than the rural court, there is one commodity which is very rare in the city, *time*. The metropolitan courts are faced with an enormous volume of cases: court B, the extreme example, handled some 14,000 cases (mostly misdemeanors) in 1962. In these circumstances, and with limited numbers of court officers, individual attention to a single case is usually not feasible.

The second condition concerns political pressure. In both rural and metropolitan courts there is considerable public sentiment about cases in which the judge or other official errs by releasing a person whom subsequent events prove should have been retained. There is considerably less sentiment against the opposite error, of retaining a person who should have been released. Officials therefore appear much more careful about erroneously releasing than they are about erroneously retaining. Our impression, however, was that this is less of an issue in rural areas. The absence of sensational treatment of mistakes in the newspapers, and the generally greater personal familiarity with facts of the case, makes for less political pressure on the rural judge.

Court officials in rural areas also usually have greater personal familiarity with the situation than do urban judges. In the typical rural case the judge will personally know the person alleged to be mentally ill, or at least a member of his family. This greater familiarity may lead to delay and investigation that would be absent in the urban court, where virtually every person who comes before the court is a stranger.

Personal familiarity with the patient affects not only the official's knowledge about the patient, but also his attitude. From our interviews, we gained the impression that it was much easier for the officials to consider cases using the impersonal framework of mental illness if they did not know the patient personally. This consideration operated in conjunction with the fact that the rural judges tended to be less psychiatrically sophisticated than the judges in the metropolitan courts, and to use a commonsense framework in most cases.

A fourth condition is also related to the ideological framework within which the officials considered the case. The greater psychiatric sophistication of the metropolitan judges reduces the rationality of their decision procedures in two ways. By establishing the assumption that the person alleged to be mentally ill is "sick" and in "need of help," extra-legal humanitarian considerations are introduced, and tend to break down the investigatory and adjudicatory nature of the court procedures. Introduction of the idea of disease also diffuses the responsibility for a final decision between the judge, who has the legal authority for the decision, and the psychiatrist, whom the judge assumes to have authority by virtue of his technical knowledge. We received the impression that the consequence of this diffusion of authority is that neither the judge nor the psychiatrist assumes the responsibility for decision to continue hospitalization, but each believes that his own decision is unimportant, since the real authority rests with the other.

A final condition is related to the resources of the patient. We formed the impression that an articulate patient, who knew his rights and who had the ability to retain his own lawyer, had a much better chance to obtain summary release from the hospital than the patient who was inarticulate, was unaware of his legal rights, and did not have the money or knowledge to retain a lawyer to represent him.

The Incidence of Mental Illness

To summarize these five conditions, we found that in jurisdictions characterized by a small volume of cases, only moderate public pressures against releasing patients erroneously, personal acquaintance with the patient or his family, little psychiatric sophistication, and where the patient has resources for defending himself against the allegations about him, substantial rationality is a characteristic of civil commitment procedures. In jurisdictions with large numbers of cases, strong public pressures against erroneous releases, lack of personal acquaintance with the persons alleged to be mentally ill, and few resources for patients to defend themselves against the allegations, hospitalization and treatment are virtually automatic once the complaint has been made to the court.

To the extent that all five of the latter conditions are present, hospitalization, far from being a rational decision, becomes an irreversible process. Since the procedures used in the metropolitan areas account for the majority of patients coming to the mental hospitals, the irreversibility of hospitalization has implications which deserve more attention than can be given them here. First, this discussion suggests that the well-established relationship between urban areas and high rates of mental illness may be a product less of greater incidence of mental illness than of the absence of official screening in urban areas.

Secondly, and more generally, since the entire legal and medical decisionmaking process in metropolitan areas appears to be largely ceremonial, the important decision in hospitalization is that which is made before the complaint comes to the court, i.e., in the community, and particularly in the family. The crucial decision of diagnosis, hospitalization, and treatment is thus made usually not by an expert, but by a layman: the relatives or others who bring the case before the court. This suggests that understanding of the incidence of mental illness requires study of the operation of social control in the community.

Conditions for Rationality in other Settings

Turning from the topic of decision-making in mental illness to broader concerns, it might be worthwhile to consider some of the conditions discussed here in connection with rationality in other areas. The recent New York bail studies suggest that much of the same situation applies to the handling of criminal deviants in the New York legal system as was discussed here.[8] Decisions concerning scientific matters may also be usefully considered within this framework. The decisions of an advisory board evaluating research findings, or, more frequently, research proposals, might be analysed in this way,

[8] Charles E. Ares, Ann Rankin, and Herbert Sturz, "The Manhattan Bail Project: An Interim Report on the Use of Pre-Trial Parole," *New York University Law Review,* 38 (January 1963), 67–95.

to ascertain the effect of volume of cases, political pressure because of erroneous decisions, the ideological framework of the members of the board, the diffusion of responsibility, the effect of personal acquaintance with the applicants, and the power and resources available to the applicants.

A pair of examples will illustrate one of the many parallels between judicial and scientific decision-making which bear on the issue of the conditions for rationality. The diffusion of responsibility between the judge and the psychiatrist, discussed above, puts the judge in the position of having the legal, but not the technical, authority to make final dispositions in hospitalization and commitment. Apparently, however, this conflict is consciously used by some judges who privately have doubts about the seriousness of the psychiatric examination. These judges justify their decisions by referring to the recommendations of the psychiatrists, and thus use the psychiatrists as "fronts" for their own purposes.

Apparently, like psychiatry, the name of science is regularly invoked as a bureaucratic mechanism of defense. The following testimony is by a missile expert, Werner von Braun, before a congressional investigating committee:[9]

> . . . a physics professor may know a lot about the upper atmosphere, but when it comes to making a sound appraisal of what missile schedule is sound and how you can phase a research and development program into industrial production, he is pretty much at a loss. . . . When confronted with a difficult decision involving several hundred million dollars, and of vital importance to the national defense, many Pentagon executives like to protect themselves. It helps if a man can say, "I have on my advisory committee some Nobel prize winners, or some very famous people that everybody knows." And if these famous people then sign a final recommendation, the executive feels, "Now, if something goes wrong, nobody can blame me for not having asked the smartest men in the country what they think about this."

The parallel suggested by these two examples points to regularized organizational techniques for manipulating avowedly rational means to serve non-rational ends, and suggests the need for studies explicitly formulated to determine the social conditions for substantial rationality. Although rationality is a difficult and elusive concept, such studies could help to clarify it and bring empirical materials to bear on an important problem.

---

[9] U.S. Senate Hearings, *Inquiry into Satellite and Missile Programs,* 1958, quoted in Merton J. Peck and Frederick M. Scherer, *The Weapons Acquisition Process: An Economic Analysis* (Boston: Harvard U. Press, 1962), p. 245.

ERVING GOFFMAN

The Insanity of Place

[We] turn now to a specific matter: the parallel drawn between medical and mental symptoms.

Signs and symptoms of a *medical* disorder presumably refer to underlying pathologies in the individual organism, and these constitute deviations from biological norms maintained by the homeostatic functioning of the human machine. The system of reference here is plainly the individual organism, and the term "norm," ideally at least, has no moral or social connotation. (Of course, beyond the internal pathology there is likely to be a cause in the external environment, even a social cause, as in the case of infectious or injurious situations of work; but typically the same disorder can be produced in connection with a wide variety of socially different environments.) But what about *mental* symptoms?

No doubt some psychoses are mainly organic in their relevant cause, others mainly psychogenic, still others situational. In many cases etiology will involve all of these causal elements. Further, there seems no doubt that the prepatient—that is, the individual who acts in a way that is eventually perceived as ill—may have any of the possible relations to intentionality: he may be incapable of knowing what he is doing; or he may know the effects of his acts but feel unable to stop himself, or indifferent about stopping himself; or, knowing the effects of certain acts, he may engage in them with malice aforethought, only because of their effects. All of that is not at issue here. For when an act that will later be perceived as a mental symptom is first performed by the individual who will later be seen as a mental patient, the act is not taken as a symptom of illness but rather as a deviation from social norms, that is, an infraction of social rules and social expectations. The perceptual reconstituting of an offense or infraction into a medical, value-free symptom may come quite late, will be unstable when it appears, and will be

Source: Erving Goffman, "The Insanity of Place," pp. 357–388 in *Relations in Public* (New York: Harper Colophon Books, 1971). Erving Goffman, "The Insanity of Place," *Psychiatry,* 32, IV (November, 1969), pp. 357–388. Reprinted by special permission of the copyright holder, The William Alanson White Psychiatric Foundation, Inc., and Erving Goffman.

entertained differently, depending on whether it is the patient, the offended parties, or professional psychiatric personnel doing the perceiving.[1]

This argument, that mentally ill behavior is on its face a form of social deviancy, is more or less accepted in psychiatric circles. But what is not seen —and what will be argued in this paper—is that biological norms and social norms are quite different things, and that ways of analyzing deviations from one cannot be easily employed in examining deviations from the other.

The first issue is that the systems regulated by social norms are not biological individuals at all, but relationships, organizations, and communities; the individual merely follows rules or breaks them, and his relation to any set of norms that he supports or undercuts can be complex indeed—as we shall see, more of a political issue than a medical one.

The second issue has to do with the regulative process itself. The biological model can be formulated in simple terms: deviation; restorative counteractions; reequilibration (associated with the destruction or extrusion of the pathogenic agent); or disorganization, that is, destruction of the system. A realistic picture of social regulation is less tidy.

The traditional sociological answer to the question of regulation and conformance is found in the normative sense of the term "social control" and the corrective cycle that presumably occurs when an offense takes place.

As suggested, through socialization the individual comes to incorporate the belief that certain rules are right and just, and that a person such as himself ought to support them and feel remorse and guilt if he does not. He also learns to place immediate value on the image that others might obtain of him in this regard; he learns to be decently concerned about his reputation.

Taking the notion of personal incorporated norms as central, one can distinguish three basic forms of normative social control. First, and no doubt most important, there is "personal control": the individual refrains from improper action by virtue of acting as his own policeman. Finding that he has acted improperly, he takes it upon himself to admit his offense and volunteer such reparative work as will reestablish the norms and himself as a man respectful of them.

Second, there is "informal social control." When the individual begins to offend, the offended parties may warn him that he is getting out of line, that disapproval is imminent, and that deprivations for continuation are likely. As a result of this more-or-less subtle warning, amplified and sustained until the offense is corrected, the offender is brought to his senses and once again acts so as to affirm common approved understandings. As Parsons has remarked, this corrective feedback is constantly occurring in social life, and is in fact one of the main mechanisms of socialization and learning.[2]

Third, the threat that an offender introduces to the social order is managed through "formal" social sanction administered by specialized agents designated for the purpose. Criminals certainly break social rules, but there

[1] Of course, some personal conditions, such as loss of memory or intense anxiety or grandiose persecutory beliefs, are very quickly shifted from offense to symptoms, but even here it is often the case that social rules regarding how a person is properly to orient himself or feel about his situation may be what are initially disturbed.

[2] Talcott Parsons, *The Social System* (New York: The Free Press, 1951), p. 303.

is an important sense in which they do not threaten the social order, and this by virtue of the risk they accept of apprehension, imprisonment, and harsh moral censure. They may find themselves forced, as we say, to pay their debt to society—the price presumably adjusted to the extent of the offense—which in turn affirms the reasonableness of not breaking the rules at all. In any case, they often try to conceal the act of breaking the law, claim to be innocent when accused, and affect repentance when proven guilty—all of which shows that they know the rules and are not openly rebelling against them. Note that the efficacy of informal and formal social control depends to a degree on personal control, for control that is initiated outside the offender will not be very effective unless it can in some degree awaken corrective action from within.

Personal control, informal control, and formal control are the moral means and the main ones by which deviations are inhibited or corrected and compliance to the norms is assured. But taken together, these means of control provide a very narrow picture of the relation between social norms and social deviations.

For one thing, the agencies of control that have been reviewed can be as effective as they are not because of the offender's moral concern, but because of his expediential considerations. The good opinion of others may be sought in order to render these persons vulnerable to exploitation. A fine may be viewed not as a proclamation of guilt but as a routine cost to be figured in as part of operating expenses.[3] The point here, of course, is that often what looks like automatic and dependable conformance is to be expected from the actor only over a strictly limited range of costs to him.

Further, the norms may be upheld not because of conscience or penalty, but because failure to comply leads to undesired, unintended complications which the offender was unaware of when first undertaking his offensive action.[4]

But even this expanded base for normative social control provides a partial view. The control model that is implied—a model that treats social norms somewhat like biological norms—is itself too restrictive. For when an offense occurs it is by no means the case that sanctions are applied, and when negative sanctions or penalties *are* applied, or when unanticipated penalizing consequences occur—that is, when the corrective cycle is begun—it is by no means generally true that diminution of the deviation results.

When the offense occurs, the offended parties may resolve the situation simply by withdrawing from relevant dealings with the offender, placing their social business with someone else. The threat of this sort of withdrawal is, of course, a means of informal social control, and actual withdrawal may certainly communicate a negative evaluation, sometimes unintended. But the process just as certainly constitutes something more than merely a negative sanction; it is a form of management in its own right. As we shall see, it is

[3] When the agencies of control take the same expediental view, then we might better speak of social direction rather than social control. It is thus, for example, that a subsidy policy directs crop allocation without reliance on the factor of moral sensibility.
[4] This is a functionalist argument. See, for example, S. F. Nadel, "Social Control and Self-Regulation," *Social Forces* XXXI (1953): 265–273.

just such withdrawal which allows those in a social contact to convey glaringly incompatible definitions and yet get by each other without actual discord.

If the offense is such as to make legal action possible, the offended person may yet desist (and withdraw) for practical reasons which sharply limit the application of formal control: the cost and time required to make a formal complaint and appear in court; the uncertainty of the legal decision; the personal exposure involved in taking official action; the reputation that can be acquired for being litigious; the danger of reprisal later by the offender.

There are still other contingencies. The individual who offends expectations can prevail, causing his others to accept him on his new terms and to accept the new definition of the situation that this implies. Children growing up in a family are constantly engaged in this process, constantly negotiating new privileges from their keepers, privileges which soon come to be seen as the young person's due. Some of the mutinies that occur in schools, prisons, and ghettos illustrate the same theme. The social changes produced by the labor movement and the suffragette movement provide further examples.

And even when withdrawal from the offender or submission to him does not occur, social control need not result. The negative moral sanctions and the material costs of deviation may further alienate the deviator, causing him to exacerbate the deviation, committing him further and further to offense. And as will be later seen, there may be no resolution to the discord that results thereby. The foreign body is neither extruded nor encysted, and the host does not die. Offended and offender can remain locked together screaming, their fury and discomfort socially impacted, a case of organized disorganization.

These limitations on the social version of the homeostatic model are themselves insufficient, for they are cast in the very assumptions that must be broadened. The issue is that the traditional social control approach assumes an unrealistically mechanistic version of the social act, a restriction that must be relaxed if the close analysis of social control is to be achieved.

As the law suggests, our response to an individual who physically performs an offensive act is radically qualified by a battery of interpretive considerations: Did he know about the rule he was breaking, and if so, was he aware of breaking it? If he did not appreciate the offensive consequences of his act, ought he to have? And if he did anticipate these offensive results, were they the main purpose of his act or incidental to it? Was it within his physical competence to desist from the offense, and if so, were there extenuating social reasons for not doing so?

The answers to these questions tell us about the actor's *attitude* toward the rule that appears to have been violated, and this attitude must be determined before we can even say what it is that has happened. The issue is not merely (and often not mainly) whether he conformed or not, but rather in what relationship he stands to the rule that ought to have governed him. Indeed, a significant feature of *any* act is what it can be taken to demonstrate about the actor's relation to such norms as legitimately govern it.

However, the actor's attitude toward a rule is a subjective thing; he alone, if anyone, is fully privy to it. Inevitably, then, an important role will be played by the readings others make of his conduct, and by the clarifying expressions that he contributes, whether to ensure that a proper purpose is not misinterpreted or an improper one is not disclosed. It follows, for example, that if a deviator is suitably tactful and circumspect in his violations, employing secrecy and cover, many of the disruptive consequences of the violation in fact will be avoided. A particular application of the rules is thwarted, but the sancity of the rule itself is not openly questioned.

A reorientation is therefore to be suggested. An actual or suspected offender is not so much faced with an automatic corrective cycle as with the need to engage in remedial ritual work. Three chief forms of this work are available to him: accounts, apologies, and requests. With accounts he shows that he himself did not commit the offense, or did it mindlessly, or was not himself at the time, or was under special pressure, or did what any reasonable man would have done under the circumstances;[5] with apologies he shows that if indeed he had intended the offense, he now disavows the person that he was, bewails his action, repents, and wants to be given a chance to be what he now knows he should be; with requests he seeks the kind of offer or permission which will transform the act from his offense into the other's boon. With this ritual work, with explanations, propitiations, and pleas, the offender tries to show that the offense is not a valid expression of his attitude to the norms. The impiety is only apparent; he really supports the rules.

Once we see that ritual work bears on the very nature of social acts and considerably loosens what is to be meant by social equilibrium, we can re-address ourselves to the crucial difference between medical symptoms and mental symptoms.

The interesting thing about medical symptoms is how utterly nice, how utterly plucky the patient can be in managing them. There may be physical acts of an ordinary kind he cannot perform; there may be various parts of the body he must keep bandaged and hidden from view; he may have to stay home from work for a spell or even spend time in a hospital bed. But for each of these deviations from normal social appearance and functioning, the patient will be able to furnish a compensating mode of address. He gives accounts, belittles his discomfort, and presents an apologetic air, as if to say that in spite of appearance he is, deep in his social soul, someone to be counted on to know his place, someone who appreciates what he ought to be as a normal person and who is this person in spirit, regardless of what has happened to his flesh. He is someone who does not *will* to be demanding and useless. Tuberculosis patients, formerly isolated in sanitaria, sent home progress notes that were fumigated but cheerful. Brave little troops of colostomites and ileostomites make their brief appearances disguised as nice clean people, while stoically concealing the hours of hellish toilet work required for each appearance in public as a normal person. We even have our Beckett player buried up to his head in an iron lung, unable to blow his own nose, who yet somehow expresses by means of his eyebrows that a full-fledged person is present who knows how to behave and would certainly behave that way were he physically able.

[5] A discussion of accounts is available in Marvin Scott and Stanford Lyman, "Accounts," *American Sociological Review* XXXIII (1968): 46–62.

And more than an air is involved. Howsoever demanding the sick person's illness is, almost always there will be some consideration his keepers will *not* have to give. There will be some physical cooperation that can be counted on; there will be some task he can do to help out, often one that would not fall to his lot were he well. And this helpfulness can be *absolutely* counted on, just as though he were no less a responsible participant than anyone else. In the context, these little bits of substantive helpfulness take on a large symbolic function.

Now obviously, physically sick persons do not always keep a stiff upper lip (not even to mention appreciable ethnic differences in the management of the sick role); hypochondriasis is common, and control of others through illness is not uncommon. But even in these cases I think close examination would find that the culprit tends to acknowledge proper sick-role etiquette. This may only be a front, a gloss, a way of styling behavior. But it says: "Whatever my medical condition demands, the enduring me is to be dissociated from these needs, for I am someone who would make only modest reasonable claims and take a modest and standard role in the affairs of the group were I able."

The family's treatment of the patient nicely supports this definition of the situation, as does the employer's. In effect they say that special license can temporarily be accorded the sick person because, were he able to do anything about it, he would not make such demands. Since the patient's spirit and will and intentions are those of a loyal and seemly member, his old place should be kept waiting for him, for he will fill it well, as if nothing untoward has happened, as soon as his outer behavior can again be dictated by, and be an expression of, the inner man. His increased demands are saved from expressing what they might because it is plain that he has "good" reasons for making them, that is, reasons that nullify what these claims would otherwise be taken to mean. I do not say that the members of the family will be happy about their destiny. In the case of incurable disorders that are messy or severely incapacitating, the compensative work required by the well members may cost them the life chances their peers enjoy, blunt their personal careers, paint their lives with tragedy, and turn all their feelings to bitterness. But the fact that all of this hardship can be contained shows how clearly the way has been marked for the unfortunate family, a way that obliges them to close ranks and somehow make do as long as the illness lasts.

Of course, the foregoing argument must be qualified. In extreme situations, such as the military, when it can be all too plain that the ill person has everything to gain by being counted sick, the issue of malingering may be seriously raised and the whole medical frame of reference questioned.[6] Further, there is the special problem caused by illness directly affecting the face and the voice, the specialized organs of expression. An organic defect in this equipment may be a minor thing according to a medical or biological frame of reference, but it is likely to be of tremendous significance socially. There is no disfigurement of the body that cannot be decorously covered by a sheet

---

[6] Here see the useful paper by Vilhelm Aubert and Shelden Messinger, "The Criminal and the Sick," *Inquiry* 1 (1958): 137–160.

and apologized for by a face; but many disfigurements of the face cannot be covered without cutting off communication, and cannot be left uncovered without disastrously interfering with communication. A person with carcinoma of the bladder can, if he wants, die with more social grace and propriety, more apparent inner social normalcy, than a man with a harelip can order a piece of apple pie.

With certain exceptions, then, persons have the capacity to expressively dissociate their medical illness from their responsible conduct (and hence their selves), and typically the will to do so. They continue to express support of the social group to which they belong and acceptance of their place therein. Their personality or character will be seen to remain constant in spite of changes in their role. This means that the illness may tax the substantive resources of the group, make tragic figures of well members, but still not directly undermine the integrity of the family. In brief, ritual work and minor assistance can compensate for current infractions because an important part of an infraction is what it can be taken to symbolize about the offender's long-range attitude toward maintaining his social place; if he can find alternate ways of conveying that he is keeping himself in line, then current infractions need not be very threatening. Note that the efficacy here of excusing expressions (with the exceptions cited) is due to that fact that medical symptoms involve behavior which is either not an infraction of social norms at all —as in the case of internal tumors of various kinds—or only incidentally so. It is the incidental side effects of the physical deviation that disqualify the person for compliance. When an amputee fails to rise to greet a lady, it is perfectly evident that this failure is only an incidental and unintentional consequence of his condition; no one would claim that he cut off his legs to spite his courtesies. Almost as surely, his disqualification for jobs that require rapid movement can be seen as a side effect of his deviance and not its initial expression. He is a deviator, not a deviant. Here is incapacity, not alienation.

Now turn to symptoms of mental disorder as a form of social deviation. The most obvious point to note is that since there are many kinds of social deviation that have little to do with mental disorder, nothing much is gained by calling symptoms social deviations.[7]

The position can be taken that mental illness, pragmatically speaking, is first of all a social frame of reference, a conceptual framework, a perspective that can be applied to social offenses as a means of understanding them. The offense, in itself, is not enough; it must be perceived and defined in terms of the imagery of mental illness. By definition one must expect that there always will be some liberty and some dissensus in regard to the way this framework is applied. Many important contingencies are known to be involved, some causing the imagery to be applied to psychologically normal behavior with the consequence of reconstituting it into a mental symptom. But given this necessary caveat, we can ask: In our society, what is the nature of the social offense to which the frame of reference "mental illness" is likely to be applied?

The offense is often one to which formal means of social control do not

[7] I omit considering the popularists who have tried to establish the psychogenesis of everything that is interesting, from crime to political disloyalty.

apply. The offender appears to make little effort to conceal his offense or ritually neutralize it. The infractions often occur under conditions where, for various reasons, neither the offended nor the offender can resolve the issue by physically withdrawing from the organization and relationship in which the offense occurs, and the organization cannot be reconstituted to legitimate the new self-assumptions of the offender—or, at least, the participants strongly feel that these adaptations are not possible. The norms in question are ones which frequently apply and which are constantly coming up for affirmation, since they often pertain to expressive behavior—the behavior which broadcasts to all within range, transmitting warnings, cues, and hints about the actor's general assumptions about himself. Finally, with the exception of paranoia of primary groups (*folie à deux, trois,* etc.), the offense is not committed by a set of persons acting as a team, but rather—or so it is perceived—by an individual acting on his own. In sum, mental symptoms are willful situational improprieties, and these, in turn, constitute evidence that the individual is not prepared to keep his place.[8]

One implication of the offense features I have mentioned should be stressed. Mental symptoms are not, by and large, *incidentally* a social infraction. By and large they are specifically and pointedly offensive. As far as the patient's others are concerned, the troublesome acts do not merely happen to coincide partly with what is socially offensive, as is true of medical symptoms; rather these troublesome acts are perceived, at least initially, to be intrinsically a matter of willful social deviation.

It is important now to emphasize that a social deviation can hardly be reckoned apart from the relationships and organizational memberships of the offender and offended, since there is hardly a social act that in itself is not appropriate or at least excusable in some social context. The delusions of a private can be the rights of a general; the obscene invitations of a man to a strange girl can be the spicy endearments of a husband to his wife; the wariness of a paranoid is the warranted practice of thousands of undercover agents.

Mental symptoms, then, are neither something in themselves nor whatever is so labeled; mental symptoms are acts by an individual which openly proclaim to others that he must have assumptions about himself which the relevant bit of social organization can neither allow him nor do much about.

---

[8] Although much of mental symptomatology shares these offense features—thereby allowing us to answer to the argument that mental symptoms are not merely any kind of social deviation—it is the case that many social deviations of the situational kind do not qualify as signs of mental illness. We have been slow to learn this, perhaps because mental wards once provided the most accessible source of flagrant situational improprieties, and in such a context it was all too easy to read the behavior as unmotivated, individually generated aberrancy instead of seeing it as a form of social protest against ward life—the protest having to employ the limited expressive means at hand. In the few years the non-psychiatric character of considerable symptomlike behavior has become much easier to appreciate because situational improprieties of the most flagrant kind have become widely used as a tactic by hippies, the New Left, and black militants, and although these persons have been accused of immaturity, they seem too numerous, too able to sustain collective rapport, and too facile at switching into conventional behavior to be accused of insanity.

It follows that if the patient persists in his symptomatic behavior, then he must create organizational havoc and havoc in the minds of members. Although the imputation of mental illness is surely a last-ditch attempt to cope with a disrupter who must be, but cannot be, contained, his imputation in itself is not likely to resolve the situation. Havoc will occur even when all the members are convinced that the troublemaker is quite mad, for this definition does not in itself free them from living in a social system in which he plays a disruptive part.

This havoc indicates that medical symptoms and mental symptoms are radically different in their social consequences and in their character. It is this havoc that the philosophy of containment must deal with. It is this havoc that psychiatrists have dismally failed to examine and that sociologists ignore when they treat mental illness merely as a labeling process. It is this havoc that we must explore.

DONALD T. DICKSON

Bureaucracy and Morality:
An Organizational Perspective
on a Moral Crusade

The occurrence of a moral commitment within a bureaucratic setting is not an uncommon phenomenon, especially in our federal bureaucratic system. Examples abound, including the Federal Bureau of Investigation, the Bureau of Narcotics, the Selective Service System, the Central Intelligence Agency, the Internal Revenue Service, and—on a different scale—the Departments of State and Justice. In fact, one could argue that some sort of moral commitment is necessary for the effective functioning of any bureaucratic body. Usually this moral commitment is termed an "ideology" and is translated into goals for the bureaucracy. Anthony Downs suggests four uses for an ideology: 1) to influence outsiders to support the bureau or at least not attack it; 2) to develop a goal consensus among the bureau members; 3) to facilitate a selective recruitment of staff, that is, to attract those who will support and further the goals of the bureau and repel those who would detract from those goals; and 4) to provide an alternative in decision making where other choice criteria are impractical or ambiguous.[1]

While most if not all bureaucracies attempt to maintain this moral commitment or ideology for the above mentioned reasons, some go further and initiate moral crusades, whereby they attempt to instill this commitment into groups and individuals outside their bureaus. The Narcotics Bureau in its efforts to mold public and congressional opinion against drug use is one

[1] Anthony Downs, *Inside Bureaucracy*, Boston: Little, Brown, 1967.

The author gratefully acknowledges the assistance of Professors John Lofland and Leon Mayhew for both their encouragement and their critical comments on previous drafts, and of Professor Albert J. Reiss, Jr., whose several suggestions strengthened the focus of the paper.

Source: Donald T. Dickson, "Bureaucracy and Morality: An Organizational Perspective on a Moral Crusade," *Social Problems*, 16, II (Fall, 1968), pp. 143–156. Copyright © 1968 by The Society for the Study of Social Problems. Reprinted by permission of the Society and Donald T. Dickson.

bureaucratic example, the F.B.I. in its anti-subversive and anti-communist crusades another.[2] The question then becomes, under what conditions does this transference of ideology from the bureaucracy to its environment or specific groups within its environment take place? Howard S. Becker supplies one answer to this, suggesting that this is the work of a "moral entrepreneur," either in the role of a crusading reformer or a rule enforcer.[3] In either role, the moral entrepreneur as an individual takes the initiative and generates a "moral enterprise."

This explanation has appeal. It is reminiscent of Weber's charismatic leader, and can be used to account for the genesis of most moral crusades and entire social movements. Further, it is very difficult to refute. A complete refutation would not only have to indicate an alternative, but also demonstrate that the bureaucratic leader is not a "moral entrepreneur"—is not a major factor in this transference of ideology. The purpose of this paper is to accomplish the former only—to provide an equally if not more persuasive alternative based upon organizational research and theory. The difficulty in separating the two approaches is similar to the historian's dilemma of whether the historical incident makes the man great or the great man makes the historical incident. Here the question becomes: does the moral crusader create the morally committed bureaucracy or is he a product of that bureaucracy?

The difference between the moral entrepreneur situation and a situation wherein the moral crusade results primarily from a bureaucratic response to environmental factors, is that in the latter instance moral considerations are secondary to bureaucratic survival and growth, while in the former instance moral considerations are primary. Further, the end results of either of these crusades may vary considerably since each is in response to different stimuli. Other conditions being equal, the bureaucratic crusade will continue only as long as bureaucratic considerations dictate, while the moral crusade will continue as long as the individual moral crusader's zealotry requires.

In this paper, the work of the Bureau of Narcotics and its former commissioner, Harry J. Anslinger, are examined in light of Becker's conclusion that Anslinger was a moral entrepreneur who led his Bureau on a moral crusade against the use of marihuana, culminating in an Anslinger-instigated publicity campaign that persuaded first the general public and then Congress that marihuana use was a vicious habit that should be outlawed and severely penalized.[4] Given the short time span Becker chose and his individualized focus, this seems to be a logical explanation of the Bureau's efforts. Given a broader organizational perspective, however, the passage of the Marihuana Tax Act and the Bureau's part in that passage appear to be only one phase of a larger organizational process, that of environmental change. Using this focus it is necessary first to examine briefly the relationships between organizations and their environments with special emphasis on adaptation and to discuss a special case of these organizations, the public bureaucracy. The results of

[2] Fred J. Cook, The FBI Nobody Knows, New York: Macmillan, 1964.
[3] Howard S. Becker, The Outsiders: Studies in the Sociology of Deviance, New York: Free Press, 1963, esp. pp. 147–163.
[4] Becker, op. cit., pp. 135–146.

this analysis are then applied to the Narcotics Bureau and narcotics legislation in conjunction with an examination of Becker's findings. Finally, the implications of this analysis are examined.

Organizations and Environments

One on-going problem an organization must cope with is its relationship with its environment.[5] For the incipient organization this means an initial decision as to the type of relationship it desires to establish with its environment, an assessment of the type of relationship it is able to establish, and the working-out of some acceptable compromise between the two. For the established organization, this means maintaining this relationship either through normal boundary defenses or through other means, or establishing a more favorable one. The consequences of these—decision, assessment, and compromise—for the organization are far reaching; for if the organization wishes to grow and expand or even continue to exist, it must come to terms with its environment, and where necessary insure acceptance by it. No doubt a few organizations with substantial resources may exist for some time in a hostile environment, but the more normal case seems to be that an organization must at least establish an environmentally neutral relationship if not an environmentally supportive one.

Of course when the organization is in its incipient stages, the problems are magnified. Environmental support is more necessary, environmental hostility more of a threat to survival. Usually the organization will adapt to the demands of the environment, but occasionally Starbuck's observation, "Adaptation is an obvious precondition of survival,"[6] is ignored and the organization either chooses to attempt to alter these demands, or chooses to ignore them. Not uncommonly such a decision results in drastic consequences for the organization. The Women's Christian Temperance Union failed in its efforts to gain wide acceptance for its programs and has only been able to continue with its operations severely curtailed. The counseling organization at Western Electric that grew out of the Hawthorne Studies felt it could not function properly if it adapted to the requirements of the larger organization and was eventually discontinued, though adaptation was part of a more complex problem.[7]

An organization may attempt to alter the demands of its environment when such an attempt would not draw too heavily upon the organization's resources, or when the alternative, adaptation to the environment, would mean

[5] See especially Peter M. Blau and W. Richard Scott, *Formal Organizations: A Comparative Approach,* San Francisco: Chandler, 1962, pp. 222–254; William H. Starbuck, "Organizational Growth and Development," in James G. March, editor, *Handbook of Organizations,* Chicago: Rand McNally, 1965, pp. 450–533; and Phillip Selznick, *TVA and the Grass Roots: A Case Study in the Sociology of Formal Organizations,* Berkeley: U. of California, 1949.

[6] W. Starbuck, *op. cit.,* p. 468.

[7] William J. Dickson and F. J. Roethlisberger, *Counseling in an Organization: A Sequel to the Hawthorne Researches,* Boston: Harvard Business School, 1966, Chap. 14 and 16.

a substantial loss to the organization or perhaps dissolution. Selznick's study of the TVA and Clark's study of adult education in California are examples of organizations which chose to try to alter their environments rather than adapt to them.[8] In Selznick's case, the organization itself was altered through these efforts. Clark argues that a number of organizations undergoing a similar value transformation may alter the values of the society in which they exist. He focuses on what he calls "precarious values" and discusses under what conditions these may be changed.

It is clear then that some attempts to alter the environment succeed and others fail. Why is this so? An organization's environment may be very simple or highly complex, but in general every environment when viewed as a system will contain the following elements: 1) pragmatic day-to-day decisions categorized as policies or practices; 2) long-range goals; 3) a clearly defined normative system; and 4) a generalized value system.[9]

If placed in a hierarchy in this order, each succeeding category would influence its predecessors. That is, values in the environment are in part the basis of the other three, norms influence both goals and policies and practices, and so forth. Further, any member of any category may be strongly or weakly held. Some of the reasons for weakness are outlined by Clark—that is, not legitimated, undefined, or not widely accepted.[10]

Any organization that chooses to alter its environment will have to make a decision as to where along the hierarchy to focus its efforts. Attempts to alter some policy of an environmental element may be more successful and less costly than attempts to alter some value of an environment, but the latter might result in a long-term change while the former might be the more unstable—since the goals, norms, and values underlying it were not changed. A change in the value system, where possible, would eventually result in changes throughout the system.

Organizational attempts at environmental change will depend upon a number of factors:

1. The necessity for change—is environmental change a prerequisite for organizational survival, or is it not necessary but merely desirable?
2. The amount of resources available—can the organization afford to attempt the change effort?
3. The size and complexity of the environment—would change be necessary in only a small element in the environment, or would a whole complex of elements need to be altered?
4. The extent to which change must take place—is it necessary to change only some environmental policy or practice, or is it necessary to totally revamp the environmental structure from values on down?
5. Is the policy, goal, norm, or value to be changed, strongly or weakly held—is it firmly entrenched and legitimated, or is it "precarious?"

[8] Selznick, op. cit.; Burton Clark, "Organizational Adaptation and Precarious Values," American Sociological Review, 21 (1956), pp. 327–336.
[9] Adapted from Talcott Parsons, "An Outline of the Social System," in Talcott Parsons, Edward Shils, Kasper D. Nagele, and Jesse N. Pitts, editors, Theories of Society: Foundations of Modern Sociological Theory, New York: Free Press, Vol. I, pp. 30–79.
[10] Clark, op. cit., pp. 328–329.

It is clear, then, that when one is talking about organizations changing their environment, one should make explicit what elements in the environment are being focused upon, how extensively they are being changed, and how strongly held they were to begin with. Clark's adult education study was concerned with weakly-held values. The W.C.T.U. as discussed by Gusfield was concerned with strongly-held values and this may in some degree account for its failure.[11] In his discussion of the Marihuana Tax Act as a "moral enterprise," Becker was concerned with a weakly-held value, as will be shown, though he did not discuss it in these terms.

A Case Study: The U.S. Bureau of Narcotics

The Bureau as a Public Bureaucracy

This case study will be limited to an analysis of the policies of the Narcotics Bureau and the effects of these policies on salient elements of its environment. This approach is preferable to a more general organizational analysis of the Bureau—examining its structure, recruitment, boundary defenses, and myriad environmental transactions—because in these respects the Bureau is not unlike most other governmental bureaucracies. Further, in its efforts to mold public opinion in support of its policies, it is not unlike many organizations, especially those with a moral commitment. The W.C.T.U. carried on the same sort of campaign—including propaganda, attacks on its critics, and legislative lobbying. What makes the Bureau unique from many other organizations which have tried to influence their environments is that the campaign was and is carried out by a governmental organ.

Several ramifications of this difference are immediately apparent. There is the element of legitimation. The public is far more likely to accept the pronouncements of a federal department than a voluntary private organization. There is the element of propaganda development. Due to its public nature, a federal department is more skilled in dealing with the public and in preparing propaganda for public consumption. There is the element of communication. A federal organization has far more means available for the dissemination of the information than a private one—by press releases, publications, or lectures and speeches—and it is likely to have representatives based in major population centers to disseminate the information. There is the element of coercion. A federal department can bring a wide range of pressures to bear on its critics.

Finally, at a different level, a federal bureau differs in the area of survival. Private organizations have considerable control over their future. They may decide to expand, continue as before, disband, merge, alter their aims, or reduce their activities. The attitude of their environments will have great bearing on this decision, to be sure, but the final decision rests with the organization. A federal department may go through any of the above stages, but frequently the final decision does not rest within the department but with

[11] Joseph R. Gusfield, *Symbolic Crusade: Status Politics and the American Temperance Movement,* Urbana: U. of Illinois, 1963.

the congressional, executive, or judicial body that created it. A bureau created by congressional enactment will continue to be unaltered except by internal decision only as long as Congress can be convinced that there is no need to alter it. Although there may be some question of degree, there is no question that public opinion will be a major factor in the congressional decision.

Therefore the federal department must convince the public and Congress: 1) that it serves a useful, or if possible, a necessary function; and 2) that it is uniquely qualified to do so. The less the department is sure of its future status, the more it will try to convince Congress and the public of these.

Background to Environmental Change: The Emergence and Development of the Bureau

In the late nineteenth and early twentieth centuries, narcotics were widely available: through doctors who indiscriminately prescribed morphine and later heroin as pain killers, through druggists who sold them openly, or through a wide variety of patent medicines.

> The public . . . (in the early twentieth century) had an altogether different conception of drug addiction from that which prevails today. The habit was not approved, but neither was it regarded as criminal or monstrous. It was usually looked upon as a vice or personal misfortune, or much as alcoholism is viewed today. Narcotics users were pitied rather than loathed as criminals or degenerates. . . .[12]

In 1914 Congress through the passage of the Harrison Act attempted to exert some control over the narcotics traffic. This act remains today the cornerstone of narcotics legislation. Rather than eliminate the use of narcotic drugs, the act was passed in order to honor a previous international obligation stemming from the Hague Convention of 1912, and to control the criminal encroachments into the drug trade. Nowhere in the act is there direct reference to addicts or addiction.

> Its ostensible purpose appeared to be simply to make the entire process of drug distribution within the country a matter of record. The nominal excise tax (one cent per ounce), the requirement that persons and firms handling drugs register and pay fees, all seemed designed to accomplish this purpose. There is no indication of a legislative intention to deny addicts access to legal drugs or to interfere in any way with medical practices in this area.[13]

Medical practices were specifically exempted:

[12] Alfred R. Lindesmith, *Opiate Addiction,* Bloomington, Ind.: Principia, 1947, p. 183.
[13] Alfred R. Lindesmith, *The Addict and the Law,* Bloomington, Ind.: Indiana U., 1965, p. 4. See also Rufus King, "The Narcotics Bureau and the Harrison Act: Jailing the Healers and the Sick," *Yale Law Journal,* 62 (1953), p. 736; and William B. Eldridge, *Narcotics and the Law,* New York: American Bar Foundation, 1961. The Act is placed in a statutory perspective in "Note: Narcotics Regulation," *Yale Law Journal,* 62 (1953), pp. 751–787.

Nothing contained in this section . . . shall . . . apply . . . [t]o the dispensing or distribution of any drugs mentioned . . . to a patient by a physician, dentist, or veterinary surgeon registered under section 4722 in the course of his professional practice only.[14]

Thus, the act did not make addiction illegal. All it required was that addicts should obtain drugs from registered physicians who made, a record of the transaction.

A narcotics division was created in the Internal Revenue Bureau of the Treasury Department to collect revenue and enforce the Harrison Act. In 1920 it merged into the Prohibition Unit of that department and upon its creation in 1927 into the Prohibition Bureau. In 1930 the Bureau of Narcotics was formed as a separate Bureau in the Treasury Department.

Legitimation: The Process of Changing an Environment

After 1914 the powers of the Narcotics Division were clear and limited: to enforce registration and record-keeping, violation of which could result in imprisonment for up to ten years, and to supervise revenue collection. The large number of addicts who secured their drugs from physicians were excluded from the Division's jurisdiction. The public's attitude toward drug use had not changed much with the passage of the Act—there was some opposition to drug use, some support of it, and a great many who did not care one way or the other. In fact, the Harrison Act was passed with very little publicity or news coverage.[15]

Thus at this time the Narcotics Division was faced with a severely restricted scope of operations. Acceptance of the legislation as envisioned by Congress would mean that the Division would at best continue as a marginal operation with limited enforcement duties. Given the normal, well-documented bureaucratic tendency toward growth and expansion, and given the fact that the Division was a public bureaucracy and needed to justify its operations and usefulness before Congress, it would seem that increased power and jurisdiction in the area of drug control would be a desirable and, in fact, necessary goal. Adaptation to the Harrison Act limitations would preclude attainment of this goal. Operating under a legislative mandate, the logical alternative to adaptation would be to persuade the Congress and public that expansion was necessary and to extend the provisions of the Harrison Act.

Also at this point, the public's attitude toward narcotics use could be characterized as only slightly opposed. Faced with a situation where adaptation to the existing legislation was bureaucratically unfeasible, where expansion was desirable, and where environmental support—from both Congress and the public—was necessary for continued existence, the Division launched a two-pronged campaign: 1) a barrage of reports and newspaper articles

14 26 *U.S.C.* 4705(c) (1954 Code).
15 The *New York Times Index* for 1914 lists only two brief articles on the federal legislation, one in June and one in August when the Senate adopted the Act. It should be noted that there was also discussion of a broadened New York State narcotics act and articles publicizing the arrest of violators of an earlier New York statute at that time.

which generated a substantial public outcry against narcotics use, and 2) a series of Division-sponsored test cases in the courts which resulted in a re-interpretation of the Harrison Act and substantially broadened powers for the Narcotics Division.[16] Thus the Division attained its goals by altering a weakly-held public value regarding narcotics use from neutrality or slight opposition to strong opposition, and by persuading the courts that it should have increased powers.[17]

Though the resources of the Division were limited, it was able to accomplish its goals because it was a public bureaucracy and as such had the afore-mentioned advantages which arise from that status. Since the ability to develop propaganda and the means to communicate it were inherent in this status, as was the propensity by the public to accept this propaganda, environmental support could be generated with less resource expenditure. Further, the Division as a public bureaucracy would be assumed to have a familiarity with governmental processes not only in its own executive branch, but also in the congressional and judicial branches as well. This built-in expertise necessary for the Division's expansion might be quite costly in time and resources for the private bureaucracy but again was inherent in the Division's status.

One typical example of the public campaign was a report cited and re-lied upon by the Narcotics Division for some years. It is an interesting com-bination of truth, speculation, and fiction, a mix which the Division and the Bureau which succeeded it found to be an effective public persuader for many years. In a report dated June, 1919, a committee appointed by the Treasury Department to study narcotics reported *inter alia* that there were 237,665 addicts in the United States treated by physicians (based upon a 30 percent response by physicians queried), that there were over one million addicts in the country in 1919 (a figure based upon a compromise between projections based on the percentage of addicts in Jacksonville, Florida in 1913 and New York City in 1918), that there was extensive addiction among children, that narcotics were harmful to health and morals, and that they were directly con-nected with crime and abject poverty. Among the physical effects noted were insanity; diseased lungs, hearts, and kidneys; rotting of the skin; and sterility.[18]

This "scholarly report" is an interesting example of the propaganda ef-fort, for it appears to the casual reader to be credible (especially given its source), and contains charges which seem to be designed to generate wide-spread public disgust toward narcotics users and support for the Division and its efforts. Many of the same charges were applied to marihuana when the Bureau campaigned against its use.

While the Division was carrying out its public campaign, it was also busy in the courts. Between 1918 and 1921 the Narcotics Division won three im-portant cases in the Supreme Court and persuaded the Court, essentially, to

[16] King, *op. cit.*, pp. 737–748; Lindesmith, *The Addict . . .*, pp. 5–11.

[17] In focusing on judicial expansion of existing legislation rather than on further Congressional action, the Division was able to avoid the lobbies of doctors and pharma-cists who strongly opposed the Harrison Act in the first place and who successfully lob-bied for the medical exception. See the *New York Times*, June 28, 1914, Sec. II, p. 5.

[18] U.S. Treasury Department, *Report of Special Committee to Investigate the Traf-fic in Narcotic Drugs* (April 15, 1919).

delete the medical exception from the Harrison Act thereby broadening its position as an enforcement agency. In the first case, *Webb v. United States*,[19] the court held that a physician could not supply narcotics to an addict unless he was attempting to cure him and in so doing made illegal the work of a large number of physicians who were supplying addicts with drugs under the registration procedures of the Harrison Act. This decision was supported in the two following cases: *Jin Fuey Moy v. United States*[20] and *United States v. Behrman.*[21] In *Behrman,* it was held that physicians could not even supply drugs to addicts in an attempt to cure them. The medical exception was nullified. The cases were skillfully chosen and presented to the court. Each was a flagrant abuse of the statute—in *Webb,* the physician's professional practice seemed to be limited to supplying narcotics to whoever wanted them. In the other two cases, the physicians supplied huge amounts of drugs over short periods of time to a small number of patients—patently for resale at a later time. Yet the Division did not argue for and the court did not rule on the cases as violations of the statute as it was intended, but instead regarded all of these as normal professional practices by physicians and held that, as such, they were illegal.

Three years after *Behrman,* the court somewhat reversed itself in *Linder v. United States.*[22] Here the doctor supplied a small dosage to a patient who was a government informer. The court rejected the government's case in a unanimous opinion, holding:

> The enactment under consideration . . . says nothing of "addicts" and does not undertake to prescribe methods for their medical treatment, and we cannot possibly conclude that a physician acted improperly or unwisely or for other than medical purposes solely because he has dispensed to one of them, in the ordinary course and in good faith, four small tablets of morphine or cocaine for relief of condition incident to addiction.[23]

The court went on to warn the Division:

> Federal power is delegated, and its prescribed limits must not be transcended even though the ends seem desirable. The unfortunate condition of the recipient certainly created no reasonable probability that she would sell or otherwise dispose of the few tablets entrusted to her and we cannot say that by so dispensing them the doctor necessarily transcended the limits of that professional conduct with which Congress never intended to interfere.[24]

Though *Linder* might have reintroduced doctors into the area, the Narcotics Division successfully prevented this by refusing to recognize *Linder* in its regulations, thus creating a situation where few would accept the risks involved in testing the doctrine, and by launching an all-out campaign against

[19] 249 *U.S.* 96 (1918).
[20] 254 *U.S.* 189 (1920).
[21] 258 *U.S.* 280 (1921).
[22] 268 *U.S.* 5 (1924).
[23] 268 *U.S.* 5 at 15 (1924).
[24] 268 *U.S.* 5 at 20 (1924).

doctors—closing the remaining narcotics clinics, imprisoning rebellious doctors, and publicizing records and convictions of physician addicts.[25]

Rufus King comments on this period of growth:

> In sum, the Narcotics Division succeeded in creating a very large criminal class for itself to police . . . instead of the very small one Congress has intended.[26]

The success of this campaign was reflected not only in the increased number of potential criminals, but in financial growth as well. Between 1918 and 1925, the Bureau's budgetary appropriations increased from $325,000 to $1,329,440, a rise of over 400 percent.[27]

The Marihuana Tax Act of 1937: A Bureaucratic Response

There are many other examples of efforts by the Bureau to create and maintain a friendly and supportive environment—through other publicity campaigns, through lobbying in Congress, and through continued and diligent attacks upon and harassments of its critics—which have been amply chronicled by others, although not as part of an organizational process.[28]

The Bureau's efforts to induce passage of the Marihuana Tax Act deserve special mention, however, in light of Becker's finding that the legislation was the result of what he terms a "moral enterprise."[29] Becker concludes that Narcotics Commissioner Anslinger and his Bureau were the motive forces behind the original 1937 legislation and the increasingly severe penalties which have since been imposed. This is readily conceded.[30] But he argues that the motivation behind this desire for the marihuana legislation was a moral one. He presents a picture of a society totally indifferent to the use of marihuana until Anslinger, in the role of a moral entrepreneur, "blows the

[25] King, *op. cit.*, pp. 744–745; "Note: Narcotics Regulation . . .," pp. 784–787. The Bureau's yearly report *Traffic in Opium and Other Dangerous Drugs* carries numerous reports of addiction among physicians during this period. See also Lindesmith, *The Addict . . .*, pp. 135–161.

[26] King, *op. cit.*, p. 738.

[27] See Table 1. During this period, two pieces of legislation were enacted that affected the Bureau's scope of operation: The Revenue Act of 1918, and the Narcotic Drug Import and Export Act of 1922.

[28] Along with the works of Lindesmith and King above, see the Bureau's publication, *Comments on Narcotic Drugs* (Undated), the Bureau's reply to the A.B.A.— A.M.A. committee interim report "Narcotic Drugs." This publication was described by DeMott as "perhaps the crudest publication yet produced by a government agency . . ." and was later taken out of print. Benjamin DeMott, "The Great Narcotics Muddle," *Harpers Magazine*, March, 1962, p. 53. For a vivid account of the Bureau's methods with its critics, see Lindesmith, *The Addict . . .*, pp. 242–268.

[29] Becker, *op. cit.*, p. 135.

[30] It seems clear from examining periodicals, newspapers, and the *Congressional Record* that the Bureau was primarily responsible for the passage of the act, though Becker's almost exclusive reliance on the claims of the Bureau in its official publication *Traffic in Opium and Other Dangerous Drugs* does not seem warranted given the previously discussed tendency of a public bureaucracy to emphasize its necessity and successful functioning.

whistle" on marihuana smoking. Again, it is conceded that Commissioner Anslinger throughout his long career with the Narcotics Bureau has opposed drug and narcotics use on moral grounds. This theme runs consistently through his writings.[31] What Becker ignores is that Anslinger was also a bureaucrat and thus responsive to bureaucratic pressures and demands as well. The distinction between these roles is difficult to make but it is fundamental in analyzing the legislation.

To understand whether the marihuana legislation was to a large degree the result of bureaucratic processes similar to the Bureau's expansion after the Harrison Act or whether it was instead the result of an individual's moral crusade, it is necessary to focus not only on the individual, as Becker has done, but upon the Bureau and its environment during this period. Through this method, certain parallels with the post-Harrison Act period become evident.

The Marihuana Tax Act which imposed a prohibitively costly tax on the sale of marihuana was passed by both houses of Congress with practically no debate[32] and signed into law on August 2, 1937. While Becker seems to argue that the Bureau generated a great public outcry against marihuana use prior to the passage of the Act, his data supporting this argument are misleading if not erroneously interpreted.[33] While marihuana use seems to have increased since the early 1930's, there appears to have been little public

[31] See especially Harry Anslinger and Will Osborne, *The Murderers: The Story of the Narcotic Gang,* New York: Farrar, Straus, 1961, Chap. 1; and also the other writings of the Commissioner, among them: Harry Anslinger and William F. Tompkins, *The Traffic in Narcotics,* New York: Funk and Wagnalls, 1953; and Harry Anslinger and J. Gregory, *The Protectors: The Heroic Story of the Narcotic Agents, Citizens and Officials in Their Unending, Unsung Battle Against Organized Crime in America,* New York: Farrar, Straus, 1964.

[32] This is not unusual in the area of moral legislation, as Becker points out. Furthermore, unlike non-criminal legislation where the losing party still has a variety of remedies available to challenge the law, few remedies are available to those who are legislated against in criminal areas. Legitimate lobbies cannot be formed and test cases are dangerous.

However, Becker gives the impression that the only opposition to the marihuana legislation came from hemp growers, and that no one argued for the marihuana users (*Outsiders,* pp. 144–145). This is erroneous. The legislative counsel for the A.M.A., Dr. William C. Woodward, challenged the Bureau's conclusions that marihuana use was harmful to health and widespread among children, and demanded evidence to support these assertions. While he was not representing the marihuana users, he was certainly arguing their case and questioning the need for the legislation. See *Taxation of Marihuana,* Hearings Before the Committee on Ways and Means of the House of Representatives, 75th Congress, 1st Session, on H.R. 6385, April 27–30 and May 4, 1937, esp. p. 92. It should be noted that this opposition was ignored by the comittee members.

[33] Becker's data consist of a survey of the *Readers Guide to Periodical Literature,* in which he found that no magazine articles appeared before July, 1935; four appeared between July, 1935 and June, 1937; and 17 between July, 1937 and June, 1939 (*Outsiders,* p. 141). While this is correct, it is misleading due to the time intervals used. The four articles in the second period all appeared before 1937, no articles appeared in the five months preceding the House committee hearings on the act in late April and early May, one appeared in July, 1937, and the rest appeared after the bill was signed into law on August 2, 1937. In short, of the articles which Becker asserts provided the impetus to Congressional action, only one appeared in the seven months of 1937 before the marihuana bill was signed into law.

concern expressed in the news media, even in 1937. Few magazine articles were written about the subject, and if the *New York Times* is any indication, newspaper coverage was also slight.[34] The final presidential signing of the act received minimal coverage from the *Times*.[35] In short, rather than the Bureau-generated public turmoil that Becker indicates, it seems that public awareness of the problem, as well as public opposition to it, was slight.

While it cannot be shown conclusively that the Marihuana Tax Act was the result of a bureaucratic response to environmental conditions, similarities between this period and the post-Harrison Act period are evident. Marihuana opposition, like narcotics opposition before, appears to have resulted from a weakly held value. In both situations, publicity campaigns were launched. In both cases, one through the courts and one through Congress, efforts were exerted to expand the power of the Bureau. In both cases, there were substantial numbers of potential criminals who could be incorporated into the Bureau's jurisdiction.

Perhaps more convincingly than similarities are the budgetary appropriations for the Bureau from 1915 to 1944 presented in Table 1. In 1932, when the Bureau's appropriations were approaching an all time high, the Bureau stated:

> The present constitutional limitations would seem to require control measures directed against the intrastate traffic of Indian hemp (marihuana) to be adopted by the several State governments rather than by the Federal Government, and the policy has been to urge the State authorities generally to provide the necessary legislation, with supporting enforcement activity, to prohibit the traffic except for bona fide medical purposes. The proposed uniform State narcotic law . . . with optional text applying to restriction of traffic in Indian hemp, has been recommended as an adequate law to accomplish the desired purpose.[36]

At this time, according to the Bureau, sixteen states had enacted legislation in which "the sale or possession (of marihuana) is prohibited except for medical purposes."[37] One year later, 18 more states had enacted the desired legislation, and by 1936, it appears that the Bureau's policy had succeeded completely for all 48 states had enacted legislation which governed the sale or possession of marihuana.[38]

Despite this apparent success and despite former questions concerning

[34] A survey of the *New York Times Index* shows: one article discussed marihuana in 1936 and eight discussed the subject between January and August 1937. There were no articles about or coverage of any of the Congressional hearings. Contrary to Becker's assertion, perhaps the most significant thing about this period was the lack of publicity involved.

[35] The total coverage by the *New York Times* consisted of a four line AP dispatch near the bottom of page four, titled "Signs Bill to Curb Marihuana" and reading in its entirety: "President Roosevelt signed today a bill to curb traffic in the narcotic, marihuana, through heavy taxes on transactions." (August 3, 1937.)

[36] U.S. Bureau of Narcotics, *Traffic in Opium and Other Dangerous Drugs For the Year Ending December 31, 1932,* Washington: Government Printing Office, p. 43.

[37] *Ibid.,* p. 43.

[38] U.S. Bureau of Narcotics, *Traffic in Opium and Other Dangerous Drugs . . .,* Washington: Government Printing Office, 1932–1936.

Table 1 Budgetary Appropriations for the
U.S. Narcotics Bureau (1915–1944)*

Year**	Total Appropriation
1915	$ 292,000
1916	300,000
1917	325,000
1918	750,000
1919	750,000
1920	750,000
1921	750,000
1922	750,000
1923	750,000
1924	1,250,000
1925	1,329,440
1926	1,329,440
1927	1,329,440
1928	1,329,440
1929	1,350,440
1930	1,411,260
1931	1,611,260
1932	1,708,528
1933	1,525,000
1934	1,400,000
1935	1,244,899
1936	1,249,470
1937	1,275,000
1938	1,267,000
1939	1,267,600
1940	1,306,700
1941	1,303,280
1942	1,283,975
1943	1,289,060
1944	1,150,000

* Source: Appropriations Committee, U.S.
Senate, *Appropriations, New Offices, etc., State-
ments Showing Appropriations Made, New Of-
fices Created, etc.,* 1915–1923; U.S. Bureau of
the Budget, *The Budget of the United States
Government,* Washington: Government Printing
Office, 1923–1945.
** Fiscal year the appropriation was made.
Each sum was appropriated for the following
fiscal year.

the constitutionality of the measure, the Bureau in 1937 pressed for the enactment of the federal marihuana act. For Anslinger, the moral entrepreneur,
1936 should have been a year of victory. In every state the marihuana menace

was subjected to statutory control.[39] But for Anslinger, the bureaucrat, 1936 seems to have been another year of defeat. His budgetary appropriation remained near a low point that had not been seen in over a decade, which to some extent reflected the general economic conditions of the time. His request for fiscal 1933 had been cut $100,000 below the general Treasury Department reduction for all bureaus.[40] In succeeding years, reductions in actual operating expenses were greater than those reflected in Table 1, for varying sums were deducted from the appropriations and held in a general trust fund as part of the government's anti-depression program. The Bureau's actual operating funds remained at about one million dollars from fiscal 1934 to fiscal 1936.[41] In his appearances before the House Subcommittee of the Committee on Appropriations that considered the Treasury Department budget, Anslinger repeatedly warned that the limited budget was curtailing his enforcement activities.[42] By 1936, his budget had decreased over $450,000 from its high four years before, a fall of almost 26 percent.

Again in 1937 Anslinger, the moralist, would be expected first to convince the general public that marihuana use was evil and immoral, while Anslinger, the bureaucrat, would be more concerned with attaining passage of legislation which would increase the Bureau's powers and then proceed to generate environmental support for these powers. In fact, the latter occurred. The great bulk of Bureau-inspired publicity came after the passage of the act, not before.[43]

Faced with a steadily decreasing budget, the Bureau responded as any organization so threatened might react: it tried to appear more necessary,

[39] It can be argued that a federal measure was still necessary because: (1) state legislation was poorly drawn, or 2) state enforcement was inadequate. The former is doubtful since by 1937, 39 states (as compared to four in 1933) had enacted the Uniform Narcotic Drug Act, the very legislation the Bureau felt would best control marihuana use. The latter situation, even if true, could have been rectified by means other than federal legislation.

[40] *Hearings Before the Subcommittee of the House Committee on Appropriations,* 72nd Congress, 1st Session, in charge of the Treasury Department Appropriations Bill for 1933, January 14, 1932, pp. 375–393.

[41] *Hearings Before the Subcommittee of the House Committee on Appropriations, op. cit.,* for fiscal 1934: 72nd Congress, 2nd Session, November 23, 1932, pp. 171–180; for fiscal 1935: 73rd Congress, 2nd Session, December 18, 1933, pp. 178–198; for fiscal 1936: 74th Congress, 1st Session, December 17, 1934, pp. 201–225.

[42] Thus in the hearing for the 1935 appropriation:

Mr. Arnold: How are you getting by with that $1,000,000 after those deductions? Comm. Anslinger: I am getting by, but I have had to cut back enforcement activities so sharply that it has reached a point where I think it has been harmful . . . (1935 Hearings, *op. cit.,* p. 189).

In his opening statement at the hearing for the 1936 appropriation, Anslinger stated "Mr. Chairman, and distinguished members of the committee, during the past fiscal year we have been operating under a very restricted appropriation. Our enforcement did not fall off too much although it did suffer somewhat." (1936 Hearings, *op. cit.,* p. 201). A decrease in seizures and fines levied was attributed to the limited budget, *ibid.,* pp. 213–214.

[43] See footnote 32.

and it tried to increase its scope of operations. As a result of this response, the Marihuana Tax Act of 1937 was passed.[44] Whether the Bureau's efforts were entirely successful is questionable. One beneficial result for the Bureau was that violations and seizures under the Marihuana Tax Act contributed substantially to the Bureau's totals, which had been declining for some time. (When arrests, convictions, and seizures were on the increase, these were faithfully reported to the House Subcommittee as evidence of the Bureau's effective use of funds.) In 1938, the first full year under the Marihuana Tax Act, one out of every four federal drug and narcotic convictions was for a marihuana violation.[45]

Financially, the enterprise was less successful. Though the budgetary decline was halted, expected increases for enforcing the new legislation did not immediately materialize. Anslinger pointed out this problem in a 1937 subcommittee hearing in connection with the fiscal 1939 appropriation:

> *Comm. Anslinger:* We took on the administration of the marihuana law and did not get any increase for that purpose. The way we are running we may have to request a deficiency of $100,000 at the end of the year; but I sincerely hope you will not see me here for a deficit. Beginning the first of the year, Mr. Chairman, I shall control all travel out of Washington. That is a hard job. I have to do that to make up some of this money. We went ahead at high speed and broke up ten big distributing rings, and now we find ourselves in the hole financially.
> *Mr. Ludlow:* You have to find some way to recoup?
> *Comm. Anslinger:* Yes; and keep the enforcement of the Marihuana Act going. Not a dollar has been appropriated in connection with the enforcement of the Marihuana law. We have taken on the work in connection with the Marihuana Act in addition to our other duties.[46]

While the Bureau's budgetary appropriation since that time have in general increased, the period of the late 1930's and early 1940's, where increases might be expected to be the largest, was a period of small advances and then a gradual decline. Of course the major factor in that period was the massive redirection of funds from nonmilitary areas, and thus these figures do not accurately reflect the Bureau's enterprise.

In conclusion, it should be reiterated that this paper does not presume to refute the moral entrepreneur approach—for in many instances it is a valid and useful means of analysis—but rather it attempts to demonstrate an alternative explanation that may frequently be appropriate. It would be either naive or presumptuous to deny that some combination of both moral and bureaucratic factors exist in any given crusade. The problem for analysis is to

[44] While Commissioner Anslinger as leader of this bureaucratic response might be characterized as a "bureaucratic entrepreneur," such characterization would be misleading, for similar to Becker's characterization it still simplifies the problem by emphasizing the individual's importance rather than that of the Bureau and its environment.

[45] U.S. Bureau of Narcotics, *Traffic in Opium and Other Dangerous Drugs For the Year Ending December 31, 1938,* Washington: Government Printing Office, pp. 77–79.

[46] *Hearings Before the Subcommittee of the House Committee on Appropriations, 75th Congress,* 3rd Session, in charge of the Treasury Department Appropriations Bill for 1939, December 14, 1937, p. 380.

determine the relative importance of each, and the consequences stemming from a particular combination. The utility of the organizational approach lies in that it can be extended to other similar moral crusades or to entire social movements, where the emphasis so far has been on the work of individual crusaders rather than on the organizations and their environments. Further, to the extent these movements follow the general societal pattern and become increasingly complex, organized, and bureaucratic, the organizational approach will become even more important in analysis and prediction.

J. J. BERRY

Deviant Categories and Organizational Typing of Delinquents

Introduction

What is any juvenile's chance of being successfully defined as an official deviant? The traditional response would be that it will depend primarily on the individual's behavior. An emerging response would include some statement about the size, goals, and efficacy of organizations that deal with juveniles (Turk, 1969). As responsibility for social solidarity has passed from primary groups to the larger secondary groups the successful definition of deviance has become, in large part, a function of the characteristics of the responsible agencies. Some researchers have attempted to clarify the picture by investigating such factors as the power potential of agencies *vis-à-vis* clients and other agencies (Quinney, 1970; Duster, 1970; Stoll, 1968), moral indignation towards the behavior they deal with (Becker, 1963), and the dynamics of the organizations in their attempts to remain viable (Dickson, 1968; Turk, 1970). It is this dynamic quality that is of interest in this paper.

Two basic problems must be faced by these organizations. First, the definitions of deviance that are used are of paramount importance. They must be accepted as meaningful, must identify individuals in need of intervention, and must have some public support. Second, it is equally important to be able to locate and identify individuals who fit the definitions. That is, no matter how well-defined deviance is, individuals cannot be dealt with until identified.

Definitions

The organizational application of collective definitions requires decisions as to which behavior categories should be included as relevant to that organization. The decisions must take into account the probabilistic nature of deviance and the capacity of the organization to legitimize its "responsibilities" and claims to expertise. Four important factors are at least under the partial control of the organizations. A decision to alter a definition of deviant behavior on one or all of the parameters is sometimes instrumental to the survival or failure of the organization itself. At a minimum, such decisions help determine relative status, resources, and authority within the network of deviance control.

Range of Categorical Responsibilities

A fairly successful adaptation for organizations has been an extension of the range of definitions under their responsibility. For instance, the Federal Bureau of Narcotics did not deal with the use of marijuana until 1937 when, after a newspaper campaign, they successfully obtained the responsibility with the Marihuana Tax Act [note the Bureau's spelling for the drug] for dealing with a new population of drug users (Lindesmith, 1965). Another example of a successful adaptation can be found in the March of Dimes, which conquered polio and faced the loss of purpose. They respond by including under their definition of medical deviance the areas of birth defects and arthritis, thus adding new populations of individuals for whom they became "responsible" (Sills, 1957).

Range of Assessment of Seriousness

The probability of a label's being successfully applied also depends upon the perceived relative seriousness of the behavior associated with the definition. A change in the public assessment of the seriousness can be very effective in increasing the probability that the agency concerned will improve its effectiveness in the definitional process. For example, the use of opium was fairly widely spread in the United States prior to the Harrison Act (1913). Many patent medicines derived their benefits from opium. Withdrawal symptoms were associated with old age or illness (these being the reasons for the use in the first place). But with the medical evidence showing the addictive properties of opium and heroin, the situation changed dramatically. Addiction became an "important problem" (Lindesmith, 1965). The seriousness of the behavior-condition is problematic and will come under review from time to time. Changes in the assessment of seriousness may reflect societal changes or needs of organizations.

Range of Target Population

Sometimes it is possible to alter the power of and the applicability of definitions by changing the population parameters of the definition. Compulsory education became widespread in the 1900's and represented the culmination of several diverse movements (Swift, 1971). The Child Savers were concerned with the abuse and neglect of children and began the attempt to pass protective legislation as well as setting up "safe houses" for juveniles in trouble (Platt, 1969). At the same time, adults become quite concerned about the competition of children for jobs on the assembly line. At first, compulsory education was limited to a few states and extended only through primary grades. Over time it was extended to include all nonadults in all states through high school (Swift, 1971). The label of truant became meaningful as the change took place, and today truancy is very strongly associated with juvenile delinquency as well as other forms of "sociopathic behavior."

Range of Treatment

Finally, probabilities of successful definition can be affected by changing the range of treatment offered by the organization. For example, if an organization offers one treatment, it will be forced to deal with all its cases in the same fashion. It will be unable to differentiate between individuals and will either misapply treatment or be forced to send some of its cases to other agencies. Obviously, the fewer treatments it can offer the more the cases that must be sent out. Juvenile corrections has seen an explosion of treatments in the last twenty years, ranging from forest camps (minimum security, work-oriented programs) to behavior modification or token economy programs. As the range of treatment increases, so does the overall viability of the corrections organization. Critics of one program will be informed of a different one. Professionals in a given discipline can be informed of a program that will satisfy their theoretical orientations. Overall, juvenile corrections has been strengthened and legitimatized by the diversification of the treatment offered.

Identification

The intraorganizational dynamics of decision-making and the utility of definitions are influenced by oganizational characteristics. There is the problem of locating and identifying those persons deemed the organization's responsibility. That is, once the appropriate definitions have been created and legitimatized, the organization must fulfill its obligation of treatment. This requires information and identification of clients, which in turn requires agents responsible to the organization. The factors discussed below are integral to the development of an adequate network of agents who will produce the necessary identifications and apprehension.

Size

There is a truism with regard to mental illness that summarizes this factor rather well. The number of individuals defined as mentally ill in a community is highly correlated with the number of psychiatrists in the communtiy (Srole, 1962). In police work it is also known that if you increase the number of patrol cars in a given area the number of crimes reported will go up. The larger the number of people responsible for any particular set of definitions, the larger will be the number of people successfully identified as deviant.

Dispersal

All other things being equal, the most effective screen of agents will be the one that covers the target area most completely. An organization that concentrates its agents in one limited area will be ineffective in locating a continuous supply of clients and may disrupt its own activities by overdoing these restricted harvests. The broader the base population they work from, the more able they will be to insure the continuity of their operations. If the base is broad enough it will probably not be necessary to deal with changes in the definitions of deviance. Thus, dispersal of agents offers an alternative to the potentially dangerous activity of changing definitions and risking the interorganizational conflicts that are often engendered.

Coordination

There is an alternative way in which efficiency and effectiveness of identification can be accomplished without changing organizational size or dispersal. This is through a network of agencies acting in coordination with each other. The relationships between agencies can range from open conflict and competition (for scarce resources, status, and authority) through accommodation and coordination. To the degree that the relationships approach coordination, the identification process will be that much improved. In the area of juvenile delinquency Sophia Robison (1936) found that the number of delinquents dealt with by the juvenile courts in New York City made up slightly more than one half of the juvenile delinquents dealt with by some public social work agency in New York. When you consider the range of organizations now concerned with juvenile deviance, the possibilities of identification are impressive. Agencies that work separately have only the power of their own agency to lend authenticity to their attempts to identify deviants, but members of a network of organizations have the full weight of their collectivity to work with. In the very process of referring there is a built-in assumption of legitimacy and an indication that this individual is really in need of some kind of help. Once involved with such a network the individual's chances of avoiding identification as a deviant are small indeed. This "piling up" effect of coordinated service agencies creates a very strong and relatively persistent definition of deviance.

An Empirical Example

The Setting

The observations recorded here were made in a cornbelt county which will be referred to as Agri County. The main urban center is a twin-city complex we will call Alpha-Beta. The total population of the county is 105,000, with Alpha having 40,000 and Beta about 30,000. Within this relatively small area there are eight agencies whose primary function is dealing with preadults:

Family Court (juvenile court)
Youth Service Agency
Department of Child and Family Services
Department of Public Education
Tri-County Special Education
Truant Officer

A Detention Home for Girls
A Detention Home for Boys

Plus an additional twelve agencies with a major interest in pre-adults:

Police
State's Attorney
Probation Office
Department of Mental Health Zone Center
Agri County Mental Health Clinic
Department of Public Aid
Department of Public Health
Family Services
PATH Crisis Center
YWCA
YMCA
Catholic Social Services

Approximately half of these agencies are sponsored by the state, county, or other public sources with the remainder being private. The services range from the juvenile courts to voluntary programs like the PATH Crisis Center. Their orientations range from control and prevention to rehabilitation and salvation.

This list is not complete, though it does include all the major agencies. There are others which are marginal to the control of juveniles, but whose main emphasis is on other populations.

Definitions

It would be impossible to list all the operant definitions of youth deviance for even as limited an area as Agri County. There are, however, some general classifications which probably account for the majority of such definitions. They are: (1) problem persons, (2) persons with problems, and (3) problem situations. Some agencies deal only with one of these categories while others deal with all three. It is interesting to note that some of these definitions are relatively new, or newly enforced.

Table 1 Definitions of Youth Deviance

Problem Persons	Persons with Problems	Problem Situations
Delinquent (violates law)	Mental or Emotional Problems	Neglected
Minor in Need of Supervision	Retardation	Abused
Suicide–Drug–Alcohol Crisis	Poor Academic Performance	Dependent
Social/Personal		

Clearly some of these categories overlap, with the same organization dealing with more than one aspect of the "problem" while in other cases more than one agency deals with the same problem or different aspects of it. In any case, the range of potential deviant definitions is vast and the need for intervention paramount from the perspective of those with the responsibility to do so.

Location of Juvenile Deviants

Given the number and range of deviant definitions available to the control agencies in this area, the limiting factors for discovering and dealing with juvenile deviants are money and personnel. It is almost impossible to discover the exact number of individuals involved in youth control because of such questions as, do teachers count? Clergymen, Boy Scout leaders, and so forth could also conceivably be included. Leaving these latter two out, the figure ranges from some 200 control agents to some 3,000 (including teachers). The total amount of money spent is also difficult to determine, though on the basis of fragments of information available from some of the organizations it would appear to range from $100,000 to $1,000,000 (including schools) per year. The total client population (those actually treated) ranges from 2,000 to 4,000 individuals per year.

In interviewing spokesmen for the various organizations it became clear that they consider this number to be just the tip of the iceberg of juvenile deviance. Most of the spokesmen indicated that a truly efficient location system (coordinated community system) could easily triple the number of juveniles in need of intervention. Almost all of the spokesmen claimed they would approve of fuller cooperation with other agencies at the same time all of them expressed reservations concerning the sharing of authority, prestige, and money to that end.

Two Illustrative Organizations

In order to assess the impact of changes in agencies on their viability, two organizations were examined that had recently undergone or been prepared for major changes in their *modus operandi*. The first, Youth Service Agency, changed its range of definitions, range of target population, and range of treatment within a six-month span. The second agency, Department of Child Family Services, was ordered to prepare for changes regarding their target population within one year. The consequence for both of these organizations was substantial.

Table 2 Characteristics of Youth Service Agency and Department of Child–Family Services

Agency	Personnel	Client Population (month)	Areas of Deviance Defined	Origin of Cases	Agency Referred To
YSA	5	80	Drugs, Suicide, Alcohol, Family Problems	AR = 79%, SR = 21%	OA = 59%, YSA = 34%, CP = 7%
DCFS	27	20	Neglected–Abused, Parent–Child Conflict	AR = 51%, SR = 49%	OA = 22%, DCFS = 78%

AR = Agency Referral   SR = Self-Referral   OA = Other Agencies   CP = Cases Pending

In 1972, a private agency was established in the community of Alpha, with the specific function of coordination of referrals for juveniles with problems and problem juveniles. Its title was the Youth Service Agency. It was funded for two years and given a staff of five workers.

As originally designed YSA was supposed to locate individuals in need of help by maintaining contact with the various agencies already in the field. In this community there were twenty separate agencies (some private and some public). YSA was to operate as a sort of clearing house for all these services and attempt to place individuals with the agency most able to handle the evolving problems. The difficulties with this arrangement began with the discovery that many of the agencies in the area did not maintain contacts with any of the surrounding small communities in the county. That is, their services were primarily reserved for those members of the immediate community, most of whom referred themselves to particular officials. Thus, the first change that took place was the attempt to establish contact with the "gatekeepers" in the small towns in the area. This meant members of YSA went to these areas and spent time trying to locate individuals with problems. It also meant that these individuals were located, their names were passed on to the appropriate agency in Alpha.

This created the second problem. The members of YSA made themselves available on a 24-hour basis in order to be available for crisis intervention. On several occasions, individuals contacted YSA and were referred to one of the relevant agencies, say DCFS. The individual was admitted as a client and given what treatment seemed relevant and released. Unfortunately, many of these crises were recurrent, and some of the clients were unsuccessful in recontacting their treatment officer. Several of them then recontacted YSA asking for direct intervention from the staff. After a few of these experiences YSA began to deal directly with more and more of their contacts, many of whom came to them directly rather than through any referral system. The summary of statistics after six months of operation shows that of the 102 individuals who contacted YSA and received some form of treatment, 37% were dealt with exclusively by the YSA staff. The same statistics show that 25% of their referrals did not come from other agencies. The two largest referral sources were the public schools and the juvenile justice system.

The other agencies in the area began to express concern at the change in function by YSA, and they now claim that it no longer has a purpose to serve. Some agency heads objected from the beginning and at the end of six months claimed that YSA was not only irrelevant but was preventing their offices from receiving sufficient funds to improve their operations. The agencies that seem most unhappy with the operations of YSA are those established by the state (DCFS, probation, Mental Health), while those that have maintained and in some cases improved relationships tend to be made up primarily of the volunteer organizations such as PATH and the YWCA.

In summary, YSA did manage to alter several aspects of its defined responsibilities:

1. Where YSA had originally had no responsibilities other than the coordination of decisions made by others, they now include much of the crisis clientele among young people (suicides, drug overdoses, and the like).

2. The same comments can be made with regard to range of target population, where this segment of society has now been enlarged to be inclusive of all youth in the area who have "problems."
3. Whereas the original treatment was indirect and through the auspices of other agencies, YSA now offers direct treatment based primarily on counseling.

There were also changes made in terms of the organizational characteristics:

1. While size was relatively unaffected by the changes in organizational decisions, the dispersal of agents was dramatically increased to include most of the surrounding small towns and communities.
2. A coordinated net work of gatekeepers extended the location of clientele markedly.

At this time it seems quite likely that YSA will become a permanent member of the control-treatment network of the area with activities organized around the treatment of youth problems. Undoubtedly its directors will sharpen the focus on the areas of responsibility and will probably concentrate on the new ecological areas open to them in the outlying communities.

A second agency has undergone an involuntary change in its range of responsibilities. In January, 1974, the Department of Child Family Services will become responsible for a new category of clients. Under the new Juvenile Court Act, juveniles placed on probation who violate the conditions of their probation, drug addicts, and habitual truants will automatically be redesignated Minors in Need of Supervision and will become the responsibility of DCFS. To this point in time most of the children dealt with by this state agency were neglected, dependent, and abused children. Most of these children are rather young, and very few are children in trouble with the law.

This change in categorical responsibilities will also force changes in ranges of treatment. DCFS wil be required, by law, to locate appropriate treatment facilities and place their wards therein. While DCFS will not have direct control over all of these treatment centers, they will be responsible for maintenance of records and updating of such records with regard to outcomes and further treatment recommendations. At this time, it is unclear as to how these changes will affect the assessment of seriousness or the range of the target population.

It is clear, however, that there will be some increase in coordination of activities with other state agencies. The forced relationship with the Department of Corrections will increase sources of information and legitimize the decisions of DCFS. It will also limit autonomy by increasing accountability to other state agencies, at least in terms of record keeping. Locally, the relationship between DCFS and the Court will also be altered. Presently, this relationship would be best described as strained. Increased responsibility and the increased coordination of activities will require more cooperaton and assumptions of expertise (in this case authority) between the judge and the agency. While individual antipathy may survive, the formal requirements of bureaucracy will mandate such a change.

Finally, it should be noted that this change was not sought by the agency. In fact, it was strongly opposed. The objections arise out of the fear that they would be required to deal with a larger clientele without an increase in staff and that this new clientele represents a group of individuals that they are not prepared to deal with. These fears are probably justified, given the state of the State. In the long run, however, the results should prove most beneficial to organizational viability.

Conclusion

Social work agencies come and go, though few without some struggle. As more and more agencies make successful adaptations or become members of networks or systems of intervention, there is improvement in detection systems as well as an increased viability in the definitions of deviance. To the degree that this is true there is an increase in official deviance and an associated increase of importance of the consequence of deviance. As the definitions are more widely used and as the definitions become more viable, the need for treatment becomes prominent in the mind of the public. These definitions, because of their official nature, become methods by which individuals are located in the opportunity structure and carry with them permanent or at least long-term consequences.

To the degree that coordination becomes a reality, increased attention is paid to accountability and record keeping. To the degree that records are kept accurately the ability of an individual to "forget" and be "forgotten" becomes less possible. As agencies are held more directly accountable they become more careful in maintenance of records and quite concerned with "passing on" those individuals whom they have little hope of "handling" (Garfinkel, 1967). Under tight accountability and efficient record keeping the definitions become more sharply distinct, resulting in increased efficiency and success in labeling. This does not necessarily mean that individuals receive more "correct" treatment, but that they will be more efficiently located, identified, and treated (Szasz, 1970).

It is hardly surprising to read in the F.B.I. Crime Reports or the local paper that juveniles in this country are the worst in the world and today's juveniles the worst in our history. In other times and other places, it was and is downright difficult to be labeled a deviant. Today in the United States it is not difficult at all. Pre-adults who enjoy almost none of the protections of the Constitution, mental defectives, and powerless minorities are easy to label and unlikely to put up much effective resistance. New emphasis, new definitions, and new methods of identification and location lead to changes in the probability of individuals' being defined as official deviants. This is true for juveniles as well as adults.

Increases in the viability and legitimacy of deviance-controlling organizations focus public attention on particular "problems" and emphasize particular recommendations for control. As YSA extends its activities into the hinterlands, the public view that deviance is an urban phenomenon will be at least strained. As DCFS extends its activities to include problem pre-adults, the public will be forced to enlarge its perception of the extent to which deviance has enveloped children. The impact of changes in organizational responsibilities, as well as the general characteristics of organizations, strongly influences the collective definitions of deviance.

References

BECKER, HOWARD
1963   The Outsiders. New York: The Free Press.
DICKSON, DONALD
1968   "Bureaucracy and Morality: An Organizational Perspective on a Moral Crusade." Social Problems 16 (Fall): 143–157.
DUSTER, TROY
1970   The Legislation of Morality. New York: The Free Press.
GARFINKEL, HAROLD
1967   "Good Organizational Reasons for 'Bad' Clinic Records." Studies in Ethnomethodology. Englewood Cliffs, N.J.: Prentice-Hall, Inc.
LINDESMITH, ALFRED R.
1965   The Addict and the Law. New York: Vintage Books.
PLATT, ANTHONY M.
1969   "The Rise of the Child Saving Movement: A Study in Social Policy and Correctional Reforms." The Annals. 381 (January): 21–38.
QUINNEY, RICHARD
1970   The Social Reality of Crime. Boston: Little, Brown and Company.
ROBISON, SOPHIA
1936   Can Delinquency Be Measured? New York: Columbia University Press.
SILLS, DAVID
1957   Bureau of Applied Social Research. Glencoe, Illinois: The Free Press.
SROLE, LEO, et al.
1962   Mental Health in the Metropolis. New York: McGraw-Hill, Inc.
STOLL, CLARICE S.
1968   "Images of Man and Social Control." Social Forces 47(December): 119–126.
SWIFT, DAVID W.
1971   Ideology and Change in the Public Schools. Columbus, Ohio: Charles E. Merrill Books.
SZASZ, THOMAS
1970   "Mental Health Services in the School." Pp. 167–189 in Ideology and Insanity. Garden City, N.Y.: Anchor Books.
TURK, AUSTIN
1969   Criminality and the Legal Order. Chicago: Rand-McNally.
TURK, HERMAN
1970   "Interorganizational Networks in Urban Society: Initial Perspectives and Comparative Research." American Sociological Review 35(February): 1–18.

HARRISON M. TRICE
PAUL MICHAEL ROMAN

Delabeling, Relabeling, and Alcoholics Anonymous

An increasing amount of research emphasis in social psychiatry in recent years has been placed upon the rehabilitation and return of former mental patients to "normal" community roles (Sussman, 1966). The concomitant rapid growth of community psychiatry as a psychiatric paradigm parallels this interest, with community psychiatry having as a primary concern the maintenance of the patient's statuses within the family and community throughout the treatment process so as to minimize problems of rehabilitation and "return" (Pasamanick et al., 1967; Susser, 1968). Despite these emphases, successful "delabeling" or destigmatization of mental patients subsequent to treatment appears rare (Miller, 1965; Freeman and Simmons, 1963). It is the purpose of this paper to explore an apparent negative instance of this phenomenon, namely a type of social processing which results in *successful* delabeling, wherein the stigmatized label is replaced with one that is socially acceptable.

The so-called labeling paradigm which has assumed prominence within the sociology of deviant behavior offers a valuable conceptualization of the development of deviant careers, many of which are apparently permanent (Scheff, 1966). In essence, labeling theory focuses upon the processes whereby a "primary deviant" becomes a "secondary deviant" (Lemert, 1951: 75–76). Primary deviance may arise from myriad sources. The extent and nature of the social reaction to this behavior is a function of the deviant's reaction to his own behavior (Roman and Trice, 1969), the behavior's visibility, the power vested in the statuses of the deviant actor, and the normative parameters of tolerance for deviance that exist within the community. Primary

Presented to the Section on Medical Sociology, Southern Sociological Society, New Orleans, April 11, 1969. Support of the Christopher D. Smithers Foundation and the Office of General Research of the University of Georgia is gratefully acknowledged.

deviance that is visible and exceeds the tolerance level of the community may bring the actor to the attention of mandated labelers such as psychiatrists, clinical psychologists, and social workers.

If these labelers see fit "officially" to classify the actor as a type of deviant, a labeling process occurs which eventuates in (1) self concept changes on the part of the actor and (2) changes in the definitions of him held by his immediate significant others, as well as the larger community. Behavior which occurs as a consequence of these new definitions is called secondary deviance. This behavior is substantively similar to the original primary deviance but has as its source the actor's revised self concept, as well as the revised social definition of him held in the community.

Previous research and theoretical literature appear to indicate that this process is irreversible, particularly in the cases of mental illness or so-called residual deviance (Miller, 1965; Myers and Bean, 1968). No systematic effort has been made to specify the social mechanisms which might operate to "return" the stigmatized secondary deviant to a "normal" and acceptable role in the community. In other words, delabeling and relabeling have received little attention as a consequence of the assumption that deviant careers are typically permanent.

Conceptually, there appear to be at least three ways whereby delabeling could successfully occur. First, organizations of deviants may develop which have the primary goal of changing the norms of the community or society, such that their originally offending behavior becomes acceptable (Sagarin, 1967). For example, organized groups of homosexuals have strongly urged that children be educated in the dual existence of homosexuality and heterosexuality as equally acceptable forms of behavior.

Secondly, it is possible that the mandated professionals and organizations who initially label deviant behavior and process the deviant through "treatment" may create highly visible and explicit "delabeling" or "status-return" ceremonies which constitute legitimized public pronouncements that the offending deviance has ceased and the actor is eligible for re-entry into the community. Such ceremonies could presumably be the reverse of "status degradation" rituals (Garfinkel, 1957).

A third possible means is through the development of mutual aid organizations which encourage a return to strict conformity to the norms of the community as well as creating a stereotype which is socially acceptable. Exemplary of this strategy is Alcoholics Anonymous. Comprised of 14,150 local groups in the United States in 1967, this organization provides opportunities for alcoholics to join together in an effort to cease disruptive and deviant drinking behavior in order to set the stage for the resumption of normal occupational, marital, and community roles (Gellman, 1964).

The focus of this paper is the apparent success in delabeling that has occurred through the social processing of alcoholics through Alcoholics Anonymous and through alcoholics' participation in the A.A. subculture. The formulation is based chiefly on participant observation over the past 15 years in Alcoholics Anonymous and data from various of our studies of the social aspects of alcoholism and deviant drinking. These observations are supplemented by considerable contact with other "self-help" organizations. These experiences are recognized as inadequate substitutes for "hard" data; and the following points are best considered as exploratory hypotheses for further research.

The "Allergy" Concept

The chronic problem affecting the re-acceptance into the community of former mental patients and other types of deviants is the attribution of such persons with taints of permanent "strangeness," immorality, or "evil." A logical method for neutralizing such stigma is the promulgation of ideas or evidence that the undesirable behavior of these deviants stems from factors beyond their span of control and responsibility. In accord with Parsons' (1951) cogent analysis of the socially neutralizing effects of the "sick role," it appears that permanent stigmatization may be avoided if stereotypes of behavior disorders as forms of "illness" can be successfully diffused in the community.

Alcoholics Anonymous has since its inception attempted to serve as such a catalyst for the "delabeling" of its members through promulgating the "allergy concept" of alcohol addiction. Although not part of official A.A. literature, the allergy concept plays a prominent part in A.A. presentations to non-alcoholics as well as in the A.A. "line" that is used in "carrying the message" to non-member deviant drinkers. The substance of the allergy concept is that those who become alcoholics possess a physiological allergy to alcohol such that their addiction is predetermined even before they take their first drink. Stemming from the allergy concept is the label of "arrested alcoholic" which A.A. members place on themselves.

The significance of this concept is that it serves to diminish, both in the perceptions of the A.A. members and their immediate significant others, the alcoholic's responsibility for developing the behavior disorder. Furthermore, it serves to diminish the impression that a form of mental illness underlies alcohol abuse. In this vein, A.A. members are noted for their explicit denial of any association between alcoholism and psychopathology. As a basis for a "sick role" for alcoholics, the allergy concept effectively reduces blame upon one's *self* for the development of alcoholism.

Associated with this is a very visible attempt on the part of A.A. to associate itself with the medical profession. Numerous publications of the organization have dealt with physicians and A.A. and with physicians who are members of A.A. (*Grapevine,* 1968). Part of this may be related to the fact that one of the co-founders was a physician; and a current long time leader is also a physician. In any event, the strong attempts to associate A.A. with the medical profession stand in contrast to the lack of such efforts to become associated with such professions as law, education, or the clergy.

Despite A.A.'s emphasis upon the allergy concept, it appears clear that a significant portion of the American public does not fully accept the notion that alcoholism and disruptive deviant drinking are the result of an "allergy" or other organic aberration. Many agencies associated with the treatment of alcohol-related problems have attempted to make "alcoholism is an illness" a major theme of mass educational efforts (Plaut, 1967). Yet in a study of 1,213 respondents, Mulford and Miller (1964) found that only 24 percent of the sample "accepted the illness concept without qualification." Sixty-five percent of the respondents regarded the alcoholic as "sick," but most qualified this judgment by adding that he was also "morally weak" or "weak-willed."

The motivation behind public agencies' efforts at promulgating the "illness" concept of behavior disorders to reduce the probability of temporary or permanent stigmatization was essentially upstaged by A.A. Nonetheless, the data indicate that acceptance of the "illness" notion by the general public is relatively low in the case of alcoholism and probably lower in the cases of other behavior disorders (cf. Nunnally, 1961). But the effort has not been totally without success. Thus it appears that A.A.'s allergy concept does set the stage for reacceptance of the alcoholic by part of the population. A more basic function may involve the operation of the A.A. program itself; acceptance of the allergy concept by A.A. members reduces the felt need for "personality change" and may serve to raise diminished self-esteem.

Other than outright acceptance of the allergy or illness notion, there appear to be several characteristics of deviant drinking behavior which reduce the ambiguity of the decision to re-accept the deviant into the community after his deviance has ceased.

Unlike the ambiguous public definitions of the causes of other behavior disorders (Nunnally, 1961), the behaviors associated with alcohol addiction are viewed by the community as a direct consequence of the inappropriate use of alcohol. With the cessation of drinking behavior, the accompanying deviance is assumed to disappear. Thus, what is basically wrong with an alcoholic is that he drinks. In the case of other psychiatric disorders the issue of "what is wrong" is much less clear. This lack of clarity underlies Scheff's (1966) notion of psychiatric disorders as comprising "residual" or relatively unclassifiable forms of deviance. Thus the mentally ill, once labeled, acquire such vague but threatening stereotypes as "strange," "different," and "dangerous" (Nunnally, 1961). Since the signs of the disorder are vague in terms of cultural stereotypes, it is most difficult for the "recovered" mental patient to convince others that he is "cured."

It appears that one of the popular stereotypes of former psychiatric patients is that their apparent normality is a "coverup" for their continuing underlying symptoms. Thus, where the alcoholic is able to remove the cause of his deviance by ceasing drinking, such a convincing removal may be impossible in the case of the other addictions and "mental" disorders. Narcotic addiction represents an interesting middle ground between these two extremes, for the cultural stereotype of a person under the influence of drugs is relatively unclear, such that it may be relatively difficult for the former addict to convince others that he has truly removed the cause of his deviance. This points up the fact that deviant drinking and alcoholism are continuous with behavior engaged in by the majority of the adult population, namely "normal" drinking (Mulford, 1964). The fact that the deviant drinker and alcohol addict are simply carrying out a common and normative behavior to excess reduces the "mystery" of the alcoholic experience and creates relative confidence in the average citizen regarding his abilities to identify a truly "dry" alcoholic. Thus the relative clarity of the cultural stereotype regarding the causes of deviance accompanying alcohol abuse provides much better means for the alcoholic to claim he is no longer a deviant.

To summarize, A.A. promulgates the allergy concept both publicly and privately, but data clearly indicate that this factor alone does not account for the observed success at "re-entry" achieved by A.A. members. Despite ambiguity in public definitions of the etiology of alcoholism, its continuity with "normal" drinking behavior results in greater public confidence in the ability to judge the results of a therapeutic program. An understanding of A.A.'s success becomes clearer when this phenomenon is coupled with the availability of the "repentant" role.

The Repentant Role

A relatively well-structured status of the "repentant" is clearly extant in American cultural tradition. Upward mobility from poverty and the "log cabin" comprises a social type where the individual "makes good" for his background and the apparent lack of conformity to economic norms of his ancestors. Redemptive religion, emergent largely in American society, emphasizes that one can correct a moral lapse even of long duration by public admission of guilt and repentance (cf. Lang and Lang, 1960).

The A.A. member can assume this repentant role; and it may become a social vehicle whereby, through contrite and remorseful public expressions, substantiated by visibly reformed behavior in conformity to the norms of the community, a former deviant can enter a new role which is quite acceptable to society. The re-acceptance may not be entirely complete, however, since the label of alcoholic is replaced with that of "arrested alcoholic;" as Gusfield (1967) has stated, the role comprises a social type of a "repentant deviant." The acceptance of the allergy concept by his significant others may well hasten his re-acceptance, but the more important factor seems to be the relative clarity by which significant others can judge the deviant's claim to "normality." Ideally the repentant role is also available to the former mental patient; but as mentioned above, his inability to indicate clearly the removal of the symptoms of his former deviance typically blocks such an entry.

If alcohol is viewed in its historical context in American society, the repentant role has not been uniquely available to A.A. members. As an object of deep moral concern, no single category of behavior (with the possible exception of sexual behavior) has been laden with such emotional intensity in American society. Organized social movements previous to A.A. institutionalized means by which repentants could control their use of alcohol. These were the Washingtonians, Catch-My-Pal, and Father Matthews movements in the late 1800's and early 1900's, which failed to gain widespread social acceptance. Thus not only is the repentant role uniquely available to the alcoholic at the present time, but Alcoholics' Anonymous has been built on a previous tradition.

Skid Row Image and Social Mobility

The major facet of Alcoholics Anonymous' construction of a repentant role is found in the "Skid Row image" and its basis for upward social mobility. A central theme in the "stories" of many A.A. members is that of downward mobility into Skid Row or near Skid Row situations. Research evidence suggests that members tend to come from the middle and lower middle classes (Trice, 1962; Straus and Bacon, 1951). Consequently a "story" of downward mobility illustrates the extent to which present members had drastically fallen from esteem on account of their drinking. A.A. stories about "hitting bottom" and the many degradation ceremonies that they experienced in entering this fallen state act to legitimize their claims to downward mobility. Observation and limited evidence suggests that many of these stories are exaggerated to some degree and that a large proportion of A.A. members maintained at least partially stable status-sets throughout the addiction process. However, by the emphasis on downward mobility due to drinking, the social mobility "distance" traveled by the A.A. member is maximized in the stories. This clearly sets the stage for impressive "comeback accomplishments."

Moral values also play a role in this process. The stories latently emphasize the "hedonistic underworld" to which the A.A. member "traveled." His current status illustrates to others that he has rejected this hedonism and has clearly resubmitted himself to the normative controls and values of the dominant society, exemplified by his A.A. membership. The attempt to promulgate the "length of the mobility trip" is particularly marked in the numerous anonymous appearances that A.A. members make to tell their stories before school groups, college classes, church groups, and service clubs. The importance of these emphases may be indirectly supported by the finding that lower-class persons typically fail in their attempts to successfully affiliate with A.A., i.e., their social circumstances minimize the distance of the downward mobility trip (Trice and Roman, 1970; Trice, 1959).

A.A. and American Values

The "return" of the A.A. member to normal role performance through the culturally provided role of the repentant and through the implied social mobility which develops out of an emphasis upon the length of the mobility trip is given its meaning through tapping directly into certain major American value orientations.

Most importantly, members of Alcoholics Anonymous have regained self control and have employed that self control in bringing about their rehabilitation. Self control, particularly that which involves the avoidance of pleasure, is a valued mode of behavior deeply embedded in the American ethos (Williams, 1960). A.A. members have, in a sense, achieved success in their battle with alcohol and may be thought of in that way as being "self-made" in a society permeated by "a systematic moral orientation by which conduct is judged" (Williams, 1960: 424). This illustration of self control lends itself to positive sanction by the community.

A.A. also exemplifies three other value orientations as they have been delineated by Williams: humanitarianism, emphases upon practicality, and suspicion of established authority (Williams, 1960: 397–470). A definite tendency exists in this society to identify with the helpless, particularly those who are not responsible for their own afflictions.

A.A. taps into the value of efficiency and practicality through its pragmatism and forthright determination to "take action" about a problem. The organization pays little heed to theories about alcoholism and casts all of its literature in extremely practical language. Much emphasis is placed upon the simplicity of its tenets and the straightforward manner in which its processes proceed.

Its organizational pattern is highly congruous with the value, suspicion of vested authority. There is no national or international hierarchy of officers, and local groups maintain maximum autonomy. Within the local group, there are no established patterns of leadership, such that the organization proceeds on a basis which sometimes approaches anarchy. In any event, the informality and equalitarianism are marked features of the organization, which also tend to underline the self control possessed by individual members.

A.A.'s mode of delabeling and relabeling thus appears in a small degree to depend upon promulgation of an allergy concept of alcoholism which is accepted by some members of the general population. Of greater importance in this process is the effective contrivance of a repentant role. Emphasis upon the degradation and downward mobility experienced during the development of alcoholism provides for the ascription of considerable self control to middle-class members, which in turn may enhance their prestige and "shore up" their return to "normality." The repentance process is grounded in and reinforced by the manner in which the A.A. program taps into several basic American value orientations.

A.A.'s Limitations

As mentioned above, A.A. affiliation by members of the lower social classes is frequently unsuccessful. This seems to stem from the middle-class orientation of most of the A.A. programs, from the fact that it requires certain forms of public confessions and intense interpersonal interaction which may run contrary to the images of masculinity held in the lower classes, as well as interpersonal competence.

Perhaps an equally significant limitation is a psychological selectivity in the affiliation process. A recent followup study of 378 hospitalized alcoholics, all of whom had been intensely exposed to A.A. during their treatment, revealed that those who successfully affiliated with A.A. upon their re-entry into the community had personality features significantly different from those who did not affiliate (Trice and Roman, 1970). The successful affiliates were more guilt prone, sensitive to responsibility, more serious, and introspective. This appears to indicate a definite "readiness" for the adoption of the repentant role among successful affiliates. To a somewhat lesser extent, the affiliates possessed a greater degree of measured ego strength, affiliative needs, and group dependency, indicating a "fit" between the peculiar demands for intense interaction required for successful affiliation and the personalities of the successful affiliates. Earlier research also revealed a relatively high need for affiliation among A.A. affiliates as compared to those who were unsuccessful in the affiliation process (Trice, 1959).

These social class and personality factors definitely indicate the A.A. program is not effective for all alcoholics. Convincing entry into the repentant role, as well as successful interactional participation in the program, appear to require middle-class background and certain personality predispositions.

Summary

In summary, we shall contrast the success of A.A. in its delabeling with that experienced by other self help groups designed for former drug addicts and mental patients (Wechsler, 1960; Landy and Singer, 1961). As pointed out above, the statuses of mental patients and narcotic addicts lack the causal clarity accompanying the role of alcoholic. It is most difficult for narcotic addicts and former mental patients to remove the stigma since there is little social clarity about the cessation of the primary deviant behavior. Just as there is no parallel in this respect, there is no parallel in other self-help organizations with the Skid Row image and the status-enhancing "mobility trip" that is afforded by this image. The primary deviant behaviors which lead to the label of drug addict or which eventuate in mental hospitalization are too far removed from ordinary social experience for easy acceptance of the former deviant to occur. These behaviors are a part of an underworld from which return is most difficult. On the other hand, Alcoholics Anonymous possesses, as a consequence of the nature of the disorder of alcoholism, its uniqueness as an organization, and the existence of certain value orientations within American society, a pattern of social processing whereby a labeled deviant can become "delabeled" as a stigmatized deviant and relabeled as a former and repentant deviant.

References

ANONYMOUS
    1968   "Doctors, Alcohol and A.A." Alcoholics Anonymous Grapevine, October, 1938, entire number.
FREEMAN, H., and O. SIMMONS
    1963   The Mental Patient Comes Home. New York: Wiley.
GARFINKEL, H.
    1957   "Conditions of Successful Degradation Ceremonies." American Journal of Sociology 61 (November): 420–425.
GELLMAN, I.
    1964   The Sober Alcoholic. New Haven: College and University Press.

GUSFIELD, J.
   1967 "Moral Passage: The Symbolic Process in Public Designations of Deviance." Social Problems 15 (Winter): 175–188.
LANDY, D., and S. SINGER
   1961 "The Social Organization and Culture of a Club for Former Mental Patients." Human Relations 14(January): 31–40.
LANG, K., and G. LANG
   1960 "Decisions for Christ: Billy Graham in New York City." Pp. 415–427 in M. Stein et al. (eds.), Identity and Anxiety. New York: The Free Press.
LEMERT, E.
   1951 Social Pathology. New York: McGraw-Hill.
MILLER, D.
   1965 Worlds That Fail. Sacramento, California: California Department of Mental Hygiene.
MULFORD, H.
   1964 "Drinking and Deviant Drinking, U.S.A., 1963." Quarterly Journal of Studies on Alcohol, 25(December): 634–650.
MULFORD, H., and D. MILLER
   1964 "Measuring Public Acceptance of the Alcoholic as a Sick Person." Quarterly Journal of Studies on Alcohol, 25(June): 314–323.
MYERS, J., and L. BEAN
   1968 A Decade Later. New York: Wiley.
NUNNALLY, J.
   1961 Popular Conceptions of Mental Health. New York: Holt, Rinehart and Winston.
PARSONS, T.
   1951 The Social System. Glencoe, Ill.: The Free Press.
PASAMANICK, B., et al.
   1967 Schizophrenics in the Community. New York: Appleton, Century, Crofts.
PLAUT, T.
   1967 Alcohol Problems: A Report to the Nation. New York: Oxford University Press.
ROMAN, P., and H. TRICE
   1969 "The Self Reaction: A Neglected Dimension of Labeling Theory." Presented at American Sociological Association Meetings, San Francisco.
SAGARIN, E.
   1967 "Voluntary Associations among Social Deviants." Criminologica 5 (January): 8–22.
SCHEFF, T.
   1966 Being Mentally Ill. Chicago: Aldine.
STRAUS, R., and S. BACON
   1951 "Alcoholism and Social Stability." Quarterly Journal of Studies on Alcohol 12(June): 231–260.
SUSSER, M.
   1968 Community Psychiatry. New York: Random House.

SUSSMAN, M. (ed.)
   1966   Sociology and Rehabilitation. Washington: American Sociological Association.
TRICE, H.
   1959   "The Affiliation Motive and Readiness to Join Alcoholics Anonymous." Quarterly Journal of Studies on Alcohol 20(September): 313–320.
   1962   "The Job Behavior of Problem Drinkers." Pp. 493–510 in D. Pittman and C. Snyder (eds.), Society, Culture and Drinking Patterns. New York: Wiley.
TRICE, H., and P. ROMAN
   1970   "Sociopsychological Predictors of Successful Affiliation with Alcoholics Anonymous." Social Psychiatry 5(Winter): 51–59.
WECHSLER, H.
   1960   "The Self-Help Organization in the Mental Health Field: Recovery, Inc." Journal of Nervous and Mental Disease 130(April): 297–314.
WILLIAMS, R.
   1960   American Society. New York: A. A. Knopf.

V

THE SOCIAL AND CULTURAL CONTROL OF DEVIANT BEHAVIOR

Introduction

Assuredly the most difficult problem of macrosociology is to conceptualize with richness the historical and contemporary relationships between the social and cultural systems. Collective definitions of deviance and techniques for controlling deviant behavior have to be viewed as a social and cultural ensemble in order for us to perceive their larger significance. What then are the structures of the social and cultural control of deviant behavior and how do they penetrate each other?

Stivers' article, "Social Control in the Technological Society," is an application of Jacques Ellul's description and analysis of modern society to the social control of deviant behavior. For Ellul (1964), technique is the single most important social phenomenon of modern existence. Technique dominates civilization as its infrastructure, its underlying logic. Technique, obeying no other law than that of efficiency in the interest of order, molds social control efforts according to its necessary unfolding. Modern society, characterized by the onslaught of technique, the growth of and centralization of power within the state (Ellul, 1967), and the persuasiveness of propaganda (Ellul, 1965), justifies itself through a neo-Marxist and/or behavioristic ideology and concomitantly compensates for this development by permitting and even encouraging a humanistic ideology which stresses individual man's autonomy if not his omnipotence (Ellul, 1968).

Related to this broad humanistic ideology has been the vast movement to treat the deviant offender rather than to punish him. Hence, rehabilitation as a justification for control purports a primary interest in the individual offender and his welfare. But such efforts, dependent as they are on technique, state control, and an ideological view of man in harmonious relationship to society, serve only to adjust man to his immediate situation and thus benefit society. Therefore, the rehabilitation of man conceals the fact that what is being reformed is society (as the institutionalized abstraction of man) and what is being destroyed is culture.

No one speaks to this latter point better than Philip Rieff in "The Triumph of the Therapeutic." Rieff's major works (1961; 1968; 1973) represent an attempt to construct a theory of culture and of cultural change. Rieff (1968: 232) is quick to point out that "to speak of culture as moral would be redundant" because the essence of any culture is the organization of demands it makes upon members of society. These demands are either controls or remissions. Cultural controls are essentially authoritative definitions of what should and should not be done, which make it appear there is no choice. Cultural remissions are institutionalized releases from the controls,

372

that is, socially accepted ways of getting around the controls without appearing to violate them directly. The controls and remissions are unequal during periods of stability (with controls dominant most of the time historically), while during a period of change they become more nearly equal. Today they have moved toward equality, perhaps even in the direction of remissions (Rieff, 1968:234–237). Insofar as remissions and controls are both demands that culture necessitates, their relationship is dialectical (Rieff, 1968:22):

> Self-knowledge again made social is the principle of control upon which the emergent culture may yet be able to make itself stable. Indeed, with the arts of psychiatric management enhanced and perfected, men will come to know one another in ways that could facilitate total socialization without a symbolic or communal purpose. Then the brief historic fling of the individual, celebrating himself as a being in himself, divine and therefore essentially unknowable, would be truly ended—ending no less certainly than the preceding personification of various renunciatory disciplines. Men already feel freer to live their lives with a minimum of pretense to anything more grand than sweetening the time.

Of course, social and cultural controls intersect most profoundly today in propaganda. Informed by the human sciences, propaganda's form is that of technique, while its content is ideological and mythical. Dependent upon an individualistic/mass society for its very existence and effectiveness, propaganda is a human technique which aims at the total integration of the individual into the group through the promulgation of facts interpreted through ideology and myth (Ellul, 1965). The trick is to convince people that what is necessary is what they desire after all. Social necessity is translated into individual autonomy. Ideology, in its justification of and compensation for what is, supplants culture when social control becomes autonomous from culture.

Societies can be distinguished according to whether they rely on institutions informed by culture and its derivative, authority, or whether they rely on "systems of purposive-rational action" (instrumental-utilitarian action) to control behavior (Habermas, 1971: 91–97). The former is a traditional society, the latter a modern society. About modern society's methods of control, Habermas (1971: 96) argues, "What is new is a level of development of the productive forces that makes permanent the extension of subsystems of purposive-rational action and thereby calls into question the traditional form of the legitimation of power." Increasingly all of life becomes organized for purposes of production and consumption and the necessities imposed by such administration makes conscious consensus about belief and morality superfluous. Hence, ideology which conceals reality rises not to exercise direct control on man's acts as with culture but to distract man from the real purpose and consequences of his acts, thereby rendering them irrational.

The implication of Rieff's theory of a culture of therapy and of Ellul's exegesis of the commonplace, "cultivate your personality: be a person" (Ellul, 1968: 269–279), is that one must be honest, that is, accept both one's limitations and one's desires and bare one's innermost life for public scrutiny (Rieff, 1961: 329–360). The metamorphosis of private to public is accomplished in the modern concept of "person," wherein a therapeutic morality of two, each one a role-playing therapist to himself and the other, governs interaction. Thus, therapy as propaganda works to adjust man while providing him with the illusion of self-actualization.

In one sense, then, there exists an inverse relationship between social and cultural control systems. To the degree to which culture decays and authority disappears, power increases in society to meet the need for social order, as witnessed by the growth of technique, the state, and propaganda. Traditionally, culture largely determined the institutional control of behavior, while today ideology conceals social control and thus permits its autonomy from culture. Social control is molded by the efficiency needs of an increasingly abstract society.

The upshot of all this is certain dialectical occurrences. Paradoxically there is both an increase and a decrease in what is defined as deviant. Each new fact, each new "problem" of society requires a rule or a law to regulate man's behavior; hence there is proliferation of administrative regulations and laws (Ellul, 1964: 296–300). Coeval with the increase in the number of administrative and civil laws (remember that much of what would have been formulated as criminal law in the past is now handled through civil law proceedings of the therapeutic and welfare states) are efforts at "decriminalization"—that is, the repeal of certain criminal laws for which there are both little consensus and widespread violation, making enforcement extremely difficult. The moral underpinning of criminal laws becomes irrelevant next to pragmatic considerations of enforceability and public opinion. In fact, the inefficient or unsuccessful is the modern definition of deviance (Ellul, 1969: 185–198; Habermas, 1971: 92).

As consensus about the traditional definitions of the absolutely good and evil disappear, the single-minded norm of efficiency replaces them. Thus, a multitude of criteria underlying traditional definitions of the good are reduced to but one criterion, the efficient; yet this criterion is increasingly applied to all behavior, eventually insuring man no respite from control.

Thus, modern society permits more (a release from absolute traditional morality) at the same time it restricts more (all behavior falls under the province of the successful or efficient). Nothing will have to be prohibited when everything and nothing are deviant. When techniques (which guarantee success) for every action are fully institutionalized, nothing and nobody will be capable of being deviant or at least of remaining so. But from the vantage point of traditional culture everything will be deviant, for man's freedom to be wrong will have vanished. When social control is total, cultural definitions of deviance will be unnecessary save only to distract man from his immediate situation.

References

ELLUL, JACQUES
    1964   The Technological Society. New York: Vintage Books.
    1965   Propaganda. New York: Alfred Knopf.

1967   The Political Illusion. New York: Vintage Books.
1968   A Critique of the New Commonplaces. New York: Alfred Knopf.
1969   To Will and To Do. Philadelphia: Pilgrim Press.
HABERMAS, JURGEN
1971   "Technology and Science as 'Ideology.'" Pp. 81–122 in Toward a Rational Society. Boston: Beacon Paperback.
RIEFF, PHILIP
1961   Freud: The Mind of the Moralist. Garden City, New York: Anchor Books.
1968   The Triumph of the Therapeutic. New York: Harper Torchbooks.
1973   Fellow Teachers. New York: Harper and Row.

RICHARD STIVERS

Social Control in the
Technological Society

Recently a work by three British sociologists, in a critique of historical and contemporary schools of criminological thought, has called for a "political economy" of both crime and the societal reaction to crime (Taylor, Walton, and Young, 1973: 270–274). Like Mills and Marx they recognize that few sociologies, whether of crime and social control or of some other social issue, have a clear view of social structure, which can be grasped only through historical and comparative research.

Not stridently Marxist, they reject Marx's dismal view of the *Lumpenproletariat* (Taylor, Walton, and Young, 1973: 217), the degraded and dangerous among the lower class. However, they do observe that Marx's full view of crime and social control remains unstated, because Marx was more concerned with the class struggle between the bourgeoisie and the proletariat than with the class "beneath" the proletariat.

In many other ways, however, they are avowedly Marxist, especially with respect to the utopian element of the Marxist ideology:

> Close reading of the classical social theorists reveals a basic agreement; the abolition of crime is possible under certain social arrangements. . . . It should be clear that a criminology which is not normatively committed to the abolition of inequalities of wealth and power, and in particular of inequalities in property and life-chances, is inevitably bound to fall into correctionalism. . . . the task is to create a society in which the facts of human diversity, whether personal, organic or social, are not subject to the power to criminalize (Taylor, Walton, and Young, 1973: 281–282).

The quest for the perfect society is obvious here. Hayek (1952) and Popper (1964) have linked Marxism, with its historicism, collectivism, and scientism, to the positivism of the nineteenth century. As Gouldner (1970) has observed, positivistic sociology after Comte was bifurcated into opposing ideological camps: one version, academic sociology, stressed the positive methods for the social sciences, that is, the scrupulous application of quantitative methods developed in the natural sciences to the study of man and society; the other version, Marxist sociology, focused more on practice, the positive rebuilding of society, according to Marx's philosophy of history.

Ellul's (1968; 1971) critique of Marx and the Marxist ideology is pertinent. First of all he observes that Marx was himself bourgeois in the following respects: (1) his belief in work as the ultimate good, as the bourgeois were considered parasitical for living off the fruits of other men's labors; (2) his belief in progress, as evidenced by his philosophy of history whose dialectic culminated in the final utopian synthesis; (3) his unrealistic conception of power as a more or less constant historical force and his uncertainty about the role of the state. Marx certainly looked with disdain upon the state as a vehicle for bourgeois oppression of the proletariat; yet he regarded the state as subordinate to social class. Thus, even though evolution would necessarily lead to a greater concentration of power in the new state, necessary to overthrow the old regime, the new state would be temporary; the state would cease to exist as power came to reside in the proletariat as a whole. Marx's mistake, according to Ellul (1971: 164–167), was to regard class conflict as the basis for the unfolding of history when in fact class conflict was actually the form that the conflict between the state[1] and society assumed in the nineteenth century and continued into the present century. Thus the state was superordinate and not subordinate to social class. The bourgeoisie unwittingly increased the power of the state and assuredly reaped the major benefits of the "welfare state," but they did not control it.

DeJouvenal (1963: 43–59) has noted that whenever a dominant ideology conceptualized society as an organism superior to and more important than the individual and regarded power as justly residing within the social whole, one could be sure that power was growing and becoming concentrated within the state. Marx, as we know, first and foremost conceptualized man as collective man, refusing to make a distinction between the individual and society (Lowith, 1967: 309–313).

Marx was, however, to the point in much of his analysis of bourgeois society and its ideology; moreover, he developed a remarkable dialectical method of analysis. But for the reasons just given, Marx's philosophy of history is not sufficient to grasp the social structure of modern technological societies. Therefore a political economy of crime and social control will be inadequate if it remains only a political economy. That is, differences between the political economies, whether democratic-capitalist, socialist, or communist, are less important than their similarities. Political economies in modernized societies all possess both an expansionist and eminently powerful state and a vast technological apparatus whose infrastructure is technique. The work of the French sociologist Jacques Ellul (1964; 1965; 1967; 1968; 1971) offers, I think, the clearest view of our very complex social structure in western civilization. He has performed the same service of social criticism

[1] Ellul (1967: 141) maintains that "A modern state is not primarily a centralized organ of decision, a set of political organs. It is primarily an enormous machinery of bureaus. It is comprised of two contradictory elements: on the one hand, political personnel, assemblies, and councils, and, on the other, administrative personnel in the bureau—whose distinction, incidentally, is becoming less and less clear."

for our twentieth-century technological societies that Marx did for the industrializing societies of the nineteenth-century without grounding his analysis in a philosophy of history and obfuscating its cogency with ideological diatribe. Ellul's perspective will form the background for our discussion of the social control of deviant and dependent behavior.

In *The Technological Society* Ellul attempts to describe modern societies as they actually exist. To an ever greater degree modern societies are dependent upon technique for their survival (defined in terms of a higher level of production and consumption). Technique is the *"totality of methods rationally arrived at and having absolute efficiency* (for a given stage of development) in *every* field of human activity" (Ellul, 1964: xxv). His definition is, he warns, not a "theoretical construct" but a description of a real phenomenon. Technique is a "sociological phenomenon," and Ellul describes its effect on social, political, and economic structures and relationships (Ellul, 1964: xxvi). The end of technique is efficiency and order, and its use in human affairs results in the adjustment of man to his environment. Technique is the realm wherein means becomes ends and facts become values.

Men have always employed techniques in the course of their attempts to control nature, but in the past technique was never beyond man's spiritual and esthetic control. Technique served man; it was not the *raison d'être* of his civilization. Technique could be absorbed within the civilization without dominating it. All of this has changed, Ellul argues.

The principal characteristics of modern technique are: (1) rationality, (2) artificiality, (3) automatism, (4) self-augmentation, (5) monism, (6) universalism, and (7) autonomy (Ellul, 1964: 77–147).

The rationality of technique involves the reduction of the spontaneous to logic, to a method. Rationality exhibits itself in bureaucracy, the division of labor, production norms, roles, and so on. A human act is reduced to an operation with the most efficient and effective method set out in advance.

Technique is likewise artificial; it stands in contradistinction to the natural, subverts and even destroys it. Environment increasingly becomes a technological environment as the natural environment is exploited for the purpose of economic production.

Automatism of technique refers to the fact that when a method superior in efficiency to competing methods exists, it is automatically employed. In addition, when the still nontechnical dimensions of human life come into contact with technique, they become subject to it. Thus, in criminal law, guilty-plea negotiation gains ascendancy over the criminal trial. Technique in all its forms becomes "self-directing." Once the capability is developed, it will be employed.

The self-augmentation of technique has been formulated by Ellul (1964: 89) into two laws: "1. *In a given civilization, technical progress is irreversible. 2. Technical progress tends to act, not according to an arithmetic, but according to a geometric progression.*" Each new technique creates problems (just as surely as the technique is itself a solution to some problems) that have to be solved technically. Thus, the city was a solution to man's greater demands for material aggrandizement, but it generated a host of problems for which urban planning becomes a solution. Even though pollution was created by industrial technology, we look to technology for the way out.

Technique is monistic, that is, all the specific techniques work to form a totality, a whole. All techniques have essentially the same characteristics. Technique as a "method of action" cannot be distinguished from its uses. Technique and use are one; the means become the end. All of this happens without one individual or elite directing it. Rather it is the constant application of the "best" means created by experts and employed by workers unaware of techniques developed in every other sphere of work and leisure.

Universalism is a further trait of technique. Insofar as man's happiness, defined in terms of material production and consumption and realized by technique, is the unquestioned goal of modernized societies, those countries who wish to modernize and make "progress" must technologize at a rapid rate. Technology is becoming the universal language.

The autonomy of technique refers to man's being controlled by technique in his use of it. "The technique which takes man for its object," human technique, "becomes the center of society" (Ellul, 1964: 127). Techniques of human control boomerang to control their users. Man conquers time by inventing the clock and then finds his whole life is ruled by the clock, that he has become a slave to time-tables, appointments, and schedules. Or similarly man conquers space, pacifies the wilderness, builds cities, and subsequently becomes entrapped within small home dwellings built increasingly closer together in densely populated areas.

The final result is a technical civilization originally set in motion to free man but which in turn has enslaved him. Yet Ellul (1971: 233–300) is no absolute determinist and has broadly outlined what an individual might do who refuses to accept this objective reality as final; but, of course, the first step entails correctly diagnosing the situation.

Equally important and related to the emergence of a technical civilization is the growth of and centralization of power within the state. "From the political, social and human points of view, this conjunction of state and technique is by far the most important phenomenon of history," claims Ellul (1964: 233).

Ellul (1964: 233–239) has suggested at least three causes for this historical and sociological conjunction of technique and state. First was the lightning-quick development of techniques which affected the masses, among which were transportation, education, and welfare. These techniques produced obviously efficacious results, and because they were generally applicable, they become public and not just private concerns. The state whose domain is the public was quick to pick them up. For example, education as technique helped to create not only universities but also free and compulsory public education.

Second and related is the expense of these techniques. Increasingly the state supports them. Gradually increasing state support of private education is a ready example.

The third cause is the enlarged role of the state and its varied conceptualizations. The state then becomes the "nation-state," the director and formulator of the public domain, which is identified with the nation. Ellul (1964: 238) describes this development:

> . . . the state seeks to organize national life and to govern its various collectivities most often because natural communities have disappeared and it is necessary to create new ones. Second, the state seeks to fashion the "individualist" society (the role the twentieth century has elected to play) and to penetrate into men's private lives on the ground that they are no longer able materially to manage their own affairs. Finally, all kinds of theories, both socialist and non socialist, are influential, but whatever their nature, they all appeal to the state to secure a greater degree of justice and equality. In all these ways the state assumes functions which were formerly the province of private groups.

Ultimately, however, the state becomes dependent upon techniques and experts to fulfill its obligations, while the widespread diffusion of technique is contingent upon a highly developed state (Ellul, 1964: 271). Each one feeds the other.

The Rise of the Therapeutic State

Parallel to and really part of the growth of the state and the proliferation of techniques has been the emergence of the therapeutic state (Kittrie, 1973). The therapeutic state is legally derived from the concepts of *parens patriae*— the state's right to help those unable to care for themselves—as is the welfare state. Criminal justice on the other hand receives legal sustenance from the police power of the state—the state's right to defend itself from dangerous individuals. The chief differences between the therapeutic state and the welfare state can be summarized as follows: the welfare state has been and remains concerned with the poor, whether the poverty be due to mental impairment, physical handicap, widowhood, orphanhood, or some other cause; the therapeutic state has concerned itself with the socially deviant who fall under its aegis not simply for a criminal act but for criminal behavior thought to be a by-product of an emotionally unstable status. The therapeutic state contains legal sanctions for handling the mentally ill, psychopath, drug addict, alcohol addict, and juvenile delinquent. The middle three categories broadly refer to the mentally ill who have also committed a crime, i.e., sex crimes, public drunkenness, drug offenses. Take the case of alcohol-related offenses. A criminal law largely concerns itself with behavior and not status or character and because of the constitutional guarantee against cruel and unusual punishment, it has declared unconstitutional several legal decisions which had the effect of making it illegal to be an alcoholic (Kittrie, 1973: 279–285). The juvenile delinquent on the other hand is held not to be criminally responsible because of his immaturity.

Prior to the eighteenth century little distinction was made between those who fell under the control of the state: the criminal deviant, and pauper (Kittrie, 1973: 358). They often ended up together in workhouses and almshouses and later in asylums (Rothman, 1971; Foucault, 1965). The dominant religious world view made crime, deviant behavior, and dependency quite intelligible; they were within God's providence. Those predestined to hell often gave evidence of their future station through deviant acts or financial failure. The criminal, deviant, and pauper would always be with us and even became the occasion for the practice of private charity by the well-to-do. In this sense, then, nonconformity did not constitute a social problem (Erikson, 1966; Rothman, 1971).

With the rise of science and humanism, especially liberalism, in the eighteenth century, reforms of various agencies of social control were introduced. Inveighing generally against the arbitrary exercise of power by Church and Crown, and specifically against a tyrannical criminal justice system, reformers of the time reworked the foundation and principles of criminal law (Radzinowicz, 1966). Starting with an abstraction of man as a rational, hedonistic animal (natural man), they invoked the principles of freedom, justice, and equality defined with man and not God as their end. Criminal laws were now to be formally stated with advance warning, punishment was to be fair and in accord with the nature and seriousness of the offense, and the legal rights of the accused were to be scrupulously protected.

For the liberal, prevention and freedom were not antithetical. Freedom and prevention could both be institutionalized in law. The number of laws should be kept to a minimum in the interest of freedom, but concurrently the punishment which accrues to criminal law should be just severe enough to deter the potential criminal. A criminal justice system perceived as just and equitable would likewise deter the commission of those crimes which were principally attempts to escape an unpredictable and severe punishment for a previous crime. The assumption about man and society underlying the view was that man as a rational being would respond favorably to a criminal justice system perceived as fair and in his best interest or, in other words, that rational man would be good (rational) in a rational environment.

However, the liberal-utilitarian reliance upon law freed from its traditional religious origins produced a dilemma. Law was now to be judged according to its usefulness in attaining human happiness. But then there exists no restraint upon law except power, because objective morality has been replaced by a morality of consequences. De Jouvenal (1963: 307) has described this dilemma:

the modern problem is here posed for us. When law has ceased to be a thing in its essential parts untouchable, a thing sustained by the beliefs held in common by the whole of society, when it has become, even in respect of fundamental morals, a thing modifiable at the pleasure of the legislator, one of two consequences must follow: either a monstrous spawning of laws at the bidding of every interest which agitates and of every opinion which stirs, or else their planned economy by a master who knows his mind and wills society to accept whatever rules of comduct he thinks it necessary to prescribe.

Our own criminal justice system as well as our constitution owes much to the liberal revisions of the eighteenth century. Yet where the liberal advocated a modicum of law, we witness an endless proliferation of law by statute and especially by administrative dictate according to various interests. Each new fact, each new problem creates a law (Ellul, 1964: 297).

The legal and philosophical architects of the modern criminal justice system in the West were not only opposed to the proliferation of law but also to enforced rehabilitation, the development of a therapeutic state (Radzinowicz, 1966: 11–12). Yet the liberal approach unwittingly contributed to the institutionalization of the therapeutic state, just as it led to the proliferation of law by stressing the prevention of undesired behavior in purely utilitarian terms. Deterrence theory professes to deter the general populace from crime while concomitantly maximizing individual freedom. Thus, citizens were to be prevented from crime by the threat of punishment before the fact or by the example of an offender being punished after the fact. Punishment is an evil but a necessary evil if general adherence to the law is its consequence.

While general deterrence was historically enmeshed in a free-will model of human behavior, logically it need not be. Packer (1968: 40–45) has noted that the deterrence theory can be reconciled to the findings of the behavioristic social sciences. Thus, one might accentuate the unconscious socializing or reinforcing effect of criminal justice as an institution on the individual. Beccaria, the intellectual engineer of criminal law reform in the eighteenth century, in claiming that the prevention of crime was superior to its punishment, mentioned education and the reward of virtuous behavior as supplementary modes of deterrence to the establishment of precisely measured and well-publicized sanctions (Radzinowicz, 1966: 13).

But in their emphasis on consequences, the usefulness of an act for the collective happiness, the utilitarians laid the basis for the separation of prevention from individual freedom. For if wholesale crime appeared imminent and the general welfare were in danger, prevention would become an increasingly paramount consideration. Freedom and prevention would be in harmony only when a conjunction of rational men and just and equitable environments occurred. In the liberal equation, human nature and social order would not conflict, since the former was rational and the latter capable of being made rational.

Convergent with the rise of the modern criminal justice system was the expansion of and specialization within the welfare system (Kittrie, 1973: 358). As early as the late eighteenth century, poor relief had become "a major institution" (Piven and Cloward, 1971: 21), but more importantly special services for the insane, the delinquent, and the retarded were being provided by the state. In contradistinction to the compulsory criminal justice system, the welfare system was presumed to be voluntary. Criminal justice and welfare, previously hopelessly intertwined, still did not effect a disengagement. The poor without job or residence could still be prosecuted as vagrants or vagabonds on the one hand or could be obligated to work, make restitution, or rehabilitate themselves on the other hand. The obligations the receipt of welfare entailed harken to an earlier period when private charity predominated (Kittrie, 1973: 358–359). However, since the client could still refuse the money, goods, and services, welfare was regarded as "voluntary." Furthermore, for several centuries a certain link between poverty and crime had been perceived, whether stated in religious or secular terms. In the nineteenth century, however, crime came to be seen as concentrated in the recalcitrant among the lower class, and subsequently mere poverty became tantamount to potential criminality.

By the middle of the nineteenth century a strong reaction against classical criminology was generated by reformers supportive of deterministic theories of human behavior. Positivistic social science, at least initially, perceived the causes of deviant and dependent behavior to be man's larger social environment—social organization (Radzinowicz, 1966: 29–46). Statistical regularities in the incidence of crime according to social characteristics, i.e., age, sex, race, social class, provided the basis for this approach. Positivistic criminology strove to explain differing rates of crime so as to maximize the control and prevention of crime.

As positivistic criminology began to look to individual constitution and personality for the answer to the crime problem, the criminal justice system became the object of intense criticism. The free-will model underlying criminal justice was in direct conflict with new findings about man's highly determined existence. If man's behavior really was determined, a realistic criminal justice would take this into account.

"Criminal responsibility," the determinists contended, "should not be based on free will but upon the needs of society. It should be concerned not with the guilt of the offender but with his potential danger to the community" (Radzinowicz, 1965: 52). Therefore, social responsibility was conceived of as the individual's obligations and duties toward the state. Furthermore, the state's legal responsibility was the social defense of its citizenry, which entailed calculations about the offender's propensity for future crime and his therapeutic malleability. If he could not be safely reformed, he must be eliminated from society.

At this time there was a modicum of sentimentality directed to the offender. The deterministic reformers recognized that the defense of society lay behind their concern with the individual offender. Hence, rehabilitation was only one of several possibilities for defense; corporal and capital punishment were considered necessary alternatives.

The deterministic position made inroads on the liberal-utilitarian criminal justice system insofar as criminal law, recognizing insanity as the dividing line between responsible and nonresponsible individuals (Packer, 1968: 131–135), allowed for the gradual expansion of the definition of insanity. Yet criminal law still retains most of the liberal trappings it acquired in the eighteenth century.

The deterministic premises of positivistic social sciences have created their own field of social control, independent to some extent of criminal justice—the therapeutic state. Beginning in the eighteenth century with the mentally ill, continuing into the nineteenth century with the juvenile delinquent, and finally into the twentieth century with the psychopath, drug addict, and alcoholic, the therapeutic state has siphoned off clients previously dealt with through the criminal justice system.

These offenders, judged to lack *mens rea* (a set of legal concepts dealing with what constitutes a guilty state of mind) are nevertheless deemed dangerous to the rest of society. A hearing in a civil court or juvenile court is usually a prerequisite for their institutionalization. The result is a quasi-criminal justice system without a concern for individual legal guilt but instead for social dangerousness. However, the social dangerousness of the mentally ill has to be demonstrated according to strict legal standards. Proof for social dangerousness often entails overt acts, deviant if not criminal; thus, the therapeutic state, just as the criminal justice system, becomes dependent upon offensive acts to demonstrate its legal right to control. Kittrie (1973: 40) has described the synthesis of formal controls instituted to deal with those perceived as socially dangerous but who are also regarded as not criminally responsible:

> When the concepts of determinism are grafted onto the classical model of criminal justice, two important shifts occur that cause the role of treatment to ascend in the hierarchy of sanctions. First, since the deterministic theory is selectively adapted to offenders who are considered to lack *mens rea,* those who benefit thereby are designated ill, immature, unbalanced, or in some other way deficient. This designation was unnecessary in a pure determinist system of social defense—but it was mandatory to facilitate the hybridization of the criminal system. Second, logically following the thesis of "illness," came the notion that the only proper thing to do with those deficiencies is to treat and hope to cure them. This ascension of treatment and cure as the primary goals of the state in those areas in which the determinist theory was acknowledged has been one of the main factors in the development of the therapeutic state.

Thus, the therapeutic state was forced to look to treatment for social defense because the criminal justice system already utilized the alternative sanctions of imprisonment and capital punishment; yet, the therapeutic state was still called upon to demonstrate its case against the offender in a civil court. The therapeutic state "found" its clientele by developing categories of deviance which reflected an assumption of illness. Psychopath, alcoholic, and drug addict are categories applied to those whose sexual, drinking, and drug behavior is thought to be beyond their control. The therapeutic state developed the idea that certain repeated criminal offenses actually constitute ill or sick status.

The rise of the therapeutic state, however, must not be thought of as only the legal norms and procedures for the control of dangerous deviants. There are many additional modes of control. A variety of social reform movements to eliminate and control social deviance burgeoned in the latter half of the nineteenth century. Although Hofstadter (1955) calls the period from the 1890's to the 1940's *The Age of Reform,* it would appear to be possible to date it even earlier. Among these movements the temperance movement (Gusfield, 1963) and the child-saving movement (Platt, 1966) have attracted attention from sociologists in recent years. These various movements all shared a common concern—the revitalization of society by means of the creation of a standardized culture. But outstanding among these movements, because of its implications for the convergence of the police power and *parens patriae* functions of the state, was the advent of the asylum.

In the United States in the 1830's and 1840's, mental institutions, penitentiaries, juvenile reformatories, and public asylums for the poor began to proliferate. Until this time local communities had dealt with the deviant and dependent through community jails, almhouses, and work-houses supplemented by corporal punishment, capital punishment, and banishment (Rothman, 1971).

Americans had become ambivalent about social mobility, immigration, urbanization, and industrialization. Some had come to enjoy a greater measure of material comfort as a result, but they could not understand how competition and mobility could produce a social order. Having lost, in part, their previous religious view of social hierarchy and hence social order, they did not as yet possess a new cosmology, something Social Darwinism would subsequently provide. The deviant behavior they perceived then was a sign of social disorganization, but simultaneously in their tautological thinking social disorganization, especially the lack of family discipline and the presence of temptations in the community (taverns and brothels), caused deviant behavior.

The asylum as an agency of reform was a logical sequel to their deterministic theories of deviant behavior. The asylum was to create a model family which would resocialize the offender away from the hubbub and temptations of city life. Surrogate parents on the asylum staff and "decent" citizens from the community would instruct the erring inmate. Rothman (1971) suggests that the asylum represented a somewhat unconscious attempt to create order in American society at a time when disorder, i.e., mobility, seemed omnipresent. The asylum as a model of good family living would become contagious for the rest of society. Therefore, the concern was for order and stability and rehabilitation became the means to accomplish it.

Ironically the asylum quickly became a factory-like enterprise dominated by bureaucratic organization. As the end of the asylum is order and efficiency, reformation itself had to become efficient. Thus, what was an attempt to reconstruct the community and family of the past became a futuristic organization characterized by hard work and deprivation (Rothman 1971).

Of course, Americans were not always aware of this. Objectively the asylum represented an efficient means of disposing of those displaced by industrialization and immigration. Subjectively the asylum was intended to rehabilitate the recalcitrant as a means to a more perfect social order.

By the middle of the nineteenth century, the asylum, claiming as it did the criminal, pauper, and social deviant, signified the synthesis of criminal justice, public welfare, and the therapeutic state. Each of the three systems had as its main function the police power, of the state and each with greater or lesser success concealed that real function under the guise of *parens patriae*. The asylum as a common element among the three systems of control is of greater sociological import than the systems' divergent legal criteria for judging and evaluating the offender prior to his institutionalization. The asylum both as a total institution (Goffman, 1961) and as an agency of rehabilitation is an overriding consideration for an understanding of social control in the nineteenth century. If the liberalism of classical criminology and its free-will model of human behavior remains the philosophical underpinning of our criminal justice system, the determinism of positivistic criminology inspires much of the rhetoric for the reformation of criminals.

The asylum was *the* social fact of social control in the nineteenth century; in the twentieth century it is succeeded by the techniques of social prevention. By social prevention is meant the prevention of undesired behavior both by manipulating social structure—as with community psychiatry, applied behavioral analysis, social planning, and community organization— and by manipulating individuals as with psychotherapy, social casework, behavior therapy, and the like. Various helping professionals, utilizing the research findings of behavioral scientists, apply human techniques and a whole array of technology to prevent deviant behavior before it can occur. This represents the logical conclusion of social defense. Our thesis can be illustrated by an analysis of three types of techniques: organization, treatment, and communication.

Techniques of Organization

Bureaucracy is the modern technique of organization. Both in recent history (Rothman, 1971) and in the contemporary situation (Goffman, 1961) asylums for the reformation of the deviant and dependent have been bureaucratically organized, thereby geared toward efficient and orderly control. But recent studies have also indicated how important bureaucracy is to an understanding of police control methods (Skolnick, 1966), criminal courts (Blumberg, 1967), and the civil commitment proceedings for the mentally ill (Scheff, 1968: 172–185). Evaluation, promotion, or salary increment for the police is in part dependent upon the number of arrests made, for the criminal prosecutor upon the number of convictions, and for the court-appointed psychiatrist upon the number of commitments to mental institutions.

The criminal justice system is a large bureaucracy which employs even the public defender: guilty-plea negotiation is its major strategy. The accused is placed in a vulnerable position—either he pleads guilty with the guarantee of a reduction in the seriousness of the charge or in the severity of the punishment or he faces the risk of severe punishment for a more serious crime if convicted. Guilty-plea negotiation becomes an efficient means, in avoiding the time and cost of a trial, for a bureaucratically organized and over-burdened system to appear effective by obtaining a high percentage of convictions.

Moreover, all our major agencies of law enforcement, social work, and psychological and psychiatric services are bureaucratically organized. However, as Goffman (1961) and others have observed, the bureaucracy serves its own needs and those of the larger society often at the expense of its client's needs.

Techniques of Treatment

Modern treatment methods contain a myriad of human techniques: lobotomy, electroshock, brainwashing, hypnosis, drugs, behavior therapy, eugenics, sterilization, applied behavior analysis, community psychiatry and psychology, community organization, encounter groups, social group work, group counseling, and self-help societies, to name just a few (London, 1971; Kennedy and Kerber, 1973).

Although many of these are techniques for treating the individual as such, some are techniques for restructuring, coordinating, or planning man's social environment. All of the techniques of human intervention are ideologically defended as in man's best interest, to help him adjust and conform, often in ways in which he is led to feel that he is expressing his individuality: underlying such techniques are the assumption of and preference for a basic compatibility between if not total synthesis of man and society—the complete absorption of man into society. Examples of such techniques are encounter groups and self-help societies, two highly popular forms of treatment.

The encounter group provides a lush example of a human technique to adjust man to his society through the social group. Encounter group advocates correctly perceive that men are often isolated, anxious, less than honest with themselves and others; yet in their sincere effort to free man from inhibition they subject man to the tyrany of the group. Group pressure helps to break down his facade, to strip the individual of his defenses; then he is compelled to state his "real" feelings toward the others. The individual has become more dependent upon the group, more subject to collective irrationality. Group leaders reconstruct the weaker members according to their own predilections.

Take also the proliferation of self-help societies (Sagrarin, 1969) for the socially stigmatized. These associations for the dwarf and the obese, the ex-alcoholic and ex-schizophrenic, represent a growing trend of using those who are or have been stigmatized to treat themselves. Whatever their ideological stance (Goffman, 1963) their end result is to adjust the individual to the group with the ideology serving as a secular religion for group members. The ideological posture may be obstreperous in its demand that the public change its attitude or in its assertion that the deviant act or status is actually superior to the normal, or it may be acquiescent in its attempt to help the stigmatized accept his stigma and the public accept the stigmatized.

Encounter groups and self-help societies are a phenomenon of mass society. The efforts of the eighteenth and nineteenth centuries to create an individualist society—to free the individual from the constraints of natural groups such as community and extended family—actually resulted in the development of a mass society. As the individual was freed and set on his own, he felt a greater need to identify with something beyond himself. He then became vulnerable to integration through propaganda into the larger collectivity—the nation-state—and into associations such as encounter groups and self-help societies (Ellul, 1965: 90–99). In the dialectic of the individual and society, of the ideal and the real, an idealistic liberal individualism fostered actual technological collectivism.

Techniques of Communication

The most efficient technique of communication and the one most prevalent today between collectivities is propaganda. Ellul (1965: 61) defines propaganda as "a set of methods employed by an organized group that wants to bring about the active or passive participation in its actions of a mass of individuals, psychologically unified through psychological manipulation and incorporated in an organization." Most writers restrict their definition of propaganda to political propaganda, but Ellul's conceptualization includes public and human relations and advertising as additional forms of propaganda, specifically sociological propaganda, which "is the penetration of an ideology by means of its sociological context" (Ellul, 1965: 63). The ideology in question is middle-class or bourgeois (see the introduction to Part II).

The helping professions and their agencies and organizations, most of which are state-supported, sell their services to the public. Advertising against alcoholism, drug addictions, and mental illness as well as advertising in favor of seeking "professional" help for almost every "problem," are presented as public service messages on radio and television. Moreover, state agencies employ public relations experts to create and maintain a good public image and to gain public support for new programs and additional funds.

The techniques of organization, treatment, and communication for the social control of deviant and dependent behavior are related to other human techniques such as education, industrial relations, and leisure. Taken together they form a massive attack on human individuality. Ellul (1967: 227–228) has described this onslaught:

> To want man to be, means to want him to exist despite propaganda and psychological techniques of influence, and surely despite the hypocritical "sciences of man," which claim to act on him in order to lift him to the level of his destiny in society, to the level on which he can exercise his responsibilities, but which, in reality, dispossess him of himself in order to possess him more thoroughly. Himself? Yes, a mediocre, maladjusted, uncertain, fragile "himself." Still, himself. Undoubtedly with our psychological therapy, we will do much better, and create a nice, extraverted, responsible, adjusted, efficient man. I always hear that famous objection: you think you should defend this man? Go on, he is just a product of chance, family influences, his mileu, profession, tradition, climate . . . why should that "himself" be repeated?" The answer is simple. To be sure, all these determining factors exist. And because they are quite heavy, constraining, and numerous, one should not add on top of them, complementary determinants stemming from "scientific" inroads made by other people. All the less because it is possible to struggle to some extent against the first-named orientations, which are the fruit of chance and circumstance. But gripped by such proved, rational, and profound techniques, how can man escape? And if he tried, would he not immediately be regarded as abnormal or as a dangerous anarchist? What is more, in the name of what authority, what virtue, what certainty, are we interfering with his life? We have the means to make this man conform, but are we sure we know all the consequences such action entails? Are the psychologists and sociologists supermen, and therefore entitled to "treat" the vulgar herd? Is this new aristocracy quite certain what its wisdom will turn them into? . . . But to demand that the soul of this clumsy, badly adjusted, mediocre man should not be lanced, to demand that he should be respected and permitted to evolve spontaneously, also means to favor a political type that is the opposite of what the combined mechanisms of technology, or-

ganization and propaganda tend to produce automatically. One can no longer opt in favor of man without making this choice; it is evident that regimes created by these techniques will lay their hands on man in order to adjust and conform him.

As society becomes more rigidly organized, new kinds of behavior become a threat to that increased organization and hence must be dealt with. This fact is not grasped simply by an examination of the number of criminal laws formulated and applied, the number of social control agents and the increased efficiency of their intervention techniques, or the number and size of institutional facilities but rather by the incursion of "treatment" into areas of people's lives previously untouched. The extent of deviance is not measured by rates of deviant behavior and official definitions of deviance but by what behavior is actually subject to the control of the state. The existence and popularity of encounter groups and well-being programs for individuals generally assessed as normal is an example. As agencies, services, and techniques of treatment expand, more maladjustment will be "discovered."

Yet certain changes suggest that just the opposite is occurring, that there is a liberalization of our control efforts. Thus, in the early 1970's in Illinois was begun a concerted effort to extricate the mentally ill from total institutions portrayed as villainous, totalitarian abodes and to move them back into the community. But "back into the community" meant residence in a nursing home, work at an occupational development center, and a personality rendered docile by a massive ingestion of drugs. Total institutions for the treatment of deviants can be discarded when society begins to approximate a total institution.[2]

This is why Kittrie's (1973: 372–410) solution to the problem of the therapeutic state, while necessary, is really only a formal and relatively unimportant step. He has suggested that we develop a therapeutic bill of rights, legally guaranteeing both the individual's right to treatment and his defense against arbitrary intrusions upon his personality. Kittrie does not realize that today the former necessarily implies the latter. The ideological defense of even voluntary therapy is part of an attack on inherited culture; it is the new anticulture which frees man from the old cultural constraints only to leave him at the mercy of his own instincts, collective manipulation, and the power of the state (Rieff, 1966; 1973). Furthermore, Kittrie shares a political illusion of our age—that the state, as it is, actually operates or can be readily made to operate according to principles embodied in constitutions.

The problem with the therapeutic state is its insatiable desire to restructure our social and cultural environments under the banners of prevention and rehabilitation both through the co-option of the potentially malad-

---

[2] The totalitarian nature of modern technological societies characterized by the growth of technique, the centralization of power within the state, and the widespread utilization of propaganda is not readily observable, however. One might recall that "The Brave New World" of Huxley did not appear oppressive to most of its inhabitants. Ideology, transmitted by techniques of propaganda, can create illusions, including that of freedom.

justed at an earlier and earlier age and the sponsorship of therapy for everyone. Each person becomes patient and therapist to himself and to others (Rieff, 1966; 1973). The real issue is not the growth of the therapeutic state but rather the growth of and centralization of power within the state which itself has become totally therapeutic.

References

BLUMBERG, ABRAHAM S.
　　1970　Criminal Justice, Chicago: Quadrangle Books.
DE JOUVENAL, BERTRAND
　　1963　On Power. Boston: Beacon Press.
ELLUL, JACQUES
　　1964　The Technological Society. New York: Vintage Books.
　　1965　Propaganda. New York: Alfred A. Knopf.
　　1967　The Political Illusion. New York: Vintage Books.
　　1968　A Critique of the New Commonplaces. New York: Alfred A. Knopf.
　　1971　Autopsy of Revolution. New York: Alfred A. Knopf.
ERIKSON, KAI T.
　　1966　Wayward Puritans. New York: John Wiley.
GOFFMAN, ERVING
　　1961　Asylums. Garden City, N.Y.: Anchor Books.
　　1963　Stigma. Englewood Cliffs, N.J.: Prentice Hall.
GOULDNER, ALVIN W.
　　1970　The Coming Crisis of Western Sociology. New York: Basic Books.
GUSFIELD, JOSEPH R.
　　1963　Symbolic Crusade. Urbana, Ill.: University of Illinois Press.
HAYEK, F. A.
　　1952　The Counter-Revolution of Science. Glencoe, Ill.: The Free Press.
HOFSTADTER, RICHARD
　　1955　The Age of Reform. New York: Vintage Books.
KENNEDY, DANIEL B., and AUGUST KERBER
　　1973　Resocialization: An American Experiment. New York: Behavioral Publications.
KITTRIE, NICHOLAS N.
　　1973　The Right to be Different. Baltimore: Penguin Books.
LONDON, PERRY
　　1971　Behavior Control. New York: Perennial Library.
LOWITH, KARL
　　1967　From Hegel to Nietzche. Garden City, N.Y.: Anchor Books.
PACKER, HERBERT L.
　　1968　The Limits of the Criminal Sanction. Stanford, Cal.: Stanford University Press.
PIVEN, FRANCES FOX, and RICHARD A. CLOWARD
　　1971　Regulating the Poor: The Functions of Public Welfare. New York: Vintage Books.

PLATT, ANTHONY M.
  1969   The Child Savers. Chicago: The University of Chicago Press.
POPPER, KARL R.
  1964   The Poverty of Historicism. New York: Harper Torchback.
RADZINOWICZ, LEON
  1966   Ideology and Crime. New York: Columbia University Press.
RIEFF, PHILIP
  1966   The Triumph of the Therapeutic. New York: Harper Torchbooks.
  1973   Fellow Teachers. New York: Harper and Row.
ROTHMAN, DAVID J.
  1971   The Discovery of the Asylum. Boston: Little, Brown.
SAGARIN, EDWARD
  1969   Odd Man In. Chicago: Quadrangle Books.
SCHEFF, THOMAS J.
  1968   "Screening Mental Patients," Pp. 172–185 in Earl Rubington and
         Martin S. Weinberg (eds.), Deviance: The Interactionist Perspective.
         London: The Macmillan Co.
SKOLNICK, JEROME H.
  1966   Justice Without Trial. New York: John Wiley.
TAYLOR, IAN, PAUL WALTON, and JOCK YOUNG
  1973   The New Criminology: For a Social Theory of Deviance. London
         and Boston: Routledge and Kegan Paul.

PHILIP RIEFF

The Triumph of the Therapeutic

There is a whole civilization to be remade.
—Camus, *Notebooks**

Lawrence, Reich, and Jung made representative efforts to go beyond the analytic attitude. They exhibit, in their writings, various uses of faith in a culture populated increasingly by psychological men. Each attacked the connection between morality and a culture about which they expressed strong disapprovals.

To speak of a *moral* culture would be redundant. Every culture has two main functions: (1) to organize the moral demands men make upon themselves into a system of symbols that make men intelligible and trustworthy to each other, thus rendering also the world intelligible and trustworthy; (2) to organize the expressive remissions by which men release them-

* That he tried seriously and with high artistry to clarify a post-Christian symbolic that could combat the emergent culture, measures the great contemporary importance of Albert Camus as a writer. Camus accepted the possibility that spiritual preceptorship in modern culture has fallen to the literary intellectual. Without a language of faith, Camus wrote in a mood far more "conservative" than that of many advanced and enlightened Christians, who have a genius for accepting almost any position, so to say, that is grossly anti-Christian or simply vulgar—especially in sex and art. On sexual life, Camus wrote, in his *Notebooks,* that it "was given to man, perhaps, to turn him aside from his true path. It is his opium. In it everything goes to sleep. Outside it things take on life again. At the same time chastity puts an end to the species which is, perhaps, the truth. Sexuality leads to nothing. It is not immoral, but it is unproductive. One can give oneself to it for a time when one does not wish to produce. But chastity alone is connected with personal progress. There is a time when sexuality is a victory—when it is released from moral imperatives. But it quickly becomes a defeat afterwards—and the only victory is won over it in its turn: that is chastity." On poverty, Camus is nearer the classical tradition than the modern therapeutic. "What can a man better desire than poverty? I have not said misery nor the hopeless toil of the modern proletariat. But I do not see what more can be desired than poverty linked with an active leisure." (See "A Writer's Notebook," *Encounter,* Vol. 24, No. 3, March, 1965, pp. 28–29.)

Source: Philip Rieff, "The Triumph of the Therapeutic," pp. 232–261 in *The Triumph of the Therapeutic: Uses of Faith after Freud* (New York: Harper & Row, Publishers, Inc., 1966). Copyright © 1966 by Philip Rieff. Reprinted by permission of Harper & Row, Publishers, Inc.

selves, in some degree, from the strain of conforming to the controlling symbolic, internalized variant readings of culture that constitute individual character. The process by which a culture changes at its profoundest level may be traced in the shifting balance of controls and releases which constitute a system of moral demands.

Those who transmit the moral demand system are a cultural elite, exemplifying those demands in their character and behavior. But an elite cannot merely teach or write of the moral demand system without acting out some part of it. However the labor of exemplary enactment is divided, no culture survives long without its elite, those cadres which demonstrate the particular balance of control and remission in the culture itself.

No culture of which we are aware has yet escaped the tension between the modalities of control and release by which every culture constitutes itself. Cultures achieve their measure of duration in the degree that they build releasing devices into the major controls. These are the devices that modern psychotherapy seeks to develop; it is this development which gives to psychotherapy its present importance in the history of our culture.

There remains a tension between controls and releases, even when the releases are devised cleverly (or dialectically) enough to allot to the controls their superordinate function. A cultural revolution occurs when the releasing or remissive symbolic grows more compelling than the controlling one; then it is that the inherent tensions reach a breaking point. Roman culture may have been moving toward such a breaking point when Christianity appeared, as a new symbolic order of controls and remissions.

At the breaking point, a culture can no longer maintain itself as an established span of moral demands. Its jurisdiction contracts; it demands less, permits more. Bread and circuses become confused with right and duty. Spectacle becomes a functional substitute for sacrament. Massive regressions occur, with large sections of the population returning to levels of destructive aggression historically accessible to it.[1] At times of impending transition to a new moral order, symbolic forms and their institutional objectifications change their relative weights in that order. Competing symbolisms gather support in competing elites; they jostle each other for priority of place as the organizers of the next phase in the psychohistorical process.

In all cultures before our own, the competing symbols took the form of languages of faith. A language of faith is always revelatory, communicating through some mouthpiece of the godterm a system of interdicts—a pattern of "thou shalt nots," or taboos. The language of science is not revelatory but analytic; for this reason, the scientist can never claim that his own terms have a prophetic function. His work is non-moral, that is,

[1] As in the case of Germany during the Nazi period, or ancient Rome when it became less a city than a mob. Jung noted, in 1912, that "We can hardly realize the whirlwinds of brutality and unchained libido that roared through the streets of Imperial Rome. But we would know that feeling again if ever we understood, clearly and in all its consequences, what is happening under our very eyes. The civilized man of today seems very far from that. He has merely become neurotic. For us the needs of the Christian community have gone by the board; we no longer understand their meaning. We do not even know against what it is meant to protect us." "Symbols of Transformation," *Collected Works*, Vol. 5 (New York, 1956), pp. 70–71.

without interdictory purpose. So far as the therapist casts himself in the role of a social scientist (e.g., Freud), he seeks to analyze interdictory symbolisms, not to assert them. Yet, as we have seen, modern therapists must use a language of faith. So far as their languages are "scientific" and yet moralizing, they depend upon counter-interdictory symbolism, "heretical" or negative conceptions of the interdictory symbolism itself, releasing rather than controlling. Jung was a prophet of the "subterranean God," as opposed to the "Heavenly Father." Reich's energic "Orgone" opposes all "spiritual" principles. A language of faith may be, therefore, controlling or releasing, interdictory or counter-interdictory. It contributes vitally to what Mannheim called "collective definitions," not mere hypotheses or replaceable theories but rather a "source of collective habits and actions."[2]

A language of hypothesis is culturally neutral. Commitment to hypothesis is made to be abandonable. The scientific psychologist, as clinician, aspires to be neither interdictory nor counter-interdictory. Because the clinical attitude aspires to moral neutrality, its therapeutic effect is culturally dubious. Clinicians continue to vacillate between interdictory and counter-interdictory symbolisms, depending upon a diagnosis of the individual patient's own conditional relation to these symbolisms. No culture has yet produced a third type of symbolic—one that would embrace that historic contradiction in terms: a "scientific culture." If, and only if, a neutralist symbolic becomes operative, may we speak of a scientific culture. For the present, clinical psychologists often try to produce an interdictory effect with counter-interdictory analytic symbols, an ambivalence Freud himself did not have the genius to overcome, except at the expense of an already weakened interdictory symbolic. Neither Jung nor even more conservative therapists have known how to resolve this ambivalence except by tempering their radical attitude toward culture with an obdurate conservatism toward the social order.

Every system of moral demands must operate within some social order. No less than its predecessors, the neutralist symbolic would have to create institutions appropriate to its expression, and even enter into shifting class alliances. As in the history of the Christian culture, a symbolic may be carried to power by a class very differently positioned in the social structure from that class in which it originated.

The next culture, with its component symbols, and with institutions embodying these symbols arranged in a normative working order, probably will require, in order to establish itself, (1) a new institutionalized inequality of demand and remission, (2) an ideal character type designated in these studies as the "therapeutic." Under foreseeable ideological and technological conditions, this emerging moral ideal is unlikely to be a workingman; on the contrary, the therapeutic will be a man of leisure, released by technology from the regimental discipline of work so as to secure his sense of well-being in highly refined alloplastic ways.

The term "inequality" of demand and remission is used advisedly. Every culture has hitherto required that the modalities of control dominate, that expressions of the "unwitting part of it" be disciplined and rendered in-

2 Karl Mannheim, *Essays on the Sociology of Culture* (London, 1956), p. 97.

stitutional. Whenever a releasing symbolic increases its jurisdiction to the point where it no longer serves to support the incumbent moral demands, but rather contradicts them, that culture is in jeopardy. Such freedoms were signatures on the death warrant of previous cultures.

At the close of a culture, the releasing modalties themselves begin to look and sound like controls. They are harbingers of the next culture. Some fresh imbalance is required before the succeeding system of culture can be born, bringing into being a new symbolic of expectations, and, moreover, institutions appropriately organized to enact those expectations, translating the high symbolic into rules of social conduct. In the realm of culture, equality of controlling and remissive functions, rather than inequality, is the mother of revolution. When the cross becomes a symbol of power or beauty, suppressing the historical reminder of a particularly brutal instrument of humiliation and death, then its own moral authority, under the Christian rubic of "cross-bearing," is threatened. Remissive components within some psychohistorical moral demand system may be underdeveloped, or overdeveloped. All symbolic and institutional devices balancing remission and control must be examined within multiple perspectives of historical change before the examiner can arrive at any judgment about the fixed moralities of a culture. But precisely those fixed moralities cannot remain permanently fixed. There are particular historical moments of imbalance in a dialectical order of controls and releases. The imbalances are subject to "correction" in the very process of maintaining themselves. Thus even the most stable moral demand systems are inherently liable to change. The primary process of cultural change refers to shifting jurisdictions over categories of social action by controlling and remissive symbolisms of communal and individual purposes.

One distinctive characteristic of modern remissive symbolisms, such as have been examined in the preceding three chapters, is that none has yet had the power to organize the erotic illusions that hold together aggregates of men for communal purposes. Doctrines of release in a culture cannot, of themselves, develop into new modalities of purpose unless they are subtly transformed and institutionally elaborated, as for example in the case, now all but closed, of Christianity.

In modern culture, there is a major question about the motor by which new purposive energies might be generated. Only with respect to nature does physical science produce transformative control devices. With respect to culture, it is still unclear whether the social sciences will produce control devices, as Comte hoped, or in what sense they may help create and install fresh convictions of communal purpose. Scientific psychotherapies often consist in attacks upon control-release systems which have failed as motors of communal purpose, according to criteria set up by patient, profession, or society. A judgment by psychotherapy upon itself as a remissive device itself in modern culture depends on how it conceives a preferable control-release system. Yet this is precisely the level of conceptualization with respect to its functions within a culture which psychotherapy tries, when understood as a science, to avoid.[3]

[3] See Freud, *Standard Edition*, XXI, p. 144.

We have some clues about the functional imperatives of psychoanalysis—desired and realized—in modern culture. Freud considered that his symbols were exempt from the cultural process by which remissive modalities become controlling, although rationally ordered ego controls are intended to operate remissively. Being analytic rather than remissive, the Freudian doctrine was never to be put in systemic service to either interdiction or release, under pain of ceasing to be analytic. Because Freud's doctrine was anti-communal, it could be used as a theoretical basis for elaborating a strategy of self-realization for the therapeutic. Americans, in particular, have managed to use the Freudian doctrine in ways more remissive than he intended, as a counter-authority against any fresh access of communal purpose.

By mid-century, the controls and the remissions from those controls have grown so nearly equal that the one works no better than the other. More precisely, the old established controls are enunciated so vacuously, and in such hollow voices, that they sound like remissions; and the remissions have become so elaborately stated, by some of the most charming voices in our culture, that they seem rather like controls. Such are the contrarieties of a revolutionary epoch. No one knows the internal voice, or external look, of the new devices of control and release that will succeed our failing ones. That even Freud expected them indicates the hold of the inherited configuration of culture over even the most radically inquiring minds.[4]

On the other hand, a heavily remissive psychotherapy may become a permanent institutional fixture of modern culture—a kind of secular methodism for those who remain obstinately uncomfortable in their pleasures. Structurally induced conditions, such as the decline of an ethic of work, may, like individual neuroses, seek their own pathological resolution. The new saving symbolic may never arrive, although from time to time, in various places, its arrival has been announced and new remissions experimentally tried. What appears now fairly certain is that the control-release system inherited from an older, mainly agrarian, culture into our technologically advanced, urban one cannot renew itself. Whether or not an innovation will occur is likely to be determined by the requirements of affluence accumulating in the hands of the therapeutic himself. With their secondary needs automatically satisfied, men may no longer need to have something in common, as an end, to love. The organization of indifference may well succeed the organization of love, producing a culture at lower cost to individual energies. Indeed, by this reorganization the interior life would cease to press its sickening claim to superiority.

The strange new lesson we have begun to learn in our time is how not to pay the high personal costs of social organization. The revolution continues in a remissive direction, beyond that rational Max Weber called "disenchantment," toward the dissolution of old systems of moral demand, with their requirements of almost total social cooperation in order to survive hard reality in a world characterized by scarcity. The present swing in the direction of release may not be orbital but more extended and historically more per-

4 *Ibid.*, p. 143.

manent, based on the automaticity and ease with which an infinity of created needs can now be satisfied.

Remissive motifs other than sexual have dominated earlier phases of the psychohistorical process, expressing the ideological breakup of great communities, but always at the same time preparing the ground for fresh internalizations of control. But the modern cultural revolution has built into itself a unique prophylaxis: it is deliberately not in the name of any new order of communal purpose that it is taking place. On the contrary, this revolution is being fought for a permanent disestablishment of any deeply internalized moral demands, in a world which can guarantee a plenitude produced without reference to the rigid maintenance of any particular inter-dictory (and counter-interdictory) system. This autonomy has been achieved by Western man from common and compelling mobilizations of motive. Stabilizing the present polytheism of values, there is the historic deconversion experience of the therapeutic, proposing an infinity of means transformed into their own needs.

Interdictory systems are still deeply rooted within us, of course. A cultural revolution does not occur as a discernible event, or as a plurality of events, nor does it occur swiftly within a few years, as does a political revolution; only afterwards, when the revolution itself has been incorporated into the new system of controls, do such mythic condensations of cultural change occur. Moreover, in significant ways, a cultural revolution may run with or against the indicated direction of political change. For example, the first Christian culture revolution accommodated itself from the beginning to the ruling classes of its time.[5] Christian doctrine began by distinguishing between culture and politics, concentrating its efforts at change upon the former, thus preparing a theoretical way for the Constantinean accommodation.

Cultural revolution is usually distinguishable from political revolution, which may assault the social order and leave the moral demand system fundamentally unaltered. Our cultural revolution has been made from the top, rather than from the bottom. It is anti-political, a revolution of the rich by which they have lowered the pressure of inherited communal purpose upon themselves. Seen in this way, the Negro protest movement in the United States will have to become more profoundly cultural if it is to succeed politically. Yet the American Negro is himself limited in his demands by the successful revolution of the rich. Being an American, the poor Negro believes that he too can live by bread alone. What the Negro asks, essentially, is a place at the American trough. But to gain that place, he is constrained to ask for something more than his share of places. His moralizings become an em-barrassment, for they hint at the acquisition of something greater than a place in a vaster suburbia.

Indeed, cultural revolutions before our own have asserted some limit on the race for status and satisfaction, and have promoted interdicts to limit and displace the dynamics of acquisitive appetite. Western culture has been dominated by an ascetic modal personality. Even the Calvinist bourgeois was to have his capital as if he had it not. Ours is the first cultural revolu-

[5] Probably as a result of the lesson learned from the disastrous Jewish attempt to maintain an identity of culture and society.

tion fought to no other purpose than greater amplitude and richness of living itself. Is this not what is meant by the "revolution of rising expectations"?

Our revolution is more Freudian than Marxist, more analytic than polemic, more cultural than social. There is no reason why, as the reluctant leader of moral revolutionaries, Freud should have threatened the social order. Of course, he knew that a revolution, to be thorough, must transform the property relations in society.[6] Nevertheless, his diagnosis of our "communal neurosis" takes no account of property relations. Culture, not the social order, takes the point of Freud's analytic attack, as it does of Jung's reconstructions in terms of religious psychology. Attacking the culture, such insights as the subjects of this volume propose could be adapted as safeguards against all inherited therapies of commitment. For the culturally conservative image of the ascetic, enemy of his own needs, there has been substituted the image of the needy person, permanently engaged in the task of achieving a gorgeous variety of satisfactions.

What is the logic of choice by which one symbolic begins to displace another? How do god-terms change? The present volume is not meant to be a history of our cultural revolution. That work will have to be done in monographic bits and pieces. We are too close to the subject. Moreover, a theory of the psycho-historical process has not yet been worked out. What has been attempted here, rather, is a tentative prospect of the revolution, drawing first some implications from various attacks on the failing cultural super-ego. Nor is this meant to be a defense of that inherited culture. Under the circumstances of a shifting balance of controls and releases, the classical internalizations of social authority, as an unconscious conscience, may be indefensible anyway. That it has been so ardently defended indicates not the eternal necessity of an unconscious conscience but rather that the initial cost of the modern cultural revolution has been a feeling of symbolic impoverishment.

The religiously inclined therapists are themselves engaged in the absurd task of trying to teach contented people how discontented they really are. Many would-be patients are recovering, it seems, from a pervasive feeling of impoverishment, so emphatically stated in the literature of the nineteenth century and of the first half of the twentieth. One main lesson is being more and more widely learned: that all compelling symbols are dangerous, threatening the combined comfort of things as they are. Even the religiously inclined grow more diffuse in their self-demand, praising "faith in life." And those without even this general faith—as, for example, Samuel Beckett, with his effort to be an artist working ultimately with a silent mankind, because the "silent God" has been used up—are hailed as most religious because they can find nothing to obey or await. All binding engagements to communal purpose may be considered, in the wisdom of therapeutic doctrines, too extreme. Precisely this and no other extreme position is stigmatized as a neurotic approach to paroxysms of demand for a more fundamental revolutionary dogma. It is in this sense that the contemporary moral revolution is anti-political; more precisely, it serves the purposes of the present anti-politics, representing a calm and profoundly reasonable revolt of the private man

[6] *Op. cit.,* p. 143.

against all doctrinal traditions urging the salvation of self through identification with the purposes of community.

In its reasonableness, the triumph of the therapeutic cannot be viewed simply as a break with the established order of moral demand, but rather as a profound effort to end the tyranny of primary group moral passion (operating first through the family) as the inner dynamic of social order. Crowded more and more together, we are learning to live more distantly from one another, in strategically varied and numerous contacts, rather than in the oppressive warmth of family and a few friends.

A culture of contacts is, at last, an historically accomplishable fact. Everything conceivable can be made universally available. Variety has become a term of control as well as remission. Confronted with the irrelevance of ascetic standards of conduct, the social reformer has retreated from nebulous doctrines attempting to state the desired quality of life to more substantial doctrines of quantity. The reformer asks only for more of everything—more goods, more housing, more leisure; in short, more life. This translation of quantity into quality states the algebra of our cultural revolution. Who will be stupid enough to lead a counter-revolution? Surely, even the rich are now emanicpated enough from ascetic symbol systems to concede more of everything to everyone, without serious loss of themselves. They cannot be threatened by a doctrine that merely asks for more, for this presupposes that quantity determines the quality of life—and this very assumption expresses the religion of the rich.

To ever-diminishing restrictive effect, lip service is still being paid to the ascetic principle that "more" does not translate into "better." Nevertheless, our suspicions fade that the quality of life may not be a synonym for the standard of living, after all. At least, a high standard of living, in our post-ascetic culture, is considered the permitting condition for attaining a higher quality of life. That "more" equals "better" has been an idea supported by the failure of the Russian revolution to say anything more original. Carried though it was by the Marxist-Leninist doctrine, that most recently ascendant variety of the Western commitment, therapy, the Russian revolutionary movement attracted many of the religious by its promise to change fundamentally the self-serving character of modern social relations. Militant socialism developed in its most powerful variety as a secular version of militant asceticism. Viewed in terms of its place in the history of culture, the Russian revolution carried a conservative bias, even in its apparently releasing initial phase, preaching the ethic of self-salvation through identification with communal ends in secular terms. The present course of the Russian Communists appears set toward an ironic convergence of a culture growing less conservative and a politics growing less radical. An understanding of the dynamics of such a convergence would illuminate at once the study of both culture and politics.

Cultural revolutions may be viewed more as typical recurrences rather than as unique occurrences. Like a planet, a culture may move around in an elliptical course, slowly changing its moral direction. In this classical view, all revolutions are repetitions; certainly, there is nothing surprising in the advent of a revolution. It is to be expected, like a change of seasons. But there is another view: that a culture may reach a definite close. This may well be the closing time of ascetic culture in the West; releasing modalities have enlarged their jurisdiction, demobilizing moral motivation, opening up possibilities suppressed during the long tutelary struggle of that culture against nature.[7] In fact, Western culture may now be so divorced from nature that revolution has lost its earlier cyclical implication. A truly unique revolution would be one that would not generate any compelling therapies of commitment. In our urban technological culture, it seems both archaic and dispensable already to organize men into compassionate communities by what Freud called "erotic illusions." Instead, the therapeutic is more adapted to organization into administrative units, with what used to be called "indifferentism," or, more recently, "nihilism," as the general rubric describing social emotion. Not trained in a symbolic of obedience—indeed, entertaining the category merely as a convenience—Western man could be free at last from an authority depending upon his sense of sin. Even now, sin is all but incomprehensible to him inasmuch as the moral demand system no longer generates powerful inclinations toward obedience or faith, nor feelings of guilt when those inclinations are over-ridden by others for which sin is the ancient name.

Compassionate communities, as distinct from welfare states, exist only where there is a rich symbolic life, shared, and demanding of the self a hard line limiting the range of desires. The symbolic impoverishment of the Western communities cannot be corrected by analysis, nor by analysis of other analysts. Rather, the present correction of this impoverishment amounts to an effort to change the criteria of impoverishment. Perhaps the issue thus formulated can help us judge more accurately the continuing changes in the character of our culture.

The history of a culture—and of its social organization—may be written as a dialectic of the shift from evaluative to expressive symbolisms. Ethical despair becomes, in such a history, a transitional feeling. Earlier transitions have been felt as painful. In the degree that an ethos of control (that is, an evaluative symbolic) loses force, just so does a pathos of release (that is, an expressive symbolic) revenge itself in social analogues of individual symptoms. But from the classical repressive-sublimative organization of motive, our culture has veered toward an expressive-impulsive organization.[8] The way in which the inherited culture was structured by internalized love and externalized hatred describes the ambivalence in its therapies of commitment. Opposing commitments depend upon the same dual therapeutic modes.

[7] There is a resemblance between revolutions in culture and social systems. In culture, too, a revolution may be taken to represent the overthrow of an established order, a substitution of some new ruling symbolism of personal sacrifice for the old. Social change is heralded, or accompanied, by ideological or cultural movements that are themselves training schools for some new therapy of commitment. The socialist movement existed as a cultural and psychological phenomenon long before it became politically significant. We do not know from what dynamic element of contemporary culture the next political thrust will develop—the two systems may now be experimenting with a trial separation leading to permanent divorce.

[8] The cultural significance of advertising, for example, has been usefully analyzed under this general rubric. See Jules Henry, *Culture Against Man* (New York, 1963), pp. 3–99, also p. 317, *et pass.*

Paralleling those commitments that are the symbolic structure of community is the social structure. No therapy before the analytic has produced salvations or cures except through a social system penetrated by organizational commitments—these commtiments legitimizing the order of vocation and personal relation from which the sense of community is derived. We are privileged to be participant observers of another great experiment by Western humanity upon itself: an attempt to build upon the obsolescence of both love and hatred as organizing modes of personality.

In every vital community there has been a cultural elite, sometimes distinct from political or social elites, carrying doctrines of communal purpose as its motivating characteristics. The test for the cultural elite has been its capacity to express, in a symptomatic language of faith, the self-effacing moral demands. Western society nowadays scarcely even pretends to produce a cultural elite in the sense indicated; it boasts many highly educated and gifted people, but none are therapists of commitment.[9] No successor therapists to the religious professionals have emerged. It is conceivable that therapists of commitment grow less and less necessary to the imaginations modern men have of each other.

A cultural elite may have either a critical or a supporting relation to the upper classes, politically or economically defined; historically, that relation has been supporting in the main. By "cultural elite" are not meant intellectuals, necessarily; rather, such an elite may be either anti-intellectual or fiercely intellectual, aesthetically sophisticated or hostile to the arts. The significance of these or other characteristics can only be established when the contents of the moral demands shaping the elite's general plan of life and its impress upon the social class structure have been studied. That intimate connections develop between social classes (that is, aggregates defined in terms of property and status), on the one hand, and culture classes (that is, aggregates defined in terms of moral demand), on the other, has been a proposition accepted in general by liberals and conservatives alike, as well as by democratic and aristocratic theorists. It is characteristic of power to be associated with culture. To rule is to become exemplary or, at least, to sponsor cadres practicing the praise of rulers as far as decorum, in that culture, would allow.

Yet, there have been periods in history when a cultural elite, opposing refinement with aesthetically coarse moral demands, has risen in critical passion from both the lower social orders and from disaffected members of the higher.[10] Culture in its primary sense, a moral demand system, is not the equivalent of a technical education or of aesthetic refinement. To take yet another step in the development of this historical perspective: Culture classes have been ambivalently related to social classes throughout Western history. The upper social classes rarely preserve a strict moral demand system. Associated with them, an elite culture class grows less strict. Moral re-

[9] Not excepting the discouraged professionals of the old normative institutions, themselves more than half persuaded that they are protected remnants of a dying culture, struggling to find avenues of relevance to the present age.

[10] The four first centuries of the Christian era were such a period.

form, no less than social, must push up from below. Even in Nietzsche's pejorative variation on this theory, the dialectic holds: the cultivated, with their high arts and literature, are too comfortable to deploy righteous indignation; and the lowly are sunk too far into their peculiar resorts of comfort. Moralizing belongs to the ambitious middle range of the Western social structure, if it may be properly located anywhere at all. But the proper locus is more ideological than structural, it seems. Not class position but creedal preoccupation, as an alternative to refinement and aesthetic perception, is the driving force of moralizing movements. In all the writings of Calvin there is scarcely a reference to the beauty of the landscape surrounding Geneva. He was far too busy regulating the manners of Genevans, including the exact length of the ladies' skirts.

That social and cultural classes may be ambivalently related is, of course, an empirical generalization, and thus subject to a run through the gantlet of historical objections. But, until practically our own time, this generalization can be substantiated over and over again. Some evidence of sustained opposition between social classes and culture classes may be cited.

In the seventeenth century, some artisans and sections of the lower middle social classes in Western Europe developed powerful motifis of control, complete with normative institutional modes for exercising these controls, as in the case of the English Puritans or the Dutch bibliolaters. The leadership of these movements entertained the ambition of a cultural elite, offering their resolutions of ambiguous moralities as fresh options for the organization of consensus. On the other hand, at times a group or movement competing for elite status would withdraw from the struggle to alter the culture system, so as to maintain the purity of the moral demand for itself alone. This describes the basic difference between sects of withdrawal and sects of militancy in Western cultural history. Yet even sects of withdrawal may preserve a certain militancy and aspirations of catholicity. By maintaining their community as a whole as an exemplary institutional embodiment of their proclaimed moral demand system, the withdrawn sect would preach a prescriptive remedial lesson to the society external to it; this society is treated pejoratively as "the World," an immoral system of remissions, as opposed to the correct conduct of the corporate life.

So far as it offers counter-interdicts, aiming first at release from (or radical reform of) the established moral demands, a challenging elite[11] appears deviant or even downright immoral to the cultural establishment which is carrying out the maintenance functions of the dominant demand system incorporating the official scientific wisdom of the period. Yet, by offering

[11] The probability of "youth" as an emergent Western cultural elite would seem quite high in the light of this tendency, for intergenerational tension becomes greater as industrialization—and the concomitants of this process as it has been experienced—progresses. However, as products of the analytic attitude, today's youth may attack the culture system but rarely the social, thus precluding its involvement in the creation or propagation of new (or old) commitment systems. The historical trend of youth as cultural elites is, today, almost entirely a non-Western phenomenon. For a more detailed analysis of the role of youth in American society, see Erik Erikson (ed.) *Youth: Change and Challenge* (New York, 1963), especially the chapters by Talcott Parsons and Kenneth Keniston.

modes of release, a challenging cultural elite may become the spiritual preceptor of the moral demand system that is thus being born. There is a hint of this ambition in Freud, when he proffered, as a successor to both the established psychiatrists and to the pastors of the older dispensation, the psychoanalyst in the role of a "secular spiritual guide."

Who are those who now are spiritual preceptors? The affluent and powerful often have not been the morally supportive class. What happens if an entire society grows rich, technologically loaded with bribes, and is dominated by preoccupations that may be best defined as anti-creedal? What cadres offer a powerful rationale of abandonment of the disintegrating cultural super-ego?

Certainly, Freud hoped the psychoanalyst would be the one to have some legitimate claim to spiritual perception. Yet Freud himself was reluctant to tamper radically with the cultural superego. As we have seen, his orthodox successors have become even more strictly client-centered.

In the sequence of Western spiritual preceptors, the psychotherapist came before the professional revolutionary. Committed Communists claimed they possessed a spiritual perception that was in fact the propaedeutic necessary to the creation of a new moral order. And before the Communists, there were, of course, the Christians. Indeed, the entire effort of Christian socialism can be best explained as an attempt to renew the spiritual perceptions of the Christian doctrine by transfusions from the outside—from a competing and hostile therapy of commitment. The tragicomic fate of Christian socialism was that it became more aesthetic than ascetic. In another respect, the failure of Christianity resembles that of Communism: both have been wrecked by success; neither could resist incorporation into social orders that were partly their own creation. In the doctrine of the Church, however, Christianity still preserved its capacity for spiritual perception. That the Church is, supposedly, *in* but not wholly *of* this world supplied a critical principle of renewal which is basic to all Christian therapies of commitment. The Church, as an institution, is vital only inasmuch as its symbolic is detached from the established soical order, thus preserving its capacity for being the guardian critic of our inherited moral demand system.

The Leninist doctrine of the Party maintained no doctrinal reserve about the social order, over which it developed a stewardship in theory and practice more complete than that ever claimed or practiced by the churches. No director of the faith has proved less perceptive spiritually than the professional revolutionary turned Party functionary. Having lost the nimbus of resistance to the precedent social order, he operates more in terms of bureaucratic self-interest than in those of communal purpose. More precisely, Party interest becomes identical with communal purpose. The Gletkins have no gods, and usually cannot be driven therefore to personal despair by a Party which devours its own members. For those in search of new gods, after 1914–1919, the attractive pull of the professional revolutionary was accounted for, probably, by a residue of his earlier charisma as a spiritual preceptor proposing, in his political acts and thought, a new moral order. Nowadays, that charisma is rarely to be found, because the Communist moral order appears anything but new. As a Party functionary, the Western or Russian Communist no longer represents a cultural elite. Nevertheless, the Marxist political functionary remains *culturally* conservative—he is a "Hebraist," as compared with the "Hellenes" that dominate the national politics of the West.

There persists a revolutionary impulse throughout the West; but it is cultural rather than political, and therefore more difficult to describe than the political revolutions of the East. That revolutionary impulse is in evidence not only in the writings of those specimen therapeutics examined in preceding chapters but in the writings and conversations of significant numbers of the educated. One British technologist has enunciated the doctrine of the therapeutic in a language so simple and clear that it is well worth while to quote him at length, to stand for countless other utterances heard and read: "Any religious exercise is justified only by being something men do for themselves, that is, for the enrichment of their own experience." Attached as he is to the word "Christian," the writer even seeks to make Jesus out to be a therapeutic, as Lawrence and Reich did before him. "Jesus," we learn, "used the word 'God' to . . . refer to the vital energy of personal life itself, the energy of love." Living in a culture no longer religious, "people who center their lives on ritual, sacrament, and constant reference to some supposed plan underlying experience are just as cut off from vital personal contact with others . . . as is the individual neurotic." The technical psychological term, this writer concludes, following Freud, for "such a way of living," carried over from the previous culture, is "paranoid fantasy-obsession."

What, then, should churchmen do? The answer returns clearly: become, avowedly, therapists, administrating a therapeutic institution—under the justificatory mandate that Jesus himself was the first therapeutic. For the next culture needs therapeutic institutions. "Society as a whole needs patterns of community life which will help ordinary people to fulfill themselves in much the same sort of way that psychiatrists help those who are specially troubled. Building up such community life would surely be a directly Christian activity, in my sense; but the training for those who are needed for it would be rather different from any sort of training clergy at present receive." The writer understands that churchmen will be able to become professional therapeutics "only if they break away radically from almost all, if not all, of their traditional religious pursuits."[12] Here speaks the therapeutic, calmly con-

---

[12] John Wren-Lewis, "What Are Clergy For?" *The Listener*, LXXI, No. 1824 (March 12, 1964), pp. 418–19. Argument for the therapeutic has entered strongly into the higher reaches of journalism. See, for example, David Gourlay, "The Churches," in the *Manchester Guardian*, May 21, 1964, p. 9. Gourlay is speculating on just what will be going on in churches a hundred years hence, assuming they will exist at all. "The church of tomorrow will be a place for the celebration of life, and its characteristics will be spontaneity and acceptance; the spontaneity of abandoned righteousness and the acceptance of the self-rejected. It will be a place of colour, movement, and vitality where young and old will not only look at what men of past ages have painted, listen to what they have written and the music they have made, but where they themselves will be free to paint, dance, talk, and express themselves in ways no longer easy in an age of automation, non-employment, space sickness, and leisure lostness. Few, if any, places in the new society will offer such arresting and beckoning horizons of human creativity. Political leaders will be glad to discover in the churches centres where somehow man's place and dignity in the world is mysteriously maintained in spite of all evidence to the

fident that community life no longer needs "some supposed plan underlying experience," that is, no longer needs doctrinal integrations of self into communal purposes, elaborated, heretofore, precisely through such "supposed plans." It is in "traditional religious pursuits" that such plans are reinforced and the self integrated into a saving corporate purpose. Without such incorporating plans, the self has found fulfillment in an even more elusive condition.

Both East and West are now committed, culturally as well as economically, to the gospel of self-fulfillment. Yet neither the American nor the Russian translations of the gospel can be transformed into a spiritual perception. Both the United States and the Soviet Union are cultures of the new-rich—the United States, perhaps, even more so than the Soviet Union. Though it has begun to catch up culturally, the Soviet Union remains the more conservative system, with the Party, directly descended from the Church, striving to maintain a doctrine which asserts, at once, its social viability and truth. The Communist therapy of commitment must contend precisely with the new-rich of its own creation. In the United States, the rich have already adopted, it appears, the character structure of the therapeutic. No exemplary social stratum, above, restrains its elaborate and infinite sense of personal need. On the contrary, the Soviet Union and the United States are engaged in a common race to appeal to, and increase, the new-rich.

The leisured, or non-working, classes are the main sources from which the therapeutic, as a character type, is drawn. Emancipated from an ethic of hard work, Americans have also grown morally less self-demanding. They have been released from the old system of self-demands by a convergence of doctrines that do not resort to new restrictions but rather propose jointly the superiority of all that money can buy, technology can make, and science can conceive.

Certain naïve ascetic doctrines, which once did contain spiritual perceptions of great depth, such as that of holy poverty, now embarrass the churches, competing as they do for pride of place in a culture of affluence. Such perceptions are practically taboo subjects, specially among Americans, except negatively, when clergymen complain that they do not receive salaries commensurate with their status as professional men. Nor does the present ferment in the Roman Catholic Church seem so much like a renewal of spiritual perception as a move toward more sophisticated accommodations with the negative communities of the therapeutics. Grudgingly, the Roman churchmen must give way to their Western laity and translate their sacramental rituals into comprehensible terms as therapeutic devices, retaining just enough archaism to satisfy at once the romantic interest of women and the sophisticated interest of those historical pietists for whom the antique alone carries that lovely dark patina they call faith.

The religious psychologies of release and the social technologies of affluence do not go beyond release and affluence to a fresh imposition of restrictive demands. This describes, in a sentence, the cultural revolution of

contrary. Somewhere in the midst of all this there will be a small group of men and women helpers who, by dedication and training, will be able to serve and unite the community church in its life and interests."

our time. The old culture of denial has become irrelevant as a manipulable experience to a world of infinite abundance and reality. Carrying along inapplicable residues of "mystery" culture into the present scientific one, the ascetic labors in vain before the triumphant therapeutic to define a positive spiritual perception—except rejection of the therapeutic ethos. On the other hand, the therapeutic has arisen out of a rejection of all therapies of commitment, precisely by persuading halfway the recalcitrant among those who submitted to the old commitment therapies that they have acted out denials of knowledge and pleasure that no longer contribute to their spiritual health but, rather, to their mental dis-ease. So recently deconverted, the once-committed is unlikely to preach seriously against himself, except in terms of a historical drama, so that the therapeutic may enjoy his triumph. The obsolescent old-model man, representing a dying culture of scarce goods and absent gods, is losing popularity, even as a subject of didactic art. Ingmar Bergman's tormented souls are a bore, even more so than Antonioni's; at least the movie-Italians have progressed beyond the fantasy-obsessions of a disintegrating moral demand system for which Bergman has developed the image of the "spider-God." The anxieties of the ascetic were fit subjects for the art of, say, William Hale White, or George Eliot. The boredom of the therapeutic[13] fascinates Antonioni, Fellini, and the *nouvelle vague*—because they cannot escape the dying clutch of the old culture. American novels still agonize about pleasure as a way of life—but it is the agonizing, not the pleasure, which seems fraudulent.

In summary, each major contending cadre requires analysis in terms of its relation to contemporary character ideals. The deconverted is affected as much as the recalcitrant by the withdrawal of motive from economic and political life as the permitting condition of any spiritual perception that may develop to alter, toward a more operable imbalance, the present balance of controls and remissions. Thus far, no fresh carriers of a renunciatory symbolic have appeared able to establish themselves as serious claimants to a cultural elite status in Western society. Such a claimant may appear tomorrow, to capture the public modes of obedience; the dynamics of modern culture, however, militate against this possibility. There can develop no new (or renewed) system of interdicts from the therapeutic parody of a moral demand system; in consequence, all attempts at connecting the doctrines of psychotherapy with the old faiths are patently misconceived. At its most innocuous, these psychotherapeutic religiosities represent a failure of nerve by both psychotherapists and clergymen.[14] Finally, the professionally religious custodians of the old moral demands are no longer authoritative; although they still use languages of faith, that mode of moral communication has lost its ties with either the controls or the remissions valid among their adherents; preaching, which once communicated revelatory messages, is a dead art, wrapping empty packages in elaborate solecisms. The preachers have little of either controlling or releasing functions and retain therefore little power seriously to affect or alter the emergent control system. It is in this

[13] See, for example, the characters in *La Dolce Vita, Eclipse,* or *Les Cousins.*

[14] For an analysis of psychotherapeutic religiosity, see, in particular, the chapter "The Religion of the Fathers," in *Freud: The Mind of the Moralist,* pp. 281–328.

sense that the Christian and Jewish professionals have lost their spiritual preceptorships. Any functional equivalents to the old internal interdicts, whatever they may be, struggling to stabilize themselves and as yet without institutional conveyances, take on meaning insofar as they prove capable of providing a trained prudence to the therapeutic, anxious to increase his psychological capital without incurring dangerous risks.[15]

After the clergy, the political revolutionaries, and the psychoanalysts— there remain the artists and the scientists, as serious aspirants to the title of secular pastoral guide.

The scientists are a curious case. By tradition and training they are intractably modest. Claims to spiritual perception rarely occur explicitly in their work. Profoundly as that work has affected modern culture, the scientists have been non-combatants in the culture class war. With rare exceptions, they still accept the Ritschlian distinction between statements of fact and judgments of value. They make fact statements; the task of making value judgments belongs to other specialists, those elites that won exclusive custody over culture even as they gave up pretending they had authoritative knowledge of nature.

Notice the context within which Albrecht Ritschl, following Kant, had made his famous distinction. In Ritschlian theory, value judgments can only be made in reference to a communal perspective. According to Ritschl, Christian perceptions make sense only within the framework of a historic Christian community. The modern scientist has had quite another conception of himself; *qua* scientist, he has tried to extricate himself from all normal demands except those imposed upon him by the internal logic of his transformative endeavor directed against the natural world, all designed to overcome those gross miseries and necessities nature imposes upon mankind. The scientfic community aspires to be supra-cultural, and is not qualified therefore to supply a creedal dynamic to that new laity, the non-scientists. In this sense, the scientific endeavor in its entirety, representing as it does the effort to create a non-moral culture, embodies the moral revolution. With a commitment that is strictly vocational, the scientist personifies the latest phase in the Western psychohistorical process, one that refrains from laying down guidelines of moral intervention for the society as a whole. Whatever his professed intention, the scientist acts, therefore, as a spiritual preceptor to modern man. The therapeutic has everything—and nothing—to learn from the scientist, for in the established sense of the word, the scientist, as such, has no culture.[16]

[15] The Roman Catholic Church, practiced as she is for over a thousand years in rationalizing experience, seems far more likely to survive as a provender of prudence well into the age of the therapeutic, rather than those Protestant polities in the tradition of the free church, with their modalities of militant conscience.

[16] Sir Charles (now Lord) Snow has called for a new class of savants, able to establish the culture of the therapeutic. See *The Two Cultures and the Scientific Revolution* (Cambridge, England, 1960). In doing so, he is echoing positivist proposals, elaborated more fully by Auguste Comte, in his essay of 1821, entitled "Plan of the Scientific Operations Necessary for Reorganizing Society," which provides a brief but complete pendant to Snow's call. See Introductory, p. 9, footnote 7.

The Comtean ambition appears again in Reich's effort to combine Marxism and

The modern artist, too, has had the role of a spiritual preceptor thrust upon him. And, indeed, because modern artists move in the direction of release, there is a religious pretension inherent in the work of the moderns, reacting as they do to a situation in which nature has been taken out of their purview by science and technology. They have deliberately created alternative realities to those put in jeopardy by science. The inherent interest of modern art is not chiefly in experimenting with the representation of some microscopic reality, or in some correspondence with a presumed macrocosm, but, more importantly, in the production of a picture that would suggest, within its frame, the multiple and alternative realities through which the modern may enliven an existence divorced from both nature and faith. The artist represents what we are trying to become, the shape we are trying to take in our effort to escape the pressures of timeworn inwardness while also escaping the bondage of new internalities. It is for his professional effort at unfixed externalizations, valid first to his own psychological economy, that the modern artist has been handed a spiritual preceptorship. By exploring the range of presentable realities, quite apart from the "natural" or the "socially acceptable," the modern artist has broken his vocational connection with moral demand systems, beginning with that of the middle classes. In achieving an impersonality no less impressive than that achieved by modern science, painting, in particular, augured the emancipation from the classical moral demand system, rejecting the *person* as an object of aesthetic interest and concentrating on the self-fulfilling function of the work of art itself. Thus the art work has become, in a strict sense, a therapeutic mode.

To this quality of impersonality in our future togetherness, reference was made repeatedly, throughout the present volume, beginning with the Introduction. Freud had proposed this rejection of attachment to an inner experience no less than Lawrence. The latter wrongly accused Freud of encouraging a new outbreak of that sickly modern religiosity by which modern men turn further in upon themselves, either under the cover of Christian psychologizing or under that of humanism. This further turning in is precisely the opposite of what the present volume intends to convey by the therapeutic. His sense of well-being operates under the aegis of a technology aimed ultimately at his own emotions, so as to destroy the tension between the inner and outer life.

If yesterday's analytic thrust is to become part of tomorrow's culture super-ego, it must take on an institutional form, defend itself not only as true but also as good and dig into personality as a demand system. Yet it is precisely this that the new arts and social sciences, in their very nature, cannot accomplish. They cannot create the ardent imaginations necessary to

psychoanalysis into the theoretical predicate for a vast reorganization of society. See his *Dialektischer Materialismus und Psychoanalyze* (Copenhagen, 1934). In this sense, Reich aspired to be spiritual preceptor to a post-Christian culture. Since the neuroses suffered by millions are a result of the patriarchal, authoritarian education in which Western culture consists, the final issue, for Reich, was cultural change. And cultural change was tantamount to the prevention of neuroses, and, moreover, to the elimination of the "empty niceties of a false liberalism." (*The Mass Psychology of Fascism,* p. xi.)

the forming of new communities; although they may prepare the way for a new public mode of existence, for the present they make life all the more private. Like the old cultural super-ego, the negative communities of the next culture, so far as we can discern them in this respect, rarely utter hosannas; therapeutics, not yet settled in their mode, speak to each other mainly in harsh tones. Our spiritual preceptors practice their unkindnesses upon each other. A spiritual perception must have built into its releasing insight a vision of new stability, a promise of some settling pattern or supposed plan, and not merely the energy to reject the prevailing cultural super-ego; that latter sort of wisdom comes more and more "naturally" in contemporary culture. The "id" has always had "energy"; the cultural "super-ego" has aged into a fussy critic of the energetic. This moral revolution is occurring by default, not so much under the leadership of id-energy doctirnes as under the bankruptcy of super-ego energies. It is the impotence of the cultural super-ego rather than the potency of the id that is the crucial fact of our time. For this reason, however, "nothing" can succeed the imperative mood—nothing except the therapeutic mood itself.

Historically, the Christian spiritual perception, which had attacked the established moral demands of its time, took on an institutional form, and, moreover, had a revolutionary effect on some aspects of the social system—for example, on the status of women. At the same time, the Church was incorporated into the social system and survived, powerful and yet defeated in its ideal intention by that very incorporation. Something similar may happen to the present revolutionary effort to transform the culture. Psychotherapy may be arrested at its present stage by a reconciliation with contemporary remissive religiosity, sanctioned mainly as a post-religious science of moral management. This seems to be the present state of psychotherapy in America.

There is an ambiguity in the very function of psychotherapy as the chief among those arts interpreting the deconversion experience of Western man to himself. To investigate all instances of failed mastery of moral energy raises the possibility of controlling the moralizing process itself. Among those who followed Freud were some more willing to entertain the possibility of such a moral revolution. The range and quality of these varying theories, Jung's included, cannot be easily dismissed. Each constructed an explicit doctrine of release from the failing old controls upon some aspect or other of their intellectual encounter with Freud. None worked out the doctrine consequentially enough to become the founder of a new dispensation.

At this time, culture revolutionaries can be described mainly in terms of their ideas about the culture against which they are reacting. Revolutions have been known to press in either direction, toward control or release. Most revolutions restore an imbalance of controls and releases at a new point. It is a telling indication of Freud's own ambivalence that the revolutionaries who most interested him were the great protagonists of control, not of release.[17] Freud's revolutionary attack on the European Christian culture

[17] Most of all, Freud was interested in Moses, the founder of the cultural elite from which Freud considered he derived.

as a system of moral demand makes more sense, however, when understood in the context of his larger theory of the dynamics of culture as a system of unwitting renunciations. Seen thus, his therapeutic interest is revolutionary, a tremendous argument for expressive remissions from failed controls, re-stablilizing the moral demands that are culture at a fresh locus of imbalance between controls and remissions. In this aspect, Freud represents the climax of the nineteenth-century tradition of scientific prophecy as a functional sub-stitute for religious prophecy. His was the subtle climax of a rationalism in which a more modest moral demand system could use a prophylactic analysis intended to prevent an oppressive elaboration of those controls, which are always irrational precisely in their destructively reactive production of counter-imbalancing (that is, neurotic) remissions. Freud's analytic intricacies thrust the culture toward an apparent simplicity of controls, while elaborating the range of remissions, thus exactly reversing the normative order. Proscrip-tive symbols give way to prudential ones; but the prudent man cannot, as Freud thought, take his morality for granted—for that security derives from the proscriptive dynamics upon which he had trained his great analytic weaponry. What is moral is *not* "self-evident," as Freud declared in a letter to James Putnam.[18] What is moral becomes and remains self-evident only within a powerful and deeply compelling system of culture.

The new releasing insights deserve only a little less respect than the old controlling ones. One may expect official clamor for a renewal of the old demand system, which may well have no further plans of self-integration, but function instead to disguise a terrifying ignorance of the distinction between our present inwardness and ancient faith. The therapeutics must be under-stood precisely in their efforts to go beyond the analytic attitude, as the articulate representatives of a sharp and probably irreparable break in the continuity of the Western culture. None of their doctrines promises an authentic therapy of commitment to communal purpose; rather, in each the commitment is to the therapeutic effort itself. As Jung insisted, the therapeutic cannot claim more than a private value for his moral science. The therapy of all therapies is not to attach oneself exclusively to any particular therapy, so that no illusion may survive of some end beyond an intensely private sense of well-being to be generated in the living of life itself. That a sense of well-being has become the end, rather than a by-product of striving after some superior communal end, announces a fundamental change of focus in the entire cast of our culture—toward a human condition about which there will be nothing further to say in terms of the old style of despair and hope.

18 Ernst L. Freud (ed.), *Letters of Sigmund Freud* (New York, 1960), p. 308.

Name Index

Abrams, M. H., 22*n*
Acton, John E. E. D., 177
Adams, John, 132
Anderson, V. V., 102*n*
Anshen, Ruth, 26*n*
Anslinger, Harry, 98*n*, 335, 343–44, 346–48
Antonia, Robert, 256
Arendt, Hannah, 69*n*, 70*n*
Ares, Charles E., 323*n*
Arnold, Thurman W., 42*n*
Aubert, Vilhelm, 55, 58, 90*n*, 330*n*
Auerbach, Carl A., 43*n*
Ausubel, David, 97–98*n*
Averbach, Albert, 190*n*

Bacon, Selden D., 239, 365, 368
Banfield, Edward, 27*n*
Barbarosa-Dasilva, Fabio, 256
Bartell, Gilbert D., 161
Barth, K., 171*n*
Bean, L., 361, 368
Beaumont, Gustave de, 145*n*
Beccaria, Cesare, 132–33, 382
Beck, F. (pseud.), 241, 245–47, 249, 251–52*n*, 254
Becker, Howard S., ix–xii, 13*n*, 85, 97*n*, 175–76, 251, 254, 261–62, 266, 292, 294, 296*n*, 315*n*, 335, 338, 343–45, 348*n*, 350, 359
Beebe, Maurice, 22*n*
Beecher, Charles, 239
Beecher, Lyman, 226–27
Bell, Daniel, 29*n*, 32*n*, 38*n*, 239
Belli, Melvin M., 190*n*
Bendix, Reinhard, 213*n*
Benson, Lee, 30*n*, 32*n*
Berelson, Bernard, 28*n*, 38*n*
Berger, Peter, 4, 9
Berry, J. J., 293–94, 350–59
Billings, John Shaw, 96*n*
Billington, Ray, 94*n*, 239
Bittner, Egon, xi, xii, 292, 294, 296*n*
Black, G. F., 305*n*, 311*n*
Blacker, C. P., 205*n*, 206*n*
Blain, D., 125*n*
Blaisdell, Donald C., 41*n*

Blanchard, P., 102*n*, 103*n*
Bland, Joan, 95*n*
Blau, Peter M., 336*n*
Blumberg, Abraham S., 386, 390
Blumer, Herbert, 287*n*
Boaz, Franz, 150
Bodin, Jean, 184, 185*n*, 299, 302*n*
Bodo, J. R., 239
Boorstin, Daniel J., 77, 81, 83, 147–61
Boulding, Kenneth, 202*n*, 203*n*
Bradford, William, 132*n*, 133
Bradshaw, F., 270*n*, 273*n*
Brant, Irving, 190*n*
Bremner, Robert H., 198*n*, 201*n*, 203*n*, 221*n*
Breslauer, George W., 249, 251
Briar, Scott, 89*n*, 292, 294
Bridenbaugh, C., 239
Brill, A. A., 285–86*n*
Brodsky, Iosif, 116–17, 119, 127
Bromberg, W., 99*n*
Brosin, Henry, 120
Brown, Katya, 117*n*
Bruce, Maurice, 212, 218*n*
Brzezinski, Zbigniew K., 241, 250–51, 254
Buber-Neumann, Margarete, 254
Bukharin, Nikolai, 200*n*
Burke, Edmund, 216
Burke, Kenneth, 5, 9, 22, 25, 35, 60*n*, 70*n*, 88*n*
Burnham, W. J., 102*n*
Burr, G. L., 300*n*, 308–309*n*
Bushard, B. L., 319*n*.
Bustamante, Jorge A., 174–76, 256–66
Bye, Raymond T., 134*n*

Calkins, Raymond, 96*n*
Calvin, John, 226, 299, 402
Cameron, Norman, 80, 83
Campbell, Angus, 38*n*
Campbell, C. M., 108*n*
Campbell, Macfie, 108*n*, 112*n*, 113*n*
Camus, Albert, 392*n*
Caplan, Gerald, 82, 83, 119–21
Cardenas, Gilbert, 266
Cavan, Ruth Shonle, 50, 58

411

Gable, Richard W., 41*n*
Galdston, Iago, 183*n*
Gamio, Manuel, 257–58, 266
Gamson, William, 264, 266
Garceau, Oliver, 41*n*
Garfinkel, Harold, 19*n*, 28, 358–59, 361, 367
Garner, John Nance, 265
Geis, Gilbert, 41*n*, 42, 268*n*
Gellman, I., 361, 367
Gerth, Hans, 47*n*
Gesell, Arnold L., 153–55
Gibbs, Jack P., x-xii
Ginsberg, Allen, 98*n*
Ginsburg, Evgeniia Semenovna, 246, 254
Gladwin, Thomas, 199*n*
Glaser, Frederick G., 189–90*n*
Glass, Albert J., 319*n*
Glazer, Nathan, 215*n*
Godin, W. (pseud.), 241, 245–47, 249, 251–52*n*
Goffman, Erving, 18*n*, 25*n*, 28*n*, 36, 88*n*, 293–94, 296*n*, 325–33, 385–87, 390
Goldschmidt, Walter, 239
Goodal, Kenneth, 81, 83
Goode, William, 4, 9
Gordon, John E., 319*n*
Gorman, Michael, 119–20
Gould, James S., 144*n*
Gouldner, Alvin W., 74, 75, 83, 376, 390
Gourlay, David, 404–405*n*
Grant, Madison, 257
Grebler, Leo, 257, 266
Gregory, J., 344*n*
Groves, E. R., 102*n*, 103*n*
Gusfield, Joseph R., 2, 5, 6–7, 9, 22–39, 31*n*, 85–98, 87*n*, 88*n*, 92*n*, 95*n*, 174–76, 222–38, 239*n*, 338, 364, 367–68, 384, 390

Habermas, Jurgen, 373–75
Hadley, Eleanor M., 258*n*, 259–60, 263, 266
Haines, W. H., 285*n*
Hall, G. Stanley, 148–53, 156–57
Hall, Jerome, 268, 274*n*, 279
Hall, Thomas, 239
Halsbury, Earl of, 276–77
Hammond, Paul Y., 42*n*
Handlin, Oscar, 94*n*, 204–205, 239
Hansen, Marcus Lee, 94*n*, 212*n*, 239
Hardin, Charles M., 41*n*
Harley, Robert, 203
Harrington, Michael, 198
Harris, Charles, 281–82*n*
Harris, Neil, 131*n*
Harrison, Jane Ellen, 62, 63*n*, 64–66
Hart, Henry M., Jr., 46*n*
Harvey, William, 312*n*

Haskins, George Lee, 44*n*
Hayek, Friedrich A., 77, 83, 190*n*, 376, 390
Haynes, F., 239
Henderson, Lawrence J., 65
Henry, Jules, 400*n*
Hess, John H., 318*n*
Hirsch, Bernard D., 190*n*
Hitler, Adolph, 6, 248
Hobsbawm, E. J., 207*n*
Hoebel, E. Adamson, 42*n*, 46*n*
Hoffman, H. R., 285*n*
Hofstadter, Richard, 9, 32, 222, 239, 384, 390
Hole, Christina, 195–96
Holmes, Oliver Wendell, Jr., 42*n*
Hoover, J. Edgar, 281*n*
Hopkin, C. Edward, 162*n*
Hopkins, M., 306*n*, 310–11
Horney, Karen, 112*n*, 113*n*
Horowitz, Irving Louis, 5, 9
Horton, Donald, 239
Horton, John, 3–5, 9
Hourwich, Isaac A., 257, 266
Howard, John, 18*n*
Howe, Samuel Gridley, 141, 144*n*
Hunter, Robert, 202, 206*n*
Hurst, J. Willard, 42*n*
Huxley, Aldous, 17, 389*n*

Ingraham, W., 239

Jackson, Andrew, 30, 130–32, 140–46, 225–27
Jackson, John A., 215*n*
Jaffe, Herbert J., 318*n*
Jahoda, Marie, 79, 83
James, William, 148, 149
Jeffery, C. Ray, 45*n*
Jenks, William, 144*n*
Johnson, Guy B., 307*n*
Johnson, Virginia E., 160–61
Johnston, Norman, 307*n*
Jones, Lamar B., 258*n*, 265–66
Jung, Carl G., 392–94, 398, 409–410

Kahl, Joseph A., 206
Keller, Mark, 93*n*
Keniston, Kenneth, 402*n*
Kennedy, Daniel B., 387–88, 390
Kennedy, John F., 27, 119, 187
Kerber, August, 387–88, 390
Key, V. O., Jr., 41*n*
King, Albion Roy, 239
King, Rufus, 339*n*, 341*n*, 343
Kinsey, Alfred C., 157–61, 167, 286*n*
Kitano, Harry H. L., 257, 266
Kitsuse, John I., x, xii, 13*n*, 56, 58, 85, 292, 294, 296*n*
Kittredge, G. L., 299*n*, 311*n*

Subject Index

Abortion, 51, 54–55, 87, 98
Adolescence, 151–52, 156
Aging, 56–57, 209–210
Alcoholics Anonymous, 97, 293, 361–67
Alcoholism, 13, 53, 96–97, 163, 238, 380, 383, 388; *see also* Drinking
Alienation, 5, 18, 206–207, 235, 237–38
Anomie, xi, 5, 209
Antisemitism, 66–71, 178–80
Asceticism, 100, 103
Asylums, 79–80, 185–87, 384–86; *see also* Mental hospitals

Behavior modification, 81–83, 164–65, 170n
Beliefs, cognitive, 3, 8, 52–59, 75–76, 134–46, 149–55, 158–60, 177, 181–84, 188–96, 211, 241, 257, 264, 281–84, 287–88, 292, 298–99, 305–306, 309–310n, 312, 351, 362–64, 383, 385; *see also* Ideology; Morality, lived
Beliefs, value, 3, 8, 33–34, 51–59, 74–83, 99–113, 116, 121, 124–25, 148–55, 161–71, 198, 200–207, 224, 227–29, 236–38, 257, 337, 365–67, 378, 399, 407; *see also* Ideology; Morality, lived
Biology, 157–58, 160; *see also* Social Darwinism
Blacks, 7, 111, 215, 221, 277, 307n, 397
Blind, the, 56–57, 147
Bourgeois, 75–81, 162–63, 167–69, 377; *see also* Marx, Karl; Social class
Bureau of Narcotics, 98n, 334–49, 351
Bureaucracies, 55–57, 79–80, 120, 124, 127–28, 241–54, 293–94, 307–309, 313–16, 324–59, 374, 385–86; *see also* Deviance, control agencies; Voluntary associations

Capitalism, 75, 100–104, 127–28, 225, 229–31
Catholic, Roman, 7, 75, 94, 160, 178–81, 216, 232–34, 298–300, 301n, 405
Ceremonies, 6, 19, 26, 28, 62–65, 71, 318, 323, 361

Child training, 147–55, 205–206
Child welfare, 147–48, 150, 205–206, 230, 351, 384; *see also* Social welfare
Christianity, 61–62, 66–67, 69–72, 74–79, 93, 142, 149, 162–63, 168, 229, 393–97, 403–410; *see also* Catholic, Roman; Protestant; Reformation; Inquisition
Civil liberties, 29, 33–34; *see also* Totalitarianism
Civil rights, 27, 91; *see also* Blacks
Clinic, 153; *see also* Medical model; Community psychiatry
Collective bargaining, 24, 86
Communism, 29, 33–34, 74, 129, 167–68, 200–203, 403–404; *see also* Soviet Union
Community psychiatry, 71, 78, 81–82, 118–25, 129, 360, 386, 389
Competition, 102–104
Conformity, 11–12, 20–21, 50–51, 116–18, 121–25, 129, 164–66, 175, 361, 373, 387; *see also* Repentant role
Correctional institutions, 133, 145–48, 214, 352
Crime, 11, 13, 19–20, 49, 110, 130–46, 297, 376
  statistics, 56, 139n, 181, 242–43, 283, 352, 383, 386
Crimes without victims, 50, 54–55, 87, 90–91, 98, 190–91; *see also* Abortion; Drug use; Prostitution
Criminal law, 6, 13, 40–49, 53–55, 132–34, 139n, 174–75, 183–84, 188–92, 216–18, 241–54, 268–89, 299–316, 323, 334–49, 374, 378, 380–86

Democracy, 100, 102, 125–29, 149–50, 153–55, 225, 293
Deterrence, 282, 381–82; *see also* Criminal law
Deviance
  as dangerous, 50–51, 60–61, 64–72, 80–82, 139, 146, 175, 178, 186–91, 195, 281–84, 308, 318–19, 351, 384
  careers in, x–xi, 18, 146, 360–61

417